MUSLIM MENTAL HEALTH IN NORTH AMERICA

In the Name of Allāh
the Most Gracious, Most Merciful

DEDICATION

To all who struggle in silence and their supporters, particularly those facing unique cultural challenges, your voices deserve to be heard. Speak up, your experiences matter.

The first editor would like to dedicate this book to his deceased parents

SYED FAZAL & SAFIA HAQUE

who taught me the value of hard work and to serve others selflessly

The second editor would like to dedicate this book to her brother

ARSHAD ABID ABBASI, MD

who gave me the zest to live fully, dream big, and soar high

MUSLIM MENTAL HEALTH
IN NORTH AMERICA

Edited by

Amber Haque & Farha Abbasi

**Muslim Mental Health
Conference & Consortium**
Department of Psychiatry

This book first published 2025
Michigan State University
Muslim Mental Health Conference & Consortium
East Lansing, Michigan, USA
Copyright © 2025 by Department of Psychiatry,
Michigan State University

All rights for this book reserved. No part of this book may be reproduced, stored in a retrieval system, or transmitted, in any form or by any means, electronic, mechanical, photocopying, recording, or otherwise, without the prior permission of the copyright owner.

CONTENTS

ACKNOWLEDGMENTS	i
CONTRIBUTORS	iii
INTRODUCTION	xv

Amber Haque

SECTION ONE

MUSLIM MENTAL HEALTH CONFERENCE	1

History of Muslim Mental Health Conferences (2008-2025)

Farha Abbasi

SECTION TWO: CONCEPTS & CULTURE

CHAPTER ONE	33

Breaking the Silence: Mental Health Stigma and the American Muslim Experience

Rukhsana Chaudhry

CHAPTER TWO	49

Culturally Relevant Diagnostic Considerations and Treatment Interventions

Samar Harfi

CHAPTER THREE	75

Strategies for Community-Based Mental Health Interventions in Islamic Institutions

Osman M. Ali, Wadud Hassan

CHAPTER FOUR	95

Islamic Psychology: The Missing Link in Muslim Mental Health

Fahad Khan

SECTION THREE: FAMILIES & AGE GROUPS

CHAPTER FIVE — 117
Muslim Youth: Modern Day Challenges and Approaches

Suzy Ismail

CHAPTER SIX — 139
Muslim Women's Mental Wellbeing: A Focus on North American Muslims

Venus Mahmoodi, Maeve Winter, Yukti Bhatt, Maryam Gani

CHAPTER SEVEN — 165
Overcoming Challenges in Marriage and Family: The Case of South Asian Muslims

Afshana Haque, Saman Essa

CHAPTER EIGHT — 195
Comprehensive Mental Health Care For Elderly Muslims: Cu[lturally] Competent Approaches And Strategies

Asif Khan

SECTION FOUR: SPECIAL POPULATIONS

CHAPTER NINE — 207
Reverted and Converted Muslims Mental Health in North Am[erica]

Sarah Mohr, Anisah Bagasra

CHAPTER TEN — 229
Incarcerated Muslims' Mental Health in North America

Ibrahim Y. Z. Mohammad, Jennah Shagan, Rami Nsour, Rani[a]

CHAPTER ELEVEN — 265
Muslim Mental Health: From Trauma-Informed to Healing-C[entered]

Javeed Sukhera

CHAPTER TWELVE — 285
Muslims with Disabilities and Mental Health

Joohi Tahir

CHAPTER THIRTEEN 307
Disabilities: A Literature Review
Tarek D. Zidan

CHAPTER FOURTEEN 323
Drug Addiction in Muslim America
Ibrahim M. Sablaban

SECTION FIVE: CONTEMPORARY ISSUES

CHAPTER FIFTEEN 345
First/Second Generation Immigrants in North America: Perspectives from Theory and Lived Experiences
Hanan Hashem, Waleed Sami, Somer Saleh

CHAPTER SIXTEEN 367
Islamophobia and Mental Health in North America
Rania Awaad, Kubra Tor-Cabuk, Maram Saada

CHAPTER SEVENTEEN 389
Media and Muslim Mental Health
Anisah Bagasra, Burton Speakman

CHAPTER EIGHTEEN 413
Workplace Mental Health in North America with Muslim E
Raymond H. Hamden, Aysha Mazoon

CHAPTER NINETEEN 443
Digital Frontiers in Muslim Mental Health
Aurra Startup, Omar Khan, Iqra Ashfaq, Wadud Hassan, Subhaan Ashrafi, Athraa Fakier

SECTION SIX: HUMANITARIAN & SOCIAL SERVICE ORGANIZATIONS

CHAPTER TWENTY 471
Mental Health Services in Muslim NGOs: Challenges and Solutions
Somer Saleh, Sarah Murad, Danyal Khan

ACKNOWLEDGMENTS

The editors would like to express their gratitude to all the chapter authors who believed in the value of this project and contributed their chapters wholeheartedly. This is the first comprehensive book dedicated to Muslim mental health, and each author has made a pioneering contribution to raising awareness about issues specific to the Muslim community.

A special thank you goes to Dr. Jed Megan, Head of the Psychiatry Department, for not only recognizing the importance of an edited volume that represents diverse perspectives on various topics related to Muslim mental health but also for continuously supporting this field, especially through the annual conferences.

We would also like to acknowledge other publications, such as the Journal of Muslim Mental Health, for promoting research on Muslim mental health around the world.

We are particularly grateful to MMH Secretary Lisa Olivia and our proofreader and typesetter, Raabia Haque, for their invaluable assistance throughout the book publication process. We could not have published this book without the sincere cooperation of everyone who worked as a team.

The editors are truly thankful to all of you!

Book Editors

CONTRIBUTORS

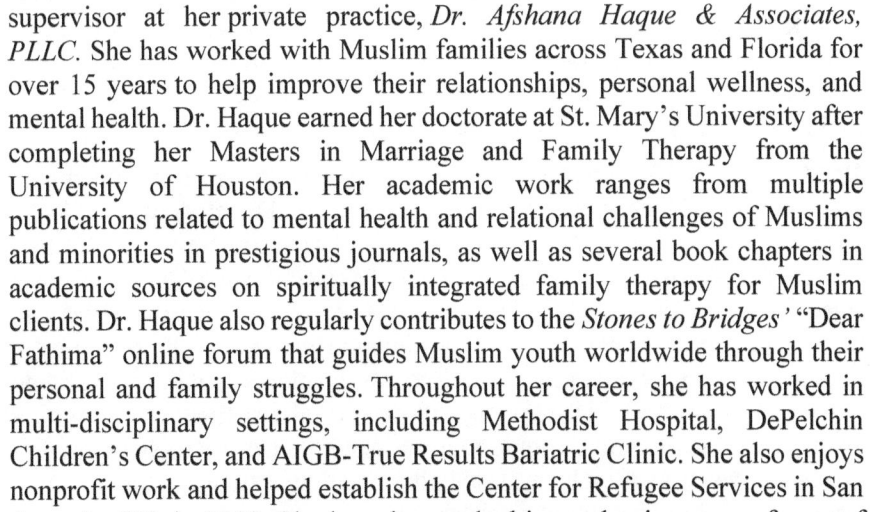

Dr. Afshana Haque is a licensed marriage and family therapist & supervisor at her private practice, *Dr. Afshana Haque & Associates, PLLC*. She has worked with Muslim families across Texas and Florida for over 15 years to help improve their relationships, personal wellness, and mental health. Dr. Haque earned her doctorate at St. Mary's University after completing her Masters in Marriage and Family Therapy from the University of Houston. Her academic work ranges from multiple publications related to mental health and relational challenges of Muslims and minorities in prestigious journals, as well as several book chapters in academic sources on spiritually integrated family therapy for Muslim clients. Dr. Haque also regularly contributes to the *Stones to Bridges'* "Dear Fathima" online forum that guides Muslim youth worldwide through their personal and family struggles. Throughout her career, she has worked in multi-disciplinary settings, including Methodist Hospital, DePelchin Children's Center, and AIGB-True Results Bariatric Clinic. She also enjoys nonprofit work and helped establish the Center for Refugee Services in San Antonio, TX, in 2010. She has also worked in academia as a professor of marriage and family therapy at the University of Houston, Clear Lake, before going into full-time private practice in 2021. She is a regular speaker in the Houston Muslim community and provides education and awareness courses periodically to her community.

Dr. Amber Haque is a psychologist and the National Director of Muslim Family Services at ICNA Relief USA. He is affiliated with the Muslim Mental Health Consortium at Michigan State University and serves as a nonresident research faculty member at Cambridge Muslim College, UK. Previously, he held the position of full professor and director of clinical psychology programs in Qatar and the UAE and led the psychology department in Malaysia. Dr. Haque also practiced psychology in Michigan for over a decade. He earned his Ph.D. in psychology from Western Michigan University and his MS in clinical psychology from Eastern Michigan University. Additionally, he has been a visiting scholar at Cornell University and the University of Pennsylvania, taught in Bosnia, and is involved with the editorial boards of several international journals, reviewing for over forty peer-reviewed journals and several international institutional review boards. Dr. Haque has published extensively on mental health and Islamic psychology.

Dr. Anisah Bagasra, from Saybrook University, is an Associate Professor in the Department of Psychological Science at Kennesaw State University specializing in behavioral health research in the Muslim American and African American faith communities. She teaches a wide range of psychology courses and mentors students engaged in undergraduate research with a focus on culturally competent research in minority communities. Her recent publications include three edited volumes, "Working with Muslim Clients in the Helping Professions," "The Changing Faces of Higher Education: From Boomers to Millennials," and "The Impact of HBCUs in the 21st Century". She also conducts CE workshops in religious and spiritual competencies for psychologists.

Dr. Asif Khan is an Assistant Professor of Psychiatry at Central Michigan University College of Medicine and serves as Director of Residency Training and Inpatient Adult & Geriatric Psychiatric Services at CMU Health. He is also the President of the Pakistani American Psychiatric Association of North America (PAPANA). He is board-certified in psychiatry, geriatric psychiatry, and addiction medicine. Dr. Khan has a special interest in resident education and has developed several educational curricula for trainees. He is a recipient of several Excellence in Teaching Awards and has mentored numerous residents and medical students. His areas of interest also include psychopharmacology, aging, neurocognitive impairments, and movement disorders.

Athraa Fakier - Content writer, Sabr App. Athraa is a registered Social Worker from South Africa. Having graduated from the University of Cape

CONTRIBUTORS

Town in 2020, she spent the first years of her career in counseling, working with issues related to addictions and mental health. Athraa's approach is to learn and share information and experiences of mental health and wellbeing for the benefit of all. She believes creating safe spaces for people to feel heard and validated is integral to building healthy communities. In addition, Athraa contributes her time and expertise as a content writer for the Sabr App. In her free time, she is practicing her kata as a Karate student, painting, or learning a language.

Aurra Startup - PhD Student, Restorative Justice Practitioner. Aurra Startup is a PhD student in the Education program at York University, focusing on how the conceptualization of restorative justice (RJ) shapes its practice in both school and community-based settings. As a Service Coordinator for Restorative Responses to Harm and Crime (RRHC) with Community Justice Initiatives, Aurra bridges theory and practice by supporting individuals and communities affected by harm and guiding them through the complexities of the criminal legal system. Aurra is currently completing an internship with Ruh as a Policy and Practice Researcher, investigating best practices for user engagement and approaches to addressing the unique mental health needs of Muslim communities through digital tools. She volunteers with the Wijhah Initiative, where she supports the "Wellness Within" program, a mental health initiative designed for BIPOC Muslim youth aged 18-25. Through this program, community members can access bi-weekly educational sessions and support groups, while connecting with culturally sensitive mental health professionals. Prior to this, Aurra coordinated programs addressing the mental health needs of Muslim communities, focusing on areas such as suicide prevention, resilience-building, positive psychology, and many more.

Aysha Mazoon is an advocate for de-stigmatizing mental health concerns among minority communities, with a specific interest in how spiritual and cultural identity intersect with psychological resilience and employee engagement. She has partnered with healthcare organizations, educational institutions, and private-sector companies to develop evidence-based mental health strategies that respect religious values while aligning with corporate goals. With intellectual curiosity and a commitment to applied psychological practice, she demonstrates cultural sensitivity with organizational behavior to culturally responsive mental health frameworks.

Dr. Burton Speakman is Associate Professor of communication at Kennesaw State University. His research focuses primarily on the impact and effects of partisan media. With Dr. Bagasra, he is the recipient of a Facebook Content policy grant to study Islamophobic rhetoric and imagery.

Danyal Khan is a nonprofit consultant and personal development coach with a bachelor's in psychology and a master's in social work, specializing in nonprofit management. He has held leadership roles like the National Director of Muslim Family Services at ICNA Relief USA and CEO of the Islamic Association of Raleigh (IAR). Now serving as the Executive Director of the Islamic Education Center of Pennsylvania (IECPA), Danyal is passionate about building stronger communities and creating spaces for Muslims to grow and thrive. Outside of work, he is active on social media as @growingwithdanyal, where he shares anecdotes on mental health, personal development, and community organizing. In his downtime, he enjoys connecting with nature and having whimsical adventures with his children.

Dr. Fahad Khan is a Licensed Clinical Psychologist with a Doctorate in Clinical Psychology and a master's in biomedical sciences. As Deputy Director at Khalil Center, he leads clinical and research efforts for North America's largest Muslim mental health provider. He also teaches at the undergraduate and graduate levels, focusing on Muslim mental health and Islamic psychology. A fellow of the International Association of Islamic Psychology, Dr. Khan actively contributes to peer-reviewed journals and professional organizations, including the American Psychological Association, which recognized him with Early Career awards in 2020 and 2021.

Dr. Farha Abbasi is a psychiatrist and a leader in mental health for minorities and newcomers. She founded the Annual Muslim Mental Health Conference, which held its seventeenth session in Detroit in 2025 and directs the Muslim Mental Health Consortium at Michigan State University. Dr. Abbasi has received multiple awards for her community service, including the National Alliance on Mental Illness Award and the American Psychiatric Association (APA) Foundation Award for Promoting Minority Mental Health, the Assembly Award for Courage in Profile, and Crain's Detroit 2024 Health Heroes Award. She serves on various boards, including the APA Council on Minority Mental Health and Health Disparities. She was recognized by Secretary Becerra as one of the nation's top women leaders of faith. Currently, she chairs the Mental Health Task Force for the Mayor of Lansing and is the Director of the American Psychiatric Association Foundation.

Dr. Hanan Hashem is an Assistant Professor in the Clinical Psychology Department at William James College and an Adjunct Professor at Michigan State University. Hanan's core research and clinical interests include intergenerational trauma, youth development, and spiritually integrated interventions and care. She has published numerous peer-

CONTRIBUTORS

reviewed empirical research on the mental health of Muslims in the United States. Hanan has worked in various clinical settings throughout her clinical training, including community health centers, university counseling centers, and a youth shelter. She is currently licensed as a psychologist in the Commonwealth of Massachusetts. Hanan is also a community organizer focused on community education and mental health consultancy, including her role on the Board of Directors for the Muslim Mental Health Conference.

Dr. Ibrahim Mohammad is a second-year psychiatry resident at the University of Toronto. His experiences in community organizing, particularly the Justice for Soli movement, led him to develop an interest in Muslim mental health. He has twice helped organize the annual Canadian Muslim Mental Health Conference held jointly by UofT and the Muslim Medical Association of Canada. He has also hosted numerous psychoeducational workshops at local mosques. He is additionally a Research Mentee at the Stanford Muslim Mental Health and Islamic Psychology Lab, where he is currently leading a study investigating the experiences of formerly incarcerated Muslims.

Dr. Ibrahim Sablaban serves on the National Board of Directors of American Muslim Health Professionals (AMHP) and is a dual-boarded psychiatrist and addiction medicine physician specializing in acute care and consultation. He has expertise in mood disorders, psychosis, and substance use and currently directs a clinical academic service at Metropolitan Behavioral Health Hospital in Dearborn, Michigan, where he treats a significant number of Muslim patients. In addition to his clinical work, Dr. Sablaban is an educator, holding academic positions at Oakland University William Beaumont School of Medicine, Michigan State University, and Wayne State University. He is heavily involved in teaching and curriculum development. Since 2017, he has also served as the psychiatric liaison for the Islamic Center of Detroit, where he lectures and disseminates information regarding mental health and substance use disorders to Muslim communities throughout Southeast Michigan. Over the years, Dr. Sablaban has received multiple awards for his academic and clinical contributions and has participated in the development of several opioid addiction toolkits and treatment protocols.

Iqra Ashfaq - Iqra Ashfaq is the Co-Founder and CEO of Noor Meditation, a groundbreaking app that fuses Islamic principles with mental and spiritual wellness. With a rich academic background in Psychology, Neuroscience, & Behavior, Iqra earned her master's degree studying the physiological effects of listening to the Qur'an and guided mindfulness meditation, along with a graduate diploma in Neuroscience. She also serves as the

Implementation and Innovation Lead at Princess Margaret Cancer Centre and is a professor in the Mental Health and Addictions program at Durham College. Under her leadership, Noor Meditation has become a pioneering platform with built-in artificial intelligence that answers questions about Islam and guides users to the perfect meditation session tailored to their needs. Iqra's passion for mental health has led to a thrilling collaboration with the Centre for Addiction and Mental Health, where Noor Meditation is being put under the microscope through a research study. This study will examine the real-world impact of the app in a lab setting, offering groundbreaking insights into how it supports users' mental wellbeing.

Dr. Javeed Sukhera is the Chair of Psychiatry at the Institute of Living (IOL) and Chief of Psychiatry at Hartford Hospital in Hartford, Connecticut. He is also the Founding Director of the Center for Research on Racial Trauma and Community Healing. He is a Professor of Psychiatry at the Frank H Netter MD School of Medicine at Quinnipiac University, an Associate Clinical Professor of Psychiatry at the Yale School of Medicine and Associate Professor in the Department of Psychiatry at the University of Connecticut School of Medicine. He is an internationally recognized health professions education researcher and thought leader. His research program explores novel approaches to addressing stigma and bias among health professionals, and he has also been involved in advocacy and cross-sectoral work in education, policing, and community services.

Jennah Shagan is a graduate student at Palo Alto University, pursuing a master's in forensic psychology. She is also a Research Mentee at the Stanford Muslim Mental Health and Islamic Psychology Lab. Her experience includes serving as a Crisis Counselor in the Bay Area, focusing on individuals with developmental disabilities and psychiatric disorders. She has experience as a Case Manager in Sacramento, working with the homeless dual-diagnosis population. Her research centers on trauma in Middle Eastern, North African, and Muslim populations.

Joohi Tahir, Co-Founder & Executive Director, MUHSEN. As a graduate of Boston University with a degree in Business Management and having spent over 20 years excelling in the corporate world, speaking globally about strategies in the Marketing field in the UK, Saudi Arabia, Dubai, Malaysia, and Turkey, Joohi turned her talents to become a national advocate for Muslims with Disabilities. This led to her involvement in Co-Founding and appointment as Executive Director of Muslims Understanding & Helping Special Education Needs (MUHSEN) with Founder Shaykh Omar Suleiman. MUHSEN is a revolutionary organization implementing Programs and Services across North America promoting the inclusion of all members of the community impacted by special needs

CONTRIBUTORS

through awareness, accommodation, and acceptance. With her own family being affected by disability, Joohi has been outspoken over the past 15 years, specifically about the need for inclusion for her daughter, who is on the Autism Spectrum. She has been a recipient of the MWA 2015 Inspiring Women's Award and the Top 7 Muslim American Women to Celebrate 2017. MUHSEN.org

Kubra Tor-Cabuk, MA, is an incoming Assistant Professor of Psychology at Central Connecticut State University. She is also a research mentee at Stanford University's Muslim Mental Health and Islamic Psychology Lab. She received her MA in Clinical Psychology and is currently a PhD candidate in Applied Psychology and Prevention Science at the University of Massachusetts Lowell. Her research and teaching interests focus on women's health, discrimination in medical settings, and utilization of health services.

Maeve Winter is a Clinical Psychology MA candidate at Teachers College Columbia University, specializing in women's health. She is actively involved in research at the Muslim Perinatal Lab at Teachers College and the Nurture Science Lab at Columbia Medical Center. Maeve's work focuses on the complex interplay between reproductive health, religiosity and spirituality, and close intimate relationships, and how these factors influence health and wellbeing. She aims to advance the field by deepening the understanding of the connection between physical and psychological health and by designing accessible interventions that promote positive outcomes and engage new populations in psychology. In her free time, Maeve practices and teaches hatha yoga and loves exploring the museums and parks of NYC!

Maram Saada earned a bachelor's degree in psychology from the University of California, Davis, and is pursuing an MS in clinical psychology at San Jose State University. She is also a Branch leader at the Stanford Muslim Mental Health and Islamic Psychology Lab. Maram's research interests include community-based participatory research, culturally responsive therapy practices, and exploring the mental health experiences of Muslim and other marginalized communities.

Maryam Gani is based in Greater Chicago and is pursuing an MA in Clinical Psychology and Counseling Practice at Roosevelt University. Her work focuses on Muslim women's mental health, with a special interest in Islamically integrated psychotherapy. Passionate about blending faith and evidence-based practices, Maryam is dedicated to advancing culturally competent mental health care for underserved communities.

Omar Khan - Co-Founder & CEO of Ruh, a Muslim Online Therapy

Platform. Ruh also hosts an Islamic mindfulness app and the world's largest directory of Muslim therapists, with over 900 therapists offering support across 23 countries. Previously, Omar served as an Advisory Product Manager at IBM and volunteered with several nonprofit and charitable organizations, such as Islamic Relief, Yaqeen Institute, and more. He is currently a Master of Divinity candidate at The Islamic Seminary of America and holds an MBA and a bachelor's in computer systems engineering. Omar's work, advocating for Muslim mental health on the global stage, has mobilized the community and received international recognition, including awards from the G20 Young Entrepreneurs Alliance Summit in Germany, the Visionary Leadership Award from the Islamic Seminary of America, the Continuum Spark Award in Qatar, winning first place amongst over 330 Muslim social impact initiatives from across 28 countries, and recently the Beacon Award from the Muslim Mental Health Conference held at Stanford University as an emerging leader in Muslim Mental Health.

Dr. Osman M. Ali is an Associate Professor in the Department of Psychiatry at the University of Texas Southwestern Medical Center (UTSW). He graduated from Cornell University with a B.A. in Neurobiology and Behavior in 1994 and from the Medical College of Ohio (University of Toledo) with an M.D. in 1999. He trained in psychiatry at Cornell's Payne Whitney Clinic in Manhattan and completed a Public Psychiatry Fellowship at Columbia, New York State Psychiatric Institute. He served as a Medical Director at Bellevue Hospital and established the first Public and Community Psychiatry Fellowship at UTSW. He is a Board Certified general adult psychiatrist working full-time serving veterans at the Plano VA Community Based Outpatient clinic. He is a Distinguished Fellow of the American Psychiatric Association (DFAPA). He was a co-founder and president of Muslim Mental Health, Inc. Some of his publications include articles related to the imam's counseling role and book chapters related to the mental health of Muslims.

Rami Nsour is a scholar, counselor, public speaker, teacher, and translator of Islamic texts. Spending over 10 years within the Mauritanian tradition (mahdara) system of studying Islam, Shaykh Rami received licensure (ijaza) to share his wisdom with students. Further enhancing his extensive study of Fiqh, Nsour completed an extraordinary 'in-residence' experience, allowing him to research questions (fatawa) of Islamic faith, law, and practice. He co-founded the Tayba Foundation, the first organization in the United States to offer a distance-learning program in Islamic Education to incarcerated men and women. Shaykh Rami has extensive experience in curriculum development, specifically in character (akhlaq), and holds a BA in Human Development with a focus on Early Childhood. He also obtained

CONTRIBUTORS

an MA in Educational Psychology. A resident of the San Francisco Bay Area, he lives with his wife and three children.

Dr. Rania Awaad is a clinical associate professor of psychiatry at the Stanford University School of Medicine and director of the Stanford Muslim Mental Health and Islamic Psychology Lab. Her research is focused on mental healthcare in Muslim communities and the history of mental health and wellbeing in Islam. At Stanford, she teaches a groundbreaking course on Islamic Psychology, exploring the relationship between culture, religion, and medical care. Dr. Awaad was the first female professor of Islamic Law at Zaytuna College in Berkeley, California.

Dr. Raymond H. Hamden is a clinical and forensic psychologist with over 50 years of experience consulting across more than 30 countries on five continents. He has served as Director of the Human Relations Institute & Clinics in Dubai and currently chairs The Foundation for International Human Relations in Washington, D.C. His expertise spans political psychology, crisis intervention, and trauma. He has contributed to academic and governmental discussions on terrorism and radicalization, including presentations before the US Congress.

Dr. Rukhsana M. Chaudhry is the Director of Mental Health Programming for the American Muslim Health Professionals (AMHP). She has developed several mental health advocacy and educational initiatives, including the "Muslim Youth Identity" series in which American Muslim speakers delivered TED-style talks about combating stereotypes and prejudice. She spearheaded and convened the first-ever National Interfaith Anti-bullying Summit with steering committee partners in December 2017. She currently serves as a psychologist at The World Bank, practices in behavioral medicine, and is a senior clinical advisor. In 2016, she received the Leadership Recognition Award for service in Mental Health Programming from the Muslim Mental Health Conference and Michigan State University Department of Psychiatry. In 2019, she established the first asylum and human rights clinic in the Department of Professional Psychology as an Assistant Professor of Clinical Psychology at George Washington University. Dr. Chaudhry received her Doctorate from George Washington University in 2010. She completed her postgraduate training at Harvard University's Global Mental Health Program, specializing in Trauma and Recovery.

Dr. Saman Essa is a licensed psychologist specializing in resilience promotion among immigrants, refugees, and asylum-seekers. She has undergone formal training in trauma and is currently completing her post-doctoral fellowship at the Lucine Center and the Trauma and Grief Center at the Meadows Mental Health Policy Institute. Dr. Essa holds a Bachelor's

Degree in Psychology and a Master's of Education in Counseling, both from the University of Houston. She graduated from the University of Houston's Counseling Psychology Doctoral program and completed her APA-accredited pre-doctoral internship at the Cincinnati VA Medical Center.

Dr. Samar Harfi (Albalawi) is a licensed clinical psychologist specializing in trauma, Islamic Psychology, multicultural counseling, and liberation psychology. She earned her Doctorate from the Illinois School of Professional Psychology and is a fellow of the International Association for Islamic Psychology (IAIP). Dr. Harfi works at Khalil Center, where she provides clinical supervision and Islamically-integrated mental health services. She has presented, trained, and published on mental health issues relevant to Muslim communities. She co-authored The Islamic Workbook for Religious OCD. Bilingual in Arabic and English, she has received presidential recognition for her contributions to refugee services in Chicago.

Sarah Mohr, born and raised in the SF Bay Area, the traditional territory of the Ohlone people, is passionate about serving her community. She is a certified drug and alcohol counselor and LCSW. She earned her MSW from CSU East Bay (2017). She also has a master's in religion and psychology from the GTU with a Certificate in Islamic Studies (2009) and is a visiting scholar at the GTU. She has published in various formats on liberation psychology, conversion, addiction treatment, mindfulness, and a variety of other topics. Her most recent book is Islamic Liberation Psychology: The Transformational Force of Self-Development, Community Empowerment, and Revolutionary Change.

Somer Saleh, LMFT, is a Licensed Marriage and Family Therapist practicing in New York and New Jersey. She serves individuals, couples, and families. In addition to her private practice, she serves as an adjunct professor at Mercy University and co-leads the Social Services department at the Muslim American Society. Somer is deeply engaged in community spaces, focusing on addressing the intersectional gap between mental health and the Muslim community. She has developed programming and events on mental wellness for Muslims and regularly advocates for culturally sensitive mental health care.

Dr. Suzy Ismail is the Founding Director of Cornerstone Marriage & Family Intervention, a global nonprofit organization providing relational, spiritual, psycho-socio-emotional wellness services at 27 locations across the US and several international sites. She is the author of many articles, research studies, and practical books focusing on achieving holistic emotional resilience, building healthier families, and rebuilding relationships. Dr. Ismail has taught in the field of communication at several universities and developed in-depth training programs using evidence-

CONTRIBUTORS

based collectivist approaches that she has delivered extensively both nationally and internationally. She has also traveled to the border of Syria, Jordan, and Turkey to serve in refugee camps and continues to work closely with national resettlement agencies in providing integration intervention and wellness programming. Dr. Ismail holds dual master's degrees in communication and human services and a PhD in Human Services specializing in Family Studies and Intervention Strategies. She currently resides in New Jersey with her husband and three children.

Sarah Murad has been a Clinical Counselor at ICNA Relief's Chicago office since 2020, where she strives to provide Islamically integrated psychotherapy. She graduated in 2018 with a master's degree from the University of Chicago in Social Service and Administration, focusing on Psychodynamic Clinical Practice. Before that, she received her bachelor's degree in psychology from DePaul University. Sarah pursued a career in social work because she wanted to work proactively, meeting the unique needs of American Muslims, especially those who have experienced trauma, hardship, and suffering. Her passion lies in one-on-one therapy and connecting with others, she hopes to impact on the wider American-Muslim community through her work.

Subhaan Ashrafi - Founder & CEO of Sabr App. In 2011, the entrepreneur, die-hard basketball fan, and high school junior, SubTheGamer, launched his own YouTube channel dedicated to playing and talking about sports video games. The then-teenager grew his audience to more than 265,000 subscribers (with 65 million views), ultimately launching a career that has given him exclusive access to the 2K Sports and Mortal Kombat studios, invitations to various NBA arenas, and even a featured role in an NBA Finals commercial featuring NBA MVP Kevin Durant. Beyond sports, games, and YouTube, Subhaan wants to use his influence to make a difference. Subhaan is a motivational speaker, the founder of Brandsposure, a digital agency helping companies with their marketing efforts, and the founder & CEO of the Sabr App.

Dr. Tarek Zidan is an Associate Professor at the Indiana University School of Social Work (IUSSW) in Indianapolis (IUI). He worked for several years serving clients with severe mental illnesses, intellectual/developmental disabilities, and immigrants and refugees. His research interests include Muslim/Arab Americans' mental health and wellbeing. He received his BSW from the Higher Institute of Social Work in Aswan, Egypt, MSW from the Brown School of Social Work at Washington University in St. Louis, MO, and Ph.D. in social work from Howard University in Washington, D.C. He teaches research and practice evaluation in the BSW and MSW programs.

Dr. Venus Mahmoodi is an Assistant Professor at Columbia University in the Department of Psychiatry, focusing on reproductive mental health. She sees patients in the Women's and Reproductive Mental Health Program, and her research focuses on trajectories of depression from pregnancy to postpartum. Her work with Muslim women approaches their wellbeing from both an Islamic psychology and a Muslim mental health perspective. She is interested in identifying Islamic conceptualizations of womanhood and motherhood, while also understanding factors that influence their mental health and mothering. Her research and clinical training include specialization in women's neuroscience and maternal mental health.

Wadud Hassan - Co-founder of the Muraqaba app. He has also contributed to a few publications.

Waleed Sami, PhD is an assistant professor in the psychology department at The City College of New York and focuses on the graduate program in mental health counseling. Waleed's research interests examine how social and political determinants function as barriers and facilitators of health, mental health, and equity. Within this framework, the goal is to examine systemic contributors to health and wellbeing, such as political economy, income inequality, religious affiliation/culture (specifically in the Muslim-American community), and family/relational dynamics (specifically the developmental role of rough and tumble play in aggression).

Yukti Bhatt, a graduate of Rutgers University with a Bachelor of Arts in Psychology, is advancing her academic journey by pursuing a master's degree in clinical psychology at the prestigious Teachers College, Columbia University. Her research interests are centered around mood disorders and their associated treatment outcomes, with a specific focus on populations that have been historically under-researched and underserved. She is interested in the complex interplay between culture and depression, particularly as it manifests among minority groups. Ultimately, she aspires to improve access to high-quality mental health care for underrepresented communities.

INTRODUCTION

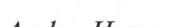

Amber Haque

Islam is the third largest religion in the US after Christianity and Judaism, yet Muslims are only 1% compared to Christians (62%) and Jews (2%) in the United States (Pew Research Center, 2023). One of the earliest records of Islam's possible presence in North America dates back to 1528, when an enslaved Moroccan, Mustafa Azemmouri, was shipwrecked in what is now Galveston, Texas (Manseau, 2015), but an estimated 10-20% of Muslims were known to have arrived in America as enslaved people from West Africa during the Atlantic slave trade (Diouf, 1998). In the late nineteenth and early twentieth century, several thousand Muslims came from the former Ottoman Empire and British India territories (Curtis, 2009). Most Muslims came to North America in the second half of the 20th century after the passage of the Immigration and Nationality Act of 1965, which abolished previous immigration quotas. Under the ruler Mohammed ben Abdullah, Morocco was the first to recognize the US as an independent nation in 1776 (Hufbauer & Brunel, 2009). The wave of Muslims coming into North America continued over the years from Muslim Majority countries, and a Gallup Poll from 2009 described Muslims as one of the most racially diverse religious groups in America (Gallup, 2009).

Despite the long history of Muslims in America, there is very little discussion about their mental health. This issue is particularly complex due to various factors, including the legacy of enslavement for some groups, the challenges of immigration and acculturation for others, and the experiences of those born in the U.S. but raised with cultural perspectives from their families. Additionally, there is a growing number of reverts or converts to Islam, especially among individuals in prison.

Islam has been a recognized practice in North America, and the Muslim population is steadily increasing. Consequently, various issues emerge within the community, impacting families, youth, the elderly, and other demographic groups. These challenges include mental health stigma within the community, drug addiction, Islamophobia, workplace issues, negative media portrayals, the role of Muslim NGOs, and recent developments in the digital landscape related to Muslim mental health. A review of the literature on Muslim mental health in North America revealed limited findings, particularly in the form of peer-reviewed journal articles.

The first issue of the Journal of Muslim Mental Health (JMMH) was published in 2006 and was an impetus for articles related to Muslims. Several articles related specifically to Muslim mental health in America appeared in the initial issues of JMMH (Rippy & Newman, 2006; Abu-Ras & Abu-Bader, 2008; Abu-Ras, Gheith, & Cournos, 2008; Aloud & Rathur, 2009; Kiely-Froude & Abdul-Karim, 2009; Ciftci, Jones, & Corrigan, 2012; Amri & Bemak, 2013; Bagasra & Mackinem, 2014).

Even before the establishment of JMMH, an article on the mental health of Muslim Americans appeared in the Journal of Religion and Health (Haque, 2004), and on Arab American mental health post-September 11 era appeared digitally (Amer, 2005). Subsequently, the mental health of Muslim Americans started to appear in different journals (Khuwaja et al., 2007; Abu-Ras et al., 2010; Basit & Hamid, 2010; Amer & Hovey, 2012; Ahmed & Reddy, 2007; Padela et al., 2013; Phillips & Lauterbach, 2017). A unique and more recent publication addressing the formation, operation, and evaluation of a community advisory board of Muslims to address local Muslim mental health needs is very encouraging (Ali et al., 2023). Islamophobia and mental health articles also surfaced, including the effects on Muslim children (Farooqui & Kaushik, 2021; Lajevardi &

INTRODUCTION

Oskooii, 2018). A few articles appeared on the Canadian scene, like trauma and religious coping among Afghan refugees (Gokani et al., 2023), women's mental health (Islam et al., 2024), and a dissertation on collaborative inquiry into discrimination and Muslim women's mental health (Hunt, 2019).

Although there are more publications on Muslim mental health in North America, the overall numbers remain unimpressive. The increasing population and numbers of Muslims and their myriad challenges have left the community at a loss and looking for answers. North American Muslims represent a resilient group facing social and political challenges, yet they are often overlooked in discussions about mental health. Despite ongoing efforts to address cultural sensitivities in academia and practice for minority populations, there is a lack of emphasis on understanding and improving the mental health of American Muslims.

The Department of Psychiatry at Michigan State University has played a key role over the years in promoting Muslim mental health by organizing and supporting annual conferences for the last 17 years. These conferences have gained significant traction, attracting scholars and academics, researchers, practitioners, students, and other stakeholders worldwide. The editors of this volume have carefully selected topics revealed as crucial from past conferences, ensuring that the book's content is comprehensive. While some important topics were omitted due to unavailable contributors, this book covers most of them. We hope to include missing topics on Muslim mental health in a future volume.

This volume aims to explore the multifaceted nature of mental health within the larger American Muslim community. It examines how faith, cultural identity, sociopolitical challenges, and personal experiences shape mental health experiences. The book brings together perspectives from academics, researchers, clinicians, religious leaders, and community activists, providing a comprehensive overview of the mental health landscape for Muslims in America.

Section One

This section of the book contains reflections of the second editor on many years of her experiences organizing the annual conferences, starting from a table in the mosque in Michigan, to where the conferences have reached today, with hundreds of scientific papers, panels, workshops, posters and registrants joining in person and online from across the globe. From having minimal or no support at the beginning, the conference is now sponsored by multiple major organizations, highlighting the importance of continuing mental health conferences on Muslims.

Section Two

This section contains four chapters. Chapter one highlights the importance of breaking the silence on mental health stigma. While Islamic teachings emphasize the importance of mental well-being, the stigma surrounding mental illness in the Muslim world has extended into American Muslim communities, often creating barriers to seeking help and treatment. The author discusses the need for culturally sensitive methods and strategies for promoting mental health awareness within the Muslim community.

Chapter two highlights the importance of culturally relevant diagnoses and treatments, demonstrating case studies unique to Muslims and illustrating the interplay of cultural values and belief systems. It also addresses how clinicians can avoid misdiagnosis and be culturally informed about Muslim conceptualizations of mental illness and treatment practices, including culture-bound syndromes.

Chapter three discusses strategies for community-based mental health interventions in Islamic institutions, such as mosques and Islamic schools, and outlines pragmatic solutions to develop and sustain meaningful and effective mental health interventions.

Chapter four's author highlights how Islamic Psychology is the missing link in Muslim mental health. For this author, psychological well-being is hidden in spiritual and religious dimensions; thus, mental health must incorporate rich Islamic traditions and practices to develop a more holistic approach to care. He discusses the dilemma of secular versus sacred knowledge and builds a case for understanding and implementing Islamic psychology in academia, research, and practice.

Section Three

This section contains four chapters, beginning with chapter five, which focuses on the challenges faced by Muslim youth and their impact on identity and faith, often leading to negative mental health outcomes. An appendix to this chapter provides commonly asked questions and answers on taboo topics.

INTRODUCTION

Chapter six addresses the mental well-being of Muslim women, emphasizing that biological, psychological, social, and spiritual factors are essential for a comprehensive understanding of health. The authors argue that an intersectional approach is crucial for recognizing the diverse realities experienced by Muslim women, shaped by unique factors and lived experiences. This approach helps in developing culturally sensitive and inclusive mental health interventions.

Chapter seven addresses the challenges faced by South Asian Muslim American marriages and families. It discusses how socio-cultural factors, historical trauma, Islamophobia, and the difficulties related to immigration and acculturation have affected family life and mental health. The author emphasizes the unique circumstances of South Asian Muslim families and offers recommendations for mental health professionals working with this community.

Chapter eight is on the mental health of elderly Muslims, highlighting the importance of cultural competence in geriatric care. It presents an interesting examination of the differences between immigrant and U.S.-born older Muslims and the impact of a geocentric culture in Islam. The author provides a brief overview of mental health conditions specific to this age group, the unique challenges faced by older Muslims, protective factors that may help alleviate these conditions, and strategies to promote awareness, culturally competent care, and discussions on end-of-life care.

Section Four

This section is the book's largest, consisting of six chapters. It begins with chapter nine, which discusses the mental health of reverted and converted Muslims. For many, the conversion experience is life-changing, requiring significant adjustments to a new lifestyle, relationships and radical changes in belief and value systems. The authors explore the implications for clinical practice and highlight how Muslim converts may differ from those born into the faith.

Chapter ten focuses on incarcerated Muslims, a topic that has received little attention in existing literature. The authors discuss the systemic factors that affect the mental health of this overlooked population, emphasizing the need for what they call "contextual sensitivity." They provide demographic data, case examples, and an analysis of the effects of institutionalization and post-incarceration syndrome. The chapter also examines barriers to care, ways to support incarcerated Muslims, the role of religious leaders, specialized mental health care, and policy recommendations. Additionally, the authors highlight successful programs that assist Muslims during their incarceration and reentry into society.

Chapter eleven addresses trauma-informed and healing-centered care for Muslims. It discusses the repercussions of oppression and discrimination, which manifest as psychological distress due to personal experiences or exposure to racism, Islamophobia, and other forms of bias in American society. Trauma-informed approaches integrate an understanding of trauma into service delivery. In addition to a critical review of existing literature on the effects of trauma on mental health, a framework for a healing-centered approach for Muslim clients is presented, drawing from the principles of liberation psychology to enhance culturally affirming mental health care for Muslims.

Chapter twelve explores the connection between disabilities and mental health, presenting insights from MUHSEN, an organization co-founded by Shaykh Omar Suleiman that focuses on the needs of this unique population. The author analyzes disabilities and mental health from an Islamic perspective while providing data on research specific to Muslims with disabilities. This chapter features an in-depth discussion of stigma, stereotypes, and their effects on parents and caregivers, along with details on how MUHSEN addresses these challenges. It also offers recommendations for interventions and advocacy for this population and plans for future initiatives.

Chapter thirteen builds on the discussion of disabilities by providing a literature review highlighting current research areas. This includes demographics, cultural attitudes towards disability, the effects of immigration and acculturation, the role of spirituality and religious beliefs, and the necessity for culturally sensitive skills and services for this vulnerable group.

Chapter fourteen addresses the challenges associated with accurately characterizing drug use among Muslims, primarily due to underreporting driven by social and religious stigmas. Despite efforts to gather information on perceptions of drug addiction and treatment within the Muslim community in the Metropolitan Detroit area, the author had limited success. As a result, the data were primarily sourced from the Substance Abuse and Mental Health Services Administration (SAMHSA) and the National Surveys on Drug Use and Health (NSDUH). This chapter

INTRODUCTION

discusses the demographics of Muslims, and the prevalence of substance use disorders, and proposes practical paths forward.

Section Five

This section addresses contemporary issues in mental health and is divided into five chapters. Chapter fifteen focuses on the experiences of first and second-generation immigrants, specifically examining how acculturation impacts their mental health processes, behaviors, and outcomes. The authors share personal narratives that reflect their acculturation journeys and how they navigate their identities across different times and places. The chapter concludes with research, clinical practice, and policy development recommendations.

Chapter sixteen explores the historical roots of Islamophobia across various contexts, including the impact of policies, and examines how it affects the mental health and identity of Muslims. It emphasizes the need to identify risk and protective factors that can help foster resilience, highlighting the implications for theory and practice in support of Muslims' mental health.

Chapter seventeen focuses on the portrayal of Muslims in the media and its impact on mental health and well-being. Negative framing through selective news coverage, which associates Muslims with terrorism and depicts Islam as a threat to Western values, has resulted in bias, discrimination, hate crimes, and unjust policies against Muslims. The authors examine these issues in depth and discuss how mental health professionals can effectively support Muslim clients affected by negative media exposure.

Chapter eighteen focuses on mental health in the workplace. It highlights early patterns of discrimination against Muslims and the unique challenges they face, such as burnout, discrimination, and psychological stress linked to their Muslim identity. The chapter also discusses current issues, referencing data from the Council on American-Islamic Relations (CAIR), which illustrates the mental health disparities experienced by Muslims in the workplace. These challenges significantly impact employee performance and necessitate targeted support, improved coping skills, and inclusive practices. The authors propose effective solutions and future directions to foster workplace inclusivity and create a supportive work environment. Additionally, an appendix provides readers with information about US government policies and laws related to workplace mental health for employees.

Chapter nineteen discusses the digital frontiers in Muslim mental health, highlighting the transformative potential of modern digital tools in meeting the unique needs of Muslims in a way that is both culturally and spiritually aligned. Muslims can anticipate the development of mental health apps and AI technologies that are culturally tailored and seamlessly incorporate Islamic principles for personalized care. The authors advocate for collaborative efforts from academics, mental health professionals, and policymakers to address existing gaps in technology and to create effective, accessible care for Muslim communities. The chapter envisions a future where technology and spiritual competence work together to support holistic mental health care across diverse Muslim populations.

Section Six

This section on Muslim humanitarian and social service organizations contains a chapter that discusses the mental health services provided by Muslim NGOs, focusing on their historical development and the unique needs of diverse Muslim communities. It emphasizes the growing demand for culturally relevant and Islamically integrated services. The authors share insights from interviews with leaders of various organizations, highlighting common challenges such as the lack of a professional mental health infrastructure, funding issues, and the reliance on untrained Imams for mental health support. As employees of Muslim NGOs, the authors draw on their extensive experience and insights from these interviews to recommend steps for overcoming barriers to service improvement and organizational growth.

A primary goal of this book is to provide practical insights for mental health professionals working with Muslim clients. Cultural competence in mental health services is essential to ensure that Muslim clients feel understood and respected in therapeutic settings. As awareness of the need for increased services for Muslim Americans grows, the editors anticipate the establishment of an online certification program in Muslim Mental Health. The Muslim Mental Health Conference and Consortium, along with the Department of Psychiatry at MSU, aim to pursue this initiative in the near future.

The book Muslim "Mental Health in North America" could have been published by any publisher, but the editors chose to self-publish

INTRODUCTION

through the Department of Psychiatry at MSU to recognize their support for the MMHC over the past seventeen years. The proceeds from the book sales will go to MMHC. This partnership has led to many successful initiatives, and we are grateful for the support from our friends and especially the authors who contributed to this book. We hope to see more partnerships and initiatives like this throughout North America, as we strive to be change agents for the mental health of all Americans.

References

Abu-Ras, W., & Abu-Bader, S. H. (2008). The impact of the September 11, 2001, attacks on the Well-Being of Arab Americans in New York City. *Journal of Muslim Mental Health*, *3*(2), 217–239. https://doi.org/10.1080/15564900802487634

Abu-Ras, W., Gheith, A., & Cournos, F. (2008). The imam's role in mental health promotion: a study at 22 mosques in New York City's Muslim community. *Journal of Muslim Mental Health*, *3*(2), 155–176. https://doi.org/10.1080/15564900802487576

Abu-Ras, W., Ali, O. M., Ansari, B., Hamid, H., Haque, S., Mahmood, O., et al. (2010). Addressing mental health issues among American Muslims in the military. Institute for Social Policy and Understanding. Retrieved from https://www.ispu.org/addressing-health-issues-among-american-muslims-in-the-military/

Ahmed, S., & Reddy, L. A. (2007). Understanding the mental health needs of American Muslims: Recommendations and considerations for practice. *Journal of Multicultural Counseling and Development*, *35*(4), 207–218. https://doi.org/10.1002/j.2161-1912.2007.tb00061.x

Ali, S. S., Mahoui, I., Hassoun, R., Mojaddidi, H., & Awaad, R. (2023). The Bay Area Muslim mental health community advisory board: evaluation of a community based participatory approach. *Epidemiology and Psychiatric Sciences*, *32*. https://doi.org/10.1017/s2045796022000786

Aloud, N., & Rathur, A. (2009). Factors affecting attitudes toward seeking and using formal mental health and psychological services among Arab Muslim populations. *Journal of Muslim Mental Health*, *4*(2), 79–103. https://doi.org/10.1080/15564900802487675

Amer, M. M. (2005). Arab American mental health in the post-September 11 era: Acculturation, stress, and coping. Retrieved at the University of Toledo Digital Repository. https://utdr.utoledo.edu/cgi/viewcontent.cgi?article=2424&context=theses-dissertations

Amer, M. M., & Hovey, J. D. (2012). Anxiety and depression in a post-September 11 sample of Arabs in the USA. *Social Psychiatry and Psychiatric Epidemiology*, *47*(3), 409–418. https://doi.org/10.1007/s00127-011-0341-4

Amri, S., & Bemak, F. (2013). Mental Health Help-Seeking Behaviors of Muslim Immigrants in the United States: Overcoming social stigma and cultural mistrust. *Journal of Muslim Mental Health*, *7*(1). https://doi.org/10.3998/jmmh.10381607.0007.104

Bagasra, A., & Mackinem, M. (2014). An exploratory study of American Muslim conceptions of mental illness. *Journal of Muslim Mental Health*, *8*(1). https://doi.org/10.3998/jmmh.10381607.0008.104

Basit, A., & Hamid, M. (2010). Mental health issues of Muslim Americans. *Journal of the Islamic Medical Association of North America*, *42*(3). https://doi.org/10.5915/42-3-5507

Ciftci, A., Jones, N., & Corrigan, P. W. (2012). Mental health stigma in the Muslim community. *Journal of Muslim Mental Health*, *7*(1). https://doi.org/10.3998/jmmh.10381607.0007.102

INTRODUCTION

Curtis, E. E. (2009). Muslims in America: A Short History.
Diouf, S. A. (1998). *Servants of Allah: African Muslims Enslaved in the Americas.*
Farooqui JF and Kaushik A (2021). Understanding Islamophobia through the eyes of American Muslim children: religious bullying and school social work interventions. *Child & Family Social Work* 26, 454–466.
Gallup (2009). *Muslim Americans Exemplify, Diversity, Potential.* Muslim Americans exemplify diversity, potential - Euro-islam.info
Gokani, R., Wiebe, S., Sherzad, H., & Akesson, B. (2023). "We're Looking for Support from Allah": A Qualitative Study on the Experiences of Trauma and Religious Coping among Afghan Refugees in Canada Following the August 2021 Withdrawal. *Religions, 14*(5), 645. https://doi.org/10.3390/rel14050645
Haque, A. (2004). Religion and Mental Health: The Case of American Muslims. *Journal of Religion and Health, 43,* 1, 45-58.
Hufbauer, G. C. & Brunel, C. (Eds.) (2009). Capitalizing on the Morocco-US Free Trade Agreement: A Road Map for Success. Peter Institute for International Economics, Pg. 1. Retrieved April 10, 2025. Capitalizing on the Morocco-US Free Trade Agreement: A Road Map for Success - Google Books
Hunt, B. (2019). The Muslimah Project: A Collaborative Inquiry Into Discrimination And Muslim Women's Mental Health In A Canadian Context" (2019). Theses and Dissertations (Comprehensive). 2206. https://scholars.wlu.ca/etd/2206
Islam, F., Qasim, K., Qutub, A., Ali-Mohammed, S., Abdulwasi, M., Shakya, Y., Hynie, M., & McKenzie, K. (2024). Mental health at the intersections: understanding South Asian Muslim youth mental health in Peel Region, Toronto, Canada. *International Journal of Migration Health and Social Care, 20*(4), 613–633. https://doi.org/10.1108/ijmhsc-04-2024-0046
Kiely-Froude, C., & Abdul-Karim, S. (2009). Providing culturally conscious mental health treatment for African American Muslim women living with spousal abuse. *Journal of Muslim Mental Health, 4*(2), 175–186. https://doi.org/10.1080/15564900903245824
Khuwaja, S. A., Selwyn, B. J., Kapadia, A., McCurdy, S., & Khuwaja, A. (2006). Pakistani Ismaili Muslim Adolescent Females Living in the United States of America: Stresses Associated with the Process of Adaptation to U.S. Culture. *Journal of Immigrant and Minority Health, 9*(1). https://doi.org/10.1007/s10903-006-9013-y
Lajevardi, N., & Oskooii, K. (2018). Old-Fashioned racism, contemporary Islamophobia, and the isolation of Muslim Americans in the age of Trump. *The Journal of Race Ethnicity and Politics, 3*(1), 112–152. https://doi.org/10.1017/rep.2017.37
Manseau, P. (2015). The Muslims of Early America. The New York Times. Retrieved April 10, 2025. Opinion | The Muslims of Early America - The New York Times
Padela, A. I., Killawi, A., Heisler, M., Demonner, S., & Fetters, M. D. (2010). The role of imams in American Muslim health: Perspectives of Muslim community leaders in Southeast Michigan. *Journal of Religion and Health, 50*(2), 359–373. https://doi.org/10.1007/s10943-010-9428-6

PEW Research Center, Washington, D.C. (2023). Muslims | Religious Landscape Study | Pew Research Center

Phillips, D., & Lauterbach, D. (2017). American Muslim immigrant mental health: The role of racism and mental health stigma. *Journal of Muslim Mental Health, 11*(1), 39–56. https://doi.org/10.3998/jmmh.10381607.0011.103

Reich, M., Jarvis, G. E., & Whitley, R. (2024). Examining recovery and mental health service satisfaction among young immigrant Muslim women with mental distress in Quebec. *BMC Psychiatry, 24*(1). https://doi.org/10.1186/s12888-024-05940-8

Rippy, A. E., & Newman, E. (2006). Perceived Religious Discrimination and its Relationship to Anxiety and Paranoia Among Muslim Americans. *Journal of Muslim Mental Health, 1*(1), 5–20. https://doi.org/10.1080/15564900600654351

SECTION ONE

MUSLIM MENTAL HEALTH CONFERENCE

HISTORY OF MUSLIM MENTAL HEALTH CONFERENCES (2008-2025)

Farha Abbasi

Introduction

It all began in an empty booth with a single table, a silent crowd, and a moment of clarity. What felt like failure that day turned out to be the start of something much larger: a journey to break the silence, build trust, and reimagine what care means in our communities.

"You should go sit with her," a man said, urging his wife while gesturing toward me sympathetically. I was sitting alone in an abandoned booth at the local Islamic center, where a small sign reading "Depression Screening" hung above the table. His words captured the discomfort and reluctance that filled the air—no one wanted to be seen approaching a booth associated with mental health.

Nearly two decades ago, during a health fair at the Islamic center, I first encountered the deep-rooted stigma surrounding mental health in the Muslim community. I had hoped to engage people in conversations about emotional well-being, but instead, I found myself sitting in silence, feeling ignored.

A few weeks later, the importance of addressing this issue became urgent. I was called to an Islamic center in Michigan to assist a family in crisis. Their son was experiencing a severe psychotic episode and had expressed homicidal thoughts, threatening his own family. The police were already involved, and the situation was dire.

We soon learned that the young man, in his delusional state, had gone to the Islamic center for Jummah prayer, which provided a rare opportunity for him to be admitted safely to the hospital. However, the family felt paralyzed—not by fear for their son's life, but by the fear of judgment from their community.

"We cannot admit him in front of everyone," they pleaded. "What will others think of us?"

I was stunned. In a moment that demanded compassion and medical intervention, the family prioritized their reputation over safety. To them, psychosis wasn't seen as a medical emergency; it was regarded as a shameful secret. This incident made it clear to me that the issue was not just clinical; it was cultural. The shame and stigma surrounding mental illness were so deeply ingrained that they overshadowed love, logic, and even self-preservation.

That day, something changed within me. I had long been aware of the existence of stigma, but I had underestimated its power—how deeply it could penetrate and how it could override even the most fundamental instinct to protect one's child.

It became clear to me that mental health issues cannot be addressed in isolation. We cannot treat individuals without also considering the needs of the community. Silence, shame, and fear are all integral parts of the illness.

For real change to happen, it needs to begin in places that often resist it the most. Mosques, Islamic centers, and community gatherings serve not only as places of worship but also as the cultural heart of Muslim life. By engaging in meaningful conversations within these spaces, we can heal individuals, families, neighbors, and future generations.

What initially began as frustration transformed into a call to action. I reached out to colleagues, scholars, counselors, and community leaders. What if we brought all these voices together? What if we created an environment where mental health was not considered taboo, but rather a central topic of discussion? This idea became the foundation for the Muslim Mental Health Conference.

Visibility to Viability

When I first began to address mental health issues within the Muslim community, I encountered significant silence, resistance, and even hostility. The stigma surrounding these topics was overwhelming, and the message was clear: being Muslim in post-9/11 America meant remaining invisible, laying low, and avoiding attention—essentially navigating life in the shadows. Speaking out about mental health was not only considered taboo; it was viewed as an act of defiance.

The idea of becoming invisible was not new to us. In the years following September 11, 2001, Muslims in the United States were often advised to blend in: to refrain from speaking our native languages in public, avoid traditional dress, and keep our heads down. The fear was palpable, as was the social pressure to disappear. However, for me, the urgency to speak outgrew increasingly pressing.

I observed that many individuals were suffering in silence, bearing the dual burden of religious discrimination and unrecognized mental health challenges. We lacked safe spaces—places where we could openly discuss anxiety, trauma, depression, and grief without the fear of judgment or alienation. Our pain remained invisible, and our solutions felt out of reach.

This realization inspired the idea for the Muslim Mental Health Conference. I envisioned a gathering where academics, clinicians, faith leaders, and community members could come together to identify problems and promote healing. The conference would be rooted in cultural and spiritual relevance, serving as a forum for connection, compassion, and action.

A conference meeting the highest academic standards will showcase peer-reviewed research presentations, training sessions, and community discussions that emphasize religious sensitivity.

At that time, establishing such a space seemed unattainable. "Muslim mental health" had not yet been acknowledged as a distinct field. There was no existing blueprint, no established infrastructure, and only a handful of pioneering researchers and clinicians working in this area.

I reached out to researchers such as Mona Amer, a scholar specializing in stigma within Arab American communities, and Hamada Altalib, the Chief Editor of The Journal of Muslim Mental Health. I was encouraged to find that research was being conducted and that some practitioners genuinely cared. However, I noticed that their work was fragmented and not effectively translated into the care our community needed.

In 2008, I was awarded a SAMHSA Minority Fellowship and Grant through the American Psychiatric Association. I submitted a proposal to establish a Muslim Mental Health Conference, which was accepted.

The post-9/11 era presented significant challenges for initiating an initiative focused on the Muslim community. Islamophobia was increasing, leading to widespread suspicion and scrutiny of anything related to Muslim identity. Starting a mental health movement in such an environment demands vision and courage. However, it was precisely within this context that the need for culturally competent mental health care became even more critical.

From the beginning, I encountered backlash and resistance. Many people questioned the relevance of this initiative, asking why we needed a Muslim Mental Health Conference. Some colleagues argued, "There's no such thing as a Christian or Jewish mental health conference. Why should there be one for Muslims? Why not just hold an inclusive mental health conference?"

When the first conference was announced, I received two very different emails. One was from a Muslim imam who expressed deep concern over the use of the terms "Muslim" and "mental" in the same sentence. He feared that this association would pathologize Muslims and lead to further discrimination. The other email came from someone who thanked me for "finally fixing them," suggesting that Muslims were inherently broken. It became clear that this conference was essential—not only to address mental health issues but also to bridge the gap of misunderstanding and stigma surrounding Muslims.

The Muslim community faces unique challenges that require culturally responsive mental health care, a need that was previously unaddressed. The conference aimed not only to discuss academic research but also to translate that research into practical support for Muslims struggling with mental health issues in an often hostile and stigmatizing environment. It focused on breaking the silence, fostering understanding, and creating a space conducive to healing.

The Muslim Mental Health Conference (MMHC) has sparked a transformative movement, placing mental health at the forefront of discussions within Muslim communities. Its rapid evolution from a small local event to a global movement highlights a significant and previously overlooked demand for culturally competent mental health resources in these communities.

The field of Muslim mental health has evolved significantly and is now recognized as a legitimate discipline. Islamic psychology has gained acceptance as a valid framework for providing care.

The MMHC is a leading initiative focused on addressing mental health issues within faith-based communities. It brings together faith leaders, researchers, and community members, along with academic partners such as Michigan State University, to address the specific needs of these communities. MMHC is not only the longest-running conference of its kind but also the most comprehensive and sustained global initiative in this area.

For the past 17 years, Michigan State University (MSU) has generously hosted the conference. This event has showcased the university's dedication to diversity, equity, and inclusion, establishing MSU as a leader in addressing the mental health needs of marginalized communities. The conference has become essential to the university's mission of promoting social justice and equity, particularly in communities where discussions about mental health have historically been considered taboo.

Vision

The conference aimed to create a space that is both Islamic in sensibility and rigorous in its academic approach. The goal was not to proselytize or teach religion; rather, it was to develop a culturally and religiously appropriate model of care that truly resonates with our community. At the same time, the conference was designed to be secular and accessible, welcoming a diverse range of religious beliefs and cultural practices among Muslims.

We intentionally scheduled the conference to begin on Friday to bring everyone together for congregational prayer. The khutbah (sermon) was meant to reinforce the message of mental wellness, using this platform to raise awareness and destigmatize struggles with mental health. Striking a balance between faith and scholarship was challenging but essential for creating the safe, inclusive space we envisioned.

Mission

When I founded the MMHC, I had specific goals in mind: to combat stigma, create a safe space, and translate research into practical care. These objectives have guided the conference and continue to shape its mission today.

Early on, I framed these goals as the "3 A's" of our conference proposal: Awareness, Acceptance, and Access.

Awareness is about educating our communities that mental illness is not a sign of spiritual weakness. While faith can serve as a powerful source of healing, facing mental health challenges does not indicate a lack of faith. It is crucial to break the silence, challenge harmful narratives, and engage in open discussions about mental health issues.

Acceptance means recognizing that our close-knit, family-oriented communities are not immune to mental illness. We face the same struggles as other groups, often made worse by marginalization and discrimination. Acknowledging our vulnerabilities is a vital step toward healing.

Access has concentrated on improving the availability of culturally and religiously competent mental health care. We needed to identify the barriers that prevent people from seeking help and ensure that services are relevant and respectful of Muslim values and identities.

In recent years, I have added a fourth "A": advocacy. Addressing mental health in the Muslim community must go beyond education and clinical care; it must also involve pursuing structural change. In a time when Islamophobia is still widespread, advocating for the mental well-being of our communities is not just helpful; it is essential. This work extends beyond conferences and research labs; it includes engaging in public policy, championing systemic equity, and recognizing that the mental health of marginalized communities is inherently political.

Early Years: Building a Foundation

MMHC started with modest goals, but it has since evolved into a global movement that has transformed the approach to mental health issues within the Muslim community. What began as a small, uncertain gathering of interdisciplinary professionals has become a robust platform that unites scholars, clinicians, and community leaders worldwide.

2009 Conference

Islam and Medicine: Treating Muslims from a Mental Health Perspective

The goal of the event was clear: to bring together professionals from various disciplines to discuss the relationship between Islam, mental health, and wellness. Hamada Altalib, the Chief Editor of the Journal of Muslim Mental Health, which we recently began hosting at Michigan State University, helped identify the speakers and topics that would be presented at the conference. The gathering was small and intimate, consisting of 30 to 40 attendees. We also provided a complimentary dinner for this one-day event.

The inaugural keynote speaker was Mouhanad Hammami, MD. He delivered an eloquent and impactful presentation titled "Mental Health in the Muslim and Arab World: Now and Then," which explored the connection between Islam and health models. His talk left a lasting impression on the attendees. The ambience of the conference was relaxed, fostering enriching conversations.

James Hillard, Provost for Health at Michigan State University, began the event with a welcoming speech. Other presenters included Rania Awaad, Hend Azhary, Adnan Hammad, Cynthia Arfken, Ibrahim Kira, Brian Smith, Sameera Ahmed, Aneesah Nadir, Osman Ali, and Wahiba Abu Ras.

The topics discussed at the conference included attitudes and barriers to mental health services, substance abuse among Arab Americans, refugee mental health, adolescent mental health, premarital and marital counseling, the role of imams, and the needs assessment of Islamic chaplain services.

The inaugural conference marked a significant milestone. At that time, many believed it would be a one-time event with a limited future—an ambitious idea that would come and go. Few recognized its potential or believed that it could evolve into a sustained and impactful movement.

It Takes a Village: Building Sustainability

As the conference progressed, I realized that sustaining a long-term initiative required more than just passion and dedication—it demanded a collective effort. Keeping the vision alive relied on a network of allies, supporters, and strategic partners. In the early years, the MMHC primarily depended on grant funding. However, when that funding ran out, I knew I had to pivot. I focused intensely on building relationships, engaging in networking, and forming meaningful partnerships. I began to present on Muslim mental health wherever possible—at cultural events, academic forums, and diversity panels—ensuring that the conversation remained visible and relevant.

The presentations led to the establishment of important relationships, particularly with Norma Baptista, a Medical Education Specialist and the Director of Faculty Development at Michigan State University's College of Osteopathic Medicine. Norma recognized the significance of this work and played a vital role in hosting the conference as part of the Statewide Campus System at the College of Osteopathic Medicine. Her support was essential in providing the MMHC with a formal academic home, which enhanced its credibility within the medical education community.

2010 Conference

The Myths and Realities of the Relationship Between Mental Health, Violence, and Muslims.

The keynote address was delivered by David Schazner, JD, from the Sanford School of Public Policy at Duke University. His presentation was titled "Anti-Terror Lessons of American Muslims." Amin A. Gadit discussed "Terrorism and Mental Health: The Global Misery." Neil Aggarwal presented on "Forensic Evaluation for Guantanamo Detainees." Chaplain Abdul Rashid, the first Muslim chaplain to serve in the American Army, spoke about "Lessons from Fort Hood." Psychoanalyst Aisha Abbasi gave a talk titled "Whose Side Are You On? Muslim Psychoanalyst - Non-Muslim Analysis." Wahiba Abu Ras presented on the "Muslim Perception of Discrimination and PTSD Symptoms Post 9/11." Janine Sinno discussed "Refugee Health," while Batool Kazim addressed "Breaking the Silence on Domestic Violence." Daniel Tutt presented on the "Impact of Media."

This conference marked a significant turning point, with broader and more diverse participation. Key figures, such as Hamada Altalib and Zareena Grewal, made important contributions to the discourse. Anelle Primm, the Director of the Minority Fellowship at the American Psychiatric Association, introduced the Minority Fellowship to the community.

2011 Conference: ACCEPT

Learning the Art of Coexistence and Resilience in Conflicting Times

The 2011 conference focused on resilience in the face of adversity, particularly in the decade following September 11, 2001. Our special guest, Congressman André Carson, one of the few Muslims elected to Congress, highlighted the importance of destigmatizing mental health issues and promoting unity within the American community. His inspirational speech on personal struggle and resilience deeply resonated with a community in search of its identity, leaving a lasting impact.

The keynote address was delivered by Juan R. Cole, on the topic "Going Beyond Islamophobia: Challenges of Pluralism in 21st Century America." He emphasized the media's misrepresentation of Muslims and advocated for greater Muslim involvement in fields such as journalism and public office.

Farha Abbasi and Zain Shamoon addressed the psychological impact of these issues on Muslim American students. Zain Shamoon, a specialist in human development and family therapy, highlighted the challenges of identity and discrimination that adolescents encounter during this critical phase of psychological growth.

Key figures such as Sameera Ahmed, Hamada Altalib, Khalida Zaki, Professor Emeritus of Sociology, and Halim Naeem led panels that discussed the growth of Muslim mental health professionals. Frank Ochberg, a pioneer in trauma science, delivered a keynote address on the unique traumatic effects of cruelty. Juan Cole emphasized the media's misrepresentation of Muslims and advocated for increased Muslim participation in journalism and public office.

During this time, I noticed a shift in the nature of the conversations emerging at the conference. Attendees began to express important concerns about the lack of diversity, particularly regarding the underrepresentation of Black Muslims.

This feedback led to meaningful changes within our community. Pioneers in Black Muslim psychology, such as Cheryl El-Amine and Halim Naeem, took on greater leadership roles at the conference, which helped create a more inclusive and representative environment. Kameelah Mumin, who is now the leader of the Black Muslim Psychology Conference, conducted an Imam training session in Detroit. This marked the beginning of a formal collaboration with Black Muslim leaders.

Around the same time, Aneesah Nadir, a prominent Black Muslim social worker from Islamic Social Services Association, joined our efforts. Her involvement significantly enriched our programming. Today, she remains an essential member of our annual planning committee, ensuring that our work is grounded in diversity, equity, and cultural authenticity.

As we made steady progress, we encountered a significant challenge in our third year: we ran out of funding. This was a critical moment that jeopardized the future of the conference. Fortunately, Jose Herrera, who was my junior resident at the time, stepped up to help. He had been awarded the same minority fellowship that had previously supported me and made a bold and generous decision to use his fellowship grant funds to keep the MMHC running for two more years. His dedication and belief in our mission were instrumental in ensuring the conference could continue when it seemed we were at a standstill.

2012 Conference

Empowering Community Workers- Training Of Imams, Chaplains and Community Leaders as Mental Health workers

The 2012 conference highlighted the vital role of faith leaders in promoting mental health awareness within Muslim communities. Wahiba Abu-Ras delivered a talk on the involvement of imams in mental health promotion and was awarded a certificate in recognition of her contributions. Sameera

Ahmed discussed the challenges faced by at-risk Muslim adolescents, emphasizing the need for effective pastoral interventions. Additionally, a significant panel led by Imam Jones, Chaplain Negedu, and Chaplain Yahya examined the collaboration between imams and chaplains, addressing the relationship between counseling, mental health, and religious leadership.

Virg Bernero, the Mayor of Lansing, delivered a keynote speech highlighting the importance of mental health awareness and the necessity of addressing the stigma associated with it. Chaplain Abdul-Rasheed Muhammad, the first Islamic chaplain in the U.S. Armed Forces, spoke about the significance of having spiritual advisors who can empathize with communities that are often viewed as "other."

2013 Conference

Promoting access to Mental health care and Mental Health First Aid (MHFA) training for Imams and Community leaders

The conference was organized in partnership with the Common Bond Institute's "Compassion for Others" program. Sponsored by Michigan State University, the event focused on addressing depression as a significant social issue. It took place at the DoubleTree Hotel in Detroit.

First Aid training was provided by Jean Wright and Kameelah Mu'min, and it was attended by 50 Imams from Michigan, including Imam Mohammad Ali Elahi.

The Fight for Financial Stability

As the conference expanded, so did the need for consistent funding. I began reaching out to various departments at MSU to request modest contributions that would help sustain the MMHC. Each year, I delivered nearly 200 presentations on Muslim mental health, viewing each one as an opportunity to raise awareness and attract potential donors.

Initially, there was some hesitation. Many people did not fully understand the importance or urgency of our work. However, as awareness grew, we started to receive small donations—$500 here, $250 there. Gradually, MSU began to recognize the value of the conference. Unbeknownst to them, the university became the primary source of support for the survival of the MMHC.

By the third year, the College of Osteopathic Medicine awarded us a $5,000 grant, which became a crucial financial foundation for the conference. Other departments contributed smaller amounts, allowing us to operate on a tight but sustainable budget. This collective effort, along with strategic partnerships and a shared sense of purpose, helped the conference thrive in its early years.

In the ninth year, we introduced a small registration fee to help cover expenses. Despite this change, the conference continued to grow in both size and reputation, solidifying its status as an essential gathering for those committed to Muslim mental health.

2014 Conference

Promoting Access to Mental Health Care, Challenging Stigma in the Muslim Community, Eliminating Barriers to Seeking Services

The 2014 conference focused on eliminating barriers to mental health services for Muslim Americans. Congressman John Dingell, a prominent advocate for healthcare reform, served as the keynote speaker and emphasized the importance of access to mental health care. Senator Debbie Stabenow, another key supporter, highlighted her commitment to mental health through legislation such as the Patient Protection and Affordable Care Act.

Halim Naeem shared personal stories of resilience, emphasizing that respect, reconciliation, and resilience are essential pillars for mental health. Imam Mohammad Ali Elahi also participated, offering religious support for the discussion on mental health.

2015 Conference

Faith and Healing: Moving from Trauma to Empowerment

The conference opened with a powerful message from US Surgeon General Vice Admiral Vivek H. Murthy. For the first time, childhood trauma and the impact of Adverse Childhood Experiences (ACEs) were discussed by Tina Hahn. Sponsored by the Department of Health and Human Services - Center for Faith-Based and Neighborhood Partnerships, an interfaith training on trauma-informed congregations was presented.

Other notable presentations included Jeff Putthoff, SJ, who explored emerging models in congregations, focusing on ACEs and vicarious trauma while introducing the Sanctuary model. Chaplain Asma Hanif, Executive Director of *Muslimat al Nisa, Inc.*, spoke about creating a shelter for homeless women in the Muslim community. Nicole Wood from the US Department of Homeland Security addressed human trafficking, while Kimberly Konkel, Associate Director of the US Department of Health and Human Services, discussed domestic violence. Finally, Reverend Talitha Arnold and David A. Litts presented on preventing suicide and the active role faith communities can take in this effort.

Prominent presenters included Hooman Keshavarzi, Sameera Ahmad, Maryam Qureshi, Olubunmi Oyewuwo-Gassikia, Rami Nsour, Rania Awaad, Hanan Hashem, Nadia Bazzi, Kameelah Mu'min Rashad, and Halim Naeem.

Melody Moezzi, JD, MPH, an award-winning author, activist, and UN global expert, delivered a TED-style talk about her personal journey with bipolar illness. Aisha Abbasi, a psychoanalyst and the president of the Michigan Psychoanalytic Institute, also presented on the topic "You Are Welcome to My Heart: The Trials, Tribulations, and Triumphs of Living With and Loving My Mother." Congressional greetings were presented by Debbie Dingell.

The 7th Annual Conference in 2015 was significant for launching the "Narratives of Pain" program, which emphasized personal stories of suffering and healing within the Muslim community through performance art. Congresswoman Debbie Dingell was honored for her ongoing advocacy for mental health. Additionally, Alean Al-Krenawi and Imam Magid participated in discussions about the intersection of faith and mental health. Notable institutions involved included Ben Gurion University of Negev, Shaheed Benazir Bhutto Women University of Peshawar, and Professor Unaiza Niaz from Pakistan.

2016 Conference

Peace and Justice: Building Harmony Between Psyche and Law

In 2016, the theme centered on the intersection of law and mental health, particularly regarding substance abuse. Farha Abbasi, along with Cynthia Arfken and Judge Linda Davis, led a workshop specifically focused on opioid dependence and treatment for imams. They examined the biological and psychological impacts of addiction and discussed how legal systems can better collaborate with medical professionals to support recovery. Notable attendees included Barb McQuade, a former U.S. Attorney, and Cheryl El-Amin.

2017 Conference

Understanding addiction among Muslim Populations

At this conference, there was a Mental Health First Responder Certification Training offered by Khalil Center, with presentations by Hooman Keshavarzi and Fahad Khan. The 2017 conference was groundbreaking due to its focus on the psychology of Black Muslims. Halim Naeem led a session that addressed the unique psychological challenges faced by this community, which included discussions by Sylvia Chan-Malik and Donna Auston.

The Islamic Psychology panel featured presentations by Carrie York Al Karam, Fyeqa Sheikh, and Mutal Khan. Notable attendees included Senator Curtis Hertel and Farhan Bhatti. William Slaughter from Harvard University delivered a talk on refugee mental health, emphasizing the importance of a global perspective on mental well-being. Additionally, Cynthia Arfken presented on substance abuse and its implications for global public health, another key session at the conference.

Prominent presenters included Alean Al-Krenawi, Afifa Anjum, Zubaida Laota, Neil Vincent, Khadijah Khudeira, Tarek Zidan, Hikmat Jamil, and Fatima Salman, the Executive Director of the Muslim Students Association in America. Rukhsana Chaudry from the American Muslim Health Professionals, Nahid Aziz, Cheryl El Amin, and Aneesah Nadir also contributed. Furthermore, Rabia Toor and Sneha Antony showcased their documentary on Muslim mental health.

2018 Conference

Out of the shackles: Pursuit of Civil Justice in the face of Psychological Trauma

The 2018 conference at the U.S. Institute of Peace attracted more than 300 participants. Congresswoman Debbie Dingell served as the keynote speaker, highlighting the importance of compassion and mental health advocacy at both local and federal levels. Kameelah Mumin-Rashad from the Muslim Wellness Foundation addressed the issue of racism within Muslim communities, particularly focusing on the experiences of Black Muslims. Talat Hamdani gave a heartfelt talk about her son, a Muslim-American first responder who lost his life during the 9/11 attacks.

The conference also featured a Black Muslim Psychology Panel with prominent speakers including Halim Naeem, Kameelah Mumin-Rashad, and Ulrick Vieux. Mona Amer provided the keynote address. Sarah Mohr described the event as follows: "The 10th Annual Muslim Mental Health Conference is a platform for Muslim mental health professionals to gather, collaborate on new ideas and goals, and strengthen our ties to each other in our shared vision of mental health for our community."

2019 Conference

Putting in the Work, Service and Advocacy for Mental Health in Muslim Communities

The 2019 conference held in Tempe, Arizona, focused on the psychological effects of Islamophobia on Muslim Americans. Imman Musa presented research demonstrating that Islamophobia contributes to increased symptoms of depression, anxiety, and stress among this community. The research proposed a therapeutic approach that includes educating individuals about systemic oppression and reinforcing Muslim identity as a protective factor. The keynote address, titled "Mental Health, Religion, and Spirituality," was delivered by Marwa Azab. Additionally, the Islamic Social Services Association celebrated its 10th anniversary at the conference.

2020 Conference

Islamic Psychology and Muslim Mental Health

Due to the COVID-19 pandemic, the 2020 conference was held virtually, attracting over 500 attendees from around the world, including a significant group of 40 participants from Ibn Haldun University (IHU) in Turkey. Recep Senturk, Rector of IHU, delivered the keynote address on integrating Islamic psychology with modern therapeutic practices. The conference featured a general Muslim mental health track that included sessions on cultural competence, trauma healing, and interpersonal violence. Additionally, the Islamic psychology track focused on Islamic cognitive interventions and faith-based psychotherapy approaches.

2021 Conference

Restorative Healing and Liberation

The theme of the 2021 conference was healing and liberation. Notable presentations included "From Healing to Liberation" by Shamaila Khan and Tahirah Abdullah. Jabbar R. Bennett, Vice President and Chief Diversity Officer at Michigan State University, participated in discussions about diversity and inclusion in mental health. A key session led by Julie Rostina and Marnaria Martinis explored the psychological needs of individuals living with HIV/AIDS in Muslim communities. Additionally, Sufi music therapy was introduced as an innovative mental health intervention for mild to moderate depression.

2022 Conference

Fragility Unmasked, Emerging from Social Isolation, Social Inequality and Covid

The unprecedented challenges posed by the COVID-19 pandemic and the resulting global lockdowns have revealed our vulnerabilities and longstanding social inequalities. These challenges have profoundly affected society and our mental health as we navigate ongoing transitions. Our understanding of the pandemic's impact is evolving and will continue to grow, highlighting the lessons we've learned about adaptation.

In this year's conference, we invited discussions on how COVID-19 has influenced professional practices: what insights have been gained, how practices have shifted, what research has emerged, and what visions we have for the future of the mental health field in the COVID-19 era. We welcomed perspectives from practitioners, community organizations, researchers, and religious leaders, seeking diverse viewpoints on how COVID-19 has reflected our vulnerabilities and how we have responded to rise to the occasion.

Yale University hosted the 14th Annual MMHC, marking its first hybrid format, allowing participants to attend either in person or virtually. Juliane Hammer delivered the keynote address, which focused on the dual role of Islam as both a resource and an obstacle in addressing domestic violence within Muslim communities. Substance abuse in the Arab American community was a significant theme, emphasized by presentations from mental health practitioners Hala Mallah and Mona Hijazi. Additionally, Sheeza Mohsin discussed the challenges of bicultural identity faced by Muslim families and how these stressors impact mental wellness.

2023 Conference

Honoring Legacies, Reflecting on Progress, and Envisioning New Horizons

The 2023 conference was held as a hybrid event, with both in-person and virtual attendance at Michigan State University. The theme centered on recognizing Muslims' historical contributions to the field of mental health while also exploring future advancements. Notable presentations included Amber Haque's discussion on the role of spiritual and culturally-based counseling by early Islamic scholars, as well as a session on Islamic-based psychological therapy led by Abdur Rasjid Skinner and Zakia Jabeen. These sessions underscored the importance of integrating Islamic principles with modern psychological practices.

2024 Conference

Tech-NO or Tech-YES: The Digital Divide Between Muslims and Their Mental Health

The 16th Annual Muslim Mental Health Conference, held at Stanford University in 2024, focused on the important theme of "The Digital Divide Between Muslims and Their Mental Health." This sold-out event drew over 500 participants, including leading experts, mental health professionals, trainees, and community leaders from more than 30 countries.

The conference examined the intersection of technology and mental health within the Muslim community, highlighting both the challenges and opportunities the digital world presents for mental health care. With a diverse lineup of speakers, the event fostered engaging discussions on how digital tools can either bridge or exacerbate gaps in mental health support for Muslims. Topics covered included Islamic psychology and various broader issues related to Muslim mental health.

Overall, the conference served as a platform for collaboration and innovation, providing participants with valuable insights to help them navigate the digital landscape in their professional practices.

2025 Conference
Building Resilience Through Resistance and Collective Care

The 17th Annual MMHC was held at the Muslim-owned SoHo Banquet Hall in Metro Detroit, marking a significant evolution for the event. This year's theme, "Building Resilience Through Resistance and Collective Care," showcased MMHC's growing influence as a national platform for culturally relevant dialogue, clinical innovation, and transformative community care.

In a strategic decision, MMHC relocated off-campus to improve safety, accessibility, and autonomy. This change fostered an environment where meaningful discussions and academic excellence could thrive. Michigan State University played a crucial role as a host and supporter by providing sponsorship and a strong faculty presence, which contributed to the conference's growth while maintaining its independence.

More than 460 attendees participated in over 115 sessions, which featured a keynote address by Su'ad Abdul Khabeer, a legacy panel honoring the resilience of Black Muslim Americans, an interfaith panel sponsored by the American Psychiatric Association Foundation, and specialized training for imams led by the Peaceful Families Project. Another highlight was the presence of Congresswoman Rashida Tlaib, who stands as the epitome of resilience and leadership, having transformed adversity into purpose and challenges into collective progress for the community. These key moments reflected MMHC's commitment to providing care that is integrated with faith and responsive to the community's needs.

This year, MMHC made significant strides in both content and creativity. We introduced new art abstracts alongside beloved staples such as the "Narratives of Pain" and the "Artist Declarations Gala." Our sponsor engagement increased significantly, with 40 sponsors and over 118,000 digital impressions, resulting in a rise in CME/CEU participation. Additionally, 84% of users engaged with the WHOVA app, demonstrating MMHC's effectiveness in hybrid engagement design.

The MMHC has proven to be a catalyst for growth beyond just the sessions it hosts. This year, twenty-three attendee-driven meetups were facilitated by WHOVA, featuring activities such as book signings, leadership retreats, rebranding initiatives, and the launch of new projects. These events illustrate how ideas born at MMHC take root and flourish long after the conference concludes. Whether sparked by a quiet moment of reflection or a bold announcement, MMHC continues to foster innovation in the field of Muslim mental health.

Driven by the collective efforts of its participants and partners, the MMHC sets new standards each year in leadership, scholarship, and transformative practices within the domain of Muslim mental health. The conference has evolved into more than just a platform; it has become a stronghold and a powerful force within a growing ecosystem of individuals, initiatives, and institutions dedicated to advancing the field. MMHC welcomes, supports, and amplifies the voices of everyone who engages with it.

Expanding Reach: From Michigan to Global Influence

In the seventh year, we established a crucial partnership with Adnan Hammad, Senior Director and founder of ACCESS (Arab Community Center for Economic and Social Services). This collaboration enabled us to bring MMHC to a wider audience in Dearborn, Michigan. It represented a significant evolution for the conference. Previously, we had maintained a strong relationship with MSU, hosting the conference on campus and later in Detroit. However, partnering with ACCESS allowed us to extend our reach beyond the academic environment and bring the conference directly into the heart of the community, where it truly belonged.

The tenth MMHC was a significant milestone. It marked the first-ever Spartan event held at the esteemed U.S. Institute of Peace in Washington, D.C., and it came with an unprecedented budget of $100,000. I still remember walking out of the institute after signing the contract and telling myself, "I can manage this—I think I can do it."

That year, the conference attracted international attendees from countries such as Saudi Arabia, Malaysia, Indonesia, Qatar, and beyond. It became clear that the MMHC had evolved into a global movement.

In the same year, we made significant progress by signing a Memorandum of Understanding (MOU) with the University of Putra Malaysia to launch the inaugural Global Muslim Mental Health Conference. This partnership strengthened our international presence and reinforced our mission to foster connections across borders, cultures, and communities.

Challenges and Overcoming Obstacles

Creating a global platform for Muslim mental health involves several challenges that must be overcome to ensure the sustainability of our efforts. Two of the most significant obstacles are limited funding and resources, as well as cultural and societal barriers.

Funding Challenges and the Power of Community

One of the most persistent challenges we have faced in promoting Muslim mental health is securing consistent funding and resources. Unlike mainstream mental health initiatives that often benefit from institutional support and public investment, specific areas like Islamic Psychology and culturally tailored programs for Muslim communities rarely receive the same level of assistance—especially in countries like the United States, where Muslim populations are minorities and mental health infrastructures are already underfunded. Much of the success of the Muslim Mental Health Coalition (MMHC) relies on the dedication of volunteers who have selflessly devoted their time, energy, and resources to this cause, often without compensation. It truly takes a village.

The conference has not only endured but thrived thanks to the steadfast support of a broad network of organizations and allies who share our mission. Michigan State University has been our most significant and consistent institutional supporter. Key sponsors include the College of Osteopathic Medicine, the Office of the Associate Dean for Diversity and Campus Inclusion, the MSU College of Human Medicine, MSU International Studies and Programs, the Office for Inclusion and Intercultural Initiatives, and the Office of the Provost. Additionally, we have received generous backing from the University of Michigan's Center for Middle Eastern and North African Studies and the Center for South Asian Studies.

Looking ahead, I am dedicated to establishing sustainable partnerships to ensure the longevity of the MMHC and securing the necessary funding to support this vital work for future generations.

Navigating Cultural Barriers and Personal Resistance

Throughout this journey, I faced significant obstacles both within institutional settings and my community. Some individuals questioned my intentions and credibility, accusing me of promoting Western ideologies or suggesting that I was "not Muslim enough" to lead this effort, particularly because I chose not to wear the hijab. When I first announced the Muslim Mental Health Conference, I received emails accusing me of pathologizing the Muslim community. These accusations underscored the resistance I encountered while trying to initiate conversations about mental health within Islamic contexts.

Cultural and societal barriers make it challenging to address mental health in Muslim communities. In many areas, mental illness remains a taboo topic, often viewed as a sign of spiritual weakness or moral failure rather than a legitimate medical condition. This stigma can silence individuals and families, discouraging them from seeking help and allowing symptoms to go untreated. Social reputation often takes precedence over mental well-being, and religious leaders, who are frequently the first point of contact, may lack the training to recognize or respond adequately to mental health concerns.

The traditional divide between spiritual and medical approaches to wellness further complicates the issue. Many individuals turn to imams or religious scholars for faith-based healing methods, which, while valuable, may delay or even replace necessary psychological treatment. As mental health practitioners working in Muslim contexts, we must navigate these dynamics with cultural sensitivity and humility. Our goal is not to replace faith but to integrate it into care, ensuring that our treatment is clinically sound and aligned with the values and beliefs that are central to our patients' identities.

Strategies for Overcoming Challenges

Integrating The Islamic Model

In response to cultural and societal barriers, an innovative approach has been to integrate Islamic teachings into therapeutic models. By creating frameworks that align with the religious and spiritual beliefs of Muslim patients, mental health professionals can help reduce resistance to psychological treatment. For example, Islamic Psychology combines traditional therapeutic techniques with principles derived from the Quran and Hadith, making mental health care more relatable and acceptable for patients.

Support from the Community and Stakeholders

Community involvement is crucial in overcoming barriers to mental health care for Muslims. Collaborating with religious leaders, such as imams and scholars, has proven effective in reducing stigma and promoting mental health awareness within our communities. These leaders are trusted figures who can advocate for mental health and guide individuals toward professional help when necessary. To support this initiative, we developed an Imam training program. These training sessions equip religious leaders with the skills to recognize signs of mental distress and provide appropriate referrals, fostering a more integrated approach to mental health care.

Impact and Outcomes

The global expansion of the Muslim Mental Health Conferences has increased outreach and raised awareness of mental health challenges within the Muslim community. The growing international presence of this conference series underscores the urgent need for ongoing global dialogue and collaboration to address mental health issues among Muslims.

We have made an impact across various fields, from academia to the establishment of new mental health centers both nationally and internationally. Additionally, we have promoted mental health awareness through performance art.

Key Partners in Mental Health

Michigan State University's Role in the Legacy of MMHC

Michigan State University (MSU) has played a crucial role in the history and success of the Muslim Mental Health Conference (MMHC). At a time when publicly supporting Muslim-led initiatives carried political and social risks, MSU demonstrated courage by hosting this groundbreaking effort. The university provided not just a platform, but also a safe and empowering academic environment where ideas could develop without censorship or compromise. MSU offered MMHC a unique combination of creative freedom, academic independence, and institutional legitimacy, allowing the conference to grow into a nationally recognized leader in faith-based mental health.

Through consistent support from various departments, faculty, and administrative leadership, MSU exemplified what true allyship looks like in academic-community partnerships. Their commitment not only fostered a successful conference but also nurtured a movement. There is no comparable example in U.S. academia of such enduring and principled support for a Muslim mental health initiative. MSU's involvement is not just a chapter in MMHC's story; it is foundational to its existence and lasting impact. I extend my deepest gratitude to the College of Osteopathic Medicine, the College of Human Medicine, the Muslim Studies Center, and the South Asian Studies Center.

I would also like to express heartfelt thanks to the amazing and supportive staff over the years who went above and beyond to sustain this work: Barb Flannery, Rita Peffers, Dana Moore, Mary Firdawsi, Laura Large, Lisa Olivia, and Hilari Rhodabeck.

Journal of Muslim Mental Health

The *Journal of Muslim Mental Health* has been instrumental in advancing research and publications in the field by providing a platform for researchers and mental health professionals worldwide. This platform facilitates contributions to the growing body of literature on mental health within Muslim communities. The recent conference supported the journal and expanded its overall impact, increasing its readership both nationally and globally. By bringing together diverse voices from around the world, the journal helps shape the narrative around mental health issues specific to Muslim populations, effectively bridging cultural and scientific knowledge.

The Institute for Muslim Mental Health

The Institute of Muslim Mental Health (IMMH), founded by Hamada Hamid Altalib, has played a significant role in the development and academic growth of the MMHC. As one of the first organizations dedicated exclusively to promoting research, training, and collaboration in the field of Muslim mental health, IMMH has been essential in establishing the scholarly framework for this area of study. Their early and ongoing support has provided crucial guidance, networking opportunities, and legitimacy, which have helped transform the MMHC from a local initiative into a nationally and internationally recognized platform.

Islamic Psychology as a Specialized Field

A significant outcome of the Muslim Mental Health Conference is the establishment of Islamic psychology and Muslim mental health as distinct fields of study in North America. The conference sparked important discussions among mental health providers, who are now fully committed to initiatives supporting Muslim mental health. This growing movement has also resulted in an increase in the number of Muslim mental health professionals dedicated to providing culturally relevant care to their communities.

Khalil Center

One significant impact of the Muslim Mental Health Conference has been its support for initiatives like the Khalil Center, which was founded by Hooman Keshavarzi in the U.S. and Canada. The Khalil Center provides mental health services based on Islamic principles and offers post-doctoral fellowships and educational programs in Islamic psychology for practitioners. In addition to providing clinical care, the center is dedicated to educating the Muslim community about mental health, breaking down stigmas, and promoting culturally sensitive approaches to well-being.

Stanford's Role in Islamic Psychology

Rania Awaad at Stanford University is a leading figure in the field of Islamic psychology and mental health. The Stanford Muslim Mental Health & Islamic Psychology Lab serves as a central hub for academic research on these subjects. It offers valuable resources for clinicians, researchers, trainees, educators, and religious leaders who work with Muslim communities. The lab's academic framework promotes a deep understanding of how mental health can be aligned with Islamic teachings, thereby providing culturally competent mental health services to Muslim populations.

Maristan

Maristan is an organization dedicated to advancing mental health through an Islamic psychological framework. Founded by Rania Awaad at Stanford University, Maristan plays a crucial role in reimagining mental health care with an approach that integrates spirituality. The organization focuses on Muslim mental health by combining academic rigor, faith-based insights, and community-centered care. Their collaboration with the MMHC has significantly elevated Islamic Psychology as a legitimate and essential discipline in clinical, educational, and grassroots settings.

The Family & Youth Institute (FYI)

Sameera Ahmad, the Director of FYI, has played a vital role in promoting research-based and culturally relevant mental health support for Muslim families, youth, and communities. Through its publications, workshops, and community engagement efforts, FYI has made significant contributions to shaping conversations and providing resources that align with the mission of the Muslim Mental Health Conference.

The Black Muslim Psychology Conference (BMPC)

The Black Muslim Psychology Coalition (BMPC), founded by Kameelah Mumin Rashad and the Muslim Wellness Foundation, is a pioneering initiative that amplifies the voices and experiences of Black Muslims within mental health spaces. The BMPC has established essential frameworks for understanding the intersection of race, faith, and psychology. Its collaboration with the MMHC has enhanced efforts to create inclusive and justice-oriented models of mental health care for Muslims.

Narratives of Pain: Expanding the Conversation Beyond Academia

The Narratives of Pain event, led by Zain Shamoon, presents a unique and creative approach to discussing mental health. Held annually at the MMHC, this performance art event goes beyond the traditional academic emphasis on journals and research. It encourages individuals to share their personal stories through performance, poetry, or storytelling. The event creates an inclusive space where people can express their struggles with mental health in emotionally and culturally resonant ways, fostering a sense of shared experience and promoting healing.

The Ruh App: Culturally Sensitive Mindfulness

The Ruh App, the first app specifically designed for Muslims, represents a significant advancement in mindfulness. The app effectively meets Muslim users' unique spiritual and psychological needs by combining Islamic principles with modern mindfulness practices. It provides mindfulness techniques that are firmly grounded in their faith.

The ADAMS Center (All Dulles Area Muslim Society)

Acknowledging the pioneering work done by the ADAMS Center under the visionary leadership of Imam Maged and social worker Sue Kafri is important. As the first wellness center established within an Islamic center, it has become a valued partner in promoting mental health in Muslim communities. Renowned for its proactive community engagement and leadership in interfaith dialogue, the ADAMS Center has been instrumental in integrating mental health awareness into faith-based settings. Their collaboration with the MMHC has bridged the gap between religious leaders and mental health professionals, furthering the conference's mission of providing holistic, culturally competent care.

Islamic Circle of North America: ICNA Relief, USA

The Muslim Family Services (MFS) program was established in Detroit, Michigan, in 1998 and expanded nationally under ICNA Relief in 2005. The MFS program focuses on providing mental health counseling for youth, families, residents of transitional homes, refugees, seniors, and anyone in need. Amber Haque, the national program director with extensive experience in mental health, raises awareness by producing various mental health booklets, which are available in multiple translations at the Resources section of the Muslim Family Services website. ICNA Relief operates in 42 states across the U.S., and its counselors provide culturally competent counseling services free of charge.

Global Expansion of Muslim Mental Health

What started as a local initiative has now evolved into a global movement, extending its impact far beyond its original intent. The MMHC has brought together experts and practitioners from around the world, resulting in international collaborations and new programs focused on Islamic psychology. For instance, there have been partnerships with institutions such as Ibn Haldun University in Turkey and Cambridge Muslim College in the United Kingdom.

Motivation for International Expansion

The decision to expand the Muslim Mental Health Conferences internationally was motivated by the need for a global dialogue on Muslim mental health, highlighting the diverse experiences and challenges faced by Muslim communities around the world. Since mental health issues transcend borders, it became essential to encourage discussions considering various cultural, religious, and societal contexts. Strategic planning enabled these global conferences to be tailored to the specific needs of local populations, all while aiming to destigmatize mental health within the Muslim community.

Global Muslim Mental Health Conferences

The 1st Annual Global Muslim Mental Health Conference was held in Malaysia in 2017, attracting over 100 participants from 20 countries. This groundbreaking event focused on the relationship between mental health and Islamic values to establish a unified framework for mental health support tailored to Muslims' needs. With its blend of modernity and deep-rooted Islamic culture, Malaysia served as the perfect setting for discussions on integrating mental health care into Islamic traditions.

The 2nd Annual Global Muslim Mental Health Conference took place in Cambridge, UK, in 2019 at Clare College. A variety of topics were addressed, with keynote speaker Professor Jonas Kunst from Norway discussing the mental health effects of Islamophobia. The conference featured significant contributions from Jed Magen, Chair of the MSU Psychiatry Department, as well as other notable figures, including Afifa Anjum and Rafia Rafique from Pakistan, and Rashid Zaman and Ahmed Hankir from the UK. High Commissioner Nafees Zakaria of Pakistan delivered an impactful speech that highlighted the mental health challenges faced in Pakistan, drawing international attention to the issue.

Acknowledgments

Dr. Aneesah Nadir, through her pioneering work with the Islamic Social Services Association (ISSA), has played a pivotal role in the Muslim mental health movement, establishing the foundation for culturally competent care and advocating for mental health awareness in North American Muslim communities long before the issue received wider recognition. The association's dedicated service over the past 25 years was recently celebrated. Aneesah Nadir continues to be a key leader and a guiding force for the new generation of practitioners in the field.

Halim Naeem has significantly expanded the reach and inclusivity of the MMHC. As a long-standing advocate for mental health within Black Muslim communities, he was instrumental in recruiting volunteers, many of whom were students and young professionals. His influence helped establish connections between the MMHC and Black Muslim communities, which have historically been underrepresented in broader Muslim spaces. Additionally, he encouraged the participation of imams and faith leaders, particularly those serving diverse inner-city congregations. Through his personal networks and deep community engagement, Halim Naeem helped normalize conversations about mental health among religious leaders and community members who previously viewed the topic with skepticism or discomfort. His leadership ensured that the conference was academically rigorous, spiritually grounded, and focused on the community's needs.

Hamad Ali introduced the Whova app, a digital platform transforming the conference's organization and experience. His leadership in implementing Whova enabled MMHC to streamline registration, manage speaker sessions, facilitate networking among attendees, and provide real-time updates during the event. This innovation significantly enhanced participant engagement, particularly during the hybrid and virtual formats adopted in response to the COVID-19 pandemic.

By adopting the Whova app, he helped elevate the professionalism of the conference, making it more accessible and user-friendly, especially for international attendees and tech-savvy younger professionals. His contribution marked a significant step in integrating technology into the MMHC experience.

Dr. Jed Magen, DO, MS. Every transformative movement needs a patron—someone who recognizes its value before the world does and supports it during its most vulnerable moments. For the Muslim Mental Health Conference, that steadfast champion has been Dr. Jed Magen, Chair of the Department of Psychiatry at Michigan State University. From the conference's earliest days, Dr. Magen has not only provided his support but also offered his vision, guidance, and active involvement. His unwavering belief in the importance of culturally and spiritually grounded mental health care remained strong, even when the journey was politically challenging or institutionally uncertain. Through his relentless advocacy and leadership, he has ensured that the Muslim Mental Health Conference has both a place at the academic table and the protection it needs to thrive. His contributions have been invaluable—not just to the conference, but to the broader movement for equity, inclusion, and healing within Muslim communities. In many ways, the conference would not be what it is today without Dr. Magen's courage and commitment.

Dr. Annelle Primm, MD, MPH, served as the Director of Minority and National Affairs for the American Psychiatric Association from 2004 to 2015. Among the many influential figures in the development of the Muslim Mental Health Conference (MMHC), Dr. Primm stands out as a mentor who not only believed in its mission but also actively contributed her time, wisdom, and resources to help it succeed.

As a nationally respected psychiatrist and advocate for mental health equity, Dr. Primm provided more than just professional support; she offered mentorship that was both personal and profoundly impactful. She dedicated time to nurture emerging leaders, strategically shaped the conference's direction, and ensured that the MMHC remained grounded in clinical excellence and cultural humility. Her commitment to mental health frameworks focused on marginalized communities helped legitimate MMHC within broader professional circles.

Dr. Primm's mentorship was not merely about guidance; it was a catalyst for change. Her generosity, integrity, and insight left a lasting impression on the spirit and sustainability of the MMHC movement.

Dr. Altha Stewart, MD, is the first African American President of the American Psychiatric Association. As a trailblazer in psychiatry and a dedicated advocate for justice in mental health, her support has always been genuine and deeply personal. It is rooted in shared values of equity, resilience, and community healing. Dr. Stewart has helped navigate complex institutional landscapes, provided critical insights during uncertain times, and never hesitated to lend her voice in support of our vision. In a movement that often felt isolating or challenging, her presence reminded me that I was never alone. To this day, she remains a beacon of hope and inspiration.

Amy Porfiri, MBA, Managing Director of the APA Foundation, has been a steady hand and has an unwavering presence, supporting me every step of the way.

Rawle Andrews, Jr., Esq., Executive Director of the American Psychiatric Association. Throughout our journey, we faced moments of doubt when the weight of our work felt overwhelming and the path ahead seemed uncertain. In these times, the unwavering strength and belief of Rawle Andrews Jr. sustained us. As a seasoned advocate for mental health equity and a powerful voice for underserved communities, Rawle provided not just encouragement, but also fortitude. His presence served as a grounding force, and his words offered clarity and conviction. Whenever we questioned our ability to continue, he reminded us of the importance of our mission. His steadfast support, strategic guidance, and strong moral compass helped stabilize MMHC during its most fragile moments. Rawle didn't just stand by us; he lifted us up. His strength became our strength, and his belief in our mission propelled us forward when our own resolve was tested.

We extend our heartfelt thanks to the American Psychiatric Association Foundation, the Health and Human Services Center for Faith-Based Neighborhood Partnerships, and the Substance Abuse and Mental Health Services Administration (SAMHSA) for their continued and invaluable support and guidance.

IN MEMORIAM

The late Cheryl El-Amin was crucial in institutionalizing the MMHC by introducing Continuing Medical Education (CME) and Continuing Education Units (CEUs) for participants. Her efforts added academic and professional credibility to the conference, attracting more healthcare professionals, clinicians, and educators by allowing them to earn credits toward their licensure and professional development.

By formalizing the MMHC educational value, Cheryl El-Amin established it as a serious platform for scholarly engagement and clinical advancement. This initiative elevated the conference's reputation and ensured its continued relevance within academic and healthcare systems.

Malik Badri - Michigan State University collaborated with the University of Putra Malaysia to host the 1st International Muslim Mental Health Conference. Malik Badri often called the "father of modern Islamic Psychology" was the keynote speaker. We were very fortunate to host this esteemed scholar.

Laleh Bakhtiar - In 2020, Carrie York Al-Karam, President of Alkaram Institute, interviewed Laleh Bakhtiar for Annual Muslim Mental Health Conference on the topic, "Islamic Psychology and a Life Well Lived."

Dean of Congress John Dingell - In 2014, Congressman John Dingell honored us with his presence. He put his complete support behind this movement and in a personal handwritten note appreciated the conference "God Bless you and your good works for your kindness, hospitality and friendship, with every good wishes." - John Dingell.

The Future of MMHC: Youth Engagement and Emerging Leadership

As the MMHC looks to the future, its foundation is built on the strength of youth and the rise of a new generation of leaders. The conference has increasingly attracted students, early-career professionals, and young activists who are transforming the mental health landscape through innovation, cultural awareness, and a strong dedication to justice and healing.

Youth-led panels, intergenerational dialogues, and leadership development sessions have become fundamental aspects of MMHC. Young attendees are participants, speakers, organizers, and movement builders. Their voices amplify diverse experiences, introduce innovative therapeutic models, and advocate for inclusive mental health approaches that reflect the changing realities of Muslim communities worldwide.

Looking ahead, MMHC aims to formalize its commitment to youth leadership by establishing mentorship pipelines, fellowships, and opportunities for collaborative content creation. By setting up advisory councils, expanding student scholarships, and creating year-round engagement platforms, MMHC is positioning itself as an incubator and launchpad for the next generation of Muslim mental health leaders.

The future of the MMHC will be influenced by emerging changemakers equipped with clinical knowledge and possess lived experiences, creative strategies, and a year's steadfast commitment to collective care.

This year's conference was a success due in large part to the visionary leadership and passionate service of the Executive Committee: Bunmi Oyewuwo, Hanan Hashem, Aquila Hussain, Hamad Ali, Sana Ali, and Shabaz Khan. Their dedication, collaboration, and unwavering commitment were crucial in shaping an event that addressed urgent mental health needs while fostering community, resilience, and hope. They are paving the way for the future of MMHC, ensuring that its legacy of support, advocacy, and innovation continues to thrive for generations.

Conclusion: The Legacy and Future of MMHC

The MMHC journey from its humble beginnings to its current status as a global leader in advocating for mental health in Muslim communities demonstrates the power of vision, resilience, and community engagement.

Each year, the conference expands its reach by bringing together diverse voices—from academics and clinicians to faith leaders and community organizers, helping ensure that mental health is no longer a taboo subject but a central topic of discussion and action.

HISTORY OF MUSLIM MENTAL HEALTH CONFERENCES

As the MMHC moves forward, it carries a legacy of progress, empowerment, and a commitment to creating lasting change. The seeds planted at each conference have led to global collaborations, new partnerships, and innovative mental health programs that continue to evolve and shape the future of mental health within Muslim communities.

MMHC is not just an event; it is a movement. This movement, driven by dedication, compassion, and a shared purpose, will continue to promote greater mental health awareness, support, and healing within Muslim communities worldwide.

Here's to growth and many more years ahead—there are miles to go and promises to keep before I sleep.

SECTION TWO

CONCEPTS AND CULTURES

BREAKING THE SILENCE: MENTAL HEALTH STIGMA AND THE AMERICAN MUSLIM EXPERIENCE

Rukhsana Chaudhry

Mental health is a crucial aspect of the spiritual essence of being a Muslim, yet it remains a challenging topic within the Muslim community. This chapter explores the multifaceted issue of mental health stigma among American Muslims, highlighting its impact on individuals and the community. The stigma surrounding mental illness, often rooted in religious and cultural beliefs, leads to negative attitudes, stereotypes, and discrimination, which hinder individuals from seeking necessary mental health care. The chapter emphasizes the need for culturally sensitive methods to address mental health stigma, drawing on empirical research and recommendations from scholars. It discusses the unique challenges faced by American Muslims, including the intersection of mental illness stigma with racial and ethnic discrimination and the compounded effect of "double stigma." Strategies for promoting mental health awareness within the Muslim community, including community workshops, collaboration with religious leaders, and educational campaigns will be discussed. The paper calls for a collective effort to embrace mental well-being, break down barriers, and build bridges within the Muslim community.

Introduction

Defining Mental Health Stigma and Its Impact on Individuals

Mental health is a critical aspect of the spiritual essence of being a Muslim, yet it remains a challenging topic for many in the Muslim community. Addressing mental health is essential to ensure that individuals can lead fulfilling lives, free from the burden of untreated mental health issues, while also maintaining their sense of faith. The American Muslim population is a community of diverse beliefs, cultural backgrounds, and values in terms of mental health. Therefore, it is not simple to understand the causes of stigma grounded in one area alone. Muslims in America also have varying degrees of faith-based understanding, making it complex to surmise that Islamic faith beliefs do not lend themselves to acceptance of mental health concerns. Unfortunately, stigma and a lack of awareness often hinder progress in this area. This chapter aims to shed light on the importance of mental health, the prevalence of stigma, and the urgent need for education and action.

Phillips and Lauterbach (2017) found that mental health stigma consists of negative attitudes, stereotypes, and discrimination against individuals with mental illnesses. This stigma affects various communities and can lead to poor mental health outcomes. In American Muslim communities, beliefs that attribute mental illness to religious causes contribute significantly to this stigma. Stigma manifests on both societal and individual levels, resulting in social isolation and internalized self-stigma, which are linked to conditions such as PTSD, anxiety, and depression. However, strong resistance to stigma is associated with better mental health outcomes.

There is a belief that somatoform disorders—physical symptoms without a medical cause—are also prevalent among American Muslims, partly due to the stigma associated with mental health. However, empirical evidence supporting this idea is limited. Individuals in these communities may face "double stigma" stemming from both mental illness and racial or ethnic discrimination. This compounding effect can worsen mental health issues. Philips and Lauterbach (2017) stress the need for further empirical research to better understand the extent and impact of stigma, as well as to develop culturally informed interventions aimed at addressing and reducing this stigma.

Addressing mental health stigma in Muslim communities requires culturally sensitive approaches. In 2013, Ayse Ciftci, Nev Jones, & Patrick W. Corrigan noted that stigma hinders individuals from seeking mental health care, leading to negative outcomes and called for more research on stigma in Muslim communities and recommended interventions that consider race, ethnicity, gender, class, and religion (Ciftci, Jones, & Corrigan, 2013).

Finding innovative ways to understand stigma and its manifestations within American Muslim communities is crucial for developing effective strategies to combat it. Understanding stigma involves a cyclical process that moves from "inside out" to "outside in." Individuals may experience stigma due to social and environmental factors while also internalizing beliefs about mental health prevalent in the community. This internalization can lead to a reluctance to accept mental health issues.

Stigma often operates unconsciously in our minds, yet it still has a significant limiting effect on us. Research highlights that Muslims face various psychosocial challenges in five key areas: globally, within the broader community, locally, interpersonally, and at the intrapersonal level (Tanhan & Francisco, 2019). Studies have demonstrated that American Muslims are more susceptible to mental health issues compared to other minority groups due to these challenges (Chaudhry & Li, 2011; Tanhan & Strack, 2020). Despite these difficulties, the American Muslim community remains underserved in terms of mental health resources (Ahmed & Reddy, 2007).

Cultural Factors Specific to the Muslim Community that Contribute to Stigma

The stigma surrounding mental health in American Muslims is complex, often stemming from a widespread reluctance to seek formal mental health services within this diverse community. The lack of culturally appropriate services frequently discourages individuals from asking for help. Many cultures hold the belief that discussing family challenges can lead to embarrassment or hurt feelings among relatives if those issues come to light. This can complicate significant decisions related to marriage or finances. Additionally, some family members may fear or mistrust clinicians due to concerns about potential exposure and the risk of being judged or shamed.

While this sentiment may not apply to every American Muslim family, it's important to recognize the diversity within the Muslim population in the U.S., which encompasses various cultural backgrounds and immigration histories. This diversity complicates the ability to study mental health trends on a broader scale. Moreover, developing effective mental health approaches can be time-consuming due to the variety of cultural perspectives involved. Traditional Western psychotherapy, which often emphasizes cognitive behavioral therapy, may not be adequate without integrating cultural norms and faith-based views on mental health.

Skinner (2010) advocated for the development of better culturally sensitive methods to serve Muslims. Over the past two decades, Muslims—particularly in Western countries like the USA—have garnered more attention, often in a negative light. Given the prevalent misconceptions about Muslims, it is essential to understand their impact on the mental health of American Muslims. Integrating mental health into the lives of Muslims is vital for combating stigma and increasing awareness within the community. This approach can also foster understanding among non-Muslims regarding the mental health of Muslims without further stigmatizing mental health issues. Therefore, addressing stigma and lack of awareness is the primary path toward integrating mental health with our spiritual well-being.

Help-Seeking Behavior

Levels of religiosity influence help-seeking behaviors, but it remains unclear whether higher or lower levels of religiosity encourage or discourage help-seeking among Muslim groups. Alharbi, Farrand and Laidlaw (2021) found that higher levels of religiosity are generally associated with more positive attitudes toward seeking help for mental health issues. It is important to note that religiosity itself is not necessarily a barrier to help-seeking behavior; rather, the stigma surrounding mental illness acts as a moderator in this relationship. At low and moderate levels of stigma, higher religiosity is significantly linked to more favorable help-seeking attitudes.

Ciftci, Jones, and Corrigan (2012) indicated that the prevalence of psychiatric disorders is similar among Muslim Americans and non-Muslims. While help-seeking was generally low in both groups, Muslims with a lifetime history of PTSD were less likely than their non-Muslim counterparts to seek help through self-help groups. Additionally, Muslims with mood disorders reported lower mental health scores compared to non-Muslims with similar conditions.

In another study by Ali et al. (2022), 1,222 Muslim women participated in an anonymous online survey regarding their cultural and religious beliefs about mental health, the stigma associated with mental health issues, and their familiarity with professional mental health services. The study found that higher levels of religious and cultural beliefs, greater societal stigma, and lower familiarity with professional mental health services were linked to more negative attitudes toward seeking professional mental healthcare. Stigma accounted for the most variation in rejection attitudes, followed by cultural and religious beliefs about mental health and familiarity with mental health services. While the study examined some factors influencing Muslim women's attitudes toward professional mental health care, further research on their perceptions and attitudes is needed (Ali et al., 2022).

A Growing Crisis: The Urgent Need for Action

The mental health landscape within the Muslim community is characterized by a silent struggle, often concealed by stigma and cultural pressures. Although Islam emphasizes the importance of mental well-being, the widespread stigma surrounding mental illness frequently prevents individuals from seeking the help they need. This chapter explores the complex challenges faced by Muslim individuals in accessing mental health support, highlighting the urgent need for education, awareness, and culturally sensitive interventions.

Recent trends in mental health concerns within the Muslim community underscore the seriousness of the situation. In 2021, two young brothers in Allen, Texas, tragically took their own lives after killing family members, attributing their actions to depression, mental illness, and generational conflicts within their home. This event profoundly impacted the American Muslim community, highlighting the urgent need to address these critical issues. Furthermore, years earlier, a Muslim woman in Fairfax, Virginia, died by suicide after murdering her young sons. These tragedies are not isolated incidents; suicide is increasingly becoming a significant concern within our community.

A research letter titled "Suicide Attempts of Muslims Compared with Other Religious Groups in the US," published on July 21, 2021, reveals a troubling statistic: American Muslims exhibit a significantly higher rate of suicide attempts compared to other religious groups in the US. Specifically, nearly 8% of Muslims reported having attempted suicide in their lifetime, compared to 6% of Catholics, 5% of Protestants, and 3.6% of Jewish respondents (Awaad et al., 2021). In the wake of such tragedies, it is clear that we must break the taboo surrounding discussions of suicide in the American Muslim community.

The Roots of the Problem: Unique Challenges Faced by Muslim Individuals

The disparity among religious groups and the prevalence of suicidal ideation among Muslims stem from a complex interplay of factors. Since 2021, perceptions of Muslims in the United States have significantly changed, leading to mental health challenges both collectively and individually for this community (Institute for Social Policy and

Understanding, 2016). Many Muslims experience discrimination based on their faith, which can lead to feelings of isolation, marginalization, and stress. These experiences can contribute to mental health issues and create barriers to seeking help. Cultural obstacles, financial constraints, and a shortage of culturally competent mental health providers often hinder Muslims from accessing the services they need. This lack of access can further aggravate their mental health problems (CAIR, 2015).

The Impact of Stigma: A Multifaceted Challenge

The stigma surrounding mental illness poses a significant barrier to seeking help within the Muslim community. One major concern is that Muslims may delay treatment due to the fear of being labeled as "crazy" in their own language or cultural context. Additionally, individuals may turn to professionals or religious leaders who lack the knowledge or resources to provide adequate support. Feelings of shame and guilt associated with mental illness can lead to self-harm or increased isolation, as individuals may feel "less than" other Muslims or believe they are failing in their faith.

Community rejection often occurs when someone discloses their mental health struggles, leading to public ostracism. When individuals witness others being ostracized for their mental health issues, they may hesitate to seek help themselves, further isolating themselves during difficult times.

Discrimination in healthcare settings is also prevalent. Implicit biases and assumptions about cultural backgrounds can result in denial of treatment or inadequate care, which further erodes trust in the healthcare system. Many clinicians struggle to understand the nuances of various cultural and religious beliefs, which can hinder the therapeutic process.

The Impact of Immigration and Displacement

For immigrant and refugee Muslim communities, the challenges they face are intensified by the trauma of displacement and the complexities of adapting to a new culture. These individuals often grapple with the effects of trauma and displacement for years after arriving in the United States. For instance, many Muslims from Syria and Iraq report that they have not fully recovered from their experiences in their home countries. As a result, they frequently experience depression alongside other trauma-related disorders.

The language and understanding surrounding refugee mental health remains underdeveloped for many individuals and families, which limits their access to culturally competent mental health care. Additionally, the process of navigating a new language and culture can be overwhelming and isolating, contributing to prolonged feelings of stress and loneliness. Recent

Afghan refugees, who arrived in the U.S. after being evacuated in 2021, encountered significant language barriers that hindered their access to medical treatment and psychosocial assistance. Unfortunately, very little mental health treatment was provided during their adjustment to U.S. society.

Immigrants, refugees, and asylees often face discrimination and racism, which adversely affect their mental well-being. Furthermore, the lack of culturally competent mental health services in community and hospital settings leads to underutilization of available care. Financial difficulties add another layer of complication, making affording mental health treatment a challenge for many. There is also a noticeable gap in mental health programming tailored to these specific groups. Moreover, fears related to deportation or other immigration consequences may prevent individuals from seeking the help they need.

The impact on children is increasingly concerning. According to a 2018 report published in the American Journal of Community Psychology by the Society for Community Research and Action (Division 27), researchers reviewed three decades of scientific literature on U.S. immigration policy and its psychosocial and economic effects. They found that children who lose parent to sudden, forced deportation often experience a range of emotional and behavioral issues, such as anxiety, anger, aggression, withdrawal, heightened fear, disturbances in eating and sleeping, isolation, trauma, and depression.

Promoting Awareness

To promote awareness of mental health within the Muslim community, several effective strategies can be implemented. First, organizing community workshops and seminars on mental health topics, led by experts, can provide valuable resources. These events should ideally take place at mosques, community centers, or schools, which serve as key hubs for connection and collaboration among diverse Muslim populations.

Collaboration with religious leaders, such as imams, is also essential. Discussing mental health issues during sermons and community gatherings can help reduce stigma and encourage open conversations. Additionally, educational campaigns that include brochures, videos, and social media content addressing mental health from an Islamic perspective should be widely distributed within the community, particularly during congregational times like Ramadan.

Establishing support groups where community members can share experiences and receive peer support, facilitated by trained professionals or volunteers, is another beneficial approach. It is crucial to develop a comprehensive plan and action strategy for the Muslim community to sustain efforts in promoting mental health awareness.

Key Strategies for Increasing Awareness within the Muslim Community

Partnerships with mental health organizations are essential for the success of mental health programs and initiatives aimed at American Muslims. Collaboration among organizations is crucial for developing both broad and localized programming for Muslim communities. Sharing knowledge between organizations enhances the available resources and training focused on addressing mental health issues within the broader U.S. context, while also respecting the role of faith in these communities.

Youth Engagement: Developing programs that provide a safe and supportive environment for young people to discuss mental health is essential. Schools and youth groups play a crucial role in this effort.

Implementing cultural competency training for a wider population of therapists and clinicians is important, alongside the creation of Muslim-specific therapist groups and resources. Offering training for mental health professionals will help them better understand the cultural and religious context of the Muslim community. This approach can enhance the quality of care and improve accessibility to mental health services.

Media Outreach: Engage local media, such as community radio stations and newspapers that specifically target Muslim Americans in their communities, to raise awareness about mental health issues and the resources available.

Community Workshops and Seminars: Organize workshops and seminars on mental health topics, inviting experts to speak and providing resources. These events can be held at mosques, community centers, or schools.

Collaboration with Religious Leaders: During sermons and community gatherings, engage imams and other religious leaders to discuss mental health issues. Their influence can help reduce stigma and promote open conversations.

Educational Campaigns: Create educational materials such as brochures, videos, and social media content that address mental health from an Islamic perspective. Distribute these materials widely within local communities.

<u>Support Groups:</u> Establish support groups where community members can share experiences and receive peer support, facilitated by trained professionals.

Challenges to Implementation

Implementing mental health awareness strategies within the Muslim community can be challenging due to several factors. Stigma and misconceptions about mental health often prevent individuals from seeking help and discussing their mental health openly. Effective mental health interventions require cultural and religious sensitivity, necessitating a deep understanding of the community's beliefs, values, and practices.

There is often a lack of awareness and education regarding mental health issues and available resources, making it difficult for community members to recognize mental health problems and know where to seek help. Access to culturally competent mental health services can be limited, resulting in insufficient care and support. Resource constraints, including funding, trained professionals, and infrastructure, can also limit the scope and effectiveness of mental health programs.

Engaging the community and gaining their trust is crucial for the success of mental health initiatives, but this can be challenging, especially if there is a history of mistrust or negative experiences with mental health services. Addressing these challenges requires a multifaceted approach that includes education, community engagement, collaboration with religious leaders, and the development of culturally sensitive mental health services.

Education and Training

Education and training require a dual approach to consistently deliver mental health awareness in the community. Both psychoeducational programs and training for imams and community leaders are essential to advance mental health awareness in the Muslim community and emphasize its importance while encouraging individuals to seek help.

Providing training to imams and community leaders on mental health challenges and disorders prevalent in the community helps change the language surrounding these issues and enables them to support their community members more effectively.

The American Muslim Health Professionals (AMHP) offers programs designed to help individuals navigate mental health concerns within their families and communities. One such program is the Mental Health First Aid (MHFA) training for community leaders, educators, and activists. This training equips participants with skills to identify and respond to mental health crises, trauma, and substance abuse issues. By training over

1,600 individuals, AMHP has established a foundation for communities to effectively support mental health.

Additionally, AMHP conducts webinars and awareness campaigns to educate communities about mental health issues and reduce the stigma associated with mental illness, fostering a more supportive environment for those facing mental health challenges.

AMHP also integrates Islamic teachings into mental health practices, promoting resilience and creating environments that prevent crises. This approach helps individuals find strength and support within their faith community. Furthermore, AMHP advocates for accessible, affordable, and equitable healthcare for everyone. Their health policy and advocacy efforts aim to address health disparities and improve mental health services for underserved communities.

AMHP's Mental Health First Aid (MHFA) programming has been impactful, as evidenced by testimonials that highlight how the training has enabled individuals to recognize and effectively respond to mental health crises. They continue to push for accessible, affordable, and equitable healthcare, leveraging their network of Muslim health professionals to serve local communities and advance health equity.

Muslim Organizations Addressing Mental Health

Several organizations are making significant progress in addressing mental health issues within the Muslim community.

The American Muslim Health Professionals (AMHP) partnership with Mental Health First Aid trains community members to recognize and respond to mental health concerns. The Khalil Center serves as a psychological and spiritual wellness center that integrates traditional Islamic spiritual healing with modern psychology. It offers counseling, workshops, and educational programs aimed at addressing mental health issues specific to the Muslim community.

The Family and Youth Institute (FYI) focuses on research and education to support the mental health and well-being of Muslim families and youth. They provide resources, workshops, and training for individuals and professionals.

The Muslim Wellness Foundation seeks to reduce the stigma associated with mental illnesses, addiction, and trauma in the American Muslim community. They offer mental health first aid training, support groups, and community education initiatives.

The Institute for Muslim Mental Health (IMMH) provides resources and support for mental health professionals who work with Muslim clients. They conduct research and offer training to enhance mental health services for the Muslim community.

Additionally, the Muslim Family Services Program of ICNA Relief USA provides free counseling services, conducts workshops on mental health and well-being, and publishes educational booklets to raise public awareness on various topics.

These programs are designed to be culturally sensitive and address the unique challenges faced by the Muslim population in the U.S., such as stigma and cultural mistrust of mental health services. Looking ahead, initiatives like Project Taqwa and the Naseeha Call Lines are offering confidential support and counseling services to the Muslim community.

Future efforts to reduce stigma within the American Muslim community should prioritize the integration of mental health language in Islamic schools. It is essential to develop culturally sensitive mental health programs that address the unique needs of students in these schools. Training teachers and staff on mental health awareness, identification, and intervention strategies is crucial. Additionally, expanding access to mental health services for students, both within the school and in the surrounding community, is necessary.

Encouraging open discussions about mental health within the school community can help reduce stigma and create spaces for individuals to share their mental health struggles. This is particularly important for pre-teen and teenage students, as this is when their understanding of mental health begins to develop and the importance of safe disclosure becomes apparent.

Recommendations

Enhancing mental health programs within the Muslim community requires addressing specific cultural and religious needs. Here are some important directions to consider:

Cultural Competency and Sensitivity: It's essential for mental health professionals to receive training in cultural competency, which enables them to understand and respect Islamic beliefs and practices. This understanding can help build trust and reduce the stigma associated with mental health issues.

Integration with Religious Practices: Programs should be developed that integrate mental health support with religious practices. For instance, incorporating teachings from the Quran and Hadith that emphasize mental well-being can make these programs more acceptable to the community.

1. Community Engagement and Education: Conduct outreach initiatives to educate the community about mental health, reduce stigma, and encourage individuals to seek help. This can involve workshops, seminars, and collaboration with local mosques and community leaders.
2. Accessible Services: It's important to provide easily accessible mental health services, such as hotlines, online counseling, and community-based clinics. These services should be available in multiple languages to accommodate the diverse Muslim population.
3. Support for Specific Groups: Tailored programs should be created to address the unique needs of specific community groups, including youth, women, and refugees. These programs can help address the unique challenges faced by these populations.
4. Partnerships with Faith Leaders: Collaborating with imams and other religious leaders to provide mental health training can enhance their ability to support their congregations and refer individuals to professional help when necessary.
5. Research and Data Collection: Conduct research to understand the specific mental health needs and challenges within the Muslim community. This data can inform the development of more effective programs and policies.

By concentrating on these areas, mental health programs can become more effective and culturally relevant, thereby enhancing the well-being of the Muslim community.

The Path Forward: Breaking Down Barriers and Building Bridges

Addressing the mental health crisis within the Muslim community requires a comprehensive approach. This includes raising awareness about mental illness and its effects, dispelling misconceptions, and encouraging open dialogue. It is essential to develop culturally competent mental health services that respect religious beliefs and cultural values. Educating healthcare providers about the unique needs and experiences of Muslim patients is crucial for delivering culturally sensitive care. Ultimately, building trust and improving access to mental health services through active engagement with Muslim communities, religious leaders, and community organizations is key to effectively reducing stigma.

A Call to Action: Embracing Mental Well-being as a Collective Responsibility

The mental health crisis within the Muslim community is a serious issue that cannot be ignored. It serves as a call to action—to break down barriers and to collectively embrace mental well-being as a shared responsibility. By fostering understanding, promoting awareness, and providing culturally sensitive support, we can empower Muslim individuals to seek help, overcome stigma, and lead fulfilling lives.

Conclusion

As we strive to improve our community's approach to mental health challenges within the American Muslim community, we can gain valuable insights from other countries facing similar issues. In her article "Exploring Canada's Muslim Mental Health Landscape," published in the September/October 2024 issue of *Islamic Horizons*, Marwa Mahmod discusses the mental health challenges experienced by the Muslim community in Canada.

Mahmod highlights the cultural stigmatization and denial surrounding mental health issues, which hinder individuals from seeking help. She calls for increased awareness, support, and resources, emphasizing the need for education, culturally sensitive interventions, training for healthcare professionals, and community engagement to effectively address these challenges.

Additionally, it is essential to promote mental health awareness within the Muslim community continuously. More research is needed to measure improvements and develop effective strategies.

References

Ahmed, S., & Reddy, L. A. (2007). Understanding the mental health needs of American Muslims: Recommendations and considerations for practice. *Journal of Multicultural Counseling and Development, 35*(4), 207–218. https://doi.org/10.1002/j.2161-1912.2007.tb00061.x

Ali, S., Elsayed, D., Elahi, S., Zia, B., & Awaad, R. (2022). Predicting rejection attitudes toward utilizing formal mental health services in Muslim women in the US: Results from the Muslims' perceptions and attitudes to mental health study. *International Journal of Social Psychiatry, 68*(3), 662-669. https://doi.org/10.1177/00207640211001084

Alharbi, H., Farrand, P., & Laidlaw, K. (2021). Understanding the beliefs and attitudes towards mental health problems held by Muslim communities and acceptability of cognitive behavioral therapy as a treatment: Systematic review and thematic synthesis protocol. *BMJ Open, 11*(6), e044865. https://doi.org/10.1136/bmjopen-2020-044865

Antora, S. (2022). Muslim Americans in the fight against mental health stigma. ICNA Relief USA. Retrieved from ICNA Relief USA

Awaad, R., El-Gabalawy, O., Jackson-Shaheed, E., Zia, B., Keshavarzi, H., Mogahed, D., & Altalib, H. (2021). Suicide attempts of Muslims compared with other religious groups in the US. *JAMA Psychiatry, 78*(9), 1041-1044. https://doi.org/10.1001/jamapsychiatry.2021.1813

Aftab, A., & Khand, C. (n.d.). Resource prepared by APA Division of Diversity and Health Equity. APA Division of Diversity and Health Equity.

Chaudhry, S., & Li, C. (2011). Is solution-focused brief therapy culturally appropriate for Muslim American counselees? *Journal of Contemporary Psychotherapy, 41*(2), 109–113. https://doi.org/10.1007/s10879-010-9153-1

Ciftci, A., Jones, N., & Corrigan, P. W. (2012). Mental health stigma in the Muslim community. *Journal of Muslim Mental Health, 7*(1). https://doi.org/10.3998/jmmh.10381607.0007.102

Council on American–Islamic Relations (CAIR). (2015). Confronting fear: Islamophobia and its impact in the United States. Retrieved from https://ca.cair.com/publications/2013-2015-cair-national-islamophobia-report-confronting-fear-islamophobia-and-its-impact-in-the-united-states/

Institute for Social Policy and Understanding. (2016). Young adult American-born Muslims and mental health. Retrieved from https://www.ispu.org/wp-content/uploads/2016/12/young-adult-american-born-muslims-and-mental-health.pdf

Islamic Horizons. (n.d.). Exploring Canada's Muslim mental health landscape. Retrieved from https://islamichorizons.net/exploring-canadas-muslim-mental-health-landscape

Khan, R. (2023). Faith in mind: Islam's role in mental health. Yaqeen Institute. Retrieved from https://yaqeeninstitute.org/read/paper/faith-in-mind-islams-role-in-mental-health

Kumar, M., & Huang, K. Y. (2024). Considerations for addressing trauma in Muslim communities. *JAMA Network Open, 7*(8), e2429605. https://doi.org/10.1001/jamanetworkopen.2024.29605

Mahmod, M. (2024). Exploring Canada's Muslim mental health landscape. *Islamic Horizons, Sep/Oct 2024.*

Phillips, D., & Lauterbach, D. (2017). American Muslim immigrant mental health: The role of racism and mental health stigma. *Eastern Michigan University, 11*(1).

Skinner, R. (2010). An Islamic approach to psychology and mental health. *Mental Health, Religion & Culture, 13*(6), 547–551. https://doi.org/10.1080/13674676.2010.488441.

Society for Community Research and Action: Division 27 of the American Psychological Association. (2018). Statement on the effects of deportation and forced separation on immigrants, their families, and communities. https://doi.org/10.1002/ajcp.12256

Tanhan, A., & Francisco, V. T. (2019). Muslims and mental health concerns: A social ecological model perspective. *Journal of Community Psychology, 47*(4), 964–978. https://doi.org/10.1002/jcop.22166

Tanhan, A., & Strack, R. W. (2020). Online photovoice to explore and advocate for Muslim biopsychosocial spiritual wellbeing and issues: Ecological systems theory and ally development. *Current Psychology, 39*(6), 2010–2025. https://doi.org/10.1007/s12144-020-00692-6

Tanhan, A., & Young, J. S. (2021). Muslims and mental health services: A concept map and a theoretical framework. *Journal of Religion and Health, 61*(1), 23-63. https://doi.org/10.1007/s10943-021-01324-4

Therapy for Muslims. (n.d.). Therapy for Muslims. Retrieved January 31, 2025, from https://therapyformuslims.com/

CHAPTER TWO

CULTURALLY RELEVANT DIAGNOSTIC CONSIDERATIONS AND TREATMENT

Samar Harfi

This chapter explores how culture, religion, and psychosocial factors impact the mental health of Muslims in North America. It identifies challenges such as systemic barriers, cultural stigma, and misunderstandings about religion that obstruct access to quality care. The chapter highlights the diverse cultural landscape of this population and emphasizes the importance of cultural competency and humility in diagnosis and treatment. It utilizes case studies and evidence-based insights to illustrate the relationship between cultural values, religious beliefs, and mental health. Additionally, the chapter proposes strategies for culturally sensitive approaches and provides a framework for mental health professionals to engage effectively with Muslim clients, ensuring that care is equitable and respectful of their unique identities.

Introduction

Like the stars that shape the journey through the deserts of Arabia– culture is the constellations we follow, the compass that directs us on our path, often unnoticed yet profoundly influential. Like the rhythm of the caravan and the stories shared under the night sky, culture quietly weaves its way into our beliefs, actions, and the paths we choose to take.

Culture shapes individuals' beliefs, values, and behaviors, influencing how they understand and experience mental health issues (Office of the Surgeon General et al., 2001). Therefore, it can be understood as the values, beliefs, language, rituals, traditions, and other behaviors passed from one generation to another in any social group (American Psychological Association, 2023). DSM-5 notes that "Culture provides interpretive frameworks that shape the experience and expression of the symptoms, signs, and behaviors that are criteria for diagnosis. Culture is transmitted, revised, and recreated within the family and other social systems and institutions" (p. 14).

The experiences of Muslims in North America are significantly shaped by cultural and religious influences, which call for a nuanced approach to mental health as their diverse community evolves. This community is rich in cultural, historical, and socio-political threads (Bagasra & Mackinem, 2014). The need for such an approach is evident not only in the diversity of Muslim communities in North America but also in the unique environments and social contexts they encounter. For some, these environments may provide refuge and comfort, while for others, they can present challenges such as misunderstandings, a lack of accommodation, or unwelcoming attitudes. These factors can create additional obstacles to accessing mental health care.

Despite the various psychosocial challenges faced by Muslims in North America, they often utilize mental health services far less than necessary (Tanhan & Young, 2022). Several systemic barriers contribute to this issue, including stigma within their communities, the fear of "double stigma" as members of an already marginalized group (Çiftçi, Jones & Corrigan, 2012), a preference for religion-based counseling, cultural misconceptions held by healthcare providers (Ahmed & Reddy, 2007), a general lack of mental health awareness (Altuwairqi, 2023), and insufficient access to culturally competent resources. These barriers and delays in seeking treatment can lead to worsening mental health conditions, misdiagnoses, and ineffective treatment (Altuwairqi, 2023). Therefore, it is crucial to develop diagnostic frameworks and therapeutic approaches that consider the religious, cultural, and social contexts of Muslim clients in North America.

CULTURALLY RELEVANT DIAGNOSTIC CONSIDERATIONS AND TREATMENT INTERVENTIONS

Cultural Competence & Cultural Humility

Cultural competence has become essential in training programs and healthcare systems to address disparities in healthcare services (Lekas et al., 2020). It encompasses a provider's knowledge, attitudes, and application of cultural information about various groups, aiming to enhance the effectiveness of the services provided (DeAngelis, 2015; Kirmayer, 2012). However, the static, content-focused approach and the assumption of a final endpoint have received criticism for neglecting individual differences, intra-cultural variations, intercultural complexities, and intersecting identities (Tervalon & Murray-García, 1998; Lekas et al., 2020).

In their 2020 article "Rethinking Cultural Competence: Shifting to Cultural Humility," Lekas and colleagues criticize the ineffective, content-oriented approach to cultural competency. They advocate for cultural humility—an ongoing process of self-reflection, learning, and recognizing biases that were introduced in 1998. This approach emphasizes the importance of humility, compassionate curiosity, openness to clients' perspectives, and self-awareness. Providers are encouraged to acknowledge their limitations in cultural knowledge rather than claim expertise.

By adopting cultural humility when working with Muslims in North America, clinicians can move beyond a rigid understanding of expertise. This fosters trust, empathy, and collaboration in therapy, which is associated with stronger therapeutic alliances, higher client satisfaction, and improved outcomes.

Ethnic, Sectarian, and Cultural Subgroups

But You don't look Muslim!

The Muslim population in the United States is ethnically and racially diverse, with no single group making up the majority. Approximately 41% identify as White (including Arabs, Iranians, and North Africans), 28% as South Asian, 20% as Black, and smaller percentages identifying as Hispanic, multiracial, or Indigenous (Pew Research Center, 2017). Religiously, most Muslims identify as Sunni (55%), followed by Shia (16%), while others simply identify as Muslim (Pew Research Center, 2011). This diversity highlights the importance of avoiding assumptions that generalize the Muslim community and emphasizes the need to consider how race, ethnicity, and sectarian identity intersect with acculturation and mental health.

Given the wide range of backgrounds and the rich, multifaceted culture that Muslims represent, it is crucial to recognize the intersectionality of various influences—including racial, ethnic, gender, and other identities—and how they play a significant role in mental health care (Ahmed & Amer, 2012). Each individual brings unique stories, meanings, and sociopolitical histories that affect their interactions with mental health services and influence how they experience and express mental health concerns.

The degree of acculturation and adoption of Western values likely affects how traditional Islamic values and lifestyle shape a person's mental health service experience and engagement, necessitating that professionals account for this cultural interplay to deliver effective, sensitive care (Ahmed & Amer, 2012; Bagasra & Mackinem, 2014).

To effectively integrate knowledge about Islam and the culture of Muslims in North America into mental health services, it is crucial to recognize that information alone does not guarantee cultural competency. A culturally competent approach involves being person-centered, process-oriented, and practicing cultural humility. It also requires thoughtful engagement with individuals.

This section explores the importance of culturally relevant diagnostic considerations and treatment interventions for Muslims in North America. It examines how cultural values, religious beliefs, and community customs shape the understanding, experience, and expression of mental health symptoms. Additionally, it provides a framework for mental health professionals to practice cultural humility, ensuring that they deliver sensitive care that respects the unique experiences and needs of Muslim clients in North America.

A Tale of Two Approaches

Jameela

Jameela, a 32-year-old African American Muslim woman who wears the *hijāb*, sought therapy for anxiety and depression following a difficult divorce. She reported low confidence and feelings of undesirability. Though she selected her therapist through her insurance network, the non-Muslim provider lacked cultural competence and humility, struggling to understand Jameela's values. During intake, Jameela described her Islamic faith as a source of strength. The therapist, however, suggested that "dressing more freely" might improve her mood—failing to recognize that *hijāb* was an empowering spiritual choice, not a source of distress.

In discussing family dynamics, Jameela mentioned that she consults her father and siblings when making major decisions. The therapist interpreted this as an overreliance on male figures, failing to consider the cultural and religious significance of strong familial ties. The therapy sessions focused on promoting individual autonomy through a Western perspective, encouraging Jameela to distance herself from her family's influence—advice that clashed with her communal values. Feeling increasingly misunderstood and stigmatized, Jameela chose to discontinue therapy after just four sessions, feeling disheartened and discouraged.

Reflections

This case illustrates the potential harm that can occur when therapists lack cultural and religious sensitivity. The therapist failed to acknowledge and validate key aspects of Jameela's identity, including her faith, *hijab*, and family values. This oversight ultimately compromised the therapeutic alliance. Without a culturally responsive approach, therapy turned into a source of alienation instead of healing, resulting in premature termination of the process and increased distress for Jameela.

Omar

Omar, a 41-year-old Arab Muslim man, sought therapy for overwhelming anxiety, obsessive thoughts, and compulsive behaviors related to his religious practices. Although deeply committed to his faith, his rituals had become rigid and distressing—he spent hours in prayer and repeatedly performed *wudu'* out of fear that it was incorrect, leading to emotional exhaustion and avoidance of prayer.

His therapist, who is a culturally informed Muslim clinician, identified that his symptoms aligned with religious OCD, also known as **scrupulosity**. This specific form of OCD is characterized by excessive moral or religious concerns. The therapist explained that, unlike general OCD, scrupulosity is closely linked to a person's spiritual identity and often manifests through rituals and moral anxieties. Acknowledging Omar's distress, the therapist reassured him that Islam was not the source of his symptoms and framed treatment as a way to help him restore balance in his faith.

The treatment included culturally and Islamically relevant approaches from a religious OCD workbook, featuring *Islamically guided Exposure and Response Prevention (ERP)*. With Omar's consent, the therapist consulted a religious scholar knowledgeable about OCD and Islamic practices. Together, they addressed cognitive distortions that were inconsistent with Islamic teachings, highlighting the importance of moderation and self-compassion in worship. Their discussions also emphasized that imperfections in worship are a natural and spiritually acceptable part of the experience.

Reflections

Through this faith-integrated and culturally responsive intervention, Omar gained insight into how anxiety was influencing his religious behaviors. He started participating in worship with a better sense of balance and less fear of imperfection. By framing religious scrupulosity as a clinical condition and aligning the treatment with Omar's values, the therapist built trust, prevented misdiagnosis, and provided effective and culturally appropriate care.

The Impact of Cultural Incompetence

Cultural incompetence can lead to diagnostic errors, including both underdiagnosis and overdiagnosis of certain conditions. Research has shown that African American and Latino clients are often misdiagnosed with schizophrenia when they are actually experiencing mood disorders. This misdiagnosis is partly due to clinicians' lack of cultural understanding regarding expressions of distress within these communities (Alarcón, 2009).

Cultural insensitivity also contributes to higher dropout rates among minority clients, who may feel misunderstood, judged, or disrespected because of their cultural identity and experiences (Sue et al., 2009). Additionally, religious behaviors such as prayer, fasting, or reliance on faith-based coping mechanisms can be mistakenly viewed as either pathological or insignificant if clinicians are unfamiliar with Islamic customs (Haque & Keshavarzi, 2014).

Therefore, cultural sensitivity and competence are essential for accurate diagnosis, effective treatment, and equitable mental health opportunities.

Western psychology is influenced by the cultural values of Western societies, especially individualism. This emphasis on individualism may not resonate with the communal orientations and worldviews of many Muslims in North America. Consequently, therapeutic models based on Western frameworks may not effectively address the cultural and spiritual needs of Muslim clients (Basit & Hamid, 2010).

Research has also highlighted an antireligious sentiment within psychology training programs (Gartner, 1986). During my graduate training, I remember a peer dismissively saying, "How can someone be in graduate school and still believe in God?" Another classmate referred to religion as "a scam that people keep buying into." These attitudes reflect a broader skepticism that can alienate clients and trainees who are religiously committed.

Practitioners must reflect on how their cultural backgrounds, beliefs, and biases regarding religion, spirituality, Islam, and Muslims may influence clinical interactions. Foundational Western psychological theories have often addressed religion in ways that can feel dismissive or pathological. For instance, Freud famously characterized religion as an "illusion" similar to "childhood neurosis," which may be experienced as invalidating by clients for whom faith is central to their lives and meaning. However, a growing body of research highlights the positive connections between religion and mental health, challenging earlier deficit-based narratives and emphasizing the value of collaboration between religious leaders and mental health professionals (Ibrahim & Whitley, 2021).

Cultural sensitivity involves a conscious effort to unlearn ingrained biases, assumptions, and binary notions of "good" and "bad" that shape our understanding. This process allows us to engage more authentically with a client's lived experience by viewing it from their perspective. By doing so, we can avoid inadvertently dismissing or redirecting clients away from values and practices that are deeply rooted in their cultural and spiritual beliefs. This approach fosters a therapeutic alliance based on respect, humility, and genuine connection, which are essential for effective and culturally attuned care.

Culturally Relevant Diagnostic Considerations: Misdiagnosis and Missed Diagnoses

Understanding the Question is Half of The Answer

As the Arabic saying goes, *understanding the question is half the answer.* Recognizing the presenting concern and the individual behind it is essential in mental health treatment. Assessment and treatment are dynamic and interdependent processes. For Muslim clients, it is crucial to sensitively explore their values, worldviews, spirituality, religiosity, cultural influences, experiences of discrimination, and acculturative stress, as these elements are integral to providing effective care (Ahmed & Reddy, 2007). Acknowledging the central role of Islam in the lives of many Muslims promotes cultural curiosity and enhances clinical understanding. This approach, supported by self-education through training, consultations, and relevant resources, fosters culturally informed practice.

Cultural consideration starts from the very first meeting, especially during the intake process. Clients may feel hesitant to share sensitive information due to feelings of shame or stigma. Effective engagement involves not only gathering information but also how questions are framed to promote trust and understanding. Even culturally informed professionals should avoid assuming expertise over a client's spiritual or cultural experiences. Instead, an open and exploratory approach is beneficial. For example, asking questions like, "Can you share how your faith or culture relates to what you are experiencing?" or "Do you find strength in your faith? If so, how?" can help clients feel recognized and understood without imposing assumptions.

Mental Health Measures: Keeping Culture in Mind

When utilizing standardized psychological assessments, clinicians need to be aware of potential cultural biases that may arise from several factors. These include the philosophical foundations of the tests, the lack of diverse representation in normed samples, and the presence of culturally loaded items (Washington et al., 2016; Reynolds & Suzuki, 2013). Historically, psychological research and test development have predominantly relied on samples that are white, Western, and socioeconomically advantaged (Croizet, 2012).

Personality assessments, such as the Minnesota Multiphasic Personality Inventory (MMPI), are often used with various Muslim populations; however, their cultural validity has not been thoroughly examined. Research shows that minority groups may score differently on various scales. For instance, Bagby et al. (2020) found that Muslims who hold strong Islamic values tend to have a more positive self-image. These findings emphasize the need for culturally adapted assessments that are normed specifically for diverse Muslim populations in North America. In the meantime, clinicians who use these tools for diagnostic, academic, legal, or parenting decisions should be aware of potential biases and consider relevant cultural factors when interpreting the results.

Cultural Threads in the Mental Health Experiences of Muslims in North America

According to a 2017 report by the Pew Research Center, approximately two-thirds of Muslims in the United States consider their religion to be very important, and around 60% pray daily. There are no significant differences in these practices across age groups or immigrant status. However, religiosity is not a simple concept; it encompasses belief, practice, and engagement with the Muslim community (Umarji & Islam, 2024). The Qur'anic discourse highlights this complexity by emphasizing both internal belief and outward behavior. Understanding this multifaceted nature helps prevent oversimplified assumptions about Muslim religiosity.

CULTURALLY RELEVANT DIAGNOSTIC CONSIDERATIONS AND TREATMENT INTERVENTIONS

Muslims emphasize different aspects of their faith, which can lead to varying perceptions of religiosity. For instance, a woman who wears the *hijāb* may be viewed as more religious than another woman who does not, even though both may engage deeply with their faith. Recognizing that religious identity includes internal beliefs, external expressions, and cultural influences can help facilitate a more accurate understanding of how faith intersects with mental health.

When non-Muslim providers work with Muslim clients, they may misinterpret specific religious practices—such as daily prayers, fasting during Ramadan, or modesty norms—as rigid or obsessive if they lack an understanding of the religious context. However, these practices are integral to the lives of many Muslims and should not be confused with symptoms of mental illness. It is crucial to differentiate between normal religious observance and expressions of mental illness. For example, feelings of distress over missing a prayer may not be unusual for practicing Muslims, given the importance of the prescribed prayers (ṣalāh) that must be performed at specific times. Unlike the more flexible concepts of prayer found in many non-Muslim traditions—and even within Islam through duʿāʾ—Islamic prayer (ṣalāh) consists of obligatory rituals and intentionally skipping them is considered a serious sin.

Understanding this distinction can help clinicians more accurately assess expressions of distress and avoid misdiagnosis caused by cultural misunderstandings.

Islamic practices, such as fasting during Ramadan and dietary restrictions—including the avoidance of pork, non-halal animal products, and alcohol-derived substances—can influence the choices of psychiatric medications, particularly for individuals with eating disorders. While Islam teaches that healing comes from Allah, it also emphasizes the importance of seeking treatment and preserving life (Attum et al., 2023).

Scholars generally permit the use of medications containing prohibited substances if they are necessary for life-saving treatments. However, opinions vary about using such medications for preventative or "life-enhancing" purposes (Khokhar et al., 2015). Some Muslims may choose to consult an Imam before making these decisions.

Clinicians who possess a basic understanding of these practices and are willing to collaborate with client-approved religious leaders can

The Dimensions of Shame

Ḥayā', Toxic Shame & Honor

In Western psychology, shame is often viewed as a negative emotional experience linked to feelings of inadequacy, self-loathing, and diminished self-worth (Budiarto & Helmi, 2021). For Muslims in North America, this negative form of shame can lead to similar adverse mental health consequences. However, within an Islamic framework, there is another understanding of shame, known as ḥayā', which carries a profoundly different meaning and impact.

Ḥayā' (Healthy Shame)

Ḥayā' can be translated as "modesty" or "humility" and reflects moral consciousness, self-respect, and a keen awareness of accountability before Allah. This form of shame is not viewed as self-condemnation but rather as a positive, virtuous trait that promotes self-awareness and ethical behavior. Unlike the destructive shame often emphasized in Western psychology, ḥayā' encourages self-improvement while upholding an individual's inherent dignity. It motivates individuals to align their actions with moral and spiritual values without undermining their self-worth.

The Prophet Muhammad (peace be upon him) highlighted the importance of ḥayā', describing it as a branch of faith (Imān). He said, *"Faith consists of more than sixty branches, and haya (modesty) is a part of faith"* (Ṣaḥīḥ al-Bukhārī, Vol. 1, Book 2, Hadith 9).

Toxic Shame & Honor

Many Muslims in North America belong to collectivistic communities and often identify as part of the *Ummah*, which represents a unified and interconnected collective. In many predominantly Muslim cultures, the concepts of *shame* and *honor*—such as family social standing and the need to save face—are deeply significant. These concepts influence how individuals experience and express distress, particularly among those who strongly identify with their in-group (Corrigan & Watson, 2002).

Feelings of shame, especially the fear of bringing dishonor to one's family, can lead individuals to avoid seeking psychiatric services or to conceal family members who have mental illnesses (Aloud & Rathur, 2009)

For some Muslims, shame related to mental health struggles may manifest as excessive worry about how their mental state could reflect on their family or community, which can affect their willingness to seek help (Haque & Keshavarzi, 2014).

Understanding these cultural constructs is essential for accurately interpreting the hesitations Muslims may express when facing psychological distress.

Death & Suicide

Despite the increasing involvement of Imams in suicide prevention efforts, discussing suicide remains taboo in many Muslim communities. Guilt and shame often suppress open conversations about suicidal thoughts, leading individuals to respond to direct questions with resistance or passivity (Elzamzamy et al., 2023). Using culturally sensitive language, such as asking, "Have you prayed that Allah would let you die?" in addition to "Have you thought about killing yourself?" can help promote openness.

In Islam, suicide is considered a prohibited sin (Qur'ān 4:29). While wishing for death during difficult times is discouraged, the Prophet Muhammad (peace be upon him) advised believers to maintain humility and trust in Allah's wisdom: "None should wish for death due to calamity; if compelled, say: 'O Allah, keep me alive if life is better, and let me die if death is,'" (Ṣaḥīḥ al-Bukhārī, Vol. 7, Book 70, Hadith 575).

Muslims may struggle with the religious status of someone who has died by suicide, but fatwas state that these individuals remain within Islam and retain their communal rights (Elzamzamy et al., 2023).

The remembrance of death in Islamic tradition is not necessarily a sign of clinical depression or suicidal risk. Rather, it is encouraged as spiritual practice to foster humility and detachment from worldly distractions. The Prophet Muhammad (peace be upon him) stated, "Frequently remember the destroyer of pleasures," referring to death (Sunan Ibn Mājah, Vol. 5, Book 37, Hadith 4258, narrated by Abū Hurayrah). Although this may seem harsh, it serves as merciful guidance, offering perspective on the temporary nature of life and encouraging focus on the afterlife. A nuanced and culturally informed understanding of a Muslim's thoughts about death can help distinguish between ideation stemming from mental health issues and reflections that are tied to spiritual practice and deeper religious engagement.

Language

Verbal communication is the primary method through which clinicians assess symptoms, evaluate severity, and determine functional impairment (Office of the Surgeon General et al., 2001). Muslims in North America come from diverse linguistic backgrounds and possess varying levels of English proficiency. It is essential to provide therapy in a language that the client is fluent in, as this facilitates effective communication, emotional processing, and the development of a strong therapeutic alliance. Language barriers can impede engagement and significantly contribute to the underutilization of mental health services, highlighting the importance of linguistically and culturally competent care (Ohtani et al., 2015).

Use of Islamic-Based Psychotherapy

"The central role that Islam plays in the lives of adherent Muslims throughout the world calls for more spiritually oriented methods of approaching psychological treatment with this group" (Keshavarzi & Haque, 2013).

A meta-analysis comparing religious and spiritual psychotherapies to secular approaches found that clients who received religious or spiritually accommodating therapies experienced comparable outcomes and, in some cases, even superior results (Worthington et al., 2011). Abdullah (2007) emphasizes that effective counseling with Muslim clients requires an understanding of their cultural and religious frameworks, respect for Islamic principles, and the integration of faith-based support with professional psychological practices. Therapeutic adaptations aligned with Islamic teachings—such as cognitive reframing through an Islamic perspective, reflection on Qur'anic verses or ḥadīth, guided self-talk rooted in Islamic values, and the incorporation of prayer and supplication—have been encouraged in some settings and shown to be effective across several studies (Keshavarzi & Haque, 2013).

Some Muslims may not prefer certain therapeutic approaches; others may be unfamiliar with what these methods entail, while some may actively reject them. There is considerable diversity among Muslims regarding their religious identities, levels of observance, and views on the role of religion in mental health. This diversity also extends to ethnicity, culture, and race. A gentle, exploratory approach combined with culturally sensitive listening can help clinicians connect with clients in a way that respects their individual beliefs, including openness to Islamically integrated methods. The International Association of Islamic Psychology offers guidance for individuals seeking clinicians certified in Islamic Psychology and provides a roadmap for clinicians pursuing certification in this field.

Inclusion of Prayer in Therapy

Despite the increasing secularization of psychology in the West, belief in God remains prevalent, with 81% of Americans reporting belief in God

(Gallup, 2022). Much of the existing research on prayer in therapy originates from Christian-based contexts. While some evidence suggests that clients may prefer therapists to incorporate prayer, further research is needed across specific religious groups. Preferences for prayer in therapy often correlate with clients' self-reported levels of spiritual and religious commitment (Saenz & Waldo, 2013).

In Islam, prayer is a central act of worship that can be performed both privately and publicly. Congregational prayer, whether in the form of formal ritual (ṣalāh) or informal supplication (duʿā'), fosters feelings of unity, belonging, and spiritual growth. Praying for one another is a common expression of care, safety, and communal support among Muslims.

When incorporating prayer into therapy, it is essential to do so intentionally and with a strong ethical foundation. Care must be taken to avoid crossing boundaries—such as a client asking what they should pray for regarding the therapist—or intrusions, like a therapist praying for a client without considering the client's own beliefs. We should also avoid spiritual bypassing, which occurs when religious practices are used to evade psychological work and be careful not to undermine the client's autonomy.

When prayer is used thoughtfully, it can enhance the therapeutic alliance, affirm the client's experiences, and promote psychological healing and spiritual growth.

Conceptualization of Mental Illness

The central role of religion in the lives of Muslims often leads to the belief that mental health issues may arise from neglecting religious practices, perceived as a "punishment" for moral or spiritual failings, or as a result of supernatural influences (Haque, 2008; Haque & Keshavarzi, 2014). Some Muslims may view mental and psychological distress as a test from Allah, or a manifestation of God's will, which must be patiently endured (Husain, 1998). These views can be traced back to Quranic verses. For example, the verse: *"And whoever turns away from My remembrance – indeed, he will have a miserable (or depressed) life"* (Quran 20:124) reflects this belief. Conversely, faith and closeness to Allah are also understood within the Islamic tradition to provide psychological and emotional benefits, as highlighted in the verse: *"Verily, in the Remembrance of Allah do hearts find rest/tranquility"* (Quran: 13:28).

This understanding may lead some Muslims to avoid mental health services, opting instead to be patient or to engage in spiritual practices and seek spiritual atonement. Recognizing the role and interplay of spirituality in the expression and alleviation of psychological distress among Muslims is important for fostering a more authentic engagement in therapy, which can lead to a more accurate understanding and treatment of mental illness and emotional distress.

While prayer and acts of worship are encouraged during times of distress, Islamic teachings also highlight the importance of seeking treatment. The Prophet Muhammad (peace be upon him) stated, *"Make use of medical treatment, for Allah has not created a disease without appointing a remedy for it, except for old age"* (Sunan Abī Dāwūd). Nevertheless, some Muslims may downplay their symptoms or avoid mental health services due to feelings of shame or the belief that they should rely solely on patience (*ṣabr*) for spiritual reward. This can create an internal conflict with their faith (Sabry & Vohra, 2013).

At Khalil Center, one of the largest providers of mental health services for Muslims in North America, clients often ask, "Are my mental health difficulties a punishment from Allah or a hardship meant to draw me closer to Him?" Addressing such questions in a manner that is sensitive to the client's psychological and spiritual context can enhance therapeutic engagement. It is important to explore how clients arrive at these interpretations, how each perspective shapes their experiences, and how they view the clinician's role in addressing these concerns. This approach offers valuable insights into their understanding of mental health and the spiritual meanings they assign to their struggles.

Engaging with Muslim clients requires a thoughtful approach that embraces the idea that it's not an either-or situation, but rather a combination of both and more. This framework acknowledges that mental health challenges can be understood simultaneously as a test from Allah, a clinical issue, and an opportunity for proactive self-care alongside spiritual practices such as patience (*ṣabr*). Clinicians can facilitate discussions about how mental health struggles may affect spiritual engagement. For example, depression can decrease motivation for prayer or hinder expressions of gratitude, while anxiety can disrupt *tawakkul* (trust in Allah), potentially leading to feelings of guilt—like thinking, "I believe in relying on Allah, but I can't feel its benefit."

Islamic teachings emphasize that individuals play an active role, through their free will and intentional spiritual orientation, in shaping how they experience hardship. When one seeks closeness to Allah, difficulties may be viewed as opportunities for growth and spiritual empowerment; conversely, if one turns away, the same challenges may be seen as punishment.

CULTURALLY RELEVANT DIAGNOSTIC CONSIDERATIONS AND TREATMENT INTERVENTIONS

Mental Health and Supernatural Beliefs in Muslims

Jinn Possession & Zaar

Belief in supernatural entities inhabiting human bodies exists across various cultures (Cohen, 2008). In Islamic tradition, Jinn are supernatural beings mentioned in both the Qur'an and Hadith, with an entire chapter (Sūrat al-Jinn) dedicated to them. Jinn are believed to inhabit a parallel realm and, like humans, are created to worship Allah. However, they differ in their origin: Jinn are created from "the smokeless flame of fire" (Qur'an 55:15), whereas humans are created from clay (Qur'an 15:26).

Jinn possession is thought to occur through black magic (siḥr) or by provoking Jinn, either knowingly or unknowingly. While Jinn are attributed certain powers, Islamic teachings emphasize Allah's ultimate authority and discourage seeking protection from Jinn. Instead, they recommend the recitation of specific Qur'anic verses for spiritual safeguarding.

Muslims hold diverse beliefs about Jinn, particularly regarding possession. Some fully attribute mental and behavioral changes to Jinn, while others are skeptical of its existence. It is essential to engage clients in exploring their beliefs. Symptoms associated with Jinn possession may include personality changes (such as mood swings or uncontrollable laughter), physical alterations (like convulsions or psychosomatic pain), cognitive shifts (for example, speaking unknown languages), and spiritual reactions (such as an aversion to reciting the Quran) (Lim et al., 2018). Those who believe in possession often seek spiritual remedies like ruqyah, which involves Quranic recitation and prayers aimed at expelling Jinn. Unfortunately, this focus on spiritual solutions can lead to neglecting biomedical or psychiatric explanations, which may exacerbate untreated mental health issues and feelings of helplessness (Haque & Keshavarzi, 2014).

Zaar is a term used in Arab and North African regions, such as Sudan, Egypt, and Ethiopia, to refer to spirit or Jinn possession. It is considered a culture-bound syndrome that is more prevalent among women and is characterized by dissociative, somatic, and affective symptoms. These symptoms can include shouting, laughing, apathy, and a refusal to carry out daily tasks (American Psychological Association, 2023; Şar, 2022).

Zaar is often triggered by prolonged stress or unresolved conflicts. In response, some communities seek out pseudo-religious figures and engage in healing ceremonies that involve music, dance, incense, and chants. These practices are rooted in cultural traditions rather than Islamic teachings and provide emotional release and social support.

Witchcraft (black magic) and Evil Eye

Witchcraft and the evil eye are mentioned in both the Quran and Hadith. The evil eye (*al-'ayn*) refers to harm caused by jealousy or envy, which is believed to result in various mental, emotional, and physical afflictions. This belief is widespread in Muslim-majority cultures and is rooted in a Hadith: "The evil eye is real, and if anything were to overtake the divine decree (*al-qadar*), it would be the evil eye" (Sahih Muslim, Book 26, Hadith 5427, narrated by Ibn 'Abbas).

The Quran also emphasizes seeking refuge in Allah from harm, including envy and black magic (*Quran 113:1-5*).

Individuals may attribute illnesses, marital issues, financial losses, or mental health symptoms to the evil eye. These concerns often intensify after successes, such as purchasing a new home, gaining wealth, or having a child.

While the practice of using blue beads, eye-shaped charms, or amulets inscribed with Quranic verses to ward off the evil eye is common, these cultural traditions are not based on Islamic teachings.

Treatment Considerations

Although possession is classified as a dissociative disorder in the DSM, it is important to approach such beliefs with cultural sensitivity. Validating the client's experiences while providing psychoeducation can help integrate psychological and spiritual perspectives. Exploring the client's interpretation of their experiences and their perceived path to healing, along with incorporating practices like *ruqyah* or specific prayers, can enhance both spiritual and clinical care.

When physical symptoms, such as convulsions, are present, a medical evaluation is necessary to rule out any organic causes. Mental health professionals should maintain ethical boundaries by avoiding direct referrals to religious healers. Instead, they may encourage clients to consult trusted religious leaders who are knowledgeable about mental health, ensuring that informed consent is obtained for any collaborative communication.

Trust and Exploitation

When Fear Fuels Exploitation and Distrust

A study published in the *Journal of Muslim Mental Health* found that many Muslims feel disillusioned with conventional mental health services, leading some to seek help from alternative healers (Amri & Bemak, 2013).

Unfortunately, unverified "healers" may take advantage of vulnerable individuals by charging high fees and using questionable methods that lack support from recognized Islamic scholarship. These practices can spread misinformation, exacerbate untreated psychological conditions, and increase feelings of isolation and helplessness. As a result, they can undermine trust in both mainstream mental health services and qualified Muslim practitioners who provide ethical, culturally sensitive care.

Religious-Specific Expressions of Mental Illness

Waswasa (Scrupulosity)

Waswasa refers to intrusive and obsessive thoughts that often focus on issues of religious purity, correctness, or self-worth. This phenomenon is commonly observed in Muslims who experience scrupulosity-type OCD, known as *Al-Waswās al-Qahri*. This specific form of religious OCD frequently manifests as intrusive doubts related to rituals, such as *ṭahāra* (purification), marriage and divorce, blasphemy or apostasy (*'aqīdah*), and moral character (*akhlāq*). These doubts can lead to compulsive behaviors, including repeated *prayers (ṣalāh), ritual ablution (wuḍū')*, or affirmations of faith (*shahāda*).

Islamically integrated psychotherapy—incorporating elements from cognitive-behavioral therapy (CBT), exposure and response prevention (ERP), and spiritually informed interventions—has proven effective in treating religious OCD. Collaborating with knowledgeable religious leaders, such as imams and scholars, ensures that the care provided is both ethically sound and theologically appropriate. *The Islamic Workbook for Religious OCD* by Keshavarzi et al. (2022) is a valuable resource for clinicians working with clients who experience this condition.

Somatization and Physical Expressions of Psychological Distress

Somatization refers to the way psychological distress is expressed through physical symptoms (Kirmayer & Young, 1998). It was once believed to be more prevalent in non-Western cultures due to the stigma surrounding mental health, but research has shown that it is a universal phenomenon that occurs across various cultural contexts (Kirmayer, 2001). Somatization can lead to the underdiagnosis and undertreatment of conditions when emotional distress is overlooked. Clinicians need to consider the social and emotional significance of bodily symptoms to avoid misdiagnosis. This means they should not attribute these symptoms solely to biomedical causes or prematurely conclude that they are purely psychological without first ruling out possible medical conditions (Kirmayer & Young, 1998).

Sensitivity to Gender Roles and Influences

Muslims who adhere to strong cultural and religious gender norms often prefer to work with therapists of the same gender. Islamic guidelines dictate certain interactions between genders, including restrictions on physical contact and private communication in specific contexts. If a provider is unfamiliar with these norms, they may be viewed as intrusive or inappropriate (Keshavarzi & Haque, 2013).

In the United States, many practitioners lack an understanding of how Islam influences the daily lives of Muslim women, which can negatively impact the quality of care they provide (Saherwala, Bashir, & Gainer, 2021). In medical settings, some Muslim women—especially those with conservative values and lower levels of acculturation—may prefer that their husbands communicate on their behalf. This preference reflects modesty norms and traditional gender roles rather than a lack of engagement. Acknowledging and respecting these preferences can help build trust and strengthen the therapeutic alliance (Attum et al., 2023).

A few important sub-considerations here:

Conservatism among Muslim women refers to the adherence to traditional Islamic interpretations and cultural norms, such as modest dress, defined gender roles, and family structures. This is distinct from extremism, which involves politicized and rigid views that may promote intolerance or violence, contradicting mainstream Islamic teachings.

In Western contexts, this form of conservatism is often misunderstood or equated with extremism, leading to harmful stereotypes. However, it manifests differently in each individual. For example, wearing the hijāb is often a reflection of personal choices related to spirituality, cultural identity, or modesty, and does not uniformly indicate a conservative viewpoint. Many hijāb-wearing Muslim women hold diverse social, political, and religious perspectives.

Each woman's relationship with her faith and culture is unique, shaped by various factors including personal beliefs, family upbringing, and societal influences.

Abuse vs. Conservatism: Providers must be vigilant about potential controlling or abusive dynamics in marital or family relationships. When a husband speaks on behalf of his wife, it may sometimes result from coercion rather than her personal preference or cultural/religious values. It is essential for providers to balance cultural sensitivity with an awareness of power imbalances, ensuring that Muslim women have the opportunity to voice their concerns privately, if necessary. This approach not only protects their autonomy but also respects cultural values, ultimately fostering more nuanced and compassionate care.

Modesty Among Men: Modesty in Muslim men often reflects religious and cultural norms. For instance, beards may carry religious significance, leading some men to avoid shaving unless necessary (Attum et al., 2023). During a mental status examination (MSE), clinicians should differentiate between religious grooming practices and potential indicators of mental health concerns, such as a disheveled appearance associated with depression or psychosis. Significant changes in grooming or modesty that deviate from an individual's baseline may suggest underlying clinical issues, including mania, histrionic personality disorder, or a history of trauma. Recognizing these distinctions is crucial for accurate diagnosis and culturally sensitive care.

Involving family members in therapy, when appropriate, can improve treatment outcomes. Family therapy models that align with Islamic familial structures—where parents or elders often play central roles—can help reduce conflict and strengthen cohesion. This is vital for the collective identity of many Muslim families (Carter & Rashidi, 2019).

Culturally Bound Syndromes and Conditions

Culturally bound syndromes (CBS) refer to mental health phenomena that are rooted in specific cultural contexts, where symptoms and meanings are shaped by cultural beliefs and practices. These syndromes represent a combination of psychiatric and physical symptoms that are recognized only within certain cultures (Haque, 2008, p. 685). Understanding CBS is essential for clinicians, as it helps them better contextualize their clients' symptoms and labels.

For example, *Dhat syndrome*, which derives its name from the Sanskrit word for semen, is common in South Asian Muslim communities and is also observed in some Arab Gulf regions. It involves anxiety and distress related to the perceived loss of semen, often associated with nocturnal emissions or masturbation. In these cultures, Dhat syndrome is connected to notions of masculinity and vitality (Uvais, 2017). Clinicians should view Dhat syndrome as a culturally embedded phenomenon shaped by societal beliefs about health, gender, and bodily function, rather than solely as a psychological disorder.

The term "amok" originates from the Malay phrase *"meng-amok,"* which means "to make a furious and desperate charge." It is identified as a culturally bound syndrome characterized by sudden, violent outbursts that often follow a period of brooding or depression and conclude with exhaustion (Saint Martin, 1999). Historically, these episodes were linked to spirit possession, but today, they are more commonly associated with underlying personality traits, mental illness, and psychosocial stressors. To effectively prevent and treat this syndrome, it is crucial to identify contributing factors, such as a history of violent behavior or significant personal loss (Saint Martin, 1999).

Latino cultures may exhibit conditions such as *"nervios"* or *"ataque de nervios,"* which are culturally rooted expressions of emotional distress characterized by anxiety, irritability, and intense episodes of crying or trembling. These conditions are often linked to stressors such as immigration challenges, family conflict, or cultural dislocation.

Another condition is "susto," which translates to "soul loss." This belief holds that trauma can cause symptoms like fatigue, weakness, and depression, which are attributed to the soul leaving the body due to shock. *Additionally, the concept of "mal de ojo,"* or the "evil eye," suggests that envy or harmful intentions can lead to physical or mental symptoms such as vomiting, fever, or anxiety (Bayles & Katerndahl, 2009).

In Malay culture, psychological issues are often interpreted through physical or spiritual perspectives in order to avoid the stigma associated with mental illness. For example, conditions like the loss of *semangat* (soul substance) or disturbances caused by *angin* (wind in the body) are linked to psychological distress. Additionally, possession by Jinn or the influence of black magic is frequently mentioned as well (Haque, 2008).

Matching Clients and Practitioners

It is advisable to match Muslim clients in the US with practitioners who share their faith or cultural background when it is appropriate and desired (McLaughlin et al., 2022). While many clients prefer Muslim clinicians, others may feel more comfortable with culturally competent non-Muslim providers, especially when discussing sensitive topics. This preference may arise from concerns about feelings of shame or guilt associated with disclosing personal issues to a practitioner who is known within their community (Keshavarzi & Haque, 2013).

Collaboration with Religious Leaders

Imams and religious leaders play a crucial role in shaping the attitudes and help-seeking behaviors of individuals and families facing mental illness (Padela et al., 2012; Abu-Ras, Gheith & Cournos, 2008). In a study that included 62 imams from different regions in the U.S., researchers found that an overwhelming majority—95%—regularly participated in counseling activities for their congregations (Ali, Milstein, & Marzuk, 2005).

CULTURALLY RELEVANT DIAGNOSTIC CONSIDERATIONS AND TREATMENT INTERVENTIONS

Building trust through collaborative and respectful engagement with religious leaders can create effective partnerships that support the psychological and spiritual well-being of clients. Practically, this might involve clinicians conducting workshops or presentations at mosques or Islamic schools, or—upon gaining client consent—consulting with trusted religious leaders to better understand the intersection of spiritual, psychological, and medical issues.

Muslims in North America hold a variety of perspectives on Islam and community, but enhancing mental health awareness among religious leaders can benefit the wider community. Collaboration with imams, scholars, teachers, and parents can improve understanding of mental health, reduce stigma, and encourage positive help-seeking behaviors (Padela et al., 2012). Services that respect and integrate spirituality—rather than merely acknowledge it—are consistent with Islamic principles, which prioritize the preservation of intellect, one of the five core objectives of Islamic law, alongside the preservation of religion, life, lineage, and wealth. Therefore, seeking mental health treatment can be considered an essential part of one's spiritual journey and worldly responsibilities.

Conclusion

Practitioners are not required to share their clients' beliefs, but they must make an effort to understand and respect their cultural and value systems. By honoring these differences without imposing their own views, practitioners can build trust and provide culturally sensitive care that aligns with the client's identity. It's important to remember that culture and religion are not uniform; a client's identity is shaped by a combination of their faith, ethnicity, gender, acculturation, and personal experiences. Practitioners should avoid making assumptions, stay open to individual nuances, and engage each client with curiosity and humility. Ongoing training in cultural competence and religious literacy, grounded in cultural humility, is essential for delivering care that is appropriate, respectful, and effective.

References

Abdullah, S. (2007). Islam and counseling: Models of practice in Muslim communal life. *Journal of Pastoral Counseling, 42,* 42–55.

Abu-Ras, W., Gheith, A., & Cournos, F. (2008). The imam's role in mental health promotion: A study at 22 mosques in New York City's Muslim community. *Journal of Muslim Mental Health, 3*(2), 155–176. https://doi.org/10.1080/15564900802487576

Ahmed, S., & Amer, M. M. (2012). *Counseling Muslims: Handbook of mental health issues and interventions.* Taylor & Francis.

Ahmed, S., & Reddy, L. A. (2007). Understanding the mental health needs of American Muslims: Recommendations and considerations for practice. *Journal of Multicultural Counseling and Development, 35*(4), 207–218.

Alarcón, R. D. (2009). Culture, cultural factors, and psychiatric diagnosis: Review and projections. *World Psychiatry, 8*(3), 131–139.

Ali, O. M., Milstein, G., & Marzuk, P. M. (2005). The imam's role in meeting the counseling needs of Muslim communities in the United States. Psychiatric Services, 56, 2-5. http://dx.doi.org/10.1176/appi.ps.56.2.202

Aloud, N., & Rathur, A. (2009). Factors affecting attitudes towards seeking and using formal mental health and psychological services among Arab Muslim populations. *Journal of Muslim Mental Health, 4,* 79–103. http://dx.doi.org/10.1080/15564900802487675

Altuwairqi, Y. (2023). Factors influencing delay in seeking care for mental illness among a sample of adult Saudi Arabian patients. *Cureus, 15*(11), e49438. https://doi.org/10.7759/cureus.49438

Amri, S., & Bemak, F. (2013). Mental health help-seeking behaviors of Muslim immigrants in the United States: Overcoming social stigma and cultural mistrust. *Journal of Muslim Mental Health, 7*(1). https://doi.org/10.3998/jmmh.10381607.0007.104

American Psychiatric Association. (2013). *Diagnostic and statistical manual of mental disorders* (5th ed.). https://doi.org/10.1176/appi.books.9780890425596

American Psychological Association. (2023). Culture. In *APA dictionary of psychology.* Retrieved October 10, 2024, from https://dictionary.apa.org

Attum, B., Hafiz, S., Malik, A., et al. (2023). Cultural competence in the care of Muslim patients and their families. In StatPearls. Treasure Island, FL: StatPearls Publishing. Retrieved January 2025, from https://www.ncbi.nlm.nih.gov/books/NBK499933/

Bagasra, A., & Mackinem, M. (2014). An exploratory study of American Muslim conceptions of mental illness. *Journal of Muslim Mental Health, 8*(1), 57–76.

Bagby, R. M., Onno, K. A., Mortezaei, A., & Sellbom, M. (2020). Examining the "traditional background hypothesis" for the MMPI-2–RF L-r scores in a Muslim faith–based sample. *Psychological Assessment, 32*(10), 991–995. https://doi.org/10.1037/pas0000941

Basit, A., & Hamid, M. (2010). Mental health issues of Muslim Americans. *The Journal of IMA, 42*(3), 106–110. https://doi.org/10.5915/42-3-5507

Bayles, B. P., & Katerndahl, D. A. (2009). Culture-bound syndromes in Hispanic primary care patients. *The International Journal of Psychiatry in Medicine, 39*(1), 15–31. https://doi.org/10.2190/PM.39.1.b

Budiarto, Y., & Helmi, A. F. (2021). Shame and self-esteem: A meta-analysis. *Europe's Journal of Psychology, 17*(2), 131–145. https://doi.org/10.5964/ejop.2115

Carolan, M. T., Basherinia, G., Juhari, R., Himelright, J., & Mouton-Sanders, M. (2000). Contemporary Muslim families: Research and practice. *Contemporary Family Therapy, 22*(1), 67–79.

Carter, A. M., & Rashidi, A. (2019). Family dynamics in Muslim communities: Implications for therapy. *Journal of Family Therapy, 41*(2), 254–269.

Çiftçi, A., Jones, N., & Corrigan, P. W. (2012). Mental health stigma in the Muslim community. *Journal of Muslim Mental Health, 7*(1), 17-32.

Cohen, E. (2008). What is spirit possession? Defining, comparing, and explaining two possession forms. *Ethnos, 73*(1), 101–126. https://doi.org/10.1080/00141840801927558

Corrigan, P. W., & Watson, A. C. (2002). The paradox of self-stigma and mental illness. *Clinical Psychology: Science and Practice, 9*(1), 35–53. https://doi.org/10.1093/clipsy.9.1.35

Croizet, J.-C. (2012). *The racism of intelligence: How mental testing practices have constituted an institutionalized form of group domination*. In L. D. Bobo et al. (Eds.), *The Oxford Handbook of African American Citizenship, 1865-present* (online ed.). Oxford Academic. https://doi.org/10.1093/oxfordhb/9780195188059.013.0034

DeAngelis, T. (2015). In search of cultural competence. *APA Monitor on Psychology*. Retrieved from https://www.apa.org/monitor/2015/03/cultural-competence

Elzamzamy, K., Owaisi, R. B., Elayan, H., & Elsaid, T. (2023). Muslim experiences and Islamic perspectives on suicide: A qualitative analysis of fatwa inquiries. *International Review of Psychiatry*. https://doi.org/10.1080/09540261.2023.2295475

Gallup. (2022, June 24). How many Americans believe in God? *Gallup*. https://news.gallup.com/poll/268205/americans-believe-god.aspx

Gartner, J. D. (1986). Antireligious prejudice in admissions to doctoral programs in clinical psychology. Professional Psychology: Research and Practice, 17(5), 473–475. https://doi.org/10.1037/0735-7028.17.5.473

Hamdan, A. (2008). Cognitive restructuring: An Islamic perspective. *Journal of Muslim Mental Health, 3*(1), 99–116. https://doi.org/10.1080/15564900802035268

Haque, A. (2008). Culture-bound syndromes and healing practices in Malaysia. *Mental Health, Religion & Culture, 11*(7), 685–696. https://doi.org/10.1080/13674670801958867

Haque, A., & Keshavarzi, H. (2014). Integrating indigenous healing methods in therapy: Muslim beliefs and practices. *International Journal of Culture and Mental Health, 7*(3), 297–314.

Hassan, G., Ventevogel, P., Jefee-Bahloul, H., Barkli-Oteo, A., & Kirmayer, L. (2016). Mental health and psychosocial wellbeing of Syrians affected by armed conflict. *Epidemiology and Psychiatric Sciences, 25,* 129–141. https://doi.org/10.1017/S2045796016000044

Hook, J. N., Davis, D. E., Owen, J., Worthington, E. L., & Utsey, S. O. (2013). Cultural humility: Measuring openness to culturally diverse clients. *Journal of Counseling Psychology, 60*(3), 353–366.

Husain, S. A. (1998). Religion and mental health from the Muslim perspective. In H. G. Koenig (Ed.), *Handbook of religion and mental health* (pp. 279–291). Academic Press. https://doi.org/10.1016/B978-012417645-4/50087-0

Ibrahim, A., & Whitley, R. (2021). Religion and mental health: A narrative review with a focus on Muslims in English-speaking countries. *BJPsych Bulletin, 45*(3), 170–174. https://doi.org/10.1192/bjb.2020.34

Keshavarzi, H., & Haque, A. (2013). Outlining a psychotherapy model for enhancing Muslim mental health within an Islamic context. *International Journal for the Psychology of Religion, 23*(3), 230–249. https://doi.org/10.1080/10508619.2012.712000

Keshavarzi, H., Harfi, S., Elzamzamy, K., Khan, F., & Kaban, E. (2022). *The Islamic workbook for religious OCD: A guide for overcoming intrusive thoughts and compulsions.* Claritas Books.

Khokhar, W. A., Dein, S. L., Qureshi, M. S., Hameed, I., Ali, M. M., Abbasi, Y., ... Sood, R. (2015). When taking medication may be a sin: dietary requirements and food laws in psychotropic prescribing. BJPsych Advances, 21(6), 425–432. doi:10.1192/apt.bp.114.012534

Kirmayer, L. J. (2001). Cultural variations in the clinical presentation of depression and anxiety: Implications for diagnosis and treatment. *Journal of Clinical Psychiatry, 62*(Suppl. 13), 22–28.

Kirmayer, L. J. (2012). Rethinking cultural competence. *Transcultural Psychiatry, 49*(1), 149–164. https://doi.org/10.1177/1363461512444673

Kirmayer, L. J., & Young, A. (1998). Culture and somatization: Clinical, epidemiological, and ethnographic perspectives. *Psychosomatic Medicine, 60*(4), 420–430. https://doi.org/10.1097/00006842-199807000-00006

Lekas, H.-M., Pahl, K., & Lewis, C. F. (2020). Rethinking cultural competence: Shifting to cultural humility. *Health Services Insights, 13,* 1178632920970580. https://doi.org/10.1177/1178632920970580

Lim, A., Hoek, H. W., Ghane, S., Deen, M., & Blom, J. D. (2018). The attribution of mental health problems to Jinn: An explorative study in a transcultural psychiatric outpatient clinic. *Frontiers in Psychiatry, 9,* 89. https://doi.org/10.3389/fpsyt.2018.00089

McLaughlin, M. M., Ahmad, S. S., & Weisman de Mamani, A. (2022). A mixed-methods approach to psychological help-seeking in Muslims: Islamophobia, self-stigma, and therapeutic preferences. *Journal of Consulting and Clinical Psychology, 90*(7), 568–581. https://doi.org/10.1037/ccp0000746

Office of the Surgeon General (US), Center for Mental Health Services (US), and National Institute of Mental Health (US). (2001). *Mental health: Culture, race, and ethnicity: A supplement to mental health: A report of the Surgeon General*. Rockville, MD: Substance Abuse and Mental Health Services Administration. Retrieved from https://www.ncbi.nlm.nih.gov/books/NBK44249/

Ohtani, A., Suzuki, T., Takeuchi, H., & Uchida, H. (2015). Language barriers and access to psychiatric care: A systematic review. *Psychiatric Services, 66*(8), 798–805. https://doi.org/10.1176/appi.ps.201400351

Padela, A. I., Gunter, K., & Killawi, A. (2012). Religious values and healthcare accommodations: Voices from the American Muslim community. *Journal of General Internal Medicine, 27*(6), 708–715.

Pew Research Center. (2011, January 27). The future of the global Muslim population. Retrieved from http://www.pewforum.org/The-Future-of-the-Global-Muslim-Population

Pew Research Center. (2017, July 26). US Muslims concerned about their place in society but continue to believe in the American dream. Retrieved from https://www.pewresearch.org/religion/2017/07/26/findings-from-pew-research-centers-2017-survey-of-us-muslims/

Reynolds, C. R., & Suzuki, L. A. (2013). Bias in psychological assessment: An empirical review and recommendations. In J. R. Graham, J. A. Naglieri, & I. B. Weiner (Eds.), *Handbook of psychology: Assessment psychology* (2nd ed., pp. 82–113). John Wiley & Sons.

Sabry, W. M., & Vohra, A. (2013). Role of Islam in the management of psychiatric disorders. *Indian Journal of Psychiatry, 55*(Suppl. 2), S205–S214. https://doi.org/10.4103/0019-5545.105534

Saenz, R., & Waldo, M. (2013). Clients' preferences regarding prayer during counseling. *Psychology of Religion and Spirituality, 5*(4), 325. https://doi.org/10.1037/a0033711

Şar, V. (2022). Dissociation across cultures: A transdiagnostic guide for clinical assessment and management. *Alpha Psychiatry, 23*(3), 95–103. https://doi.org/10.5152/alphapsychiatry.2022.21556

Saherwala, Z., Bashir, S., & Gainer, D. (2021). Providing culturally competent mental health care for Muslim women. *Innovations in Clinical Neuroscience, 18*(4–6), 33–39.

Saint Martin, M. L. (1999). Running amok: A modern perspective on a culture-bound syndrome. *Primary Care Companion to the Journal of Clinical Psychiatry, 1*(3), 66–70. https://doi.org/10.4088/pcc.v01n0302

Sue, S., Zane, N., Hall, G. C., & Berger, L. K. (2009). The case for cultural competency in psychotherapeutic interventions. *Annual Review of Psychology, 60*, 525–548. https://doi.org/10.1146/annurev.psych.60.110707.163651

Tanhan, A., & Young, J. S. (2022). Muslims and mental health services: A concept map and a theoretical framework. *Journal of Religion and Health, 61*(1), 23–63. https://doi.org/10.1007/s10943-021-01324-4

Tervalon, M., & Murray-García, J. (1998). Cultural humility versus cultural competence: A critical distinction in defining physician training outcomes in multicultural education. *Journal of Health Care for the Poor and Underserved, 9*(2), 117–125.

Umarji, O., & Islam, F. (2024). The role of holistic religiosity on mental health and mental illness: A global study of Muslims. *Psychology of Religion and Spirituality, 16*(4), 378–387. https://doi.org/10.1037/rel0000522

Uvais, N. A. (2017). Dhat syndrome among the Islamic populations of India and Pakistan. *Oman Medical Journal, 32*(5), 442. https://doi.org/10.5001/omj.2017.84

Velott, D., & Sprow, F. K. (2019). Toward health equity: Mindfulness and cultural humility as adult education. *New Directions for Adult & Continuing Education, 2019*(161), 57–66. http://dx.doi.org/10.1002/ace.20311

Washington, K., Malone, C., Briggs, C., & Reed, G. (2016). Testing and African Americans: Testing monograph from the Association of Black Psychologists.

Worthington Jr., E. L., Hook, J. N., Davis, D. E., & McDaniel, M. A. (2011). Religion and spirituality. *Journal of Clinical Psychology, 67*(2), 204–214.

CHAPTER THREE

STRATEGIES FOR COMMUNITY-BASED MENTAL HEALTH INTERVENTIONS IN ISLAMIC INSTITUTIONS

Osman M. Ali, Wadud Hassan

The mental health of Muslim communities depends upon the availability of culturally and religiously compatible professional services and their willingness to access such services when needed. Mosques and Islamic schools have the potential to serve as avenues to reduce barriers to mental health care for Muslims. However, these institutions lack the resources and expertise to fulfill this role. A pragmatic solution, including actionable guidance consistent with findings from the academic literature and Islamic principles, is proposed to assist the leadership of their respective institutions in developing and sustaining meaningful and effective mental health interventions.

Introduction

A public health model views mental health as a spectrum, ranging from mental well-being to mental illness. It emphasizes the need for interventions that include epidemiological surveillance, health promotion, disease prevention, and access to services (Satcher, 2000). The stress-diathesis model suggests that individuals with lower resilience are more likely to transition from mental health to mental illness with less exposure to adversity. Resilience is influenced by a person's biological predispositions, contributing factors, psychological traits, and coping mechanisms (Ingram, 2005). Adversity can vary widely, from everyday stressors to life-threatening trauma, and can occur as both one-time events and chronic situations. Therefore, a community-based intervention aimed at strengthening resilience to stress and improving the identification and early clinical intervention for emerging or existing mental health issues would promote overall mental well-being and enhance mental health outcomes.

Muslims in America face a variety of stressors that can negatively impact their mental health (Kathawalla & Syed, 2021). Islamophobia contributes to poor mental health outcomes, unhealthy behaviors, and unfavorable health care-seeking practices (Samari et al., 2018). Additionally, the specific stresses experienced can vary based on cultural backgrounds. Some Muslims belong to indigenous minorities who encounter racial discrimination. Even indigenous Muslims from the majority race experience challenges as reverts, as they must navigate changes in their identities, practices, social circles, and familial relationships (Catic, 2024). Immigrant and first-generation Muslims also confront intergenerational stressors related to migration and the process of acculturation. Refugees and migrants often experience stress due to the traumatic situations that forced them to leave their homes, along with the challenges they face in meeting their basic needs upon arrival in a new country. Among this population, factors such as hope, faith, relationships, and societal connections are linked to increased resilience (Lindert et al., 2023).

Additionally, there is a lesser-known source of stress that can affect Muslims: the emotional distress felt in relation to other Muslims who are experiencing traumatic situations around the world. These individuals may be family members, but many also feel a deep connection to their fellow Muslims, inspired by Islamic teachings. According to the Holy Qur'an and Sunnah, Muslims are encouraged to empathize with the suffering of others and to support one another, reflecting their moral responsibilities and emotional ties to the larger Muslim community, or Ummah (Maidugu & Sadeeq, 2024).

There are significant barriers that prevent Muslims from seeking and receiving mental health services. These barriers include stigma around seeking mental health care, a lack of mental health literacy, and a shortage of culturally informed providers (Ciftci et al., 2013; Amri & Bemak, 2013; Muse, 2024). Best practices suggest "engaging with the local Muslim community to provide education and information about mental health conditions and services" and "working with community and faith leaders," according to the American Psychiatric Association (Abassi & Paulsen, 2024).

Locations most frequented by Muslims, such as mosques, Islamic community centers, youth centers, and Muslim educational institutions, would be ideal for implementing mental health-related interventions in the Muslim community. This chapter examines population-based mental health prevention interventions at Islamic institutions, particularly mosques and Islamic schools, and proposes actionable strategies for leaders of these centers to develop community-based interventions.

Mosques

The majority of mosques in the United States lack comprehensive mental health services that address the entire spectrum of preventative health. A study called "Mosque in America," conducted by Bagby, Perl & Froehle (2001), found that 45% of mosques had no full-time staff. This study estimated that around 31,700 children and teens attended full-time schools associated with mosques, yet no mental health services were offered at these locations.

In a follow-up study from 2012, it was reported that half of the mosques still had no full-time staff. However, there was significant growth in full-time Islamic schools: 32% of all full-time Islamic schools were K-12, compared to just 13% in 2000, and 31% were K-8/9, up from 6% in 2000. Additionally, 84% of mosques reported providing counseling services, primarily focused on marriage counseling. No mental health services were reported because the question was not specifically included in the survey. According to the 2020 American Mosque Survey, approximately 45% of mosques reported having no staff members. There was also a slight decrease in the provision of family and marital counseling, dropping from 86% in 2012 to 78% in 2020. The authors concluded that there is a growing reluctance among mosques to offer counseling services through non-professional counselors, as well as a hesitation to burden imams with an excessive number of counseling cases. A new question regarding mental health counseling revealed that 32% of participants provided either in-house counseling or referrals for mental health services. This statistic does not imply that mental health counseling is absent, or that in-house clinics do not exist; rather, it indicates that this topic is being explored more directly. There is clearly a need for these services in masajid and Islamic centers. Research suggests they would be more welcomed if staff have previous experience in mental health (Ali & Milstein, 2012).

Descriptions of mental health services on mosque websites suggest that some mental health and related services are offered; however, information about their utilization and effectiveness is not widely reported. A scoping review of the literature conducted by Abu-Ras et al. (2024) explored mosques as venues for health-related interventions. The authors identified three primary categories: mental health, prevention, and communication. Based on these findings, mosques are recognized as important institutions where community-based mental health interventions can help address existing barriers. However, the feasibility of implementing specific interventions in individual mosques depends on the leadership within those communities. Further research is needed to understand and customize these interventions to meet the unique cultural needs of different Muslim populations.

In one article, the authors analyzed a community-based psychoeducation intervention held at a mosque (Mushtaq et al., 2020). This intervention was a half-day educational symposium conducted at a large Islamic center. It featured lectures, didactic sessions, small group discussions, and panel discussions with Muslim patients sharing their experiences with psychiatric illnesses. The event also included insights from religious leaders and experts in both mental health and Islamic teachings. The goal of the symposium was to reduce stigma and promote positive attitudes regarding the compatibility of religion and mental health care. After analyzing the pre- and post-intervention questionnaires from 31 out of 56 attendees, the authors discovered that participants were "very willing to discuss mental health concerns with imams" and had "high levels of agreement regarding psychiatric illness as a medical condition" even before the intervention. Additionally, their willingness to take psychotropic medications increased significantly after the intervention. The authors concluded that collaboration with religious leaders was essential for facilitating this change.

To effectively adjust the services provided in a community, it is important to study the community members and understand how they respond to various interventions. A community advisory board, which includes a large mosque and a local academic institution, facilitated a research study involving 37 mosque attendees—17 women, 10 men, and 10 mixed-gender youth (Ali et al., 2022). The researchers organized focus groups that were presented with vignettes to investigate the barriers and facilitators to seeking mental health support both from the mosque and from one another.

The study findings highlighted the mosque as a crucial venue for offering various mental health services, including "support groups, psychosocial activities, community social workers, virtual support, and family-oriented services." It also addressed several barriers, such as community stigma, the exclusion of racial minorities, misconceptions linking religiosity to mental illness, explanations of mental illness based on supernatural causes, and challenges faced by vulnerable groups. The researchers concluded that the mosque's ability to provide these programs depends on its size, financial resources, and the sustained commitment of its leadership. They also recommended that mosque leaders receive training in grant writing to support these efforts.

Building trusting relationships with religious and community leaders is essential for both one-time and ongoing mental health interventions, research, and evaluations conducted within mosques. Compared to other religious groups in America, Muslim communities lag behind in these areas. Therefore, innovative strategies are necessary to improve the delivery of services and assess their impact within the mosque (Ali, 2016).

Islamic Schools

Both ethical and scientific justifications support the integration of mental health programming into education in high-income countries (Fazel et al., 2014). According to the United States Department of Education, during the 2021–2022 school year, 49 percent of public schools reported providing diagnostic mental health assessments, while 38 percent reported offering treatment for mental health disorders (National Center for Education Statistics, 2024). Despite this evidence, translating research into schools faces several challenges. To address barriers to implementing evidence-based practices in under-resourced schools, it is essential to provide staff training, individual support, consultation, quality improvement efforts, and cost-effective sustainability strategies (Eiraldi et al., 2015). Models for effectively implementing mental health programming in schools and communities should: a) integrate theory, research, and practice; b) consider individual cultural factors; c) engage partners and stakeholders, such as teachers and parents; d) offer a continuum of care that ranges from prevention to treatment; and e) include program evaluation to assess acceptability, integrity, and effectiveness (Nastasi, 1998).

Mosques often operate Islamic schools, but there are also independent Islamic schools that cater to students from Pre-Kindergarten through High School, as well as a few Colleges and Seminaries. In 2002, it was estimated that there were around 200 to 600 Islamic schools in the United States, with enrollments exceeding 30,000 students (Strauss & Wax,

2002). According to a 2024 report by the Institute for Social Policy and Understanding (ISPU), which included data from the Islamic Schools League of America (ISLA), there are nearly 300 full-time Islamic schools serving an estimated 60,000 to 70,000 students (Steward-Streng et al., 2024). This report also highlighted challenges in recruiting and retaining qualified teachers in full-time Islamic schools. Additionally, Islamic schools in America face various funding and staffing challenges, making it difficult to provide comprehensive ancillary services (Merry & Driessen, 2005). The academic literature is limited in its discussion of the implementation of mental health education or evaluation and referral services within Islamic schools in the United States.

Some organizations are starting to address various aspects of prevention, as indicated by their websites. The Islamic Schools League of America offers resources for crisis management related to potential threats to schools (Faisal, 2024). The Council of Islamic Schools of North America features a course on bullying (CISNA, 2021). Additionally, the American Islamic College provides a page on wellness and counseling services that includes hotlines. They also mention that a "Student Services Coordinator" will complete an intake form to offer support and, when necessary, refer students to the listed organizations or to mental health professionals from an approved and regularly updated list.

In 2024, the authors of this chapter launched a formal survey to assess mental health in Islamic schools both in the United States and abroad. While we await the results, we wish to share some insights based on the personal experiences and communications of one author, W.H. This author has had teaching and leadership roles in four Islamic schools and has witnessed the complexities surrounding student mental health firsthand.

Through discussions and informal questionnaires gathered from fellow school leaders and teachers who have received training in Social Emotional Learning (SEL), Character Coaching, and Prophetic Tarbiyah, W.H. identified emotional and behavioral dysregulation as the most common challenge faced by students. This was followed by mental health-related issues such as anxiety, depression, and potential Attention Deficit Hyperactivity Disorder (ADHD) or distractions. He recognized that community cohesion and support are among the greatest strengths of Islamic schools. Additionally, he noted that the spiritual dimension of these schools provides students with coping mechanisms and fosters resilience through their faith, including practices such as reflection, prayer, and reliance on Allah (SWT). While most staff and administration are dedicated to the holistic well-being of their students, few have formal training in mental health or even Mental Health First Aid. Importantly, there is a lack of formal policies in schools for identifying and referring students who need mental health support. Without clear guidelines, staff often feel uncertain about how to handle situations involving emotional or behavioral challenges, despite their willingness to make referrals. Although mental health awareness is increasing, cultural stigmas and misunderstandings persist—such as the misconception that mental health struggles indicate a lack of effort or signs of weak faith. School leaders overwhelmingly acknowledge the need for training staff to manage specific behaviors, assist students in regulating their emotions, integrate social-emotional learning into the classroom, and provide Mental Health First Aid training. Collaboration with a network of mental health professionals is essential as it brings expertise that aligns with the Islamic ethos of schools, ensuring culturally and religiously sensitive support. Additionally, educating parents and the community about mental health can help address lingering stigmas. Factors such as the political climate, global conflicts, Islamophobia, and discrimination can exacerbate internal struggles like anxiety, depression, and emotional dysregulation. Many Islamic schools operate on tight budgets, making it challenging to hire trained counselors or implement comprehensive mental health programs. As a result, staff can become overburdened and may lack the necessary tools to effectively meet student needs.

Considerations for Interventions

A review of 300 published articles on Muslims and mental health identified eleven key factors to consider when designing mental health services for Muslim populations (Tanhan & Young, 2022).

1. Cultural and Religious Understanding: It is essential to appreciate the religious and cultural beliefs regarding the origins of mental illness.

2. Education about Mental Health Services: There should be education on the available mental health providers, interventions, and treatments from biopsychosocial, spiritual, and economic perspectives to encourage the utilization of services before crises escalate.

3. Addressing Negative Attitudes: It is important to address the negative attitudes toward mental health services.

4. Combating Stigma: Stigma surrounding mental health services should be tackled.

5. Enhancing Self-Efficacy: Efforts should be made to enhance individuals' perceived self-efficacy in seeking mental health services.

6. Reducing Institutional Barriers: Engaging more with the community can help reduce institutional barriers to accessing mental health services.

7. Promoting Traditional Resources: The use of traditional resources, such as recitation of the Qur'an, prayer, and consultation with imams, should be encouraged alongside formal mental health services.

8. Enhancing Acculturation: Efforts are needed to support the acculturation of Muslims into the broader community.

9. Recognizing Variability: It is important to recognize the variability in research related to control variables (such as education, sex, past behaviors, race/ethnicity, economic factors, length of stay in Western countries, and age) and to call for further research in these areas.

10. Understanding Intentionality: The role of intention from an Islamic perspective should be studied and utilized to promote gradual acceptance of mental health services.

11. Mandating Action: Islam emphasizes the importance of seeking "contextually sensitive biopsychosocial-spiritual appropriate mental health services" when needed.

Partnerships between faith communities and mental health providers, as reported in the literature, generally lead to positive outcomes regarding mental health symptoms, literacy, stigma reduction, and increased referrals (primarily one-directional toward mental health providers). However, there are potential weaknesses, such as the need for evidence of sustainability and the reporting of both processes and mental health outcomes (Perez et al., 2024).

Creating lasting collaborations between community-based clinical care providers, academic researchers, and religious community organizations is challenging, even when the leadership of these organizations shares personal or professional relationships and similar mindsets.

For instance, one paper describes lessons learned from an 18-month project focused on community-based participatory research initiatives within a large and established Muslim community that includes several mosques. The authors highlight the extensive conversations and efforts required to build partnerships with mosque leaders, multiple community organizations, and an academic institution.

They conducted semi-structured interviews with community stakeholders, followed by focus groups and surveys with mosque congregants. The paper offers several recommendations to enhance research in mosque communities, including:

COMMUNITY-BASED MENTAL HEALTH INTERVENTIONS

1. Address challenges in establishing trust by engaging religious and cultural insiders to connect with mosque leadership and recruit participants.

2. Make announcements during prayer services and community events to increase participation.

3. Recognize the likelihood of limited sustainability and set realistic expectations for the involvement of community partners.

4. Create opportunities for relationship building among the community-academic team to enhance rapport and group cohesiveness.

Non-Muslim schools and religious institutions are generally more advanced in integrating mental health services. There is an urgent need for practical advice and guidance to help mosques and Islamic schools implement effective strategies for addressing the emerging mental health needs of their communities. Muslim leaders and community stakeholders must recognize that, from an Islamic perspective, it is within the scope of Muslim organizations to support the mental health of their members.

However, religious leaders are often hesitant to endorse programs that do not align with Islamic principles. Similarly, some Muslims seeking mental health services at Islamic institutions may be looking for religious or spiritual solutions, or for approaches that are acceptable within Islam. To address these needs, Muslim mental health providers must build strong, long-term relationships with community leadership and other professionals.

Individual donors, government funders, and sponsoring organizations are more likely to support initiatives if they can see the tangible impacts of their contributions. Often, when organizations provide services, the standards they meet can be overshadowed by the belief that any service is better than none. This is not always the case, as services that lack evidence or are ineffective can divert people from quality care, potentially worsening their situation. Even when services are consistent and of high quality, the impact on the community is often not measured or reported. This lack of evaluation prevents others from learning what works and what does not.

Given the limited resources of mosques and Islamic schools, leadership should consider collaborating with established organizations that already provide the desired services or resources. These organizations can assist not only in educating community members but also in training leaders and professionals, as well as providing referrals for counseling services. This overview highlights the services offered by several prominent organizations.

The Islamic Social Services Association USA, established in 2000, provides "Table Talks" online, which are discussions with experts on various topics relevant to Muslims.

In 2005, the Islamic Circle of North America (ICNA) Relief launched Muslim Family Services, offering a range of social services and counseling at no cost. They have also developed an educational series on mental health covering several high-interest topics, which have been translated into multiple languages.

Since 2006, the Institute of Muslim Mental Health has focused on developing an academic journal, creating a professional network, and providing training for imams and Islamic chaplains. They also engage in community outreach and education, regularly offering professional webinars, known as "Meet the Expert," along with online support groups.

The Family & Youth Institute, established for education and research in 2006, provides online and print materials, "toolkits," workshops, and podcasts aimed at supporting families and youth.

The Khalil Center, founded in 2010, offers community education on various topics including parenting, family cohesion, marriage, pre-marital awareness, character development, social-emotional well-being for children, youth development, and individual resilience. They also provide training for mental health professionals on integrating Islamically-oriented care and have been expanding their clinical services nationwide. Established in 2017, Maristan offers Suicide Response Training for religious and community leaders, along with educational videos, online "Learning Circles," and "Pop-Up Healing Circles." Additionally, they engage in community research collaborations and offer clinical services to Muslims.

The American Muslim Health Professionals began offering Mental Health First Aid trainings in 2017. They have tailored this evidence-based practice to the Muslim community, conducting over fifty events in more than 28 cities and certifying over 1,600 community members. All of these organizations maintain consistency with respect to best practices, and many provide online options for training. Mental Health First Aid is considered one of the most effective turnkey solutions for in-person education and training.

An Actionable Strategy

One proposed solution emphasizes a common methodology that highlights four key components: education, collaboration, training, and evaluation. This framework aims to support the conceptualization, practical implementation, and ongoing provision of mental health programming and services at mosques in the United States (Ali, 2018). A fundamental principle of this framework is that any discussion regarding psychological, mental, or social stress and their interventions must be understood within the context of the Muslim perspective on the centrality of Islam in their lives. This principle is reflected in the acronym for the four main components: Resiliency Enhancement, Collaborative Involvement, Training, and Evaluation, collectively known as RECITE. This emphasizes that reciting the Quran or listening to others recite it, along with engaging in supplication, are daily practices for Muslims that can be particularly beneficial during times of distress (Rozali et al., 2022).

Resiliency Enhancement

Resiliency Enhancement is an educational and support initiative designed to engage individuals who may not have a diagnosed mental health condition, as well as those who are currently receiving treatment elsewhere. This program offers education and workshops directly to community members who attend mosques, employing a preventive health model to combat stigma and improve mental health literacy within the community. A systematic review of resilience-enhancing programs indicates that mental health promotion initiatives focusing on resilience and coping skills positively impact students' abilities to manage daily stressors (Fenwick-Smith et al., 2018). Unfortunately, mental health resources are absent in most Muslim organizations. Many smaller organizations concentrate on their primary missions and may not prioritize developing and sustaining healthcare interventions. They often need to first recognize such interventions as essential and aligned with their mission. In contrast, larger, more established organizations are more likely to understand the necessity of these interventions and possess the economic and human resources needed to integrate mental health programming into their services.

Collaborative Involvement

In times of distress, Muslims may seek support from imams, religious scholars, family members, or mental health professionals, preferably those who understand the role of Islam in their lives. However, some individuals do not seek or receive the help they need due to community stigma or other factors. Collaborative involvement emphasizes the importance of professionals from various backgrounds working together to ensure that individuals in need of help are quickly connected to the appropriate resources. The first step in fostering collaboration should involve the organizational leadership working alongside an internal referral service or navigator. Together, they can create opportunities for the navigator to connect with individuals seeking mental health assistance. The second area of collaboration involves the navigator and the service provider that can address the individual's identified needs. This could be a professional outside the organization or a religious scholar within it. The third area focuses on collaboration between mental health professionals and religious scholars, both of whom a Muslim patient or client may consult. This collaboration can be enhanced through the development of a resource directory and regular consultation sessions or presentations where professionals can seek guidance from one another. It is important to note that collaboration is not a one-way process from the religious institution to secular service providers. Instead, follow-up with the referring provider is essential to ensure ongoing collaboration.

Training

While the knowledge and attitudes of congregants, students, and parents can be enhanced through education, professionals need to acquire new skills or improve their existing ones to better serve those in need. Training is provided for primary care providers, mental health professionals, social service workers, and others so they can recognize the crucial role of Islam in the lives of Muslims and offer culturally appropriate care. Educating religious scholars, faculty, and organizational leaders about the mental health system, the roles of clinical professionals, and the signs that a congregant or student may need additional support can help share the responsibilities of care and services. Several core competencies recommended for imams, religious leaders, or faculty include the ability to identify and refer individuals in need, establishing boundaries, practicing self-care, and addressing the religious and spiritual support needs of individuals while encouraging appropriate professional interventions when necessary.

Evaluation

All aspects of this programming are guided by processes and measures to ensure quality, safety, and value. At the core of this model is evaluation. This includes initial and ongoing community needs assessments, as well as qualitative and quantitative feedback from both service consumers and providers. Additionally, it involves analyzing data to effectively develop, reallocate, and manage resources—such as human, capital, and programming—efficiently. The lack of data collection and utilization is a common issue among Islamic organizations. Promoting standardized measures and shared educational and training resources can help pool data, allowing for a better understanding of the needs of different communities and highlighting their similarities and differences. This public health approach not only facilitates resource sharing but also enhances the effectiveness of interventions by demonstrating to potential funders the measurable differences their contributions can make. While one-time events or timely khutbahs can be beneficial, having data is essential for making a compelling case to donors or grant providers for ongoing support. Additionally, this aspect includes vetting individuals or organizations that offer education, training, or services to ensure they adhere to best practices and align with Islamic values.

Next Steps to Implement RECITE

For the leadership of mosques and Islamic schools looking to develop mental health programs at their institutions, the following steps are suggested:

Step 1: Arrange an initial meeting with key stakeholders, including other board members, mental health providers affiliated with the organization or within the local community, and religious leaders. The purpose of this meeting is to discuss the establishment of a mental health initiative called RECITE, which will focus on the elements of Resiliency Enhancement, Collaborative Involvement, Training, and Evaluation.

    A. It is important to emphasize the Islamic alignment of this effort. Key talking points may include the importance of maintaining a positive mental state in order to practice one's faith, the significance of education in Islam, and the Prophetic tradition of solving problems through **mashwara** (consultation). Collaboration with experts and careful planning are also essential, as is the concept of reducing the burden on teachers and clergy, along with minimizing liability for the organization. Additionally, it is important to note that we utilize a medical model for mental health, so any scrutiny regarding its compatibility with Islamic principles would also apply to physical health issues. It is essential to recognize that multiple approaches can coexist based on proximate versus ultimate mechanisms. For instance, an individual experiencing depression with psychotic features may require medication to address the proximate (biological) contributors. At the same time, practices such as Quranic recitation can be used to address intermediate contributors, like Djinn, while prayer and supplication can seek assistance from Allah, who ultimately controls all matters. These interventions should not be seen as mutually exclusive.

    B. Encourage individuals to make a firm commitment to ensure that their primary objective is to please the Almighty by serving the community. While they may also experience personal satisfaction and rewards that help sustain their efforts, this should be secondary. It's important for them to commit to this service for at least one year. Additionally, programs that rely too heavily on individual involvement, rather than clearly defined roles and missions, can lead to limitations and increased risk of burnout for those individuals. Therefore, participants should begin considering potential mentees who can assist them and eventually take over when they can no longer serve. Clear roles and responsibilities must be assigned to ensure the program's sustainability.

Step 2: Create and support the RECITE committee

A. The board appoints three individuals as either volunteers or paid employees. One person will be designated as the head of Education and Training, another will oversee Collaboration, and the third will focus on Evaluation. These three individuals will meet regularly and consult with religious leaders and a board liaison. During their meetings, they will discuss each person's assignments, their plans, any barriers they may encounter, and the support they need to achieve their goals.

B. The Education and Training liaison should ideally be a community member who can provide education on mental health topics and appreciate the contributions of Islamic perspectives related to mental health and wellness. Their focus should be on established, evidence-based medical and professional resources.

C. The ideal Collaboration Liaison is a Muslim mental health provider in the community. Their role involves triaging questions from community members and staff, establishing professional relationships, and building trust with religious and other leaders. They should meet regularly with these leaders to provide informal consultations on challenging topics that arise each week. Additionally, the liaison needs to maintain a resource list that includes various levels and types of interventions.

D. The Evaluation Liaison is responsible for collecting data on the programs offered, including attendance and satisfaction metrics. They should conduct a needs assessment to identify the challenges faced by the community. Additionally, they need to compile organized reports for regular presentations to the board. Ideally, the liaison will have an academic background that equips them to provide essential information for grant writing.

Step 3: Sustain the initiative through fundraising, grant writing, and succession planning.

To ensure the long-term success of the initiative, focus on fundraising, grant writing, and succession planning. Utilize the data generated from the programs to inform your efforts. Share this data with other organizations to foster collaboration. Recruit talented individuals to get involved in the program. The board can start with simple tasks to build momentum through increased awareness and volunteer involvement. While a few dedicated volunteers can coordinate initial activities, larger organizations may require paid staff for sustainability.

By establishing the program as an academically sound best practice, complete with built-in accountability and potential for further development and adaptation, you can facilitate the achievement of all these goals.

Discussion and Conclusion

Muslims in the United States face several barriers to accessing essential mental health services, including stigma, lack of awareness, and a shortage of providers who are familiar with Islamic beliefs and practices. Established Islamic organizations may serve as an entry point to address some of these barriers by providing religiously appropriate care. However, these organizations often lack the resources necessary to effectively tackle the issue of mental health in their communities, despite recognizing the problem. One-time events can provide temporary relief and generate excitement, but they are infrequent and do not ensure ongoing support. Communities are eager for any mental health discussions, even if they do not adhere to best practices. Conversely, religious interventions that overlook the medical aspects of mental health care can be introduced, but they may fail to meet the actual healthcare needs of individuals. Collaboration between large mosques, schools, and academic or professional communities is often challenging to achieve. With lofty goals and a variety of opinions from religious and mental health professionals, projects may stagnate unless there are a few individuals who can navigate politics and possess the necessary connections and expertise. Unfortunately, most organizations do not have this advantage.

To address these challenges, a pragmatic approach known as RECITE has been proposed as a strategy to initiate and sustain mental health education, training, and referral services. While implementing this solution may present challenges, it provides a way to move beyond the deadlock caused by limited resources and expertise. RECITE emphasizes the initiative rather than individual leaders, helping to mitigate issues of burnout and ensuring that the program can thrive independent of specific individuals. It is scalable, allowing for adaptation regardless of the size of the organization, and it has the potential to foster collaboration among organizations with similar goals.

By utilizing consistent metrics, organizations can consolidate, share, and present data to learn from one another, exchange resources, compare their populations, and tailor services to meet the unique needs of their communities. Although there is no straightforward solution to improving the mental health of Muslims, implementing the RECITE program in some Islamic institutions could help transform aspirations into a reality, gaining momentum and support to develop comprehensive programming and services.

References

Abbasi, F. and Paulsen, E. (2024). *Working with Muslim Patients*. Retrieved from https://www.psychiatry.org/psychiatrists/diversity/education/best-practice-highlights/working-with-muslim-patients on November 13, 2024. American Psychiatric Association, Washington, DC.

Abu-Ras, W., Aboul-Enein, B. H., Almoayad, F., Benajiba, N., & Dodge, E. (2024). Mosques and public health promotion: A scoping review of faith-driven health interventions. *Health Education & Behavior*, 51(5), 677-690.

Ali, O. M., & Milstein, G. (2012). Mental illness recognition and referral practices among imams in the United States. *Journal of Muslim Mental Health*, 6(2).

Ali, O. M. (2016). The imam and the mental health of Muslims: Learning from research with other clergy. *Journal of Muslim Mental Health*, 10(1).

Ali, O. M. (2018). Promoting a common framework for developing mental health programming at Islamic centers. Presented at the Islamic Society of North America Annual Convention, September 2018, Houston, Texas.

Ali, S., Mahmood, A., McBryde-Redzovic, A., Humam, F., & Awaad, R. (2022). The Role of Mosque Communities in Supporting Muslims with Mental Illness: Results from CBPR-Oriented Focus Groups in the Bay Area, California. *Psychiatric Quarterly*, 93(4), 985-1001.

Amri, S., & Bemak, F. (2013). Mental Health Help-Seeking Behaviors of Muslim Immigrants in the United States: Overcoming Social Stigma and Cultural Mistrust. *Journal of Muslim Mental Health*, 7(1).

Awaad, R., Obaid, E., Kouser, T., & Ali, S. (2023). Addressing Mental Health through Community Partnerships in a Muslim Community. Psychiatric Services, 74(1), 96-99.

Bagby, I. A. W., Perl, P. M., & Froehle, B. (2001). *The mosque in America, a national portrait: A report from the Mosque Study Project* (pp. 1-63). Washington, DC: Council on American-Islamic Relations.

Catic, N. (2024). Persuaded by the Qur'an: Converting to Islam in Canada. *Religious and Socio-Political Studies Journal*, 2(1), 33-77.

Ciftci, A., Jones, N., & Corrigan, P. W. (2013). Mental health stigma in the Muslim community. *Journal of Muslim Mental Health*, 7(1).

CISNA. (2021, December 13). *The Educator's Toolkit - CISNA*. CISNA - Council of Islamic School of North America. https://cisnausa.org/toolkit/

Ingram, R. E. (2005). Vulnerability-Stress Models. In *Development of Psychopathology: A Vulnerability-Stress Perspective*. Sage Publications Inc.

Eiraldi, R., Wolk, C. B., Locke, J., & Beidas, R. (2015). Clearing hurdles: The challenges of implementing mental health evidence-based practices in under-resourced schools. *Advances in School Mental Health Promotion*, 8(3), 124–140.

Faisal, A. (2024, March 20). *Crisis Toolkit | ISLA*. ISLA. https://theisla.org/crisis-toolkit/).

Fazel, M., Hoagwood, K., Stephan, S., & Ford, T. (2014). Mental health interventions in schools in high-income countries. *The Lancet Psychiatry*, 1(5), 377–387.

Fenwick-Smith, A., Dahlberg, E. E., & Thompson, S. C. (2018). A systematic review of resilience-enhancing universal, primary school-based mental health promotion programs. *BMC Psychology*, 6, 1–17.

Kathawalla, U. K., & Syed, M. (2021). Discrimination, life stress, and mental health among Muslims: A preregistered systematic review and meta-analysis. *Collabra: Psychology*, 7(1), 28248.

Lindert, J., Samkange-Zeeb, F., Jakubauskiene, M., Bain, P. A., & Mollica, R. (2023). Factors contributing to resilience among first-generation migrants, refugees, and asylum seekers: A systematic review. *International Journal of Public Health*, 68, 1606406.

Maidugu, U. A., & Sadeeq, A. A. A. (2024). Islam and morality: The teachings of Al-Ihsan from the Qur'an and Hadith and their effects on the Muslim Ummah. *Solo Universal Journal of Islamic Education and Multiculturalism*, 2(03), 181-194.

Merry, M. S., & Driessen, G. (2005). Islamic schools in three Western countries: Policy and procedure. *Comparative Education*, 41(4), 411-432.

Muse, R. A. (2024). Breaking the barriers: Enhancing mental health care for Muslim communities through cultural proficiency and community awareness.

Mushtaq, S. B., Ayvaci, E. R., Hashimi, M., & North, C. S. (2020). Bringing psychiatry into the mosque: An analysis of a community psychoeducation intervention. *Journal of Psychiatric Practice*, 26(3), 249-257.

Nastasi, B. K. (1998). A model for mental health programming in schools and communities: Introduction to the mini-series. *School Psychology Review*, 27(2), 165-174.

National Center for Education Statistics. (2024). Prevalence of mental health services provided by public schools and limitations in schools' efforts to provide these services. *Condition of Education*. U.S. Department of Education, Institute of Education Sciences. https://nces.ed.gov/programs/coe/indicator/a23

Samari, G., Alcalá, H. E., & Sharif, M. Z. (2018). Islamophobia, health, and public health: A systematic literature review. *American Journal of Public Health*, 108(6), e1-e9.

Satcher, D. S. (2000). Executive summary: A report of the Surgeon General on mental health. *Public Health Reports*, 115(1), 89.

Steward-Streng, N., Khan, S., & Al-Majaideh, S. (2024). Improving Islamic schools: Attracting and retaining qualified teachers in U.S. full-time Islamic schools through analysis of compensation. June 26, 2024. https://ispu.org/improving-schools-1/

Strauss, V., & Wax, E. (2002). Muslim schools in America: Where two worlds collide. *Washington Post*, 25 February.

Tanhan, A., & Young, J. S. (2022). Muslims and mental health services: A concept map and a theoretical framework. *Journal of Religion and Health*, 61(1), 23-63.

Perez, L. G., Cardenas, C., Blagg, T., & Wong, E. C. (2025). Partnerships Between Faith Communities and the Mental Health Sector: A Scoping Review. *Psychiatric Services, 76*(1), 61-81.

Rozali, W. N. a. C. W. M., Ishak, I., Ludin, A. F. M., Ibrahim, F. W., Warif, N. M. A., & Roos, N. a. C. (2022). The impact of listening to, reciting, or memorizing the Quran on physical and mental health of Muslims: Evidence from Systematic review. *International Journal of Public Health, 67*. https://doi.org/10.3389/ijph.2022.1604998

Yusufali, S. S. (2021). A values-based, holistic approach towards school mission in a U.S. Islamic school.

CHAPTER FOUR

ISLAMIC PSYCHOLOGY: THE MISSING LINK IN MUSLIM MENTAL HEALTH

Fahad Khan

The global mental health landscape is filled with complex challenges that go beyond cultural and geographical boundaries. As we see an unprecedented rise in mental health issues worldwide, it is increasingly important to understand these challenges from various perspectives. This understanding is essential for creating effective interventions and support systems. According to the World Health Organization (2022), nearly one billion people worldwide live with diagnosable mental disorders, and most lack access to effective services and care. The rising rates of mental illnesses—such as depression, anxiety, stress-related disorders, and substance use disorders—have turned mental health into a global concern (Kieling et al., 2024). For instance, 23.4% of American women suffer from anxiety (Harvard Medical School, 2007), while 20% of British children aged 8 to 16 are likely to have a mental disorder (Newlove-Delgado et al., 2022). In Australia, 3% of the population grapples with substance use disorders (Australian Institute of Health & Welfare, 2023), and 34.9% of Indonesian adolescents exhibit symptoms of mental disorders (Wahdi et al., 2023). In Pakistan, over 20 million individuals experience various mental health conditions, with only one psychiatrist available for every half a million people (Nisar et al., 2019; WHO, 2009). Both the Western and Muslim worlds have experienced a decline in mental health, influenced by distinct cultural, social, and economic factors that shape the nature and expression of mental illness.

Mental Health Challenges

In the Western world, mental health challenges are often understood within the context of fast-paced, industrialized societies. Key contributors to the rising prevalence of mental health issues include chronic stress, isolation, substance abuse, and work-related burnout (Moss, 2021). Despite advancements in therapeutic methods, many populations in the West continue to struggle with anxiety disorders, depression, and suicidal thoughts.

For several decades, the limitations of the secular biomedical framework of Western psychology have been critiqued by scholars (Haque, 1998; Al-Issa, 2000). This reductionist approach has drawn criticism not only from Muslim scholars but also from Western researchers who recognize its shortcomings in addressing the spiritual and cultural dimensions of mental health (Richards & Bergin, 2005; Koenig, 2012). Early critiques pointed out how the secular orientation of Western psychology often clashes with religious worldviews and healing traditions (Haque & Keshavarzi, 2014). Some recent analyses also demonstrate that this framework can marginalize non-Western concepts of psychological well-being (Keshavarzi & Haque, 2013; Kaplick & Skinner, 2017).

The reductionist perspective often overlooks the spiritual and existential aspects of human suffering, which many individuals deem essential for their well-being. Consequently, there has been a growing movement to integrate holistic and Eastern practices, such as mindfulness and meditation, into Western mental health care (Keng et al., 2011). Acknowledging this critical gap, the American Psychological Association (APA) has made significant institutional changes, including the establishment of Division 36 (Society for the Psychology of Religion and Spirituality) and the development of guidelines for addressing religious and spiritual issues in psychological practice (Vieten et al., 2013).

The APA's increasing focus on religious and spiritual competencies formally recognizes that culturally competent care requires an understanding and respect for clients' spiritual beliefs. These developments reflect a broader shift in Western psychology toward more inclusive and culturally responsive approaches to mental health care.

The Muslim world faces a distinctive set of challenges related to mental health. In many Muslim-majority countries, mental health issues are still heavily stigmatized. As a result, individuals often hesitate to seek professional help due to fears of being labeled as "possessed" or believing that mental health symptoms are a curse or punishment from God. Additionally, seeking psychiatric services may be viewed as a sign of spiritual weakness (American Psychiatric Association, 2019; Khan, 2019). Furthermore, the situation is worsened by underdeveloped mental health services, a shortage of professionals providing culturally appropriate care, economic hardships, and ongoing political instability in various regions. These factors contribute to a growing mental health crisis within Muslim societies (Islam et al., 2022).

The Missing Link

Islam emphasizes the importance of psychological well-being through the concepts of balance (*I'tidal*) and the purification of the soul (*tazkiyat al-nafs*) (Keshavarzi et al., 2020). The Quran highlights that success is linked to the purification of the soul (91:9). In the Muslim world, modern psychology is largely influenced by Western models, which may not fully address the spiritual or religious aspects of mental health. While contemporary Western psychology has started to incorporate Eastern contemplative practices like mindfulness and meditation, this shift requires careful historical consideration. The early development of Western psychology was closely linked to religious and spiritual exploration. This connection is notably illustrated in William James's influential work, "The Varieties of Religious Experience" (1902), as well as in Carl Jung's extensive writings on spirituality. However, as the field sought scientific credibility during the early to mid-20th century, there was a conscious effort to distance psychology from spiritual matters (Nelson, 2009).

This secularization occurred despite the West's rich tradition of Christian psychology and pastoral counseling. The subsequent acknowledgment and integration of Eastern practices reflect not only a response to psychology's materialistic limitations but also a complex institutional evolution shaped by various factors. These include emerging empirical evidence supporting contemplative practices (Keng et al., 2011), an increasing awareness of multiculturalism, and changing societal attitudes toward spirituality (Pargament, 2011). The American Psychological Association's gradual reintegration of spirituality—through Division 36 and the establishment of religious competency guidelines—demonstrates this intricate trajectory (Vieten et al., 2013).

Following the trends of spiritual integration in Western developed countries, Muslim-majority nations have begun to explore how the rich Islamic tradition can be incorporated into mental health care (Haque & Keshavarzi, 2013). Practices such as *dhikr* (remembrance of God), *salat* (prayer), and fasting are being revisited not only as religious obligations but also as tools for promoting mental well-being (Irawati et al., 2023; Sulistyawati et al., 2019). There is an increasing emphasis on character development, virtue cultivation, and psychological wellness (Keshavarzi et al., 2024; Rothman et al., 2024). This intersection of psychology and spirituality offers an opportunity to create a more holistic approach to mental health care that addresses both the body and the soul. Furthermore, it fills a significant gap in modern psychology, benefiting both Muslims and non-Muslims alike.

The Development of Psychological Models

Modern-day Western psychology emerged as a formal discipline in the late 19th century, shaped by the intellectual currents of that era. To gain acceptance in the contemporary post-modern landscape, psychology distanced itself from its philosophical roots, obscuring its original identity as the "Study of the Soul" (Textor, 2021). This shift occurred under the influence of various untrained theorists, each shaped by their own worldviews, resulting in the loss of a potentially limitless source of human creativity.

Sigmund Freud, often regarded as the father of psychology, was a physician whose psychodynamic theory was developed from observations in clinical practice, primarily involving wealthy, white patients. Erik Erikson, who proposed the widely influential theory of psychosocial development, became a psychotherapist without formal academic training beyond high school. John Bowlby is known for his attachment theory, and Jean Piaget was a philosopher and biologist who concentrated on cognitive development. Lev Vygotsky, a key figure in sociocultural theory, began his career as a lawyer before shifting to philosophy and eventually to developmental psychology (Watson, 2002).

The contributions of these individuals also highlight key issues related to power and its impact on knowledge production and societal acceptance. Research indicates that Western psychological interventions, which are not culturally adapted, often demonstrate reduced effectiveness in clinical settings (Sue & Sue, 2015). This limited cross-cultural validity, along with documented implementation challenges, has led to increasing skepticism regarding the universal applicability of Western psychological frameworks (Kim et al., 2006).

Furthermore, it's crucial to acknowledge that research practices, clinical approaches, and even public policies and perceptions are often shaped by power dynamics and the influence of privileged groups (Collins & Stockton, 2018; Kincheloe et al., 2017). These limitations have propelled the indigenous psychology movement, especially in mental health, where local healing traditions and cultural frameworks have demonstrated promising outcomes in addressing psychological distress within their specific cultural contexts (Hwang, 2019).

The Mechanistic vs. The Organismic Worldviews

John Locke's mechanistic worldview, rooted in empiricism, posits that the mind begins as a blank slate (*tabula rasa*) and that all knowledge is derived from sensory experience (Locke, 1975). This perspective laid the groundwork for behaviorism, a school of thought that prioritizes the study of observable behaviors rather than internal mental processes. By emphasizing empirical evidence and measurable data, Locke's mechanistic approach reinforced a reductionist view of human beings as passive recipients of environmental stimuli (Watson, 1913). Subsequently, the dominance of this perspective in Western psychology marginalized other ways of understanding, including holistic and spiritual approaches to human behavior.

In contrast to Locke, Jean-Jacques Rousseau's organismic worldview emphasized the inherent nature and potential of human beings. Rousseau believed that individuals are born free and capable of growth, but that society often corrupts their natural development (Rousseau, 1921). This organismic perspective significantly influenced humanistic psychology, which emerged in the mid-20th century as a response to the limitations of both behaviorism and psychodynamic theories.

Paving the Path for Theories

Psychological paradigms developed over the last century are based on fundamental assumptions about human nature, behavior, and mental processes. Each paradigm provides a unique perspective for psychologists to understand and address human behavior. These paradigms often react to one another, evolving as critiques of previous beliefs and addressing perceived gaps in knowledge.

The psychodynamic paradigm, originally developed by Sigmund Freud and later expanded by figures such as Carl Jung and Erik Erikson, assumes that humans are born with innate, often unconscious tendencies that drive them toward seeking pleasure and avoiding pain. Freud famously proposed that human behavior, although largely irrational, is influenced by deep-seated unconscious forces, which he categorized as the Id (instinctual desires), the Ego (rational self), and the Superego (moral compass) (Freud, 1915). As a result, mental illness is seen as stemming from unresolved inner conflicts between these desires and societal expectations. While later theorists like Erikson highlighted the importance of developmental stages and social factors, the psychodynamic paradigm ultimately presents a somewhat pessimistic view of human nature at its core.

The humanistic paradigm, developed by Rogers and Maslow, emerged as a reaction to the deterministic and often pessimistic views of human nature presented by the psychodynamic approach. It suggests that humans are born with an innate capacity for self-actualization, characterized by a drive to grow, improve, and reach their full potential (Maslow, 1954; Rogers, 1961). Unlike the psychodynamic perspective, which posits that unconscious forces govern human behavior, humanists believe that individuals possess the ability for rational thought, self-reflection, and conscious decision-making. Consequently, the humanistic paradigm offers a more optimistic view of human nature, emphasizing potential, self-growth, and positive psychological health.

On the other hand, the behaviorist paradigm, championed by figures such as Watson and Skinner, emerged in the early 20th century as a response to the lack of scientific rigor in psychology at that time. Behaviorists argued that psychology should focus exclusively on observable behavior, as this is the only aspect of human nature that can be objectively measured and studied (Watson, 1913; Skinner, 1953). They contended that behavior is conditioned by external stimuli rather than by unconscious forces, innate desires, or a drive for self-actualization.

The cognitive paradigm, led by Piaget and Vygotsky, shifted the focus to internal mental processes like perception, memory, language, and problem-solving (Piaget, 1954; Vygotsky, 1978). This approach views thought processes as central to understanding behavior, suggesting that the mind functions as an information processor seeking to understand how individuals acquire, store, and retrieve information. The cognitive and behaviorist movements eventually merged into what we now call Cognitive Behavioral Therapy (CBT), partly due to their shared emphasis on measurable phenomena—specifically, thoughts and behaviors—which provide a systematic way to observe, measure, and modify human functioning.

The final blow to the field of psychology has been struck by an emphasis on neurochemical imbalances, genetic predispositions, and observable changes in brain structures that are central to the biomedical model. Consequently, treatment approaches have increasingly focused on pharmacological interventions, such as antidepressants, antipsychotics, and mood stabilizers. This shift often comes at the expense of addressing the psychological, emotional, and social dimensions of mental illness. Neuroimaging studies have shown that the field has become preoccupied with measurable phenomena, such as thoughts and behaviors, as well as observable changes in brain activity. While these measurable aspects offer valuable insights, they tend to marginalize the deeper emotional and existential experiences that are essential to human psychology.

Current State of Affairs

Each psychological paradigm has attempted to address the shortcomings of others, often in reactionary ways. This tendency continues among followers of different theoretical orientations, who frequently reject and criticize opposing schools of thought. Positive psychology, rooted in the work of humanistic psychologists, seeks to highlight the metaphysical and spiritual aspects of human experience by focusing on strengths, virtues, and overall wellbeing (Seligman & Csikszentmihalyi, 2000). This movement emphasizes flourishing and wellbeing as more than just the absence of mental illness. It represents an effort to reconnect with the "study of the soul," which early psychology had distanced itself from in its pursuit of scientific credibility.

The rise of third-wave cognitive behavioral therapy (CBT), which incorporates mindfulness and acceptance, alongside an increase in experiential approaches such as Emotion-Focused Therapy (EFT), aims to deepen human experience through experiential connection (Greenberg, 2011). Additionally, a more recent trend in therapeutic settings involves the use of psychedelics, which have garnered attention for their potential to induce states of consciousness often described as spiritual or transcendent (St. Arnaud & Sharpe, 2023). However, these "pseudo-spiritual" experiences are considered superficial, as they are induced by substances rather than achieved through authentic spiritual practices (Elcock et al., 2017). While the insights or emotional breakthroughs obtained from psychedelic experiences can be profound, they may not lead to lasting spiritual transformation without proper integration.

This shift in Western psychology mirrors broader social changes, with growing recognition of the limitations of Eurocentric models of mental health. Psychology, which historically distanced itself from metaphysical aspects, is now grappling with the incorporation of spirituality while striving to maintain its scientific integrity. This may explain the recent rise in spiritual approaches and religiously integrated psychotherapy within the field. The increasing appeal of these spiritually integrated methods likely arises from a desire for a deeper understanding of human experience that transcends the confines of secular or materialist models, addressing both emotional and spiritual dimensions of well-being (Richards et al., 2023).

The Case for Islamic Psychology

The need for Islamic Psychology arises from the lack of spirituality in modern psychological frameworks and the growing recognition that the deeper, mystical, and experiential dimensions of human existence must be addressed to achieve true mental well-being. Muhammad Iqbal, a renowned Muslim philosopher and poet, emphasized the significance of the inner self (*khudi*) and the journey of self-realization as essential components of human development, much like his predecessors in the rich Islamic tradition (Awaad et al., 2021; Khan & Malik, 2021). For Iqbal, true selfhood involves individual autonomy and experiencing the Divine within, which leads to profound personal transformation (Iqbal, 1930).

Islamic Psychology can offer this inner, mystical journey by focusing on more than just surface-level psychological well-being; it aims to cultivate a deeper, spiritually connected self. This framework resonates with the existential and spiritual needs of both Muslims and non-Muslims alike.

In the rich tradition of Islam, mental health has historically been approached through a spiritual and moral lens. This perspective emphasizes the cultivation of character virtues (*tahdhib al-akhlaq*) and the purification of the soul (*tazkiyat al-nafs*). These concepts originate from the belief that the soul, mind, and body are interconnected, and that well-being is achieved by aligning one's actions, emotions, and intentions with spiritual and ethical principles (Keshavarzi et al., 2020; Rothman & Coyle, 2018; Skinner, 2019). Islamic psychology aims to address the full spectrum of human experiences by considering the cognitive and emotional dimensions, as well as the spiritual and ethical implications of human behavior (Rothman & Coyle, 2018).

Islamic scholars have contributed significantly to understanding mental health and psychology through the work of philosophers, theologians, and clinicians. Pioneers like Al-Balkhi, Al-Ghazali, and Al-Razi provided early insights into mental and physical health relationships. These polymath pioneers laid the foundation for a holistic approach to mental health in Islamic thought, which addressed both the spiritual and psychological dimensions of human existence long before modern psychology emerged (Haque, 2004; Keshavarzi et al., 2020).

The Dilemma of Sacred vs The Secular

The current global culture has been shaped largely by the intellectual, cultural, and political changes that have occurred over the last four to five centuries. The Enlightenment emphasized reason and rationality over religious ideals, a theme that was further developed by post-modernism, which fostered skepticism toward grand narratives, objective truth, and universal values. The post-truth era, along with the sexual revolution, encouraged individuals to construct their own truths based on personal understanding and experiences. This shift prioritized self-serving, hedonistic values over the objective religious tenets that traditionally served society as a whole.

Recent changes in modern thought have created a divide between secular and sacred knowledge by separating religious beliefs from scientific inquiry. As a result, secular psychological theories have become dominant, often overlooking or downplaying the spiritual aspects of human experience. In the Western world, psychology has increasingly taken a reductionist approach that focuses primarily on observable behaviors and cognitive processes, while neglecting the deeper existential and spiritual dimensions of life. This disconnection has posed challenges for the Muslim world, which has adopted Western models but often disregards its own cultural healing traditions. Consequently, there is a lack of mental health care that is culturally and religiously appropriate.

Current psychological theories often do not adequately address the specific needs of Muslims. These models typically overlook the significant role that spirituality and religion play in the lives of Muslims, leaving a gap in addressing the spiritual distress and existential concerns many individuals experience. Additionally, the emphasis on individualism and autonomy in Western psychological models can conflict with the communal and religious values held by many Muslims. As a result, these psychological theories may not resonate fully with Muslim clients and may fall short in addressing the full range of mental health concerns, particularly those that include spiritual and religious dimensions.

Islamic psychology provides a comprehensive and culturally relevant approach to mental health for Muslim populations by integrating spiritual, psychological, and physical aspects of well-being. It emphasizes that mental health is not just about managing symptoms or changing behaviors; it also involves addressing the needs of the soul, aligning with moral and spiritual values, and fostering a connection with the divine. This framework reflects the holistic understanding of human beings found in Islamic teachings, which assert that mental well-being cannot be separated from spiritual fulfillment and moral development.

Furthermore, Islamic psychology offers an alternative to the Western secular models that dominate the mental health field. By incorporating Islamic principles, this approach creates a more meaningful and authentic therapeutic process for clients. It has the potential to address spiritual and character issues that often precede or coexist with psychological symptoms.

From Theoretical to Practical

In recent decades, Islamic Psychology has shifted from theoretical discussions to practical applications in academic, research, and clinical settings. Organizations such as the International Association of Islamic Psychology (IAIP) and the International Association of Muslim Psychologists (IAMP) have actively promoted the field and provided support for those pursuing careers in this area. Additionally, the International Students of Islamic Psychology (ISIP) focuses specifically on assisting the growing number of students interested in Islamic Psychology by offering didactic training, resource exchange, and supervision opportunities.

Academia

The presence of Islamic Psychology in academia has been steadily increasing, with numerous institutions now offering courses, degrees, and certification programs in this field. Notably, the International Islamic University in Malaysia has been providing graduate degrees in Psychology that emphasize Islamic integration. Recently, more academic institutions have started to offer diplomas and certifications in Islamic Psychology as well.

The establishment of Islamic Psychology training in Western institutions marks an important step in addressing the mental health needs of Muslims (York, 2021). The Khalil Center has been at the forefront of this movement in the United States, offering a certification program called Traditional Islamically Integrated Psychotherapy (TIIP), which combines Islamic principles with clinical practice (Keshavarzi et al., 2020). In the United Kingdom, academic programs like the Diploma in Islamic Psychology at Cambridge Muslim College have emerged, effectively bridging traditional Islamic sciences with contemporary psychological theory and practice.

Other structured academic programs include:

- Applied Islamic Psychology Program (126 hours) from Avicenna Academy in Indonesia, led by Bagus Riyono.

- Graduate Certificate in Islamic Psychology (6 months) from Charles Sturt University in Australia.
- Introduction to Islamic Psychology (9 months) from The Al Karam Institute in the United States, led by Carrie York.
- Islamic Counselling and Psychology – Two levels (approximately 1 year) from Al Balagh Academy in the United Kingdom, taught by Abdur Rasjid Skinner, Mahbub Khan, G. Hussein Rassool, and others.

Research Advancements

Research on the applications of Islamic Psychology remains limited and requires more attention, particularly through increased publications in peer-reviewed journals. In their 2016 literature review, Haque et al. noted that studies on clinical applications were the least represented in research and academic publications. While this is still the case, the field has seen a rise in studies focused on the applications of Islamic Psychology (IP). Since Keshavarzi et al. introduced their model in 2020, there have been additional publications on the application of the Theory of Islamic Integrative Psychology (TIIP) (Khan & Keshavarzi, 2023; Khan et al., 2023a; Khan et al., 2023b).

Rothman and Coyle (2021) expanded upon their previous work by developing a model for the clinical scope of Islamic psychotherapy. This model provides guidelines that help clinicians distinguish between Islamically integrated therapy and general religious guidance. This clarification is intended to assist clinicians in navigating these areas effectively. Saged et al. (2022) contributed evidence-based findings on an Islamic-based intervention for treating depression and anxiety, highlighting the benefits of faith-centered approaches.

In 2023, a special issue of the APA journal *Spirituality in Clinical Practice*, edited by York & Awan, was dedicated to Islamic spirituality in clinical contexts, featuring several significant studies. Weisman de Mamani et al. (2023) presented a pilot study on a transdiagnostic, culturally informed therapy that incorporates religious and spiritual components. Additionally, the issue included case series on integrating Islamic spirituality in the treatment of grief following pregnancy loss across different stages (Mahmoodi et al., 2023).

Clinical Practice

Islamic Psychology has been effectively integrated into therapeutic settings, with various models and interventions yielding positive outcomes for clients. The Khalil Center, the largest provider of Muslim mental health services in the West, has successfully demonstrated the integration of Islamic spiritual practices in addressing mental health concerns among Muslims. Their 2023 publication in the APA's Journal of Spirituality in Clinical Practice shows a reduction in clinical and functional distress in routine evaluations over time, providing preliminary evidence for the efficacy of the Therapeutic Islamic Integrative Practice (TIIP) (Khan et al., 2023b).

Additionally, research conducted in Malaysia on Islamic-based interventions for depression and anxiety, such as the work by Saged et al. (2022), illustrates significant improvements in clients' mental health, supporting the broader applicability of Islamic Psychology principles.

Other studies have also focused on specific Islamic interventions and their effectiveness. Notable examples include dhikr (the remembrance of God), which has been shown to reduce depression and anxiety (Sulistyawati et al., 2019; Wahyuni et al., 2018), as well as Quranic therapy (Lismayanti et al., 2021; Mashitah, 2020).

Case Study: Ahmed

Ahmad is a 45-year-old married professional and father of three who sought therapy at the Khalil Center to improve his parenting skills and create a more nurturing family environment. Over the course of more than a dozen therapy sessions, he gained valuable insights into the underlying factors that contributed to his recurring anger outbursts toward his wife and children.

Ahmad's upbringing in an emotionally distant household instilled deeply rooted beliefs about his self-worth, which led to patterns of emotional avoidance and interpersonal isolation. These patterns not only affected his family relationships but also influenced his spiritual life. Ahmad struggled to develop a meaningful connection with Allah, as his relationship with the Divine felt largely transactional. It was focused on fulfilling religious obligations rather than experiencing a deeper sense of presence, trust, and reliance (tawakkul).

Ahmad faced challenges in engaging emotionally within his marital and familial relationships. He found it difficult to express vulnerability and affection. When his wife and children tried to connect with him on an emotional level, these interactions often triggered unresolved emotional wounds. Instead of experiencing and processing feelings of sadness, Ahmad instinctively responded with anger, which further reinforced his cycle of emotional detachment.

His difficulty in trusting emotional connections with his family reflected his struggle to cultivate a trusting relationship with Allah. Ahmad often viewed hardships as punishments rather than opportunities for growth and spiritual development.

Through the therapeutic process, Ahmad developed a greater awareness of his emotions and identified unhealthy patterns that were hindering his ability to connect with his family and with Allah. He engaged in structured interventions aimed at fostering emotional expression, increasing distress tolerance, and cultivating deeper relational bonds. As he worked on regulating his emotions and embracing vulnerability, he began to view his relationship with Allah in a new light—focusing on compassion and closeness instead of rigidity and obligation. By reflecting on the divine attributes of mercy (*rahma*) and gratitude (*shukr*), he was able to reframe his perspective on family relationships as a spiritual responsibility and an opportunity for personal growth.

Strengthening his connection with Allah had a transformative effect on his family dynamics. As Ahmad deepened his spiritual practice—not just as ritual acts but as moments of connection and reliance on the Divine—he became more patient, empathetic, and emotionally available to his wife and children. His renewed faith helped him cultivate humility, allowing him to accept his shortcomings without defensiveness and work toward becoming a more present and compassionate husband and father.

Ahmad continues to focus on his psychospiritual development, demonstrating significant progress in his capacity for emotional intimacy, self-awareness, and relational fulfillment. His ongoing commitment to therapy highlights the transformative potential of integrating psychological interventions with Islamic principles to promote holistic well-being.

Challenges to Islamic Psychology

Islamic Psychology faces significant challenges in academic settings due to a lack of acceptance and recognition for religiously based models and spiritually integrated interventions. In the West, the field of psychology has historically prioritized secular frameworks, focusing on evidence-based approaches and standardized models that adhere to conventional scientific rigor. This emphasis on secular methods often excludes or marginalizes therapeutic models that incorporate spirituality or religious concepts, leading to skepticism about Islamic Psychology as a credible field. Academic institutions typically require psychological interventions to conform to empirically validated methods, which makes it difficult for Islamic Psychology to gain institutional support, secure funding, or achieve recognition for research and clinical work that addresses the cultural and spiritual needs of Muslim clients.

The challenges in research arise from the fact that integrative practices (IP) often employ experiential and process-oriented therapeutic approaches that do not easily align with the randomized controlled trials (RCTs) typically used to demonstrate treatment efficacy. Many IP interventions are inherently individualized and deeply experiential, resisting the structured and replicable processes that RCTs require. Additionally, therapies rooted in spirituality and religion tend to be fluid and responsive to individual experiences rather than strictly manualized, making their assessment through traditional scientific methods more complex.

A practice-based evidence (PBE) approach, which gathers data from actual therapeutic settings, presents a more appropriate alternative (Margison et al., 2000). Furthermore, mixed-methods research—which combines quantitative data with qualitative insights—can capture the nuanced, subjective experiences of clients. This allows for the evaluation of IP interventions in a way that respects their spiritual dimensions while also providing empirical evidence. This flexible and holistic approach would facilitate a deeper understanding of the effectiveness of IP in both clinical and academic contexts, broadening its acceptance and supporting its integration into mainstream psychological practice.

Conclusion

In conclusion, Islamic Psychology serves as a valuable framework for addressing the unique mental health challenges faced by the American Muslim community. It offers a potential solution to the limitations found in the broader field of psychology today. Modern psychology often focuses on a secular and reductionist approach, prioritizing measurable phenomena such as neurochemical imbalances and observable behaviors. This focus can lead to the marginalization or neglect of the spiritual and existential aspects that are essential for overall well-being. While various psychological paradigms—such as psychodynamic, cognitive-behavioral, and biomedical approaches—provide valuable insights, they often view human behavior through a reductionistic lens. This perspective has created a disconnect from the deeper, metaphysical dimensions of mental health. Islamic Psychology is positioned uniquely to bridge this gap by integrating these important aspects into the understanding of mental well-being. The evolution of the current field reflects a significant tension between scientific rigor and spiritual integration. Modern psychology, with its secular foundations, poses considerable challenges for Muslim populations seeking culturally appropriate mental health care. Islamic Psychology aims to bridge this gap by providing an evidence-based framework that combines spiritual dimensions with psychological principles. This approach offers a more comprehensive strategy for mental well-being that aligns with Islamic values and community orientations. Through ongoing research, education, and clinical application, Islamic Psychology has the potential to improve mental health care delivery while ensuring both scientific credibility and spiritual authenticity.

Recommendations for Future Development

The advancement of Islamic Psychology requires systematic development across several important areas:

Research Priorities:

Establish empirical validation through:

- Controlled outcome studies of Islamic psychological interventions.
- Systematic evaluation of treatment efficacy across diverse populations.
- Development of culturally validated assessment tools.

Academic Integration:

- Develop standardized curricula for training in Islamic Psychology.
- Create evidence-based guidelines for clinical supervision.
- Establish quality metrics for evaluating programs.

Clinical Implementation:

- Design manualized treatment protocols.
- Create frameworks to integrate Islamic practices within existing healthcare systems.
- Develop professional competency standards.

Islamic Psychology serves as a vital link between scientific rigor and spiritual integration in mental healthcare. While its theoretical foundations and initial clinical applications show promise, greater acceptance requires a continued commitment to empirical validation and professional development. Through systematic research and structured implementation, Islamic Psychology can enhance the field's capacity to serve diverse populations while maintaining scientific credibility and spiritual authenticity.

References

Al-Issa, I. (2000). *Al-Junūn: Mental Illness in the Islamic World*. International Universities Press.

American Psychiatric Association. (2019). *Treating Muslims*. In *Stress & Trauma Toolkit for Treating Historically Marginalized Populations in a Changing Political and Social Environment*. American Psychiatric Association.

Australian Institute of Health and Welfare. (2023). *Australian Burden of Disease Study (ABDS) 2023*. Retrieved from https://www.aihw.gov.au/reports/burden-of-disease/australian-burden-of-disease-study-2023.

Awaad, R., Elsayed, D., Ali, S., & Abid, A. (2021). Islamic psychology: A portrait of its historical origins and contributions. In H. Keshavarzi, F. Khan, B. Ali, & R. Awaad (Eds.), *Applying Islamic Principles to Clinical Mental Health Care: Introducing Traditional Islamically Integrated Psychotherapy* (pp. 69–95). Routledge/Taylor & Francis Group.

Collins, C., & Stockton, C. (2018). The central role of theory in qualitative research. *International Journal of Qualitative Methods, 17*, 1-10.

Elcock, C., Shipley, M., Richards, W. A., & St. John, G. (2017). Psychedelics and religious experience. [Review of *Psychedelic Mysticism: Transforming Consciousness, Religious Experiences, and Voluntary Peasants in Postwar America; Sacred Knowledge: Psychedelics and Religious Experiences; Mystery School in Hyperspace: A Cultural History of DMT*]. *Nova Religio: The Journal of Alternative and Emergent Religions, 20*(4), 94–99.

Freud, S. (1915). The unconscious. In J. Strachey (Ed. & Trans.), *The Standard Edition of the Complete Psychological Works of Sigmund Freud* (Vol. 14, pp. 159–190). Hogarth Press.

Greenberg, L. S. (2011). *Emotion-Focused Therapy*. American Psychological Association.

Haque, A. (1998). Psychology and religion: Their relationship and integration from an Islamic perspective. *American Journal of Islamic Social Sciences, 15*(4), 97–116.

Haque, A. (2004). Psychology from an Islamic perspective: Contributions of early Muslim scholars and challenges faced by contemporary Muslim psychologists. *Journal of Religion and Health, 43*(4), 357–377.

Haque, A., & Keshavarzi, H. (2014). Integrating indigenous healing methods in therapy: Muslim beliefs and practices. *International Journal of Culture and Mental Health, 7*(3), 297–314.

Haque, A., Khan, F., Keshavarzi, H., & Rothman, A. E. (2016). Integrating Islamic traditions into modern psychology: Research trends over the last ten years. *Journal of Muslim Mental Health, 10*(1), 75–100.

Harvard Medical School. (2007). National Comorbidity Survey (NCS). Retrieved August 21, 2017, from https://www.hcp.med.harvard.edu/ncs/index.php.

Hwang, K. (2019). Enhancing cultural awareness through the construction of culture-inclusive theories. *Journal of Theoretical and Philosophical Psychology, 39*(2), 67–80.

Iqbal, M. (1930). *The Reconstruction of Religious Thought in Islam*. Oxford University Press.

Irawati, K., Indarwati, F., Haris, F., Lu, J. Y., & Shih, Y. H. (2023). Religious practices and spiritual well-being among individuals with schizophrenia: A Muslim perspective. *Psychology Research and Behavior Management, 16*, 739–748.

Islam, Z., Gangat, S. A., Mohanan, P., Rahmat, Z. S., El Chbib, D., Marfani, W. B., & Essar, M. Y. (2022). The mental health impacts of Lebanon's economic crisis on healthcare workers during COVID-19. *The International Journal of Health Planning and Management, 37*(2), 1160–1165.

James, W. (1902/2002). *The Varieties of Religious Experience: A Study in Human Nature*. Dover Publications.

Kaplick, P. M., & Skinner, R. (2017). The evolving Islam and psychology movement: Contemporary perspectives. *European Psychologist, 22*(3), 198-204.

Keng, S. L., Smoski, M. J., & Robins, C. J. (2011). Effects of mindfulness on psychological health: A review of empirical studies. *Clinical Psychology Review, 31*(6), 1041–1056.

Keshavarzi, H., & Haque, A. (2013). Outlining a psychotherapy model for enhancing Muslim mental health within an Islamic context. *International Journal for the Psychology of Religion, 23*(3), 230–249.

Keshavarzi, H., Khan, F., Ali, B., & Awaad, R. (Eds.) (2020). *Applying Islamic Principles to Clinical Mental Health Care: Introducing Traditional Islamically Integrated Psychotherapy*. Routledge.

Keshavarzi, H., Yanık, M., Keçeci, E., & Cinisli, M. F. (2024). A reclassification of al-Ījī's *Akhlāq al-ʿAḍudiyya* into a model of traditional Islamic virtues (TIV). *Journal of Muslim Mental Health, 18*(1), 75-90.

Khan, F. (2019). Challenges of Islamophobia: Psychiatric considerations for effectively working with Muslim patients. In Moffic, H. S., Peteet, J., Hankir, A., & Awaad, R. (Eds.), *Islamophobia and Psychiatry: Recognition, Prevention, and Treatment* (pp. 171–181). Springer International Publishing.

Khan, F., Aycan, S., & Keshavarzi, F. (2023a). Clinical applications of the Traditional Islamically-Integrated Psychotherapy (TIIP) model: A case study of a Turkish female. In Haque, A. & Rothman, A. (Eds.), *Clinical Applications of Islamic Psychology*. International Association of Islamic Psychology.

Khan, F., Keshavarzi, H., Ahmad, M., Ashai, S., & Sanders, P. (2023b). The application of Traditional Islamically Integrated Psychotherapy (TIIP) and its outcomes on psychological distress among American Muslims in outpatient therapy. *Spirituality in Clinical Practice*. Advanced online publication.

Khan, F. & Keshavarzi, H. (2023). The theoretical foundations and clinical applications of Traditional Islamically Integrated Psychotherapy (TIIP). In Richards, S., Kawika, G., & Judd, D. (Eds.), *Handbook of Spiritually Integrated Psychotherapies*. American Psychological Association Press.

Khan, F. & Malik, K. (2021). Tarbiyat-e-Khudi: A model of self-development from the poems of Muhammad Iqbal in Asrar-i-Khudi. *Bahria Journal of Professional Psychology, 20*(1), 14-26.

Kieling, C., Buchweitz, C., Caye, A., Silvani, J., Ameis, S. H., Brunoni, A. R., Cost, K. T., et al. (2024). Worldwide prevalence and disability from mental disorders across childhood and adolescence: Evidence from the Global Burden of Disease Study. *JAMA Psychiatry, 81*(4), 347–356.

Kim, U., Yang, K. S., & Hwang, K. K. (2006). *Indigenous and cultural psychology: Understanding people in context*. Springer.

Kincheloe, J. L., McLaren, P., Steinberg, S. R., & Monzó, L. (2017). Critical pedagogy and qualitative research: Advancing the bricolage. In N. K. Denzin & Y. S. Lincoln (Eds.), *The SAGE Handbook of Qualitative Research* (5th ed., pp. 235–260). Thousand Oaks, CA: Sage.

Koenig, H. G. (2012). Religion, spirituality, and health: Research and clinical implications. *ISRN Psychiatry, 2012*, 278730.

Lismayanti, L., Ariyanto, H., Azmi, A., Nigusyanti, A. F., & Andira, R. A. (2021). Murattal Al-Quran Therapy to reduce anxiety among operating patients. *Genius Journal, 2*(1), 9-15.

Locke, J. (1975). *An Essay Concerning Human Understanding* (P. H. Nidditch, Ed.). Oxford University Press.

Mahmoodi, V., Akhavan, A., & Virk, Z. (2023). Integration of Islamic spirituality in the treatment of grief for pregnancy loss: A case series of losses during early, mid-, and late pregnancy. *Spirituality in Clinical Practice*, 10(1), 52-61.

Margison, F. R., Barkham, M., Evans, C., McGrath, G., Clark, J. M., Audin, K., & Connell, J. (2000). Measurement and psychotherapy: Evidence-based practice and practice-based evidence. *British Journal of Psychiatry, 177*(2), 123–130.

Mashitah, M. W. (2020). Quran recitation therapy reduces the depression levels of hemodialysis patients. *International Journal of Research in Medical Sciences, 8*(6), 2222–2227.

Maslow, A. H. (1954). *Motivation and Personality*. Harper & Row.

Moss, J. (2021). *The Burnout Epidemic: The Rise of Chronic Stress and How We Can Fix It*. Harvard Business Review Press.

Nelson, J. M. (2009). *Psychology, Religion, and Spirituality*. Springer Science & Business Media.

Newlove-Delgado, T., Marcheselli, F., Williams, T., Mandalia, D., Davis, J., McManus, S., Savic, M., Treloar, W., & Ford, T. (2022). *Mental health of children and young people in England, 2022*. NHS Digital, Leeds.

Nisar, M., Mohammad, R. M., Fatima, S., Shaikh, P. R., & Rehman, M. (2019). Perceptions pertaining to clinical depression in Karachi, Pakistan. *Cureus, 11*(7), e5094.

Pargament, K. I. (2011). *Spiritually Integrated Psychotherapy: Understanding and Addressing the Sacred*. Guilford Press.

Piaget, J. (1954). *The Construction of Reality in the* Child (M. Cook, Trans.). Basic Books.

Richards, P. S., Allen, G. E. K., & Judd, D. (Eds.). (2023). *Handbook of Spiritually Integrated Psychotherapies*. American Psychological Association.

Richards, P. S., & Bergin, A. E. (2005). *A Spiritual Strategy for Counseling and Psychotherapy (2nd ed.)*. American Psychological Association.

Rogers, C. R. (1961). *On Becoming a Person: A Therapist's View of Psychotherapy*. Houghton Mifflin.

Rothman, A. & Coyle, A. (2018). Toward a framework for Islamic psychology and psychotherapy: An Islamic model of the soul. *Journal of Religion and Health, 57*, 1731–1744.

Rothman, A. & Coyle, A. (2021). The clinical scope of Islamic psychotherapy: A grounded theory study. *Spirituality in Clinical Practice*, online first publication.

Rothman, A., Yücesoy, Z. B., & Yalçın, E. (2024). Early Muslim scholars' conceptions of character development and contemporary applications in mental health and well-being. *Journal of Muslim Mental Health, 18*(1), 62-74.

Rousseau, J.-J. (1921). *Emile, or Education* (B. Foxley, Trans.). J. M. Dent and Sons; E. P. Dutton.

Saged, A. A. G., Sa'ari, C. Z., Abdullah, M., Al-Rahmi, W. M., Ismail, W. M., Zain, M. I. A., & Al-Shehri, N. (2022). The effect of an Islamic-based intervention on depression and anxiety in Malaysia. *Journal of Religion and Health, 61*(1), 79-92.

Seligman, M. E. P., & Csikszentmihalyi, M. (2000). Positive psychology: An introduction. *American Psychologist, 55*(1), 5–14.

Skinner, B. F. (1953). *Science and Human Behavior*.

Skinner R. (2019). Traditions, Paradigms and Basic Concepts in Islamic Psychology. *Journal of religion and health, 58*(4), 1087–1094.

St. Arnaud, K. O., & Sharpe, D. (2023). Entheogens and Spiritual Seeking: The Quest for Self-Transcendence, Psychological Wellbeing, and Psychospiritual Growth. *Journal of Psychedelic Studies, 7*(1), 69-79.

Sue, D. W., & Sue, D. (2015). *Counseling the Culturally Diverse: Theory and Practice (7th ed.)*. John Wiley & Sons.

Sulistyawati, R. A., Probosuseno, & Setiyarini, S. (2019). Dhikr Therapy for Reducing Anxiety in Cancer Patients. *Asia-Pacific Journal of Oncology Nursing, 6*(4), 411–416.

Textor, M. (2021). Psychology, the Science of the Soul. In *The Disappearance of the Soul and the Turn Against Metaphysics: Austrian Philosophy 1874–1918* (pp. 150–180). Oxford University Press.

Vieten, C., Scammell, S., Pilato, R., Ammondson, I., Pargament, K. I., & Lukoff, D. (2013). Spiritual and Religious Competencies for Psychologists. *Psychology of Religion and Spirituality, 5*(3), 129–144.

Vygotsky, L. S. (1978). *Mind in Society: Development of Higher Psychological Processes* (M. Cole, V. Jolm-Steiner, S. Scribner, & E. Souberman, Eds.). Harvard University Press.

Wahdi, A. E., Wilopo, S. A., & Erskine, H. E. (2023). The Prevalence of Adolescent Mental Disorders in Indonesia: An Analysis of the Indonesia

National Mental Health Survey (I-NAMHS). *Journal of Adolescent Health, 72*(3S), S70.

Wahyuni, S., Anies, A. S., Soejoenoes, A., Putra, S. T., & Syukur, M. A. (2018). Spiritual Dhikr Reduces Stress and Depression Symptoms in Primigravidas. *Pakistan Journal of Medical and Health Sciences, 12*(3), 1368-1371.

Watson, J. B. (1913). Psychology as the Behaviorist Views It. *Psychological Review, 20*(2), 158–177.

Watson, M. W. (2002). *Theories of Human Development* (Part I). The Teaching Company.

Weisman de Mamani, A., Lopez, D., McLaughlin, M. M., Ahmad, S. S., & Altamirano, O. (2023). A Pilot Study to Assess the Feasibility and Efficacy of a Transdiagnostic, Religiously/Spiritually Integrated, Culturally Informed Therapy. *Spirituality in Clinical Practice, 10*(3), 233.

World Health Organization. (2009). *WHO-AIMS Report on the Mental Health System in Pakistan*. World Health Organization.

World Health Organization. (2022). *World Mental Health Report: Transforming Mental Health for All*. World Health Organization.

York Al-Karam, C. (2021). Islamic Psychology in the United States: Past, Present, and Future Trajectory. In A. Haque & A. Rothman (Eds.), *Islamic Psychology Around the Globe* (p. 224). International Association of Islamic Psychology.

York, C. M., & Awan, H. (Eds.). (2023). Islamic spirituality in clinical practice [Special issue]. *Spirituality in Clinical Practice, 10*(1).

SECTION THREE

FAMILIES AND AGE GROUPS

CHAPTER FIVE

MUSLIM YOUTH: MODERN-DAY CHALLENGES AND APPROACHES

Suzy Ismail

This chapter explores the many challenges that Muslim youth face today and the impact of those challenges on identity and faith perspectives, often resulting in adverse mental health outcomes. Each section opens with a dramatized narrative that captures several common themes that can be found among the challenges faced by Muslim youth today. The narratives are followed by an explanation of the main challenges faced in the narrative and how academic research in the field helps inform strategies and interventions that can be applied in each case. The chapter includes an appendix that lists commonly asked questions in their original format and the answers given during a Taboo Topic talk and texted to the author during and after a youth conference held in 2021. The answers are rooted in the Cornerstone Marriage & Family Intervention approach to modern-day youth challenges.

Introduction

According to recent post-pandemic research, Muslim youth in America are facing greater challenges today in terms of identity, relationships, and mental health outcomes than before the Covid-19 pandemic period (Dyer, Crandall, & Hanson, 2023; Shidhaye, 2023). These challenges can be seen as often increasing anxious outcomes related to questions of identity, relationships, social media usage, parental pressure, academic challenges, substance abuse, and many more struggles (Farooqui & Kaushik, 2022). These difficulties have resulted in mental health outcomes of great concern for families living in the West, primarily the US, Australia, Europe, and Canada, that are often not addressed (Kayrouz, 2022). While some preteens, teens, and young adults may receive diagnoses and treatments for mental health outcomes such as anxiety and depression by mental health practitioners, many others may not receive any form of psychological or psychiatric intervention due to parental stigmatization of mental healthcare (Tineo, Bonumwezi, & Lowe, 2021). The following chapter explores the difficulties that often lead Muslim youth in Western countries to both diagnosed and undiagnosed mental health outcomes rooted in struggles with identity, relationships, social media, substances and addictions, academic and school pressures, mental health stressors and issues of family instability and lack of emotional control.

Challenges of Identity

Topics Explored:

- Culture and faith: Navigating a fragmented identity
- Who am I? Stuck between two worlds
- What is my worth? Issues of self-esteem

Narrative: A Tale of Two

Meena feels torn. She has a boyfriend in school, is among the most popular girls in high school, hikes up her skirts, and takes off her hijab. She can often be found at parties and trap houses when her parents think she is staying with a friend who covers for her. During one of these "friend visits," Meena got a small tattoo of her boyfriend's name in a place she knew her parents would never look. She is sexually active and recently found out that she is pregnant. At home, she is known to be a very "good girl" who wears a hijab, goes to the mosque, helps her siblings, and is well-known in the community as a student leader. Her mom has just stumbled upon text messages on her phone of very inappropriate picture exchanges between her and her boyfriend, messages about the pregnancy and contemplation of abortion, threatening notes from the boyfriend about breaking up with her, and Meena threatening to end her life.

Identifying the Challenges

Meena's story is, unfortunately, one that many Muslim teens raised in Western countries can potentially identify with to varying degrees. Navigating personal identity at home and social identity outside of the home can result in a complicated view of the self (Cheah, Gürsoy, & Balkaya-Ince, 2021). It can, at times, result in actions that cause harm to oneself physically, mentally, and emotionally. In the narrative above, one may posit that a potentially undiagnosed mental health struggle exists in the form of split personality syndrome (Driezen, Verschraegen, & Clycq, 2021). However, the desire for Meena to fit in and to be accepted by her surrounding non-Muslim peers may play an even larger role in motivating the character's actions and resultant outcomes.

In the brief narrative shared above, there are multiple struggles at hand. Issues of self-esteem may also play a role in the character's engagement in unprotected sexual relations and in changing the way she dresses around her family and home community as opposed to how she may dress around her peers and school community. Self-esteem and self-valuation can often be a common challenge for Muslim youth when navigating culture, faith practice, and contextualization in vying for greater social credibility and acceptance among peers (Ahmed, 2014). Feeling torn between worlds can often result in questioning young Muslims' value, likeability, and self-worth navigating their identity projection (Sirin & Balsano, 2007). The need for connection and affirmation may also be at the heart of the character's dilemma, particularly if home life does not provide affirmation or emotional support in the way the character desires (Ahmed, 2014). There may also be intense shame or guilt surrounding the character's actions and resulting outcomes. The parental response to finding out about Meena's behavior is critical regarding what may happen next in this scenario.

Towards a Positive Approach

While many parents may feel a sense of betrayal upon learning that their child acts or dresses differently when they are not around, the reality is that growing up is inclusive of experimentation in identity formation. Parents should not respond with intense emotion but should instead seek to understand and converse openly with their child when learning of what may appear to be a split personality in action (Cheah, Gürsoy, & Balkaya-Ince, 2021). Parents can facilitate ways to connect with their children and manage their responses to create a sense of safety and security at home and speak honestly about realistic options and approaches (Bisati, 2021).

In the case of the character in the narrative, a chronological approach to well-being must be established by tackling the most harmful situations first (Ahmed & Ezzeddine, 2009). The first element that needs to be addressed in Meena's case would be the teen's safety: mentally, emotionally, and physically. This would mean approaching the discovery of the messages, first by establishing the level of threat in the statements of self-harm or suicide ideation, followed by addressing the physical ramifications of teenage pregnancy, then addressing the unhealthy relationship dynamic, followed by the issues of identity fluctuation. Often, the first parental response to a Muslim teen's behavior that is contrary to expectations and *Tarbiyah* (Islamic upbringing) is reactionary and rooted in anger, followed by a purely religious approach centered on the *haram* (that which is impermissible in Islam), which neglects the important safety elements that need to be addressed first and then followed by ensuring the emotional and mental wellness of the teen.

While this narrative takes an exacerbated approach to issues of identity, the reality is that any of the situations described above, even to a much lesser extent, would cause parental concern. However, the response should not be harsh or rooted in rejection since that may be at the core of the behaviors to begin with. Sometimes, the issues of identity are more closely related to changing a name, deviating away from *Haya*, telling an untruth, engaging with the wrong friends, or other common types of struggles of character development for Muslim youth growing up in the West. (Cheah, Gürsoy, & Balkaya-Ince, 2021). In any of these cases, the parental approach must be one of calm, understanding, engagement, and solution-orientation rather than negative reactionary responses in a way that alienates the teens and pushes them further away from the home and the family.

Challenges of Relationships/Sexuality

Topics Explored:

- Parental/Family Communication
- Friends/Same & Opposite Gender Attraction
- Understanding Struggles of Sexual Orientation

Narrative: Self-harm and Self-doubt in Sexuality

Amir is 16 years old and is struggling with his sexuality. He identifies as pansexual, and although he has not acted on his sexual identification, he feels confusion and self-doubt regarding his faith and his identity as rooted in sexual orientation. The school guidance counselor has learned that Amir is cutting because it was brought to her attention by a teacher who saw marks on his wrist. After being called by the school and told of the situation, Amir's parents are hesitant to bring him to see a traditional mental health professional and have been urging him not to talk to anyone because they are embarrassed by his feelings and his actions. They are angry at him and have been shaming him regarding his behavior.

Identifying the Challenges

The concept of *satr* (covering of sins) can be problematic for Muslim teens who grow up in homes in which topics they may be struggling with are considered off-limits for discussion. In this narrative, the character is a 16-year-old child trying to better understand his human desires and inclinations toward attraction to people regardless of gender identification or sexual orientation. Due to the cultural sexualization of even the most platonic of relationships and the movement of emotional connection towards the intimate and romantic, many young people struggle with understanding what they are feeling towards their peers of the same and the opposite gender as they grow and develop greater sexual awareness (Farooqui & Kaushik, 2022).

For many Muslim community members, topics surrounding sex and sexuality are often considered taboo and are not talked about openly in homes, mosques, or any other safe spaces (Kosar, Akhtar, & Selim, 2022). Thus, these same topics that often result in tongue-tied parents and red-faced religious leaders are not given outlets for healthy discussion for youth who are already socially exposed to these concepts through a variety of mediums. In neglecting the discussion of these topics, Muslim youth are left instead with an affluence of curiosity and a desire to learn about sexuality from the many sources that do offer open dialogue: namely friends, books, magazines, school, television, and, of course, the Internet (Farooqui & Kaushik, 2022). While the information may be plentiful and easily accessible, without guidance, a Muslim teenager in the West may be left to their own devices to make sense of very grown-up topics. Yet, the Islamic faith indicates that conversations are critical in preparing youth and adults to deal with the real world. As the Prophet Mohamed (peace be upon him) instructed in an authentic narration, there should be no shyness in matters of religion when legitimately seeking knowledge (Mohamed, 2001).

The loneliness that often results in youth who feel like they are committing an act of *haram* by potentially misnaming feelings of sexual attraction and being unable to discuss these feelings with anyone can lead to mental health outcomes such as depression and anxiety that may result in self-harm behaviors (Kayrouz, 2022; Shidhaye, 2023). Tackling the problem of self-harm must take precedence prior to taking a *haram*-centric approach. If the parents remain focused on the idea of hiding their child's actions and feelings, the child will likely not be able to seek the help needed to guide him toward understanding his emotions and the actions of frustration and lack of self-acceptance that may be leading to self-harm behaviors. As parents, shaming him and expressing anger will likely only lead to greater guilt-laden actions and struggles for the child.

Towards a Positive Approach

The first step in adopting a positive approach to the situation presented in the narrative involves talking to teens (Bisati, 2021). Communication is a critical component in connecting with young people in a way where they can feel heard and understood. Parents can also seek avenues of their learning regarding labels that surround sexual orientation and gender identity and how to address topics of LGBTQIA+ struggles among our youth (Cheah, Gürsoy, Balkaya-Ince, 2021). Part of this parental education requires an understanding of the affirmation that can be enticing to youth when they feel a sense of inclusion within a "love is love" community that stands in stark contrast to a home life in which Islam may be presented in a way that is restrictive, unforgiving, and even judgmental. Guiding youth toward an understanding of the Islamic conceptualization of love is critical to counter-narratives that frame non-Islamically aligned approaches to love as more authentic or humanly satisfying than human and spiritual love expressed within Islamic parameters (Zahrin, Ibrahim, & Fadzil, 2020).

Challenges of Social Media and Gender Expression

Topics Explored:
- Gender Identity and Exploration
- Social media influence
- Self-image and identity construction

Narrative: Gender Expression

Dunia is a first-year college student who has asked her friends and professors at school to call her "Danny" and has identified her pronouns as "they/them." Dunia's parents do not know about these requests, but they do recognize that she is moving away from faith and questioning whether she is even Muslim anymore. Dunia is a commuter at college but spends long hours on campus since she is resentful towards her parents for not allowing her to dorm because she is a girl. Her brothers live with roommates at out-of-state schools and often travel with friends. When Dunia is home, she is often in her room scrolling through TikTok or spending much time on Instagram. Her parents notice that she spends excessive time online on multiple platforms and has started an overly familiar texting relationship with one of her professors. Due to this relationship, she is constantly quoting the professor's challenges to Islamic ideals and a binary gender approach and is often quick to argue these points. During a masjid event, Dunia insists on praying in line with males. However, the males in the line feel uncomfortable praying next to someone who externally presents as female despite adopting a gender nonconformist identity.

Identifying the Challenges

Struggles with gender expression and identification are becoming more prevalent among Muslim youth in the West (Driezen, Verschraegen, & Clycq, 2021). More and more youth are turning to social media consumption as a source through which they define self-valuation, worth, beauty standards, gender expressions, and many other self-concepts, which can result in negative mental health outcomes through social media influence (Kayrouz, 2022). Fluidity in gender identity has become a rapidly growing expression among many Muslim youths in the West who create comparisons between love and acceptance in secular society and contrast that with their misperception of a lack of love and acceptance in Islam-- particularly along gender lines (Farooqui & Kaushik, 2022). Mischaracterizations of cultural conceptualizations of gender roles and expectations often become conflated with Islamic ideals by well-meaning parents using the *haram*-centric approach when it is often inapplicable (Cheah, Gürsoy, & Balkaya-Ince, 2021). This approach may result in a desire to control that which feels like it can be controlled for the youth. Thus, when gender identity becomes fluid, it may feel like a teenager or young adult can now exert some form of control over their lives, much like what is often described by youth who use self-harm as a coping mechanism and means of controlling pain in dealing with posttraumatic outcomes (Tineo, Bonumwezi, & Lowe, 2021).

Towards a Positive Approach

The prevalence of social media and its impact on Muslim youth and on negative mental health outcomes is a reality that cannot be ignored, particularly post-pandemic, when increased social media usage and virtual education have drastically changed the landscape of mediated communication (Dyer, Crandall, & Hanson, 2023). Rather than trying to ban social media or declare it as a poison, parents should work towards understanding its application and influence in the lives of Muslim youth.

Offering alternative avenues of connection and communication is critical for youth craving spaces where they can feel heard and understood.

In the narrative above, the character clearly struggles with cultural conceptualizations of gender and what is perceived as unfair treatment between the males and the females in the household. This may lead to social dysphoria in which cultural components of gender approach disillusion the individual. Often, this social dysphoria is mislabeled or misunderstood as gender dysphoria in which the individual assumes their gender identification must be changed rather than the social circumstances that surround the desire for this change (Yazdanpanahi, Ebrahimi, Badrabadi, & Akbarzadeh, 2022).

Parental awareness of their role in propagating gender divisions and equating these divisions to Islamic perspectives rather than cultural or family norms can cause youth to question faith and steer away from both religious principles and gender identity as aligned with biological sex traits. Often, disillusionment in the home may lead to seeking sources of comfort externally, whether with peers or an influential mentor who may take a more secular approach or to online resources that feel like safer spaces (Ahmed & Ezzeddine, 2009). Understanding the pervasiveness of cisgender challenges, pronoun use, and the motivation behind changing views of gender is a good starting point for parents to seek an understanding of what their children may be struggling with in terms of gender identity.

Challenges of Substances/Behavioral Addictions

Topics Explored:

- Behavioral addictions/Substance abuse
- Adopting unhealthy coping mechanisms
- Desire driving action in identity and addiction

Narrative: Addiction or Distraction

Ra'ed has been kicked out of high school for using and selling marijuana. He grew up in a tight-knit masjid community, with his father as the imam and his mother as an active community volunteer. He has three older sisters who still live at home. He spends most of his time playing video games and is disinterested in schoolwork, prayer, or other activities. He does not see a problem with his behavior as many of his friends use harder drugs and are involved in what he sees as much worse activities. His parents are frustrated with his disinterest in life and are unsure how to proceed. His parents have caught him watching pornography online many times, in addition to finding out about his marijuana use following his suspension from school.

Identifying the Challenges

Western society tends to promote a more individualistic rather than collectivist view, which incorporates a disproportionate emphasis on fulfilling the desires of the self over prioritizing the well-being of others (Inglehart & Oyserman, 2004). From a young age, Western approaches in books, movies, popular culture, online, and in other avenues may encourage Muslim youth to feed the *nafs al-Amara* (base, lower self) and to satisfy all worldly desires regardless of moral or religious reservations rather than refrain from gratification and practice self-restraint towards those desires (Rothman, 2020). This message of always satisfying the self at any cost is a problematic contradiction for Muslims who believe in controlling the desires of *dunia* (earthly life) as the ultimate form of submission to the will of *Allah* (God). However, this message pales for many young people compared to the glitzy appeal of a world that advocates for the unfettered attainment of all desires rather than adherence to Islamic ethics (Mohamed, 2001). Consistently raising the bar on what will satisfy the *nafs* becomes a major factor in the lack of contentment pervading youth seeking out various vices as coping mechanisms.

Behavioral addictions and substance abuse may both be outcomes of dissatisfaction with the self or reality. They may be rooted in a response to many internal and external factors of home and environment (Shidhaye, 2023). The rampant rise in vaping, marijuana use, and gaming addictions post-pandemic is problematic as being cited as stress-relievers among many teens and young adults in the West (Dyer, Crandall, & Hanson, 2023). The challenges in the narrative above encompass substance use, behavioral addictions, apathy, and a lack of motivation, which are everyday struggles that have long plagued Muslim youth and youth in general, albeit at increased levels in more recent years with the legalization of weed usage in many states and the prevalence of vaping at young ages (Ahmed, 2014).

Towards a Positive Approach

Guiding Muslim youth towards understanding the differences between desire and action is a critical component to improved mental health outcomes in how young Muslims in the West approach the many challenges they face (Rothman, 2020). When responding to the desires of the basest self, whether in terms of behavior or substance use, teens will often become entangled in turning to negative coping mechanisms as an outlet that they think may help but only causes further harm (Tineo, Bonumwezi & Lowe, 2021). Both Islamic and public schools have tried cracking down on students who are caught vaping with detentions and suspensions, but this often results in increased rebellion and a desire to push the envelope even more.

Promoting mental health care as a positive approach to dealing with stressors and difficult challenges should be a more normalized approach among Muslim families (Kayrouz, 2022). Having open dialogue that is rooted in love and understanding is also critical in guiding Muslim youth away from harmful substances and behavioral addictions that can lead to a sense of apathy and a lack of motivation (Sirin & Balsano, 2007). Pornography and video game addictions are also mind-altering behavioral actions that can sustain psychosocial and spiritual harm. Parental education, teen education, encouragement, and alternative outlets are all critical components in working through these challenges.

Challenges in Academics and Home Issues Impacting Faith

Topics Addressed:

- Peer pressure and stress management
- Family expectations and impact
- When faith is called into question

Narrative: Family and School Pressure

Maha and Mai are twin sisters in their senior year in high school. Their mom recently remarried, and they struggled to adjust to the new family dynamic. Maha wants to move back in with her dad, and Mai wants to stay with her mom and new stepdad. This causes a great deal of tension between the girls and their parents. The girls' biological father puts much pressure and emphasis on academics, while their mom tends to focus more on religious practice. Mai does not perform as well as Maha academically, so she feels distant from her dad and rejects a relationship with him. Mai also feels closer to her mom because she is more religiously inclined, while Maha is beginning to question her faith. Recently, Mai told her mom that Maha wrote a post online stating, "I don't believe in God" and that she does not identify as Muslim any longer. Maha responds by telling their dad that Mai is failing several classes in school and may not even apply to college.

Identifying the Challenges

Turbulence in home life can be a factor that threatens mental health and stability in terms of adolescence (Sirin & Balsano, 2007). The stress of parental expectations can severely impact mental health outcomes, whether these expectations are academic or religiously focused (Ahmed, 2014). In the narrative above, both sisters are experiencing extreme stress from their home situation but may be responding in different ways. Questioning faith can also be a common part of growing up, such as the question of academic trajectory. Although it may call into question deeper concerns, parental approach to any deviation from expectations from their children should again not be reactionary but should instead be approached from a place of open dialogue and discussion. Parents maintaining a similar approach regardless of marital status is also critical in not sending conflicting messages to children as they navigate their worlds.

Towards a Positive Approach

Although the initial approach to questioning faith or failing classes at school may be one of anger, the parental temperament should be measured and calm in approaching what may seem to be a crisis in upbringing (Bisati, 2021). Stress, anxiety, anger, fear, and uncertainty may all affect how each teenager responds to the major transitions impacting the home. The questioning of faith and the lack of positive academic performance may stem from the internal turmoil that the girls in the narrative are experiencing.

Whether articulated or not, the reality is that many Muslim youths today do question their faith. At the same time, many others struggle academically despite their parent's best efforts to push them toward faith practices and academic success that may sometimes be too demanding (Kayrouz, 2022). Unlike parents' fears regarding raising their children, a lack of faith can go unnoticed initially since the teen might outwardly continue to share in the religious rituals. However, internally, they may feel their faith fading (Driezen, Verschraegen, & Clycq, 2021). Parents and community members often look for overt signs or indications that a teen is rebelling, such as failing classes, not praying or fasting, using drugs or alcohol, or evidence of dating or inappropriate relationships. However, the complexity of losing one's religion lies more in the state of the heart rather than in outward rebellion of behavior (Kayrouz, 2022).

In both situations, parents should not immediately jump to a place of reprimand. Instead, guidance should be offered, and questioning of faith or future direction should be accepted as a rite of passage for many. The Islamic tradition has many examples of prophets who sought solitude to question themselves about the direction of their faith. Through questioning in ethical and sound ways, they came to a greater sense of awareness and appreciation for monotheistic faith and beliefs (Mohamed, 2001). This same form of critical thinking rooted in seeking knowledge should be fostered in young Muslims so that their faith is rooted in their solid belief systems rather than just following what they are being told.

An Islamic analogy that can be applied to youth struggling with faith and identity stems from the Quranic example of the Prophet Moses (may God be pleased with him) and how he had many questions about the *hikmah* (wisdom) of *Allah* [18:61-83]. In the narration in the Quran in *Suratul Kahf* (the chapter of The Cave), adherents to the faith learn about Prophet Moses traveling with *Al-Khidr* (believed to be a saintly man). In this chapter of the Quran, Moses is told not to ask Al-Khidr about anything that occurs. However, from a place of curiosity and wanting to understand his faith, Moses does ask questions. In the Quranic narration, he is not turned away nor told never to ask questions. By the end of their travels together, Al-Khidr answered all of Moses' questions, and Moses came to understand that the knowledge of God far exceeds any human knowledge (Mainiyo, 2015). There is much to be learned as parents from using Quranic principles to foster greater openness and connection with Muslim youth.

Conclusion

This chapter provides a brief glimpse of some of the challenges Muslim youth face in the West today, followed by some approaches to tackling these challenges. The areas explored included identity, sexual orientation, gender expression, addictions, academic stress, family turbulence, and questions of faith. All of these challenges can contribute to negative mental health outcomes if not addressed with patience, compassion, and open communication. Seeking the counsel of mental health professionals is critical in ensuring the well-being of Muslim youth as they navigate through many of these struggles. While the topic of Muslim youth challenges impacting mental health can be explored much further, the chapter offers an introduction to some modern-day situations and scenarios seen in intervention sessions, schools, and interactions with youth. The appendix that follows provides a more practical exploration of some of the questions asked and the more prevalent topics that come up as challenges for Muslim youth today. Issues of identity, dating, gender, relationships, school concerns, mental health inquiries, and much more are explored in both the previous content of this chapter and in the questions answered in the appendix.

References

Ahmed, S. (2014). *Religion, spirituality, and emerging adults: Processing meaning through culture, context, and social position.* In McNamara-Barry, C. & Abo-Zena, M. M. (Eds.), *Emerging adults' religiousness and spirituality.* Oxford University Press.

Ahmed, S., & Ezzeddine, M. (2009). Challenges and opportunities facing American Muslim youth. *Journal of Muslim Mental Health, 4*(2), 159–174.

Bisati, A. A. (2021). Parenting is Counseling: The Relationship of the Parent Child in Islam. *Hamdard Islamicus, 44*(2).

Cheah, C. S., Gürsoy, H., & Balkaya-Ince, M. (2021). Parenting and social identity contributors to character development in Muslim American adolescents. *International Journal of Intercultural Relations, 81,* 68-78.

Cornerstone. (n.d.). Cornerstone. https://www.cornercounseling.com/

Driezen, A., Verschraegen, G., & Clycq, N. (2021). Negotiating a contested identity: Religious individualism among Muslim youth in a super-diverse city. *International Journal of Intercultural Relations, 82,* 25-36.

Dyer, W. J., Crandall, A., & Hanson, C. L. (2023). COVID-19 stress, religious affiliation, and mental health outcomes among adolescents. *Journal of Adolescent Health, 72*(6), 892-898.

Farooqui, J. F., & Kaushik, A. (2022). Growing up as a Muslim youth in an age of Islamophobia: A systematic review of literature. *Contemporary Islam, 16*(1), 65-88.

Inglehart, R., & Oyserman, D. (2004). Individualism, autonomy, self-expression: The human development syndrome. In *Comparing cultures* (pp. 73-96). Brill.

Kosar Altinyelken, H., Akhtar, Y., & Selim, N. (2022). Navigating contradictory narratives on sexuality between the school and the mosque in four Muslim communities in the Netherlands. *Sexuality & Culture, 26*(2), 595-615.

Kayrouz, R. (2022). Muslim adolescent mental health in Australia: A cross-cultural comparison of the risk of developing clinically significant psychological problems. *Journal of Child and Family Studies.*

Mainiyo, A. S. (2015). Relevance of Surah Al-Kahf in the Search of Knowledge. *Research on Humanities and Social Sciences, 5*(7), 175-180.

Mohamed, Y. (2001). The Evolution of Early Islamic Ethics. *American Journal of Islam and Society, 18*(4), 89-132.

Rothman, A. (2020). The levels of the *nafs* and their impact on youth behavior. *Islamic Psychology Journal.*

Sirin, S. R., & Balsano, A. B. (2007). Editors' Introduction: Pathways to Identity and Positive Development Among Muslim Youth in the West. Applied Developmental Science, 11(3), 109–111. https://doi.org/10.1080/10888690701454534

Shidhaye, R. (2023). Global priorities for improving access to mental health services for adolescents in the post-pandemic world. *Current Opinion in Psychology,* 101661.

Tineo, P., Bonumwezi, J. L., & Lowe, S. R. (2021). Discrimination and posttraumatic growth among Muslim American youth: Mediation via posttraumatic stress disorder symptoms. *Journal of Trauma & Dissociation, 22*(2), 188-201.

Yazdanpanahi, Z., Ebrahimi, A., Badrabadi, N., & Akbarzadeh, M. (2022). Gender Dysphoria, Its Causes and Symptoms: A Review. *Journal of Health Science and Medical Research, 41*(1), 2022883.

Zahrin, S. N. A., Ibrahim, M. H., & Fadzil, F. A. (2020). The Psychology of Love in Islam and Implications for Education. *International Journal of Business and Social Science, 11*(12).

Appendix

Q: What do you do if your parents look down on depression as being "crazy," and you can't truly get therapy?

A: First, try speaking to your parents. Share with them different Islamic lectures, books, and articles that explain counseling in a way they can understand. Seek the help of local organizations that could provide you with materials to help you communicate with your parents about how important it is to get help. If you are in college, most campuses offer free or low-cost counseling services, which may be an avenue you can explore with your parents. If you're in high school, speak to your school counselor for support and have them talk to your parents about what you may need regarding therapy. If those resources aren't available, reach out to someone in the masjid, like an Imam or trusted community leader, who can talk to your parents about the importance of mental health care. Encourage your parents to investigate different resources with you that can ease their worries and concerns and provide you with the help you seek.

Q: I struggle with bad anxiety, and next week I'm forced to see a therapist because of it. I don't know what to expect, and I'm so against it. Any advice?

A: Be open-minded. Therapy is meant to help, not harm. If the therapist uses techniques like Dialectical Behavior Therapy (DBT) or Cognitive Behavioral Therapy (CBT), these are excellent ways to learn how to manage your anxiety and regain control over your thoughts and feelings. Remember, this is an opportunity for healing. Don't close the door but also recognize that it may take a few tries to find the right counselor who is the best fit for your concerns.

Q: I have trouble expressing my thoughts, and when I argue with my mother, I get frustrated and begin to stutter. How do I improve my communication skills?

A: Sometimes, expressing yourself through writing can help when speaking is difficult. Try writing down your thoughts in a letter or text message. It allows you to process what you want to say without the pressure of an immediate response and allows you to communicate your feelings more clearly.

Q: What can I do to help a Muslim friend of mine who is depressed?

A: Talk to your friends about whether they have approached their parents or trusted mentors. If not, ask them if they need help talking to their parents about their feelings. Their parents may not be aware of the severity of the situation. Even if your friend thinks it's hard to talk to their parents initially, if they are minors, they will hopefully get them the help they need. You could also suggest accompanying your friend to speak with their parents, offering support as they take that step. Encouraging professional help is critical. Be sure to remind your friend that seeking help is part of healing.

Q: What if your friend has a secret boyfriend? What can you do?

A: I suggest having an honest conversation with your friend. Explain how detrimental this situation can be to her faith and emotional well-being. If she continues down this path, it's important to let her know that you care for her and that you want her to stop exhibiting behavior that compromises her faith.

Q: Is music haram, and if so, why?

A: "*Haram*" is a term we should use carefully. Rather than focusing on whether something is strictly *haram* (impermissible), reflects on the type of music you listen to and ask yourself: Does it bring me closer to *Allah*, or does it pull me away? Music that encourages you to indulge in worldly pleasures or detracts from your purpose may not align with Islamic principles. Intentions matter, so ensure that your actions align with your spiritual goals.

Q: What do you do if you like a guy, and how can you find the right man if you can't date?

A: Finding the right person starts with knowing yourself and understanding what you want in a partner. Islam provides guidelines to help you form a relationship based on compatibility and faith without the need for dating in the traditional sense. Find a spouse who complements your life, not just your desires.

Q: Why is dating haram?

A: Dating, as is commonly practiced, leads to situations that may bring one closer to *zina* (fornication). Islam encourages us to safeguard our hearts and bodies from any paths that could lead to inappropriate physical intimacy. Dating often blurs these boundaries and can lead us away from *Allah*'s commands.

Q: Why don't men cover up like women do?

A: The commandments for modesty differ for men and women. In the Quran, men are commanded to lower their gaze in verse 30 of *Surat an-Nur* (chapter of Light), while women are instructed to cover in verse 31. While the requirements are different, both commandments are acts of worship. Modesty is not just about physical coverings; it's about character, behavior, and humility before *Allah* in your interactions with others and in your own thoughts with yourself.

Q: Is it haram to go to homecoming or prom?

A: Reflect on the environment of such events. Is it one where your faith, modesty, and values are preserved? In answering that question, you will likely be able to answer the question you asked.

Q: What are the parameters for talking to someone when you're looking to get married?

A: When you are seeking a spouse, focus on compatibility, not completion. Make sure to involve a guardian and keep interactions purposefully, public, and professional within the boundaries of modesty and respect. Seek out premarital and compatibility counseling as an avenue of education and preparation for a very important step in life.

Q: Is there such a thing as "halal dating"?

A: Dating, in its common form, often leads to emotional intimacy, which can open the door to inappropriate behavior in the form of physical intimacy. Islam provides ways to get to know a potential spouse within a *halal* (permissible) framework, involving family and a *wali* (guardian) and maintaining modesty throughout the process.

Q: Is Fortnite or RPG dating bad?

A: I would ask the same question about "Roblox girlfriends." These interactions might seem harmless but can lead to inappropriate feelings or behaviors. It's important to question whether such interactions align with Islamic values of modesty and purpose.

Q: What do you do if a boy says that he likes you and wants to date you, and he's Muslim?

A: Be confident and firm in your response. Let him know that dating isn't an option if he wants to honor his faith. You can express that you prioritize your relationship with *Allah* over pleasing another person, even if it's hard at first. If he truly respects you, he will respect your boundaries as well.

Q: Is it haram to text a boy?

A: Ask yourself why you are texting him. Is it necessary, and do your intentions align with your purpose? Remember, casual communication can often blur boundaries, so it's important to keep interactions professional, public, and limited, especially regarding gender interactions.

Q: I like to wear "loud" clothes like red and orange camo pants, but my parents are against it. I feel like this is how I express myself. What should I do if they force me to wear a hijab?

A: Try to have an open and respectful conversation with your parents. Explain that while you respect their views, you also value expressing yourself in a modest but unique way. You might suggest a compromise, like wearing more "quiet" colors or traditional clothing at family gatherings or religious events but continuing to dress the way you feel comfortable in other situations. If speaking directly doesn't help, you might involve a trusted family member or community leader who can mediate.

Q: I took my hijab off because of bullying, and I have been diagnosed with PTSD, depression, and anxiety. My parents don't support me. What should I do?

A: This is a very difficult situation, and I'm sorry that you are experiencing this. Mental health is a priority, and your feelings matter. I would encourage you to continue seeking professional help and to find a trusted community leader or mental health advocate to help communicate your struggles to your parents. They may not fully understand the impact of your experience, so having someone else explain it might help. Also, remember to make *dua* (prayer) and ask *Allah* for strength and healing.

Q: I'm a convert and have been dating someone for a long time. We want to get married, but I know dating is haram. What should I do?

A: First, *Masha Allah* on your commitment to your faith. This is a difficult situation, and I understand your feelings. I would suggest taking a step back and pausing the relationship. Use this time to focus on your relationship with *Allah* and encourage your partner to learn more about Islam. When we leave something for the sake of *Allah*, He always replaces it with something better. Trust in the process, and with time, things will become clearer, *Insha'Allah* (God willing).

Q: How do you get to know a potential future husband if dating is haram?

A: You can get to know a potential spouse through *halal* (permissible) means. Involve a *wali* (appointed guardian), keep interactions public and limited, and focus on compatibility rather than romantic feelings. Seeking a spouse is not about fulfilling temporary desires but about building a lifelong partnership rooted in faith.

Q: How would you safely reject a girl?

A: Be respectful and honest. If you don't feel the same way or are not interested (assuming this

is related to marriage intentions), it's important to express that kindly but firmly. No means no, whether it's coming from a man or a woman. Let her know that you appreciate her feelings but that you are striving to follow what pleases *Allah* and do not see compatibility between you.

Q: Can I hang out with a mixed group of friends in public?

A: Reflect on whether it's necessary and aligns with Islamic values of modesty and gender interaction. Public, professional, and limited interactions are key to maintaining proper boundaries. Ask yourself if these situations bring you closer to *Allah* or pull you away.

Q: What should you do if a guy says he likes you and stares at you?

A: Be strong and confident. If someone's behavior makes you uncomfortable, let them know. Kindly but firmly tell him that his behavior isn't appropriate and that you are not interested in pursuing anything that conflicts with your faith.

Q: How do you tell someone off in an Islamic way?

A: You can express yourself respectfully yet firmly. If someone's behavior makes you uncomfortable or crosses boundaries, let them know directly but politely. There's no need for harshness, but confidence in setting your limits is key.

Q: Is it haram to "smash"?

A: The term "smash" is slang for inappropriate behavior that is clearly against Islamic teachings. Think about the concept of *Haya* and the importance of purity in interactions. Any action that leads to *zina* (fornication) is not permitted in Islam, and we should strive to stay far from it.

Q: Is it haram to have guys on Snapchat? If you are depressed, does it mean Allah is mad at you?

A: Having guys on Snapchat isn't inherently *haram*, but it can lead to inappropriate conversations or behaviors. Reflect on why you need to interact with them and ensure your intentions are aligned with your faith. As for depression, it's not a sign that *Allah* is angry with you. Depression is a real illness that requires care and treatment. *Allah* tests us in different ways, and mental illness is an opportunity to grow closer to Him.

Q: What if you can't control it, and a bunch of girls like you won't leave you alone?

A: Be strong and confident. You are not obligated to entertain anyone's advances. Politely set boundaries and let them know you are not interested. Your commitment to your faith should come first, and they will eventually respect your decision.

Q: What should someone do if the opposite gender asks them out on a date?

A: Be strong and confident. Let them know you aren't interested in dating because it conflicts with your beliefs. Politely but firmly explain that you want to align your actions with your faith and try to stay away from behaviors that don't please *Allah*.

Q: I'm having such a hard time with my mom. She always says negative things to me, and it's hurtful. I used to talk back, but now I just listen, and it's really hard to keep it all inside. What can I do?

A: I'm so sorry to hear that you're going through this. It's important to take care of your mental and emotional well-being in these situations. Try to have an open, calm conversation with your mom about how her words are affecting you. If you struggle to express yourself verbally, try writing her a letter. If the situation doesn't improve, seek advice from a trusted family member or counselor who can help mediate the conversation.

Q: I was wondering if it's haram or halal to have friends of the opposite gender.

A: Reflect on why you need to have a close friendship with someone of the opposite gender. It's important to maintain professional, public, and limited interactions with the opposite gender to preserve modesty and respect for Islamic values. Friendships can often blur boundaries, so it's best to be mindful of the nature of your interactions.

Q: If someone isn't straight on earth and they continue to act the right way, in Jannah, will they be able to freely express that? (I'm straight by the way.)

A: In *Jannah* (Heaven), our desires and needs will be different. It's important to understand that *Jannah* is a place where everything we experience will be pure and pleasing to *Allah*. The pleasures of this world, including struggles with desires, will no longer be an issue. In *Jannah*, we will be in a state of contentment that transcends our worldly concerns. Everything we experience there will be in complete harmony with *Allah*'s will, and it will bring us the greatest satisfaction without any of the negative consequences we face in this world.

Q: How do you deal with someone who keeps bothering you?

A: Be firm and set clear boundaries. If the person continues to disrespect those boundaries, don't hesitate to distance yourself. Make it clear that their behavior is unacceptable and that you won't tolerate it. Always prioritize your well-being and respect. Speak to a parent, teacher, or mentor if the situation continues and adult intervention is needed.

Q: Is it wrong to consider a guy your close friend?

A: Close friendships with the opposite gender can lead to emotional attachments and blurred boundaries. Ask yourself if it's necessary and aligns with Islamic principles of modesty and respect. If friendship is leading to situations that compromise your faith, it's best to re-evaluate and maintain professional, public, and limited interactions.

Q: Is it wrong to tell someone you have feelings for them? Or even just tell your friends?

A: Before expressing your feelings, ask yourself if it's necessary and aligns with your values. Sharing feelings with someone can complicate matters, especially if it leads to behavior that strays from Islamic guidelines. It's important to guard your heart and intentions and to avoid unnecessary emotional entanglements that may cause more struggle.

Q: Can we hug a guy, even without feelings for him?

A: Ask yourself why you feel the need to hug a guy, even if there are no romantic feelings. Physical contact can blur boundaries and lead to behavior that may not align with Islamic values of modesty. It's often best to maintain respectful distance in interactions.

Q: Why do women have to wear hijab, but men don't?

A: Modesty is required of both men and women, but the expressions of that modesty differ. Men are commanded to lower their gaze and dress modestly, while women are commanded to cover more physically. Both are acts of worship, but they manifest in different ways. Men have their own set of obligations, such as attending Friday prayer in the masjid and providing for their families, while women's obligations, including hijab, are unique acts of devotion that differ.

Q: What if your mom is forcing you to wear a hijab? Is it bad if you have a boy best friend?

A: As Allah has commanded, there should be no compulsion in religion. It's important to have an open conversation with your mom and try to express your feelings. As for having a boy best friend, it's important to ask yourself if the friendship is necessary and whether it aligns with Islamic guidelines of modesty and respect. To maintain *Haya*, it may be better to maintain professional, public, and limited interactions with the opposite gender.

Q: Is it haram to have a relationship without physical contact? Is it haram to have a guy friend? What do you do if you like two guys?

A: Even without physical contact, a relationship can lead to emotional attachment and inappropriate interactions, which can distance you from your faith. Islam encourages us to safeguard our hearts and minds.

Friendships with the opposite gender can also blur boundaries, so it's important to ask yourself if friendship is truly necessary and if it aligns with your values. When you like someone, especially two people, it's important to step back and ask whether these feelings are leading you toward or away from *Allah*. Involve a *wali* (guardian) if you are of marriageable age and trying to decide between two marital proposals. Make sure any interactions with the potential proposals are public, professional, and purposeful.

Q: Is hanging out with boys in a group or playing basketball with them, okay?

A: Reflect on why you feel the need to hang out with boys in a group. Is it necessary, and can you maintain modesty and respect in those interactions? While casual group settings may seem harmless, they can sometimes lead to situations that blur boundaries. As for playing sports together, think about whether this environment allows you to maintain *Haya* (modesty). Engaging in activities that align with your values and preserve your modesty is always best.

Q: Is it wrong to have a gay friend of the opposite gender?

A: Regardless of someone's sexual orientation, maintaining appropriate boundaries with the opposite gender is important. Reflect on why you want or need to have a close friendship with someone of the opposite gender and whether it aligns with Islamic guidelines of modesty and respect. Regardless of sexual orientation, with any friend, maintaining professional, public, and purposeful interactions are key to nurturing healthier relationships.

Q: How do you deal with mental illness when it may be connected to a lack of belief in religion?

A: Sometimes, working on our mental health first is necessary before we can get back to a better spiritual path. Your mental and emotional well-being are closely linked, so addressing one can improve the other.

CHAPTER SIX

MUSLIM WOMEN'S MENTAL WELLBEING: A FOCUS ON NORTH AMERICAN MUSLIMS

Venus Mahmoodi, Maeve Winter, Yukti Bhatt, Maryam Gani

The mental wellbeing of Muslim women in North America is shaped by intersecting biological, psychological, social, and spiritual factors. This chapter utilizes an intersectional framework to examine how these domains contribute to mental health outcomes. Biologically, hormonal fluctuations associated with menstruation, pregnancy, and menopause influence mood and wellbeing, while cultural and religious practices interact with these processes. Psychologically, Muslim women experience heightened risks of depression and anxiety due to Islamophobia, gender discrimination, and acculturative stress, although strong familial and community support networks serve as protective factors. Social structures, including family dynamics, marital relationships, and faith-based community support, play a critical role in mental health. While spirituality and religious coping mechanisms, such as prayer and dhikr, provide resilience, over-reliance on spiritual practices instead of professional intervention may impede access to mental health care. Cultural stigma, gender norms, and the preference for gender-concordant providers further influence healthcare utilization. Effective mental health interventions for Muslim women require a bio-psycho-social-spiritual approach that integrates Islamic values and addresses structural barriers to care. Culturally competent treatment strategies, such as Islamically adapted cognitive-behavioral therapy and collaborative models involving religious leaders, can enhance accessibility and efficacy. Addressing systemic disparities and fostering inclusive mental health frameworks are essential to improving outcomes for this population. Future research should focus on developing and evaluating tailored interventions that align with Muslim women's unique cultural and religious contexts in North America.

Introduction

This chapter focuses on the mental well-being of Muslim women in North America. It aims to build an understanding of how these women navigate their biological, psychological, social, and spiritual functioning. Biological health determinants, including hormonal changes and reproductive health experiences such as menstruation, pregnancy, and menopause, can significantly influence both mental and physical health (Allison & Hyde, 2011; Sharp & De Giorgio, 2023). Psychological risk and protective factors shape how Muslim women manage mental health challenges and their consequences (Budhwani & Hearld, 2017; Jasperse et al., 2012). Social influences are also crucial, encompassing the quality of intimate relationships, family dynamics, and community resources, all of which contribute to resilience and well-being (Ahmed & Mao, 2024). Finally, spirituality plays a central role in understanding the health of Muslim women, as it provides meaning, purpose, and emotional balance (Koenig & Shohaib, 2014; Mohr et al., 2019).

This chapter employs an intersectional framework to account for the diverse identities of Muslim women. Intersectionality examines how overlapping social identities and systems of oppression interact to shape individual experiences. This concept emerged to highlight the overlooked experiences of Black women, as race and gender were often treated as separate categories (Crenshaw, 2014). Intersectionality emphasizes that individuals do not experience discrimination or privilege in isolation but rather through the interaction of multiple identity factors, including race, gender, religion, and class (Steele et al., 2023).

For Muslim women, an intersectional approach recognizes their diverse realities, shaped by factors such as immigration status, racial and ethnic background, religious adherence, and cultural identity. Each of these intersecting factors influences lived experiences in different ways. By acknowledging these complexities, researchers and practitioners can move beyond monolithic assumptions and develop culturally sensitive and inclusive mental health interventions (Padela et al., 2017; Callender et al.,

2022). This understanding is essential for creating effective support systems that cater to the unique needs of Muslim women.

Demographics of Muslims in North America

The Muslim population in North America has seen significant growth over recent decades, along with notable demographic changes. As of 2020, approximately 4.5 million Muslims lived in the United States, making up about 1.34% of the total US population (Pew Research Center, 2021). This represents a substantial increase from previous decades, driven primarily by immigration and higher birth rates within Muslim communities.

The Muslim population is racially and ethnically diverse. According to a 2014 study, **38%** of US Muslims identified as non-Hispanic white (which includes Arabs and Iranians), 28% as Asian (primarily South Asians), 28% as Black, 4% as Hispanic, and 3% as mixed or other races (Pew Research Center, 2014). Additionally, 36% of Muslims in the US were born in the country, while 64% are first-generation immigrants. The largest Muslim populations are found in states such as New York, Illinois, New Jersey, and Maryland, with New York City hosting the highest number of Muslims among US cities (Pew Research Center, 2021).

In Canada, the Muslim population has experienced significant growth. According to the 2021 Canadian Census, Muslims made up 4.9% of the national population, a rise from 2.0% in 2001 (Statistics Canada, 2022). This increase is primarily due to immigration from Muslim-majority countries. The Muslim community in Canada is notably young, with a median age of 30, compared to 41 for the overall Canadian population. Ontario has the largest Muslim population, especially in the Greater Toronto Area, where Muslims account for 10% of the population. Quebec also has a considerable Muslim presence, with Muslims constituting 8.7% of the population in the Greater Montreal Area (Statistics Canada, 2022). The Canadian Muslim community is highly diverse, including significant representation from South Asian, Arab, West Asian, and Black communities.

These demographic trends highlight the increasing diversity of Muslim populations in both the United States and Canada, reflecting broader immigration patterns, cultural integration, and generational changes.

Islam and mental health

Muslim women come from a variety of racial and ethnic backgrounds, but they are united by their faith and shared identity as Muslims. Islamic teachings influence many aspects of their lives, including significant events such as marriage, motherhood, and death, as well as everyday activities like eating, sleeping, and social interactions. These teachings also shape their roles within families and society. Given that Islam influences all facets of their lives, it is important to incorporate these values into the understanding of mental health and treatment approaches.

Early Islamic scholars recognized mental illness, often referring to it as "amrad al-qalb," which means "diseases of the heart," to describe psychological distress. This terminology reflects the belief in a connection between emotional, spiritual, and physical well-being (Bagasra & Mackinem, 2014). In Islam, health is viewed holistically, emphasizing the balance among the physical, mental, and spiritual dimensions. The Qur'an highlights this interconnectedness, stressing the importance of caring for both the body and the soul to achieve overall wellness (Afiya).

The Islamic understanding of mental health and well-being is based on teachings from the Qur'an, Hadith, and centuries of Islamic scholarship. These sources offer a comprehensive framework that integrates the body, mind, and spirit, influencing attitudes toward mental health and its treatment. Historically, these perspectives have shaped how Muslim communities perceive psychological disorders and seek treatment, often combining spiritual, social, and medical interventions.

Mental health conditions in Islamic contexts are understood to have biological, psychological, and spiritual causes (Mitha, 2020). These foundational beliefs greatly influence Muslim women's preferences and attitudes toward treatment options. For instance, women may prefer to consult practitioners of the same gender or seek providers who show sensitivity to Islamic values. Programs that do not consider cultural or religious sensitivities tend to be less effective (Padela et al., 2017).

Islamic teachings emphasize modesty, family responsibilities, and community support, which significantly influence Muslim women's mental health and their attitudes toward treatment. Cultural norms related to gender roles and motherhood can contribute to stressors such as anxiety and postpartum depression. However, concerns about social stigma and family expectations may prevent women from seeking professional help. While Islam encourages individuals to pursue medical care, the effectiveness of mental health interventions often relies on their alignment with religious and cultural values.

Biological Determinants

Biological differences among Muslim women are attributed to their racial, ethnic, and geographic backgrounds, rather than their religious identity. Variations in health are influenced by cultural, social, and environmental factors that affect reproductive health, mental health, and overall well-being. For example, genetic predispositions to conditions like diabetes or cardiovascular disease can be worsened by lifestyle factors such as diet and physical inactivity, but these issues can often be addressed through preventive measures.

Health disparities among North American Muslim women, including higher rates of certain conditions, are more closely related to access to healthcare, education, socioeconomic status, and experiences of discrimination than to any inherent biological differences.

Cultural and religious practices also intersect with biological factors, shaping the mental health and well-being of Muslim women. Social expectations surrounding menstruation, fertility, and pregnancy—along with practices like fasting and modesty—interact with hormonal changes throughout their lives. These dynamics present both challenges and strengths, uniquely influencing the mental health and emotional well-being of Muslim women in North America.

Menstrual Cycle

The menstrual cycle significantly impacts various aspects of health, particularly hormone levels such as estrogen and progesterone. These fluctuations can influence mood, energy levels, and overall physical health (Allison & Hyde, 2013; Sharp & De Giorgio, 2023). Despite being chronic understudies and often misunderstood, the menstrual cycle serves as an important indicator of women's reproductive health. Menstruation can be utilized as a valid diagnostic tool (Critchley et al., 2020) and has been recognized by the NIH as the "fifth vital sign," since menstrual irregularities can signal hormonal imbalances, gynecological diseases, or infections (ACOG Committee, 2006).

Globally, menstruation is frequently stigmatized and misunderstood. These misconceptions are particularly prevalent in Muslim communities in North America, resulting in negative effects on women's physical, mental, and social well-being (Critchley et al., 2020). Mental health disorders, such as depression, anxiety, and psychotic disorders, are often exacerbated during periods of hormonal fluctuation—including the menstrual cycle, pregnancy, and menopause (Nolan & Hughes, 2022; Cirillo et al., 2012).

Premenstrual Syndrome (PMS) and Premenstrual Dysphoric Disorder (PMDD) are conditions influenced by hormonal changes, affecting both mental and physical health. Although the prevalence of menstrual disorders among Muslim women in North America is not well-documented, a study involving 3,856 English-speaking premenopausal

Asian, Latina, and Black women found that 3.3% experienced PMDD at some point in their lives, with an increased risk associated with longer residency in the U.S. (Pilver et al., 2011). These findings suggest that acculturation to American culture, rather than biological differences, may contribute to the higher likelihood of PMDD among ethnic minority women.

Pregnancy and Childbirth

Biological changes during pregnancy, including hormonal shifts and increased blood volume, can significantly impact mental health. For instance, conditions such as gestational diabetes mellitus (GDM) disproportionately affect women from South and Southeast Asian backgrounds, raising their risk of developing type 2 diabetes later in life (Yuen & Wong, 2015).

For Muslim women, the practice of fasting during Ramadan interacts with these physiological changes. Although research on the effects of fasting has produced mixed results, some studies suggest a potential link between fasting and neonatal risks, such as preterm birth (Tith et al., 2019).

Furthermore, chronic stress and depressive symptoms during pregnancy can lead to increased inflammation, which may adversely affect mental health after childbirth (Yim et al., 2015). Cultural practices such as breastfeeding and avoiding alcohol may provide protective benefits (Khorasgani & Beikzadeh, 2023). However, the acculturative stress experienced by many in North America can negate these advantages by elevating inflammation levels (Fang et al., 2014).

Menopause

The transition to menopause, characterized by declining levels of estrogen and progesterone, has a significant impact on mental health by affecting neurotransmitter systems such as serotonin and GABA (Alblooshi et al., 2023). Common symptoms during perimenopause include hot flashes, insomnia, and mood disorders, including depression and anxiety. Limited research suggests that Arab women may experience more severe symptoms, influenced by cultural perceptions (Freeman & Sherif, 2007). Additionally, health risks associated with menopause, such as osteoporosis and cardiovascular disease, further complicate mental health challenges for Muslim women in North America.

Biological processes like menstruation, pregnancy, and menopause have a profound effect on women's mental health, intersecting with cultural and environmental factors. For Muslim women, addressing mental health issues requires integrating cultural and religious contexts into healthcare practices. There is a critical need for more research and culturally tailored interventions to reduce health disparities and enhance mental well-being within this population.

Psychological Factors

Muslim women in North America encounter distinct mental health challenges arising from the intersection of their religious, gender, and ethnic identities. Factors such as discrimination, especially Islamophobia, gender-based prejudice, and acculturative stress—significantly contribute to higher rates of depression and anxiety (Budhwani & Hearld, 2017). In addition, cultural and familial pressures within their communities can further complicate these issues. As a result of these intertwining factors, Muslim women often face complex forms of oppression both within their communities and in the broader society, which intensifies their mental health struggles.

Prevalence Rates

The mental health of Muslim women in North America has become an increasingly important area of study due to the growing population and the unique challenges they face. This situation calls for a more nuanced understanding of their experiences and the factors that impact mental health outcomes.

Recent research indicates that the rates of depression among Arab American women are significantly higher than those of non-Hispanic white women, with estimates ranging from 30-40% compared to 10-15% (Budhwani & Hearld, 2017; Jasperse et al., 2012; Suleiman et al., 2021). One explanation for these elevated rates is discrimination, particularly in the form of Islamophobia and religious-based prejudice, which are closely associated with depressive symptoms (Hodge et al., 2015).

Depression is particularly prevalent among Muslim women who are navigating societal and familial pressures or who are especially sensitive to religious-based discrimination (Jasperse et al., 2012). Additionally, research shows that Muslim college students—primarily women—report experiencing more anxiety symptoms than their peers, a situation that is exacerbated by perceived discrimination (Tineo et al., 2021).

Some women are more vulnerable to mood symptoms during hormonal changes, as previously discussed. Research shows that postpartum depression (PPD) is twice as common among immigrant women compared to non-immigrant women (Falah-Hassani et al., 2015). Although specific data on Muslim women is limited, studies indicate that Arab American and immigrant women are particularly at risk. For instance, 36%

of Arab participants in the U.S. were identified as high-risk for PPD (Alhasanat et al., 2017). This prevalence rate aligns with a systematic review by Haque et al., which found that the rate of PPD among Arab and Middle Eastern women ranges from 10% to 51% (Haque et al., 2015). These findings suggest that Muslim women of Arab descent and immigrant women experience higher rates of depression and anxiety compared to their white counterparts, primarily due to increased psychosocial pressures and challenges, despite having similar biological factors.

Factors Influencing Mental Health

Discrimination and Acculturation

Muslim women encounter multiple forms of discrimination that stem from both their gender and religious identity. Visible signs of faith, such as the hijab, increase their vulnerability to stereotypes and marginalization, particularly in public and professional environments (Murrar et al., 2024; Hashem & Awad, 2024). This perceived discrimination often leads to psychological distress, especially for women who have a strong identification with their faith (Steele et al., 2023).

Furthermore, acculturative stress adds to these challenges as Muslim women adapt to cultural differences, language barriers, and feelings of exclusion from mainstream society. For instance, Saudi Arabian international students report experiencing high levels of acculturative stress, which are associated with increased symptoms of depression and anxiety (Al-Krenawi et al., 2021). These stressors impact not only recent immigrants but also U.S.-born Muslim women as they navigate their dual identities (Nagra, 2018).

Solo Status

"Solo status" refers to the experience of being the sole representative of a social group, which can heighten psychological stress for Muslim women, especially those who wear the hijab (Hashem & Awad, 2024). Younger Muslim women often report feeling isolated or alienated due to their visibility as both Muslims and women. These feelings, combined with pressures to assimilate, can worsen their sense of marginalization and lead to mental health challenges (Wang et al., 2020).

Sexism

Within their communities, Muslim women often encounter a form of ambivalent sexism, which encompasses both hostile sexism—characterized by negative attitudes toward women—and benevolent sexism, which involves paternalistic attitudes that reinforce traditional gender roles (Glick & Fiske, 1996). These dynamics contribute to gender inequality and mental health challenges. Research indicates that Muslim men in Western societies are more likely to express hostile attitudes toward women, while Muslim women may internalize benevolent sexism due to a stronger identification with religious fundamentalism (Hannover et al., 2018; Mastari et al., 2021).

Ironically, anti-sexism movements in Western countries sometimes use the rhetoric of gender equality to promote discriminatory views against Islam, further marginalizing Muslim women (Van Oost et al., 2023).

The intersecting challenges of discrimination, acculturative stress, and internalized sexism significantly impact the mental health of Muslim women in North America. Addressing these issues requires a nuanced, intersectional approach that considers both societal and cultural pressures. Efforts to support Muslim women should focus on reducing systemic discrimination while fostering inclusive environments that affirm their complex identities.

Societal Domains

Relational and social factors, such as intimate relationships, family dynamics, and community support, profoundly influence the mental health and well-being of North American Muslim women. These elements shape their coping mechanisms in response to societal pressures. Family and romantic relationships provide emotional support, helping to buffer stress and foster resilience. Strong family dynamics are essential for identity formation and a sense of belonging, especially for Muslim women navigating multiple cultural contexts. Additionally, community support networks play a crucial role in reducing isolation and stigma, significantly contributing to their mental well-being (Ahmed & Mao, 2024).

This section examines the psychosocial factors affecting Muslim women's well-being, focusing on mosques, marital roles, and peer support within communities. These elements create a comprehensive framework of emotional, spiritual, and practical support, enhancing resilience in the face of the unique challenges experienced by Muslim women in North America. While this chapter aims to address inequities within social domains through Islamic perspectives, it is not exhaustive and cannot capture all the complexities of Muslim women's experiences.

Faith-Based Community Support

Community support plays a vital role in the psychological well-being of Muslim women, especially those from collectivist and immigrant backgrounds where interdependence is highly valued. In the United States, mosques serve not only as places of worship but also as community hubs that provide educational programs, health services, and women's support initiatives (Bagby et al., 2001). These spaces foster a sense of belonging, which is essential for coping with the stress associated with being a religious minority (Mohr et al., 2019).

However, some mosques have physical designs and organizational structures that reflect traditional practices, which can marginalize women. Women's prayer areas are often less accessible, poorly maintained, or segregated in ways that limit their participation, reinforcing feelings of exclusion and invisibility (Eskandari, 2011).

Despite these challenges, inclusive mosques are crucial for enhancing women's spiritual and emotional well-being. The strong peer relationships that develop in these spaces provide psychological support, helping women navigate the complexities of their religious identity in a Western context (Nguyen et al., 2023; Buckley & Carland, 2023).

Evolving Roles and Dynamics in Muslim Families

A Muslim woman's identity is influenced by religious, cultural, and societal factors, with Islam emphasizing equity and mutual responsibility in marriage. While cultural practices often impose gender-specific expectations, Islamic teachings highlight that spouses should share responsibilities to contribute to the wellbeing of the family (Trask, 2011). According to Islamic principles, a woman's ultimate purpose is to worship God, and acts of service to her family are considered extensions of that worship rather than obligatory gender roles (Maqbool, 2023). However, in many Muslim communities, women are socialized into roles focused on familial service, often at the expense of their own worship and personal development.

This presents several challenges:

1. Women may find it challenging to cultivate a personal relationship with Allah, as their faith is frequently linked to their roles as caregivers.
2. Gender expectations can vary based on human interpretation rather than divine decree, resulting in inconsistent and culturally driven obligations.
3. Additionally, limited access to religious knowledge prevents many women from challenging incorrect cultural norms.

To address these issues, it is crucial for Muslim women to engage in traditional Islamic scholarship, ensuring that they understand their roles through an Islamic rather than a purely cultural lens.

The Role of Husbands in Emotional and Mental Wellbeing

In Muslim families, a husband's role in alleviating emotional burdens is crucial for maintaining his wife's mental health, as exemplified by the practices of the Prophet Muhammad ﷺ (Maqbool, 2023). Research shows that spousal support significantly reduces depression among Muslim American wives, often providing more benefits than social support from extended family or friends (Aroian et al., 2017).

Islamic marriage is viewed as a partnership based on shared responsibilities, where both spouses have complementary roles. A husband's active participation in household duties and emotional support helps reduce his wife's stress and enhances her overall well-being (Alghafli et al., 2017). The Prophet Muhammad ﷺ offered emotional, physical, and financial support to his wives, actively helping to alleviate their burdens during challenging times. This challenges the misconception that household and caregiving responsibilities rest solely on women (Maqbool, 2023).

Extended Family Dynamics and Mental Health

In many Muslim societies, extended family relationships play a significant role in shaping familial responsibilities and mental well-being. The concept of *birr al-walidayn*, which refers to dutifulness to parents, applies equally to both sons and daughters. This challenges cultural norms that often place a heavier burden of caregiving on women (Maqbool, 2023). Traditional expectations that women should assume primary caregiving roles can conflict with Islamic teachings, which advocate for a more equitable distribution of familial responsibilities.

While extended family structures can offer emotional and logistical support, living with in-laws may also introduce stress and conflict, particularly during times of immigration and resettlement (Aroian et al., 2017). Research indicates that women who coexist with extended family members often experience higher levels of stress and family conflicts, especially when caregiving roles are not fairly shared (Aroian et al., 2017). Islamic teachings encourage husbands to adopt the Prophetic model by assisting their wives in navigating family expectations. Establishing healthy boundaries and prioritizing self-care are essential strategies for managing familial obligations while maintaining mental well-being (Maqbool, 2023).

The Concept of Qawwam: Beyond Financial Responsibility

Islamic teachings designate husbands as *Qawwam*, a term that is often misunderstood as solely referring to financial and physical protection. In reality, *Qawwam* encompasses a broader responsibility that includes ensuring the emotional and mental well-being of one's spouse. Islamic scholarship asserts that a husband who neglects his wife's emotional well-being fails in his role as *Qawwam* (Maqbool, 2023). This understanding aligns with the *Maqasid* (objectives) of *Shari'ah*, which prioritize the protection of the body, honor, intellect, wealth, and dignity.

A *Qawwam* must actively create an environment of emotional security, safeguarding his wife's psychological and spiritual welfare. This interpretation expands the traditional understanding of marital roles, emphasizing that emotional neglect contradicts Islamic principles (Maqbool, 2023).

Peer Support and Resilience

Peer relationships are crucial for supporting Muslim women, especially when coping with discrimination. Research indicates that friendships among minority women can alleviate psychological distress, enhance resilience, and foster a sense of belonging (Thelamour et al., 2019). Muslim women in predominantly white institutions often encounter unique challenges, such as Islamophobia and racial discrimination. Peer support from organizations like Muslim Student Associations has been shown to lessen the psychological impact of discrimination and promote mental health (Guerrero et al., 2022).

Women and Ramadan: Balancing Responsibilities

Ramadan offers a chance for spiritual renewal and community involvement, but it can also pose significant challenges for Muslim women. These women often juggle the responsibilities of work, family, and religious obligations (Buckley & Carland, 2023). They are frequently expected to prepare meals for their families while also engaging in spiritual acts of worship, which can lead to emotional and physical exhaustion (Buckley & Carland, 2023). Despite these difficulties, Ramadan promotes communal support, accountability, and a sense of spiritual empowerment.

The mental wellbeing of Muslim women is influenced by various social, familial, and religious factors. Support from husbands, peer networks, and inclusive community spaces is essential for fostering emotional resilience. Future research should continue to explore Islamic frameworks that encourage gender equity, emotional support, and mental health awareness (Maqbool, 2023).

Spiritual Influences on Mental Health

Spirituality plays a significant role in mental health by offering meaning, emotional stability, and a sense of purpose. Spiritual practices, such as mindfulness, meditation, prayer, and communal worship, act as protective factors against psychological distress. These practices help individuals manage stress, promote emotional regulation, and foster resilience (Koenig & Al Shohaib, 2014). Spirituality often provides a framework for understanding life's challenges, reduces feelings of hopelessness, and creates a connection to a higher purpose. Activities like prayer and mindfulness encourage introspection, self-awareness, and emotional regulation, resulting in both immediate relief and long-term benefits, such as decreased anxiety and depression (Levin, 2016). Furthermore, communal spiritual practices enhance social support and foster a sense of belonging, which further contributes to mental well-being.

For Muslim women in North America, spirituality serves as a vital framework for coping with the unique challenges of navigating their religious identity within a predominantly secular society. Spiritual practices like prayer (salat), Qur'anic recitation, and dhikr (remembrance of Allah) provide emotional grounding and personal solace. These practices not only align with universal spiritual principles but also address the specific needs of Muslim women, reinforcing their sense of collective identity and offering emotional resilience (Mohr et al., 2019).

This section examines the role of spirituality in promoting mental health among Muslim women in North America, highlighting both the protective and challenging aspects of spiritual practices. It explores how these women utilize spiritual tools to cope with social, cultural, and psychological challenges.

Spiritual Coping Mechanisms

Spirituality offers valuable coping mechanisms that significantly impact mental health and well-being. For Muslim women, practices such as prayer, Qur'anic recitation, and dhikr are essential tools for managing stress and maintaining emotional balance. Research has shown that prayer provides comfort and helps Muslim women reframe their struggles in the context of faith, which reduces feelings of helplessness and enhances resilience (Mohr et al., 2019).

Prayer, particularly when practiced in a communal setting, fosters emotional support networks and strengthens connections within the Muslim community. It reinforces familial bonds and cultural traditions. One participant noted, "I want my children to see me when I am praying. As soon as I start praying, they start praying too. I want to be a role model for them" (Callender et al., 2022). Such practices help mitigate feelings of isolation and enhance well-being by promoting a sense of shared identity and community.

Islamic teachings, such as *tawakkul* (trusting Allah's plan) and *muraqaba* (mindfulness of Allah's presence), further contribute to resilience by helping Muslim women cope with uncertainty and daily stressors. These practices encourage emotional regulation and composure in stressful situations (Ibrahim & Whitley, 2021. Regular engagement with dhikr and muraqaba cultivates a mindset of surrender to Allah's will, which alleviates the mental burden of feeling personally responsible for life's uncertainties.

In a fast-paced world where external pressures often collide, spiritual reflection provides a meaningful pause. Practices like dhikr and mindfulness not only alleviate stress but also strengthen trust in divine wisdom, empowering Muslim women to maintain emotional balance in the face of adversity.

Religiosity and Mental Health

Religiosity plays a complex role in the mental health of Muslim women in North America, offering both emotional support and stability in the face of challenges like discrimination, marginalization, and cultural adaptation. Religious practices provide a framework for understanding life's difficulties, which can contribute to resilience (Koenig & Al Shohaib, 2019).

Research indicates that intrinsic religiosity—marked by personal conviction and devotion—is associated with better mental health outcomes, such as lower levels of anxiety and depression (Gulamhussein & Eaton, 2015). For many women, intrinsic religiosity allows them to reframe adversity as part of a divine plan, thereby fostering resilience and emotional stability (Callender et al., 2022).

On the other hand, extrinsic religiosity, which is driven by external cultural or societal expectations, can sometimes create internal conflict, particularly in secular or Islamophobic environments. While this form of religiosity may offer community support, it is not as consistently linked to positive mental health outcomes (Ghorbani et al., 2008). However, engagement in communal religious practices can potentially lead to deeper personal connections to faith, highlighting the intricate relationship between religiosity and mental well-being.

Resilience, Tolerance of Uncertainty, and Adaptability

Resilience is essential in understanding the mental health of Muslim women, particularly when facing intersecting challenges like discrimination and cultural expectations. Spiritual practices, along with the ability to adapt to new environments, enable these women to navigate life's uncertainties while maintaining emotional stability (Callender et al., 2022).

A key aspect of this resilience is the concept of *tawakkul,* or trust in Allah's plan. This belief helps women cope with uncertainty and fosters a sense of hope and agency. For example, women in the San Francisco Bay Area have shared that their faith in submitting to Allah's will provides them with patience and emotional strength during difficult times (Mohr et al., 2019).

Challenges in Balancing Spirituality and Mental Health

While spirituality can be a vital source of resilience, challenges arise when cultural and community expectations complicate the balance between spirituality and mental health care. For some Muslim women, the belief that spiritual devotion alone can resolve emotional distress may delay or prevent them from seeking professional psychological help (Ahmad et al., 2023). Additionally, stigma surrounding mental health, particularly within some Muslim communities, can discourage open discussions about mental health issues (Mohr et al., 2019).

Another challenge is the phenomenon of spiritual bypassing, where spiritual practices are used to avoid addressing psychological issues. For instance, practices such as dhikr may offer temporary relief but can inadvertently replace necessary professional treatment, leaving underlying issues unresolved (Mitha, 2020).

Furthermore, Muslim women who wear the hijab or visibly express their faith may experience increased anxiety due to discrimination or the pressure of balancing religious and societal expectations. This tension can lead to significant identity conflicts, especially among adolescents and young adults grappling with the need to reconcile their religious values with Western norms (Balkaya-Ince et al., 2024).

These challenges underscore the need for culturally sensitive mental health approaches that acknowledge both the spiritual significance of religious practices and the psychological well-being of Muslim women, particularly in diasporic contexts (Callender et al., 2022; Mohr et al., 2019).

Treatment Approaches for Muslim Women in North America

The mental health preferences of Muslim women are significantly influenced by Islamic principles, which promote a holistic approach to well-being that encompasses the body, mind, community, and spirit. This comprehensive perspective on health shapes their treatment choices, as many women seek therapies that align with their cultural, spiritual, and religious values. Treatments that incorporate Islamic practices, such as prayer, Qur'anic recitation, and spiritual healing (e.g., ruqyah), are often preferred. These practices are viewed as effective, whether used on their own or in conjunction with conventional care, underscoring the importance of an integrative treatment model (Alrawi et al., 2012; Douki et al., 2007; Padela et al., 2012).

Preference for Holistic Treatment

Many Muslim women prefer mental health treatments that address their psychological, physical, and spiritual well-being. This preference aligns with the Islamic understanding of health as a balanced integration of these elements. Incorporating spiritual practices, such as prayer and mindfulness, alongside traditional therapies like cognitive-behavioral therapy (CBT), enhances the effectiveness of treatment and fosters comfort and trust between patients and therapists (Qureshi et al., 2020).

Gender-Concordant Care

Islamic teachings on modesty play a significant role in the preference for female therapists, especially when addressing sensitive issues like marital problems or reproductive health. Research has consistently shown that Muslim women in North America are more inclined to seek care from female providers (Kamimura et al., 2018; Vu et al., 2016). This preference is rooted in the cultural values surrounding gender and modesty within Islamic traditions. Providing gender-concordant care is essential for reducing barriers to treatment and improving the therapeutic relationship.

Cultural Sensitivity and Islamic Values in Treatment

Mental health treatments that integrate Islamic principles, such as patience (sabr) and trust in God's plan (tawakkul), are preferred by many Muslim women (Hassan, 2022). Therapists who respect these values are more likely to build trust and provide effective care. CBT, for example, can be adapted to incorporate these principles, helping Muslim women reframe challenges and cope more effectively (Qureshi et al., 2020). Despite recognizing these spiritual practices as part of holistic care, further research is needed to assess their effectiveness and integrate them into mainstream healthcare.

Reluctance to Use Conventional Health Services

The stigma surrounding mental health remains a barrier to care for many Muslim women. However, this stigma is complex, with factors such as the lack of female clinicians, unfamiliarity with the healthcare system, and fear of religious discrimination contributing to delays in seeking treatment (Vu et al., 2016). Furthermore, rural Muslim women may experience discomfort with the perceived authority of healthcare providers in the US, which contrasts with their experiences in Muslim-majority countries where physicians are often seen as spiritual guides (Simpson & Carter, 2008). Public health initiatives that educate Muslim communities on mental health as an act of self-care and faith are critical to overcoming these barriers.

Use of Family and Community Support

Islamic teachings highlight the importance of family and community support in promoting mental and emotional well-being. They also recognize the roles of teachers and physicians, emphasizing the need to seek guidance from knowledgeable individuals when addressing health concerns (Koenig & Al Shohaib, 2014). Many Muslims rely on trusted family members or religious leaders when making health decisions, including those related to mental health (Ali & Milstein, 2012). Thus, fostering collaboration between healthcare providers and religious leaders is essential for delivering culturally relevant mental health care. Initiatives such as training imams in mental health literacy and programs like *Clergy Outreach and Professional Engagement (COPE)* can enhance communication between religious figures and mental health professionals, thereby improving healthcare access in Muslim communities (Ali & Milstein, 2012).

However, Muslim women face unique challenges when seeking support. Research indicates that many women are hesitant to seek counseling from male imams, especially for sensitive issues such as serious mental illness, domestic violence, or family conflict. This discomfort stems from the difficulty of discussing sensitive topics with male religious authorities (Hassan, 2022; Mohr et al., 2019). Additionally, some women may perceive male imams as lacking impartiality in dealing with complex family cases, particularly when cultural expectations favor male perspectives in conflict resolution (Hodge et al., 2015).

The shortage of highly trained female religious scholars and mental health providers has been identified as a barrier to holistic recovery for Muslim women (Hassan, 2022). Increasing the number of gender-concordant mental health professionals and female Islamic scholars could significantly enhance treatment engagement, facilitate culturally sensitive interventions, and improve overall mental well-being for Muslim women (Kamimura et al., 2018; Vu et al., 2016). Strengthening interdisciplinary partnerships among mental health professionals, female scholars, and religious leaders will be crucial for advancing culturally competent care and addressing the nuanced needs of Muslim women.

Case Example: Integrating Bio-Psycho-Social-Spiritual Approaches

Amina is a 32-year-old Muslim woman facing anxiety and depression linked to cultural adaptation and work-life stress. As a recent immigrant, she struggles to balance her religious identity with the demands of a secular workplace. Amina finds comfort in regular prayer, Qur'anic recitation, and dhikr (remembrance of Allah), which provide her with moments of solace and emotional grounding. However, she also experiences feelings of isolation and inadequacy that hinder her social and professional functioning.

A bio-psycho-social-spiritual approach to treatment would integrate the following:

- **Biological:** Address any physiological factors contributing to Amina's mental health, such as sleep disruptions or stress-related physical symptoms. This can be done through a combination of cognitive-behavioral therapy (CBT) and, if necessary, medication.
- **Psychological:** Utilize Islamically oriented CBT techniques to help Amina reframe negative thoughts and develop coping strategies that align with her Islamic values. Focus on fostering patience (sabr) and trust in God's plan (tawakkul).
- **Social:** Recognize the importance of Amina's family and community support. Encourage open discussions about her mental health with close relatives and integrate her faith community into her treatment plan to help reduce feelings of isolation.
- **Spiritual:** Incorporate spiritual practices such as prayer, mindfulness, and dhikr to manage anxiety and foster emotional resilience. By embracing the Islamic principle of tawakkul, Amina can learn to trust in the divine plan, which may help alleviate feelings of anxiety and uncertainty.

Amina's spiritual, emotional, and social needs are addressed through an integrated treatment approach, promoting greater wellbeing and resilience in managing her daily life challenges. This integrative method may involve collaboration between the therapist and an Islamic scholar to create a treatment plan that addresses both mental health and spiritual concerns. Alternatively, some therapists may choose to incorporate religious coping strategies within a more traditional Western treatment framework. In such cases, the therapist can consult with an Imam or scholar to identify relevant verses from the Quran, explore religious perspectives, and incorporate spiritual practices that can help reduce stress and anxiety while effectively coping with life's challenges.

Conclusion

The mental wellbeing of Muslim women in North America is influenced by a complex interaction of biological, psychological, social, and spiritual factors. This chapter highlights how these domains intersect, affecting mental health experiences and treatment preferences. Biologically, hormonal changes throughout a woman's life—particularly during menstruation, pregnancy, and menopause—can impact mental health.

These changes are often compounded by cultural and religious expectations (Allison & Hyde, 2013; Sharp & De Giorgio, 2023). Psychologically, Muslim women face unique challenges such as Islamophobia, gender-based discrimination, and acculturative stress, which can increase the risk of depression and anxiety (Budhwani & Hearld, 2017; Jasperse et al., 2012). However, protective factors like family support, peer networks, and spiritual coping mechanisms help mitigate these risks, fostering resilience and emotional balance (Mohr et al., 2019; Callender et al., 2022). From a social perspective, faith-based communities, family structures, and cultural expectations play crucial roles in Muslim women's mental health. While mosques and community networks provide support, gender-specific barriers—such as the reluctance to seek guidance from male religious leaders—underscore the need for trained female Islamic scholars and gender-concordant mental health professionals (Hassan, 2022; Vu et al., 2016). Spiritually, religiosity serves as a key coping mechanism, offering both protective and potentially restrictive influences on mental health. When integrated effectively, spiritual practices such as prayer, Qur'anic recitation, and dhikr enhance wellbeing and reinforce cultural identity (Koenig & Al Shohaib, 2014; Mohr et al., 2019). Addressing the mental health needs of Muslim women requires culturally competent, intersectional, and spiritually integrated approaches. Mental health professionals must work collaboratively with religious leaders and develop gender-sensitive interventions to bridge the gap between Islamic values and conventional mental health care. Future research should explore evidence-based models that incorporate bio-psycho-social-spiritual frameworks to ensure holistic and inclusive mental health care for Muslim women in North America (Padela et al., 2017; Qureshi et al., 2020).

References

ACOG Committee on Adolescent Health Care. (2006). ACOG Committee Opinion No. 349, November 2006: Menstruation in girls and adolescents: using the menstrual cycle as a vital sign. *Obstetrics and gynecology, 108*(5), 1323-1328.

Ahmad, S. S., McLaughlin, M. M., & Weisman de Mamani, A. (2023). Spiritual bypass as a moderator of the relationships between religious coping and psychological distress in Muslims living in the United States. *Psychology of Religion and Spirituality, 15*(1), 32-42. https://doi-org.ezproxy.cul.columbia.edu/10.1037/rel0000469

Ahmed, R., & Mao, Y. (2024). An Intersectional approach to understanding beliefs and attitudes toward mental health issues among muslim immigrant women in Canada. *Health Communication, 39*(10), 2014-2025.

Alblooshi, S., Taylor, M., & Gill, N. (2023). Does menopause elevate the risk for developing depression and anxiety? Results from a systematic review. *Australasian Psychiatry, 31*(2), 165-173.

Alghafli, Z., Marks, L. D., Hatch, T. G., & Rose, A. H. (2017). Veiling in fear or in faith? Meanings of the Hijab to practicing Muslim wives and husbands in USA. *Marriage & Family Review, 53*(7), 696-716.

Alhasanat, D., Fry-McComish, J., & Yarandi, H. N. (2017). Risk For Postpartum Depression Among Immigrant Arabic Women in the United States: A Feasibility Study. *Journal of midwifery & women's health, 62*(4), 470–476. https://doi.org/10.1111/jmwh.12617

Ali, O. M., & Milstein, G. (2012). Mental illness recognition and referral practices among imams in the United States. *Journal of Muslim Mental Health, 6*(2), 3–13. https://doi-org.ezproxy.cul.columbia.edu/10.3998/jmmh.10381607.0006.202

Alimahomed-Wilson, S. (2017). Invisible violence: Gender, Islamophobia, and the hidden assault on US Muslim women. *Women, Gender, and Families of Color, 5*(1), 73-97. https://doi.org/10.5406/womgenfamcol.5.1.0073

Alimahomed-Wilson, S. (2020). The matrix of gendered Islamophobia: Muslim women's repression and resistance. *Gender & Society, 34*(4), 648–678. https://doi-org.ezproxy.cul.columbia.edu/10.1177/0891243220932156

Allison, C. M., & Hyde, J. S. (2011). Early Menarche: confluence of biological and contextual factors. *Sex Roles, 68*(1–2), 55–64. https://doi.org/10.1007/s11199-011-9993-5

Al-Krenawi, A., Alotaibi, F., & Elbedour, S. (2021). Acculturative stress among female Saudi college students in the United States. *Community mental health journal, 57*, 372-379.

Alrawi, S., Fetters, M. D., Killawi, A., Hammad, A., & Padela, A. (2012). Traditional healing practices among American Muslims: perceptions of community leaders in southeast Michigan. *Journal of immigrant and minority health, 14*(3), 489–496. https://doi.org/10.1007/s10903-011-9495-0

Aroian, K., Uddin, N., & Blbas, H. (2017). Longitudinal study of stress, social support, and depression in married Arab immigrant women. *Health care for women international, 38*(2), 100-117.

Bagasra, A., & Mackinem, M. (2014). An exploratory study of American Muslim conceptions of mental illness. *Journal of Muslim Mental Health, 8*(1), 57–76. https://doi-org.ezproxy.cul.columbia.edu/10.3998/jmmh.10381607.0008.104

Balkaya-Ince, M., Cheah, C. S. L., Gürsoy, H., & Amer, M. (2024). Time-varying and gender differences in religious socialization and associations with Muslim American adolescents' religious identity. *Psychology of Religion and Spirituality.* Advance online publication. https://doi-org.ezproxy.cul.columbia.edu/10.1037/rel0000517

Buckley, A., & Carland, S. (2023). Triple roles, worship, and "Period shaming": how Muslim women maintain belonging and connection in ramadan. *Journal for the Scientific Study of Religion, 62*(4), 869-884.

Budhwani, H., & Hearld, K. R. (2017). Muslim Women's Experiences with Stigma, Abuse, and Depression: Results of a Sample Study Conducted in the United States. *Journal of women's health (2002), 26*(5), 435–441. https://doi.org/10.1089/jwh.2016.5886

Callender, K. A., Ong, L. Z., & Othman, E. H. (2022). Prayers and Mindfulness in Relation to Mental Health among First-Generation Immigrant and Refugee Muslim Women in the USA: An Exploratory Study. *Journal of religion and health, 61*(5), 3637–3654. https://doi.org/10.1007/s10943-022-01600-x

Cirillo, P. C., Passos, R. B. F., Bevilaqua, M. C. D. N., López, J. R. R. A., & Nardi, A. E. (2012). Bipolar disorder and Premenstrual Syndrome or Premenstrual Dysphoric Disorder comorbidity: a systematic review. *Brazilian Journal of Psychiatry, 34,* 467-479.

Crenshaw, K. W. (2014). *On intersectionality: Essential writings.* The New Press.

Critchley, H. O., Babayev, E., Bulun, S. E., Clark, S., Garcia-Grau, I., Gregersen, P. K., ... & Griffith, L. G. (2020). Menstruation: science and society. *American journal of obstetrics and gynecology, 223*(5), 624-664.

Douki, S., Zineb, S. B., Nacef, F., & Halbreich, U. (2007). Women's mental health in the Muslim world: cultural, religious, and social issues. *Journal of affective disorders, 102*(1-3), 177–189. https://doi.org/10.1016/j.jad.2006.09.027

Eksheir, S., & Bowling, J. (2020). Perceived reproductive health needs among Muslim women in the southern US. *McGill Journal of Medicine, 18*(1), 1-15. https://doi.org/10.26443/mjm.v18i1.177

El-Hazmi, M. A., Al-Hazmi, A. M., & Warsy, A. S. (2011). Sickle cell disease in Middle East Arab countries. *The Indian Journal of Medical Research, 134*(5), 597–610. https://doi.org/10.4103/0971-5916.90984

Eskandari, M. (2011). *Women places and spaces in contemporary American mosque* (Doctoral dissertation, Massachusetts Institute of Technology).

Falah-Hassani, K., Shiri, R., Vigod, S., & Dennis, C. L. (2015). Prevalence of postpartum depression among immigrant women: A systematic review and meta-analysis. *Journal of psychiatric research, 70*, 67–82. https://doi.org/10.1016/j.jpsychires.2015.08.010

Fang, C. Y., Ross, E. A., Pathak, H. B., Godwin, A. K., & Tseng, M. (2014). Acculturative stress and inflammation among Chinese immigrant women. *Psychosomatic medicine, 76*(5), 320-326.

Freeman, E., & Sherif, K. (2007). Prevalence of hot flushes and night sweats around the world: a systematic review. *Climacteric, 10*(3), 197-214.

Ghorbani, N., Watson, P. J., & Shahmohamadi, K. (2008). Afterlife Motivation Scale: Correlations with maladjustment and incremental validity in Iranian Muslims. *International Journal for the Psychology of Religion, 18*(1), 22–35. https://doi-org.ezproxy.cul.columbia.edu/10.1080/10508610701719314

Glick, P., & Fiske, S. T. (1996). The Ambivalent Sexism Inventory: Differentiating hostile and benevolent sexism. *Journal of Personality and Social Psychology, 70*(3), 491–512. https://doi-org.ezproxy.cul.columbia.edu/10.1037/0022-3514.70.3.491

Glick, P., Sakallı-Uğurlu, N., Akbaş, G., Orta, İ. M., & Ceylan, S. (2016). Why do women endorse honor beliefs? Ambivalent sexism and religiosity as predictors. *Sex Roles: A Journal of Research, 75*(11-12), 543–554. https://doi-org.ezproxy.cul.columbia.edu/10.1007/s11199-015-0550-5

Guerrero, J. G., Ali, S. A. A., & Attallah, D. M. (2022). The acquired critical thinking skills, satisfaction, and self-confidence of nursing students and staff nurses through high-fidelity simulation experience. *Clinical Simulation in Nursing, 64*, 24-30.

Gulamhussein, Q.-u.-a., & Eaton, N. R. (2015). Hijab, religiosity, and psychological wellbeing of Muslim women in the United States. *Journal of Muslim Mental Health, 9*(2), 25–40. https://doi-org.ezproxy.cul.columbia.edu/10.3998/jmmh.10381607.0009.202

Hannover, B., Gubernath, J., Schultze, M., & Zander, L. (2018). Religiosity, religious fundamentalism, and ambivalent sexism toward girls and women among adolescents and young adults living in Germany. *Frontiers in Psychology, 9*, Article 2399. https://doi-org.ezproxy.cul.columbia.edu/10.3389/fpsyg.2018.02399

Haque, A., Namavar, A., & Breene, K. A. (2015). Prevalence and risk factors of postpartum depression in Middle Eastern/Arab women. *Journal of Muslim mental health, 9*(1).

Hashem, H. M., & Awad, G. H. (2024). Hijab, solo status, discrimination, and distress among Muslim women in the U.S. *The Counseling Psychologist, 52*(5), 773–801. https://doi-org.ezproxy.cul.columbia.edu/10.1177/00110000241242808

Hashem, H., Ghani, M., Hirani, S., Bennett, A., & Awad, G. H. (2022). Solo status, religious centrality, and discrimination among American Muslim women. *International Journal of Intercultural Relations, 88*, 32–41. https://doi-org.ezproxy.cul.columbia.edu/10.1016/j.ijintrel.2022.03.005

Hassan S. M. (2022). Religious practices of Muslim women in the UK during maternity: evidence-based professional practice recommendations. *BMC pregnancy and childbirth*, *22*(1), 335. https://doi.org/10.1186/s12884-022-04664-5

Hodge, D. R., Zidan, T., & Husain, A. (2015). Depression among Muslims in the United States: Examining the role of discrimination and spirituality as risk and protective factors. *Social work*, *61*(1), 45-52.

Ibrahim, A., & Whitley, R. (2021). Religion and mental health: a narrative review with a focus on Muslims in English-speaking countries. *BJPsych bulletin*, *45*(3), 170–174. https://doi.org/10.1192/bjb.2020.34

Jamal, A., Baldwin, C., Ali, W., & Dhingra, S. (2022). "I Am Not Who You Think I Am": Multiple, Hybrid and Racialized Identities of Canadian Muslim Youth in the Negotiation of Belonging and Citizenship. *Journal of Muslim Minority Affairs*, *42*(4), 393–408. https://doi.org/10.1080/13602004.2023.2191909

Jasperse, M., Ward, C., & Jose, P. E. (2012). Identity, perceived religious discrimination, and psychological well-being in Muslim immigrant women. *Applied Psychology: An International Review*, *61*(2), 250–271. https://doi-org.ezproxy.cul.columbia.edu/10.1111/j.1464-0597.2011.00467.x

Kamimura, A., Pye, M., Sin, K., Nourian, M. M., Assasnik, N., Stoddard, M., & Frost, C. J. (2018). Health and Well-being of Women Migrating from Predominantly Muslim Countries to the United States. *Journal of health care for the poor and underserved*, *29*(1), 337–348. https://doi.org/10.1353/hpu.2018.0023

Khorasgani, M. R., & Beikzadeh, B. (2023). The impact of lifestyle on the immune system: Focus on Islamic lifestyle: A narrative review. *International journal of preventive medicine*, *14*(1), 105.

Koenig, H.G. & Al Shohaib, S.S. (2019). Religiosity and Mental Health in Islam. In: Moffic, H., Peteet, J., Hankir, A., Awaad, R. (eds) Islamophobia and Psychiatry. *Springer, Cham* (pp. 55-65). https://doi.org/10.1007/978-3-030-00512-2_5

Koenig, H.G. & Al Shohaib, S.A. (2014). Religion and Negative Emotions in Muslims. In: Health and Well-Being in Islamic Societies. *Springer, Cham* (pp.125-165). https://doi.org/10.1007/978-3-319-05873-3_7

Levin, J. (2016). Prevalence and religious predictors of healing prayer use in the USA: Findings from the Baylor Religion Survey. *Journal of religion and health*, *55*, 1136-1158.

Lipka, M. (2017, April 6). *Why Muslims are the world's fastest-growing religious group*. Pew Research Center. https://www.pewresearch.org/short-reads/2017/04/06/why-muslims-are-the-worlds-fastest-growing-religious-group/

Liu, X., Wang, S., & Wang, G. (2022). Prevalence and Risk Factors of Postpartum Depression in Women: A Systematic Review and Meta-analysis. *Journal of clinical nursing*, *31*(19-20), 2665–2677. https://doi.org/10.1111/jocn.16121

Mastari, L., Droogenbroeck, F. V., Spruyt, B., & Keppens, G. (2022). Ambivalent sexism among Christian and Muslim youth. The gendered pathway of perceived pressure for religious conformity. *European Societies*, *24*(2), 154-177. https://doi.org/10.1080/14616696.2021.2012219

Maqbool, I. (2023). Education Transformation in Muslim Societies: A Discourse of Hope ed. by Ilham Nasser. *Journal of Education in Muslim Societies*, *5*(1), 113-117.

Mitha K. (2020). Conceptualising and addressing mental disorders amongst Muslim communities: Approaches from the Islamic Golden Age. *Transcultural psychiatry*, *57*(6), 763–774. https://doi.org/10.1177/1363461520962603

Mohr, S. H., & Afi, H. (2023). Islamic feminist liberation psychology and peacebuilding: Case studies of Muslim women in community organizing in restorative justice and parenting. *Peace and Conflict: Journal of Peace Psychology*, *29*(2), 155–166. https://doi-org.ezproxy.cul.columbia.edu/10.1037/pac0000651

Mohr, S. H., Wong, R., & Keagy, C. (2019). Protective factors in Muslim women's mental health in the San Francisco Bay Area. *Journal of Muslim Mental Health*, *13*(2).

Murrar, S., Baqai, B., & Padela, A. I. (2024). Predictors of Perceived Discrimination in Medical Settings Among Muslim Women in the USA. *Journal of racial and ethnic health disparities*, *11*(1), 150–156. https://doi.org/10.1007/s40615-022-01506-0

Nagra, B. (2018). Cultural explanations of patriarchy, race, and everyday lives: Marginalizing and "othering" Muslim women in Canada. *Journal of Muslim Minority Affairs*, *38*(2), 263-279.

Naseem, A., Majed, M., Abdallah, S., Saleh, M., Lirhoff, M., Bazzi, A., & Caldwell, M. T. (2023). Exploring Muslim Women's Reproductive Health Needs and Preferences in the Emergency Department. *The western journal of emergency medicine*, *24*(5), 983–992. https://doi.org/10.5811/westjem.58942

Nguyen, T. T., Criss, S., Kim, M., De La Cruz, M. M., Thai, N., Merchant, J. S., ... & Nguyen, Q. C. (2023). Racism during pregnancy and birthing: experiences from Asian and Pacific Islander, Black, Latina, and Middle Eastern women. *Journal of racial and ethnic health disparities*, *10*(6), 3007-3017.

Nolan, L. N., & Hughes, L. (2022). Premenstrual exacerbation of mental health disorders: a systematic review of prospective studies. *Archives of Women's Mental Health*, *25*(5), 831-852.

Padela, A. I., Killawi, A., Forman, J., DeMonner, S., & Heisler, M. (2012). American Muslim perceptions of healing: Key agents in healing, and their roles. *Qualitative Health Research*, *22*(6), 846–858. https://doi-org.ezproxy.cul.columbia.edu/10.1177/1049732312438769

Padela, A. I., Pruitt, L., & Mallick, S. (2017). The Types of Trust Involved in American Muslim Healthcare Decisions: An Exploratory Qualitative Study. *Journal of religion and health*, *56*(4), 1478–1488. https://doi.org/10.1007/s10943-017-0387-z

Pew Research Center. (2017, July 26). *Demographic portrait of Muslim Americans.* Pew Research Center. https://www.pewresearch.org/religion/2017/07/26/demographic-portrait-of-muslim-americans/

Pilver, C. E., Levy, B. R., Libby, D. J., & Desai, R. A. (2011). Posttraumatic stress disorder and trauma characteristics are correlates of premenstrual dysphoric disorder. *Archives of women's mental health, 14*(5), 383–393. https://doi.org/10.1007/s00737-011-0232-4

Qureshi, N. A., Khalil, A. A., & Alsanad, S. M. (2020). Spiritual and Religious Healing Practices: Some Reflections from Saudi National Center for Complementary and Alternative Medicine, Riyadh. *Journal of religion and health, 59*(2), 845–869. https://doi.org/10.1007/s10943-018-0677-0

Saeed, S., Kanaya, A. M., Bennet, L., & Nilsson, P. M. (2020). Cardiovascular risk assessment in South and Middle-East Asians living in the Western countries. *Pakistan journal of medical sciences, 36*(7), 1719–1725. https://doi.org/10.12669/pjms.36.7.3292

Sharp, G. C., & De Giorgio, L. (2023). Menarche, Menstruation, Menopause and Mental Health (4M): a consortium facilitating interdisciplinary research at the intersection of menstrual and mental health. *Frontiers in Global Women's Health, 4,* 1258973.

Simpson, J. L., & Carter, K. (2008). Muslim women's experiences with health care providers in a rural area of the United States. *Journal of transcultural nursing : official journal of the Transcultural Nursing Society, 19*(1), 16–23. https://doi.org/10.1177/1043659607309146

Statistics Canada. (2024, December 19). *The Muslim population in Canada: A demographic portrait.* https://www150.statcan.gc.ca/n1/pub/11-627-m/11-627-m2024058-eng.htm

Steele, R. R., Bengali, S., Richardson, G., Disbennett, M., & Othman, Y. (2023). Muslim women negotiating their identity in the era of the Muslim ban. *Journal of Gender Studies, 32*(7), 707–718. https://doi-org.ezproxy.cul.columbia.edu/10.1080/09589236.2021.2016382

Suleiman, A. R., Afify, O., & Whitfield, K. E. (2021). The Effect of Stress, Acculturation, and Heritage Identity on Depression in Arab Americans. *Journal of community hospital internal medicine perspectives, 11*(4), 433–438. https://doi.org/10.1080/20009666.2021.1929050

Tackett, S., Young, J. H., Putman, S., Wiener, C., Deruggiero, K., & Bayram, J. D. (2018). Barriers to healthcare among Muslim women: A narrative review of the literature. *Women's Studies International Forum, 69,* 190-194. https://doi.org/10.1016/j.wsif.2018.02.009

Thelamour, B., George Mwangi, C., & Ezeofor, I. (2019). "We need to stick together for survival": Black college students' racial identity, same-ethnic friendships, and campus connectedness. *Journal of Diversity in Higher Education, 12*(3), 266.

Tineo, P., Lowe, S. R., Reyes-Portillo, J. A., & Fuentes, M. A. (2021). Impact of perceived discrimination on depression and anxiety among Muslim college students: The role of acculturative stress, religious support, and

Muslim identity. *American Journal of Orthopsychiatry, 91*(4), 454–463. https://doi-org.ezproxy.cul.columbia.edu/10.1037/ort0000545

Tith, R. M., Bilodeau-Bertrand, M., Lee, G. E., Healy-Profitós, J., & Auger, N. (2019). Fasting during Ramadan increases risk of very preterm birth among Arabic-speaking women. *The Journal of Nutrition, 149*(10), 1826-1832.

Trask, B. S., & Hamon, R. R. (2007). *Cultural diversity and families: Expanding Perspectives.* SAGE Publications, Incorporated.

Trask, B. S. (2011). "Globalization and families: Meeting the family policy challenge." *ЛН Гумилев атындағы Еуразия ұлттық университетінің ХАБАРШЫСЫ* (2011).

Van Oost, P., Leveaux, S., Klein, O., & Yzerbyt, V. (2023). Gender inequality discourse as a tool to express attitudes towards Islam. *Journal of Social and Political Psychology, 11*(2), 690–707. https://doi-org.ezproxy.cul.columbia.edu/10.5964/jspp.9621

Vu, M., Azmat, A., Radejko, T., & Padela, A. I. (2016). Predictors of Delayed Healthcare Seeking Among American Muslim Women. *Journal of women's health (2002), 25*(6), 586–593. https://doi.org/10.1089/jwh.2015.5517

Wang, S. C., Raja, A. H., & Azhar, S. (2020). "A lot of us have a very difficult time reconciling what being Muslim is": A phenomenological study on the meaning of being Muslim American. *Cultural Diversity & Ethnic Minority Psychology, 26*(3), 338–346. https://doi-org.ezproxy.cul.columbia.edu/10.1037/cdp0000297

Yim, I. S., Tanner Stapleton, L. R., Guardino, C. M., Hahn-Holbrook, J., & Dunkel Schetter, C. (2015). Biological and psychosocial predictors of postpartum depression: systematic review and call for integration. *Annual review of clinical psychology, 11*, 99-137.

Yuen, L., & Wong, V. W. (2015). Gestational diabetes mellitus: challenges for different ethnic groups. *World journal of diabetes, 6*(8), 1024.

Yun, S., Ahmed, S. R., Hauson, A. O., & Al-Delaimy, W. K. (2021). The Relationship Between Acculturative Stress and Postmigration Mental Health in Iraqi Refugee Women Resettled in San Diego, California. *Community mental health journal, 57*(6), 1111–1120. https://doi.org/10.1007/s10597-020-00739-9

CHAPTER SEVEN

OVERCOMING CHALLENGES IN MARRIAGE AND FAMILY: THE CASE OF SOUTH ASIAN MUSLIM AMERICANS

Afshana Haque, Saman Essa

This chapter examines mental health and family dynamics within the South Asian Muslim population in the United States. The authors analyze how socio-cultural factors, historical trauma, post-9/11 Islamophobia, and the challenges of immigration and acculturation affect marital relationships, family dynamics, and intergenerational relationships in South Asian Muslim American (SAMA) communities. These complex challenges amplify the mental health issues faced by these families. It is essential for mental health professionals to understand the unique contexts of SAMA families when providing therapeutic services. The authors advocate for culturally sensitive therapeutic practices that cater to the intricate needs of SAMA families, which can enhance the effectiveness of their practice and reduce the likelihood of early termination of therapy. Additionally, this chapter highlights religious and cultural practices that foster resilience within SAMA families.

Introduction

South Asian Muslim Americans (SAMA) come from countries such as Pakistan, India, Bangladesh, Sri Lanka, Nepal, Bhutan, and the Maldives (Arshad & Falconier, 2019). Practicing SAMA individuals hold religious beliefs and guidelines that shape their marital and family lives, distinguishing them from other South Asian (SA) religious groups (Sauerheber et al., 2014). Additionally, the intersections of SAMA's historical context, South Asian identity, and Islamic culture create a unique subculture that sets SAMA families apart from other ethnic Muslim subgroups, including Arabs, Turks, Africans, and Persians.

SAMA families face distinctive challenges, particularly in post-9/11 America, which are compounded by pre- and post-immigration trauma, historical trauma, racism, and Islamophobia. These factors significantly impact their mental health and well-being (Arshad & Falconier, 2019; Chowdhury & Okazaki, 2020; Haque et al., 2019; Keshavarzi & Haque, 2013). Ignoring this intersectionality in research and practice could lead to increased stereotyping, discrimination, and ineffective mental health services for SAMA families (Chowdhury & Okazaki, 2020; Cole, 2009).

These multidimensional factors underscore the need for two key elements: 1) effective and culturally sensitive mental health services, and 2) mental health professionals who can leverage the strength and resilience of the SAMA community to help them navigate these challenges (Haque et al., 2019).

Historical Trauma, Social & Religious Contexts

The unique history of South Asian Muslims (SAMA) plays a significant role in shaping their religious, cultural, and family dynamics (Chowdhury & Okazaki, 2020). South Asians converted to Islam through various means, including foreign conquests, interracial marriages with Arab traders and merchants, and the influence of Sufi orders from Persia (Hossain, 2018). Some Hindus embraced Islam to escape the oppression of the Indian caste system, seeking to improve their social status. However, many new converts maintained connections to their Hindu past, continuing to incorporate traditional practices, ancestral customs, religious values, and Islamic teachings (Hossain, 2018).

Despite Islam's egalitarian principles, remnants of the Hindu caste system are still evident in the social hierarchy among South Asian Muslims today (Hossain, 2018). Segregation based on notions of racial superiority originated from foreign conquerors who often looked down on local converts to Islam (Momin, 1977). To enhance their status and legitimacy, converts sometimes traced their ancestry back to the early companions of the Prophet Muhammad or even to the Prophet himself.

The caste mentality and social stratification persist within various cultural and occupational groups, leading converted Muslims to marry strictly within their own groups. For instance, Patels typically do not consider it appropriate to marry Sayyids or Pathans (Momin, 1977; Hossain, 2018). Today, SAMA parents often insist that their children marry within the family, race, ethnicity, class, or skin color, discouraging inter-racial or intercultural marriages despite their Muslim backgrounds.

Intergroup divisions within SAMA communities or mosques often arise based on ethnicity, language, or religious sect. Additionally, language differences and the genocide during Bangladesh's 1971 war for independence from Pakistan may have further contributed to the separation between the two South Asian Muslim countries (Bass, 2016).

As newer immigrant generations in the U.S. become less connected to their historical backgrounds, embrace their bicultural identities, and pursue intercultural marriages, the divisions based on these factors are decreasing. However, these factors may still contribute to some intergenerational tensions. Intergenerational trauma resulting from colonization, refugee crises, poverty, immigration, and Islamophobia also influences the dynamics within South Asian and Middle Eastern (SAMA) families, as well as their mental health challenges (Chowdhury & Okazaki, 2020). Recent studies have found evidence of higher risks of suicide, self-harm, psychotic conditions, substance abuse, PTSD, and family violence within SAMA families (Badrinath & Seto, 2024; Contractor et al., 2023; Qureshi et al., 2023).

Colonization

European colonization of the South Asian subcontinent resulted in significant displacement, physical and psychological violence, exploitation, economic destruction, genocide, and cultural dispossession due to British dominance. This history disrupted social networks (Qureshi et al., 2023). Colonization officially ended in 1947 with the chaotic division of the country known as The Partition, which led to interreligious violence and extensive loss of life. The forced displacement created by The Partition destroyed communities and severed family ties across the region (Khan, 2017). These traumatic events are only one to two generations removed from the first wave of South Asian Muslim Americans (SAMA) immigrants, who carry distrust for out-group members and have limited recognition of their historical trauma (Qureshi et al., 2023).

Stressors arising from these mass trauma experiences, along with other socio-political challenges, have led to compromised mental and physical health among SAMAs. Symptoms of post-traumatic stress disorder (PTSD) manifest as increased anger and aggression, social isolation and shame, diminished self-worth, feelings of terror and fear, grief, withdrawal, and emotional numbness (Contractor et al., 2023; Shaligram et al., 2022; Sotero, 2006). Physical health issues include cardiovascular disease, diabetes, and hypertension (Paradies et al., 2007; Qureshi et al., 2023).

Poverty and Immigration

Furthermore, European imperialism and colonial exploitation created political instability and economic devastation, which drove South Asians out of their native lands (Cai & Lee, 2022). In pursuit of a better life in the U.S., immigrant generations also carry unresolved trauma and PTSD. Post-migration stressors they face include culture shock, acculturation stress, identity loss, shifting family structures, loss of social support, discrimination, racism, Islamophobia, and bullying (Shaligram et al., 2022). A primary pathway for the intergenerational transmission of trauma is through family dynamics, attachment relationships, and relational trauma (Isobel et al., 2019; Lang & Gartstein, 2018). Immigrant parents' heightened post-migration anxiety surrounding safety and economic security impacts family expectations, roles, and dynamics as well (Cai & Lee, 2022).

Islamophobia

The events of September 11th, 2001, led to an increase in xenophobia, discrimination, microaggressions, and racism against Muslims. Biased policies and media coverage regarding conflicts in the SWANA (Southwest Asia and North Africa) regions often depict all Muslims as a single, monolithic group inclined toward violent extremism, posing a threat to American safety and necessitating surveillance (Ali, 2016; Haque et al., 2019; Shams, 2020). South Asian and Middle Eastern Americans (SAMA) who wear headscarves, grow beards, or don modest cultural attire (such as saris or salwar kameez) are frequently targeted for hate crimes, which exacerbates fear and mistrust experienced before migration (Shams, 2020).

As a result of this ongoing marginalization, there has been an increase in anxiety, depression, insecurity, PTSD, disenfranchisement, and other mental health challenges within this population (Haque et al., 2019; Shams, 2020). Given that life under surveillance, along with anxiety related to discrimination and job insecurity, affects family dynamics among SAMA individuals, effective mental health treatment must take these experiences into account.

Impact of Historical Trauma and Cultural Contexts on Marital and Family Relationships

Historical and social traumas, along with religious and cultural influences, significantly impact the marital dynamics within SAMA (South Asian and Middle Eastern American) communities. Immigration to the United States has shifted traditional patriarchal values toward more equal partnerships, necessitating adaptations in marital and family life to align with new norms. Women's advancements in education and increased participation in the workforce have also heightened tensions regarding the division of household labor, childcare, financial responsibilities, adult caregiving, and living arrangements (Tariq & Syed, 2017).

Common factors contributing to marital stress include domestic violence, intergenerational conflict, social isolation, and limited support systems. Recent studies emphasize the need for further exploration of the impacts of historical trauma and PTSD on SAMA families (Badrinath & Seto, 2024; Cai & Lee, 2022; Contractor et al., 2023; Qureshi, Misra & Poshni, 2023; Shaligram et al., 2022).

Marital therapy can assist SAMA couples in processing traumatic experiences within their socio-historical contexts. It helps them develop the skills necessary to thrive in their relationships by enabling couples to tap into their strengths and navigate evolving marital needs and expectations effectively (Singh, 2017).

Patriarchal Culture

The marital dynamics of traditional, patriarchal South Asian families typically revolve around a family structure where the husband's mother takes precedence in her sons' lives. Women are expected to depend on their fathers during their early years, their husbands after marriage, and their sons once they come of age (Chaudhuri et al., 2014).

Marital expectations often dictate that sons dominate the public sphere and provide financially, while the daughter-in-law is expected to adapt to her husband's family norms and serve the family within the domestic sphere. The domestic responsibilities of a daughter-in-law include cooking, cleaning, child-rearing, maintaining relationships within the family and extended family, hosting guests, and caring for elderly family members.

Cultural norms further dictate that couples should treat their parents with a near "divine" or infallible status, often providing financial support to the husband's parents and allowing them to manage or influence their finances. In addition, women are expected to fully obey their husbands and in-laws, reside in multigenerational family homes, and align their social activities around their husbands' families (Tummala-Narra, 2013).

Failure to meet these expectations can justify abusive behavior from husbands and in-laws (Chaudhuri et al., 2014). In South Asian cultures, marriages are primarily viewed as unions between two families, which shifts the focus away from individual compatibility, sexuality, and attraction (Badrinath & Seto, 2024; Singh & Bhayana, 2015).

Islamic Perspectives

A Muslim husband is responsible for providing for his wife's and their nuclear family's financial, physical, and emotional needs. In contrast to SAMA culture, Islam emphasizes that all Muslims should care for their parents without distinction between the husband's or wife's families. A husband is expected to maintain his wife's status and lifestyle. Meanwhile, a wife is responsible for providing physical and emotional care for her husband and children (though caring for in-laws is not obligatory), and any financial contribution she makes is at her discretion.

The analogy of a husband and wife being like "garments" for one another illustrates their roles in fulfilling each other's emotional, physical, and sexual needs. This idea is exemplified in the relationship between Prophet Muhammad and his wives, who serve as role models for Muslim couples. Islamic values generally promote a more egalitarian approach compared to the patriarchal norms found in many South Asian cultures.

Islam's inherent flexibility allows for the integration of South Asian cultural norms alongside the adoption of egalitarian family dynamics often seen in Western societies. South Asian immigrants who grow up in Muslim-majority countries sometimes blur the lines between cultural practices and religious mandates. However, increased exposure to Islamic scholarship and interactions with Muslims from diverse backgrounds help second-generation immigrants clarify these distinctions. This understanding enables them to move away from cultural practices that may not align with their religious values and the new cultural norms they encounter. (al-Huraibi & Konradi, 2012)

Cultural Shift

SAMA families post-immigration may adopt Western ideals, such as marrying for individual compatibility, emotional connection, and physical attraction. They often prioritize nuclear family structures over multigenerational ones, embracing dual earnings and shared household responsibilities (Singh & Bhayana, 2015). Research indicates that some men desire progressive and educated wives but may unconsciously expect them to handle all domestic duties (Singh & Bhayana, 2015). This can lead to conflict if these expectations are not addressed and if there is ineffective communication regarding the transition to equal partnerships or dual-earner households. Success in dual-earner families requires adequate support for both partners in childcare and household labor (Farris & Haque, 2008).

Many SAMA families lose their support systems after immigrating, which can include extended family, neighbors, friends, and community members. However, some families choose to maintain multigenerational homes, which can provide significant support. Still, this family structure may pose challenges, such as disrespected boundaries and reduced autonomy for couples (Deepak, 2005).

Education of Women

SAMA families prioritize high educational achievement because their options for increasing wealth and status in South Asia are limited due to the economic devastation caused by colonization and war. Immigrant SAMA families often encourage their children to pursue careers in STEM fields, as these areas are associated with job stability, wealth, and status.

While children of both genders are motivated to excel academically, there are distinct societal expectations. Men are typically encouraged to pursue higher education and advance their careers to become providers. In contrast, women often face pressure to marry early and start families, with their education seen as a factor that makes them more desirable as mothers and spouses. Although there has been a movement to educate women, cultural expectations regarding their domestic responsibilities have not diminished. For those women who pursue careers, the heavy demand for domestic labor often makes it challenging to balance work and family responsibilities (Tummala-Narra, 2013). Many individuals sacrifice their careers to become full-time housewives and daughters-in-law. Others seek lower-tier jobs that offer flexibility, low workload, or part-time positions with limited prospects for growth or leadership roles (Tariq & Syed, 2017).

Some SAMA elders may pressure women to limit or step away from their careers to meet domestic responsibilities and reduce family conflict (Tariq & Syed, 2017). This unsolicited advice can increase the shame and guilt experienced by working mothers and continue to limit their financial independence and overall value beyond domestic chores and child-rearing. While rooted in the patriarchal aspects of South Asian culture, first-generation SAMA individuals may use religious reasons to justify women sacrificing their careers for domestic responsibilities. In contrast, second-generation SAMA individuals highlight the contributions of influential women in Islamic history, such as scholars, rulers, calligraphers, mathematicians, and astronomers, to showcase how Muslim women have positively impacted their communities beyond their roles as mothers and wives. For instance, Prophet Muhammad's wife, Khadija, was a successful businesswoman who provided for the entire Muslim community during challenging times (Rahemtulla & Ababneh, 2021). Expectations to sacrifice career prospects while taking on all domestic and childcare responsibilities are particularly scrutinized by women in abusive marriages, divorced women, and those dealing with infertility or who choose not to marry or have children.

Child Marriages

Child marriages that occurred before migration have significantly impacted marital dynamics and expectations within SAMA families. These early marriages were often driven by economic necessity for impoverished families that lacked resources to care for their children. Moreover, older brides typically demanded higher dowries than younger brides, who were considered more desirable due to their presumed ability to adapt.

However, this practice, which involves children under the age of 18, constitutes a serious human rights violation. It can lead to severe reproductive and sexual health issues for girls, hindering their overall development and well-being, while also increasing their risk of violence, exploitation, and abuse.

Furthermore, child marriages are associated with a range of negative outcomes, including higher rates of school dropouts, marital violence, maternal morbidity and mortality, and the risk of unintended pregnancies, among other risks (Subramanee et al., 2022).

Despite the negative consequences of child marriages, divorce is often impossible for these young brides due to their limited education, which hinders their ability to secure well-paying jobs. Additionally, returning to their childhood homes after a divorce would bring great shame to their families. Child marriages have occurred as recently as the generation of SAMA's grandparents or great-grandparents.

The traumatic effects of child marriages on children, who are ill-prepared to manage the physical, emotional, relational, and sexual demands of such unions, can lead to serious mental health issues including depression, anxiety, PTSD, emotional dysregulation, and unhealthy relational attachments (Subramanee et al., 2022). These difficulties, combined with the toxic family dynamics often present in child marriages, have intergenerational effects on SAMA couples. These effects include the perpetuation of family violence, physical and emotional abuse, emotional disconnection, marital rape, sexual abuse, imbalanced power dynamics between spouses, unequal distribution of household labor, and the wife's unfulfilled needs and inability to advocate for herself (Subramanee et al., 2022). Children who lose mothers due to pregnancy-related complications experience grief and trauma from this loss, in addition to potential abuse from family and stepfamily members (de Silva D. G., 2007).

Despite the significant decline in child marriages, dysfunctional patterns persist in SAMA marriages today (Chapman & Cattaneo, 2013; Ali et al., 2022; Adam & Schewe, 2007; Chen, 2024; Sabri et al., 2018; Bhandari & Sabri, 2020). SAMA culture continues to prioritize younger brides, encouraging women to marry in their early 20s to maximize fertility, beauty, chastity, adaptability, and a smoother integration into their husband's family. However, with the high rates of domestic violence and rising divorce rates in SAMA marriages, sacrificing education and career opportunities for early marriages or unplanned children can trap women in unhealthy or abusive relationships (Singh & Bhayana, 2015; Adam & Schewe, 2007; Chen, 2024; Sabri et al., 2018; Bhandari & Sabri, 2020).

Emotional Disconnection

Disconnected relationships between mothers and daughters can be attributed to various cultural factors, including child marriages. In many South Asian (SA) cultures, daughters are viewed as belonging to their in-laws and are often seen as guests in their biological homes. Raising daughters typically involves teaching them skills such as cooking, cleaning, and managing a household, in preparation for becoming submissive wives and daughters-in-law. Historically, without opportunities for women to pursue careers or earn a sustainable income, they were not encouraged to seek independence or advocate for their needs. Instead, self-sacrifice, submission, and serving their husbands and in-laws became their primary means of survival and economic security.

Preparing daughters for a life of servitude and marriage from a young age has left limited opportunities for mothers and daughters to develop meaningful and connected relationships. Additionally, a mother's financial security often depended more on her relationship with her son, leading to greater time investment in nurturing that bond rather than the mother-daughter relationship.

SAMA men face significant pressure to earn high incomes to support their families, parents, and extended relatives. They are typically raised with minimal expectations regarding household responsibilities, allowing them to focus on their education and career advancement. This avoidance of domestic tasks often carries into their marital relationships.

Responsibilities such as caretaking, childcare, and maintaining connections with family and extended relatives are generally assigned to women. As a result, men may miss valuable opportunities to build deeper emotional connections with their families and children. Fathers often limit their roles to providing financially, protecting, disciplining, and advising their children, with little emphasis placed on play or emotional engagement.

Modern Marriages

Currently, South Asian Muslim American (SAMA) couples desire companionate marriages that address the emotional connection often lacking due to historical, transgenerational, cultural, and immigration trauma. However, companionate marriages come with complex dynamics, including expectations for fulfillment in various areas, as well as the need for mutual respect, fairness, and egalitarian relationships.

Traditionally, South Asian marriages have functioned as arrangements designed to unite and expand families, with prescribed gender-based roles where wives typically defer to their husbands' leadership. In contrast, companionate marriages involve couples who expect a partnership characterized by negotiated roles and decision-making. Navigating these new dynamics can be challenging for SAMA couples, as they often lack role models from previous generations.

In addition to grappling with transgenerational trauma and dysfunction, SAMA couples face new challenges that can heighten conflicts. Issues often arise around finances, balancing careers, and the division of household labor. Differences in views regarding egalitarian marital roles, cultural backgrounds, and experiences in inter-ethnic and inter-religious relationships can also lead to complications. Furthermore, challenges related to divorce and remarriage, divergent attitudes about sexual intimacy, communication styles, emotional regulation, conflict resolution skills, infidelity, and issues related to pornography and other addictions can significantly impact these marriages. Lastly, considerations concerning LGBTQIA+ issues add another layer of complexity (Chapman & Cattaneo, 2013; Singh & Bahayana, 2015; Shaligram et al., 2022; Tummala-Narra, 2013).

The Impact of Trauma on Family and Parenting

The impact of trauma on SAMA families requires further investigation; however, we can learn from the experiences of other groups affected by historical trauma. For example, Black and Native American families have faced disruptions in the intergenerational transmission of healthy parenting relationships and behaviors due to historical trauma. This has led to impaired parental mental health and hindered positive communication within families (Evans-Campbell, 2008; Nagata, Kim, & Gone, 2024).

Specifically, when parents are exposed to trauma, it increases the risk of trauma in their children due to several factors: (1) potential maltreatment by parents, (2) difficulties traumatized parents face in relating to and communicating with their children, (3) children's vulnerability in their stress responses, and (4) children's susceptibility to stress-related neurobiological abnormalities and genetic modifications (Shaligram et al., 2022, p. 794).

Parenting. Many SAMA parents immigrated to the U.S. to escape the trauma of their homelands and to provide better lives for their families. However, they often find themselves struggling to navigate the challenges of living in a Western imperialist society. This constant state of survival impacts their ability to parent effectively, as healthy parenting requires emotional availability and attunement with their children. When parents are in a state of chronic stress, such as survival or fight-or-flight mode, they struggle to access the emotional processing centers of their brains.

Parents who are hyper-focused on safety and financial stability often make decisions based on fear and anxiety, which can hinder their children's growth and development. Many SAMA immigrant parents have not healed from their traumatic experiences and continue to live in survival mode. Additionally, it is expected within SAMA communities to suppress emotional expression and to endure hardships without appearing weak. While this emotional suppression may be useful in acute survival situations, it can lead to serious long-term consequences for physical, emotional, and relational health.

Disconnecting from emotions resulting from trauma can prevent individuals from regulating their emotional experiences effectively. Moreover, the avoidance of mental health services—often due to stigma—means that many SAMA immigrant children and young adults are raised by emotionally detached or dysregulated parents. Such emotional unhealthiness can lead to the intergenerational transmission of patterns of emotional suppression, conflict avoidance, domestic violence, and attachment issues, including anxious or avoidant styles.

Additionally, SAMA immigrant parents often grieve the loss of future generations who maintain cultural values and practices, particularly due to inter-cultural and interfaith marriages among their second-generation children (Singh, 2017). Clinicians can support these families by helping them process their grief, validate their cultural losses due to migration, and empower them to create multicultural homes that combine positive elements from both cultures they wish to retain.

Clinical Implications and Therapeutic Approaches to Marital and Family Challenges

SAMA tends to keep relational and mental health issues private in order to maintain honor and avoid the stigma associated with mental illness. This stigma can lead to struggles being manifested as physical health conditions or being attributed to sin, moral failure, the evil eye (Nazar), black magic (sihr), or possession by demons or evil spirits (jinn). Overcoming relational and mental health challenges for SAMA may require collaboration between religious healers and medical professionals (Shaligram et al., 2022; Contractor et al., 2022).

Outreach programs and educational initiatives, as well as endorsements of mental health services by religious scholars and leaders, could enhance SAMA's engagement with mental health resources. The emergence of SAMA and other Muslim mental health practitioners may also contribute to increased utilization of these services.

To provide effective support, mental health practitioners must thoroughly understand the client's historical, social, cultural, and religious contexts, as well as any relevant trauma. The focus should then shift towards leveraging individual, relational, and community strengths. Clinicians should adopt culturally responsive, psychoeducational, exploratory, collaborative, and integrative approaches when working with SAMA.

Furthermore, mental health professionals should consider incorporating indigenous healing practices and emphasize the importance of nutrition and social connectedness alongside psychotherapy (Shaligram et al., 2022). Research indicates that SAMA may prefer directive, structured, and solution-oriented therapeutic approaches that aim for symptom reduction, preferably delivered by culturally matched and bilingual clinicians (Contractor et al., 2022).

PTSD Treatment Approaches

The suppression of difficult or uncomfortable emotions in SAMA individuals can lead to emotional dysregulation, disconnection, and further detachment from unprocessed trauma, which may exacerbate PTSD symptoms. To help clients process PTSD related to intergenerational trauma, discrimination, Islamophobia, or immigration, clinicians can use approaches that foster a sense of safety, community, and connection.

Often, PTSD causes SAMA clients to feel more isolated, lonely, and silent. Strengthening healthy family connections, developing effective communication skills, and identifying supportive community networks can provide the emotional and financial support needed to heal from trauma (Hinton et al., 2004). The approaches discussed in the following paragraphs can enhance connectedness and highlight resilience.

Narrative Approach

Researchers recommend that families develop a contextualized narrative identity to foster collective healing. This can be achieved by engaging in adaptive, intergenerational communication methods such as conversations, storytelling, written narratives, and the creation of shared narratives that emphasize collective resilience (Cai & Lee, 2022; Contractor et al., 2022). Additionally, helping SAMA clients rediscover sources of motivation and purpose, incorporating their religious or spiritual beliefs and values, and highlighting their resilience can strengthen therapeutic relationships and improve treatment outcomes (Boyd-Franklin, 2010).

Culturally Adapted CBT (CA-CBT)

Adapting Cognitive Behavioral Therapy (CBT) for South Asian Muslim Americans involves several key strategies: focusing on cultural awareness, enhancing assessment and engagement methods, and tailoring therapy to address the patient's specific concerns while linking those concerns to the goals of culturally adapted CBT (CA-CBT) (Naeem et al., 2015, p. 244). This approach also emphasizes the importance of providing psychoeducation on PTSD to alleviate anxiety about the therapy process. During the assessment phase, it is crucial to recognize that South Asian Muslim Americans may describe trauma in various ways, such as feelings of sadness, physical aches, anxiety, fear, or disrupted sleep (Contractor et al., 2022).

To reduce the impact of emotional suppression and avoidance among SAMA individuals, it is important to emphasize mindfulness regarding emotions and encourage a focus on the present. This can help them process the effects of their traumatic pasts. Engaging in collective discussions and grieving of trauma through religious rituals, community clinics, and religious institutions (such as mosques and Islamic organizations) can be framed as educational programs and skills training, which may increase effectiveness and compliance (Contractor et al., 2022; Shaligram et al., 2022).

Incorporating cultural metaphors, the clients' preferred language, and religious scriptures can enhance both the effectiveness and retention of clients (Hinton et al., 2004; Otto et al., 2003). For instance, reminding clients of the deeply traumatic losses experienced by Prophet Muhammad and his expression of painful emotions through tears and grief can help normalize emotional expression and attunement.

Research has found that practicing Muslims who consider themselves religious tend to be moderately happier, healthier, and less depressed than those who are not actively involved in their faith (Alghafli et al., 2014). Encouraging SAMA individuals to connect with their religion through scholarship can lead to increased empowerment, alignment of values, and healing. Furthermore, studies indicate that spending time reading and analyzing the Quran and Hadith has helped SAMA women differentiate between genuine religious tenets and sexist cultural norms presented as Islam (al-Huraibi & Konradi, 2012).

Transgenerational Therapy

Another effective therapy model to consider when working with SAMA is transgenerational therapy. SAMA may have difficulty identifying the root causes of their challenges, especially when intergenerational trauma is present. This approach emphasizes the exploration of multiple generations and can help address family conflict patterns that span generations (Badrinath & Seto, 2024). It validates the client's needs and highlights how factors such as immigration, acculturative stress, and discrimination can worsen relational challenges (Hargrave & Houltberg, 2020).

To identify trends or explore root causes, clinicians can ask questions like:

- How would your parents have reacted to this situation?
- Can you share your experiences when you were the same age as your child?
- How were grief and loss managed in your family and extended family systems?
- What were your expectations of yourself growing up?
- How did your childhood experiences differ from those of your children today?
- How have levels of religiosity changed over time? (Badrinath & Seto, 2024).

Utilizing cultural genograms is a visual technique that can help assess cultural backgrounds and their impact on individual and relational dynamics. These genograms are particularly useful in identifying how healthy and maladaptive coping skills—such as seeking or avoiding mental health support—may be passed down through generations (Goodman, 2013).

Clinicians can explore various themes through genograms, including immigration stories, religious and spiritual beliefs, languages spoken, cultural traditions and rituals, countries of birth, and the individual values and beliefs of each family member (Badrinath & Seto, 2024, p. 195). By adopting a strengths-based perspective, clinicians can help families identify and appreciate the transmission of intergenerational strengths and values. Additionally, families can strengthen their bonds by discussing and engaging in traditions, rituals, or joyful experiences that bring them closer together (Badrinath & Seto, 2024).

Marriage & Family Therapeutic Interventions

Marital Therapy Intervention

SAMA couples may need therapeutic support to address various challenges, such as shifting roles, managing relationships with in-laws, and conflicts that arise from living in multigenerational homes, among other stressors (Chowdhury & Okazaki, 2020; Chapman & Cattaneo, 2013). Marital issues rooted in trauma can manifest as difficulties in communication and conflict resolution, often due to emotional dysregulation, irritability toward a partner, insecurity in the relationship, stonewalling, an inability to advocate for one's needs, controlling behaviors, intimate partner violence (IPV), addiction, and codependency (Bhandari & Sabri, 2020).

SAMA couples can benefit from structured and directive approaches such as the PEX Method (Atkinson, 1998). This method provides psychoeducation, practical strategies, and skills aimed at improving relationships. Additionally, it emphasizes mindfulness, which is consistent with Islamic healing practices, including the remembrance of God (dhikr) and prayer (dua). These practices can aid in grounding and emotional regulation. For clients struggling with addiction, incorporating motivational interviewing techniques can help disrupt these cycles and boost motivation for change (Cordova et al., 2001). Therapists may also combine other marital therapy models with a trauma-informed perspective, all within a culturally responsive and collaborative framework (Contractor et al., 2023).

Marital Therapy Assessment

Any marital therapy should begin with an assessment phase during the first three sessions at a minimum. In this phase, the clinician first meets with the couple together and then holds separate sessions with each partner for the following two sessions. Before starting any marital therapy, it is essential for the clinician to assess for intimate partner violence (IPV) or sexual abuse.

Therapy places partners in vulnerable positions, where heightened emotions can lead to feelings of blame, potentially triggering IPV. If IPV is identified, the therapist can assist in creating a safety plan that includes client-identified support networks, as well as providing information on emergency and mental health resources, shelters, escape strategies, and preparing an emergency bag.

After the individual sessions, the clinician should inform the clients if they do not meet the criteria for marital therapy, recommending that they continue with individual sessions instead. Additionally, clinicians can include screening tools and structured assessments for depression (PHQ-9), anxiety (GAD-7), and PTSD (PCL-5).

Muslim Clinicians

When addressing marital concerns related to spousal roles, rights, and obligations, clients from South Asian Muslim American (SAMA) backgrounds may lean towards Islamic perspectives. These clients might prefer working with a Muslim clinician who can incorporate an Islamic viewpoint into their therapy sessions or with a Desi therapist (someone of South Asian origin) who understands cultural contexts and may speak the same language.

Clinicians who are not Muslim should possess a basic understanding of Islam and SAMA culture to ensure that clients do not spend unnecessary time educating them. Additionally, Muslim or Desi clinicians should be cautious about making assumptions or drawing parallels with their clients, as the SAMA community is diverse. This diversity encompasses various levels of religiosity, bicultural experiences, socioeconomic backgrounds, education, and differing views on traditional and modern lifestyles, among other factors.

Collaboration

As discussed earlier, some members of the SAMA community may not distinguish between cultural and religious expectations regarding marital roles, assuming that their beliefs are solely rooted in religion. It can be beneficial for clinicians to understand the differences between cultural and religious norms to aid in resolving marital conflicts. Alternatively, clinicians might collaborate with trusted community Muslim scholars to clarify any concerns about the roles prescribed in Islam.

Furthermore, clinicians can facilitate a negotiation process that validates the needs and perspectives of both partners, especially on issues where there is more flexibility within the religious framework. In Islam, marriage is defined as a contract in which both partners are committed to fulfilling their agreed-upon rights and responsibilities. Therefore, negotiating the terms of their marriage during therapy sessions aligns with the foundational principles of the relationship.

Division of Household Labor

A common source of marital conflict among SAMA couples, as they transition from traditional to egalitarian households, is the division of household labor and childcare. Clinicians can help by asking each partner to identify their current roles and the division of household responsibilities, as well as how these align with or differ from their expectations as a couple.

After validating the couple's concerns, partners should work to understand each other's needs and expectations and then negotiate them. Clinicians can facilitate this negotiation process by assisting with the division of chores, childcare, and other responsibilities during sessions. It is important for clinicians to remind couples that the division of chores can be based on individual interests or capabilities rather than adhering to traditional gender norms.

Clinicians should also address any obstacles or points of contention that arise during the negotiation, such as feelings of resentment, betrayal, insecurities, or difficulties in advocating for their needs. Additionally, clinicians can help couples become aware of the cultural or intergenerational influences that shape their expectations regarding roles and responsibilities.

SAMA couples, whether in single or dual-career households, often stretch themselves too thin as they try to balance work commitments, extended family obligations, social activities, and the demands of caring for children and elderly parents. The cultural stigma surrounding paid care services makes it even more difficult for them to manage these responsibilities. Clinicians can encourage SAMA clients to broaden their support networks and consider the advantages of utilizing paid childcare or home maintenance services. This approach can help prevent unequal distribution of household labor and childcare duties, as well as reduce conflict over childcare practices imposed by extended family members. Additionally, clinicians can assist SAMA clients in processing feelings of guilt associated with seeking non-familial or paid assistance, while discussing the physical and emotional costs and benefits of these services.

Emotional Connection and Sexual Intimacy

The quality of a couple's relationship can be negatively impacted by overextension, burnout, and stress. Clinicians can assist couples in managing their schedules to prioritize rest and quality time together. High levels of stress can also lead to emotional dysregulation, conflict, and disconnection between partners. This emotional disconnection can have a significant effect on a couple's sex life, which is a crucial aspect of SAMA marriages, as it is often the only accepted outlet for sexual satisfaction.

Discussing sexual intimacy can be a complex issue for SAMA clients, as these conversations are typically meant to be private between married spouses (Ahmed & Reddy, 2007). Some clients may feel ashamed or uncomfortable addressing this topic in therapy sessions. Clinicians can reassure clients that these discussions will be handled professionally and only at the client's comfort level. They can also remind clients that talking about sexual health with a clinician is similar to discussing private matters with a medical professional.

It is important to emphasize that the main goal of these discussions is to improve both sexual and marital health. Clinicians can draw on an Islamic perspective by referencing the openness with which the Prophet Muhammad discussed sexual matters with both men and women, which can help ease discomfort around the topic of sexual intimacy and dysfunction.

In addition to using traditional sex therapy models, collaborating with religious scholars or referring to religious texts can help clarify misconceptions or address the permissibility of various sexual practices, foreplay, and female sexual satisfaction.

Effective Communication

Healthy relationships rely on key components such as compromise, negotiation, reciprocity, and emotional connection, all of which require effective communication. To mitigate marital conflict, SAMA couples must develop strong communication skills, including active listening and empathic responding (Amuta et al., 2021; Tavakolizadeh et al., 2015). In therapy sessions, clinicians can guide clients to discuss unresolved issues while teaching them how to communicate effectively. Providing a written handout for clients to review between sessions can help them practice and enhance their understanding of these skills.

The effectiveness of communication is closely linked to the couple's ability to manage their emotions. Therefore, clinicians should address trauma responses, insecurities, and resentments that may contribute to emotional dysregulation. After working through these heightened emotions, clinicians can instruct clients on how to set the emotional stage for constructive conversations. The following steps can be useful:

1. Check in with oneself and assess personal arousal levels.
2. Check in with the partner's arousal levels.

3. If both partners are in an optimal emotional state, they can begin to implement effective communication skills.
4. If either partner is not in an optimal state, they should negotiate a later time for the conversation.
5. Take time-outs during conversations if emotions escalate.

Communication styles in SAMA cultures are often more indirect compared to the more direct style found in Western cultures. It is crucial to consider this when assisting SAMA clients in creating and implementing culturally appropriate boundaries (Naeem et al., 2015). Desi-friendly boundaries emphasize behavioral and indirect strategies to express personal needs and limitations. For example, using excuses for leaving a family gathering—such as work or home obligations—can be more effective than trying to explain the importance of ensuring that children go to bed on time. Additionally, engaging in behavioral boundaries, such as excusing oneself from the conversation when uncomfortable topics arise, is often preferred over verbal interruptions. This approach helps maintain family harmony while also respecting the couple's needs.

Boundaries are essential for reducing conflict with in-laws, but discussions about these boundaries should be led by the biological son or daughter in a gentle, non-confrontational manner. Sons and daughters-in-law should avoid engaging in direct, heated, or sensitive discussions with their parents-in-law. It is also important for couples to refrain from speaking negatively or venting about family issues to their spouses. Introducing negativity into an already sensitive dynamic with in-laws can complicate conflict resolution.

Helping SAMA couples establish boundaries, improve connection, manage stress, regulate emotions, communicate effectively, and resolve conflicts not only enhances marital quality and satisfaction but also creates a positive model for their children. This approach can help mitigate the transmission of intergenerational trauma in SAMA families (Chapman & Cattaneo, 2013; Bachem et al., 2018).

Cultural and Religious Strengths to Help Mediate, Regulate, and Navigate Challenges

Community Orientation

In addition to the role of healthy couple relationships and family systems in mediating the transmission of trauma, community and religious support can offer protection and healing from intergenerational trauma. Though modern SAMA couples and families often navigate both Eastern and Western cultures, they tend to emphasize collectivistic values, such as giving back to and supporting members of their community (Singelis et al., 1995). This support may manifest in various ways, such as seasoned professionals mentoring students, prioritizing support for SAMA-owned businesses, or providing housing for extended family members until they can improve their financial situation. A community-oriented approach fosters cohesion, enhances both intra- and interpersonal well-being, and helps build social networks. These social networks can generate social capital, which encompasses access to information, socio-emotional support, and financial resources (Schulz et al., 2017).

Social capital is crucial, particularly as many SAMAs have experienced familial and community losses due to historical and migration trauma. In addition to fostering community connections, social capital can also arise from religious spaces. For SAMAs, mosques (masjids) serve as centers for information, emotional support, political engagement, education, and social gatherings, in addition to being places of worship (Nguyen et al., 2013). These spaces provide access to social services, host both religious and non-religious classes, and even offer voter registration. They are also venues for significant life events, including aqiqahs (celebrations of birth), nikkahs (weddings), and janazahs (funerals). Furthermore, mosques create opportunities for SAMAs to connect with one another, regardless of their level of religious adherence. The mosque remains a focal point for community gatherings, as giving time, resources, and support to fellow congregants is a fundamental principle in Islam (Nguyen et al., 2013).

To support SAMA clients who are experiencing isolation or disconnection, clinicians can encourage them to build community connections. They can remind clients that being charitable with resources—such as social capital, food, prayer, and money—is a fundamental principle in Islam. For example, when someone is facing a difficult time, community members often offer support through initiatives like meal trains. According to a recent survey, 67% of Asian American adults have donated money in the past year, with Muslim Asians being the most charitable group (Atske, 2024). Overall, SAMA is known for its generosity and willingness to support individuals both within and outside of their community.

Religious Values

Similar to South Asian culture, Islam values collectivism and community. In a hadith, or teaching of the Prophet Muhammad, it is stated, "Love for your brother what you love for yourself" (Al-Nawawi, Hadith 13). This emphasizes the importance of supporting those around us. It is common for South Asian Muslim Americans (SAMA) to seek support from their religious communities, particularly in the form of prayer (Sharma et al., 2020).

Support can also involve seeking advice from imams or religious leaders regarding marital issues and mental health concerns. While imams may provide guidance based on Islamic teachings, they are often not trained in professional counseling. However, the trust that SAMA place in religious leaders can be utilized to connect them with mental health professionals who can gently encourage congregants to seek mental health services.

SAMA could greatly benefit from community-based interventions, such as mental health lectures and workshops held at the masjid. These initiatives can promote community learning, healing, and destigmatization of mental health issues (Sharma et al., 2020).

Islam offers religious guidance on various aspects of a Muslim's life, including social, financial, political, moral, and spiritual matters. As such, caring for one's physical and mental health can be viewed as a religious practice. Islamic tradition also emphasizes the significance of introspection, contemplation, and self-improvement to enhance one's connection to God (Abdullah, 2014). Therefore, framing the pursuit of mental health assistance and psychoeducation within the context of Islam can help dispel the notion that it is something new, "Western," or external to Islamic beliefs.

To promote mental health care within an Islamic framework, it can be useful to educate individuals about Muslim scholars who have advocated for mental health support. For instance, Abu Zayd al-Balkhi authored a medical treatise titled "Sustenance of the Body and Soul" (Masalih al Abdan wa al-Anfus), where he explores the interconnection between the mind, body, and soul (Awaad & Ali, 2023; Balkhi et al., 2005). This concept may resonate with many Muslims who believe in the mind-body interdependence rather than viewing them as separate entities, thus reducing the stigma associated with mental health issues (Sharma et al., 2020).

Furthermore, al-Balkhi suggests that seeking therapy from external sources, such as medical professionals, wise individuals, and loved ones, is essential for obtaining sound advice, guidance, and support (Awaad & Ali, 2023; Balkhi et al., 2005). Imams could benefit from referencing these scholarly works to encourage the seeking of mental health assistance within their communities.

Family Values

Religious and cultural values such as respect, connection, loyalty, and support among family members serve as protective factors for the SAMA community (Badrinath & Seto, 2024; Patel et al., 2024). In this community, the definition of family extends beyond the nuclear family (Kurrien & Vo, 2004). Extended family members, including aunts, uncles, cousins, and grandparents, are regarded with the same respect and significance as immediate family members (Badrinath & Seto, 2024). In some cases, joint-family systems strengthen connections and family bonds to the extent that cousins are viewed as siblings and aunts are considered second mothers, providing substantial support to all household members (Ahmad et al., 2004). For example, grandparents may help with child-rearing when both parents work outside the home. From a therapeutic perspective, having multiple adults at home not only offers physical and emotional support but also reduces barriers to attending therapy, such as the need for childcare arrangements. Grandparents can receive both physical and financial support from their children and grandchildren, and children can develop positive connections and healthy attachments with multiple parental figures (Keller & Brown, 2014). Furthermore, having more adults in the household can help with daily tasks such as cooking and cleaning, and having multiple financial contributors can ease the management of household expenses. In this way, living together can alleviate various burdens and foster a true sense of community.

An important protective factor for SAMA is the cultural significance of building and maintaining family-like connections among friends. In SAMA communities, individuals who are not related by blood are often considered extensions of the nuclear family (Inman et al., 2007; Salam, 2013). For example, SAMA members refer to anyone who is around their mother's age as "Aunty" and anyone who is around their father's age as "Uncle" (Raman et al., 2014). This honorific title given to elders carries an implicit responsibility to provide family-like support to non-family members. For instance, adult SAMA individuals may check in on their parents' friends, invite family friends to celebrations, and offer meals, comfort, and advice to family friends in the same way they would for their blood relatives. By expanding SAMA support networks in this manner, individuals can navigate both joyful and challenging life experiences with the safety net provided by their community.

Work Ethic

Like other immigrant communities, SAMA has a strong work ethic and works diligently for themselves, their families, and their community. This dedication may stem from the historical impact of colonialism, as South African Muslims have worked tirelessly to recover what was lost during British rule. Even after migration, SAMA continues to strive despite facing discrimination and racism, which often results in fewer opportunities and the need to work harder than their white counterparts to achieve acceptance (Patel et al., 2024). Clinicians should leverage the strength-based qualities, such as perseverance and a strong work ethic, found in SAMA clients to promote behavioral activation, instill hope, and alleviate mental health distress. By reminding SAMA of their ancestors' resilience and ability to overcome adversity, clinicians may inspire them to pursue personal and community goals.

Education

SAMA places a high value on education and professional skills because they facilitate upward mobility and help individuals escape poverty in both the Indian subcontinent and the United States (Rahman & Witenstien, 2014). The Hart-Celler Immigration and Nationality Act of 1965 enabled the arrival of highly skilled professionals, including scientists, engineers, and doctors, from South Asia (Sharma et al., 2020). Today, South Asians from countries with large Muslim populations possess some of the highest levels of educational attainment in the United States (US Census Bureau, 2023).

To connect with SAMA's cultural emphasis on education, clinicians could use terms like "skill building" and "psychoeducation" when conducting mental health workshops and therapy sessions. Research has indicated that enrolling in psychoeducation or general psychology courses can enhance psychological coping and skill development (Holmes et al., 1999; Wallach, 2004).

Moreover, given this population's appreciation for accomplishments, clinicians might encourage participation in therapy or workshops by offering completion certificates. For example, upon reaching therapy goals, clients could receive a certificate that emphasizes their communication or conflict resolution skills, which they could then include in their resumes or curriculum vitae.

Conclusion

SAMA has a history shaped by war, colonialism, genocide, immigration, xenophobia, and discrimination. These experiences can lead to intergenerational trauma, relational dysfunction, and individual mental health challenges. Clinical approaches to improving mental health and relationships can include:

1. Conducting a trauma assessment and processing phase.
2. Helping clients understand the potential impact of intergenerational trauma on their mental health issues or relational dysfunction.
3. Building emotional attunement, connection, regulation, and adaptive coping skills.

4. Increasing relational and marital satisfaction by developing effective communication and negotiation skills, while also encouraging multigenerational healing conversations.
5. Embracing multicultural homes by processing grief related to losses and incorporating elements from both cultures that align with their religious and family values.

SAMA's strong sense of community, family, and generosity, rooted in their religious and cultural values, can act as protective factors against PTSD symptoms, mental illness, and family dysfunction. Mental health practitioners can collaborate with members of the religious community to enhance the therapeutic process and support SAMA in building community and family connections. Clinicians should also leverage SAMA's strong work ethic, religious commitment, desire for growth, and thirst for education to help overcome challenges and strengthen their resilience.

References

Abdullah, S. (2014). An Islamic perspective for strengths-based social work with Muslim clients. *Journal of Social Work Practice*, *29*(2), 163–172.

Adam N. M., Schewe P. A. (2007). A multilevel framework exploring domestic violence against Immigrant Indian and Pakistani women in the United States. *Journal of Muslim Mental Health*, 2(1), 5-20.

Ahmad, F., Shik, A., Vanza, R., Cheung, A. M., George, U., & Stewart, D. E. (2004) Voices of South Asian Women: Immigration and mental health. *Women & Health*, *40*, 113-130

Ahmed, S., & Reddy, L. A. (2007). Understanding the mental health needs of American Muslims: Recommendations and considerations for practice. *Journal of Multicultural Counseling and Development*, 35(4), 207.

al-Huraibi, N., & Konradi, A. (2012). Second-Generation Yemeni American Women at the Turn of the Century: Between Individual Aspirations and Communal Commitments. *Humanity & Society*, *36*(2), 117–144.

Alghafli, Z., Hatch, T., & Marks, L. (2014). Religion and Relationships in Muslim Families: A Qualitative Examination of Devout Married Muslim Couples. *Religions*, *5*(3), 814-833.

Ali, A. I. (2016). Citizens under Suspicion: Responsive Research with Community under Surveillance. *Anthropology & Education Quarterly*, *47*(1), 78–95.

Ali, B., Ahsan, M., Ahmed, N., Leff, H. S., Chow, C., & Khatab, Y. (2022). Domestic violence in urban American Muslim women. *Journal of Muslim Mental Health*, 16(1).

Amuta, A., Shanmugavelu, G., Parasuraman, B., Ariffin, K., Manickam, M. N., Vadivelu, M., & Kanapathy, K. (2021). Effective communication skills among married couples: An overview. EPRA International Journal of Research & Development (IJRD), 6(8).

Arshad, Z., & Falconier, M. K. (2019). The experiences of non-Muslim, Caucasian licensed marriage and family therapists working with South Asian and Middle Eastern Muslim client s. *Journal of Family Therapy*, 41(1), 54–79.

Atkinson, B. J. (1998). Pragmatic/Experiential therapy for couples. *Journal of Systemic Therapies*, *17*(2), 18-35.

Atske, S. (2024). *Asian Americans, Charitable Giving and Remittances*. Pew Research Center. https://www.pewresearch.org/race-and-ethnicity/2024/05/02/asian-americans-charitable-giving-and-remittances/

Awaad, R., & Ali, S. (2023). The original self-help book: Al-balkhi's 9th century "Sustenance of the body and soul". *Spirituality in Clinical Practice*, *10*(1), 89.

Bachem, R., Levin, Y., Zhou, X., Zerach, G., & Solomon, Z. (2018). The Role of Parental Posttraumatic Stress, Marital Adjustment, and Dyadic Self-Disclosure in Intergenerational Transmission of Trauma: A Family System Approach. *Journal of marital and family therapy*, *44*(3), 543–555.

Badrinath, A., & Seto, A. (2024). Exploring factors influencing South Asian immigrant family dynamics in the USA. *International Journal for the Advancement of Counselling*, *46*, 185–201.

Balkhi, A. S., Misri, M., & Khayyat, M. H., World Health Organization, & Institute of Arab Manuscripts. (2005). *Masalih al-abdan wa-al-anfus*. Ma'had al-Makhtutat al-Arabiyah.

Bass, G. J. (2016). Bargaining away justice: India, Pakistan, and the international politics of impunity for the Bangladesh genocide. *International Security, 41*(2), 140-187.

Bhandari, S., & Sabri, B. (2020). Patterns of abuse among South Asian women experiencing domestic violence in the United States. *International social work, 63*(1), 55–68.

Boyd-Franklin, N. (2010). Incorporating spirituality and religion Into the treatment of African American clients. The Counseling Psychologist, 38(7), 976–1000.

Cai, J., & Lee, R. M. (2022). Intergenerational communication about historical trauma in Asian American families. *Advances in Research Science, 3*(3), 233–245.

Chapman, A. R., & Cattaneo, L. B. (2013). American Muslim marital quality: A preliminary investigation. *Journal of Muslim Mental Health, 7*(2).

Chaudhuri, S., Morash, M., & Yingling, J. (2014). Marriage migration, patriarchal bargains, and wife abuse: A study of South Asian women. *Violence Against Women, 20*(2), 141–161.

Chen, Y. (2024). Domestic Violence in Asian Communities: A Scoping Review of Quantitative Literature. *Trauma, Violence, & Abuse, 25*(5), 3814-3826.

Chowdhury, T., & Okazaki, S. (2020). Intersectional complexities of South Asian Muslim Americans: Implications for identity and mental health. In G. C. Nagayama Hall (Ed.), *Mental and Behavioral Health of Immigrants in the United States* (pp. 179-200). Academic Press.

Cole, E.R. (2009) Intersectionality and research in psychology. *American Psychologist, 63*(3), 170-180.

Contractor, A. A., Rafiuddin, H. S., Kaur, K., & Asnaani, A. (2023). Asian Indians in the United States and posttraumatic stress disorder interventions: A narrative literature review. *Trauma, Violence, & Abuse, 24*(4), 2395-2411.

Cordova, J. V., Warren, L. Z., & Gee, C. B. (2001). Motivational interviewing as an intervention for at-risk couples. *Journal of marital and family therapy, 27*(3), 315–326.

Deepak, A. C. (2005). Parenting and the Process of Migration: Possibilities Within South Asian Families. *Child Welfare, 84*(5), 585–606

de Silva D. G. (2007). Children needing protection: experience from South Asia. *Archives of disease in childhood, 92*(10), 931–934.

Evans-Campbell, T. (2008). Historical trauma in American Indian/Native Alaska communities: A multilevel framework for exploring impacts on individuals, families, and communities. *Journal of Interpersonal Violence, 23*(3), 316–338.

Farris, C., & Haque, A. (2008). A Systematic Research Synthesis of the Various Adaptive Strategies Utilized by Dual-Income Couples. *Journal of Feminist Family Therapy, 20*(2), 126–141.

Goodman, R. D. (2013). The transgenerational trauma and resilience genogram. *Counselling Psychology Quarterly, 26*(3–4), 386–405.

Haque, A., Tubbs, C. Y., Kahumoku-Fessler, E. P., & Brown, M. D. (2019). Microaggressions and Islamophobia: Experiences of Muslims across the United States and clinical implications. *Journal of Marital and Family Therapy*, 45(1), 76–91.

Hargrave, T. D., & Houltberg, B. J. (2020). Transgenerational theories and how they evolved into current research and practice. The Handbook of Systemic Family Therapy, 1, 317–338.

Holmes, E. P., Corrigan, P. W., Williams, P., Canar, J., & Kubiak, M. A. (1999). Changing attitudes about schizophrenia. *Schizophrenia bulletin*, 25(3), 447-456.

Hossain, M. I. (2018). Hindu-Muslim cultural syncretism, mixed heritage, and inter-faith harmony: Some pragmatic observations from Eastern India. *Studies in Interreligious Dialogue*, 28(2), 1-21.

Hinton, D. E., Pham, T., Tran, M., Safren, S. A., Otto, M. W., & Pollack, M. H. (2004). CBT for Vietnamese with treatmentresistant PTSD and panic attacks: A pilot study. Journal of Traumatic Stress, 17(5), 429–43

Inman, A. G., Yeh, C. J., Madan-Bahel, A., & Nath, S. (2007). Bereavement and coping of South Asian families post 9/11. *Journal of Multicultural Counseling and Development*, 35(2), 101-115.

Isobel, S., Goodyear, M., Furness, T., & Foster, K. (2019). Preventing intergenerational trauma transmission: A critical interpretive synthesis. *Journal of Clinical Nursing,* 28(7-8), 1100-1113.

Kabir, A. J. (2005). Gender, memory, trauma: Women's novels on the Partition of India. *Comparative Studies of South Asia, Africa, & the Middle East*, 25(1), 177-190.

Keller, C. J., & Brown, C. (2014). Conflictual independence, adult attachment orientation, and career indecision among Asian American students. *Journal of Career Development*, 41(5), 426-444.

Keshavarzi, H., & Haque, A. (2013). Outlining a psychotherapy model for enhancing Muslim mental health within an Islamic context. *International Journal for the Psychology of Religion*, 23(3), 230–249.

Khan, Y., (2017). The great partition : The making of India and Pakistan. Yale University Press.

Kurrien, R., & Vo, E. D. (2004). Who's in charge?: Coparenting in South and Southeast Asian families. *Journal of Adult Development*, 11, 207-219.

Lang, A. J., & Gartstein, M. A. (2018). Intergenerational transmission of traumatization: Theoretical framework and implications for prevention. *Journal of Trauma & Dissociation*, 19(2), 162-175.

Momin, A. R. (1977). The Indo-Islamic tradition. *Sociological Bulletin*, 26(2), 242-258.

Naeem, F., Phiri, P., Munshi, T., Rathod, S., Ayub, M., Gobbi, M., & Kingdon, (2015). Using cognitive behaviour therapy with South Asian Muslims: Findings from the culturally sensitive CBT project. *International Review of Psychiatry*, 27(3), 233–246

Nagata, D. K., Kim, J. H. J., & Gone, J. P. (2024). Intergenerational Transmission of Ethnoracial Historical Trauma in the United States. *Annual Review of Clinical Psychology*, 20(1), 175–200.

Nguyen, A. W., Taylor, R. J., Chatters, L. M., Ahuvia, A., Izberk-Bilgin, E., & Lee, F. (2013). Mosque-based emotional support among young Muslim Americans. *Review of religious research, 55*(4), 535-555.

Otto, M. W., Hinton, D., Korbly, N. B., Chea, A., Ba, P., Gershuny, B. S., & Pollack, M. H. (2003). Treatment of pharmacotherapyrefractory posttraumatic stress disorder among Cambodian refugees: A pilot study of combination treatment with cognitivebehaviortherapy vs sertraline alone. Behaviour Research and Therapy, 41(11), 1271–1276.

Paradies, Y., Montoya, M. J., & Fullerton, S. M. (2007). Racialized genetics and the study of complex diseases: the thrifty genotype revisited. *Perspectives in biology and medicine, 50*(2), 203–227.

Patel, A., Hui, J., Havewala, M., & Wang, C. (2024). Cultural considerations for youth mental health first aid USA for South Asian and Southeast Asian American families. *Advances in Mental Health, 22*(3), 336-355. https://doi.org/10.1080/18387357.2024.2345234

Qureshi, F., Misra, S., & Poshni, A. (2023). The partition of India through the lens of historical trauma: Intergenerational effects on immigrant health in the South Asian diaspora. *SSM - Mental Health, 4*(15).

Rahman, Z., & Witenstein, M. A. (2014). A quantitative study of cultural conflict and gender differences in South Asian American college students. *Ethnic and Racial Studies, 37*(6), 1121-1137.

Raman, S., Srinivasan, K., Kurpad, A., Dwarkanath, P., Ritchie, J., & Worth, H. (2014). 'My Mother... My Sisters... and My Friends': Sources of maternal support in the perinatal period in urban India. *Midwifery, 30*(1), 130-137.

Rahemtulla, S., & Ababneh, S. (2021). Reclaiming Khadija's and Muhammad's marriage as an Islamic paradigm: Toward a new history of the Muslim present. *Journal of Feminist Studies in Religion, 37*(2), 83–102.

Sabado, J. A., Tram, J. M., Khan, A. N., & Lopez, J. M. (2023). Mental Health Seeking Behavior Among Muslims in The United States of America. The Family Journal, 31(2), 205-212.

Sabri B., Simonet M., Campbell J. C. (2018). Risk and protective factors of intimate partner violence among South Asian immigrant women and perceived need for services. *Cultural Diversity and Ethnic Minority Psychology*, 24(3), 442–452.

Salam, R. A. (2013). *Negotiating tradition, becoming American: Family, gender, and autonomy for second generation South Asians.* LBF Scholarly Publishing.

Sauerheber, J. D., Nims, D., & Carter, D. J. (2014). Counseling Muslim couples from a Bowen family systems perspective. *The Family Journal, 22*(2), 231–239

Schulz, B., Horr, A., & Hoenig, K. (2017). The position generator in the NEPS. *NEPS Survey Papers, Bamberg.*

Shaligram, D., Aga, F., Ramakrishnan, A., Iyer, S. N., Patel, S. R., & Kamath, S. (2022). Cultural considerations for working with South Asian youth. *Child and Adolescent Psychiatric Clinics, 31*(4), 789-803.

Shams, T. (2020). Successful yet precarious: South Asian Muslim Americans, Islamophobia, and the model minority myth. *Sociological Perspectives, 63*(4), 653-669.

Sharma, N., Shaligram, D., & Yoon, G. H. (2020). Engaging South Asian youth and families: A clinical review. *International Journal of Social Psychiatry, 66*(6), 584-592.

Singelis, T. M., Triandis, H. C., Bhawuk, D. P., & Gelfand, M. J. (1995). Horizontal and vertical dimensions of individualism and collectivism: A theoretical and measurement refinement. *Cross-cultural research, 29*(3), 240-275.

Singh, M., & Bhayana, R. (2015). Straddling Three Worlds: Stress, Culture and Adaptation in South Asian Couples. *Contemporary Family Therapy: An International Journal, 37*(1), 45–57.

Singh, R. (2017). Intimate Strangers? Working with Interfaith Couples and Families. *Australian & New Zealand Journal of Family Therapy, 38*(1), 7–14.

Sotero, M. (2006). A conceptual model of historical trauma: Implications for public health practice and research. *Journal of Health Disparities Research and Practice, 1*(1), 93-108.

Subramanee, S. D., Agho, K., Lakshmi, J., Huda, M. N., Joshi, R., & Akombi-Inyang, B. (2022). Child marriage in South Asia: A systematic review. *International Journal of Environmental Research and Public Health*, 19(22), 15138.

Tariq, M., & Syed, J. (2017). Intersectionality at work: South Asian Muslim women's experiences of employment and leadership in the United Kingdom. *Sex Roles*, 77(7-8), 510–522.

Tavakolizadeh, J., Nejatian, M., & Soori, A. (2015). The effectiveness of communication skills training on marital conflicts and its different aspects in women. Procedia - Social and Behavioral Sciences, 171, 214-221.

Thomas, B., Boutté, R. L., Kaur, B., & Mazzeo, S. E. (2023). "What will people say?": Mental health stigmatization as a barrier to eating disorder treatment-seeking for South Asian American women. *Asian American Journal of Psychology*, 14(1), 96–113.

Tummala-Narra, P. (2013). Psychotherapy with South Asian Women: Dilemmas of the Immigrant and First Generations. *Women & Therapy, 36*(3/4), 176–197.

U.S. Census Bureau. (2023) "Detailed Characteristics of Hundreds of Race/Ethnic and Tribal Groups" June 15, 2023, https://www.census.gov/library/stories/2023/06/detailed-characteristics-race-ethnic-tribal-groups.html accessed on February 21, 2025.

Wallach, H. S. (2004). Changes in attitudes towards mental illness following exposure. *Community mental health journal, 40*, 235-248.

CHAPTER EIGHT

COMPREHENSIVE MENTAL HEALTH CARE FOR ELDERLY MUSLIMS: CULTURALLY COMPETENT APPROACHES & STRATEGIES

Asif Khan

Introduction

As of 2020, there were approximately 3.45 million Muslims in the US, making up about 1.1% of the total population (Mohamed, 2017). Adults aged 55 and older make up approximately 14% of Muslim Americans; this age group roughly comprises 36% of the overall US population. The Muslim population in the US is diverse, with individuals from various ethnic, cultural, and linguistic backgrounds. Muslim American adults represent a diverse range of racial and ethnic backgrounds, with no single group comprising a majority. The largest group, making up 41%, is classified as white, which includes those identifying as Arab, Middle Eastern, Persian/Iranian, and others. Approximately 28% are Asian, including individuals from South Asia, while 20% are Black. Around 8% are Hispanic, and 3% identify with another race or multiple racial groups.

Around 58% of Muslim adults aged 18 and above were born outside of the US, with South Asia being the most common region of origin for Muslim immigrants. According to an estimate, about a quarter (24%) of US Muslims are natives with US-born parents, three or more generations old (Pew Research Center, 2025).

Importance of cultural competence in geriatric care

Cultural competence is essential in delivering effective care to older Muslims in the US, ensuring their beliefs, values, and cultural practices are respected and integrated into their healthcare. This approach goes beyond simply providing medical treatment; it requires healthcare providers to understand and honor the unique cultural and religious needs of Muslim patients. For example, understanding dietary restrictions, religious practices like prayer times, and family dynamics can significantly enhance the quality of care. When these factors are considered, patients feel more comfortable, respected, and understood, leading to better engagement with their care plans.

Research has consistently shown that culturally competent care improves patient satisfaction and leads to better health outcomes. When older Muslim patients feel that their cultural and religious values are acknowledged, they are more likely to follow medical advice, adhere to treatment plans, and have improved trust in their healthcare providers. This results in better health outcomes and overall well-being, making cultural competence a vital component of effective geriatric care.

Immigrants versus US-born Muslims

Immigrant older Muslims may face challenges in navigating the American healthcare system due to language barriers, limited health literacy, and unfamiliarity with available services. U.S.-born older Muslims, on the other hand, may have better access to healthcare but may still face cultural and generational differences in attitudes toward aging, mental health, and end-of-life care. U.S.-born Muslims may have more progressive attitudes toward mental health and end-of-life care compared to their immigrant counterparts, who may hold more traditional beliefs and practices.

Gerocentric Culture In Islam

The concept of aging as wisdom in Islamic teachings

Islam views aging as a biological process and a stage of life where wisdom, experience, and knowledge are accumulated. Elders are respected for the valuable insights they have gained over the years, and caring for them is seen as a virtuous act. The Qur'an and Hadith, the foundational texts of Islam, contain many teachings that emphasize the duty to honor, respect, and care for the elderly. This respect is a sign of good character and a reflection of Islamic values that cherish the dignity of every stage of life.

The role of elderly individuals in Muslim families and communities

In Muslim families and communities, elderly individuals hold a highly esteemed and respected position. Their accumulated wisdom, life experiences, and deep understanding of religious and worldly matters make them invaluable sources of guidance and support. They are often seen as the pillars of the family, offering advice and counsel in important decisions. This respect is ingrained in Islamic tradition, where elders are honored for their age and the knowledge they pass on to younger generations.

Beyond their role in the family, elders also serve as key figures within the broader community. Their opinions and perspectives are frequently sought in community matters and play a vital role in fostering intergenerational relationships. Through their experiences, they help shape the values and decisions of the younger members, ensuring continuity in the community's moral and ethical framework.

The significance of intergenerational relationships

In Islam, intergenerational relationships hold deep significance and are a fundamental part of family life. Islam emphasizes the importance of maintaining strong family bonds, with mutual respect and support between older and younger generations. These relationships are seen as a duty and a source of emotional and social strength. The younger generation benefits from the wisdom and guidance of their elders, while the older generation receives care, companionship, and a sense of purpose from their younger family members.

This exchange between generations fosters a strong sense of community and belonging. For older Muslims, these connections provide emotional support and reduce feelings of isolation, while younger members gain a deeper understanding of their cultural and religious heritage. This dynamic helps preserve family unity and ensures that values and traditions are passed down through generations.

Brief Overview Of Mental Health Conditions, Including Dementia Syndromes In The Elderly Population

Dementia Syndromes

Neurocognitive disorders are a group of conditions marked by declines in cognitive abilities, including memory, attention, language, executive function, visuospatial skills, and problem-solving. In mild cases, these disorders may not significantly interfere with daily activities, but in more severe forms, they can significantly impair one's ability to function independently, affecting overall well-being, and are therefore classified as syndromes.

There are several subtypes of dementia, with Alzheimer's disease as the most common type, followed by vascular and Lewy body dementias. According to a study, approximately 6.7 million people in the US are living with dementia (Irfan, et al., 2024).

Identification and management of dementia is critical as it can be progressive with ultimate functional impairment. Further, dementia can be associated with a significant caregiver burden, which can lead to depression and other mental and physical declines in the caregivers.

Depression

Depression is a common mental health disorder that may be underrecognized in the elderly population. It is characterized by persistent feelings of sadness, hopelessness, guilt, loss of interest or pleasure in activities, sleep disturbances, and, in severe forms, suicidal ideation. Late-life depression may have a reciprocal relationship with medical illnesses. Depression can increase the risk of obesity, frailty, diabetes, and cognitive impairment. Depression can be linked to cardiac, cerebrovascular, and peripheral arterial disease. Further, depressed individuals may have a higher risk of stroke and mortality than non-depressed individuals. Depression can ultimately lead to functional impairment, which may further worsen the depression. Studies suggest that older Muslims may be less likely to seek mental health care compared to the general population, with only 27% believing that depression is a health problem (Alexopoulos, 2019).

Anxiety Disorders

Anxiety disorders are a group of mental health conditions characterized by excessive worry, fear, apprehension, and avoidance. It can range from generalized anxiety disorder, which translates to excessive worry about almost everyday life situations, to more specific fears in the form of phobias. Anxiety disorders can also take the form of panic attacks, which can stem from fear and can further affect individuals in terms of functionality. Literature in older adults varies in terms of prevalence. However, anxiety disorders in any form could either exist independently or may be associated with other psychiatric illnesses, in particular, depression. Data on elderly US Muslims is limited about the prevalence of anxiety disorders among elderly Muslims in the US, but experiences of discrimination are associated with an increased risk of anxiety among Muslim immigrants (Canuto et al., 2018).

Posttraumatic Stress Disorder (PTSD)

The Diagnostic and Statistical Manual of Mental Disorders, 5th Edition (DSM-5), describes PTSD as a condition that can occur after experiencing or witnessing a traumatic event, such as assault, combat, or a natural disaster (American Psychiatric Association, 2022). Symptoms include intrusive thoughts (e.g., memories, nightmares), avoidance of trauma reminders, negative mood changes, and hyperarousal (e.g., irritability, heightened alertness).

Estimates of the prevalence of current posttraumatic stress disorder (PTSD) in older adults across ethnic minority and non-minority groups range from 0.4 to 4.5% (Kaiser et al., 2018). Elderly Muslim refugees in the US may be at increased risk for PTSD due to experiences of trauma and resettlement stress

Other Mental Illnesses

Similarly, many other mental health conditions, including schizophrenia, bipolar spectrum, and adjustment disorder along with others can affect the Muslim elderly. Identifying these with appropriate management may be crucial and require collaborative and culturally informed care.

Protective Factors Unique To The Muslim Elderly Population

Social support networks

Strong social support networks, including family, friends, and community organizations, play a crucial role in promoting the well-being of older Muslims. As noted above, the respect and wisdom associated with aging and the traditionally perceived responsibility of the family to care for their loved ones create an overall sense of support.

Religious practices and beliefs

Religious practices, such as prayer, fasting, and participation in community activities, provide comfort, meaning, and a sense of belonging to older Muslims. This can include Friday prayer attendance, Iftar dinners and Taraweeh in Ramadan, Eid celebrations, and other religious observances.

Challenges Facing Older Muslims

Acculturation stress

Acculturation stress, resulting from the challenges of adapting to a new culture while maintaining one's cultural identity, can negatively impact the mental and physical health of older Muslims. This acculturation stress can be associated with an increased risk of depression, anxiety, and other health problems among immigrant populations.

Discrimination and social isolation

Discrimination and social isolation are significant challenges faced by older Muslims in the US, contributing to increased risk of mental health problems and reduced quality of life. In particular, immigrants have limited family support compared to those in their home countries.

Impact of language barriers on healthcare access and quality

Language barriers can significantly impact healthcare access and quality for older Muslims in the US, leading to misunderstandings, misdiagnosis, and inadequate treatment.

Stigma associated with mental health care

Mental health is often stigmatized in many Muslim communities, with misconceptions and negative attitudes towards mental illness prevalent. In some Muslim communities, mental illness can be understood through various religious and spiritual lenses. It may be seen as the will of God, a test of faith, or even a form of punishment for past actions. Others might interpret mental health struggles as a signal to strengthen their connection with God or as a form of spiritual trial. In some cases, mental illness is thought to be caused by possession by evil spirits or supernatural influences. Social stigma around mental illness remains a significant concern within some Muslim communities. Disclosure of mental health can be associated with shamefulness and embarrassment. Women may worry about how a psychiatric diagnosis could affect their marital prospects or social standing within the community.

Strategies To Promote Awareness And Culturally Competent Care

Mental Health Awareness and Education

Lack of mental awareness and education about signs of mental disorders can lead to delays in diagnoses and subsequent treatment. Mental health awareness can be adopted locally at the community level. Community-based education programs and workshops can be held to raise awareness about mental health issues and reduce stigma. Collaborative efforts between healthcare providers and community and faith leaders are important to promote mental health awareness and destigmatize mental illness. Muslim faith leaders (Imams) can play an integral role in this regard, as Muslim

Americans may be more willing to seek help from religious leaders. about According to the American Psychiatric Association (2018), 95% of imams spend some time in counseling activities. Family and caregiver education and education about available resources are equally important.

Culturally Competent Care

Culturally sensitive care should be tailored to each individual's unique needs, beliefs, and preferences, considering their cultural background, language, and life experiences. For example, attention to food preferences, the Islamic Hijab, and the preference of same-sex providers, mainly by female patients, although this can be challenging in areas with limited specialized mental health providers. In clinical settings, behavior that may seem unusual or unfamiliar to healthcare providers could be entirely normal within the patient's cultural or religious framework. By considering the patient's cultural norms and values, clinicians can avoid misdiagnosing or pathologizing behaviors unrelated to a medical condition. Collaborating with family members or healthcare professionals who understand the patient's background helps ensure that care is both culturally sensitive and accurate, leading to better patient outcomes and stronger trust in the healthcare process. Training and educating healthcare providers in cultural competence and providing resources and support to assist with acculturation can help improve the quality of care provided to older Muslims in the US.

Overcoming Language Barriers in Geriatric Care

Providing professional interpreters and bilingual healthcare providers trained in cultural competence can help overcome language barriers and improve communication and understanding, which can play an important role in bridging the communication gap between the provider and patient. Utilizing translated materials, visual aids, and technology, such as telemedicine and translation apps, can also facilitate communication and enhance the quality of care provided.

Appropriate Dietary Counseling and Support

Providing culturally appropriate dietary counseling and support, including guidance on selecting nutritious halal foods, adapting traditional recipes to meet dietary needs, and addressing dietary restrictions related to chronic health conditions, is essential for promoting the nutritional well-being of older Muslims. Collaboration with dietitians, community organizations, and religious leaders can help ensure that dietary counseling and support are tailored to older Muslims' specific needs and preferences.

Religious Accommodations

Accommodating religious practices and rituals is crucial in providing respectful and compassionate care to older Muslims and ensuring their spiritual and emotional needs are met, such as prayer preferences, fasting during Ramadan, and other religious observances. This can enhance the therapeutic alliance and further the provider's and patient's trust. Engaging with the community can help healthcare providers gain insights into older Muslims' unique needs and preferences and develop culturally competent and holistic care plans.

Trauma-Informed Care for Refugee Population

Trauma-informed care, including screening, psychological support, and culturally sensitive mental health services, is crucial for addressing the unique needs of older Muslim refugees. Collaborating with resettlement agencies, community groups, and mental health professionals ensures compassionate, culturally appropriate care for these individuals.

End Of Life Care Discussions

Cultural perspectives on death and dying

Islam teaches that death is a natural part of life and emphasizes the importance of preparing for the afterlife through good deeds and faith. Respect for the dying and the deceased is highly valued, and specific rituals and practices are observed to ensure a peaceful transition.

Advance care planning and discussing end-of-life preferences

Advance care planning is essential in ensuring that the wishes and preferences of older Muslims are respected and honored. Medical decision-making should be consistent with Islamic ethics, considering the crucial role of family caregiving and the religious duty to care for older adults. Appointing a power of attorney and making decisions about housing should be approached with sensitivity to Islamic family dynamics, gender roles, and the central role of the family in caregiving. This consideration also extends to financial matters, such as insurance, where many Muslims aim to follow Islamic principles, including the prohibition of interest. Open and honest discussions about end-of-life care, including resuscitation preferences, life-sustaining treatments, and funeral arrangements, should be encouraged.

Religious and cultural considerations in end-of-life care

Healthcare providers should be knowledgeable about Islamic beliefs and practices related to death and dying and incorporate these into end-of-life care plans. Collaboration with religious leaders and community organizations can help meet older Muslims' spiritual and cultural needs.

Conclusion

Geriatric care for the Muslim population in the US requires a culturally competent and holistic approach that respects and integrates their beliefs, values, and practices into care plans. Addressing the unique needs and challenges faced by older Muslims, including cultural stigma, language barriers, dietary restrictions, and religious considerations, is essential in providing quality and compassionate care. Cultural competence and a holistic approach to care are fundamental in ensuring older Muslims' physical, mental, emotional, and spiritual well-being and promoting their overall quality of life. Training healthcare providers in cultural competence, collaborating with religious leaders and community organizations, and tailoring care plans to each individual's unique needs and preferences are essential aspects of providing culturally competent and holistic care to older Muslims in the US.

References

American Psychiatric Association. (2018). *Demographics, Mental Health Disparities, and Social Determinants of Mental Health among Muslim Americans in the United States*. https://www.psychiatry.org/File%20Library/Psychiatrists/Cultural-Competency/Mental-Health-Disparities/Mental-Health-Facts-for-Muslim-Americans.pdf

American Psychiatric Association. (2022). *Diagnostic and Statistical Manual of Mental Disorders*. https://doi.org/10.1176/appi.books.9780890425787

Alexopoulos, G. S. (2019). Mechanisms and treatment of late-life depression. *Translational Psychiatry, 9*(1). https://doi.org/10.1038/s41398-019-0514-6

Canuto, A., Weber, K., Baertschi, M., Andreas, S., Volkert, J., Dehoust, M. C., Sehner, S., Suling, A., Wegscheider, K., Ausín, B., Crawford, M. J., Da Ronch, C., Grassi, L., Hershkovitz, Y., Muñoz, M., Quirk, A., Rotenstein, O., Santos-Olmo, A. B., Shalev, A., . . . Härter, M. (2017). Anxiety disorders in old Age: psychiatric comorbidities, quality of life, and prevalence according to age, gender, and country. *American Journal of Geriatric Psychiatry, 26*(2), 174–185. https://doi.org/10.1016/j.jagp.2017.08.015

Irfan, B., Ankouni, G., Reader, J., Seraji-Bozorgzad, N., Giordani, B., Bakulski, K., Bhaumik, A., Hampstead, B. M., & Rahman-Filipiak, A. (2024). Alzheimer's disease and related dementias in Muslim women: Recommendations for culturally sensitive care. *Journal of Alzheimer S Disease, 99*(3), 857–867. https://doi.org/10.3233/jad-240064

Kaiser, A. P., Cook, J. M., Glick, D. M., & Moye, J. (2018). Posttraumatic Stress disorder in Older Adults: A Conceptual review. *Clinical Gerontologist, 42*(4), 359–376. https://doi.org/10.1080/07317115.2018.1539801

Mohamed, B., Smith, G. A., Cooperman, A., & Pew Research Center. (2017). U.S. Muslims Concerned About Their Place in Society but Continue to Believe in the American Dream. In *Pew Research Center*. https://www.pewresearch.org/wp-content/uploads/sites/20/2017/07/U.S.-MUSLIMS-FULL-REPORT-with-population-update-v2.pdf

Pew Research Center. 2025. 2023-24 U.S. Religious Landscape Study Dataset – Public Use File. doi: 10.58094/3kwb-bf52.

SECTION FOUR

SPECIAL POPULATIONS

CHAPTER NINE

REVERTED AND CONVERTED MUSLIMS' MENTAL HEALTH IN NORTH AMERICA

Sarah Mohr, Anisah Bagasra

This chapter discusses Muslim converts in North America and various factors that impact their mental health and well-being. Conversion is often a life-changing, enduring experience that requires adjustments to lifestyle, relationships, and radical changes in belief systems or values. In this chapter, the authors examine how the conversion experience itself, as well as interactions with non-Muslim and Muslim communities, may impact overall mental health and well-being, especially for new converts. Implications for clinical practice, focusing on how Muslim converts may differ from those born Muslim, is provided.

Introduction

Before discussing the facts about reversion and conversion to Islam, the authors feel it is important to contextualize their personal conversion experiences. Increasingly, theoretical work is being done on the significance of positionality, or the political, social, and theoretical impact of who a person is on the meaning of what they say (Foucault, 1980; Weiler, 2006). The idea that people create knowledge for a purpose, also known as the concept of knowledge creation, continues to gain credence as theories and facts from the past and present are shown to be heavily influenced by who produced them and what their intentions were at the time (Collins, 2019; Crenshaw, 1991; Delgado & Stefanic, 2017). Considering this increasing emphasis on speaking from one's social location intentionally and transparently, the authors would like to share a brief synopsis of their narratives.

In 1996, co-author A.B. converted to Islam at the age of 15. A.B. was born to an American mother and a Pakistani father who was a non-practicing Muslim then. She was raised in a secular household that neither encouraged nor discouraged the study of religion or spirituality. Around 12, she became curious about religious traditions and started learning about some. At age 13, she traveled to Pakistan to visit her father's side of the family for the first time and was exposed to Muslim practices, including the adhan (call to prayer), prayer, and Quran recitation. She read and did a book report on "The Benefactor and the Rightly Guided," a short biography of the Prophet Muhammad in Middle School. It was not until starting high school that she met and became close friends with a girl from Pakistan, with whom she started to attend the mosque. At this time, A.B. continued to read and learn about Islamic history, the Quran, and hadith. People at the mosque in New Jersey assumed the author was Muslim. When the Islamic teacher discovered she was not, she was encouraged to declare Shahadah. Like many converts, her newfound Muslim identity was a strain on her relationships with most friends and family who did not understand the decision to become a Muslim. The decision to wear the hijab (head scarf) was met with more incredulity and further strained her relationship with her mother, who believed all organized religions were corrupt. Within the Muslim community, which was a primarily South Asian community, there were some challenges, too. As a teenager, the author was viewed as a "half-breed" and not authentically Muslim or as a threat to corrupt young men because of her non-Muslim family. The author tried her best to fully assimilate and gain a sense of belonging with other Muslim college students. At 19, she married in Pakistan and faced additional challenges assimilating to Pakistani culture. Within her marriage, she was often challenged as not being devout enough or knowledgeable about Islam, despite a degree in religion with a focus on Islamic studies. An inability to fast due to medical reasons further isolated her as "not a good enough Muslim. "Muslim converts like the author often face challenges with acceptance from both Muslim and non-Muslims, challenges to their identity, adaptation to Muslim social norms, and perseverance in gaining spiritual and religious knowledge in the face of cultural and linguistic barriers. This can lead to a sense of isolation, distress, and questioning of one's adoption of a faith. The events of 9/11 and the framing of Islam and Muslims in Western media can exacerbate these challenges. American Muslim converts face unique challenges navigating the difficult landscape of being Muslim in America.

Co-author S.M. was raised a Christian and began studying world religions at a young age. She took a world religions class in junior college, and the teacher wrote "La ilaha il Allah" on the board. The author was struck that this was the solution to many of her questions about Christianity, and she looked up a Sufi center in the phone book. She began to be friends with the teacher there and regularly visited his quiet retreat in the redwoods in Marin County. As she continued to pursue her studies of religion as an undergraduate and prepared to go to graduate school in religion, the September 11 attacks occurred. She read the Quran cover to cover for the first time and decided to become more serious about Islam. Looking up a Muslim center in the phone book again, she took shahada and began about a year later to take classes at a local madrasa, pray, fast, and wear hijab. Her family was highly critical of these decisions, and when she married a much older man, became largely estranged from her. After a long journey through a lot of challenges, she reconciled with her family. However, it remained a source of stress. Some of the challenges she faced were standard for all Muslims, like Islamophobia. At the same time, many were unique to converts, such as skepticism about her motives given the timing of her conversion. It became a source of reflection and deeper commitment to sincerity in her religion, and she has gone on to reflect on conversion, including publishing on her journey.

The authors' stories reflect the wide range of experiences of Muslim converts and reverts. People decide to convert in many ways, and different paths lead to different challenges. This chapter will provide insight both into conversion/reversion to Islam in the US and into strategies for mental health support and intervention on behalf of converts. Given the substantial number of converts in the US, it is critical to intentionally support this population and understand their unique challenges and needs.

This chapter discusses numerous factors that impact the mental health of Muslim converts in North America. Conversion is often a life-changing, enduring experience that requires adjustments to lifestyle, relationships, and radical changes in belief systems or values. In this chapter, the authors examine how the conversion experience itself, as well as interactions with non-Muslim and Muslim communities, may impact overall mental health and well-being, especially for new converts.

Implications for clinical practice, focusing on how Muslim converts may differ from those born Muslim is provided.

Demographics of Revert/Convert Muslims

The number of Muslims in the US is around 3.45 million, according to a Pew Research study from 2017, are predominantly immigrants and are, in general, much younger than the overall population of the United States. Approximately 14% to 20% of all American Muslims are converts (Pew Research, 2011). Among African American Muslims, two-thirds are converts. (Pew Research, 2011). In the United States, there is a significant number of Muslims who convert while incarcerated. The Council on American Islamic Relations reports that about 15% of the US prison population is Muslim, with 35,000-45,000 people converting every year while incarcerated (CAIR, 2024). This adds another layer to the mental health challenges they may experience. Approximately 54% of converts to Islam in America are men and 46% are women (Pew Research, 2011). The Institute on Social Policy Understanding (ISPU) has conducted a decadal survey of US mosques from 2000, 2010, and 2020, showing changing demographics in the mosques in the US (ISPU, 2020). Some interesting changes include a decrease in African American converts, an increase in Latino/Latina converts, a continued greater percentage of men converts than women, and an overall plateau in the number of converts in general.

A Pew Research study indicated that the majority of converts to Islam in the United States were former Christians, with 53% identifying as formerly Protestant and 20% identifying as formerly Catholic (Mohammed & Sciupac, 2018). Another finding of this study was that while both Christianity and Islam lose members of the faith frequently, 22% and 23%, respectively, Islam is gaining converts at about the same speed as the faithful are leaving (23%), while among Christians converts are a declining percentage (6%), so for Islam the net effect roughly evens out.

Overall, converts are an important part of the US Muslim community and represent a significant number of people in the United States who practice Islam. Thus, it is important to understand this population and meet their mental health needs.

Common Causes of Reversion/Conversion

There are a variety of reasons that converts report impacted their choice of Islam as a religion, according to Pew. About a quarter prefer the teachings of Islam to their former religion, and 21% report that religious texts were influential in their decision. Others report that they wanted to belong to a community (10%), that marriage or a relationship was a primary motivating factor (9%), or that they were influenced by a friend or religious leader (9%)

(Mohammed & Sciupac, 2018). A grounded theory study based on 21 interviews on the impact of conversion on couples found a greater level of unity in the marital relationship, and this supports the logic of conversion for reasons of solidifying marital stability (Coffee, Brimhall & Smith, 2021). Among the roughly 50% of people in the US who make some form of religious conversion throughout their lives, generally, the personal aspects of religion, such as belief systems, are a more common driver of religious conversion than external factors such as marriage (Beider, 2022).

Research by Barro, Hwang, and McCleary (2010) indicates that the US has a significantly higher percentage of converts per capita than most other countries. They studied factors contributing to conversion in 40 countries and found that religious pluralism tends to contribute to higher levels of religious conversion, while factors like communism and other political factors greatly decrease conversion. This research indicates that higher social acceptability for religious tolerance heavily impacts conversion rates nationally.

Reversion or Conversion

There is a range of ways that Muslims who convert to Islam refer to themselves regarding their identity, and there are ongoing differences in terminology about conversion. The root of the word "conversion" is derived from the original Hebrew, Greek, and Latin terms meaning to turn, to return, and to turn again (as well as turning, returning, and turning about) (Paloutzian, Richardson, & Rambo, 1999). Many Muslim converts prefer the term revert. This has to do with the belief among Muslims that all people are Muslim (submit to God) at birth, though they may be socialized into different traditions. Thus, reversion is a return to the original faith rather than a change. Within sociological and psychological disciplines, conversion is the term to describe a radical change in belief typically occurring in adolescence or early adulthood. Casey (2021) defines American Muslim converts as individuals who are US citizens from any heritage or background who were born into non-Muslim families and have chosen Islam as their religion.

Types of Conversion

Researchers have been studying conversion in the US for well over 100 years. Early researchers include Starbuck's *A Study of Conversion* (1897) and William James' work on religion, including *The Varieties of Religious Experience* (1902) (Iqbal, Radulescu, Bains, & Aleem, 2019). Hood, Spilka, Hunsberger, and Gorsuch (1996) outline some of the key components of conversion processes in their text on the psychology of religion. They note that all conversions occur within social and cultural contexts, and precipitating events can always be identified leading up to the conversion experience (p. 286-288). While there is empirical research to support theories that describe conversion as a complex process that cannot easily be boiled down to simple categories (Halama, 2015), much of the traditional research describes conversion as a passive process and a response to events in a person's life, the "classic" paradigm, while often more modern research describes conversion as an active process of a search for meaning and purpose, the "contemporary" paradigm (Kahn, & Greene, 2004; Zinnbauer & Pargament, 1998). These two main types of conversion processes have been identified in literature, in other words, as those that are "sudden" conversion experiences and those that are "gradual" conversion experiences (James, 1902) paradigms that are sometimes described as conflicting (Kilbourne & Richardson, 1989). Sudden conversions are described as sudden and intense experiences of a religious nature that lead to a transformation for the individual. Typically, sudden conversions are most common in adolescence; changes to the person are dramatic, and the conversion is more emotional in nature than rational. In addition, the person starts with changes in belief and changes in behavior (such as active engagement in prayer, changes in style of dress, etc.), which will come after. Initial research suggests that sudden conversions tend to be long-lasting or permanent, but there are not enough longitudinal studies to prove these assertions. The second type of conversion is gradual conversion, which occurs slowly, tends to be more rational, occurs more in early adulthood, and involves more active seeking from the convert.

Additionally, gradual conversion usually starts with changes in behavior before full acceptance of belief. Snook and colleagues (2021) examined conversion motifs within a six-motif framework and found that most Muslim American converts fall within the intellectual motif. This motif is neither sudden nor gradual, falling between the two, and involves a search for meaning and knowledge primarily through the writings of the religious group. As the individual is an active seeker in their knowledge of the religious tradition, there is little to no social pressure involved. Affectional conversion, a conversion to form or maintain bonds with Muslims, has consistently been the second most common motif and fits more of a gradual conversion process (Kose & Loewenthal, 2000; Harder, 2015). Similarly, studies of Muslim converts in prison have found that conversion to Islam provides a moral framework that has helped individuals rebuild their lives during and after incarceration (Spalek & El-Hassan, 2007).

There are some questions about whether or not conversion is a consequence of a certain personality type and whether conversion is a good or a bad thing for people, including whether the changes inevitably produced by conversion are positive or negative, helpful or harmful, prosocial or anti-social (Paloutzian, Richardson, & Rambo, 1999). For example, early research by Starbuck (1899) showed changes in emotional states from depression, sadness, and pensiveness to exultation, peace, and joy in both men and women, documented through qualitative data gathered from autobiographical accounts. Later research on the positive effects of conversion by Paloutzian (1981) indicated an increase in purpose in life and positive life values when they compared the positive values and sense of purpose, including fear of death, among Christian converts, believers, and non-believers, with their data showing a higher level of life meaning among converts following conversion. Conversely, Kirkpatrick (1997,1998), in a longitudinal study on conversion in women, documented a connection between insecure-anxious and insecure-avoidant personality types and a greater tendency toward conversion than those with secure attachment styles. Other research supports that attachment anxiety can lead to higher tendencies for religious conversion (Greenwald, Mikulincer, Granqvist, & Shaver, 2021).

One factor in religious conversion, and Islam specifically, is familiar to many people, namely the tendency of religious conversion to accompany major lifestyle changes, particularly leaving behind a lifestyle of intensive sexual activity, substance use, and criminal behavior. While some research describes the development of pathological behaviors due to conversion, this is unsupported by the literature. Instead, the research on conversion indicates a high correlation between conversion and positive lifestyle changes that include stopping the use of illicit drugs and other self-destructive habits (Paloutzian, Richardson, & Rambo, 1999).

What is involved in becoming a practicing Muslim?

There are fundamental changes that go along with becoming a practicing Muslim. First, becoming a Muslim is very simple: taking shahada or confessing faith. The shahada, the requirement to become a Muslim, is that a person states out loud in front of two Muslim witnesses, "There is no God but Allah, and Muhammad is His Prophet and Messenger." Many people begin to make a lot of changes prior to taking shahada. Widely accepted basic requirements of conversion include refraining from alcohol, gambling, and fornication. Most Muslims agree that to be a Muslim requires establishing the five daily prayers, fasting the month of Ramadan, paying the zakat, or the obligatory poor tax, and at least once in a person's life, if circumstances permit it, making the pilgrimage to Mecca. Reading the Quran and learning about the words (hadith) and life (sunnah) of the Prophet Muhammad (PBUH) are typically expected of new Muslims. As far as beliefs, Muslims are expected to believe there is only one God, believe that

Muhammad (PBUH) is the last Prophet and messenger of God, believe in angels, all previous prophets, and revealed books, and believe in the day of judgment and divine decree. For some converts, behavioral change is easier, and they engage in behavioral conversion, but it takes longer to learn and fully embrace changes in belief. Others may study Islam for a while before converting and embrace all beliefs but find behavioral changes such as praying and fasting to be harder. Some converts will attempt to learn to read the Quran in Arabic, while others rely on translations and transliterations. Thus, it is important to understand every convert's unique circumstances and process, as their story is often central to emerging mental health concerns.

There is an increasing effort on the part of Muslim communities in the US to provide support for converts to the faith. Support groups and other organized meetings provide fellowship, guidance, and ways to learn things like prayer, which can be challenging for people who are monolingual English speakers, as it is said entirely in Arabic. As converts continue past their initial commitment of taking shahada, many people report challenges maintaining their faith. Unmet expectations, isolation, and problems maintaining religious life contribute to high levels of recidivism and a frequent pattern of converts leaving faith after their initial commitment (Hassan, 2018). While most of the writing on converts leaving Islam is anecdotal and not evidence-based, Pew does report that the number of people who convert to Islam every year is roughly equal to the number leaving the faith who were raised in the religion and gives reasons for their departure that many people familiar with those who have left Islam will recognize as similar, such as not connecting with the faith or teachings (Pew Research, 2018).

Mental Health Challenges Associated with Conversion

Family of Origin

Many individuals will experience rejection from their families when they convert to Islam (Sintang & Hambali, 2018). This has been exacerbated by increases in Islamophobia that continue to create misconceptions about Islam and Muslims. New converts, especially women, may adopt *hijab* and a change in style of dress that further alienates them from family members. Parents and siblings may feel that the individual is rejecting their upbringing and values, creating feelings of personal rejection. Refusal to partake in family activities that involve drinking can exacerbate tensions. There is a range of patterns of converts' engagement with non-Muslim families following conversion, including patterns of inclusion and support. However, the emphasis on filial piety in Islam can make tensions with family challenging to navigate, as attempts to balance religious beliefs and the need to maintain good ties with family can sometimes conflict (Sintang & Hambali, 2018). For individuals who convert to Islam after marriage and are already married to an individual who does not convert, this can create additional challenges for both the individual and/or couple (Mirza, 2017). Islamic law states that a Muslim woman should only marry a Muslim man (Elmal-Karakaya, 2022), whereas Muslim men can marry people of the book (Christian or Jewish women). Women who convert and whose spouses do not may face criticism from the Muslim community, and it may put additional pressure on their marriage.

Changes in Cultural and Social Norms

Like most other religious traditions, Islam has a set of values and norms that individuals are expected to adhere to. Depending upon the background of the new convert, they may have little to no exposure to some of these norms. Some of the norms may be explicit and conveyed to them upon their conversion. However, many are unwritten rules and often intermingled with cultural traditions and do not fully reflect Islamic norms. Examples of social norms within Muslim communities are men and women often segregating in the mosque and at social gatherings, not shaking hands with the opposite sex, not keeping dogs within one's home, dressing in loose and modest clothing, only associating with members of the opposite sex in public or with a chaperone if meeting someone to get to know them for possible marriage, and avoiding restaurants or social gatherings where alcohol is being served and consumed. Adapting to these changes in socially accepted behaviors can be challenging, cause tensions within one's social circle and workplace, and even require significant lifestyle changes. Rao (2015) examined gender differences in the adaptation of religiously acceptable practices among Muslim converts, with a focus on how male and female converts accept polygyny and modest clothing. Their case study highlights the way that Muslim religious identity is constructed as both gendered and distinct from non-Muslims. Adapting to veiling and acceptance of polygyny is usually a much more difficult process for women. It also makes Muslim women more visible in public life, making them easy targets of Islamophobia (Alimahomed-Wilson, 2017).

Acculturative Stress

Acculturative stress is often associated with the experiences of immigrants and refugees struggling to adapt to cultural norms in a new country. Conversion experiences can trigger a similar experience for new Muslims who are struggling to adapt to normative behaviors within their newly adopted religious tradition. Converts often struggle to adapt to and feel accepted in Muslim communities (Baba, 2017). Pressure to assimilate to both religious and cultural norms within the community that their conversion has occurred can lead to significant acculturative stress. Religious norms that may be challenging include gender segregation, no longer shaking hands with the opposite gender, adapting to dietary restrictions, and adapting to changes in clothing (more modest clothing). Other norms relate directly to religious behaviors such as fasting, performing wudu (ablutions), and daily prayers. Adaptation may be more challenging depending on whether the conversion was gradual or sudden. Sudden conversion in which a person immediately tries to immerse themselves in these norm changes may be especially distressing.

Casey argues that Muslim converts lack the "heritage" background-cultural, linguistic, racial, and geographic backgrounds that lend legitimacy to their Muslim identity, especially as "Muslimness" is frequently racialized in the United States (Casey, 2021). As a result of this, some Muslim converts (especially White converts) may be viewed with suspicion by Muslim communities who fear FBI infiltration post 9/11 or be viewed as not truly Muslim by non-Muslims who associate Islam with the Middle East or South Asia. Due to these challenges to their Muslim identity from both sides, white Muslim converts, in particular, might experience more distress as they try to establish legitimacy by adopting cultural norms that have nothing to do with Islam, such as food, style of dress, or other outward features that add to their "Muslimness."

Similarly, research suggests that Black American converts face issues acculturating into immigrant Muslim communities in the United States. In addition to challenges to their authenticity as Muslims, Black converts may face racial prejudice and discrimination within immigrant communities (Casey, 2022). Mosques in the United States, especially in communities where multiple mosques exist, tend to be segregated on racial and linguistic lines. Interracial marriages continue to be rare in the Muslim community, especially between Black Muslims and Muslims of other racial/ethnic backgrounds (Laird-Jackson, 2010; Grewal, 2009). Much of this is rooted in deep-seated racism and colorism found in colonized Muslim countries that have transferred to immigrant populations originating from those countries. Racial prejudice and the division of Muslim communities along racial, ethnic, and linguistic lines can cause further acculturative stress from Black Muslim converts, adding a layer to stress that may already exist from general racial discrimination faced in America. Black Muslim converts who feel they are looked down upon experience greater mental health concerns (Lateef & Umarji, 2022)

Literature associating conversion with radicalization

In addition to other challenges of being a convert in the US, there is the question of radicalization. Some literature suggests that conversion to Islam is associated with greater tendencies toward radicalization, including outright terrorism (van den Elzen, 2018). Unfortunately, much of this research is suspect, given that the Defense Department funds it, and initiatives like Countering Violent Extremism raise fundamental questions about the clarity of their research (Mohr, 2019). On the one hand, research exists that could potentially identify an outlying effect of conversion. On the other hand, the presence of this research shows the impact of government surveillance and the personal impact of the political situation in the US with the long-standing aggression towards Muslims and Islam generally. As a result, many mainstream cultural groups in US society are suspicious of people who have chosen to become Muslim, associating the change with an acceptance of terrorism and violence, "assuming converts are uniformly excitable and dogmatic" (Snook, Branum-Martin & Horgan, 2022, p. 633). This assumption involves accepting conventional wisdom that questions the validity of converts spiritual convictions. It also erases the element of personal politics and the relevance of conversion as an act that includes an element of conscious resistance to racism, colonialism, and state-sponsored violence by the US government and other Western nations (Mohr, 2024).

The research on the dangers of radicalization related to conversion states that converts are more likely to be terrorists than Muslims born into the faith, citing a variety of statistics, including that while converts are 20% of the Muslim population in the US, they make up 40% of the ISIS-related cases in the US (Fodeman, Snook, & Horgan, 2022). Fodeman, Snook, & Horgan (2022) state, "Since the turn of the 21st century, Western converts to Islam have been involved in terrorism at a disproportionately high rate relative to those born into the faith overall" (p. 3). However, other research, also funded by the Department of Defense, indicates that religious zeal among converts is less pronounced than it is among people born into Islam. Thus, conversion is not an indicator of tendencies toward religious or politically justified violence (Snook, Branum-Martin, & Horgan, 2022).

Some research suggests that converts are highly motivated to disprove stereotypes about Islam. One participant in a study that drew from qualitative interviews with six Muslim converts in Europe described wanting to fight stereotypes (Younis & Hassan, 2017). In another article based on case studies of three women Muslim converts, negative stereotypes of Islam, including terrorism, contributed to a greater desire to be good citizens and represent the best face of the religion to non-Muslims, including fighting stereotypes of Muslims as violent or terrorists (Mohr, 2024).

Mental Health Diagnoses Associated with Conversion

There are a number of mental health diagnoses that can directly be related to the stress of undergoing a conversion experience. Even though many converts will describe their conversion as a positive experience, as noted throughout this chapter, conversion can cause strain on personal relationships, lead to radical changes in a person's belief system and behaviors, and require adjustment. It is not surprising, therefore, that some converts may meet the criteria for diagnosis of adjustment disorder. Adjustment disorders triggered by the stress of conversion can lead to increased anxiety, depression, and interruptions in daily functioning. Developing adequate coping mechanisms and support systems and addressing negative thoughts are important steps to prevent an adjustment disorder from becoming a clinical depression or a long-term anxiety disorder.

The clinical category that was first introduced in the DSM-IV was the category of religious or spiritual problems (Lukoff, Lu, & Turner, 1992) in recognition of the frequent pathologizing of genuine spiritual experiences by clinicians, including diagnosis of psychosis. Religious or spiritual problems encompass a wide range of experiences and are designed to help a clinician understand the context in which symptoms may emerge. Spiritual emergence or a spiritual emergency is an experience of spiritual awakening that is traumatizing for the individual (Grof & Grof, 2017). Additionally, we see religious or spiritual imagery that may be prevalent in the descriptions of mental health crises for deeply religious and spiritual individuals. In some cases, this imagery is part of a real psychopathology, such as psychosis. In other cases, the individual attempts to come to terms with personal trauma or challenges. Through the process of assessment, it is important to distinguish between these and not lump all mention of visions or conversations with a higher being as a sign of psychosis. Belief in jinn possession, evil eye, and black magic are also common within Muslim worldviews as causation for some mental health disorders. Discussion of psycho-spiritual causation of distress, including the will of God or illness as a test or punishment from God, should also not be dismissed or ignored by helping professionals within the therapeutic setting as the way a client views their condition is important in the healing process.

Recent research has documented the phenomenon of spiritual bypassing, where individuals use spiritual practices to avoid dealing with past or present emotional issues. Sometimes described as a defense mechanism, religion or spirituality may be used by an individual to compensate for low self-esteem, isolation, or other perceived insecurities or to avoid dealing with unresolved traumas such as child abuse or relationship issues. This can become an unhealthy form of religious or spiritual coping as the individual relies heavily on a spiritual explanation for life's difficulties, making little to no effort to address their issues and typically avoiding help-seeking (Ahmad, McLaughlin & Weisman de Mamani, 2023). Few studies have sought to examine spiritual bypassing in the Muslim community thus far. Ahmad and colleagues (2023) found that individuals scoring high in spiritual bypass also had higher levels of negative religious and spiritual coping and higher on average levels of depression, anxiety, and stress. They concluded that using spirituality to explain or avoid life difficulties may have a negative impact on the mental health of Muslims and have a significant impact on the use of religious coping as well as Islamically integrated psychotherapy with Muslim clients. A much larger body of work examines the use of religious coping within the Muslim population, suggesting that positive religious coping can be beneficial when dealing with stress and life challenges. Clinicians, therefore, may need to distinguish between religious bypassing and positive religious coping among religious clients and encourage the use of positive religious coping if appropriate.

Mental Health Interventions to Support Reverts/Converts

Developing a Support Network

One of the most important parts of successfully converting to Islam is consistent with the essential element of the successful practice of any religion: community support. It is often commented on by converts that they have insufficient support once they enter the faith. As noted above, one ongoing issue for converts is the difficulty of acculturative stress; where while they have accepted the religion, and this can be learned, much of the Muslim community at large is steeped in traditional cultural practices that are much harder to learn and make a part of personal habit, practice, and life. Increasingly, the Muslim community is addressing this issue through formal support groups and organizations; Ta'leef Collective's work with "Newcomers," Khalil Center's convert groups, and countless other small initiatives at the level of local masjids provide some network for people seeking to learn and grow in Islam.

Individual Counseling

Two new developments that can be beneficial to Muslim converts are the increase in religious and spiritual competency training for counselors and psychologists and the increase in Muslims entering the field of clinical psychology, often engaging in Islamically integrated psychotherapy. The American Psychological Association recommends that all psychologists possess sixteen outlined religious and spiritual competencies within the three domains of attitudes, knowledge, and skills (Vieten & Lukoff, 2021; Vieten et al., 2013). These competencies emerge from the recognition that many Americans consider religion important in their lives, which was not previously acknowledged in the training received by counselors and psychologists. Some of these competencies broadly address religion and spirituality, and others may require learning about specific religious or spiritual views and practices of clients. Recent work has begun integrating and assessing religious and spiritual competencies in formal training (Pearce, Pargament, Oxhandler, Vieten, & Wong, 2019; Hull, Suarez & Hartman, 2016). Several RS competency training programs now incorporate Islamic religious and spiritual competencies, including training for graduate students to prepare them for working with diverse clients. This training is important as Muslim Americans often underutilize available mental health services due to stigma and fear of bias or being misunderstood by a counselor or psychologist because of their beliefs (Mclaughlin et al., 2022; Moscovitz, Bedi & Outadi, 2023; Winklejohn, Drinane & Akef, 2023). As noted in previous literature (Raiya & Pargament, 2010; Bagasra & Mackinem, 2020), asking a client about the role of religion in their life is an important first step in the initial client interview (now part of competency 12). For converts, it may be important to ask for further details such as years since conversion, self-rated level of religiosity, and any conflicts that have directly arisen that may be tied to their conversion. If the client is religious and has no complex trauma or conflicts that have arisen from their conversion, the therapist can consider incorporating forms of religious coping. All of this, of course, requires the therapist or psychologist to confront their attitudes towards Islam and Muslims first, assess their own biases, and try to obtain basic knowledge about religious beliefs and practices (part of competencies 3-9).

The second significant development is incorporating the Islamic worldview into various forms of therapy, including psychotherapy and cognitive behavior therapy (CBT) (Munawar, Ravi, Jones & Choudhry, 2023). Many highly religious Muslims view mental illness through the lens of religion (Bagasra & Mackinem, 2014). They are more likely to view a mental health issue or diagnosis as psycho-spiritual. Specifically, they may interpret their distress as a result of disobedience to their Creator, the will of God, or a test from God (Bagasra, 2023). The development, testing, and validation of such integrative therapies provide Muslims with religiously congruent options for mental health treatment, which in turn can decrease stigma toward mental health services and increase service utilization (Rothman & Coyle, 2023; Khan et al., 2023; York Al-Karam, 2018). Converts who are religious may be more interested in trying Islamically integrated interventions that reflect their worldview and believe they will experience less bias from a practitioner who incorporates spiritual or religious elements into their practice.

Spiritual Wellness Tools for Reverts/Converts

There are several primary considerations for mental health support for Muslim converts that include the personal stresses of conversion, challenging family dynamics, social challenges both within and outside of the Muslim community, and political ramifications of conversion to a religion that is associated with racialized discrimination nationally and globally. Additionally, the importance of overcoming any internalized Islamophobia presents itself for converts, as some converts come to the religion following periods of organized persecution of Muslims and have a need to deconstruct and dismantle complicated systems of belief and being that contradict their new faith.

The personal stresses of conversion include the challenges with behavior changes and internal belief systems that can have far-reaching effects on individual identity and day-to-day life experiences. These stresses have been experienced as improving through support groups. However, at least in grey literature, most converts state the importance of dedication to personal spiritual practice as the antidote for these types of challenges. Maintaining a consistent spiritual practice and patiently practicing the religion, and considering the original reasons for conversion, can be sufficient to carry converts through the challenges of being Muslim. In many cases, therapeutic support for personal stress in conversion involves simply providing sufficient room to process and integrate the experience of being a Muslim and the challenges it entails, as with other difficult emotions. In this case, solution-focused narrative therapy, narrative approaches generally, motivational interviewing, and other forms of self-exploration, motivational approaches, and therapeutic support can be helpful and beneficial (Karami, Khodabakhshi-Koolaee, Heidari, & Davoodi, 2023). Some research suggests Mindfulness-Based Stress Reduction can alleviate painful emotions (Karami, Khodabakhshi-Koolaee, Heidari, & Davoodi, 2023) and support mindfulness's usefulness generally for accepting and processing change (Baer, 2010). How to truly incorporate Islamic mindfulness practices into therapeutic support for converts remains undeveloped, mainly in English literature.

In the case of challenging family dynamics, more relational approaches may be more suitable. Couples or family therapy can help maintain open communication, resolve differences, improve understanding, and create positive dynamics where cultural or religious differences have created strain.

Social challenges both within and outside of the Muslim community, like challenging family dynamics, can be addressed through therapy. One of the recent developments that has become prevalent in the

Muslim mental health community has been the use of Healing Circles. This approach gathers Muslims with similar challenges and combines didactic and Q&A to facilitate group healing. This approach draws heavily on the fact that many Muslims view the individualism of Western European psychological approaches with skepticism and feel more connected to a collectivistic worldview (Mohr, Shaiq, & Berte, 2020). Additionally, support groups such as those mentioned above are excellent resources for concerts who often feel isolated and disoriented as new Muslims or even after practicing for quite some time.

The political ramifications of conversion to a religion that is associated with racialized discrimination nationally and globally also impact the overall wellness of converts, just as it impacts the overall wellness of the entire Muslim community. Again, organizations like the International Students of Islamic Psychology (ISIP), Maristan, and the Khalil Center frequently offer online or in-person meetings where a group of like-minded people with similar stressors come together in a group therapy-like setting to heal and offer each other support and fellowship. For individual converts who intensely feel the stress of political and social events, therapy, self-care, and continued spiritual connectedness and focus remain core tools for consistency in faith, wellness, and spiritual practice.

Conclusion

In this chapter, the co-authors offer insights into the community of converts to Islam in the United States. Many of these challenges are unique to converts, while others are challenges faced by people born Muslim. Many resources exist for mental health counseling for the Muslim community. For those clinicians who are not Muslim, one of the most important steps to being able to provide competent care for Muslim clients is to familiarize oneself with Islam (Ahmed & Amer, 2012), the Muslim community, and mental health services for converts, to read and better understand the unique strengths and challenges for people converting to Islam.

References

Ahmad, S. S., McLaughlin, M. M., & Weisman de Mamani, A. (2023). Spiritual bypass as a moderator of the relationships between religious coping and psychological distress in Muslims living in the United States. *Psychology of Religion and Spirituality, 15*(1), 32–42. https://doi.org/10.1037/rel0000469

Ahmad, S. S., McLaughlin, M. M., & Weisman de Mamani, A. (2023). Validation and test-retest reliability of the Spiritual Bypass Scale in Muslims and implications for psychological help-seeking attitudes and self-stigma. *Spirituality in Clinical Practice, 10*(1), 62–73. https://doi.org/10.1037/scp0000300

Ahmed, S. & Amer, M. (2012). *Counseling Muslims: Handbook of mental health issues and interventions*. New York: Brunner-Routledge.

Alimahomed-Wilson, S. (2017). Invisible Violence: Gender, Islamophobia, and the Hidden Assault on US Muslim Women. W*omen, Gender & Families of Color, 5*(1), 73–97. https://doi.org/10.5406/womgenfamcol.5.1.0073

Baba, H. (2017). Muslim converts wrestle with isolation and seek support. *Crosscurrents,* KALW News. https://www.kalw.org/show/crosscurrents/2017-05-08/muslim-converts-wrestle-with-isolation-seek-support

Baer, R. A. (2010). *Assessing mindfulness & acceptance processes in clients: illuminating the theory & practice of change*. Context Press.

Bagasra, A. (2023). Religious interpretations of mental illness and help-seeking experiences among Muslim Americans: Implications for clinical practice. *Spirituality in Clinical Practice, 10*(1), 20–31. https://doi.org/10.1037/scp0000299

Bagasra, A. & Mackinem, M. (2020). *Working With Muslim Clients in the Helping Professions*. Hershey, PA: IGI Global. doi:10.4018/978-1-7998-0018-7

Bagasra, A. and Mackinem, M. (2014). An exploratory study of American Muslim Conceptions of Mental Illness, *Journal of Muslim Mental Health, 8*(1), 57-76.

Barro, R., Hwang, J., & McCleary, R. (2010). Religious Conversion in 40 Countries. *Journal for the Scientific Study of Religion, 49*(1), 15–36. https://doi.org/10.1111/j.1468-5906.2009.01490.x

Behnaz Karami, A. K., Heidari, H., & Davoodi, H. (2023). The Effectiveness of Solution-focused Narrative Therapy and Mindfulness-based Stress Reduction on the Level of Expressed Emotion in Mothers of Boys With Gross Motor Disabilities. *Journal of Client-Centered Nursing Care (Online), 9*(4), 243–254. https://doi.org/10.32598/jccnc.9.4.33.21

Beider, N. (2022). Motivations and Types of Religious Change in Contemporary America. *Review of Religious Research*, https://doi.org/10.1007/s13644-022-00507-z

Casey, P. M. (2022). "They Don't Look at You as a Real Muslim": the racial exclusion of black American Muslim converts. *Muslim World, 112*(4), 404–421. https://doi.org/10.1111/muwo.12448

Casey, P. M. (2021). White Duality: The (dis)Advantage of Being a White Convert in the Muslim American Community. *Journal of Muslim Minority Affairs, 41*(4), 615–626. https://doi.org/10.1080/13602004.2022.2032902

Coffee, R. C., Brimhall, A. S., & Smith, M. (2021). Choosing between my Partner and My God: A Tentative Theory Exploring How Married Couples Navigate Relational-Religious Loyalties after Conversion. *Journal of Couple & Relationship Therapy, 20*(1), 50–75. https://doi.org/10.1080/15332691.2020.1757544

Collins, P. H. (2019). *Intersectionality as Critical Social Theory*. Durham, N.C.: Duke University Press.

Council on American Islamic Relations (CAIR). (2024). Protecting the rights of incarcerated Muslims. CAIR. https://ca.cair.com/ramadan/incarcerated-muslims-los-angeles/

Crenshaw, K. W. (1991). Mapping the Margins: Intersectionality, Identity Politics, and Violence against Women of Color. *Stanford Law Review, 43*(6): 1241–1299. Accessed February 11, 2023. https://doi.org/10.2307/1229039

Delgado, R, & Stefancic, J. (2017). *Critical Race Theory: An Introduction*. New York: New York University Press.

Elmali-Karakaya, A. (2022). Interfaith Marriage in Islam: Classical Islamic Resources and Contemporary Debates on Muslim Women's Interfaith Marriages †. *Religions, 13*(8), 726. https://doi.org/10.3390/rel13080726

Foucault, M. (1980). POWER/KNOWLEDGE Selected Interviews and Other Writings 1972 -1977. Ed, Gordon, Colin. Trans. Gordon, Colin, Marshall, Leo, Mepham, John, and Soper, Kate. New York: Pantheon Books. (Originally published in 1972).

Fodeman, A. D., Snook, D. W., & Horgan, J. G. (2020). Picking Up and Defending the Faith: Activism and Radicalism Among Muslim Converts in the United States. *Political Psychology, 41*(4), 679–698. https://doi.org/10.2307/45295270

Fodeman, A. D., Snook, D. W., & Horgan, J. G. (2022). Pressure to prove: Muslim converts' activism and radicalism mediated by religious struggle and punishing Allah reappraisal. *Behavioral Sciences of Terrorism and Political Aggression, 14*(1), 49–69. https://doi.org/10.1080/19434472.2020.1800788

Greenwald, Y., Mikulincer, M., Granqvist, P., & Shaver, P. R. (2021). Apostasy and conversion: Attachment orientations and individual differences in the process of religious change. *Psychology of Religion and Spirituality, 13*(4), 425–436. https://doi.org/10.1037/rel0000239

Grewal, Z. (2009). Marriage in colour: race, religion and spouse selection in four American mosques. *Ethnic & Racial Studies, 32*(2), 323–345. https://doi.org/10.1080/01419870801961490

Grof, C., & Grof, S. (2017). Spiritual emergency: The understanding and treatment of transpersonal crises. International Journal of Transpersonal Studies, 36 (2). https://doi.org/10.24972/ijts.2017.36.2.30

Halama, P. (2015). Empirical Approach to Typology of Religious Conversion. *Pastoral Psychology, 64*(2), 185–194. https://doi.org/10.1007/s11089-013-0592-y

Harder, E. (2015). A Muslim's Non-Conversion Story. *Journal of Mennonite Studies, 33*, 167–173.

Hassan, M. (2018). In The Age of Islamophobia, Why Reverts Are Leaving Islam. *Muslim Matters*. https://muslimmatters.org/2018/01/10/in-the-age-of-islamophobia-why-reverts-are-leaving-islam/

Hood, R. W., Jr., Spilka, B., Hunsberger, B., & Gorsuch, R. (1996). *The psychology of religion: An empirical approach* (2nd ed.). Guilford Press.

Hull, C. E., Suarez, E. C., & Hartman, D. (2016). Developing spiritual competencies in counseling: A guide for supervisors. *Counseling and Values, 61*(1), 111–126. https://doi.org/10.1002/cvj.12029

Institute for Social Policy and Understanding (ISPU) (2020). *American Muslim Poll 2020: Full Report*. https://ispu.org/american-muslim-poll-2020-full-report/

Iqbal, N., Radulescu, A., Bains, A., & Aleem, S. (2019). An Interpretative Phenomenological Analysis of a Religious Conversion. *Journal of Religion & Health, 58*(2), 426–443. https://doi.org/10.1007/s10943-017-0463-4

James, W. (1902). *Varieties of religious experience*. New York: Longmans. (Mentor ed., 1958).

Kahn, P. J., & Greene, A. L. (2004). "Seeing Conversion Whole": Testing a Model of Religious Conversion. *Pastoral Psychology, 52*(3), 233–258.

Karami, B., Khodabakhshi-Koolaee, A., Heidari, H., Davoodi H. (2023). The Effectiveness of Solution-focused Narrative Therapy and Mindfulness-based Stress Reduction on the Level of Expressed Emotion in Mothers of Boys with Gross Motor Disabilities. *Journal of Client Centered Nursing Care 9* (4) :243-254 http://jccnc.iums.ac.ir/article-1-468-en.html

Khan, F., Keshavarzi, H., Ahmad, M., Ashai, S., & Sanders, P. (2023). Application of Traditional Islamically Integrated Psychotherapy (TIIP) and its clinical outcome on psychological distress among American Muslims in outpatient therapy. *Spirituality in Clinical Practice*. https://doi.org/10.1037/scp0000350

Kilbourne, R., & Richardson, J. T. (1989). Paradigm Conflict, Types of Conversion, and Conversion Theories. *SA: Sociological Analysis, 50*(1), 1–21. https://doi.org/10.2307/3710915

Kirkpatrick, L. A. (1997). A longitudinal study of changes in religious belief and behavior as a function of individual differences in adult attachment style. *Journal for the Scientific Study of Religion, 36*(2), 207–217.

Kirkpatrick, L. A. (1998). God as a substitute attachment figure: A longitudinal study of adult attachment style and religious change in college students. *Personality and Social Psychology Bulletin, 24*(9), 961–973.

Kose, A., & Loewenthal, K. M. (2000). Conversion Motifs Among British Converts to Islam. *International Journal for the Psychology of Religion, 10*(2), 101–110. https://doi.org/10.1207/S15327582IJPR1002_03

Laird-Jackson, H. (2010). Color Blind. Azizah, 6(2), 38–41.
Lateef, H., & Umarji, O. (2022). Black American Muslims: a study of religious identity and mental health. *Mental Health, Religion & Culture, 25*(8), 802–816. https://doi.org/10.1080/13674676.2022.2116632
Lukoff, D., Lu, F., & Turner, R. (1992). Toward a more culturally sensitive DSM-IV. *Psychoreligious and psychospiritual problems.* The Journal of nervous and mental disease, 180(11), 673–682. https://doi.org/10.1097/00005053-199211000-00001
McLaughlin, M. M., Ahmad, S. S., & Weisman de Mamani, A. (2022). A mixed-methods approach to psychological help-seeking in Muslims: Islamophobia, self-stigma, and therapeutic preferences. *Journal of Consulting and Clinical Psychology, 90*(7), 568–581. https://doi.org/10.1037/ccp0000746
McLaughlin, M., Ahmad, S. S., Rodriguez, M., & Weisman de Mamani, A. (2022). Vulnerable—Not zealous: Muslim converts experience greater distress when experiencing religious struggle. *Professional Psychology: Research and Practice, 53*(4), 340–350. https://doi.org/10.1037/pro0000473
Mir, A. (2003). Chapter 4: Immigrants, Converts, and Communities. American Encounter with Islam, 14–19.
Mirza, M. (2017). Interfaith Marriages: Do Muslims realize that interfaith unions could be an existential threat to their community? *Islamic Horizons, 46*(3), 34–36.
Mohammed, B. & Sciupac, E.P. (2018). The share of Americans who leave Islam is offset by those who become Muslim. *Pew Research.* https://www.pewresearch.org/short-reads/2018/01/26/the-share-of-americans-who-leave-islam-is-offset-by-those-who-become-muslim/
Mohr, S. (In press, anticipated 2024). Islamophobia and Conversion: The Role Anti-Racism Plays in White Converts' Experience of Islam Post 9-11. *Islamophobia Studies Journal.*
Mohr, S., Shaiq, S. & Berte, D. (2020). Directive vs. non-directive clinical approaches:
Liberation psychology and Muslim mental health. *Journal of Islamic Faith and Practice. 3* (1), 31-58. https://doi.org/10.18060/24667
Mohr, S. H. (2019). Liberation Psychology from an Islamic Perspective: Some Theoretical and Practical Implications of Psychology with a *Telos* of Justice. *Journal of Religion & Society, 21.*
Moscovitz, A. M., Bedi, R. P., & Outadi, A. (2023). Examination of Perceived Religion in Muslim Women's access to counseling and psychotherapy services: An audit study. *Journal of Counseling Psychology, 70*(1), 30–40. https://doi.org/10.1037/cou0000644
Munawar, K., Ravi, T., Jones, D., & Choudhry, F. R. (2023). Islamically modified cognitive behavioral therapy for Muslims with mental illness: A systematic review. *Spirituality in Clinical Practice.* https://doi.org/10.1037/scp0000338
Paloutzian, R. F. (1981). Purpose in life and value changes following conversion. *Journal of Personality and Social Psychology, 41*, 1153–1160.

Paloutzian, R. F., Richardson, J. T., & Rambo, L. R. (1999). Religious Conversion and Personality Change. *Journal of Personality, 67*(6), 1047–1079. https://doi.org/10.1111/1467-6494.00082

Pearce, M. J., Pargament, K. I., Oxhandler, H. K., Vieten, C., & Wong, S. (2019). A novel training program for mental health providers in religious and spiritual competencies. *Spirituality in Clinical Practice, 6*(2), 73–82. https://doi.org/10.1037/scp0000195

Pew Research. (2011). Muslim Americans: No signs of growth in alienation of support for extremism. *Pew Research.* https://www.pewresearch.org/politics/2011/08/30/section-2-religious-beliefs-and-practices/

Pew Research. (2017). US Muslims Concerned About Their Place in Society but Continue to Believe in the American Dream. *Pew Research.* https://www.pewresearch.org/dataset/2017-survey-of-u-s-muslims/

Pew Research (2018). *Muslims in America: Immigrants and those born in U.S. see life differently in many ways.* https://www.pewresearch.org/religion/2018/04/14/muslims-in-america-immigrants-and-those-born-in-u-s-see-life-differently-in-many-ways/

Rao, A. H. (2015). Gender and Cultivating the Moral Self in Islam: Muslim Converts in an American Mosque. *Sociology of Religion, 76*(4), 413–435.

Raiya, H. A., & Pargament, K. I. (2010). Religiously integrated psychotherapy with Muslim clients: from research to practice. Professional Psychology, Research and Practice, 41(2), 181.

Rothman, A., & Coyle, A. (2023). The clinical scope of Islamic psychotherapy: A grounded theory study. *Spirituality in Clinical Practice, 10*(1), 4–19. https://doi.org/10.1037/scp0000282

Sintang, S., & Hambali, K. M. (2018). Double Marginality in New Muslims' Relationship With Born Muslims and Non-Muslims. *International Journal of Humanities, Arts & Social Sciences, 4*(3), 150–159. https://doi.org/10.20469/ijhss.4.10004-3

Snook, D. W., Branum-Martin, L., & Horgan, J. G. (2022). Zeal of the convert? Comparing religiousness between convert and nonconvert Muslims. *Psychology of Religion and Spirituality, 14*(4), 630–634. https://doi.org/10.1037/rel0000421

Snook, D. W., Kleinmann, S. M., White, G., & Horgan, J. G. (2021). Conversion motifs among Muslim converts in the United States. *Psychology of Religion and Spirituality, 13*(4), 482–492. https://doi.org/10.1037/rel0000276

Spalek, B., & El-Hassan, S. (2007). Muslim Converts in Prison. *Howard Journal of Criminal Justice, 46*(Issue 2), 99–114.

van den Elzen, J. (2018). Radicalisation: A Subtype of Religious Conversion? Perspectives on Terrorism, 12(1), 69–80. https://www.jstor.org/stable/26343747

Vieten, C., & Lukoff, D. (2021). Spiritual and religious competencies in psychology. *American Psychologist.* https://doi.org/10.1037/amp0000821

Vieten, C., Scammell, S., Pilato, R., Ammondson, I., Pargament, K. I., & Lukoff, D. (2013). Spiritual and religious competencies for psychologists. *Psychology of Religion and Spirituality,* 5(3), 129–144. https://doi.org/10.1037/a0032699

Weiler, H N. (2006). *Challenging the Orthodoxies of Knowledge: Epistemological, Structural and Political Implications for Higher Education.* In *Knowledge, Power, and Dissent: Critical Perspectives on Higher Education and Research in Knowledge Society,* edited by Guy Neave, 61–87. Paris: UNESCO Publishing.

Winkeljohn Black, S., Drinane, J. M., & Akef, Z. (2023). Detecting microaggressions toward a

Muslim client in psychotherapy. *Professional Psychology: Research and Practice,* 54(6), 461–469. https://doi.org/10.1037/pro0000528

York Al-Karam, C. (2018). *Islamically Integrated Psychotherapy: Uniting Faith and Professional Practice.* Templeton Press.

Younis, T., & Hassan, G. (2017). Changing Identities: A Case Study of Western Muslim Converts Whose Conversion Revised Their Relationship to Their National Identity. *Journal of Muslim Minority Affairs,* 37(1), 30–40. https://doi.org/10.1080/13602004.2017.1294377

Zinnbauer, B. J., & Pargament, K. I. (1998). Spiritual conversion: A study of religious change among college students. *Journal for the Scientific Study of Religion 37* (1), 161–180.

CHAPTER TEN

INCARCERATED MUSLIMS' MENTAL HEALTH IN NORTH AMERICA

*Ibrahim Y. Z. Mohammad, Jennah Shagan,
Rami Nsour, Rania Awaad*

This chapter explores the mental health experiences and needs of incarcerated Muslims in North America. Although there are clear gaps in research in this area, the authors discuss a number of important systemic and sociocultural factors that impact their mental health. They also highlight a number of important considerations in attempting to address the significant mental health challenges faced by this vulnerable population group. After exploring clinical implications, with an emphasis on cultural and contextual sensitivity, the chapter closes with recommendations and examples of existing successful programs that support Muslims through their incarceration and reentry.

Introduction

Mass incarceration in the USA began in the 1970s as a result of President Richard Nixon's famed "War on Drugs," which continued through the presidencies of Ronald Reagan, George H. W. Bush, and Bill Clinton (Cummings, 2012). Since then, America has consistently ranked among the top countries in the world in population imprisonment rates, with significant racial disparities (Lurigio, 2024; Enders et al., 2019). While America's northern neighbor did not incarcerate people at the same rate, Canadian prisons showed similar racial disparities, with Black and Indigenous individuals especially overrepresented (Robinson et al., 2023; Owusu-Bempah et al., 2023).

The resulting prison-industrial complex has led to direct benefits to government and private sector profits at the expense of the freedom and health of incarcerated individuals (Klein & Lima, 2021). From a mental healthcare perspective, the corrections population is one of the most vulnerable. Indeed, it is well-documented that incarceration correlates bidirectionally with mental illness, with effects that persist even after their return to the community (Beckett & Goldberg, 2022; Fitch et al., 2024; Favril et al., 2024). Muslims are overrepresented in US state prisons, comprising approximately 9% of state prisoners despite only making up 1% of the US population (Muslim Advocates, 2019). Yet, little exists in the literature on the mental health of incarcerated Muslims. What challenges do they uniquely face? What are their mental health needs? How can we improve their mental health outcomes?

This chapter is an effort to bridge this gap. This work is of timely importance, given that Islam is likely the fastest-growing religion in US prisons (SpearIt, 2014; Pew Research Center, 2012). While the primary focus will be on those currently incarcerated, we aim to explore the lasting impacts of incarceration more broadly. As such, there will also be discussions on formerly incarcerated Muslims in North America. Further, as research in this particular subpopulation is highly limited, we will often draw from studies focusing more broadly on incarcerated individuals. We will then draw parallels that allow us to better understand the experiences of Muslims behind bars in North America. This chapter is of marked relevance to anyone who works with the prison population, namely prison employees, volunteers, mental health workers, educators, chaplains, faith leaders, as well as those who work in the field of Muslim mental health.

Our chapter will begin with a couple of real-life case studies, followed by a brief overview of Muslims in US and Canadian prisons, with some commentary on the difficulty of obtaining accurate data on this population. Next, we will explore mental health in the carceral setting and significant contributors to mental illness therein, especially as it pertains to the Muslim subpopulation. This will be followed by an overview of institutional and societal barriers to care for incarcerated and formerly incarcerated Muslims. Finally, we will highlight existing, successful interventions, with further recommendations for supporting this population. As you will read in our conclusion, this chapter is an early effort at combating the health inequities faced by incarcerated Muslims, and more work—especially in the area of policy—is needed to serve this vulnerable group adequately.

Case Examples

Before we delve into the unique challenges faced by incarcerated Muslims in North America, it is worth acknowledging the immense stigma faced by this group. As you read this, you may have already identified some feelings towards incarcerated people. It is not uncommon for our minds to immediately categorize them as "criminals" long before thinking of them as "vulnerable." As you will read in our chapter, mental illness is highly prevalent in the prison system, and many incarcerated individuals get arrested *because of* mental illness. One study by Hall et al. (2019) found that a prior diagnosis of major mental illness was associated with a more than 50% increase in the risk of getting arrested for misdemeanors. Although the forensic mental health system is meant to identify those deemed not criminally responsible because of mental disorders, evidence suggests they are rarely diverted by the justice system, with many ending up incarcerated regardless (Ramsay et al., 2011).

Hence, we wish to explore two key case studies that exemplify the lived reality of incarcerated Muslims in North America. These examples will help contextualize and underscore the importance of addressing the issue of incarcerated Muslim mental health.

Case 1 – Kamau, Michigan, USA

Kamau is a 56-year-old Muslim, Black American man currently incarcerated and facing life in prison. His story was shared through the American Prison Writing Archive, where he wrote a detailed account of his experiences with posttraumatic stress disorder (PTSD). In his writings, he described growing up in Detroit, surrounded by violence, eventually being absorbed into it. This led to him serving a 17-year-long federal sentence, where he spent much of his time in solitary confinement. In 2009, he was released with "$200.00, a box containing my life in prison, the clothes on my back, and PTSD!" While he tried to get his life back on track, even attending college classes, he was battling significant mental health issues daily. He described significant insomnia, anxiety, nightmares, and panic attacks, to the extent that he would try to cope by exercising for hours on end every day to exhaust himself into sleep. Although he started to address his mental health by working with a therapist, she left that position shortly thereafter, and he was "back out into the wild."

As his mental health deteriorated, he developed significant paranoia and flashbacks. During one flashback, he assaulted a woman, erroneously believing he was attacking someone else from his memories. He was sentenced to 45 years in jail after this incident. At the end of his letter, Kamau, which is his pen name, states that he prays daily for a death, "not as in some form of suicide [...] more so... the thoughts of a better, just place awaiting one (i.e., Paradise or Heaven) is all that soothes my aching spirit." He hopes his writings will touch others, perhaps "a relative of someone who has experienced similar psychological breakdowns" (Kamau, 2018).

Case 2 – Soleiman Faqiri, Ontario, Canada

Soleiman "Soli" Faqiri was an Afghan-Canadian man who grew up in Whitby, Ontario, after coming to Canada with his family as refugees. Despite being the youngest of his siblings, he was often called the "star" of the family, with significant athletic and academic success. After a car accident in his early adult years, he was diagnosed with schizophrenia. Though this posed its own challenges, he continued to work toward self-improvement. Soli's faith was a particularly important coping mechanism for him. He taught himself how to read Arabic, memorized the Qur'an, taught his mother the Arabic language, and taught his older brother, Yusuf, how to pray.

On Dec. 4, 2016, Soli experienced a mental health crisis, leading to an altercation with a neighbor. The latter then called the police, leading to Soli's arrest. Eleven days later, on Dec. 15, 2016, Soli died after a violent confrontation with a group of correctional officers at the Central East Correctional Centre in Lindsay, Ontario. While an initial coroner's report deemed the 30-year-old's cause of death as "unascertained," after much advocacy by his family—through the Justice for Soli campaign—a coroner's inquest ruled his death a homicide. Although this has provided the family with some relief, to this day, no charges have been laid in Soli's death.

Many more questions remain: Why was Soli taken to jail instead of a hospital? Why was he denied psychiatric care while imprisoned? Could his death have been prevented if he had received the care he needed? These questions continue to haunt the family (Syed, 2017; Paradkar, 2019; Saint-Julien, 2022; Habibinia, 2023).

Demographics of Incarcerated Muslims in North America

There are over 1.2 million incarcerated individuals in US prisons (Carson & Kluckow, 2023) and just over 35,000 in Canada (Statistics Canada, 2024a; 2024b). In 2022, of the 20,807 inmates detained in Correctional Service of Canada facilities, 1,627 (8%) identified as Muslim (Public Safety Canada, 2024), despite Muslims comprising just under 5% of Canada's general population (Statistics Canada, 2022). In the US, however, it is difficult to know exactly how many of those incarcerated are Muslim. Religious affiliation is not collected as part of mandatory censuses by the US Census Bureau, including those performed in prisons, as Congress passed an Act in the 1970s preventing them from doing so (Public Law 94-521, 1976). Further, research in this population is highly regulated and challenging to perform due to incarcerated individuals' status as a vulnerable group (Binswanger et al., 2019). People impacted by the criminal justice system are also often wary of researchers due to fears that information they share as part of a study may impact their eligibility for parole or release timelines (National Institute of Justice, 2012).

Nonetheless, there are a few estimates of the number of incarcerated Muslims in certain US carceral settings. The Federal Bureau of Prisons (BOP) Chaplaincy Services Branch estimated that of the over 150,000 prisoners in custody in 2003, about 9,000 (6%) were identified as Muslim (Office of the Inspector General, 2004). By 2020, of 118,330 federal inmates who accessed chaplaincy services, 11,073 (9.4%) identified as Muslim (Office of the Inspector General, 2021) – once again an overrepresentation relative to the general population, where only 1.1% of the US population identifies as Muslim (Pew Research Center, 2017). Further, anecdotally, co-author R.N. of this article has spoken with multiple Muslim prison chaplains in the US who feel that the estimates are lower than in reality. They posit that the numbers are generated by those who explicitly request religious services and, as such, do not include a substantial number of Muslims who do not seek services from the chaplaincy department.

One important source of a growing Muslim population in North American prisons, besides disproportionate incarceration rates, is conversion to Islam behind bars. While an oft-cited estimate claims that about 30,000–40,000 incarcerated individuals convert to Islam every year in US prisons (Ammar et al., 2004; SpearIt, 2013), this number originated in a 2001 article by Dr. Siraj Islam Mufti, where he does not cite the source of this figure (Mufti, 2006). However, he was a prison chaplain and likely had first-hand evidence of this phenomenon. Indeed,

Pew Research Center (2012) surveyed prison chaplains across the US on their views of religion and religious change in prison, and most chaplains believed that the proportion of Muslims was growing. Unfortunately, this growing population has unique mental health needs, which are often unaddressed.

Incarceration and Mental Health

Prevalence and Intersectionality

A relatively high percentage of inmates in North American prisons have a diagnosed mental illness. Although estimates vary, studies consistently show that inmates in the US and Canada have higher rates of serious mental illness relative to the general population, with upper estimates exceeding 70% when including substance use disorders (Prins, 2014; Cameron et al., 2021; Beaudette & Stewart, 2016). This prevalence remains quite high at over 40%, even when substance use and personality disorders are excluded (Maruschak et al., 2021; Beaudette & Stewart, 2016). Of the mental disorders, major depression and post-traumatic stress disorder (PTSD) are the most prevalent behind bars worldwide, including in North America (Favril et al., 2024; Prins, 2014). A recent study from Iowa found that almost half of all inmates were diagnosed with a mental disorder, and just under a third had a serious mental illness (Al-Rousan et al., 2017). Interestingly, this study also found that almost all mental illness diagnoses were first made during incarceration. Many have opined that the prison system is effectively America's "largest mental hospital" (Ford, 2015).

Muslims, including those incarcerated, are certainly not immune to mental illness. For previously mentioned reasons, data around their unique mental health experiences and needs are limited. It is helpful, then, to consider data around the mental health of incarcerated minorities more broadly, where the literature is less barren. Several studies have found racial disparities in mental illness identification in US jails, where White individuals report higher rates of mental illness than racialized people (Kaba et al., 2015; Plummer et al., 2023). At the surface level, this may be interpreted as incarcerated people of color having lower rates of mental illness. However, a key limitation of these studies is their reliance on self-report measures. The lower rate is thus partly explained by the racialized stigma associated with mental illness, where it is known that some racialized groups display less professional help-seeking behavior for any mental health concerns (Morrow et al., 2020; Plummer et al., 2023; Sheehan et al., 2018). The American Muslim subpopulation similarly reports a high level of mental health stigma, leading to decreased help-seeking behaviors, though it should be noted that this relationship is influenced by perceived Islamophobia (McLaughlin et al., 2022; Ciftci et al., 2012).

It is clear then, despite the dearth of literature, that incarcerated Muslims face significant mental health challenges. To better understand how this ended up being the case, and specifically for incarcerated Muslims, it is important to examine a number of structural factors. These include the prison structure itself, difficulty in practicing one's faith, and the role that incarceration plays in shaping one's self-identity. We will explore these in detail in the following sections.

Life in Prison

Imprisonment is an independent risk factor for both physical and mental illness (Ramsay et al., 2011). Intuitively, this is due to the immense stress under which incarcerated individuals are placed. For one, living conditions in North American prisons are notoriously poor, marked by overcrowding, inadequate sanitary conditions, and poor nutrition, all being direct contributors (Massoglia & Pridemore, 2015). Daily stressors also include antagonism by correctional officers, witnessing violence, and even being victims of violence, where death is a possibility behind bars. Indeed, studies have shown that incarcerated individuals are at higher risk of mortality both during and after incarceration, with the most common cause of mortality being cardiovascular disease (Spaulding et al., 2011; Daza et al., 2020). However, violent deaths can and do occur in prison, including against those with mental illness. Soleiman Faqiri, one of the case studies discussed earlier, is only one of at least 14 Canadian individuals with schizophrenia who died after a use of force incident while incarcerated between 2001–2023 (Bradley et al., 2023). The prison environment hence exposes incarcerated individuals to acute stress, which, over time, turns into chronic stress. This can directly contribute to worse mental health (Daza et al., 2020), as it is known that chronic stress plays a psychological and neurobiological role in the development of mental illness (Cohen, 2000; Ishikawa & Furuyashiki, 2022).

One of the most severe areas of mental health disparities in prison is the use of solitary confinement. While this practice has significant adverse psychological effects (Haney, 2018) and is considered a form of torture by many human rights organizations (Fuller, 2018), it remains in use in North American prisons (Western et al., 2021). Despite Canada outlawing solitary confinement just over 5 years ago (Bill C-83, 2019), it continues *de facto* under the name "structured intervention units" (Sprott & Doob, 2021). Individuals with serious mental illness face a stigma of dangerousness and, as a result, are much more likely to be placed in solitary confinement—and held there for more days—compared to those without mental illnesses (Simes et al., 2022; Dellazizzo et al., 2020). Of course, this then leads to even worse mental health – a dangerous cycle of criminalization of the mentally ill that continues beyond the act of incarceration itself. Incarcerated Muslims, in particular, have been discriminated against with the use of solitary confinement in American prisons (SpearIt, 2022). This has resulted in a number of successful lawsuits dating as early as the 1960s (*Cooper v. Pate*, 1964), though many incarcerated Muslims—especially those with mental illnesses—do not have the resources necessary to pursue litigation.

Another important factor to consider is the role of the prison's social climate as a contributor to psychopathology (Ross et al., 2008). Studies have previously described the prominence and normalization of violence between inmates as a maintainer of social hierarchy, leading to a highly tense and fearful atmosphere (Goomany & Dickinson, 2015). Whereas social connection and safety are important components of mental wellbeing, the prison social structure catalyzes mental illness instead. Naturally, this social structure differs somewhat from prison to prison, though it is rarely, if ever, conducive to positive mental health outcomes. This leads many incarcerated individuals to adopt a highly individualistic approach to survive this threat, though this perpetuates uncertainty by preventing the development of social bonds (McKendy & Ricciardelli, 2021). This is why Islam, through providing an avenue of "brotherhood" to connect with other inmates, may play an important role in promoting the mental wellbeing of incarcerated Muslims (SpearIt, 2012). Unfortunately, despite constitutional protections for religious freedom, Muslims often face significant barriers to fully practicing their faith in prison.

Religious Identity and Accommodations

Religiosity and spirituality, including Islam, can positively contribute to mental health (Plante & Sharma, 2001; Papaleontiou-Louca, 2021). In fact, religiosity can even have physical health benefits (Mueller et al., 2001). Muslims often rely on their faith to cope with distress through prayer and reading the Qur'an (Abu-Raiya & Pargament, 2015; Asfari & Gacek, 2024). This extends to the prison setting, where incarcerated Muslims often turn to their faith when distressed. This reliance on religion as a means of coping may be protective against depression and even reduce disciplinary actions (Stansfield et al., 2018; Eytan, 2011). When their ability to practice their faith is stripped from them, however, this can prove detrimental to their mental wellbeing.

Religious discrimination and Islamophobia have significant mental health consequences (Ali & Awaad, 2019; De Nolf & d'Haenens, 2024), and anti-Islamic rhetoric, hate crimes, and discrimination have surged in the years following 9/11 (Kumar, 2021). The prison system is no exception to these pervasive phenomena (Marcus, 2015; Asfari et al., 2023), where inmates often report experiencing discrimination (LeBel, 2012). Indeed, practicing Islam in prison can be difficult due to religious discrimination, where religious accommodations are not consistently provided for incarcerated individuals (SpearIt, 2022; Slabaugh, 2023). Numerous lawsuits have been filed against American jails and prisons for failing to accommodate Muslims' religious beliefs, with allegations ranging from refusal to provide copies of the Qur'an to failing to accommodate inmates' fasting of Ramadan to not allowing them to request kosher meals even in the absence of a halal option (Jaafari, 2020a; Jaafari, 2020b). Although there are clear discrepancies in access to religious accommodations from one jurisdiction to another, the pervasive obstacles faced by incarcerated Muslims to practice their beliefs are a definite—and easily modifiable—source of distress (Muslim Advocates, 2019).

A note should be made here that there are gendered differences to the Muslim carceral experience, including in experiences of discrimination. First, there have been multiple incidents of Muslim women having their hijab (headscarf) forcibly removed or strong-armed into its removal while in custody (Ammoura, 2013). In one instance, a woman in Georgia who was accompanying her nephew for a traffic violation was held in contempt of court and jailed simply for refusing to remove her hijab prior to entering the courthouse (*Valentine v. City of Douglasville*, 2010). Although this led to an updated head covering policy, the sheer humiliation faced by Muslim women simply for practicing their faith is disheartening at best. Second, there is evidence that incarcerated Muslim women have a different religious experience than incarcerated Muslim men. Given that over 90% of incarcerated individuals in North America are male, research on incarcerated women is scarce (Bucerius & Sandberg, 2022). One important study by Purdie et al. (2021), though based in Europe, attempts to bridge this gap. They found that while Muslim men's religiosity tended to increase while incarcerated, it tended to reduce for Muslim women. They posit that this is partly explained by the absence of family having a more significant, gendered impact on Muslim women and that Muslim men tended to mobilize a shared religious identity that was not as readily accessible for incarcerated Muslim women. For example, whereas Muslim men could more consistently gather in congregation for jummah (Friday prayer), providing them with regular connection to their peers, Muslim women were less able to do this, given that praying jummah is only Islamically mandatory for Men (though many women do attend). Although this is a European study, it is based on a sample of minority Muslims in Western countries; hence, it may be decently generalizable to the North American population.

Ultimately, to truly ascertain the impact of religious discrimination on the mental health of incarcerated Muslims, it would require—at a minimum—an exploration of mental health outcomes across jurisdictions based on the degree of religious accommodations provided (for an interactive map of American prison policies for Islamic practices, see Muslim Advocates, n.d.-a). This represents a crucial area for future research, particularly in light of the above evidence.

"Prislam"

As mentioned earlier, individuals converting to Islam while incarcerated is an increasingly recognized phenomenon (Pew Research Center, 2012). While faith can play a significant role in improving mental wellbeing (Papaleontiou-Louca, 2021; SpearIt, 2012), conversion behind bars also presents with distinct challenges compared to those who were born Muslim or accepted Islam prior to incarceration. *Prislam*, a portmanteau for "prison Islam," is a term that has been used in recent years (primarily by alarmists) to describe a particular form of Islam practiced by those who accepted the faith while incarcerated (Hiller, 2015). Granted, there are certainly some unique aspects to this experience. For example, it is not uncommon for incarcerated converts to select a leader amongst themselves to provide Islamic rulings (though this is not always allowed by prison policies) or attempt to interpret primary sources themselves, given that they often have limited access to Islamic scholars (Nsour, 2015).

However, "prislam" is most often used in the context of warning against the "radical threat" born out of "extremist" ideologies harbored while in prison (Hiller, 2015). Amplified after the events of 9/11, what began as investigations into real cases of terrorism by individuals who accepted Islam while incarcerated perversely transformed into broadly painting prisons as "incubators for radical Islam" which have been infiltrated by Saudi-trained "Wahhabists" (Hiller, 2015; Hamm, 2009). Naturally, this position is deeply flawed, and the studies upon which these conclusions were built were "devoid of social science methodologies" (Hamm, 2009). Indeed, investigative efforts have found no evidence of "Wahhabist radicalization" behind bars (Hiller, 2015; Zoll, 2005). One of the co-authors of this chapter, R.N., once asked one of his students (who was in the Federal prison system at the time) if he had ever heard of Muslim inmates making terrorism-related comments. This student flatly replied, "I have been Muslim in prison for over 20 years, and I never heard one person make such comments" (Nsour, 2015). Despite the lack of evidence, these beliefs continue to be pervasive. In 2022, a training video for police and correctional officers in California was leaked, where it depicted incarcerated Muslims as being likely to produce terrorist attacks against the

US (Hatewatch, 2022). These prejudices likely contribute to the tensions and mistreatment experienced by incarcerated Muslim converts (SpearIt, 2012).

If increased scrutiny during incarceration was not enough, unfortunately, Muslims who have accepted the faith while incarcerated also face challenges post-reentry. Some converts report being shunned or alienated by family and friends due to their acceptance of Islam (Asfari & Gacek, 2024). Additionally, based on an ongoing study by the authors of this chapter, some report feeling ostracized by fellow Muslims who claim they only converted for in-group protection while incarcerated, as well as due to extant stigma surrounding incarceration (Mohammad et al., n.d.). These challenges and many more contribute to significant mental health difficulties for Muslim converts both during their incarceration as well as after their release.

Institutionalization and Post-Incarceration Syndrome

Before we delve into the reasons underlying why incarcerated individuals, including Muslims, face significant barriers to accessing mental healthcare, it is important to contextualize incarceration through the concepts of *institutionalization* and *post-incarceration syndrome*. Institutionalization (also occasionally called "prisonization" in this context) refers to the phenomenon of individuals becoming psychologically disabled by long-term incarceration, to the extent that they become accustomed to, or even reliant upon the prison (Haney, 2012). This phenomenon is not new; it was described under different terminology as early as the late 1950s (Sykes, 2007). Some incarcerated women even describe feeling "at home" after spending a long time in incarceration (Sufrin, 2017). Consequently, many then describe difficulty coping and functioning on the "outside" after their release, sometimes even intrusively wishing that they were back in prison (Crane & Pascoe, 2021).

Adjacently, post-incarceration syndrome (PICS), first described in detail at the turn of the century, refers to a constellation of symptoms experienced by some formerly incarcerated individuals (Gorski, 2001). In recent years, it has been researched as a subtype of PTSD resulting from prolonged imprisonment (Liem & Kunst, 2013). Although PICS is not officially recognized under the Diagnostic and Statistical Manual of Mental Disorders (DSM), there is growing evidence that suggests its existence as a discrete disorder (Quandt & Jones, 2021). Liem & Kunst (2013) proposed that individuals with PICS experience PTSD in addition to the following unique symptoms:

1. Institutionalized personality traits resulting from incarceration (e.g., difficulty trusting others)
2. Social-sensory deprivation syndrome (e.g., difficulty in social interactions)
3. Social/temporal alienation (e.g., thoughts that positive events can be taken away)

While there remains debate as to the exact symptoms that would encompass PICS, it is clear from an abundance of research that many incarcerated individuals present with PTSD-like symptoms post-incarceration (Goomany & Dickinson, 2015). Even in the absence of a clear PTSD/PICS-like syndrome, however, the resulting inability to function in a free society underscores the mental health consequences of institutionalization more broadly (Crane & Pascoe, 2021; Hu et al., 2020). Individuals frequently endorse significant psychological distress after reentry, with many meeting diagnostic criteria for depressive disorders (Addison et al., 2022).

It is clear then that incarcerated (and formerly incarcerated) individuals face significant mental health challenges. Unfortunately, numerous barriers prevent them from accessing the care they need. In the next section, we will explore these in detail.

Barriers to Care

Limited Access to Mental Healthcare

Mental health services are severely limited in the correctional system. Though data on the exact number of mental health professionals in this setting is scarce, there is a clear shortage of providers and services in North American prisons (Morris & Edwards, 2022; Canada et al., 2022; Scallan et al., 2021). Because of this deficiency, many incarcerated individuals never get any treatment for their mental disorders (Lupez et al., 2024; Hutchison, 2017). Significant barriers remain even when a correctional institute has an established mental health program. In the US, most prisons charge co-payments for certain health services, which makes access to care challenging—prison jobs often pay as little as a few pennies per hour (Lupez et al., 2024). While healthcare provision is publicly funded in Canada, mental health services remain limited there, too, with negative mental health outcomes (Scallan et al., 2021; Kouyoumdjian et al., 2016). As a result of the aforementioned shortage, incarcerated individuals also face significant wait times to access care, often several months long (Canada et al., 2022; Mohamed, 2024). Worse yet, access to psychiatric medications in jail is highly tenuous. Several important psychotropics are inaccessible in many prisons, such as clozapine (the only approved antipsychotic for treatment-resistant schizophrenia) and long-acting injectable antipsychotics (Burval et al., 2023; Jacobs & Giordano, 2018). The American Academy of Psychiatry and the Law acknowledges these barriers in its Practice Resource for Prescribing in Corrections, with some recommendations for providing adequate care despite these barriers (Tamburello et al., 2022). However, it is abundantly clear that the actual solution for improving mental health provision in the carceral setting involves dismantling several structural barriers, as outlined above.

Concerningly, there may also be racial disparities in access to mental healthcare in the carceral setting (Mohamed, 2024). Indeed, although we previously discussed that incarcerated minorities are less likely to self-report mental health concerns, several studies have found that when they *do* report mental illness, they are less likely than white inmates to be assessed and receive the treatment they need (Kaba et al., 2015; Martin et al., 2018). As it applies to our population of interest, certainly, Islam is not an ethnicity. However, the vast majority of Muslims in North America and its prisons are non-white and thus likely face comparable barriers. Incarcerated Muslims, hence, face several obstacles to adequate mental health care.

It should be further noted that even post-reentry, formerly incarcerated individuals have difficulty accessing mental health services. Hu et al. (2020) found that in an Ontario, Canada, sample of individuals recently released from a provincial jail, many described significant barriers to accessing mental health professionals and physicians and even getting prescriptions for the medications they were taking prior to incarceration. Other studies based in the US have made similar observations, with many describing difficulties accessing mental health providers and obtaining medication refills (Binswanger et al., 2011; Nishar et al., 2023; Addison et al., 2022). Further compounding this is that some formerly incarcerated individuals report being stigmatized by healthcare providers, which leads to both poorer mental health outcomes as well as worsening trust in the healthcare system as a whole (O'Connor et al., 2023). Many formerly incarcerated individuals, who are disproportionately racialized, also attribute this discrimination to racism (Frank et al., 2014). As previously discussed, incarcerated and formerly incarcerated Muslims face similar barriers to accessing care, which may be even more difficult due to their intersectional identity. Thus, it is clear that incarceration leads many Muslims to have limited access to mental healthcare, with this challenging reality following them even after release.

Mistrust of the System

Many marginalized groups in North America report mistrust toward the healthcare system (Bazargan et al., 2021; Hudson & Williams, 2023), including Muslims (King et al., 2023). This is partly due to Black and other racialized individuals often experiencing discrimination at the hands of healthcare professionals (Tong et al., 2022; Brown et al., 2024; Mahabir et al., 2021). One study by Cénat (2024) directly linked Black Canadians' experiences of discrimination to mistrust and even conspiracy theories about the healthcare system's attitudes towards racialized individuals. In the case of North American Muslims, experiences of Islamophobia similarly contribute to diminished trust in the healthcare system (Furqan et al., 2022; Samari et al., 2018). Although a number of initiatives in recent years aim to combat medical racism (Hall & Boulware, 2023), mistrust toward medical care is often rooted in knowledge of historical injustices inflicted upon marginalized groups in the healthcare system (Jaiswal & Halkitis, 2019).

This mistrust similarly exists for individuals impacted by incarceration. Though this is partly explained by the overrepresentation of minorities in North American prisons (Enders et al., 2019; Owusu-Bempah et al., 2023)—who may be more likely to report medical mistrust in the first place—incarcerated individuals also portray distrust towards medicine; regardless of race (Vandergrift & Christopher, 2021). Problematic institutional structures, such as those described earlier, may directly foster distrust in healthcare while incarcerated. This may lead to an even more deeply seated degree of medical mistrust, with formerly incarcerated individuals, especially those who are racialized, reporting significant mistrust toward the healthcare system even after their release (Valera et al., 2016; James, 2024). Indeed, the process of institutionalization, prior negative interactions with healthcare professionals, and discrimination may all instill a lack of trust in the healthcare system. Hence, medical mistrust represents yet another significant barrier for incarcerated and formerly incarcerated individuals to seek care, even when they need medical attention.

Lack of Culturally Competent Care

Lastly, even when an incarcerated individual can access healthcare and trusts the medical professionals in their facility, they are immediately confronted by another hurdle to adequate care – a lack of culturally competent mental health care. While an exact definition is debated, *cultural competence* may be broadly defined as having knowledge of cultural groups and their beliefs and harboring inclusive attitudes toward cultural diversity (Seeleman et al., 2009). Some prefer the term *cultural safety*, emphasizing a critical reflection on the power imbalance in the patient-physician relationship to make patients feel safe when receiving care (Curtis et al.,

2019). For this section, we will use the term cultural competence while recognizing that culturally competent care must also be culturally safe. Although cultural competence has become an axiomatic component of mental healthcare in recent years, culturally competent services and providers remain highly limited across North America (Rice & Harris, 2021; Fante-Coleman & Jackson-Best, 2020), with significant disparities in how racialized individuals perceive the degree of cultural competence of their mental health providers (Eken et al., 2021). This has notable relevance for North American Muslims, whose religious beliefs are often a core component of their identity. In the absence of culturally competent mental healthcare, Muslim patients may receive inadequate, if not harmful, care (Jabeen & Snowden, 2022; Rassool, 2015).

Naturally, as the carceral system often amplifies disparities, access to culturally competent mental healthcare is even more limited in this setting. As previously discussed, access to care is generally scarce in prisons – if incarcerated individuals cannot access medical care in general, one can only imagine how difficult it would be for them to access culturally competent care. As expected, culturally competent care is highly limited in correctional settings, with significant challenges to increasing its availability for inmates (Day et al., 2022). This also extends to limitations in accessing culturally competent mental healthcare (Mendez, 2018; Primm et al., 2005; Kapoor et al., 2013), which is arguably the field of healthcare where patients' cultural understandings and beliefs are most directly relevant to their care (Kirkmayer, 2012). Once again, incarcerated Muslims are similarly impacted by these challenges, with significant concerns about inadequate care for this subpopulation (Asfari & Gacek, 2024).

Overall, incarcerated and formerly incarcerated Muslims face numerous barriers to accessing adequate mental healthcare, some of which are extrinsic (e.g., lack of existing services) and some of which are intrinsic (e.g., mistrust toward the healthcare system). Ensuring that this vulnerable patient population is adequately supported is of utmost importance to ensure their needs are met. In the next section, we will explore how to do so.

Supporting Incarcerated Muslims

Connection to Free Society and Reentry Planning

Incarceration is a difficult experience, often leading to moral injury (van Willigenburg, 2020). Maintaining a connection with the community on the "outside," including family members, friends, and religious leaders, can help make individuals better cope with incarceration and prime them to a smoother reentry (Christian et al., 2006; Datchi et al., 2016; Liu & Visher, 2021; Frazier, 2011; Folk et al., 2019). Several studies have shown that re-

release programming and connection to family and friends—such as through visitation—can help reduce recidivism by improving individuals' social capital post-release (Rodriguez et al., 2017; McKiernan et al., 2013; Bales & Mears, 2008; Hickert et al., 2019; Mowen et al., 2018).

Specifically for incarcerated Muslims, there is some evidence that connection to their religious communities and faith-based programs are effective in reducing the risk of recidivism (Irfan, 2022; Yucel & Paget, 2017). Increasing access to faith-based programs that support incarcerated Muslims and those transitioning into reentry is, hence, an important priority. One of the simplest interventions to improve incarcerated Muslims' connection to a free society is through prisoner letter correspondence or "pen pal" programs. Letter writing can assist inmates in connecting with others outside of the carceral setting and help them develop narrative healing skills and a sense of purpose (Mejia-O'Donnell, 2019). Storytelling and communication with non-incarcerated people also serve a dual purpose of destigmatizing mental healthcare and humanizing incarcerated individuals (Bove & Tryon, 2018).

Further, it is important to include substance relapse prevention efforts as part of a successful reentry planning strategy, given the prevalence of substance use disorders in the incarcerated population (Prins, 2014; Cameron et al., 2021). A systematic review by Moore et al. (2020) evaluated 34 unique reentry interventions to address substance use. Although there was a high degree of variability across studies, they found that of the studies that did measure recidivism outcomes and/or substance use outcomes, most interventions decreased recidivism and/or substance use. Although there is a dearth of literature on substance use, particularly in reentering Muslims, inspiration may be drawn from these interventions in designing an effective program for this subpopulation.

Another successful intervention model is peer mentoring, which involves assigning a peer mentor to an individual going through reentry to promote community integration and reduce recidivism (Sell et al., 2020). While several similar Muslim-based initiatives to support incarcerated Muslims exist, there is very limited research in the literature on their efficacy. Anecdotally, faith-based organizations can be life-changing for many incarcerated Muslims in North America (Shuwekh, 2020). However, having confirmatory data can be the catalyst for the development and funding of community initiatives to continue doing their important work.

The Role of Religious Leaders

Although there is clear evidence that reentry and release planning can reduce recidivism, the prevalence of these programs is highly limited

(Bowers, 2009). One avenue through which incarcerated Muslims can directly access mentorship and mental health support is by working with prison chaplains and Imams. Despite the severe shortage of Muslim faith leaders in North American prisons, there is growing attention on the importance of their roles (Faheid, 2021; Stark, 2023). Their presence within the prison system is vital in helping inmates receive adequate resources to keep practicing their faith (Gacek & Asfari, 2024; Shamma, 2018). Additionally, they are able to impart pearls of faith that can foster a sense of resilience in incarcerated Muslims—such as helping them relate to the story of the prophet Yusuf, for example. They also play a key role in preparing them for their transition to free society once released by serving as a bridge between their community on the outside and incarceration (Gacek & Asfari, 2024). Indeed, Muslim prison chaplains and other religious leaders can aid in connecting incarcerated Muslims to social services to assist them in reentry planning and housing (Long & Ansari, 2018). As such, it is important to empower our faith leaders and encourage them to work in the prison setting, which is unfortunately often highly stigmatized in the Muslim community (Asfari & Gacek, 2024).

Dedicated Subspecialized Mental Healthcare

As previously discussed, the prison environment is conducive to mental illness, with incarcerated Muslims not exempt from its effects. We have also touched upon the lack of culturally competent mental healthcare and its need for this particular population group. One important study by Hodge et al. (2023) explored Muslim Americans' perspectives on their unique mental healthcare needs and what cultural competence looks like for them. This study identified eight central conceptual themes that would help Muslim clients better trust their therapists, particularly when the latter are non-Muslim:

1. Understanding basic Islamic values and beliefs.
2. Recognizing intragroup ethnic/cultural differences.
3. Developing self-awareness of personal biases.
4. Respecting traditional Islamic gender roles.
5. Avoiding assumptions regarding their Muslim clients' beliefs.
6. Using Islamic beliefs and practices as strengths.
7. Understanding bias in the larger culture.
8. Consulting with Muslim therapists and Imams.

Of course, these key principles inform the approach to mental healthcare with Muslim patients more broadly and are not specific to incarcerated Muslims. Naturally, due to their unique experiences and vulnerable circumstances, individuals affected by incarceration similarly require specialized approaches to mental healthcare (Coleman et al., 2024; Ellis & Alexander, 2017). In considering how these studies apply to incarcerated Muslims, their intersectional identities require a subspecialized approach that blends both concepts – culturally competent mental healthcare that is adapted to the carceral setting. As previously discussed, Muslim prison chaplains and Imams are uniquely situated in having experience in both domains. However, the work must not fall entirely on them and *cannot* fall on them, given the aforementioned shortage. Hence, community-based workshops that allow prison chaplains to share their expertise and teach other mental healthcare professionals to provide care for this vulnerable population group would allow for this gap in subspecialized care to begin to close.

Policy Recommendations

Based on everything discussed thus far, several policy changes ought to take place to address the mental health needs of this vulnerable population adequately. First, to "cut it at the root," significant reform is needed to address the race-based targeting of marginalized individuals, who often face longer sentences for the same crime as their White counterparts (Veiga et al., 2023). Additionally, protections need to be put in place to ensure that Muslims are able to practice their faith freely while incarcerated. Naturally, these beets a much larger conversation around systemic racism in North America and what "reform" would look like. At a minimum, increasing judicial diversity and establishing a watchdog board are two considerations to reduce racial disparities in policing and sentencing.

Second, existing carceral structures must be altered to improve mental healthcare access. For example, in the US, it is cruel and inhumane to charge inmates co-payments to access health services while simultaneously only paying them pennies per hour *if* they are able to work (Lupez et al., 2024). This is only legal because the Thirteenth Amendment renders involuntary servitude illegal *except* as punishment for a crime (US Const. amend. XIII). While we recognize that the degree of access to healthcare differs across US states (and Canada), Federal-level legislation in both the US and Canada addressing access to healthcare is long overdue. Additionally, in light of the clear negative mental health implications of solitary confinement (Haney, 2018), it must be outlawed entirely.

Finally, an important consideration is that community stakeholders, including those from the Muslim community, must be consulted in drafting and implementing policy reforms. While much debate can be had around the reform of the current prison system, suggesting that an abolitionist approach is a more effective route, this extends beyond the scope of our chapter. However, we acknowledge this controversial stance as worthy of conversation and not without merit.

Examples of Existing Programs

Despite the limited research on incarcerated Muslims in North America and their mental health needs, several successful programs aiming to support this subpopulation exist. The following list is not exhaustive, though it includes a few key examples of holistic organizations that support incarcerated and formerly incarcerated Muslims in North America.

The *Islamic Circle of North America Council for Social Justice (ICNA CSJ)* houses a *Muslim Prisoner Support Project* that aims to support incarcerated Muslims (Islamic Circle of North America, n.d.). The project provides them with religious furnishings such as prayer mats and Islamic books and has additionally aided in arranging for Muslim chaplains to serve at a number of prisons. The project vows that religion is a constitutional right that must be granted to the incarcerated population. It also aims to improve prison conditions and advocate for prison reform.

Muslim Advocates is a national civil rights organization that utilizes policy engagement, litigation, and communication strategies to promote the right of people to practice their faith freely (Muslim Advocates, n.d.-b). This charitable organization uses a social justice approach to protect the rights of the American Muslim community, including the incarcerated population. They ensure that incarcerated Muslims have access to religious items, a place to pray, and religiously approved food. They created the "Keeping the Faith" database of US state prison policies for religious practices (Muslim Advocates, n.d.-a).

Islamic Family is a registered Canadian charity based in Edmonton, Alberta (Islamic Family, n.d.). Though it began as a food bank, it has since grown into a holistic social services organization. It additionally works with incarcerated Muslims in Canada, aiming to better understand the spiritual and cultural services currently being offered to them and advocating for better care behind bars. It also helps connect prisons with Muslim chaplains.

Muslim Reentry Initiative (M.R.I.) is a community collective that aims to assist incarcerated and reentering Muslims, serving as a bridge between the incarcerated population and Muslims in society (Muslim Reentry Initiative, n.d.). It is a charitable organization that aims to provide "full-scale" Islamic prison chaplaincy and reentry services.

Tayba Foundation is a non-profit organization founded in 2008 by co-author R.N. (Tayba Foundation, n.d.). Its mission statement is inspired by the belief that all human beings contain goodness. The foundation serves individuals and families impacted by incarceration. Although it serves everyone, regardless of religious beliefs, it works primarily with incarcerated and reentering Muslims in America. Its work focuses on education, skill-building, and reentry.

Conclusion

Incarcerated Muslims in North America face significant mental health challenges and numerous barriers to accessing care, with these difficulties persisting post-reentry. An important contributor to their mental health challenges are experiences of discrimination behind bars and, in many cases, a limited ability to practice their faith fully. Experiences of institutionalization and traumatic experiences pose further challenges to living a fulfilling life outside of prison. While there is limited research on this vulnerable, growing population, the existing literature is not without recommendations. Destigmatization efforts and connection to a free society are vital components of reentry planning and reducing the risk of recidivism. Chaplains and Imams are trusted members of the Muslim community and are uniquely positioned to promote adequate religious education and spiritual guidance for inmates. More importantly, they can play a role in training other psychotherapists and counselors to meet this subpopulation's unique needs, including non-Muslim providers who are prepared to provide culturally competent care. Although mental health resources for incarcerated individuals, let alone incarcerated Muslims, are scarce, several existing, successful programs serve as blueprints for services that work.

As we noted at multiple points throughout this chapter, research on the mental health of incarcerated Muslims is scarce. Research efforts, both quantitative and qualitative, must be undertaken in order to understand how to best support this vulnerable subpopulation. Notably, studies focused on the mental health of incarcerated Muslims, as well as empirical investigations of existing interventions to assess their efficacy, are two crucial areas of research that urgently need to be addressed.

It should be evident to the reader that the prison system is structured to be punitive. It is, by design, the most important contributor to mental illness in those affected by the criminal justice system. As such, systemic reform and policy changes are critical to address the root of the issue (Haney, 2012). We briefly touched on a number of recommendations, including abolishing the practice of solitary confinement and removing barriers to Muslims' ability to practice their faith freely while incarcerated.

Nonetheless, we hope that this chapter serves as a starting point to support research into the mental health of incarcerated Muslims in North America. We also hope for structural changes to the correctional system to address the root cause of these challenges.

References

Abu-Raiya, H., & Pargament, K. I. (2015). Religious coping among diverse religions: Commonalities and divergences. *Psychology of Religion and Spirituality*, *7*(1), 24–33. https://doi.org/10.1037/a0037652

Addison, H. A., Richmond, T. S., Lewis, L. M., & Jacoby, S. (2022). Mental health outcomes in formerly incarcerated Black men: A systematic mixed studies review. *Journal of Advanced Nursing*, *78*(7), 1851–1869. https://doi.org/10.1111/jan.15235

Ali, S., & Awaad, R. (2019). Islamophobia and Public Mental Health: Lessons Learned from Community Engagement Projects. In H. S. Moffic, J. Peteet, A. Z. Hankir, & R. Awaad (Eds.), *Islamophobia and Psychiatry: Recognition, Prevention, and Treatment* (pp. 375–390). Springer International Publishing. https://doi.org/10.1007/978-3-030-00512-2_31

Al-Rousan, T., Rubenstein, L., Sieleni, B., Deol, H., & Wallace, R. B. (2017). Inside the nation's largest mental health institution: A prevalence study in a state prison system. *BMC Public Health*, *17*(1), 342. https://doi.org/10.1186/s12889-017-4257-0

Ammar, N. H., Weaver, R. R., & Saxon, S. (2004). Muslims in Prison: A Case Study from Ohio State Prisons. *International Journal of Offender Therapy and Comparative Criminology*, *48*(4), 414–428. https://doi.org/10.1177/0306624X03261558

Ammoura, A. (2013). Banning the Hijab in Prisons: Violations of Incarcerated Muslim Women's Right to Free Exercise of Religion. *Chicago-Kent Law Review*, *88*(2), 657–684.

Asfari, A., & Gacek, J. (2024). Muslim Mental Health in Prison: The Costs and Consequences of Inadequate Services. In N. W. Link, M. A. Novisky, & C. Fahmy (Eds.), *Handbook on Contemporary Issues in Health, Crime, and Punishment* (pp. 432–444). Routledge.

Asfari, A., Gacek, J., & Shurayadi, A. (2023). Islam, Islamophobia, and the Carceral Experience. In D. Rudes, G. Armstrong, K. Kras, & T. Carter (Eds.), *Handbook on Prisons and Jails* (1st ed., pp. 264–379). Routledge. http://doi.org/10.4324/9781003374893-29

Bales, W. D., & Mears, D. P. (2008). Inmate social ties and the transition to society: Does visitation reduce recidivism? *Journal of Research in Crime and Delinquency*, *45*(3), 287–321. https://doi.org/10.1177/0022427808317574

Bazargan, M., Cobb, S., & Assari, S. (2021). Discrimination and Medical Mistrust in a Racially and Ethnically Diverse Sample of California Adults. *Annals of Family Medicine*, *19*(1), 4–15. https://doi.org/10.1370/afm.2632

Beaudette, J. N., & Stewart, L. A. (2016). National Prevalence of Mental Disorders among Incoming Canadian Male Offenders. *The Canadian Journal of Psychiatry*, *61*(10), 624–632. https://doi.org/10.1177/0706743716639929

Beckett, K., & Goldberg, A. (2022). The Effects of Imprisonment in a Time of Mass Incarceration. *Crime and Justice*, *51*, 349–398. https://doi.org/10.1086/721018

Bill C-83: An Act to Amend the Corrections and Conditional Release Act and Another Act (2019) https://lop.parl.ca/sites/PublicWebsite/default/en_CA/ResearchPublicatio ns/LegislativeSu mmaries/421C83E

Binswanger, I. A., Maruschak, L. M., Mueller, S. R., Stern, M. F., & Kinner, S. A. (2019). Principles to Guide National Data Collection on the Health of Persons in the Criminal Justice System. *Public Health Reports*, *134*(Supplement 1), 34S-45S. https://doi.org/10.1177/0033354919841593

Binswanger, I. A., Nowels, C., Corsi, K. F., Long, J., Booth, R. E., Kutner, J., & Steiner, J. F. (2011). "From the prison door right to the sidewalk, everything went downhill," a qualitative study of the health experiences of recently released inmates. *International Journal of Law and Psychiatry*, *34*(4), 249–255. https://doi.org/10.1016/j.ijlp.2011.07.002

Bove, A., & Tryon, R. (2018). The Power of Storytelling: The Experiences of Incarcerated Women Sharing Their Stories. *International Journal of Offender Therapy and Comparative Criminology*, *62*(15), 4814–4833. https://doi.org/10.1177/0306624X18785100

Bowers, A. (2009). The Search for Justice: Islamic Pedagogy and Inmate Rehabilitation. In Y. Y. Haddad, F. Senzai, & J. I. Smith (Eds.), *Educating the Muslims of America* (pp. 179–208). Oxford University Press. https://doi.org/10.1093/acprof:oso/9780195375206.003.0009

Bradley, J., Jennings, L., & McClelland, A. (2023). *Fact Sheet: Deaths of people labeled with schizophrenia in custody in Canada.* Tracking (In)Justice.

Brown, C. E., Jackson, S. Y., Marshall, A. R., Pytel, C. C., Cueva, K. L., Doll, K. M., & Young, B. A. (2024). Discriminatory Healthcare Experiences and Medical Mistrust in Patients With Serious Illness. *Journal of Pain and Symptom Management*, *67*(4), 317-326.e3. https://doi.org/10.1016/j.jpainsymman.2024.01.010

Bucerius, S., & Sandberg, S. (2022). Women in Prisons. *Crime and Justice*, *51*, 137–186. https://doi.org/10.1086/722105

Burval, J. K., Iuppa, C. A., Kriz, C. R., Lang, S. E., Nelson, L. A., Gramlich, N. A., Elliott, E. S. R., & Sommi, R. W. (2023). Barriers to access to psychiatric medications in Missouri county jails. *The Mental Health Clinician*, *13*(5), 200–206. https://doi.org/10.9740/mhc.2023.10.200

Cameron, C., Khalifa, N., Bickle, A., Safdar, H., & Hassan, T. (2021). Psychiatry in the federal correctional system in Canada. *BJPsych International*, *18*(2), 42–46. https://doi.org/10.1192/bji.2020.56

Canada, K., Barrenger, S., Bohrman, C., Banks, A., & Peketi, P. (2022). Multi-Level Barriers to Prison Mental Health and Physical Health Care for Individuals With Mental Illnesses. *Frontiers in Psychiatry*, *13*, 777124. https://doi.org/10.3389/fpsyt.2022.777124

Carson, E. A., & Kluckow, R. (2023). *Prisoners in 2022 – Statistical Tables* (NCJ 307149). https://bjs.ojp.gov/library/publications/prisoners-2022-statistical-tables

Cénat, J. M., Farahi, S. M. M. M., Dalexis, R. D., Yaya, S., Caulley, L., & Chomienne, M.-H. (2024). COVID-19 vaccine uptake, conspiracy theories, and health literacy among Black individuals in Canada: Racial discrimination, confidence in health, and COVID-19 stress as mediators. *Journal of Medical Virology*, *96*(2), e29467. https://doi.org/10.1002/jmv.29467

Christian, J., Mellow, J., & Thomas, S. (2006). Social and economic implications of family connections to prisoners. *Journal of Criminal Justice*, *34*(4), 443–452. https://doi.org/10.1016/j.jcrimjus.2006.05.010

Ciftci, A., Jones, N., & Corrigan, P. W. (2012). Mental Health Stigma in the Muslim Community. *Journal of Muslim Mental Health*, *7*(1), 17–32. https://doi.org/10.3998/jmmh.10381607.0007.102

Cohen, J. I. (2000). Stress and Mental Health: A Biobehavioral Perspective. *Issues in Mental Health Nursing*, *21*(2), 185–202. https://doi.org/10.1080/016128400248185

Coleman, J. J., Drinane, J. M., Owen, J., Sinha, S., Porter, E. F., Agorsor, C., DeBlaere, C., & Davis, D. E. (2024). Psychotherapy with clients who are incarcerated: Therapists' multicultural orientation, alliance, and outcomes. *Professional Psychology: Research and Practice*, *55*(1), 39–47. https://doi.org/10.1037/pro0000522

Cooper v. Pate, 378 U.S. 546 (1964). https://supreme.justia.com/cases/federal/us/378/546/

Crane, J. T., & Pascoe, K. (2021). Becoming Institutionalized: Incarceration as a Chronic Health Condition. *Medical Anthropology Quarterly*, *35*(3), 307–326. https://doi.org/10.1111/maq.12621

Cummings, A. D. P. (2012). All Eyez on Me': America's War on Drugs and the Prison-Industrial Complex. *The Journal of Gender, Race & Justice*, *15*, 417–448.

Curtis, E., Jones, R., Tipene-Leach, D., Walker, C., Loring, B., Paine, S.-J., & Reid, P. (2019). Why cultural safety rather than cultural competency is required to achieve health equity: A literature review and recommended definition. *International Journal for Equity in Health*, *18*, 174. https://doi.org/10.1186/s12939-019-1082-3

Datchi, C. C., Barretti, L. M., & Thompson, C. M. (2016). Family Services in Adult Detention Centers: Systemic Principles for Prisoner Reentry. *Couple and Family Psychology: Research and Practice*, *5*(2), 89–104. https://doi.org/10.1037/cfp0000057

Day, A., Tamatea, A., & Geia, L. (2022). Cross-cultural practice frameworks in correctional settings. *Aggression and Violent Behavior*, *63*, 101674. https://doi.org/10.1016/j.avb.2021.101674

Daza, S., Palloni, A., & Jones, J. (2020). The Consequences of Incarceration for Mortality in the United States. *Demography*, *57*(2), 577–598. https://doi.org/10.1007/s13524-020-00869-5

De Nolf, A., & d'Haenens, L. (2024). Consequences of Islamophobia: A Systematic Review. *Journal of Religion & Society*, *26*, 130–163.

Dellazizzo, L., Luigi, M., Giguère, C.-É., Goulet, M.-H., & Dumais, A. (2020). Is mental illness associated with placement into solitary confinement in correctional settings? A systematic review and meta-analysis.

International Journal of Mental Health Nursing, *29*(4), 576–589. https://doi.org/10.1111/inm.12733
Eken, H. N., Dee, E. C., Powers, A. R., & Jordan, A. (2021). Racial and ethnic differences in perception of provider cultural competence among patients with depression and anxiety symptoms: A retrospective, population-based, cross-sectional analysis. *The Lancet Psychiatry*, *8*(11), 957–968. https://doi.org/10.1016/S2215-0366(21)00285-6
Ellis, H., & Alexander, V. (2017). The Mentally Ill in Jail: Contemporary Clinical and Practice Perspectives for Psychiatric-Mental Health Nursing. *Archives of Psychiatric Nursing*, *31*(2), 217–222. https://doi.org/10.1016/j.apnu.2016.09.013
Enders, W., Pecorino, P., & Souto, A.-C. (2019). Racial Disparity in US Imprisonment Across States and Over Time. *Journal of Quantitative Criminology*, *35*(2), 365–392. https://doi.org/10.1007/s10940-018-9389-6
Eytan, A. (2011). Religion and Mental Health During Incarceration: A Systematic Literature Review. *Psychiatric Quarterly*, *82*(4), 287–295. https://doi.org/10.1007/s11126-011-9170-6
Faheid, D. (2021, Jul. 12). There Are 11,073 Muslims In Federal Prisons But Just 13 Chaplains To Minister To Them. *NPR*. https://www.npr.org/2021/07/12/1014823399/muslim-chaplains-federal-prisons-islam-religion-shortage
Fante-Coleman, T., & Jackson-Best, F. (2020). Barriers and Facilitators to Accessing Mental Healthcare in Canada for Black Youth: A Scoping Review. *Adolescent Research Review*, *5*(2), 115–136. https://doi.org/10.1007/s40894-020-00133-2
Favril, L., Rich, J. D., Hard, J., & Fazel, S. (2024). Mental and physical health morbidity among people in prisons: An umbrella review. *The Lancet Public Health*, *9*(4), e250–e260. https://doi.org/10.1016/S2468-2667(24)00023-9
Fitch, K. V., Pence, B. W., Rosen, D. L., Miller, V. E., Gaynes, B. N., Swilley-Martinez, M. E., Kavee, A. L., Carey, T. S., Proescholdbell, S. K., & Ranapurwala, S. I. (2024). Suicide Mortality Among Formerly Incarcerated People Compared With the General Population in North Carolina, 2000-2020. *American Journal of Epidemiology*, *193*(3), 489–499. https://doi.org/10.1093/aje/kwad214
Folk, J. B., Stuewig, J., Mashek, D., Tangney, J. P., & Grossmann, J. (2019). Behind Bars but Connected to Family: Evidence for the Benefits of Family Contact During Incarceration. *Journal of Family Psychology*, *33*(4), 453–464. https://doi.org/10.1037/fam0000520
Ford, M. (2015, Jun. 8). America's Largest Mental Hospital Is a Jail. *The Atlantic*. https://www.theatlantic.com/politics/archive/2015/06/americas-largest-mental-hospital-is-a-jail/395012/
Frank, J. W., Wang, E. A., Nunez-Smith, M., Lee, H., & Comfort, M. (2014). Discrimination based on criminal record and healthcare utilization among men recently released from prison: A descriptive study. *Health & Justice*, *2*(1), 6. https://doi.org/10.1186/2194-7899-2-6

Frazier, B. D. (2011). Faith-Based Prisoner Reentry. In L. Gideon & H.-E. Sung (Eds.), *Rethinking Corrections: Rehabilitation, Reentry, and Reintegration* (pp. 279–306). Sage Publications.

Fuller, S. (2018). Torture as Management Practice: The Convention Against Torture and Non-Disciplinary Solitary Confinement. *Chicago Journal of International Law, 19*(1), 102–144.

Furqan, Z., Malick, A., Zaheer, J., & Sukhera, J. (2022). Understanding and addressing Islamophobia through trauma-informed care. *Canadian Medical Association Journal, 194*(21), E746–E747. https://doi.org/10.1503/cmaj.211298

Gacek, J., & Asfari, A. (2024). Islamophobia and the Benefits and Challenges for Prison Imams. *Islamophobia Studies Journal, 8*(2), 246–260. https://doi.org/10.13169/islastudj.8.2.0246

Goomany, A., & Dickinson, T. (2015). The influence of prison climate on the mental health of adult prisoners: A literature review. *Journal of Psychiatric and Mental Health Nursing, 22*(6), 413–422. https://doi.org/10.1111/jpm.12231

Gorski, T. T. (2001). *Post Incarceration Syndrome and Relapse (PICS)*. https://www.november.org/stayinfo/breaking/PICS.html

Habibinia, M. (2023, December 4). Why wasn't Soleiman Faqiri sent to hospital? Inquest reveals jailhouse dysfunction ahead of mentally ill man's death. *Toronto Star*. https://www.thestar.com/news/gta/why-wasn-t-soleiman-faqiri-sent-to-hospital-inquest-reveals-jailhouse-dysfunction-ahead-of-mentally/article_e0c8b78c-b381-535c-b798-346839d42aab.html

Hall, D., Lee, L.-W., Manseau, M. W., Pope, L., Watson, A. C., & Compton, M. T. (2019). Major Mental Illness as a Risk Factor for Incarceration. *Psychiatric Services, 70*(12), 1088–1093. https://doi.org/10.1176/appi.ps.201800425

Hall, J. E., & Boulware, L. E. (2023). Combating Racism Through Research, Training, Practice, and Public Health Policies. *Preventing Chronic Disease, 20*, E54. https://doi.org/10.5888/pcd20.230167

Hamm, M. S. (2009). Prison Islam in the age of sacred terror. *British Journal of Criminology, 49*(5), 667–685. https://doi.org/10.1093/bjc/azp035

Haney, C. (2012). Prison Effects in the Era of Mass Incarceration. *The Prison Journal, 20*(10), 1–24. https://doi.org/10.1177/0032885512448604

Haney, C. (2018). The Psychological Effects of Solitary Confinement: A Systematic Critique. *Crime and Justice, 47*, 365–416. https://doi.org/10.1086/696041

Hickert, A., Palmen, H., Dirkzwager, A., & Nieuwbeerta, P. (2019). Receiving Social Support after Short-term Confinement: How Support Pre- and During-confinement Contribute. *Journal of Research in Crime and Delinquency, 56*(4), 563–604. https://doi.org/10.1177/0022427819826302

Hiller, T. (2015). "Prislam" Myths and Realities. In N. Ammar (Ed.), *Muslims in US Prisons: People, Policy, Practice* (pp. 147–166). Lynne Rienner Publishers. https://doi.org/10.1515/9781626375505-011

Hodge, D. R., Zidan, T., & Husain, A. (2023). How to Work with Muslim Clients in a Successful, Culturally Relevant Manner: A National Sample of American Muslims Share Their Perspectives. *Social Work, 69*(1), 53–63. https://doi.org/10.1093/sw/swad048

Hu, C., Jurgutis, J., Edwards, D., O'Shea, T., Regenstreif, L., Bodkin, C., Amster, E., & Kouyoumdjian, F. G. (2020). "When you first walk out the gates...where do [you] go?": Barriers and opportunities to achieving continuity of health care at the time of release from a provincial jail in Ontario. *PLOS ONE, 15*(4), e0231211. https://doi.org/10.1371/journal.pone.0231211

Hudson, P., & Williams, M. A. (2023). People are much less likely to trust the medical system if they are from an ethnic minority, have disabilities, or identify as LGBTQ+, according to a first-of-its-kind study by Sanofi. *Fortune.* https://fortune.com/2023/01/31/people-trust-health-medical-system-ethnic-minority-disabilities-identify-lgbtq-study-sanofi-hudson-williams/

Hutchison, D. (2017). Inadequate Mental Health Services for Mentally Ill Inmates. *Whittier Law Review, 38*(1), 161–180.

Irfan, L. (2022). The Religious Community: A Space that Facilitates Successful Resettlement for Muslim Offenders. In H. Schmid & A. Sheikhzadegan (Eds.), *Exploring Islamic Social Work: Between community and the Common Good* (pp. 47–64). Springer Nature.

Ishikawa, Y., & Furuyashiki, T. (2022). The impact of stress on immune systems and its relevance to mental illness. *Neuroscience Research, 175,* 16–24. https://doi.org/10.1016/j.neures.2021.09.005

Islamic Circle of North America. (n.d.). *Muslim Prisoner Support Project.* ICNA CSJ. Retrieved Nov. 15, 2024, from https://icnacsj.org/muslim-prisoner-support-project/

Islamic family. (n.d.). *Islamic Family—Islamic Family & Social Services Association.* Islamic Family. Retrieved Nov. 15, 2024, from https://www.ifssa.ca/

Jaafari, J. D. (2020a, Jan. 7). Christians Pray At a Discount: Muslim inmates charged more for religious texts. *WITF.* https://www.witf.org/2020/01/07/christians-pray-at-a-discount-muslim-inmates-charged-more-for-religious-texts/

Jaafari, J. D. (2020b, May 15). 'They put me in solitary for having oranges'— Muslim inmates struggle during Ramadan. *WITF.* https://www.witf.org/2020/05/15/they-put-me-in-solitary-for-having-oranges-muslim-inmates-struggle-during-ramadan/

Jabeen, T., & Snowden, A. (2022). Can mental healthcare for Muslim patients be person-centered without consideration of religious identity? A concurrent analysis. *Nurse Education in Practice, 64,* 103449. https://doi.org/10.1016/j.nepr.2022.103449

Jacobs, L. A., & Giordano, S. N. J. (2018). "It's Not Like Therapy": Patient-inmate perspectives on jail psychiatric services. *Administration and Policy in Mental Health, 45*(2), 265–275. https://doi.org/10.1007/s10488-017-0821-2

Jaiswal, J., & Halkitis, P. N. (2019). Towards a More Inclusive and Dynamic Understanding of Medical Mistrust Informed by Science. *Behavioral Medicine, 45*(2), 79–85. https://doi.org/10.1080/08964289.2019.1619511

James, J. E. (2024). "We're Not Patients. We're Inmates": Older Black Women's Experience of Aging, Health, and Illness During and After Incarceration. *The Gerontologist, 64*(4), 1–9. https://doi.org/10.1093/geront/gnad114

Kaba, F., Solimo, A., Graves, J., Glowa-Kollisch, S., Vise, A., MacDonald, R., Waters, A., Rosner, Z., Dickey, N., Angell, S., & Venters, H. (2015). Disparities in Mental Health Referral and Diagnosis in the New York City Jail Mental Health Service. *American Journal of Public Health, 105*(9), 1911–1916. https://doi.org/10.2105/AJPH.2015.302699

Kamau. (2018). *I am a 50 yr old Muslim man of Afrikan descent that suffers PTSD*.C:\Users\16789\Downloads\https://prisonwitness.org/apwa-essay/i-am-a-50-yr-old-muslim-man-of-afrikan-descent-that-suffers-ptsd/

Kapoor, R., Dike, C., Burns, C., Carvalho, V., & Griffith, E. E. H. (2013). Cultural competence in correctional mental health. *International Journal of Law and Psychiatry, 36*(3), 273–280. https://doi.org/10.1016/j.ijlp.2013.04.016

King, J. K., Kieu, A., El-Deyarbi, M., Aljneibi, N., Al-Shamsi, S., Hashim, M. J., Östlundh, L., King, K. E., King, R. H., AB Khan, M., & Govender, R. D. (2023). Towards a better understanding between non-Muslim primary care clinicians and Muslim patients: A literature review intended to reduce health care inequities in Muslim patients. *Health Policy OPEN, 4*, 100092. https://doi.org/10.1016/j.hpopen.2023.100092

Kirmayer, L. J. (2012). Rethinking cultural competence. *Transcultural Psychiatry, 49*(2), 149–164. https://doi.org/10.1177/1363461512444673

Klein, D. E., & Lima, J. M. (2021). The Prison Industrial Complex as a Commercial Determinant of health. *American Journal of Public Health, 111*(10), 1750–1752. https://doi.org/10.2105/AJPH.2021.306467

Kouyoumdjian, F., Schuler, A., Matheson, F. I., & Hwang, S. W. (2016). Health status of prisoners in Canada: Narrative review. *Canadian Family Physician, 62*(3), 215–222.

Kumar, D. (2021). *Islamophobia and the Politics of Empire: Twenty years after 9/11*. Verso Books.

LeBel, T. P. (2012). If One Doesn't Get You Another One Will: Formerly Incarcerated Persons' Perceptions of Discrimination. *The Prison Journal, 92*(1), 63–87. https://doi.org/10.1177/0032885511429243

Liem, M., & Kunst, M. (2013). Is there a recognizable post-incarceration syndrome among released "lifers"? *International Journal of Law and Psychiatry, 36*(3), 333–337. https://doi.org/10.1016/j.ijlp.2013.04.012

Liu, L., & Visher, C. A. (2021). The Roles of Family, Community, and Services in the Prevention of Illicit Drug Use: Findings From a Sample of Released Prisoners. *Journal of Drug Issues, 51*(2), 358–375. https://doi.org/10.1177/0022042620984770

Long, I. J., & Ansari, B. (2018). Islamic Pastoral Care and the Development of Muslim Chaplaincy. *Journal of Muslim Mental Health, 12*(1), 109–121. https://doi.org/10.3998/jmmh.10381607.0012.105

Lupez, E. L., Woolhandler, S., Himmelstein, D. U., Hawks, L., Dickman, S., Gaffney, A., Bor, D., Schrier, E., Cai, C., Azaroff, L. S., & McCormick, D. (2024). Health, Access to Care, and Financial Barriers to Care Among People Incarcerated in US Prisons. *JAMA Internal Medicine, 184*(10), 1176–1184. https://doi.org/10.1001/jamainternmed.2024.3567

Lurigio, A. J. (2024). The Golden Anniversary of Mass Incarceration in America. *The Prison Journal, 104*(3), 271–295. https://doi.org/10.1177/00328855241240131

Mahabir, D. F., O'Campo, P., Lofters, A., Shankardass, K., Salmon, C., & Muntaner, C. (2021). Experiences of everyday racism in Toronto's health care system: A concept mapping study. *International Journal for Equity in Health, 20*, 74. https://doi.org/10.1186/s12939-021-01410-9

Marcus, K. L. (2015). Religious Rights, Religious Discrimination. In N. H. Ammar (Ed.), *Muslims in US Prisons: People, Policy, Practice* (pp. 65–78). Lynne Rienner Publishers. https://doi.org/10.1515/9781626375505-006

Martin, M. S., Crocker, A. G., Potter, B. K., Wells, G. A., Grace, R. M., & Colman, I. (2018). Mental Health Screening and Differences in Access to Care among Prisoners. *Canadian Journal of Psychiatry, 63*(10), 692–700. https://doi.org/10.1177/0706743718762099

Maruschak, L. M., Bronson, J., & Alper, M. (2021). *Indicators of Mental Health Problems Reported by Prisoners* (NCJ 252643). https://onlinelibrary.wiley.com/doi/10.1002/mpr.333

Massoglia, M., & Pridemore, W. A. (2015). Incarceration and Health. *Annual Review of Sociology, 41*, 291–310. https://doi.org/10.1146/annurev-soc-073014-112326

McKendy, L., & Ricciardelli, R. (2021). The Pains of Imprisonment and Contemporary Prisoner Culture in Canada. *The Prison Journal, 101*(5), 528–552. https://doi.org/10.1177/00328855211048166

McKiernan, P., Shamblen, S. R., Collins, D. A., Strader, T. N., & Kokoski, C. (2013). Creating Lasting Family Connections: Reducing Recidivism With Community-Based Family Strengthening Model. *Criminal Justice Policy Review, 24*(1), 94–122. https://doi.org/10.1177/0887403412447505

McLaughlin, M. M., Ahmad, S. S., & Weisman de Mamani, A. (2022). A mixed-methods approach to psychological help-seeking in Muslims: Islamophobia, self-stigma, and therapeutic preferences. *Journal of Consulting and Clinical Psychology, 90*(7), 568–581. https://doi.org/10.1037/ccp0000746

Mejia-O'Donnell, T. (2019). *Exploring Inmates' Prison Pen-Pal Soliciting Profiles* [San Diego State University]. https://digitalcollections.sdsu.edu/do/e4316863-821f-4927-9fc2-e3d216d1decd/file/fa8bbedb-0e7a-4f2d-ab3a-f28084e19a16/download/MejiaODonnell_sdsu_0220N_12924.pdf

Mendez, P. G. (2018). Imprisoned Hispanic/Latinx Individual Need Access to Culturally Competent Mental Health Treatment. *Annals Advance Directive, 28*(2), 157–172.

Mohamed, S. (2024). The State of Mental Health Services for Incarcerated Adults in Ontario: A Scoping Review. *International Journal of Offender Therapy* and Comparative Criminology, 0(0), 1–25. https://doi.org/10.1177/0306624X241228218

Mohammad, I. Y. Z., Jennah, S., Mukhtar, S., Nsour, R., & Awaad, R. (n.d.). Resilience Behind Bars: Experiences of Formerly Incarcerated Muslims in the United States [Manuscript in preparation].

Moore, K. E., Hacker, R. L., Oberleitner, L., & McKee, S. A. (2020). Reentry interventions that address substance use: A systematic review. *Psychological Services*, *17*(1), 93–101. https://doi.org/10.1037/ser0000293

Morris, N. P., & Edwards, M. L. (2022). Addressing Shortages of Mental Health Professionals in US Jails and Prisons. *Journal of Correctional Health Care*, *28*(4), 209–214. https://doi.org/10.1089/jchc.21.08.0072

Morrow, M., Bryson, S., Lal, R., Hoong, P., Jiang, C., Jordan, S., Patel, N. B., & Guruge, S. (2020). Intersectionality as an Analytic Framework for Understanding the Experiences of Mental Health Stigma Among Racialized Men. *International Journal of Mental Health and Addiction*, *18*(5), 1304–1317. https://doi.org/10.1007/s11469-019-00140-y

Mowen, T. J., Stansfield, R., & Boman, J. H. (2018). During, After, or Both? Isolating the Effect of Religious Support on Recidivism During Reentry. *Journal of Quantitative Criminology*, *34*(4), 1079–1101. https://doi.org/10.1007/s10940-017-9366-5

Mueller, P. S., Plevak, D. J., & Rummans, T. A. (2001). Religious Involvement, Spirituality, and Medicine: Implications for Clinical Practice. *Mayo Clinic Proceedings*, *76*(12), 1225–1235. https://doi.org/10.4065/76.12.1225

Mufti, S. I. (2006, November 20). *Islam in American Prisons* [Online post]. IslamiCity Forum. C:\Users\16789\Downloads\https://www.islamicity.org/forum/forum_posts.asp?TID=7640&title=islam-in-american-prisons

Muslim Advocates. (n.d.-a). *Keeping The Faith*. Muslim Advocates. Retrieved Nov. 10, 2024, from https://muslimadvocates.org/keepingthefaith/

Muslim Advocates. (n.d.-b). *Muslim Advocates—Promoting Justice & Equity*. Muslim Advocates. Retrieved Nov. 15, 2024, from https://muslimadvocates.org/

Muslim Advocates. (2019). *Fulfilling the Promise of Free Exercise for All: Muslim Prisoner Accommodation in State Prisons*. https://muslimadvocates.org/wp-content/uploads/2019/07/FULFILLING-THE-PROMISE-OF-FREE-EXERCISE-FOR-ALL-Muslim-Prisoner-Accommodation-In-State-Prisons-for-distribution-7_23.pdf

Muslim Reentry Initiative. (n.d.). *Muslim Reentry Initiative*. Muslim Reentry Initiative. Retrieved Nov. 15, 2024, from https://www.muslimreentryinitiative.org

National Institute of Justice. (2012, Mar. 25). *Challenges of Conducting Research in Prisons*. https://nij.ojp.gov/topics/articles/challenges-conducting-research-prisons

Nishar, S., Brumfield, E., Mandal, S., Vanjani, R., & Soske, J. (2023). "It's a revolving door": Understanding the social determinants of mental health as experienced by formerly incarcerated people. *Health & Justice, 11*(1), 26. https://doi.org/10.1186/s40352-023-00227-8

Nsour, R. (2015, Dec. 31). *Islam & Muslims in the US Prison System.* Tayba Foundation. https://www.taybafoundation.org/articles/2020/islam-and-muslims-in-the-us-prison-system

O'Connor, S. K., Vanjani, R., Cannon, R., Dawson, M. B., & Perkins, R. (2023). General and reproductive healthcare experiences of formerly incarcerated women in the United States: A qualitative study. *International Journal of Prisoner Health, 19*(4), 545–564. https://doi.org/10.1108/IJPH-09-2021-0094

Office of the Inspector General. (2004). *A Review of the Bureau of Prisons' Selection of Muslim Religious Services Providers.* https://oig.justice.gov/sites/default/files/archive/special/0404/index.htm

Office of the Inspector General. (2021). *Audit of the Federal Bureau of Prison's Management and Oversight of its Chaplaincy Services Program.* https://oig.justice.gov/sites/default/files/reports/21-091.pdf

Owusu-Bempah, A., Jung, M., Sbaï, F., Wilton, A. S., & Kouyoumdjian, F. (2023). Race and Incarceration: The Representation and Characteristics of Black People in Provincial Correctional Facilities in Ontario, Canada. *Race and Justice, 13*(4), 530–542. https://doi.org/10.1177/21533687211006461

Papaleontiou-Louca, E. (2021). Effects of Religion and Faith on Mental Health. *New Ideas in Psychology, 60*, 100833. https://doi.org/10.1016/j.newideapsych.2020.100833

Paradkar, S. (2019, November 13). Campaign seeks accountability for Soleiman Faqiri's death in jail. *Toronto Star.* https://www.thestar.com/opinion/star-columnists/campaign-seeks-accountability-for-soleiman-faqiri-s-death-in-jail/article_d0f37839-74dc-56ee-b04f-e3fe3d085dab.html

Pew Research Center. (2012). *Religion in Prisons – A 50-State Survey of Prison Chaplains.* https://www.pewresearch.org/religion/2012/03/22/prison-chaplains-exec/

Pew Research Center. (2017). *US Muslims Concerned About Their Place in Society, but Continue to Believe in the American Dream: Findings from Pew Research Center's 2017 survey of US Muslims.* https://www.pewresearch.org/religion/2017/07/26/demographic-portrait-of-muslim-americans/

Plante, T. G., & Sharma, N. K. (2001). Religious Faith and Mental Health Outcomes. In T. G. Plante & A. C. Sherman (Eds.), *Faith and Health: Psychological Perspectives* (pp. 240–264). Guilford Press.

Plummer, N., Guardado, R., Ngassa, Y., Montalvo, C., Kotoujian, P. J., Siddiqi, K., Senst, T., Simon, K., Acevedo, A., & Wurcel, A. G. (2023). Racial Differences in Self-Report of Mental Illness and Mental Illness Treatment in the Community: An Analysis of Jail Intake Data. *Administration and Policy in Mental Health and Mental Health Services Research, 50*(6), 966–975. https://doi.org/10.1007/s10488-023-01297-4

Primm, A. B., Osher, F. C., & Gomez, M. B. (2005). Race and Ethnicity, Mental Health Services and Cultural Competence in the Criminal Justice System:

Are we Ready to Change? *Community Mental Health Journal, 41*(5), 557–569. https://doi.org/10.1007/s10597-005-6361-3

Prins, S. J. (2014). The Prevalence of Mental Illnesses in US State Prisons: A Systematic Review. *Psychiatric Services, 65*(7), 862–872. https://doi.org/10.1176/appi.ps.201300166

Public Law 94-521, Oct. 17, 1976: An Act to Amend Title 13, United States Code, to Provide for a Mid-Decade Census of Population, and for Other Purposes (1976).

Public Safety Canada. (2024). *Corrections and Conditional Release Statistical Overview 2022* (1713–1073; p. 174). https://www.publicsafety.gc.ca/cnt/rsrcs/pblctns/ccrso-2022/indexen.aspx

Purdie, M. S., Irfan, L., Quraishi, M., & Wilkinson, M. (2021). Living Islam in Prison: How Gender Affects the Religious Experiences of Female and Male Offenders. *Religions, 12*(5), Article 5. https://doi.org/10.3390/rel12050298

Quandt, K. R., & Jones, A. (2021, May 13). *Research Roundup: Incarceration can cause lasting damage to mental health.* https://www.prisonpolicy.org/blog/2021/05/13/mentalhealthimpacts/

Ramsay, C. E., Goulding, S. M., Broussard, B., Cristofaro, S. L., Abedi, G. R., & Compton, M. T. (2011). From Handcuffs to Hallucinations: Prevalence and Psychosocial Correlates of Prior Incarcerations in an Urban, Predominantly African American Sample of Hospitalized Patients with First-Episode Psychosis. *The Journal of the American Academy of Psychiatry and the Law, 39*(1), 57–64.

Rassool, G. H. (2015). Cultural Competence in Counseling the Muslim Patient: Implications for Mental Health. *Archives of Psychiatric Nursing, 29*(5), 321–325. https://doi.org/10.1016/j.apnu.2015.05.009

Rice, A. N., & Harris, S. C. (2021). Issues of cultural competence in mental health care. *Journal of the American Pharmacists Association, 61*(1), e65–e68. https://doi.org/10.1016/j.japh.2020.10.015

Robinson, P., Small, T., Chen, A., & Irving, M. (2023). *Over-representation of Indigenous persons in adult provincial custody, 2019/2020 and 2020/2021* (85-002–X). https://www150.statcan.gc.ca/n1/pub/85-002-x/2023001/article/00004-eng.htm

Rodriguez, B. M., Kim, J. L., & Kim, Y. (2017). Evaluation of Prison Pre-Release Facility Program: What Effect Do These Programs Have on Offender Success in Texas? *Critical Issues in Justice and Politics, 10*(1), 55–70.

Ross, M. W., Diamond, P. M., Liebling, A., & Saylor, W. G. (2008). Measurement of prison social climate: A comparison of an inmate measure in England and the USA. *Punishment & Society, 10*(4), 447–474. https://doi.org/10.1177/1462474508095320

Saint-Julien, C. (2022, Apr. 28). Soleiman Faqiri, a death that cannot be explained. *La Converse.* https://www.laconverse.com/en/articles/soleiman-faqiri-une-mort-qui-ne-sexplique-pas

Samari, G., Alcalá, H. E., & Sharif, M. Z. (2018). Islamophobia, Health, and Public Health: A Systematic Literature Review. *American Journal of Public Health, 108*(6), e1–e9.   https://doi.org/10.2105/AJPH.2018.304402

Scallan, E., Lancaster, K., & Kouyoumdjian, F. (2021). The "problem" of health: An analysis of health care provision in Canada's federal prisons. *Health, 25*(1), 3–20.   https://doi.org/10.1177/1363459319846940

Seeleman, C., Suurmond, J., & Stronks, K. (2009). Cultural competence: A conceptual framework for teaching and learning. *Medical Education, 43*(3), 229–237. https://doi.org/10.1111/j.1365-2923.2008.03269.x

Sells, D., Curtis, A., Abdur-Raheem, J., Klimczak, M., Barber, C., Meaden, C., Hasson, J., Fallon, P., & Emigh-Guy, M. (2020). Peer-Mentored Community Reentry Reduces Recidivism. *Criminal Justice and Behavior, 47*(4), 437–456. https://doi.org/10.1177/0093854820901562

Shamma, S. (2018, August 20). Caring for Minds Behind Bars: The Role of the Muslim Chaplain. *Institute for Muslim Mental Health.* https://muslimmentalhealth.com/i-am-not-crazy-i-am-just-a-muslim-inmate/

Sheehan, A. E., Walsh, R. F. L., & Liu, R. T. (2018). Racial and ethnic differences in mental health service utilization in suicidal adults: A nationally representative study. *Journal of Psychiatric Research, 107*, 114–119. https://doi.org/10.1016/j.jpsychires.2018.10.019

Shuwekh, M. Y. (2020, October 25). *Teaching Islam in the US Prison System.* Tayba Foundation. C:\Users\16789\Downloads\https://www.taybafoundation.org/articles/2020/teaching-islam-in-the-us-prison-system-tayba-foundation

Simes, J. T., Western, B., & Lee, A. (2022). Mental health disparities in solitary confinement. *Criminology, 60*(3), 538–575. https://doi.org/10.1111/1745-9125.12315

Slabaugh, E. (2023). Dignity, Deference, and Discrimination: An Analysis of Religious Freedom in America's Prisons. *Brigham Young University Law Review, 49*(1), 269–308.

Spaulding, A. C., Seals, R. M., McCallum, V. A., Perez, S. D., Brzozowski, A. K., & Steenland, N. K. (2011). Prisoner survival inside and outside of the institution: Implications for healthcare planning. *American Journal of Epidemiology, 173*(5), 479–487. https://doi.org/10.1093/aje/kwq422

SpearIt. (2012). Religion as Rehabilitation? Reflections on Islam in the Correctional Setting. *Whittier Law Review, 34,* 29–53.

Spearit. (2013). Growing Faith: Prisons, Hip-Hop and Islam. *HuffPost Contributor.* https://www.huffpost.com/entry/growing-faith-prisons-hip-hop-and-islam_b_2829013

SpearIt. (2014). Muslim Radicalization in Prison: Responding with Sound Penal Policy or the Sound of Alarm? *Gonzaga Law Review, 49,* 37–82.

SpearIt. (2022). Muslims in American Prisons. *Journal of Islamic Law, 3*(1), Article 1. https://doi.org/10.53484/jil.v3.spearit

Sprott, J. B., & Doob, A. N. (2021). *Solitary Confinement, Torture, and Canada's Structured Intervention Units.* https://www.crimsl.utoronto.ca/sites/www.crimsl.utoronto.ca/files/Tortur

e%20Solitary%20SIUs%20%28Sprott%20Doob%2023%20Feb%202021%29.pdf

Stansfield, R., O'Connor, T., & Duncan, J. (2018). Religious Identity and the Long-Term Effects of Religious Involvement, Orientation, and Coping in Prison. *Criminal Justice and Behavior, 46*(2), 337–354. https://doi.org/10.1177/0093854818801410

Stark, H. (2023). Muslim Chaplains in North America. *Oxford Research Encyclopedia of Religion.* https://doi.org/10.1093/acrefore/9780199340378.013.855

Statistics Canada. (2022). *Religion by visible minority and generation status: Canada, provinces and territories, census metropolitan areas, and census agglomerations with parts.* https://www150.statcan.gc.ca/t1/tbl1/en/tv.action?pid=9810034201

Statistics Canada. (2024a). *Average counts of adults in provincial and territorial correctional programs.* https://www150.statcan.gc.ca/t1/tbl1/en/tv.action?pid=3510015401

Statistics Canada. (2024b). *Average counts of offenders in federal programs, Canada and regions.* https://www150.statcan.gc.ca/t1/tbl1/en/tv.action?pid=3510015501

Sufrin, C. (2017). *Jailcare: Finding the Safety Net for Women behind Bars.* University of California Press. https://doi.org/10.1515/9780520963559

Syed, F. (2017, Oct. 13). 'My beautiful son is dead': Family still searching for answers after Whitby man's 2016 death in prison. *Toronto Star.* https://www.thestar.com/news/gta/my-beautiful-son-is-dead-family-still-searching-for-answers-after-whitby-man-s-2016/article_6b8bef4f-8658-5304-8963-153d1d0d97c7.html

Sykes, G. M. (2007). *The Society of Captives: A Study of a Maximum Security Prison.* Princeton University Press. https://doi.org/10.1515/9781400828272

Tamburello, A., Penn, J., Ford, E., Champion, M. K., Glancy, G., Metzner, J., Ferguson, E., Tomita, T., & Ourada, J. (2022). The American Academy of Psychiatry and the Law Practice Resource for Prescribing in Corrections. *Journal of the American Academy of Psychiatry and the Law Online, 50*(4 Supplement), S1–S62. https://doi.org/10.29158/JAAPL.220082-22

Tayba Foundation. (n.d.). *Tayba Foundation—Supporting incarcerated Muslims.* Tayba Foundation. Retrieved Nov. 15, 2024, from https://www.taybafoundation.org

Tong, J. K. C., Akpek, E., Naik, A., Sharma, M., Boateng, D., Andy, A., Merchant, R. M., & Kelz, R. R. (2022). Reporting of Discrimination by Health Care Consumers Through Online Consumer Reviews. *JAMA Network Open, 5*(2), e220715. https://doi.org/10.1001/jamanetworkopen.2022.0715

US Const. Amend. XIII. Retrieved Feb. 1, 2025, from: https://www.archives.gov/milestone-documents/13th-amendment

Valentine v. City of Douglasville, 1:2010cv04056 (US District Court for the Northern District of Georgia). https://www.aclu.org/cases/valentine-v-city-douglasville

Valera, P., Boyas, J. F., Bernal, C., Chiongbian, V. B., Chang, Y., & Shelton, R. C. (2016). A Validation of the Group-Based Medical Mistrust Scale in Formerly Incarcerated Black and Latino Men. *American Journal of Men's Health*, *12*(4), 844–850. https://doi.org/10.1177/1557988316645152

van Willigenburg, T. (2020). Moral Injury, Post-incarceration Syndrome and Religious Coping Behind Bars. In S. Sremac & I. W. Jindra (Eds.), *Lived Religion, Conversion and Recovery* (pp. 171–185). https://doi.org/10.1007/978-3-030-40682-0_8

Vandergrift, L. A., & Christopher, P. P. (2021). Do prisoners trust the healthcare system? *Health & Justice*, *9*, 15. https://doi.org/10.1186/s40352-021-00141-x

Veiga, A., Pina-Sánchez, J., & Lewis, S. (2023). Racial and ethnic disparities in sentencing: What do we know, and where should we go? *The Howard Journal of Crime and Justice*, *62*(2), 167–182. https://doi.org/10.1111/hojo.12496

Western, B., Simes, J. T., & Bradner, K. (2021). Solitary confinement and institutional harm. *Incarceration*, *3*(1), 26326663211065644. https://doi.org/10.1177/26326663211065644

Yucel, S., & Paget, J. (2017). Are Faith-Based Programs Effective in Reducing Recidivism? A Case Study of Muslim Parolees in NSW. *Australian Journal of Islamic Studies*, *2*(3), Article 3. https://doi.org/10.55831/ajis.v2i3.53

Zoll, R. (2005, June 5). *U.S. prisons a religious battleground*. Times Argus.https://www.timesargus.com/news/u-s-prisons-a-religious-battleground/article_36f67328-ed02-5c9d-9257-52a2a6893ae2.html

CHAPTER ELEVEN

MUSLIM MENTAL HEALTH: FROM TRAUMA-INFORMED TO HEALING-CENTERED CARE

Javeed Sukhera

Systemic inequities have a profound impact on the mental health and overall wellness of individuals who identify as Muslim. The repercussions of oppression and discrimination manifest in psychological distress and heightened vigilance stemming from personal experiences or witnessing discriminatory acts, mistreatment, threats, violence, and intimidation. In the context of Muslim mental health, deeply ingrained and culturally sustained forms of discrimination such as structural racism, gendered Islamophobia, and other forms of bias perpetuate psychological distress among Muslim patients, community members, and health workers. Despite these challenges, the concept of trauma-informed care (TIC) has the potential to inform a paradigmatic shift towards more inclusive, affirming, and ultimately higher-quality mental health care. Trauma-informed approaches generally refer to a philosophical or cultural stance that integrates understanding and awareness of trauma into service delivery. This chapter takes a critical perspective to review the literature on trauma-informed care and how the concepts of racial trauma, minority stress, and internalized racism may influence the mental health of Muslims in direct and indirect ways. A framework is also provided for healing-centered care for Muslim patients. Healing-centered care is a concept built upon existing literature in liberation psychology and the published concept of "Radical Healing." Incorporating healing-centered care may allow existing mental health practitioners and systems to improve culturally affirming mental healthcare.

Introduction

Anti-Muslim prejudice and discrimination are associated with significant adverse physical and psychological consequences for individuals who identify as Muslim. For this chapter, the term anti-Muslim discrimination and anti-Muslim prejudice will be used interchangeably. These terms are somewhat synonymous with the concept of Islamophobia, which is defined as a combination of social stigma towards Islam and Muslims, a dislike of Muslims as a political entity, and a form of xenophobia and racism (Samari et al., 2018). Anti-Muslim prejudice and discrimination operate on individual, societal, and structural levels, manifesting in various ways (International Civil Liberties Monitoring Group, Islamic Social Services Association, & Noor Cultural Centre, 2020).

In a North American context, the impact of anti-Muslim hatred was demonstrated in a public way in 2017 when six Muslim worshippers were killed in Quebec, Canada (Senate of Canada Standing Senate Committee on Human Rights, 2023). This tragedy was followed by another act of hatred that took place on the evening of June 6, 2021, when a terrorist attack claimed the lives of four Muslim family members in London, Ontario, Canada (Senate of Canada, 2023). In North America, physical violence against Muslims occurs at alarming rates. In the United States, much of the modern discourse on anti-Muslim racism was amplified during the period leading up to the 2016 election and beyond (Samari et al., 2018). Anti-Muslim sentiment is also embedded in policies and laws, leading to frequent microaggressions, travel restrictions, and hate crimes, which have more than doubled in the past decade (Albahsahli et al., 2023). The impact of these hate crimes goes beyond the victims and their families, instilling fear, heightened alertness, and grief in entire communities (Perry & Alvi, 2012; Senate of Canada, 2023).

Research connects experiences of anti-Muslim prejudice and discrimination to poorer physical and mental health, with intersectional forms of oppression exacerbating these negative effects (Samari et al., 2018). Black Muslims and visibly Muslim women face higher rates of anti-Muslim violence and discrimination (Hassouneh, 2017). Muslim children are also affected; research on young Muslims highlighted themes of fear and identity struggles among children, especially after public acts of anti-Muslim violence (Elkassem et al., 2018). The cumulative effects of anti-Muslim prejudice and discrimination also lead to reduced help-seeking and increased mistrust in healthcare systems among Muslim patients (Samari et al., 2018).

This chapter posits that to effectively address the mental health consequences of anti-Muslim prejudice and discrimination; it is essential to recognize the manifestation of such prejudice and discrimination as a form of discrimination and/or oppression trauma. Over time, a trauma-informed framework has been offered as a comprehensive approach that may guide individuals and systems on a path forward (Substance Abuse and Mental Health Services Administration, 2014). However, trauma-informed framing and nomenclature may be insufficient as they focus on the pain of discrimination rather than an orientation toward healing, restoration, and advocacy. Therefore, a healing-centered framework is proposed. A healing-centered approach includes being trauma-informed while integrating principles from liberation psychology and diverse epistemologies to inform a more aspirational framework that foregrounds healing while honoring pain.

Discrimination Trauma and Muslim Mental Health

Studies show that the combined effects of oppression, victimization, and discriminatory experiences can significantly impact a person's mental and physical health. The concept of oppression refers to asymmetries of power that can contribute to some social groups leveraging certain forms of power and influence to contribute to discrimination or derogation of other groups (Prilleltensky & Gonik, 1996). Oppression is also self-perpetuating and tends to contribute to furthering and maintaining the domination of some groups over others (David et al., 2019). Experiencing oppression through prejudice and discrimination leads to chronic stress, which in turn raises the risk of illness and morbidity (Geronimus, 1992; Kirkinis et al., 2021).

Experience of oppression and discrimination can also contribute to victimization. Victimization is a similar construct, however, and can lead to more maladaptive outcomes. The term victim can imply a loss of agency or choice, leading to helplessness and powerlessness, perpetuating a cycle of blame rather than accountability. The language of victimization can be passive versus the active language of being a 'survivor' who shapes one's future and healing (Dunn, 2005).

Racial and Discrimination Trauma

For individuals with Muslim faith tradition, the experience of anti-Muslim prejudice and discrimination can be conceptualized as a form of discrimination trauma akin to existing literature on racial trauma. Such trauma can be defined as psychological distress that results from experiences of discrimination, threats, violence, or intimidation (Akerele et al., 2021; Carter et al., 2017; Williams et al., 2021). Racial trauma is unique as it does not stem solely from isolated racist incidents but rather from a combination of exposure to race-based traumatic stress and the interpretation of these experiences as part of the widespread presence of systemic racism (Akerele et al., 2021). In these ways, racial trauma can have parallels with the systemic nature of anti-Muslim prejudice and discrimination (Awaad, 2023), especially in the context of rhetoric that demonizes Muslims and foreign policy choices that devalue Muslim lives. A study of Muslim international students in the United States found that discrimination predicted post-traumatic stress symptoms above general stress and that less social connectedness was associated with perceived discrimination. This finding was particularly salient for visibly Muslim women (Jeevanba et al., 2024).

Discrimination trauma results in both physical and psychological consequences. Exposure to discrimination triggers the body's stress response, increasing cortisol levels and activating the autonomic nervous system. The cumulative effects of chronic stress heighten the risk of physical health issues, including cardiovascular, metabolic, and autoimmune diseases (Carter, 2017; Williams & Halstead, 2019). Psychologically, discrimination trauma can manifest with symptoms similar to post-traumatic stress disorder (PTSD), such as anxiety, mood changes, sleep disturbances, and hypervigilance. For instance, individuals may experience intrusive thoughts about discriminatory events, avoid reminders of discriminatory experiences, and undergo mood changes accompanied by feelings of self-blame, guilt, or anger (Williams et al., 2021).

Discrimination trauma can be inflicted in various ways on individuals who experience it. Direct experiences of prejudice/discrimination, indirect forms like microaggressions, hearing about discriminatory experiences faced by friends, peers, or family, witnessing trauma involving strangers we identify with, or public narratives about anti-Muslim violence can all undermine well-being and negatively affect academic and social performance. For instance, Black and Hispanic students in communities with high rates of police violence are particularly affected, with significant declines in grades following police killings of racially minoritized individuals (Ang, 2020; Bor et al., 2018). Likewise, racially minoritized individuals often face racism in work or educational settings. Workplace discrimination can involve unequal access to resources or a lack of agency, contributing to findings that suggest the workplace is particularly stressful for racially minoritized individuals (Williams et al., 2021).

Lived Experiences of Discrimination Trauma in London, Ontario, Canada

Firsthand accounts of anti-Muslim prejudice and discrimination draw attention to the many ways in which discrimination trauma can be experienced by Muslims and non-Muslims alike. From my own lived and living experience of the London, Ontario terror attack, I never imagined that my work on healing trauma and advancing equity and justice would become so personally relevant due to the loss of beloved family friends a few minutes from our home (Sukhera, 2021). The murder of the Afzaal family and the subsequent trial have had a profound emotional impact on the Muslim Mental Health community. This impact was particularly difficult for individuals who share a Muslim faith identity and serve Muslim patients.

During the trial, it was clear that the perpetrator shared views about Muslims with hate-filled stereotypes and tropes of Muslims posing a threat to Canadian society. His views were rooted in deeply embedded White supremacist ideology and a history of colonial narratives that portray Muslims as an "uncivilized" group. The effects of the crime contributed to mistrust and decreased treatment seeking, thereby worsening the overall well-being of Muslim communities. It contributed to behavioral responses to prejudicial hostility against Muslims, such as physical withdrawal, social isolation, difficulty or anxiety when accessing medical or mental health services or engagement with civil institutions or organizations. Ultimately, such mistrust also perpetuates worse health outcomes over time.

I have worked with young people who have experienced hateful crimes, but I have most often worked with young people who have lived in fear. The London, Ontario community lived and continues to live in fear. When you are in fear, it sensitizes you to perceive everything that happens. It still sensitizes me to perceive something like a black pickup truck or a revved engine as harmful. The community trauma that this crime has precipitated contributed to a sense of continuous anticipation of harassment. Heightened fears around relatively routine undertakings such as going for a walk with one's family or attending worship services. Consequently, many were too paralyzed with fear to leave their homes. After June 6, 2021, many patients I have worked with (both Muslim and non-Muslim) felt paralyzed with fear, leading them to avoid going outside or seeking services such as healthcare appointments.

Minority Stress Theory

In addition to discrimination trauma, another construct that can be applied to the mental health consequences of anti-Muslim prejudice and discrimination comes from the literature on minority stress theory. Examples of minority stress may range from discriminatory experiences that occur on a day-to-day basis to the impact of structural discrimination, such as policy and law (Frost & Meyer, 2023). Minority stress can also arise through gradually internalizing a negative self-concept (Jaspal et al., 2021; Liang & Huang, 2022). Therefore, those who internalize negative stereotypes about their own minoritized identity can be highly sensitized to stereotypes about themselves, including sensitization to rejection or social stigma (Douglass et al., 2020), leading to stress due to excessive self-censorship and concealment of their minoritized identity (Pachankis et al., 2020).

Over time, the accumulation of this process of internalization leads to an adverse impact on the health and well-being of the minoritized group (Frost & Meyer, 2023). There are several ways that minority stress may contribute to physical and psychological problems. Minority stress can contribute to emotional dysregulation and have a negative impact on social and interpersonal functioning (Sarno et al., 2020). There is also research suggesting that minority stress can become amplified within romantic and sexual relationships through minority stress contagion, thus compounding the negative effects of individual minority stress among couples (Frost et al., 2023; Menakem, 2022; Rostosky & Riggle, 2017).

Minority stress theory also connects to the concept of stereotype threat, which is a psychological phenomenon where individuals fear they may confirm negative stereotypes about their social group. Therefore, this pending threat can contribute to poor performance in related tasks (Steele, 2011). For example, consider the scenario of a visibly Muslim woman on a clinical rotation where they are being graded on their clinical performance. Their performance may be worse than non-Muslim counterparts due to anxiety or self-doubt leading to a self-fulfilling prophecy where fears of conforming to a negative stereotype impact their performance on the rotation.

In the context of anti-Muslim prejudice and discrimination, minority stress theory and stereotype threat can apply in dynamic and intersection ways related to various sociohistorical, contextual, racialized, and gendered forms of oppression and discrimination. Visibly identifiable women in healthcare professions can experience stereotypes that Muslim women are powerless victims of their religious tradition (Khan et al., 2022). Similarly, gendered stereotypes about Muslim men as intrinsically barbaric and violent (Wiemers et al., 2024) can contribute to prejudice and discrimination. Altogether, these stereotypes become pervasive and, at some level, can become internalized, leading Muslims to experience pressure to undo stereotypes and experience exclusion, lack of safety, fear, decreased job satisfaction, and burnout (Khan et al., 2022).

Trauma-Informed and Healing-Centered Care

Trauma-informed approaches generally represent a cultural or philosophical stance that incorporates an awareness of trauma into how services are delivered (Substance Abuse and Mental Health Services Administration, 2014). Such approaches have been offered as a powerful paradigm shift in delivering healthcare and other human services. Trauma-informed care (TIC) is built on tenets from trauma theory, which suggests that traumatic experiences or memories leave behind a residue that can be reactivated or manifested in an individual's present-day life (van der Kolk, 1994). A trauma-informed approach to mental health services incorporates an understanding of trauma and recognizes its impact across various settings, services, and populations. TIC considers trauma through both ecological and cultural perspectives, acknowledging that context significantly influences how individuals experience and cope with traumatic events, whether they are acute or ongoing. It emphasizes being mindful of and avoiding institutional processes or personal practices that could retraumatize those with a history of trauma.

Additionally, TIC values consumer involvement in creating, delivering, and assessing services. TIC suggests that certain ingredients can improve the quality and experience of healthcare if embedded into organizational and individual practices. The Substance Abuse and Mental Health Services Administration suggests that trauma-informed care must incorporate safety, trustworthiness/transparency, peer support, collaboration/mutuality, empowerment, and attention to cultural, historical, and gender issues (SAMHSA, 2014). Despite the promise of TIC, there has also been considerable critique. For example, there is a lack of conceptual consistency due to varying definitions of the concept and TIC practices (Bendall et al., 2021). There is also a lack of organizational metrics to effectively assess TIC initiatives' implementation (Wathen et al., 2023). In addition, existing conceptualizations of trauma-informed care may not sufficiently recognize harmful social and structural conditions like racism or other forms of discrimination (Wathen & Varcoe, 2023).

As TIC evolves, the concept of Healing Centered Care (HCC) may serve as a framework for addressing the root causes of discrimination trauma and minority stress and ultimately fostering healing from the wounds of anti-Muslim prejudice and discrimination. Given that existing mental health systems have contributed to historical trauma and injustice, those of us in the field must also work toward healing and dismantling these injustices. There is growing recognition that current systems need to shift away from solely focusing on biomedical symptom management and instead embrace diverse approaches. Promoting a healing-centered approach involves more than platitudes or buzzwords, as it encourages a holistic, intergenerational perspective on recovery from suffering. Ultimately, healing-centered organizations advance liberatory praxis, equity, and justice through restorative principles to address identity-based discrimination and injustice through community, collectivism, and cultural authenticity (French et al., 2020).

Radical Healing

The radical healing framework may offer specific strategies for integrating HCC into Muslim mental health. Amid increasing structural and racial violence, a group of psychology thought leaders emphasized that heightened exposure to discrimination leads to emotional distress and that individual healing should occur alongside collective healing. This group introduced the concept of radical healing, highlighting that "conventional healing focuses on individual symptom reduction...radical healing incorporates strategies that address the root causes of the trauma by building on the strengths of individuals and engaging the general and culture-specific practices of their community that promote resilience and well-being (Neville et al., 2019). Radical healing is built upon key principles, including (a) collectivism, (b) critical consciousness, (c) radical hope, (d) strength and resistance, and (e) cultural authenticity and self-knowledge (French et al., 2020). The core idea of the radical healing framework involves acknowledging and actively resisting oppression while envisioning possibilities for freedom and well-being rooted in pride and hope for the future.

Although research on the implementation of radical healing is still emerging, some have developed interventions for minoritized populations. For example, a radical healing therapeutic approach created by Adames et al. (2023) was used to treat clients experiencing racial trauma to resist self-blame, racism, and oppression and to develop and nurture healing. Research suggests that radical healing is a useful mechanism to validate experiences of discrimination trauma while validating how such trauma can influence mental health. Other interventions, such as the storying survival and the Blafemme Healing framework, use similar approaches. However, more research and evaluation are needed in this area (McNeil-Young et al., 2023; Mosley, 2023).

Key Components of Healing-Centered Care for Muslim Mental Health

Radical Hope

Radical hope embodies a steadfast belief that the fight against discrimination and oppression is achievable. Individuals suffering from the psychological effects of oppression often feel trapped in a state of hopelessness and helplessness. The concept of radical hope directs individuals who might be suffering towards a future state that cannot yet be felt or understood when they are experiencing the pain of their present moment. To cultivate radical hope in the context of Muslim mental health is to remain anchored to the concepts of *Iman* and *Ihsan*. Within Muslim contexts, *Iman* can translate to the concept of faith or belief in the unseen, whereas *Ihsan* refers to the actualization of goodness or virtue (Khaiyom et al., 2022). These concepts come from the Hadith of Jibril, which is a narration in Islamic tradition where the Prophet Muhammed (peace be upon him) described the concepts of Islam, Iman, and Ihsan, noting that Iman represents an individual's internal beliefs and Ihsan' represents a high standard of excellence and mindfulness in one's relationship with themselves, God, and those around them.

In Muslim faith tradition, hope is an important concept, while hopelessness is generally viewed as a negative state that is contrary to the importance of one's faith. In multiple verses in the Quran, there is the invocation of "patience" (Qur'an 39:10 and 94:6), not losing "hope" (12:87), and themes of trust, gratitude, and unwavering faith in God. Actualizing hope as part of HCC requires sharing narrative and concrete examples demonstrating how anti-Muslim prejudice and discrimination can be addressed through healing and dialogue. Foregrounding hope allows Muslims to remain anchored to a sacred belief in a future in this world and the hereafter that there will be liberation from the pain of discrimination and oppression.

When encountering prejudice and discrimination, radical hope allows Muslims to remain anchored to a central construct as part of illness narratives. For example, a study of South Asian Sikhs and Muslims in Scotland found hope was a central part of illness narratives and unfolded as an active process that enabled them to live with their illness (Kristiansen et al., 2014). Trauma-focused treatment for Muslim populations integrates cultural and religious practices, including narratives of Muslim prophets who have remained anchored to hope and faith in the context of healing from trauma (Bentley et al., 2021).

Strength and Resistance

The scholars who created the radical healing framework defined strength and resistance to highlight the significance of celebrating joy, moving away from narratives focused on deficits, and utilizing ancestral and intergenerational stories of resilience (French et al., 2020). The strength to resist oppression and discrimination goes beyond individual-level processes such as resilience and considers an individual's relationship with their community and the world. Strength and resistance are interconnected because a call for resistance recognizes the strength of those enduring discrimination or identity-based trauma and their intrinsic ability to challenge discriminatory practices and systems to pursue justice and liberation for themselves and one another (Ginwright, 2016). HCC and radical healing envision strength and resistance as a bridge to hope and future possibilities.

Muslims are encouraged to practice non-violent resistance as part of their faith tradition. For example, the Quran (4:135) calls on believers to stand "firm in justice," remain humble (25:63), and be committed to the public good (maslaha). Ultimately, Islam places a collective obligation on the Muslim community to oppose injustice, highlighting the strength of working together in the pursuit of what is right. In a published Hadith, the Prophet Muhammed (peace be upon him) stated, "Help your brother, whether he is an oppressor or oppressed." When asked how to help the oppressor, the Prophet stated that we help oppressors by preventing them from oppressing others (Sahih Bukhari, Volume 3; Book 43; 623-624).

When considering Muslim Mental Health and HCC, strength and resistance speak to a narrative that foregrounds hope and strength to heal and make a better world. Similar to survivors of trauma, the narrative becomes a therapeutic mechanism to re-story from the narrative of being a victim towards a narrative of survivorship, transcendence, and healing (Neimeyer, 2006). Re-telling trauma narratives is a common practice in many contemporary therapeutic approaches for trauma survivors. Therapeutic processes related to re-telling include witnessing injustice, meaning-making, or developing an explanatory account of traumatic experiences while identifying a sense of purpose or greater meaning related to adversity (Kaminer, 2006). Through HCC, those who experience prejudice and discrimination are encouraged to center their intrinsic worth and creator-endowed strength that allows them to resist oppression through an affirmation of their faith identity in the context of an oppressive world.

Critical Consciousness

Critical consciousness is defined as "an individual's ability to critically reflect on and take action regarding their sociopolitical surroundings (Kumagai & Lypson, 2009, p. 445). The concept of critical consciousness has its origins in transformative pedagogies. It typically involves three central components: Critical reflection on self and others and the system that involves questioning assumptions and challenging norms, and second, acting at the self, community, and system level by working with and through others for transformative change. Third, reinterpretation of situations and knowledge through growth and adaptation of how an individual interprets and makes meaning of situations and the world around them. Critical consciousness has been utilized to address cultural competence, aiming to cultivate critical consciousness across all aspects of health professional training through dialogic learning methods (Halman et al., 2017). Research in health professions education suggests that critical consciousness can enhance reflective practice, promote equity, and shed light on power dynamics (Manca et al., 2020). In educational literature, critical consciousness is fostered through establishing safety, identifying/addressing forms of oppression, building relationships, and role modeling the courage to advocate for equity, justice, and liberation (Zaidi et al., 2017).

Critical consciousness aligns with the Islamic notion of *Taqwa*, which can be interpreted as "God-consciousness." The concept of *Taqwa* calls on Muslims to be constantly aware of God's presence, conduct themselves with ethics and integrity and a means to spiritual growth and success. In contemporary Muslim Mental Health initiatives, *Taqwa* can be considered as piety and practiced as a form of spiritual and social responsibility for individuals and communities (Bhatti et al., 2015). This conceptualization considers both critical consciousness and *Taqwa* to represent a heightened awareness that is part of a Muslim's reciprocal relationship with their faith and creator (Lyngsøe & Stjernholm, 2022). Research describes this relationship as one of reciprocal agency where an individual strives for closeness to God and is then felt to be 'answered' by God, drawing them closer in a mutually reinforcing way (Lyngsøe & Stjernholm, 2022).

When considering anti-Muslim prejudice and discrimination and HCC, critical consciousness can be incorporated as a form of *Taqwa* that calls on Muslims to critically reflect on our role in perpetuating prejudice and discrimination. Critical consciousness then mutually reinforces the concepts of hope, strength, and resistance to foster a heightened awareness of injustice and a sense of agency for the individual experiencing prejudice or discrimination to be an active part of healing themselves and the world around them to be closer to their faith and their creator.

Collectivism

Collectivism is a central element of the radical healing framework and healing-centered care. This framework highlights that collectivism is vital for healing from the trauma of prejudice and discrimination. True healing requires community support where individuals can express themselves authentically, free from self-censorship or conformity to oppressive ideologies. Collectivism fosters healing by providing spaces for validation and refuge from the ongoing impacts of racism. It enables communities to reflect on and address discrimination trauma through group-based approaches, such as storytelling, which are used to promote mental health and well-being. A shared understanding of past or recent discriminatory experiences and a common racial identity within a group can facilitate healing. Community spaces build trust, encouraging open discussions about racism and fostering solidarity. Embracing collectivism can help restore self-worth, strengthen community effectiveness, and reconnect individuals with their racial identity.

An example of collectivism in Muslim mental health is the increasing use of cultural affinity or resource groups. These groups create environments where individuals with shared identities can connect, engage in community, and integrate self-reflection and well-being with theoretical frameworks. Such groups have been studied in K-12 education, higher education, and workplace settings and are now becoming more common in medical education and health systems (Lewis et al., 2023). At the University of California, San Francisco School of Medicine, affinity groups have allowed learners to explore their experiences with racism, embrace cultural authenticity, build community, and support anti-racist initiatives (Lewis, 2023).

Cultural Authenticity and Self-Knowledge

Cultural authenticity involves the therapeutic value of bringing one's authentic self into professional or educational environments, while self-knowledge refers to understanding one's ancestors, origins, and intergenerational histories. An example of promoting cultural authenticity and self-knowledge for Muslim mental health includes embracing decoloniality through decolonial epistemologies. Decoloniality offers a framework to examine how existing systems may sustain colonialism across different sociohistorical, geopolitical, and economic contexts. Decolonizing mental health also promotes healing by teaching how discrimination, trauma, and colonization affect mental health and highlighting knowledge systems that foster healing through community, relationships, and ancestral wisdom (Lokugamage et al., 2020; Naidu, 2021). Protective factors, such as family support and social connections, help buffer against the harmful effects of discrimination trauma. Research suggests that cultural affirmation serves as a buffer against anxiety and mood disorders for Black Americans, though not for European Americans (Watson et al., 2016; Williams et al., 2012).

An example of how to advance cultural authenticity and self-knowledge can be drawn from existing literature on self-authorship theory.

Self-authorship refers to the capacity for an individual to make meaning of their world and function so that they can allow the emotions and expectations of others to exist without absorbing them or taking responsibility for them (Boes et al., 2010). Self-authorship theory posits that an individual's capacity to define a belief system and identity that can help them navigate the world is a condition of self-authorship (Weinstock, 2010). Ingredients of self-authorship include trusting one's voice by controlling one's internal reaction rather than changing one's subjective reality, building a strong internal foundation that embraces one's unique relationship with one's multiple identities, and lastly, seeking commitment by opening oneself to growth (Boes et al., 2010). However, an individual's capacity for self-authorship varies greatly based on individual and cultural factors (Magolda, 2010).

For Muslims who experience prejudice and discrimination, cultural authenticity and self-knowledge require them to be the mediators of their relationship with their ethnic, cultural, religious, and other types of social identities. It allows them to create a sense of agency and empowerment by defining their faith identity through their own experiences (positive and negative) rather than through stereotyped or discriminatory narratives that can be commonplace in current society. Therefore, embracing cultural authenticity and self-knowledge will be unique to each individual and have various facets and textures depending on an individual's experience.

Conclusion

Discrimination and prejudice negatively impact Muslim mental health. Examples of such discrimination include racial/discrimination trauma and minority stress. Those working in the field of Muslim mental health can contribute to healing from identity-based discrimination by integrating healing-centered therapeutic approaches that embed cultural awareness and advocacy into mental health services through approaches such as collectivism, critical consciousness, radical hope, strength-based narratives, and cultural authenticity.

References

Adames, H. Y., Chavez-Dueñas, N. Y., Lewis, J. A., Neville, H. A., French, B. H., Chen, G. A., & Mosley, D. V. (2023). Radical healing in psychotherapy: Addressing the wounds of racism-related stress and trauma. *Psychotherapy, 60*(1), 39–50. https://doi.org/10.1037/pst0000435

Akerele, O., McCall, M., & Aragam, G. (2021). Healing Ethno-Racial Trauma in Black Communities: Cultural Humility as a Driver of Innovation. *JAMA Psychiatry, 78*(7), 703. https://doi.org/10.1001/jamapsychiatry.2021.0537

Albahsahli, B., Bridi, L., Aljenabi, R., Abu-Baker, D., Kaki, D. A., Godino, J. G., & Al-Rousan, T. (2023). Impact of United States refugee ban and discrimination on the mental health of hypertensive Arabic-speaking refugees. *Frontiers in Psychiatry, 14,* 1083353. https://doi.org/10.3389/fpsyt.2023.1083353

Ang, D. (2020). *Wider effects of police killings in minority neighborhoods.* Econofact: Crime and Criminal Justice. https://econofact.org/wider-effects-of-police-killings-in-minority-neighborhoods

Awaad, R. (2023, September 11). *The mental health effects of Islamophobia are devastating—and can last a lifetime. Time.* https://time.com/6335453/islamophobia-mental-health-effects-essay/

Bendall, S., Eastwood, O., Cox, G., Farrelly-Rosch, A., Nicoll, H., Peters, W., Bailey, A. P., McGorry, P. D., & Scanlan, F. (2021). A Systematic Review and Synthesis of Trauma-Informed Care Within Outpatient and Counseling Health Settings for Young People. *Child Maltreatment, 26*(3), 313–324. https://doi.org/10.1177/1077559520927468

Bentley, J. A., Feeny, N. C., Dolezal, M. L., Klein, A., Marks, L. H., Graham, B., & Zoellner, L. A. (2021). Islamic Trauma Healing: Integrating Faith and Empirically Supported Principles in a Community-Based Program. *Cognitive and Behavioral Practice, 28*(2), 167–192. https://doi.org/10.1016/j.cbpra.2020.10.005

Bhatti, O. K., Alkahtani, A., Hassan, A., & Sulaiman, M. (2015). The Relationship between Islamic Piety (Taqwa) and Workplace Deviance with Organizational Justice as a Moderator. *International Journal of Business and Management, 10*(4), p136. https://doi.org/10.5539/ijbm.v10n4p136

Boes, L. M., Magolda, M. B. B., & Buckley, J. A. (2010). Foundational assumptions and constructive-developmental theory: Self-authorship narratives. In M. B. B. Magolda, E. Creamer, & P. Meszaros (Eds.), *Development and assessment of self-authorship* (pp. 3–23). Routledge.

Bor, J., Venkataramani, A. S., Williams, D. R., & Tsai, A. C. (2018). Police killings and their spillover effects on the mental health of black Americans: A population-based, quasi-experimental study. *The Lancet, 392*(10144), 302–310. https://doi.org/10.1016/S0140-6736(18)31130-9

Carter, R. T., Johnson, V. E., Roberson, K., Mazzula, S. L., Kirkinis, K., & Sant-Barket, S. (2017). Race-based traumatic stress, racial identity statuses, and psychological functioning: An exploratory investigation. *Professional*

Psychology: Research and Practice, 48(1), 30–37. https://doi.org/10.1037/pro0000116

David, E. J. R., Schroeder, T. M., & Fernandez, J. (2019). Internalized racism: A systematic review of the psychological literature on racism's most insidious consequence. *Journal of Social Issues*, 75(4), 1057–1086. https://doi.org/10.1111/josi.12350

Douglass, R. P., Conlin, S. E., & Duffy, R. D. (2020). Beyond Happiness: Minority Stress and Life Meaning Among LGB Individuals. *Journal of Homosexuality*, 67(11), 1587–1602. https://doi.org/10.1080/00918369.2019.1600900

Dunn, J. L. (2005). Victims" and "survivors": Emerging vocabularies of motive for "battered women who stay. Sociological Inquiry, 75(1), 1–30.

Elkassem, S., Csiernik, R., Mantulak, A., Kayssi, G., Hussain, Y., Lambert, K., Bailey, P., & Choudhary, A. (2018). Growing Up Muslim: The Impact of Islamophobia on Children in a Canadian Community. *Journal of Muslim Mental Health*, 12(1). https://doi.org/10.3998/jmmh.10381607.0012.101

French, B. H., Lewis, J. A., Mosley, D. V., Adames, H. Y., Chavez-Dueñas, N. Y., Chen, G. A., & Neville, H. A. (2020). Toward a Psychological Framework of Radical Healing in Communities of Color. *The Counseling Psychologist*, 48(1), 14–46. https://doi.org/10.1177/0011000019843506

Frost, D. M., LeBlanc, A. J., De Vries, B., Alston-Stepnitz, E., Stephenson, R., & Woodyatt, C. (2017). Couple-level Minority Stress: An Examination of Same-sex Couples' Unique Experiences. *Journal of Health and Social Behavior*, 58(4), 455–472. https://doi.org/10.1177/0022146517736754

Frost, D. M., & Meyer, I. H. (2023). Minority stress theory: Application, critique, and continued relevance. *Current Opinion in Psychology*, 51, 101579. https://doi.org/10.1016/j.copsyc.2023.101579

Geronimus, A. T. (1992). The weathering hypothesis and the health of African-American women and infants: Evidence and speculations. *Ethnicity & Disease*, 2(3), 207–221.

Ginwright, S. A. (2016). *Hope and healing in urban education: How urban activists and teachers are reclaiming matters of the heart*. Routledge. https://doi.org/10.4324/9781315757025

Halman, M., Baker, L., & Ng, S. (2017). Using critical consciousness to inform health professions education: A literature review. *Perspectives on Medical Education*, 6(1), 12–20. https://doi.org/10.1007/S40037-016-0324-Y

Hassouneh, D. (2017). Anti-Muslim Racism and Women's Health. *Journal of Women's Health (2002)*, 26(5), 401–402. https://doi.org/10.1089/jwh.2017.6430

International Civil Liberties Monitoring Group, Islamic Social Services Association, & Noor Cultural Centre. (2020, November 30). *Islamophobia in Canada: Submission to the UN Special Rapporteur on Freedom of Religion or Belief*. https://iclmg.ca/wp-content/uploads/2020/11/Noor-ICLMG-ISSA-2.pdf

Jaspal, R., Lopes, B., & Rehman, Z. (2021). A structural equation model for predicting depressive symptomatology in Black, Asian and Minority

Ethnic gay, lesbian and bisexual people in the UK. *Psychology & Sexuality*, *12*(3), 217–234. https://doi.org/10.1080/19419899.2019.1690560

Jeevanba, S. B., Nilsson, J. E., & Berkel, L. (2024). Discrimination, Traumatic Stress, and Coping Among Muslim International Students. *Journal of College Student Mental Health*, 1–17. https://doi.org/10.1080/28367138.2024.2407427

Kaminer, D. (2006). Healing Processes in Trauma Narratives: A Review. *South African Journal of Psychology*, *36*(3), 481–499. https://doi.org/10.1177/008124630603600304

Khaiyom, J. H. A., Ariffin, A. H. T., & Rosli, A. N. M. (2022). Islam, Iman, and Ihsan: The Role of Religiosity on Quality of Life and Mental Health of Muslim Undergraduate Students in Islamic University. *IIUM Medical Journal Malaysia*, *21*(3). https://doi.org/10.31436/imjm.v21i3.2047

Khan, S., Eldoma, M., Malick, A., Najeeb, U., & Furqan, Z. (2022). Dismantling gendered Islamophobia in medicine. *CMAJ: Canadian Medical Association Journal = Journal de l'Association Medicale Canadienne*, *194*(21), E748–E750. https://doi.org/10.1503/cmaj.220445

Kirkinis, K., Pieterse, A. L., Martin, C., Agiliga, A., & Brownell, A. (2021). Racism, racial discrimination, and trauma: A systematic review of social science literature. *Ethnicity & Health*, *26*(3), 392–412. https://doi.org/10.1080/13557858.2018.1514453

Kristiansen, M., Irshad, T., Worth, A., Bhopal, R., Lawton, J., & Sheikh, A. (2014). The practice of hope: A longitudinal, multi-perspective qualitative study among South Asian Sikhs and Muslims with life-limiting illness in Scotland. *Ethnicity & Health*, *19*(1), 1–19. https://doi.org/10.1080/13557858.2013.858108

Kumagai, A. K., & Lypson, M. L. (2009). Beyond Cultural Competence: Critical Consciousness, Social Justice, and Multicultural Education: *Academic Medicine*, *84*(6), 782–787. https://doi.org/10.1097/ACM.0b013e3181a42398

Lewis, J. A. (2023). Contributions of Black psychology scholars to models of racism and health: Applying intersectionality to center Black women. *American Psychologist*, *78*(4), 576–588. https://doi.org/10.1037/amp0001141

Lewis, L., Cribb Fabersunne, C., Iacopetti, C. L., Negussie-Retta, G., McBride, D., Irving, P., & Marbin, J. (2023). Racial Affinity Group Caucusing in Medical Education—A Key Supplement to Antiracism Curricula. *New England Journal of Medicine*, *388*(17), 1542–1545. https://doi.org/10.1056/NEJMp2212866

Liang, Z., & Huang, Y.-T. (2022). "Strong Together": Minority Stress, Internalized Homophobia, Relationship Satisfaction, and Depressive Symptoms among Taiwanese Young Gay Men. *The Journal of Sex Research*, *59*(5), 621–631. https://doi.org/10.1080/00224499.2021.1947954

Lokugamage, A. U., Ahillan, T., & Pathberiya, S. D. C. (2020). Decolonising ideas of healing in medical education. *Journal of Medical Ethics*, *46*(4), 265–272. https://doi.org/10.1136/medethics-2019-105866

Lyngsøe, M. L., & Stjernholm, S. (2022). Nearness to God: Danish Muslims and Taqwa-infused faith frames. *Contemporary Islam, 16*(2), 173–191. https://doi.org/10.1007/s11562-022-00498-2

Magolda, M. B. B. (2010). The interweaving of epistemological, intrapersonal, and interpersonal development in the evolution of self-authorship. In M. B. B. Magolda, E. Creamer, & P. Meszaros (Eds.), *Development and assessment of self-authorship* (pp. 25-43). Routledge.

Manca, A., Gormley, G. J., Johnston, J. L., & Hart, N. D. (2020). Honoring Medicine's Social Contract: A Scoping Review of Critical Consciousness in Medical Education. *Academic Medicine, 95*(6), 958–967. https://doi.org/10.1097/ACM.0000000000003059

McNeil-Young, V. A., Mosley, D. V., Bellamy, P., Lewis, A., & Hernandez, C. (2023). Storying survival: An approach to radical healing for the Black community. *Journal of Counseling Psychology, 70*(3), 276–292. https://doi.org/10.1037/cou0000635

Menakem, R. (2022). *The Quaking of America: An Embodied Guide to Navigating Our Nation's Upheaval and Racial Reckoning*. Central Recovery Press, LLC.

Mosley, D. V. (2023). A biomythography introducing the Blafemme Healing framework. *American Psychologist, 78*(5), 678–694. https://doi.org/10.1037/amp0001146

Naidu, T. (2021). Modern Medicine Is a Colonial Artifact: Introducing Decoloniality to Medical Education Research. *Academic Medicine, 96*(11S), S9–S12. https://doi.org/10.1097/ACM.0000000000004339

Neimeyer, R. A. (2006). Re-Storying Loss: Fostering Growth in the Post-traumatic Narrative. In L. G. Calhoun & R. G. Tedeschi (Eds.), *Handbook of post-traumatic growth: Research & Practice* (pp. 68–80). Lawrence Erlbaum Associates Publishers.

Neville, H. A., Adames, H. Y., Chavez-Dueñas, N. Y., Chen, G. A., French, B. H., Lewis, J. A., & Mosley, D. V. (2019, March 27). *The psychology of radical healing*. Psychology Today. https://www.psychologytoday.com/us/blog/healing-through-social-justice/201903/the-psychology-radical-healing

Pachankis, J. E., Mahon, C. P., Jackson, S. D., Fetzner, B. K., & Bränström, R. (2020). Sexual orientation concealment and mental health: A conceptual and meta-analytic review. *Psychological Bulletin, 146*(10), 831–871. https://doi.org/10.1037/bul0000271

Perry, B., & Alvi, S. (2012). 'We are all vulnerable': The *in terrorem* effects of hate crimes. *International Review of Victimology, 18*(1), 57–71. https://doi.org/10.1177/0269758011422475

Prilleltensky, I., & Gonick, L. (1996). Polities Change, Oppression Remains: On Psychology and Politics of Oppression. *Political Psychology, 17*(1), 127. https://doi.org/10.2307/3791946

Rostosky, S. S., & Riggle, E. D. (2017). Same-sex relationships and minority stress. *Current Opinion in Psychology, 13*, 29–38. https://doi.org/10.1016/j.copsyc.2016.04.011

Samari, G., Alcalá, H. E., & Sharif, M. Z. (2018). Islamophobia, Health, and Public Health: A Systematic Literature Review. *American Journal of Public Health, 108*(6), e1–e9. https://doi.org/10.2105/AJPH.2018.304402

Sarno, E. L., Newcomb, M. E., & Mustanski, B. (2020). Rumination longitudinally mediates the association of minority stress and depression in sexual and gender minority individuals. *Journal of Abnormal Psychology, 129*(4), 355–363. https://doi.org/10.1037/abn0000508

Senate of Canada Standing Senate Committee on Human Rights. (2023, November). *Combatting. hate: Islamophobia and its impact on Muslims in Canada*. https://sencanada.ca/en/info-page/parl-44-1/ridr-islamophobia/

Steele, C. M. (2011). *Whistling Vivaldi: And Other Clues to How Stereotypes Affect Us (Issues of Our Time)* (1st ed). W. W. Norton & Company, Incorporated.

Substance Abuse and Mental Health Services Administration. (2014). *SAMHSA's concept of trauma and guidance for a trauma-informed approach* (HHS Publication No. SMA 14-4884). U.S. Department of Health and Human Services.

Sukhera, J. (2021, June 20). *A child psychiatrist who knew those killed in the London terror attack offers advice on helping kids deal with trauma*. The Conversation. https://theconversation.com/a-child-psychiatrist-who-knew-those-killed-in-the-london-terror-attack-offers-advice-on-helping-kids-deal-with-trauma-162761

van der Kolk, B. A. (1994). The body keeps the score: Memory and evolving psychobiology of post-traumatic stress. *Harvard Review of Psychiatry, 1*(5), 253–265. https://doi.org/10.3109/10673229409017088

Wathen, C. N., Schmitt, B., & MacGregor, J. C. D. (2023). Measuring Trauma- (and Violence-) Informed Care: A Scoping Review. *Trauma, Violence & Abuse, 24*(1), 261–277. https://doi.org/10.1177/15248380211029399

Wathen, C. N., & Varcoe, C. (Eds.). (2023). *Implementing trauma- and Violence-Informed Care: A Handbook* (1st ed). University of Toronto Press.

Watson, L. B., DeBlaere, C., Langrehr, K. J., Zelaya, D. G., & Flores, M. J. (2016). The influence of multiple oppressions on women of color's experiences with insidious trauma. *Journal of Counseling Psychology, 63*(6), 656–667. https://doi.org/10.1037/cou0000165

Weinstock, M. (2010). Epistemological development of Bedouins and Jews in Israel: Implications for self-authorship. In M. B. B. Magolda, E. Creamer, & P. Meszaros (Eds.), *Development and assessment of self-authorship* (pp. 143-160). Routledge.

Wiemers, S. A., Stasio, V. D., & Veit, S. (2024). Stereotypes about Muslims in the Netherlands: An Intersectional Approach. *Social Psychology Quarterly*, 01902725231219688. https://doi.org/10.1177/01902725231219688

Williams, M. T., Chapman, L. K., Wong, J., & Turkheimer, E. (2012). The role of ethnic identity in symptoms of anxiety and depression in African Americans. *Psychiatry Research, 199*(1), 31–36. https://doi.org/10.1016/j.psychres.2012.03.049

Williams, M. T., & Halstead, M. (2019). Racial microaggressions as barriers to treatment in clinical care. *Directions in Psychiatry, 39*(4), 265-280.

Williams, M. T., Osman, M., Gran-Ruaz, S., & Lopez, J. (2021). Intersection of Racism and PTSD: Assessment and Treatment of Racial Stress and Trauma. *Current Treatment Options in Psychiatry*, *8*(4), 167–185. https://doi.org/10.1007/s40501-021-00250-2

Zaidi, Z., Vyas, R., Verstegen, D., Morahan, P., & Dornan, T. (2017). Medical Education to Enhance Critical Consciousness: Facilitators' Experiences. *Academic Medicine*, *92*(11S), S93–S99. https://doi.org/10.1097/ACM.0000000000001907

CHAPTER TWELVE

MUSLIMS WITH DISABILITIES & MENTAL HEALTH

Joohi Tahir

Introduction

It has been my honor to serve the people of Jannah—both personally and professionally. On a personal level, I am the caregiver for my 24-year-old daughter, who is on the autism spectrum. On a professional level, ten years ago, I co-founded MUHSEN (Muslims Understanding and Helping Special Education Needs). MUHSEN may not have been born had it not been for my daughter.

The intersection of my passion for my family and work has been nothing short of a miracle. I am in awe that I have the opportunity to lead initiatives that can benefit not only my daughter but also anyone with special needs. Our experiences have taught us that this issue is not about us versus them; special needs families are part of our lives, our homes, our masajids, and our community. We are all one.

MUHSEN's founder, Shaykh Omar Suleiman, has a personal connection to this cause. He grew up witnessing his mother (may Allah have mercy on her) struggle with special needs due to cancer and multiple strokes, which resulted in severe hearing loss and difficulty speaking, among other medical challenges. This experience has made him particularly sensitive to the needs of individuals with disabilities in the masjid. Shaykh Omar frequently delivers khutbahs and speaks about issues related to special needs. He also serves as the President of the Yaqeen Institute for Islamic Research, is a professor of Islamic Studies at Southern Methodist University and is the resident scholar at the Valley Ranch Islamic Center.

Moreover, many of the founders, board members, staff, and volunteers at MUHSEN have family members with special needs. This connection drives our work, making it more than just a 9-to-5 job. Our passion for this cause is evident throughout the organization.

Through an Islamic Lens

Mental health and disabilities are not unique to any single community. However, the additional layers of faith and culture present in the Muslim community make it crucial to address this topic seriously. In Islam, individuals with special needs hold a significant status. For instance, when the Prophet Muhammad, peace and blessings be upon him, was attempting to persuade some leaders of Makkah to embrace Islam, Abdullah Ibn Umm Maktum, a blind man, approached him for guidance. The Prophet, occupied at that moment, did not pay attention to him.

Allah SWT revealed verses of the Quran to correct that. "He frowned and turned away because the blind man came to him. You never know perhaps he may be purified, or he may be mindful, benefitting from the reminder." (Quran 80: 1-2)

The Prophet took this advice to heart and always looked out for individuals with special needs. He appointed Abdullah Ibn Umm Maktum as the leader of Madinah on more than ten occasions during his absences. The Prophet was known for insisting on sharing meals and drinks with people who had special needs, as they were often viewed as burdens or misfortunes. As Muslims, it is essential to recognize the high status of those with special needs, as taught through the sunnah.

The story of Julaybib, a companion of the Prophet, is both heartwarming and enlightening. Julaybib had physical deformities, yet the Prophet always made an effort to include him. He frequently invited Julaybib to his table and referred to him as part of his family.

The Prophet would say, "*Allahumma hadha minni wa anna minhu*" (O Allah, this one is from me, and I am from him). What an honor!

However, we must ask ourselves: do we treat our brothers and sisters with special needs with the respect and dignity they deserve? Unfortunately, contrary to the teachings of our faith, being disabled and Muslim can lead to additional scrutiny and stigma. Many cultural practices within Muslim communities often marginalize those with disabilities.

Parents of children with special needs may face hurtful judgments, being told that they could have prevented the disability by praying more or committing fewer sins. Some have been bluntly told—both to their faces and behind their backs—that Allah is punishing them for some wrongdoing, and that is why they have a child who is "not normal."

At the time of the Prophet, there was a widespread misconception that people with special needs should be avoided, as it was believed they carried a contagious curse or disease. Unfortunately, this belief was not unique to seventh-century Arabs. For example, Plato referred to people with special needs as a "malicious category constituting a burden on society and a damaging factor for a republic."

Islam, however, teaches the exact opposite. Allah (SWT) chooses the parents of special children as part of a test, offering them higher rewards and elevating their ranks. Caring for those who cannot care for themselves is seen as a noble act, and Islam emphasizes the value and dignity of people with special needs.

Despite this, we must ask ourselves: do Muslims truly uphold these values in practice? Acknowledgment and recognition are important, but wholehearted inclusion and acceptance are equally vital. Our historical context also plays a significant role in shaping our attitudes.

Early Muslim Americans

The pioneering Muslims who migrated to the United States in the 1970s laid the foundation for our community as we know it today. They established masjids, Sunday schools, and halal meat stores, and made significant contributions in fields like medicine. Despite their tremendous sacrifices and investments in the community, they often viewed issues from an external perspective. For various reasons, including a lack of awareness, they neglected internal challenges, pushing important topics such as mental health, women's rights, racial diversity, and inclusivity for individuals with special needs to the background. We can appreciate that, given their limited resources and the challenges they faced as immigrants, they may not have been able to address everything simultaneously.

The American Muslim community today cannot excuse inaction anymore. We have already inherited the fundamental pillars of society from previous generations. Now, it's our responsibility to focus on the marginalized segments within Muslim communities. We must invest in resources for senior centers, women's transitional homes, and mental health and special needs services.

As Muslims, we believe that Allah (SWT) will ask us how we used our resources. What did we do with our education, large homes, fancy cars, and connections? Did we dedicate even a small portion of these assets to help the vulnerable among us? Did we only raise funds for chandeliers in mosques, or did we ensure that everyone could attend the mosque and participate in its events?

Instead of dwelling on what was not done yesterday, MUHSEN was born to make today and tomorrow better because the Muslim community is not immune from disabilities.

We're not Immune: Data on Disabilities/Research

It is unfair to group all individuals with disabilities together. This approach is both insensitive and inaccurate. With the wide range of disabilities that exist, it's crucial to recognize that someone who appears to be high-functioning may have a hidden disability. For instance, speech impediment might not seem significant at first glance, but it can profoundly impact a person's confidence. It's important to note that there is no competition regarding who has it worse among individuals with disabilities.

Roughly one in three of every community studied has a member of their immediate family with a disability, and this includes Muslims.

According to the US Census Bureau's American Community Survey (ACS) in 2019, approximately 61 million adults in the US (about 26% of the adult population) reported having a physical or mental disability. Disabilities can encompass a wide range of conditions, including mobility impairments, sensory disabilities (such as blindness or deafness), cognitive disabilities (such as intellectual disabilities or autism), and mental health disorders (such as depression, anxiety disorders, or schizophrenia). Disability rates increase with age. The ACS data indicates that around 38% of adults aged 65 and older reported having a disability, compared to about 7% of adults aged 18-44. Employment rates for people with disabilities are lower than for those without disabilities. In 2020, the employment-population ratio was 18.7% for people with a disability, compared to 62.3% for those without a disability.

In 2019, among individuals aged 25 to 64 with a disability, around 33.7% had a bachelor's degree or higher, compared to 41.1% of those without a disability. There are income disparities between individuals with and without disabilities. In 2019, the median earnings for individuals with a disability were approximately $25,787, while for those without a disability, it was $36,665. People with disabilities often face barriers in accessing healthcare services, including physical accessibility of facilities, affordability, and availability of specialized care. Social inclusion and participation can also be impacted by disability.

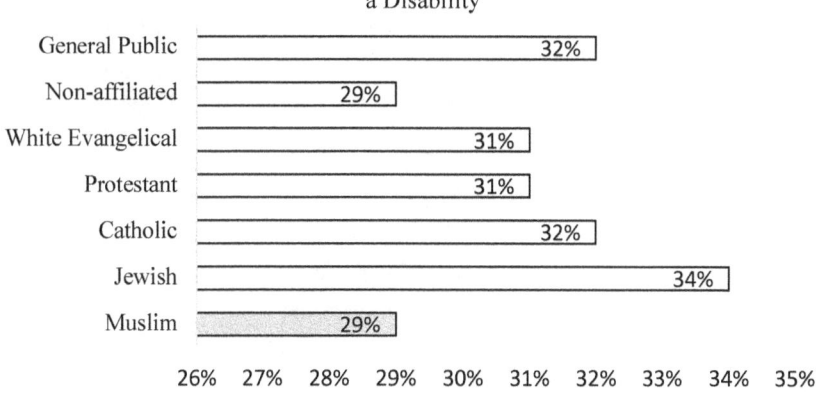

Figure 1: *Do you or does an immediate family member have a disability?* (%Yes shown) Base: Total respondents, 2020.

If 29% of Muslim households include a member that has a disability, this segment makes up a larger percentage of American Muslims than Muslims who identify as any of the following racial or ethnic groups: Arab (18%), Asian (23%), or white (23%), meaning this segment of the Muslim community cannot be ignored.

Research has shown that:

- One in thirty-six children in the US have autism.
- One in seven hundred live births have Down Syndrome.
- Cerebral palsy occurs in 1.5 to 2.5 per 1,000 live births.
- One million Americans are blind
- The deaf population in the US is 3.6%.
- About 2–3 out of every 1,000 children in the US are born with some degree of hearing loss.

For instance, around 14% of adults in the US have some form of mobility disability, such as walking or climbing stairs. Approximately 12 million adults in the US suffer from some form of vision disability, including blindness, low vision, and other visual impairments. More than 37 million Americans have varying degrees of hearing loss. More than 6 million people have cognitive disabilities that can range from intellectual disabilities to conditions affecting memory, learning, and functioning. Psychiatric disabilities include mental health conditions such as depression, anxiety disorders, bipolar disorder, schizophrenia, and others. It's estimated that approximately 20% of adults in the US experience mental illness each year, with 5% experiencing a severe mental illness that substantially interferes with or limits major life activities. Developmental disabilities typically manifest early in life and can affect physical, learning, language, or behavior areas. About 17% of children aged 3 to 17 years in the US have one or more developmental disabilities, according to CDC.

And it doesn't end here. Even beyond these categories, there is a wide range of other disabilities, such as chronic health conditions and sensory impairments.

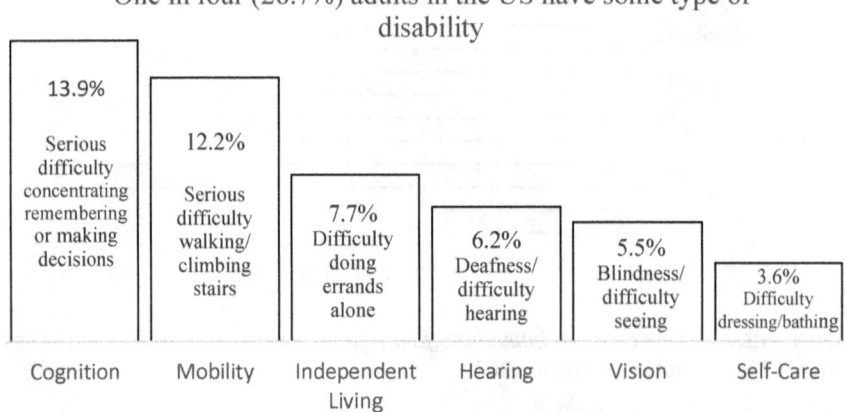

Figure 2: Percentage of U.S. adults having disability (CDC, 2020).

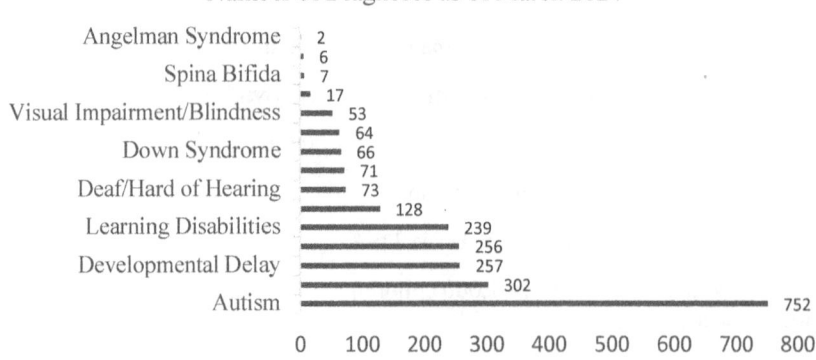

Figure 3. Needs Research Report; data collected from over 1900 participants by MUHSEN (2024).

According to the MUHSEN Needs Research Report (MUHSEN, 2024), 44% of people living with disabilities are under 18. Among 1982 respondents in North America, more than 2314 diagnoses were found. The most commonly found were Autism, ADHD, Developmental Delay, and Speech/Language Impairment.

According to the same report, the states that came out with the largest number of respondents were California (9%), Illinois (17%), and Texas (25%). The top priority for needs identified in those states were:

> California: Open house, access to programs and classes, support groups and childcare options.
>
> Illinois: Youth programs, access to programs and courses, weekend school and quiet room.
>
> Texas: Access to Programs and classes, weekend school, awareness and acceptance, and social opportunities for the child.

On a scale of 1-10, their special needs family member's acceptance in the community was rated 6.6 out of 10 overall.

How Disability Impacts Mental Health

Mental health problems are the single largest cause of disabilities in the world. Some of the major disabilities are depression, anxiety, and dementia. Adults were identified as having frequent mental distress if they reported having poor mental health for 14 or more days out of 30 days.

Disabilities and mental health are interconnected yet distinct aspects of human experience that profoundly impact individuals and societies. While disabilities refer to impairments that may affect physical, sensory, cognitive, or emotional functioning, mental health pertains to emotional, psychological, and social well-being.

People with disabilities often face significant challenges in accessing education, employment, healthcare, and social participation due to physical or structural barriers. These barriers can exacerbate feelings of isolation, frustration, and inequality, impacting their mental health. On the other hand, mental health disorders such as depression, anxiety, bipolar disorder, schizophrenia, and others can affect anyone regardless of physical ability. These conditions can be debilitating, influencing a person's thoughts, emotions, behaviors, and ability to function in daily life.

The intersection of disabilities and mental health is complex and multifaceted. Supporting individuals with disabilities and mental health concerns requires a holistic approach that addresses both their specific needs and broader systemic issues.

Stigma & Stereotypes: Impact on the Individual with the Disability

Individuals with disabilities often face stereotyping based on their conditions. These stereotypes can depict them as incapable, dependent, or less competent, leading to the perception that they cannot make significant positive contributions to society. As a result, they may experience social exclusion from community events and peer interactions, which can contribute to feelings of loneliness, depression, and low self-esteem.

Despite legal protections such as the Americans with Disabilities Act (ADA), many individuals with disabilities still encounter barriers in the workplace. Employers may hold implicit biases regarding productivity and the need for accommodations. Additionally, stigma can manifest in educational settings, negatively affecting access to inclusive education and appropriate support services.

Addressing stigma requires collective efforts to promote understanding, empathy, and inclusivity. Strategies include education, awareness, and advocacy, as well as encouraging inclusive practices in workplaces, schools, healthcare settings, and communities, which can foster environments where individuals with disabilities feel valued and respected. It is also imperative to empower individuals. Supporting self-advocacy and empowerment among individuals with disabilities to assert their rights, challenge discrimination, and participate fully in society.

No one likes to feel alienated. MUHSEN is creating that community for caregivers so no one should suffer in silence. As Muslims, we can be held accountable by God if we don't provide such a safe space for our brothers and sisters hurting. Our community needs to step up and learn. MUHSEN provides the training so there is less fear of the unknown. As awareness increases, there is more normalization. There is still a long way to go in implementation. You can read all about eating clean and exercising, but you won't see the results unless you do it.

A Perpetual Roller Coaster: Impact on Parents/Caregivers of Individuals with a Disability

As a mother of a special needs child, I often feel like I haven't had a day off in 24 years. Research has shown that the stress levels experienced by mothers of disabled children are comparable to those of combat soldiers. On top of this, we face physical, mental, and emotional stress, compounded by societal beliefs that suggest we may have done something wrong. Even if we don't fully believe it, that underlying guilt lingers in the back of our minds.

Parents, particularly mothers of children with special needs, often experience heightened anxiety stemming from the fear that something might happen to their child, as they are the primary caregivers. They face a constant juggling act of trying to prioritize their own self-care, allocating time for their marriage, giving individual attention to each child, and also nurturing the family as a whole.

In theory, it's easy to suggest that couples should establish a routine to avoid neglecting their marriage, but in practice, this can be challenging. You might not have family or trusted friends nearby, or you may find it difficult to locate or afford trained therapists for babysitting. Additionally, there might be a fear of letting go in case something goes wrong. However, with services like MUHSEN respite care, parents can receive occasional relief.

For families with special needs, maintaining a connection with your spouse is crucial, as no one understands your special needs child better than your partner, who has been alongside you from the beginning. Nevertheless, it can be easy to overlook your marriage when there are more pressing concerns.

I always suggest that families focus on what is practical. If a perfect night out at an Instagram-worthy restaurant with great ambiance isn't possible, that's okay. Instead of not doing anything for yourself or your marriage, consider ordering food delivery once the kids are asleep. It doesn't have to be anything extravagant; simply dedicating time to each other can greatly benefit your mental health and strengthen your relationship.

Additionally, MUHSEN offers respite services during Umrah, carnivals, conventions, fundraising dinners, and Eid Salah, allowing parents to enjoy activities together in peace.

Abu Hurairah reported that the Messenger of Allah said, "Whoever helps relieve a Muslim of a burden in this world, Allah will relieve him of a burden on the Day of Judgment. And whoever assists in easing difficulty in this world, Allah will grant him ease from difficulties in both this world and the Hereafter."

They Are Not OK: The Impact on Siblings

Even if a sibling of a child with special needs "looks okay," they are 100% affected in one way or another. They are not okay. Having a brother or sister with a disability is a challenge they did not choose. If the topic is not addressed appropriately from a young age, they might feel shame about their sibling. Alternatively, they might take on the role of a default parent, becoming overly protective. They may also harbor resentment due to feeling neglected when parents need to devote more time to the child with a disability. Additionally, they could experience survivor's guilt, wondering why they have opportunities—like attending college—while their sibling does not. It's possible that they could experience a combination of all these feelings. Parents often cannot choose which roles their children will assume in relation to a sibling with a disability; these roles tend to fall into place automatically. Regardless of the role they take, siblings often carry an additional layer of responsibility. It's important for parents to recognize that these children also deserve a fulfilling childhood. They should not have to live in the shadow of their sibling with a disability. This is why having a supportive community is essential. By arranging for someone to care for the child with special needs, parents can create valuable one-on-one time with their other child or children.

MUHSEN sibling support circles help families break free from feelings of isolation. Participants are encouraged to share their emotions in a manner that is appropriate for their age. Some older siblings realize that they may need to take on the role of primary caregivers for their special needs sibling once their parents are no longer able to do so, whether due to age or passing away. This responsibility can affect their life decisions, such as where to live or whom to marry. For example, they may ponder questions like, "Can I move to California if my sibling needs me to stay in Texas?" It is essential that their future partner understands this dynamic and is committed to supporting them, as he or she might also become involved in caring for the sibling with special needs. Therefore, choosing a life partner who is willing to share this long-term commitment is crucial.

MUHSEN places a high priority on creating a support system that safeguards the mental health of individuals with disabilities, as well as their families and caregivers. Our support groups are moderated by licensed social workers or therapists, ensuring a safe and understanding environment for participants. These groups allow people to come together and find meaningful support. We organize support groups specifically for siblings and caregivers, and we also train others to lead similar circles in their own towns and cities.

What MUHSEN Does to Address Mental Health (Programs and Services)

Implementing Solutions

I don't want to simply list all the programs MUHSEN offers; instead, I want to provide insights into each one to inspire other communities in the US and beyond. We need to dispel the misconception that making accommodations is difficult or expensive. Neither of these statements is true. With some planning and by following the blueprint created by MUHSEN and similar organizations, we can make accommodation and inclusivity the standard rather than the exception.

At MUHSEN, we don't just highlight the challenges faced by the community; we actively demonstrate how to address them. Rather than simply sending "thoughts and prayers" to families with special needs, we provide respite care, allowing parents to enjoy an occasional uninterrupted dinner. Instead of allowing adults with special needs to remain at home without purpose, MUHSEN has established an adult day program. This program is designed for individuals aged 18 and older who have aged out of public school services, enabling them to learn important life skills. Participants can go on outings together and receive care from trained professionals in a safe and nurturing environment.

One of the fundamental principles of our faith is to believe in Allah and perform good deeds. Belief alone is only part of the equation; Islam is a very action-oriented religion. MUHSEN embodies this principle by actively working to support the community. For example, instead of just stating that everyone is welcome to the Eid carnival at the masjid, they offer a MUHSEN fast pass that allows kids with special needs to bypass longer lines, helping them avoid unnecessary waiting. Often, making accommodations does not have to be expensive. Simply acknowledging the needs of these individuals—whether children or adults—is a crucial first step. With the right intentions, Allah provides solutions and brings the right people to help implement them.

Over the past ten years, MUHSEN has built a dedicated team where each member competes, not for accolades or awards, but to earn rewards from Allah by genuinely helping those who cannot help themselves.

Masjid Certification

Islamic Centers: MUHSEN Masjid certification efforts

During the lifetime of Prophet Muhammad (S), he welcomed everyone in the community, regardless of gender, ethnicity, or ability, ensuring inclusivity in the mosque (masjid). A blind companion served as the second muezzin following Bilal. People with disabilities were encouraged to attend the masjid and were advised not to use their disabilities as an excuse to stay away.

The saying "out of sight, out of mind" may have been convenient for those before us, but we shouldn't assume that people with special needs do not want to come to the masjid. Instead, we should work to make it a more welcoming place and see what happens. Our efforts need to go beyond merely meeting ADA legal requirements. Some improvements aren't even costly. For example, I've never had to suggest that a masjid remodel its entire bathroom; sometimes, simply adding a sprayer for wudu can significantly enhance accessibility.

Masjid certification should focus not only on adding ramps and elevators but also on elevating the conversation to include individuals with special needs in every aspect—physically, emotionally, and spiritually.

Salman al-Farisi reported: The Messenger of Allah, peace and blessings be upon him, said: "The masjid is the home of every righteous believer. Allah has guaranteed comfort and gratification of those who take the masajids as their homes..."

MUHSEN Service-Certification is a FREE program designed to help qualify organizations and community centers across North America, ensuring they are properly equipped to meet the needs of individuals with disabilities in our communities. This program is unique because we are the only organization in North America that certifies mosques and community organizations by verifying that they meet all disability-related criteria and requirements.

MUHSEN awards masajid (mosques) with certification badges based on the number of criteria they meet. You can also find a certified Islamic center on our website. However, the most important aspect is encouraging masajid to implement these changes with Ihsan (excellence). We want individuals of all abilities to feel welcomed in the masjid, allowing them to worship alongside others, connect with the community, and combat feelings of isolation.

Good Day Program

While the public school system does offer some support services, such as speech therapy and occupational therapy, this support often ceases when students age out of the system. This leaves many parents wondering: what happens next? Many students are accustomed to the routine of attending school daily and watching their siblings and parents leave the home. How can they have fulfilling days without that structure?

This gap in services inspired the creation of the MUHSEN Good Day program. Designed for young adults with disabilities aged 15 to 30, the program focuses on helping participants engage in meaningful activities that enhance their daily living skills and interests. The goal is to encourage self-esteem and personal success. Participants receive vocational training, life skills development, exercise, and opportunities for spiritual growth.

MUSLIMS WITH DISABILITIES & MENTAL HEALTH

Additionally, they take part in community service projects, such as assembling supply kits, sorting brochures, and stocking food pantries.

While the Good Day program offers many benefits for participants, we also view it as a form of dawah, as it is inclusive and not limited to Muslims. We welcome families from other faiths who bring their adult children, and they appreciate the cleanliness and professionalism with which we operate. From our name to our staff, our Muslim identity is evident and embraced.

One of MUHSEN's greatest strengths is our team of compassionate, hard-working, and dedicated individuals. Our staff and volunteers consistently prioritize the needs of others. After undergoing extensive training, we conduct background checks through third-party companies to ensure safety and peace of mind for all our families and team members.

"I believe that everything happens at the right time. I learned about MUHSEN from a friend during a challenging period in my life when Allah was testing me in many ways," said Rabab Ayyad, a single mother of a participant in our Good Day Adult Program. "I lost one of my children, separated from my husband, and faced financial difficulties. I took on full responsibility for my son, Mohammad, and I was unable to send him to school or enroll him in programs. I felt restricted and limited in every aspect of my life, spending 24 hours a day with my son without any support. In this difficult situation, I decided to seek help from MUHSEN. Alhamdulillah, it was Rizq (sustenance) that Allah provided for both of us at the right time. Allah has rewarded me and my son in a way that no one else could. Thank you from the bottom of my heart; you have uplifted our spirits and brought us happiness."

MUHSEN Weekend School

Many students with special needs are unfortunately turned away from full-time Islamic schools due to a lack of resources. As a result, weekend schools serve as a valuable alternative. MUHSEN offers a curriculum specifically designed by trained educators to make learning more accessible, teaching essential practices like wudu in a tailored way. This approach helps children feel more like their peers and fosters their connection to the masjid. Parents cherish the moments when their special needs children participate in prayers alongside their siblings—it's truly heartwarming.

The 1:1 teacher assistant provided at our weekend schools play a significant role in customizing the curriculum for each child. Stories of the prophets are adapted to suit various learning levels, and students have access to specialized arts and crafts materials.

"Alhamdulillah, I am so very pleased with the MUHSEN weekend school and grateful for the opportunity provided for my son, Zakariya," said Shaista Sharif. "I am truly delighted with how he is embraced, nurtured, and supported by the staff and teachers. He is excited to attend Sunday School and learns new things every day. Masha Allah, he has learned how to perform wudu, memorized various surahs and dua'as, and made Muslim friends. The staff at Orland Park Prayer Center is amazing, and they are earning Jannat-ul-Firdaus."

Trips and Events

MUHSEN's flagship Umrah trips, in collaboration with Dar El Salam Travel, are a tremendous blessing for people with disabilities. We provide one-on-one assistance, sign language interpretation, specialized childcare for special needs, wheelchair support, and tailored visual resources. At MUHSEN Umrah, it's evident how families connect with one another, feeling understood and supported. This sense of belonging is crucial for their mental health.

Everyone dreams of traveling with their families. While it can be more complicated for families with special needs, that doesn't mean the community assumes they wouldn't want to travel. MUHSEN demonstrates that if Allah SWT invites you to His home, we can help make that journey possible.

This isn't just a trip or any Umrah. A MUHSEN Umrah guarantees a trained volunteer for every special need child and adult, allowing parents and caregivers to perform the pilgrimage and engage in acts of worship with peace of mind. Additionally, a trained mental health counselor is available for parents to talk, vent, share experiences, and heal.

Menahal Begawala, LMHC, has served as a counselor on two MUHSEN Umrahs. She found the discomfort with the unfamiliar and the lack of awareness in the Muslim community to be startling. She believes that, historically, as a largely immigrant community, Muslims carry an added layer of cultural baggage and face a lack of resources, which has led to a mix of misconceptions. Parents were often shamed for having children with special needs and were told to recite specific duas to "fix" the problem.

During Umrah, parents have approached Menahal to share their feelings of being lost and exhausted. In some cases, spouses may be on completely different pages regarding how to handle their situation. Menahal's first step is to diagnose the underlying issues. One parent may have emotionally withdrawn, feeling resentful, blaming themselves, or grieving the loss of the expectations they had about raising their children. In other instances, there may be an uneven distribution of responsibilities.

Some parents may have suppressed their grief and become workaholics, believing that their only role is to provide financially.

Mothers often carry the majority of the responsibilities when it comes to childrearing, and this heavy burden can lead to burnout. However, many fathers are also very involved in their children's lives. An equitable sharing of responsibilities doesn't necessarily mean that fathers must change the same number of diapers. They can contribute in different ways and still be considered equal partners in parenting. For example, simply supporting a spouse and allowing her to vent can be incredibly valuable. In some cases, fathers may excel in calming down their children, which can be a significant contribution.

The situation becomes even more complex for single parents who lack a trusted partner to share the responsibilities. Many single mothers participate in the MUHSEN umrah so that they do not feel isolated on this journey.

Menahal witnessed parents mourning the loss of a dream. They experienced mixed emotions; while they felt exhilarated to be at Umrah, they also grieved the loss of what could have been. One parent asked, "If I can perform Tawaf so easily, why is it so difficult for my child?" Just hearing a trained professional assure them that experiencing these conflicting emotions is normal help lighten their burden.

Roles Professionals Can Play

Imams: Beacons of Hope

A boy with Down Syndrome gives the adhan at a masjid, while an imam encourages parents of children with special needs to attend, even if their children may cry. This is not fiction; these real-life scenarios can happen in your community.

Children will make noises, and some may not stay in one place. However, when the imam remains calm, the congregation is more likely to follow suit. When leadership demonstrates acceptance, it becomes easier to create a welcoming environment, rather than swimming against the tide.

Our children deserve a sense of belonging at the masjid. A negative experience in the House of God could lead them to feel isolated and risk losing their faith without anyone even knowing. These are serious consequences, and as a community, we have a role to play.

Tariq Musleh, imam at the Mecca Center in Willowbrook, Illinois, is passionate about supporting families with special needs. He also serves as a religious leader at MUHSEN Umrahs. He emphasizes that we should not only open the doors of the masjid but also open our hearts. The masjid is a home for all of us—whether or not someone has a diagnosed condition, everyone is welcome. Unfortunately, many special needs families feel unwelcome and distanced from the masjid, which is far from the prophetic example.

Shaykh Tariq states that while making accommodations is a good first step, it is not sufficient. Our ummah must empower our brothers and sisters with special needs. The initial experience at the masjid must be positive and welcoming, as this sets the foundation for a lifelong relationship with the House of Allah.

Imams who are trained in special needs and mental health awareness can offer comfort and hope to families facing challenges. Unfortunately, such trained religious professionals are still quite rare today. Receiving counseling from someone without proper training can be unhelpful or even detrimental. Additionally, the reactions of other congregants—such as shushing or staring at a special needs child—can lead to feelings of isolation, making families reluctant to return to the masjid.

It is essential for imams to be equipped to provide meaning and purpose, helping individuals understand their experiences and accept their circumstances. This support can be particularly valuable for those grappling with the emotional and existential aspects of disability or mental illness.

Fortunately, many Islamic scholars are becoming more aware of these issues. An increasing number are incorporating closed captioning into their videos, making their teachings accessible to individuals who may not have been able to learn from them in the past.

Decision Makers: Masjid Boards

Radwa Hafez has facilitated events for families with special needs at the Islamic Center of Naperville (ICN) in Illinois. From providing American Sign Language (ASL) interpretation at Eid prayers to organizing support groups and special needs childcare, ICN has become a pioneer in promoting inclusion.

She suggests that if others want their masajid (mosques) to provide similar arrangements, it is essential to get involved and identify influential board members who will advocate for these needs. Hafez believes that the ICN board always keeps special needs families in mind, which makes a significant difference. "Connections matter," she says. "First, they will notice; then they will empathize." She feels that regular khutbahs (sermons) about disability awareness have a powerful impact. Hafez hopes more masajid will create accommodations so that families do not have to jump through hoops or feel isolated. "The masjid should be the backbone of the family unit," she emphasizes. "MUHSEN opened my eyes. I was encouraged to volunteer and found a sense of purpose. By volunteering, we can benefit ourselves and the next generation."

However, if someone attends a masjid that does not have programs for special needs families, it is not a lost cause. Start small, find like-minded individuals, and approach the leadership. They may not be aware that these families wish to attend the masjid. Present them with solutions on how simple steps can facilitate inclusion. Approach the board not with complaints, but with proposed solutions. For instance, instead of expressing frustration about not being able to attend Eid prayers as a family, suggest ideas such as arranging respite care during the least crowded Eid prayer. Offer practical suggestions and strategies to implement them. Most likely, masajid will be receptive to these ideas; they just need community members to help put them into action.

Need for Advocacy

Academia, healthcare providers, and policymakers can collaborate with communities to reduce the frequency of mental distress among adults with disabilities. This can be achieved by promoting the importance of mental health screenings and care and by increasing access to health promotion programs, mental health screenings, clinical care, and support services, particularly for individuals with cognitive disabilities.

More than half of adults with both cognitive and mobility disabilities report experiencing frequent mental distress. This may be due to unhealthy behaviors or conditions, or unmet healthcare needs stemming from cost concerns. Many therapies are not covered by traditional insurance, and out-of-pocket expenses can add significant stress for families.

While addressing these issues requires funding, it is certainly possible. The Muslim community can mobilize resources to create more masajid, which is beneficial. However, if given the choice, we should prioritize making existing masajid more accessible to everyone, rather than focusing solely on building new houses of worship for only one segment of the community.

Interventions

Improving the mental health of individuals with disabilities requires a comprehensive approach that addresses both their specific needs related to their disabilities and the challenges they face in mental health.

Accessible Mental Health Services should ensure both physical and communication accessibility, along with accommodations for sensory impairments or cognitive disabilities.

Integrated Care Models should be implemented, involving collaborative care teams where healthcare providers—such as primary care physicians, specialists, and mental health professionals—work together to deliver comprehensive care.

Regular Screening and Assessment for mental health disorders among individuals with disabilities is essential. Early detection can facilitate timely intervention and support.

Individualized Treatment Plans should be developed, considering the specific disabilities of individuals and any potential interactions between these disabilities and their mental health symptoms or treatments.

Psychoeducation should be provided to individuals with disabilities and their caregivers, covering topics such as mental health conditions, coping strategies, and available resources. Skills training in areas like stress management, social skills, and problem-solving can empower individuals to better manage their mental health.

Peer Support Groups or group therapy sessions tailored specifically for individuals with disabilities can offer valuable social connections, validation, and shared experiences, all of which are important for mental well-being.

Community Engagement Programs should be established to combat social isolation, offering accessible recreational activities and inclusive social events. Building social connections and fostering a sense of belonging can have a positive impact on mental health.

Employment Opportunities and vocational training programs that accommodate the needs of individuals with disabilities are vital. Meaningful employment can enhance self-esteem, ensure financial stability, and improve overall mental well-being.

Anti-Stigma Campaigns are needed to challenge stereotypes and promote positive attitudes toward people with disabilities and mental health conditions. Education and awareness can help reduce barriers to social inclusion and acceptance.

The Road Ahead

We acknowledge that there is still much work to be done. We are currently working on establishing a think tank to explore the possibility of providing residential services for families with aging caregivers. Additionally, we see the value of collaboration and consistently find it beneficial to partner with other organizations that share similar goals. MUHSEN has collaborated with Maristan, Naseeha, Project Taqwa, Khalil Center, and various other professional organizations in the field of Muslim mental health.

Recent developments in the fields of disability and mental health indicate a growing awareness of these issues. There has been a strong push for inclusive education; however, full-time Islamic schools still need to improve in this area. Students with disabilities should be integrated into mainstream schools with the appropriate support and accommodations. Furthermore, advances in technology have greatly benefited individuals with disabilities and mental health conditions. Tools such as screen readers for the visually impaired, assistive communication devices for those with speech impairments, and mobile apps for managing mental health symptoms have made a significant impact.

Peer support networks and advocacy groups have become increasingly important, empowering individuals with disabilities and mental health conditions to share their experiences, advocate for their rights, and promote community engagement and awareness. Many countries, including the United States, have enacted mental health parity laws that require insurers to offer comparable coverage for both mental and physical health treatments. These laws have improved access to mental health services for individuals with disabilities.

There has also been a shift toward trauma-informed care, which recognizes the high prevalence of trauma among individuals with disabilities and mental health conditions. This approach emphasizes safety, trustworthiness, peer support, and collaboration in treatment settings. Additionally, some communities have established Crisis Intervention Teams composed of law enforcement officers trained in de-escalation techniques and mental health awareness. The goal of these teams is to reduce incidents of violence and prevent the inappropriate incarceration of individuals experiencing mental health crises, including those with disabilities.

While significant progress has been made thanks to the dedicated efforts of MUHSEN and others, there is still much work to be done. For example, many Islamic schools turn away students with special needs, citing a lack of resources. These schools often refer students who require additional assistance to public schools instead. This raises questions about priorities: Would a school board choose to invest thousands of dollars in a new gym, or would it opt to hire trained special education teachers? We recognize that the situation is complex, as many different types of therapy and support are required, but it's important to explore these options. There may be numerous Muslim families who would like to send their children to Islamic schools but are currently unable to do so.

A Bright Future

Our work is cut out for us, but we are an optimistic community. We are taught to trust in Allah, yet we are also reminded to "tie our camel first." Things are changing for the better. Mental health is no longer seen as a taboo topic. Gen Z and Millennials are unafraid to share their experiences with therapy. Youth are becoming more aware, and many celebrities have publicly discussed their own mental health struggles. They are learning to prioritize self-care and take pride in it.

What was frowned upon just a generation ago is now not only acceptable but even recognized as a form of self-care. People are beginning to understand concepts like generational trauma and the importance of setting boundaries. This understanding can be immensely beneficial in the realm of disability as well. Just because an aunt or grandparent was excluded from wedding events due to the inconvenience of accommodating their hearing or wheelchair needs doesn't mean that that practice should continue.

We can break the cycle and embrace the positive aspects of our parents' and grandparents' generation. By demonstrating that it is not only acceptable but highly encouraged to include those who might otherwise be left out, we can set a good example for our children.

Creating boundaries can greatly benefit parents and caregivers of individuals with special needs. It's important to remember that you are not obligated to interact with people who have hurt you or your child, whether that harm was verbal or expressed through body language. Even a simple eye roll can deeply affect a parent's heart. Fortunately, schools and workplaces are beginning to offer time off for mental health days, demonstrating a positive shift in societal attitudes. As Muslims, it is vital to maintain hope and not fall into despair. We cannot simply throw up our hands and believe there is no way forward.

Our journey on Earth is one of transformation. Adam and Eve, may Allah be pleased with them, repented and changed, and our Prophet Muhammad (S) brought change to his ummah. While transformation may not occur overnight, it is our purpose on this Earth; it is a long-term process requiring vision.

"Verily, Allah will not change the condition of a people until they change what is within themselves." (Quran 13:11)

We are dedicated to reviving the vision of a prophetic community. This is work that often goes unrecognized. We remind ourselves to set Allah-centric goals, not driven by fame or fortune. We believe that if we have the right intentions and put in the effort, Allah will open pathways for us.

MUHSEN has grown beyond our expectations, and yet we feel we have only scratched the surface. We cannot cease these services; the demand from this underserved community is too great. With the permission of Allah SWT, our work will continue. Will you join us?

References

Centers for Disease Control and Prevention. Disability and Health Data System (DHDS) [Internet]. [updated 2018 May 24; cited 2018 August 27]. Retrieved from: http://dhds.cdc.gov

Muslims Understanding and Helping Special Education Needs (MUHSEN). 2024. *MUHSEN Toolkit.* https://muhsen.org/wp-content/uploads/2024/08/MUHSEN_MediaKit_091224.pdf

CHAPTER THIRTEEN

DISABILITIES: A LITERATURE REVIEW

Tarek D. Zidan

Introduction

Islam is the fastest-growing religion in the world. According to the Pew Research Center (2020), approximately 3.45 million Muslims reside in the United States, making up about 1.1% of the total population. While many people associate Muslims with the Middle East, the majority (62%) live in the Asia-Pacific region, which includes countries such as Indonesia, India, and Pakistan. The Muslim American population is diverse, consisting of various nationalities, cultural backgrounds, and immigration histories. Projections suggest this population may double by 2050 (Mohamed, 2016). According to the Centers for Disease Control and Prevention (2020), approximately 61 million adults in the US — about 26%, live with a disability. The 2020 National American Muslim Poll (Institute for Policy & Understanding, 2020) revealed that 29% of Muslim Americans have an immediate family member with a disability, which is a higher proportion compared to White (23%), Asian (23%), and Arab (18%) among the American Muslims. This statistic underscores the need for more research focused on the experiences of Muslim Americans with disabilities. The World Health Organization (WHO, 2018) defines disability as impairments, activity limitations, and participation restrictions. It emphasizes the importance of social factors, such as attitudes toward disability, which can exacerbate functional impairments. Individuals with disabilities make up the largest minority group in the US, facing challenges such as exclusion, discrimination, and human rights violations globally, all of which negatively impact their quality of life (WHO, 2011). Understanding perspectives on disability, particularly at the intersections of race, religion, and culture, can help foster more positive attitudes toward individuals with disabilities across diverse communities.

Attitudes Toward Disability

Over the past two decades, the disability rights movement has made significant progress, including improvements in physical accessibility, enhanced employment and educational opportunities, and increased community integration (McCarthy, 2003). However, individuals with disabilities continue to experience systemic oppression in various areas, such as education, employment, healthcare, and housing, which negatively impacts their overall well-being (WHO, 2011).

Societal attitudes play a crucial role in these challenges, as persons with disabilities are often viewed as inferior in modern Western societies. This perception can lead to social exclusion and negative self-image (Atonak & Livneh, 2000; Seo & Chen, 2009; Abbot & McConkey, 2006; Jahoda & Markova, 2004).

Research indicates that individuals with disabilities are highly aware of the stigma associated with their condition, which can adversely affect their self-esteem and mental health (Jahoda & Markova, 2004; Caine & Hatton, 1998). Internalized stigma may result in social withdrawal and reluctance to engage with non-disabled individuals, leading to feelings of shame and isolation (Ditchman et al., 2013; Jahoda et al., 2010).

Negative societal attitudes also perpetuate stereotypes and discrimination, portraying individuals with disabilities as dependent or pitiable. This can limit their social participation and overall quality of life (Hunt & Hunt, 2000; Gilmore et al., 2003; McCaughey & Strohmer, 2005).

Ableism, which prioritizes individuals without disabilities, contributes to the discrimination faced by those with disabilities and functions similarly to other forms of oppression, such as racism and sexism (Campbell, 2009). Cultural values play a significant role in shaping the expression of disability stigma, with individuals in low-income countries often experiencing harsher stigma and suffering from consequences such as denial of fundamental rights (Sango, 2017; Tilahun et al., 2019). In Western contexts, anti-stigma interventions have been largely influenced by individualistic values, which may unintentionally reinforce stigma (Hamdani et al., 2017; Fisher et al., 2020; Boelé, 2017). This recognition has increased the emphasis on developing culturally relevant adaptations for anti-stigma initiatives (Vuuren & Aldersey, 2020).

Islam and Attitudes Towards Disability

Islamic teachings generally promote progressive attitudes toward disability, emphasizing community and equality rather than focusing solely on disabilities themselves. The Qur'an does not explicitly mention "disability," but it does discuss individuals who are unable to meet societal expectations, framing disability as something relative to social context (Al-Aoufiet al., 2012; Bazna & Hatab, 2005). The idea that perfection belongs solely to God highlights that all individuals deserve dignity and equal treatment, regardless of physical or mental capabilities (Bazna & Hatab, 2005; Ghaly, 2009). Although early Islamic scholars dismissed the beliefs of Greek physiognomy, contemporary jurists continue to engage in discussions about the rights and responsibilities of disabled Muslims.

Cultural attitudes often conflict with religious principles regarding disabilities. Many families may hold negative views about disabilities, leading to practices such as hiding children with disabilities from public view, including preventing them from attending the mosque. Some parents might interpret disabilities as divine punishment or envy, opting for spiritual treatments instead of seeking medical intervention. This cultural stigma persists despite Islamic teachings advocating for equality.

In the context of mental illness, terms like "junun" (insanity) are used to label individuals based on their behavior rather than on specific disabilities (Rispler-Chaim, 2006. Laws related to mental illness typically focus on protecting the well-being of family members rather than the rights of those with disabilities. While the Qur'an asserts that individuals with disabilities have the right to basic human needs, including marriage, debates continue regarding their capacity for responsibility in marital relationships. Some scholars argue for the right of those with disabilities to marry, while others claim that individuals with mental disabilities may not be able to fulfill marital obligations. Moreover, modern understandings of conditions like epilepsy have evolved, leading to changes in legal rulings concerning divorce and marital responsibilities (Rispler-Chaim, 2007). These discussions about the rights and capabilities of individuals with disabilities in Islamic contexts are ongoing.

The attitudes of Muslim Americans toward individuals with disabilities remain largely unexplored, with some researchers referring to them as an "invisible" or "hidden" minority in the US (Abraham & Abraham, 1983). However, following the events of 9/11, this community has become more visible and has faced significant backlash. While many studies have examined attitudes toward disability among various ethnic groups in the US, research specifically focusing on Muslim Americans is limited.

Several studies have explored attitudes toward disability in Muslim-majority countries. For instance, Al-Abdulwahab and Al-Gain (2003) found generally positive attitudes toward individuals with disabilities in Saudi Arabia, while Nagata (2007b) reported more pessimistic views among healthcare professionals in Jordan. Additionally, Nagata (2007a) conducted research with Muslim university students in Lebanon, indicating that increased knowledge and social interaction could lead to more positive attitudes toward individuals with intellectual disabilities and mental illnesses.

Furthermore, a study by Reiter, Mar'i, and Rosenberg (1986) examined Palestinian Arab families in Israel and found that these families generally held positive views toward children with developmental disabilities. Interestingly, Druze participants expressed more favorable attitudes than their Muslim and Christian counterparts.

Overall, research on attitudes toward individuals with disabilities within the Muslim American community remains limited. Given the diversity among Muslim Americans, who hold varying values, beliefs, and attitudes, it is important to understand their perspectives on disability. This understanding can contribute to developing culturally appropriate interventions to address the stigma surrounding disabilities and mental health issues (Al-Krenawi & Graham, 2000; Juvva, Sharma, & Ramanathan, 2016).

Sociodemographic Characteristics of Persons with Disabilities

Attitudes toward disability can vary significantly based on factors such as age, gender, educational level, and the type of disability (Deal, 2003). While the relationship between age and attitudes is not fully understood, some evidence suggests a developmental trend: positive attitudes generally increase from early childhood through adolescence, dip during late adolescence, and rise again from young adulthood to late adulthood (Harper & Peterson, 2001). However, other studies have found no significant correlation between age and attitudes (Lau & Cheung, 1999; Pace et al., 2010).

Research on gender yields mixed findings. Some studies indicate that females tend to be more accepting of persons with disabilities throughout their lives compared to males (Barr & Bracchitta, 2012; Hunt & Hunt, 2000; McDougall et al., 2004; Panek & Smith, 2005), while others report no significant gender differences (Tamm & Prellwitz, 2001). Laws and Kelly (2005) noted that these differences vary by disability type; females showed more favorable attitudes toward physical disabilities but expressed similar attitudes to males regarding behavioral and intellectual disabilities. A systematic review by Scior (2011) found that females, younger individuals, and those with higher education levels were more likely to have positive attitudes toward intellectual disabilities, although the impact of gender was inconsistent.

A significant limitation in existing research is the tendency to treat disability as a broad category despite evidence indicating that attitudes differ by specific disability type (Barr & Bracchitta, 2015). There is a "hierarchy of acceptance" where psychiatric, intellectual, and developmental disabilities receive less social acceptance and experience greater stigma and discrimination (Ditchman et al., 2013; Miller et al., 2009; Thomas, 2000). Individuals across age groups often express the most negative attitudes toward developmental disabilities while displaying more positive attitudes toward physical disabilities (Nowicki, 2006; Brown et al., 2011; Fevre et al., 2013). Disabilities involving communication challenges also tend to elicit more negative attitudes (Barr & Bracchitta, 2015). Therefore, understanding attitudes toward disability requires consideration of both the nature of the relationship and the specific type of disability.

Social Contact with Persons with Disabilities

Research has consistently shown that the level of contact individuals have with persons with disabilities significantly influences attitudes toward disability. For instance, Seo and Chen (2009) found that adults with more positive attitudes reported greater contact with individuals with disabilities. Numerous studies support this observation, indicating that increased contact typically leads to more favorable attitudes (Barr & Bracchitta, 2012; Kalyva & Agaliotis, 2009; McDougall et al., 2004; Hunt & Hunt, 2000).

However, recent findings suggest that contact alone is not enough to change attitudes; the quality of that contact is a more crucial factor. McManus et al. (2010) demonstrated that the quality of interactions uniquely predicted positive attitudes, while mere frequency of contact did not. Positive attitudes are more likely to develop when interactions challenge negative stereotypes and involve meaningful engagement (Smart, 2008) rather than just casual encounters (Hampton & Xiao, 2007).

Barr and Bracchitta (2012) emphasized that the nature of relationships plays a significant role in shaping attitudes. Their research found that positive attitudes are most closely associated with having friends with disabilities and engaging in shared activities. In contrast, contact with relatives or classmates did not produce the same positive effects. Therefore, the nature of relationships is a stronger predictor of favorable attitudes toward disability than the frequency of contact.

As a result, Pruett et al. (2008) recommend a multidimensional approach to assessing contact and attitudes toward disability to gain a more comprehensive understanding of disability-related biases.

Culture and Attitudes Towards Disability

Perceptions of individuals with disabilities vary significantly across cultures, influencing their inclusion in society. Orange (2009) defines culture as the behaviors and characteristics transmitted socially within a community. Phemister and Crewe (2004) note that numerous studies since the 1960s have identified diverse attitudes toward persons with disabilities among different ethnic and religious groups in the United States. Traditional cultural norms and beliefs can often lead to discriminatory practices and the alienation of individuals with disabilities (Juvva et al., 2016).

Dudley (2000) explains that negative societal attitudes and stereotypes present additional challenges, particularly impacting cognitive development and mental health. Both covert and overt stereotypes contribute to the marginalization of individuals with disabilities, resulting in exclusion and a lack of equal opportunities in education, employment, and social inclusion (Ibrahim & Ismail, 2018).

Ibrahim and Ismail (2018) argue that Muslim Americans with disabilities face unique challenges compared to their non-Muslim counterparts. These challenges are further complicated for those living as migrants in the United States, with issues related to refugee status, access to healthcare, and the assimilation process affecting their experiences.

Immigration and Acculturation

Muslim immigration to the United States has significantly increased in recent decades, contributing to the diversity of the Muslim American population and complicating the understanding of how they adopt American values (Marko, 2019; Bagasra & Mackinem, 2019). Research indicates that Islamic values are central to Muslim American identity, with many individuals embracing the intersection of their religious and national identities. However, the extent of acculturation—how Muslim Americans adopt American values—has not been extensively studied, often focusing on specific ethnic groups rather than a broader religious identity (Sirin et al., 2008; Britto & Amer, 2007; Faragallah et al., 1997).

To address this gap, Bagasra and Mackinem (2019) developed the Acculturation Scale for Muslim Americans (ASMA) to measure how individuals integrate into American culture alongside their Islamic values. Their study of 255 diverse Muslim Americans found that most respondents strongly identified with Islamic values, which reflected an identity struggle. Many resisted complete assimilations into American norms, particularly when these norms conflicted with their Islamic beliefs. The study revealed that immigrant Muslims tended to be more open to American norms than those born in the US.

The findings support a bi-dimensional and bi-directional model of acculturation, highlighting differences between immigrant and second-generation Muslims regarding their adherence to Islamic values versus American social norms (Bagasra & Mackinem, 2019; Berry, 2003; Schwartz, et al., 2010). Understanding individual levels of acculturation is crucial for exploring attitudes toward disability, as Muslim families may maintain strong Islamic beliefs that influence their perspectives on this issue. This suggests a need for resources and education for Muslim Americans with family members who have disabilities, aiming to improve their quality of life and create a supportive environment amid cultural and disability-related challenges.

Spirituality & Religious Beliefs

Muslims living in the US face unique challenges related to acculturation, cultural adaptation, and maintaining their religious identity while balancing their individuality with a sense of belonging (Wang et al., 2020). The Muslim population is diverse, encompassing various races, ethnicities, nationalities, and cultural backgrounds, and it is recognized as the fastest-growing religious group globally (Pew Research Center, 2020).

Research on children with disabilities shows that religious beliefs significantly influence how families interpret and understand disability. Although there is limited research on Muslim immigrant families with children who have disabilities, Jegatheesan et al. (2010) conducted an ethnographic study involving three South Asian Muslim families raising a child with autism in a Midwestern US city. The study revealed that Islam served as the primary framework for these families in understanding their child's diagnosis. Their faith affected their acceptance of the diagnosis, their expectations for their child's future, and their parenting behaviors. They viewed their child as a blessing and held optimistic views regarding the child's potential.

Furthermore, many Muslims rely on religious customs and practices to cope with illness, highlighting the central role of spirituality in their lives. It is essential to understand the strengths of spiritual and religious networks, cultural support systems, and the availability of educational resources for Muslim families with disabilities. This understanding is crucial for providing better support and fostering inclusive environments for those navigating cultural and disability-related challenges.

Discussion

The Muslim community in the US is growing due to immigration, religious conversion, and rising birth rates. This growth highlights the need for mental health professionals—such as psychologists, psychiatrists, and clinical social workers—to provide culturally competent and sensitive services to Muslim Americans with disabilities and their families. As the US becomes increasingly multicultural, it is essential for mental health practitioners to navigate the complex cultural differences in identity, attitudes, beliefs, and perceptions related to disability, particularly within the diverse Muslim American population (Hasnain et al., 2008).

Mental health practitioners must acquire substantial knowledge about the unique experiences of Muslims with disabilities to engage effectively with this population. Although the literature on Muslims in Western countries is limited, understanding their belief systems can help inform mental health practices and lead to the development of culturally appropriate interventions to combat the stigma surrounding mental health challenges (Al-Krenawi & Graham, 2000).

Developing culturally sensitive skills and services for spiritually diverse, minority faith-based communities is critical for effective social work practice. By understanding the sociodemographic characteristics of Muslim Americans (Abu-Habib, 1997), their level of contact with persons with disabilities (Al-Abdulwahab & Al-Gain, 2003; Nagata, 2007a, b), acculturation patterns (Amer, 2005), and their spirituality and religious beliefs (Hodge, 2003), mental health practitioners can gain insight into how these factors influence attitudes toward individuals with disabilities.

This chapter aims to address the gap in the literature regarding the attitudes of Muslim Americans without disabilities toward individuals with disabilities of all faiths. Exploring the complexities of their experiences and beliefs can enhance mental health practices. By understanding sociodemographic characteristics, acculturation patterns, and social contacts with individuals with disabilities, practitioners can gain insights into how these factors shape Muslim Americans' attitudes, particularly concerning stigma.

References

Abbott, S., & McConkey, R. (2006). The barriers to social inclusion as perceived by people with intellectual disabilities. *Journal of Intellectual Disabilities, 10*, 275–287.

Abraham, S. Y., & Abraham, N. (1983). *Arabs in the New World: Studies on Arab-American Communities* (1st ed.). Detroit, MI: Wayne State University, Center for Urban Studies.

Abu-Habib, L. (1997). *Gender and disability: Women's experiences in the Middle East.* Oxford, UK: Oxfam Publishing.

Al-Abdulwahab, S. S., & Al-Gain, S. I. (2003). Attitudes of Saudi Arabia care professionals towards people with physical disabilities. *Asia Pacific Disability Rehabilitation Journal, 14*(1), 63–70. Retrieved from http://english.aifo.it/disability/apdrj/apdrj103/attitudes-professionals.pdf

Al-Aoufi, H., Al-Zyoud, N., Shahminan, N. (2012). Islam and the cultural conceptualization of disability. *International Journal of Adolescence and Youth, 17*(4), 205-219.

Al-Krenawi, A., & Graham, J. R. (2000). Culturally sensitive social work practice with Arab clients in mental health settings. *Health & Social Work, 25*(1), 9-22. https://academic.oup.com/hsw/article-abstract/25/1/9/694024

Amer, M. M. (2005). *Arab American mental health in the post-September 11 eras: Acculturation, coping, and stress* (Doctoral dissertation) the University of Toledo. Retrieved from http://etd.ohiolink.edu/view.cgi?acc_num=toledo1115395141

Antonak, R., & Livneh, H. (2000). Measurement of attitudes towards persons with disabilities. *Disability and rehabilitation, 22*(5), 211-224.

Bagasra, A., & Mackinem, M. (2019). Assessing aspects of acculturation in a Muslim American sample: development and testing of the acculturation scale for Muslim Americans. *Religions, 10*(1), 26.

Barr, J.J. & Bracchitta, K. (2012). Attitudes toward individuals with disabilities: The effects of age, gender, and relationship. *Journal of Relationships Research, 3*, 10-17. doi:10.1017/jrr.2012.1

Barr, J. J., & Bracchitta, K. (2015). Attitudes toward individuals with disabilities: The effects of contact with different disability types. *Current Psychology, 34*(2), 223-238.

Bazna, M. S., Hatab, T. A. (2005). Disability in the Qur'an. *Journal of Religion, Disability & Health, 9*(1), 5-27.

Berry, J.W. (2003). Conceptual approaches to acculturation. In *Acculturation: Advances in Theory, Measurement, and Applied Research.* Washington, DC: American Psychological Association, 17–37.

Boelé, A. (2017). In search of community: lessons from idealized independence for adults with disabilities. *Harvard Education Review, 87*(3):380–403. https://doi.org/10.17763/1943-5045-87.3.380

Britto, P. R., & Amer, M. M. (2007). An exploration of cultural identity patterns and the family context among Arab Muslim young adults in America. *Applied Development Science, 11*(3), 137-150.

Brown, H. K., Ouellette-Kuntz, H., Lysaght, R., & Burge, P. (2011). Student's behavioral intentions towards peers with disabilities. *Journal of Applied*

Research in Intellectual Disabilities, 24, 322–332. doi:10.1111/ j.1468-3148.2010.00616.x.
Campbell, F. K. (2009). *Contours of ableism.* Basingstoke, UK: Palgrave Macmillan. http://dx.doi.org/10.1057/9780230245181
Caine, A., & Hatton, C. (1998). Working with people with mental health problems. In E. Emerson, C. Hatton, J. Bromley, & A. Caine (Eds.), *Clinical psychology and people with intellectual disabilities* (pp. 210-230). Wiley.
Centers for Disease Control and Prevention. (2020). *Disability impacts all of us.* https://www.cdc.gov/disability-and-health/articles-documents/disability-impacts-all-of-us-infographic.html
Chabeda-Barthe, J., Wambua, T., Chege, W. L., Hwaga, D., Gakuo, T., & Rotich, G. C. (2019). Child developmental disabilities, caregivers' role in Kenya and its implications on global migration. *International journal of environmental research and public health*, *16*(6), 1010. https://doi.org/10.3390/ijerph16061010.
Creswell, J.W. (2013). *Research design: Qualitative, quantitative, and mixed methods approach.* Thousand Oaks, CA: Sage.
Crocker, J., Major, B., & Steele, C. (1998). Social stigma. In D. Gilbert, S. T. Fiske, & G. Lindzey (Eds.), *The handbook of social psychology* (4th ed., Vol. 2, pp. 504–553). New York, NY: McGraw-Hill.
Deal, M. (2003). Disabled people's attitudes toward other impairment groups: A hierarchy of impairments. *Disability and Society, 18*, 897–910. doi: 10.1080/0968759032000127317
Ditchman, N., Werner, S., Kosyluk, K., Jones, N., Elg, B., & Corrigan, P. W. (2013). Stigma and intellectual disability: Potential application of mental illness research. *Rehabilitation Psychology*, *58*(2), 206.
Dudley, R. J. (2000). Confronting stigma within the services system. *Social Work, 45*(5), 449–455. doi: http://dx.doi.org/10.1093/sw/45.5.449
Durling, E., Chinn, D., & Scior, K. (2018). Family and community in the lives of UK Bangladeshi parents with intellectual disabilities. *Journal of Applied Research in Intellectual Disabilities*, *31*(6), 1133–1143. https://doi.org/10.1111/jar.12473.
Faragallah, M. H., Schumm, W. R., & Webb, F. J. (1997). Acculturation of Arab-American immigrants: An exploratory study. *Journal of Comparative Family Studies*, 182-203.
Fevre, R., Robinson, A., Lewis, D., & Jones, T. (2013). The ill-treatment of employees with disabilities in British workplaces. *Work, Employment and Society, 27*, 288–307. doi:10.1177/0950017012460311.
Findler, L., Vilchinsky, N., & Werner, S. (2007). The multidimensional attitudes scale toward people with disabilities. *Rehabilitation Counseling Bulletin, 50*, 166–176. doi:10.1177/00343552070500030401.
Fisher, M. H., Athamanah, L. S., Sung, C., & Josol, C. K. (2020). Applying the self-determination theory to develop a school-to-work peer mentoring programme to promote social inclusion. *Journal of Applied Research in Intellectual Disabilities*, *33*(2), 296–309.
Ghaly, M. (2009). *Islam and disability: Perspectives in theology and jurisprudence.* Routledge.

Gilmore, L., Campbell, J., & Cuskelly, M. (2003). Developmental expectations, personality stereotypes, and attitudes towards inclusive education: Community and teacher views of Down syndrome. *International Journal of Disability, Development and Education, 50,* 65–76. doi:10.1080/1034912032000053340

Goddard, L., & Jordan, L. (1998). Changing attitudes about persons with disabilities: Effects of a simulation. *Journal of Neuroscience Nursing, 30,* 307–313. doi:10.1097/01376517-199810000-00006

Groce, N., & Zola, I. (1993). Multiculturalism, chronic illness, and disability. *Pediatrics, 91*(5), 1048–1055. Retrieved from http://www.ntac.hawaii.edu/AAPIcourse/downloads/readings/pdf/Multiculturalism.pdf

Hamdani, Y., Ary, A., & Lunsky, Y. (2017). Critical analysis of a population mental health strategy: effects on stigma for people with intellectual and developmental disabilities. *Journal of Mental Health Research in Intellect Disabilities, 10*(2):144–61. http://dx.doi.org/10.1080/19315864.2017.1281362

Hampton, N.Z., & Xiao, F. (2007). Attitudes toward people with developmental disabilities in Chinese and American students: The role of cultural values, contact, and knowledge. *Journal of Rehabilitation, 73,* 23–32.

Harper, D.C., & Peterson, D.B. (2001). Children in the Philippines: Attitudes toward visible physical impairment. *Cleft Palate-Craniofacial Journal, 38,* 566–576. https://doi.org/10.1597/1545-1569_2001_038_0566_cotpat_2.0.co_2

Hasnain, R., Shaikh, L. C., & Shanawani, H. (2008). *Disability and the Muslim perspective: An introduction for rehabilitation and health care providers.* Center for International Rehabilitation Research Information and Exchange, United States.

Hodge, D. R. (2003). The intrinsic spirituality scale: A new six-item instrument for assessing the salience of spirituality as a motivational construct. *Journal of Social Service Research, 30*(1), 41–61. Retrieved from: https://www.tandfonline.com/doi/abs/10.1300/J079v30n01_03

Hunt, B. & Hunt, C. (2000). Attitudes toward people with disabilities: A comparison of undergraduate rehabilitation and business majors. *Rehabilitation Education, 14,* 269–283.

Ibrahim, I., & Ismail, M. F. (2018). Muslims with disabilities: Psychosocial reforms from an Islamic perspective. *Journal of disability & religion, 22*(1), 1-14.

Institute for Policy and Understanding. (2020). *American Muslim poll 2020.* https://www.ispu.org/disability-in-the-muslim-community/

Ibrahim, I., & Ismail, M. F. (2018). Muslims with disabilities: psychosocial reforms from an Islamic perspective. *Journal of Disability & Religion, 22*(1), 1-14.

Jahoda, A., & Markova, I. (2004). Coping with social stigma: People with intellectual disabilities moving from institutions and family home. *Journal of Intellectual Disability Research, 48,* 719–729.

Jahoda, A., Wilson, A., Stalker, K., & Cairney, A. (2010). Living with stigma and self-perceptions of people with mild intellectual disabilities. *Journal of Social Issues, 66,* 521-534. doi:10.1111/j.1540-4560.2010. 01660.x

Jegatheesan, B., Miller, P. J., & Fowler, S. A. (2010). Autism from a religious perspective: A study of parental beliefs in South Asian Muslim immigrant families. *Focus on Autism and Other Developmental Disabilities, 25*(2), 98-109.

Juvva, S., Sharma, P., & Ramanathan, P. (2016). People with disabilities: Strengths and Challenges. In R.S. Chathapuram, S. Juvva, S. Dutta, & K. Khaja (Eds.), *Spirituality, culture, and development: Implications for international social work practice.* (pp.157-174). New York: Lexington Books.

Kalyva, E., & Agaliotis, I. (2009). Can contact affect Greek children's understanding of and attitudes toward peers with physical disabilities? *European Journal of Special Needs Education, 24*(2), 213-220.

Kleinman, A., Wang, W. Z., Li, S., Cheng, X. M., Dai, X. Y., Li, K. T., & Kleinman, J. (1995). The social course of epilepsy: Chronic illness as a social experience in interior China. *Social Science & Medicine, 40*(10), 1319-1330. Retrieved from http://www.ncbi.nlm.nih.gov/pubmed/7638642

Lau, J. T. F., & Cheung, C. K. (1999). Discriminatory attitudes to people with intellectual disability or mental health difficulty. *International Social Work, 42*(4), 431-444. Laws, G., & Kelly, E. (2005). The attitudes and friendship intentions of children in United Kingdom mainstream schools towards peers with physical or intellectual disabilities. *Journal of Disability, Development, and Education, 2,* 79-99. doi: 10.1080/10349120500086298

Major B, Dovidio JF, Link BG, Calabrese SK. (2017). *Stigma and its implications for health: introduction and overview.* In: Major B, Dovidio JF, Link BG, editors. The Oxford handbook of stigma, discrimination, and health. Oxford University Press.

Mardiros, M. (1989). Conception of childhood disabilities among Mexican-American parents. *Medical Anthropology, 12*(1), 55-68. doi: 10.1080/01459740.1989.9966011

Marko, D.E. (2019). Nevertheless, they persist: American and European Muslim Immigrants in the era of Trump. *Journal of Muslim Minority Affairs, 39*(2), 246-258.

McCarthy, H. (2003). The disability rights movement: Experiences and perspectives of selected leaders in the disability community. *Rehabilitation Counseling Bulletin,* 46, 209-223. https://doi.org/10.1177%2F003435520304600402

McCaughey, T. J., & Strohmer, D. C. (2005). Prototypes as an indirect measure of attitudes toward disability groups. *Rehabilitation Counseling Bulletin, 48,* 89-99. doi:10.1177/00343552050480020301

McDougall, J., DeWit, D.J., King, G., Miller, L.T., & Killip, S. (2004). High school-aged youths' attitudes toward their peers with disabilities: The role of school and student interpersonal factors. *International Journal of Disability, Development, and Education, 51*, 287–313. doi: 10.1080/1034912042000259242

McHatton, P. A., & Correa, V. (2005). Stigma and discrimination: Perspectives from Mexican and Puerto Rican mothers of children with special needs. *Topics in Early Childhood Special Education, 25*, 131–142. Retrieved from http://www.eric.ed.gov/ERICWebPortal/search/detailmini.jsp?

McManus, J. L., Feyes, K. J., & Saucier, D. A. (2010). Contact and knowledge as predictors of attitudes toward individuals with intellectual disabilities. *Journal of Social and Personal Relationships, 28*, 579–590. doi:10.1177/0265407510385494.

Miller, E., Chen, R., Glover-Graf, N. M., & Kranz, P. (2009). Willingness to engage in personal relationships with people with disabilities: Examining category and severity of disability. *Rehabilitation Counseling Bulletin, 52*, 211–224. doi:10.1177/0034355209332719

Mitter, N., Ali, A., & Scior, K. (2019). Stigma experienced by families of individuals with intellectual disabilities and autism: A systematic review. *Research in Developmental Disabilities, 89*, 10-21. doi: 10.1016/j.ridd.2019.03.001.

Mohamed, B. (2016). A new estimate of the US Muslim population. Retrieved from https://www.pewresearch.org/short-reads/2016/01/06/a-new-estimate-of-the-u-s-muslim-population/

Nagata, K.K. (2007a). The measurement of the Hong Kong-based "baseline survey of students." Attitudes toward people with a disability: Cross-cultural validation in Lebanon. *International Journal of Rehabilitation Research, 30*(3), 239–241. Retrieved from http://www.ncbi.nlm.nih.gov/pubmed/17762771

Nagata. K.K. (2007b). The scale of attitudes towards disabled persons (SADP): Cross-cultural validation in a middle-income Arab Country, Jordan. *The Review of Disability Studies: An International Journal, 3*(4), 3–9. Retrieved from http://www.rds.hawaii.edu/downloads/issues/pdf/RDSv03iss04.pdf

Nowicki, E.A. (2006). A cross-sectional multivariate analysis of children's attitudes towards disabilities. *Journal of Intellectual Disability Research, 50*, 335–348. doi:10.1111/j.1365-2788.2005.00781.x

Orange, L. M. (2009). Sexuality and disability. In M. G. Brodwin, F. W. Siu, J. Howard, & E. R. Brodwin (Eds.), *Medical, psychosocial, and vocational aspects of disability* (3rd ed.) (pp. 317-328). Athens, GA: Elliott & Fitzpatrick.

Pace, J. E., Shin, M., & Rasmussen, S. A. (2010). Understanding attitudes toward people with Down syndrome. *American Journal of Medical Genetics Part A*, 152A, 2185–2192.

Panek, P.E., & Smith, J.L. (2005). Assessment of terms to describe mental retardation. *Research in Developmental Disabilities, 26*, 565–576. doi: 10.1016/j.ridd.2004.11.009

Peek, L., & Stough, L. M. (2010). Children with disabilities in the context of disaster: A social vulnerability perspective. *Child Development*, 81(4), 1260–1270. doi: 10.1111/j.1467-8624.2010.01466.x.

Pew Research Center (2020, May 30). New estimates show US Muslim population continues to grow. Pew Research Center. Retrieved from https://www.pewresearch.org/fact-tank/2018/01/03/new-estimates-show-u-s-muslim-population-continues-to-grow/

Phemister, A. A., & Crewe, N. M. (2004). Objectives self-awareness and stigma: Implications for people with visible disabilities. *Journal of Rehabilitation*, 70(2), 33–38.

Pruett, S. R., Lee, E. J., Chan, F., Wang, M. H., & Lane, F. J. (2008). Dimensionality of the contact with disabled persons scale: results from exploratory and confirmatory factor analyses. *Rehabilitation Counseling*, 51, 210–221. doi:10.1177/0034355207311310.

Raghu, R., & Small, N. (2004). Cultural diversity and intellectual disability. *Current Opinions in Psychiatry*, 17(5), 371–375. https://journals.lww.com/co-psychiatry/abstract/2004/09000/cultural_diversity_and_intellectual_disability.8.aspx

Remler, D. K., & Van Ryzin, G. G. (2011). *Research methods in practice: Strategies for description and causation.* Sage Publications, Inc.

Reiter, S., Mar'i, S., & Rosenberg, Y. (1986). Parental attitudes toward developmentally disabled among Arab communities in Israel: A cross-cultural study. *International Journal of Rehabilitation Research*, 9(4), 355–362. Retrieved from http://www.ncbi.nlm.nih.gov/pubmed/2437063

Rumbaut, R. (2008). Reaping what you sow: Immigration, youth, and reactive ethnicity. *Applied Developmental Science*, 12, 108–11.

Sandelowski, M. (2004). Using qualitative research. *Qualitative health research*, 14(10), 1366-1386.

Sango, P. N. (2017). Country profile: intellectual and developmental disability in Nigeria. *Tizard Learning Disability Review*, 22(2), 87–93. https://doi.org/10.1108/TLDR-07-2016-0019

Saetremore, C. L., Scattone, D., & Kim, K. H. (2001). Ethnicity and the stigma of disabilities. *Psychology & Health*, 16(6), 699–713. doi:10.1080/08870440108405868

Schwartz, S. J., Unger, J. B., Zamboanga, B. L., & Szapocznik, J. (2010). Rethinking the concept of acculturation: implications for theory and research. *American Psychologist*, 65(4), 237.

Scior, K. (2011). Public awareness, attitudes and beliefs regarding intellectual disability: A systematic review. *Research in Developmental Disabilities*, 32(6), 2164–2182. doi:10.1016/j.ridd.2011.07.005

Scior, K., Kan, K. Y., McLoughlin, A., & Sheridan, J. (2010). Public attitudes toward people with intellectual disabilities: A cross-cultural study. *Intellectual and Developmental Disabilities*, 48(4), 278–289. https://doi.org/10.1352/1934-9556-48.4.278

Seo, W., & Chen, R.K. (2009). Attitudes of college students toward people with disabilities. *Journal of Applied Rehabilitation Counseling*, 40, 3–8.

Sirin, S. R., Bikmen, N., Mir, M., Fine, M., Zaal, M., & Katsiaficas, D. (2008). Exploring dual identification among Muslim-American emerging adults: A mixed methods study. *Journal of Adolescence, 31*(2), 259-279.

Smart, J. (2008). *Disability, society, and the individual* (2nd ed.). Austin, TX: ProEd.

Special Olympics. (2005). Changing attitudes changing the world: Media's portrayal of people with intellectual disability. https://www.issuelab.org/resources/1159/1159.pdf

Tamm, M., & Prellwitz, M. (2001). 'If I had a friend in a wheelchair: Children's thoughts on disabilities. *Child: Care, Health and Development, 27*, 223–240.

Thomas, A. (2000). Stability of Tringo's hierarchy of preference toward disability groups: 30 years later. *Psychological Reports, 86*, 1155–1156.

Thoresen, S. H., Fielding, A., Gillieatt, S., Blundell, B., Nguyen, L. (2017). A snapshot of intellectual disabilities in Lao PDR: challenges for the development of services. *Journal of Intellectual Disabilities, 21*(3), 203–19. https://doi.org/10.1177/1744629517704535.

Tilahun, D., Fekadu, A., Tekola, B., Araya, M., Roth, I., Davey, B., ... & Hoekstra, R. A. (2019). Ethiopian community health workers' beliefs and attitudes towards children with autism: Impact of a brief training intervention. *Autism, 23*(1), 39-49. https://doi.org/10.1177%2F1362361317730298

Vuuren, J., & Aldersey, H. M. (2020). Stigma, acceptance and belonging for people with IDD across cultures. *Current Developmental Disorders Reports*, 1-10.

Wang, S. C., Raja, A. H., & Azhar, S. (2020). "A lot of us have a very difficult time reconciling what being Muslim is": A phenomenological study on the meaning of being Muslim American. *Cultural Diversity and Ethnic Minority Psychology, 26*(3), 338.

World Health Organization. (2011). *World report on disability.* Geneva, Switzerland: Author.

World Health Organization (WHO). (2018). Health topics: disabilities. Retrieved from http://www.who.int/topics/disabilities/en/

World Population Review. (2020). *Muslim population by country.* Retrieved from: https://worldpopulationreview.com/country-rankings/muslim-population-by-country

Yang, L. H., Kleinman, A., Link, B. G., Phelan, J. C., Lee, S., & Good, B. (2007). Culture and stigma: Adding moral experience to stigma theory. *Social Science & Medicine, 64*(7), 1524-1535. doi:10.1016/j.socscimed.2006.11.013

Yuker, H. E., Block, J. R., & Young, J. H. (1970). *The measurement of attitudes toward disabled persons.* Human Resources Center, Alderson, NY: Social and Rehabilitation Service, Department of Health, Education, and Welfare: 1–178. Retrieved from http://files.eric.ed.gov/fulltext/ED044853.pdf

CHAPTER FOURTEEN

DRUG ADDICTION IN MUSLIM AMERICA

Ibrahim M. Sablaban

The topic of addiction amongst Muslim Americans is a tricky one to address and usually involves a series of extrapolations and assumptions because of the void of data on the topic as a whole. Social and popular commentary usually addresses the Muslim American Community as though it were a homogenous cohort, which is a glaring oversimplification and ensures that large groups of Muslims are not represented. Although it is true that there are some aspects of drug addiction that are mitigated by a community's religiosity and social isolation (a preposition many have, in and outside of the community), it is a broad overgeneralization to assume the universality of this- and to assume that there aren't some drug addictions that may be worse in the Muslim community. This chapter will discuss drug addiction and use in the context of identity, culture, environment and treatment measures both universally American and characteristically Muslim.

Introduction

Drug use and addiction among the Muslim American population are tremendously challenging to discuss and even more difficult to characterize. Research has historically indicated that Muslim Americans tend to have lower rates of substance use disorders compared to their non-Muslim counterparts (Doukas, 2016). However, recent data from the past decade suggests that these rates are on the rise (Ragheb et al., 2023). Additionally, the accurate characterization and assessment of drug use within the Muslim American community is complicated by the religious and social stigmas associated with it. This often leads to under-reporting of substance use and an underestimation of related issues. With a rapidly growing and socially integrated population, it is reasonable to assume that trends in substance use disorders among the broader American population are also reflected within the Muslim population, albeit potentially in a more subdued manner. However, there may be an additional layer of dysfunction at play. While occasional non-pathological use of certain substances (such as alcohol) may be viewed as harmless and not associated with guilt or shame in the general American context, Muslim Americans face not only the consequences of substance use but also the social and psychological stigma surrounding the act of using those substances.

The main challenge in assessing these points is that our data is often weak, affected by reporting bias, and generally has inadequate sample sizes, making it difficult to extrapolate findings to a larger population. In my efforts to gather information on perceptions of drug addiction and treatment within the Muslim and Arab American communities in the Metropolitan Detroit area, I quickly realized how challenging it is to obtain reliably reported data. This difficulty is recognized internationally (Arfken & Ahmed, 2016). For this reason, much of the information presented will come from data collected by the Substance Abuse and Mental Health Services Administration (SAMHSA) and various iterations of the National Survey on Drug Use and Health (NSDUH). This data will be contextualized with the limited literature available on Muslim populations. Additionally, it is important to incorporate anecdotal information gathered from clinical treatment and community organizations, as this perspective is valuable given the scarcity of published data.

This chapter will primarily focus on Muslim demographics and the use of alcohol, cannabis, and opioids. While nicotine and tobacco addiction remain a significant issue in the Muslim American community, with higher usage rates (Ragheb et al., 2023), this topic will not be the focus of the chapter. For the sake of consistency, the term 'use disorder' (as defined by the Diagnostic and Statistical Manual of Mental Disorders, DSM) will be used interchangeably with 'addiction' to consolidate the limited data available. Additionally, due to the diverse sources and the span of decades from which the data is derived, terms that have fallen out of favor may be used for clarity.

The Landscape

Earlier in my career as a clinician, I found myself at the periphery of a situation that would become all too common in the Metro-Detroit Muslim community and, sadly, throughout the country. In the early 2010s, the United States was experiencing a steady increase in intravenous drug use, which ultimately evolved into the opioid epidemic we face today. Illegal opioids, such as heroin, and synthetic drugs like fentanyl gained traction amid the chaos of impulsive governmental regulations on reckless prescribing practices for opioid medications.

These prescribing practices, which were encouraged by government initiatives in the 1990s and supported by drug companies that made billions (Kolodny, 2020), marked the beginning of the epidemic. As individuals who became physiologically dependent on prescribed drugs transitioned to street drugs, addiction rates soared, leading to increased morbidity and mortality. While it may not have been perceived as common or recognized as a serious problem, it is evident that individuals and families within the Muslim community began to feel the impacts of this rapidly evolving crisis.

A young man began misusing a family member's prescription opioids for recreational purposes. After developing an addiction and facing limited access to these medications, he turned to purchasing street drugs and ultimately started using heroin. Despite being healthy, coming from a functionally intact family, and practicing Islam, his situation was surprising to many.

He was hospitalized after an accidental overdose but survived. Following this incident, he was placed on opioid replacement therapy, recognized as the gold standard of treatment in medicine. While his treatment team, and initially he, viewed this as a positive outcome, some members of the community disagreed.

In a non-medical, faith-based therapeutic setting, he was encouraged to stop taking his medication and to engage in an alternative treatment program. The underlying message was that he did not need pharmaceuticals to overcome addiction; rather, he needed support from family, community, and faith. However, in reality, he required pharmacological treatment. Unfortunately, he relapsed shortly thereafter and succumbed to another overdose.

I have kept the details vague, but the harsh reality is that this situation is often unrecognized due to its repetitive nature. The Muslim community shows a notable susceptibility to drug use and addiction; it is not prepared to confront this issue. This sentiment is common among many insular, socially religious communities in the US. The perception of drug use—ranging from cannabis to cocaine—has been viewed as a distant concern by religious leaders and much of the greater Muslim community. As a result, there is a significant unfamiliarity with both psychological and pharmacological treatment options.

Furthermore, perceptions of drug use disorders tend to be harsh, with qualitative data indicating that they are primarily viewed as moral or religious failures. Considering that over half of Muslims in the US are foreign-born first-generation immigrants, the idea that drug use is an alien issue prevails. Consequently, addressing this problem does not rank high on most people's agendas.

However, the reality is that acculturation stressors, racism, xenophobia, and generational trauma make Muslim Americans uniquely vulnerable to addiction and create additional barriers to seeking help as a Muslim.

Delineating the Muslim Cohort

Use trends in substance use vary significantly across different regions and populations in the United States, including distinctions between urban and rural areas, wealthy and low-income communities, and differences between the East and West Coast. Additionally, certain ethnicities and groups of people exhibit different patterns of addiction, influenced by a range of factors such as environment, genetic predisposition, and social context. When examining substance use among American Muslims, it is crucial to approach the topic with nuance.

Despite sharing a common faith, it would be incorrect to oversimplify the Muslim community in the United States; it is an exceptionally diverse group composed of individuals from many countries, particularly among first- and second-generation immigrants. There is also a significant native-born African American population with a unique historical background, alongside a rapidly growing group of converts who often face challenges in integrating into the Muslim community. Muslim Americans reflect the broader diversity of American society. Specific groups, such as Iraqis, Afghans, Somalis, and Syrians, have come to the US and other Western countries in distinct waves of immigration due to war and conflict, further complicating the landscape of social challenges and drug exposure within these culturally similar populations.

DRUG ADDICTION IN MUSLIM AMERICA

According to the Pew Research Survey in 2017, the largest segment of the Muslim American population consists of individuals of Southeast Asian descent (from Pakistan, India, and Bangladesh), making up over 35% of the community. This group has a wide range of linguistic, cultural, and socioeconomic diversity. The oldest segment of the Muslim community, composed of African Americans, accounts for 25-30%. American Muslims of Arab descent represents a significant minority, ranging from 20-25% of the population. Additionally, Caucasian and Latin American Muslims may comprise around 10%.

This diversity poses a significant challenge in gathering accurate data on substance use trends among Muslims. While some research does exist regarding specific groups, it is often conducted within the context of broader populations and lacks depth. Furthermore, studying the Muslim American community presents a substantial challenge in accounting for the genetic and cultural variability, even within groups that share the same demographic designation. Consequently, the extrapolation of data from other populations and regions in the US, combined with clinical and anecdotal evidence, becomes a valuable starting point for understanding which substances may be relevant to different Muslim communities.

Certain substances exhibit higher rates of use and addiction among specific ethnic demographics and geographic areas. Recognizing some general trends that may apply to Muslim Americans is crucial. For instance, non-pathological alcohol use has consistently been reported to be higher among Caucasian Americans compared to African Americans. Consequently, the rates of alcohol addiction tend to be lower in the African American community. This difference can be attributed to various genetic and environmental factors, including the higher prevalence of alcoholism in rural America compared to urban centers.

However, it is important to note that a lower rate of substance use in a community does not necessarily correlate with a lower rate of addiction or pathological use. A notable example is cocaine, which is primarily an urban drug. As a stimulant, it has led to significant negative health consequences, particularly in urban areas during the 1980s and early 1990s. According to the 2019 National Survey on Drug Use and Health (Substance Abuse and Mental Health Services Administration, 2020), 1.9% of Caucasian Americans reported using cocaine in the past year, while only 1.2% of African Americans did. Despite this lower usage rate, African Americans who used cocaine were nearly twice as likely to develop an addiction or use disorder compared to their Caucasian counterparts. Although more recent data sets indicate that rates of addiction have become more similar, these discrepancies illustrate that some communities, despite lower usage rates, may experience greater negative consequences than others with higher exposure to a particular drug. This trend can likely be extrapolated to Muslim communities, where the social stigma and seriousness surrounding drug use may make such use more psychologically and socially problematic.

Certain populations, particularly Arab Americans, present additional challenges for study. While they represent a significant minority within the Muslim American population, most Arab Americans practice Christianity rather than Islam (Arab American Institute, 2006). Consequently, the existing literature about Arabs often fails to distinguish between faiths and is generally lacking in depth.

Other substances, particularly those viewed as rural and socially unacceptable, such as crystal methamphetamine, are more prevalent in rural areas of the United States and are commonly associated with use among Caucasian men. However, rates of methamphetamine use among minority groups have steadily increased (NIH, 2021). Even though Muslim Americans typically reside in urban centers, neglecting this group could result in a small but significantly affected minority remaining unaddressed and untreated.

The Social Conundrum of Alcohol Use

The discussion about alcohol among American Muslims often feels awkward, primarily because many people are aware of a Muslim who drinks non-pathologically and have complex feelings about it. I recall an experience during medical school when I was studying with a non-Muslim friend. As we finished our work, he walked to his refrigerator, pulled out a couple of beers, and offered one to me. I declined, but he then cracked one open and began to drink. While this action seemed benign, it made me highly uncomfortable. I later explained that the feeling it evoked was akin to witnessing someone light up a crack pipe. This response is especially noteworthy, considering I am a natural-born American.

In the United States, the legal status of alcoholic beverages means that alcohol is likely the most addictive substance to which Muslim Americans are exposed, with little social stigma from non-Muslims regarding its consumption.

Over the decades, rates of alcohol consumption in the United States have increased, but they have remained relatively stable or even declined in recent years. Alcoholism continues to be a significant source of medical issues, lost income, and social disarray, with addiction rates among adults ranging from 10% to 15%. These rates vary greatly among different populations based on ethnicity and socioeconomic status. Despite this, non-pathological alcohol consumption is typical. More than half of American adults drink regularly, and over 75% of college graduates report doing the same. Higher earners tend to consume alcohol more frequently, and it is a significant part of Western culture. Alcohol is present in many celebrations, from graduations and weddings to New Year's Eve. Aged and exclusive wines are often associated with success and higher social status, and many religious and cultural ceremonies incorporate alcohol as an integral element of their rituals.

Given this context, it is not surprising that some studies suggest that around half of Muslim-identifying college students reported drinking alcohol in the past year (Abu-Ras, Ahmed, & Arfken, 2010). Although this is significantly lower than their non-Muslim peers, data indicates that about 80% of American Muslims perceive alcohol as morally wrong (Michalak, Trocki, & Katz, 2009). While this perspective may seem strange or alien to the average American clinician, it is understandable within the framework of Islam.

All mainstream branches of Islam recognize alcohol consumption as a sin and impose an absolute prohibition against it. To understand the emotional relationship Muslims have with alcohol, it is important to note that even if their consumption is clinically non-pathological, it is still viewed negatively. In the Qur'an, alcohol is mentioned alongside other sinful acts such as gambling, idolatrous divination, violence, and forgetfulness of God (Qur'an 5:90-91). Additionally, the consumption of alcohol has implications within Islam, such as rendering the ritual prayer (Salat) invalid, which implies a temporary severance of one's connection with the divine and a lack of acceptance of one's prayers.

While other religious communities in the United States, such as Baptists and Mormons, also prohibit alcohol consumption, the significantly higher rate of lifetime abstinence among Muslim Americans reflects their theological and religious beliefs about alcohol consumption. The stark contrast between the general societal views on alcohol and those held by Muslims creates emotional and psychological challenges for Muslims who drink, as well as for those who know other Muslims who do. A pertinent question is whether rates of addiction and psychopathology are higher among Muslim Americans who consume alcohol in comparison to non-Muslims. Unfortunately, there is a lack of specific data or research on this topic, and it is unlikely to emerge in the near future. However, given the conflicting views and the relative isolation a Muslim American might experience while consuming alcohol—both in terms of social acceptance and religious consequences—it is reasonable to assume that the challenges are significant. In the Western world, alcohol might be seen as a benign substance. However, for practicing Muslims, there is no such thing as a benign drink. Literature indicates that rates of alcohol use disorder among Muslim Americans are lower than those in the general population, with the lowest estimate being 10.9% (Ragheb et al., 2023). While this statistic may seem optimistic initially, it can be misleading. With the substantially lower rates of alcohol use, the likelihood of Muslims who do choose to drink becoming addicted to alcohol may be higher compared to non-Muslims.

Cannabis Contextualized

The increasing amount of data on cannabis use is among the most intriguing and concerning developments in recent years regarding drug use. Cannabis has a complex and controversial identity in American history. It was initially legal but was declared illegal with the Controlled Substances Act of 1970, despite widespread recommendations that it should not be classified as a soft (less harmful) drug (Mead, 2019). The historical persecution of minorities for minor drug offenses—particularly in impoverished urban areas and African American communities—has given this psychoactive substance significant cultural and social relevance (Ahuja, Haeny, Sartor, & Bucholz, 2022). The push for federal legalization in the US has been driven as much by a desire to confront racial bias and disparities as it has been by the drug's perceived therapeutic value and relatively benign nature. This context is crucial for understanding Muslim Americans who may use cannabis; the argument for legalization aligns with the political views of many Muslims. While cannabis has some evidence-based medical applications, the extent of these benefits is often exaggerated and misconstrued within political discussions.

Over the past decade, cannabis has increasingly been associated with various psychopathologies and mental health issues. These include diminished cognitive function (Power et al., 2021), depression, anxiety (Feingold & Weinstein, 2020; Beletsky et al., 2024), and a probable link to the development of psychosis and schizophrenia (Hasan et al., 2019a; Schoeler, Ferris, & Winstock, 2022; West & Sharif, 2023), particularly among young users. Most concerning is that the association with schizophrenia is observed not only in the United States but also in Denmark, where the legalization and increased use of cannabis have coincided with a 3 to 4-fold rise in schizophrenia rates within the population (Alzeer et al., 2021).

At the same time, public perception of cannabis has softened and even shifted towards more positive views in recent years. Between 2001 and 2022, Gallup Polls indicated that favorable perceptions of cannabis among American adults soared from 30% to nearly 70%. Furthermore, by 2021, data from the Pew Research Center revealed that over 90% of adults believed cannabis should be legal for both recreational and medicinal use. As of now, 38 US states have legalized cannabis for medicinal purposes (though not regulated by the Food and Drug Administration), and 18 have legalized it for recreational use. Usage trends are consistently on the rise, with 1 in 4 Americans aged 18 to 25 reporting cannabis use in the past month and over 50% of the same age group admitting to having used the substance at least once in their lifetime (Mattingly, Richardson, & Hart, 2024). This trend is unique in the American drug culture landscape.

It is also important to note that cannabis occupies a different space in the minds of American Muslims compared to other drugs. While there is a clear conflict between alcohol's legal status in the US and its explicit prohibition in Islamic law, cannabis is not specifically mentioned in the Qur'an or other primary Islamic texts. Historically, cannabis has had a vague status within Islamic legal and medical literature, leading to often abstract and conflicting perceptions (Nahas, 1982; Alzeer et al., 2021; Ghiabi, Maarefvand, Bahari, & Alawi, 2018). This historical variance may be related to the different cannabis strains known in the classical world, as some literature does not acknowledge the intoxicating effects of cannabis at all (Nahas, 1982).

Cannabis has been included in pharmacopeias from the Muslim world and is praised for its medicinal properties across a range of ailments (Nahas, 1982). However, it has also largely been deemed haram (impermissible) by the majority of Sunni and Shia Muslim jurists (Alzeer et al., 2021). Unlike alcohol, which is widely stigmatized in Islamic culture due to its status as an intoxicant and its legal prohibitions in Muslim-majority countries, cannabis is generally perceived as less stigmatized. It is commonly used for both recreational and medicinal purposes in conservative and Islamic countries such as Pakistan (Hasan et al., 2019b) and Bangladesh (Shaki et al., 2021), often outside the scope of government regulation. Although cannabis is typically forbidden, its status has not reached unanimous consensus (Rosenthal, 1971, p. 104), and ongoing discourse regarding its legality persists, particularly in Iran and Southeast Asian Muslim nations (Ghiabi et al., 2018; Khalid, Haseeb, Mushtaq, & Kamal, 2022).

Although there is minimal data available, it is clear that cannabis use among Muslim Americans is increasing. In response to this trend, the Fiqh Council of North America made a statement in 2018 regarding the permissibility of cannabis. They outlined two conditions under which cannabis may be used, discussed cannabis strains with low psychoactive THC content, and provided exceptions for the use of psychoactive cannabis based on commentary from two jurisprudential schools of Islam (Qatanani,

Umar, Padela, 2021). While these exceptions came with stipulations and strong warnings, one could argue for relative leniency regarding cannabis use due to the subjective nature of certain disorders, including pain and mental health issues.

However, I believe it is more important to shift our understanding of the relationship between American Muslims and cannabis away from Islamic legal rulings and toward cultural heritage and context. Several years ago, I spoke to various Islamic congregations in the Metro Detroit area about drug use, and the topic of cannabis inevitably arose. I would often ask adolescents and young adults to raise their hands if they knew any Muslims who drank alcohol. Very few, sometimes none would raise their hands, and the mood was often somber during this question. Conversely, when I asked the same groups if they were familiar with any Muslims who smoked cannabis products, approximately 90% of the attendees would raise their hands, often in a more relaxed manner and sometimes even laughing at the prevalence of use.

Cannabis has deep historical roots in Central and Southeast Asia and is used in a relatively destigmatized manner (both ritually and socially) in many parts of the Muslim world. Its use in Mughal and Persian courts is well-documented, and certain ascetic movements and Sufi Muslim practices have some associations with the drug, albeit on the fringe. From an anthropological perspective, it is not surprising that cannabis has an extensive pre-Islamic history in the region. It is ritualistically consumed as Bhang (a milled drink) and is associated with religious holidays and festivals, such as Holi, across the Indian subcontinent. This cultural context helps explain why cannabis does not carry the same negative stigma as alcohol.

This understanding also sheds light on the reported cannabis use among some conservative Muslim populations. Additionally, in the Arab countries of the Middle East and North Africa, there is both a cultural acceptance of cannabis and involvement in its production and trade.

Given this historical context, along with the fact that Southeast Asian and African American Muslims make up approximately 60-70% of the Muslim population in the US, it's reasonable to hypothesize that cannabis use rates among Muslims might be at least comparable to those of the general American population. There is no basis to assume that the rate of cannabis addiction would be lower either; approximately 4.3% of young people aged 18-25 are affected. In fact, one might suggest that due to the prohibition of other substances and the destigmatization of cannabis within the Muslim community, the rates of cannabis use, and addiction could be higher than in the broader American population.

Heroin, Fentanyl, and the Opioid Epidemic

In 2017, I treated an older, married Caucasian male, a former schoolteacher, in the hospital. He had accidentally overdosed on fentanyl-laced heroin, which he had used intranasally. The context of his addiction was both interesting and sad. After undergoing surgery, he had been prescribed high-dose opioids to manage his residual pain for nearly 15 years. However, due to increased scrutiny of prescription practices and the difficulty of managing his pain, his primary care physician eventually stopped prescribing these medications and referred him to a pain specialist. Unfortunately, the gentleman's insurance did not cover the pain specialist he was referred to, resulting in him being taken off his pain medications entirely by his physician rather aggressively.

After 15 years of physiological and psychological dependence, he began buying pills from drug dealers. As the pills became too expensive, he turned to heroin, which was a cheaper and similar substitute. Unfortunately, the heroin he purchased was often cut with fentanyl, a potent and less expensive substance that increased the dealer's profits. The man had no prior history of addiction aside from his reliance on opioids, nor did he have a history of criminal behavior or significant mental health issues. This case starkly illustrates the broader narrative of opioid addiction in America and highlights the interplay of factors that have contributed to the opioid epidemic we are currently facing.

Heroin use was relatively uncommon across the United States in the 1990s, although there were sporadic increases. Historically, it was a drug primarily used by Caucasian Americans in rural areas, but during the late 1980s and early 1990s, it experienced a spike in urban city centers followed by a decline. It was not until a policy change in 1996 that opioid addiction became widespread. This change was heavily influenced by drug companies through the American Pain Society (APS), leading the Joint Commission on Accreditation of Healthcare Organizations (JCAHO) to mandate aggressive treatment of subjective pain. As a result, hospitals and doctors began prescribing opioids more liberally (Van Zee, 2009). This period is often referred to as the First Wave of the opioid epidemic, characterized by prescription drug misuse.

As prescribing practices tightened and government regulations increased around 2010, many people turned to heroin, marking the Second Wave of the epidemic. Soon after, the rise of synthetic opioids led to worsening addiction rates and higher overdose rates, known as the Third Wave. By 2022, fatalities from opioid overdoses reached 81,000, a tenfold increase since 1999 with a terrifying increase to 114,000 deaths in the following year. Subsequently, likely due to more aggressive government initiatives and greater availability and awareness of naloxone (an overdose reversal agent administered in the community intranasally or as an injection), that number has gone down, but still provisionally sits at nearly 90,000 annual deaths (Centers for Disease Control & Prevention, 2024).

There is limited data suggesting that opioid addiction rates among Muslim Americans may be comparable to those of the general American population (Ragheb et al., 2023). However, this data is insufficient to draw definitive conclusions. Anecdotal reports from mosques and communities across the nation indicate that opioid addiction and overdose cases may be more prevalent than commonly recognized. Unfortunately, dispatch reports from areas with significant Muslim-American populations suggest that there may be less communal acknowledgment of opioid addiction, making families and community members less likely to address the issue (Herndon, 2020). Additionally, data on overdose trends in Dearborn, Michigan, a majority Arab city, show that opioid overdose deaths have more than doubled over the past decade (Hunter, 2016) and have mirrored the decline in deaths seen nationally in 2024 (City of Dearborn, 2025).

Opioid addiction and overdose rates initially were highest among Caucasian Americans. However, in recent years, there have been increases across all American demographics, likely including Muslim Americans. This trend may be influenced by several factors, such as the unclear distinction between physical and psychological pain, as well as acculturation stressors and discrimination, which can increase the likelihood of addiction to opioids prescribed for pain relief. Research from countries like Saudi Arabia (Alqahtani & Salmon, 2008), Pakistan (Minhas & Nizami, 2006; Wazir et al., 2023), and Iran (Vaziri et al., 2022) indicates that somatization—where mental stress manifests as physical pain—may be more prevalent among Middle Eastern and South Asian populations. Given the cultural disconnect and the significant number of first and second-generation Muslims in the US, it is reasonable to suggest that psychological pain is often misreported as physical pain. This misreporting is seen as a less stigmatizing and more straightforward complaint to present at a doctor's office.

For Muslim Americans who do develop opioid addiction, accessing treatment can be more challenging. According to the Institute for Social Policy and Understanding (ISPU), a Muslim research organization, its 2020 American Muslim Poll found that Muslim Americans were twice as likely as their non-Muslim counterparts to endorse a "tougher" stance on drug addiction (ISPU, 2021). The most evidence-based treatments for opioid use disorder are often opioid replacement therapies, also known as medication-assisted treatment (MAT). However, the community's perception of these treatments can be quite negative, leading patients prescribed these well-researched therapies to be still viewed as being in active addiction. This misconception was highlighted in the vignette I mentioned earlier and continues to persist within the community.

Despite the challenges, it is essential to contextualize the opioid crisis. The public perception is correct in recognizing that opioid addiction resulted from the pharmaceutical industry's lobbying of the government and the exploitation of the medical-industrial complex for profit (Kolodny, 2020; Haffajee & Mello, 2017). The clinical Muslim community must acknowledge this reality and educate our patients and communities about it.

It is also important to emphasize the effectiveness of medical treatments for opioid use disorders. Currently, the gold standard for treating opioid use disorder and addiction is Medication-Assisted Treatment (MAT), which is supported by strong data. Notably, nearly 90% of individuals who do not receive MAT will relapse within the first year (Bailey et al., 2013). Therefore, combating stigma and promoting community education around this issue is crucial. MAT for opioid addiction is not just an American phenomenon; there is substantial evidence of its efficacy internationally, including extensive data from the Arab world (Alawa et al., 2022).

Given the tendency of Muslim American parents to somaticize psychological distress and the significant stigma associated with opioid addiction, it is likely that the prevalence of opioid addiction in the US is comparable to that in other communities across the country. Although very little data on substance use disorders in Muslim populations exists (Ragheb et al., 2023), stigma and suspicion may continue to obstruct adequate and transparent research on this demographic.

The Path Forward

American Muslims, regardless of how directly they are affected by addiction, should take the lead in addressing this issue. Enjoining what is good and opposing evil and strife are cornerstones of the Islamic faith, and the community can find inspiration by looking inward. At the same time, Muslims should familiarize themselves with the resources available from both Muslim organizations and national resources regarding drug use.

Efforts have been made to enhance government engagement, and Muslim Americans have gained representation in discussions surrounding drug use disorders and addiction. Recently, initiatives by The White House, the Office of National Drug Control Policy (ONDCP), and the US Department of Health and Human Services (DHHS) have sought to engage the Muslim American community and increase their representation.

American Muslim Health Professionals (AMHP) has maintained close communication with various government departments, advocating for improvements in mental health and addiction treatment access.

In August 2023, I attended a meeting at The White House with members and leaders from several faith communities, alongside representatives from the ONDCP and DHHS, to discuss the opioid epidemic. Much of the conversation focused on supporting community engagement, utilizing government initiatives to promote local programming, and addressing the mistrust and detachment some Muslim communities feel toward governmental initiatives. Follow-up meetings and sessions were held and facilitated by SAMHSA, with which AMHP typically collaborates to receive updates and new initiatives for combating addiction. AMHP has also supported the elimination of the x-waiver, a regulation that limited the physicians authorized to prescribe Medication-Assisted Treatment (MAT) for patients with opioid addiction. This stipulation was removed at the beginning of 2023, increasing access to drug treatment. AMHP remains committed to supporting various initiatives, including increasing access to Narcan, a life-saving antidote for opioid overdoses. Additionally, AMHP is advocating for more funding for methadone clinics, which are part of a medication-assisted treatment (MAT) program that can be particularly beneficial for individuals with severe opioid addiction and higher levels of drug tolerance (Degenhardt, 2023).

It is essential to recognize the significant mistrust that the Muslim community in the US may have towards governmental organizations and initiatives, particularly given the ethically questionable foreign policy practices in Muslim countries both historically and currently.

As a result, top-down approaches to addressing addiction in Muslim communities may not be as effective as localized programs. Organizations like AMHP and other healthcare advocacy groups have been providing Mental Health First Aid (MHFA) training, with specific sessions tailored for religious clergy. For instance, AMHP offered MHFA training for Imams at Michigan's 2023 Muslim Mental Health Conference, which received excellent turnout and feedback. Since then, MHFA training has been regularly offered to Imams at various conferences all over the nation and has become a staple of the interface between the religious community and more clinically-centered psychological perspectives.

Additionally, programming explicitly designed for religious leaders and clergy has been conducted in partnership with the North American Imams Fellowship (NAIF). These seminars and training sessions focus on understanding and addressing drug use within congregations and the steps to take when conflicts arise related to this issue, including legal gray areas specifically relevant to the addressed locality. It is important to acknowledge that community leaders and clergy often have more immediate access to local problems than clinicians or academic faculty. Therefore, collaboration in tackling addiction is crucial for achieving any meaningful success.

Because of that fact, most empowering actions that can be taken at the local level revolving around education and awareness, particularly regarding the impact of "soft" drugs like cannabis and the treatment options for more stigmatized drugs like opioids. This is where the individual in the community, especially a mental health professional, can be most helpful—interfacing with Mosques and cultural centers, bringing awareness to the pathology most prevalent in that specific community and destigmatizing the conversation topic of drug use and addiction. As mentioned earlier, American Muslims are anything but homogeneous, so tailoring the approach of programming is necessary for reaching an audience and making a difference.

Every Friday as I go to pray Salat Al Juma'a at the Islamic Center of Detroit, I pass by a naloxone dispensing machine on Mosque grounds. It sits at the path to the mosque's front door, quite obvious, and loudly proclaiming the opioid epidemic in full view of attendees. It isn't there because a national organization lobbied the mosque for it to be there, or because SAMHSA or The ONDCP sent a formal request for it to be there - it is there because the community became aware of a situation and began to understand how to address it. Because a stigma was broken in favor of a solution. Misconceptions about drugs and their treatment exist across all demographics within the Muslim community, just as they do in all communities in the US. While the challenges faced by Muslim Americans concerning drugs are unique, the approaches that can effectively address these issues are not only established and clinically-proven; they also align with our Islamic heritage.

References

Abu-Ras, W., Ahmed, S., Arfken, C. L. (2010). Alcohol use among US Muslim college students: risk and protective factors. *Journal of ethnicity in substance abuse.* ;9(3). doi:10.1080/15332640.2010.500921

Afsahi, K., & Darwich, S. (2016). Hashish in Morocco and Lebanon: A comparative study. *International Journal of Drug Policy, 31,* 190–198. https://doi.org/10.1016/j.drugpo.2016.02.024

Ahuja, M., Haeny, A. M., Sartor, C. E., & Bucholz, K. K. (2022). Perceived racial and social class discrimination and cannabis involvement among Black youth and young adults. *Drug and Alcohol Dependence, 232,* 109304. https://doi.org/10.1016/j.drugalcdep.2022.109304

Alawa, J., Muhammad, M., Kazemitabar, M., Bromberg, D. J., Garcia, D., Khoshnood, K., & Ghandour, L. (2022). Medication for opioid use disorder in the Arab World: A systematic review. *International Journal of Drug Policy, 102,* 103617. https://doi.org/10.1016/j.drugpo.2022.103617

Alqahtani, M. M., & Salmon, P. (2008, April 1). *Prevalence of somatization and minor psyciatric morbidity in primary healthcare in Saudi Arabic: a preliminary study in Asir region.* https://pmc.ncbi.nlm.nih.gov/articles/PMC3377053/

Alzeer, J., Hadeed, K. A., Basar, H., Al-Razem, F., Abdel-Wahhab, M. A., & Alhamdan, Y. (2020). Cannabis and its permissibility status. *Cannabis and Cannabinoid Research, 6*(6), 451–456. https://doi.org/10.1089/can.2020.0017

Arab American Institute. (2006, June 1). Demographics. Retrieved from the Internet Archive: https://web.archive.org/web/20060601221810/http://www.aaiusa.org/arab-americans/22/demographics.

Arfken C. L., Ahmed S. (2016). Ten years of substance use research in Muslim populations: Where do we go from here? *J Muslim Ment Health.* 2016;10(1). doi:10.3998/jmmh.10381607.0010.103

Bailey, G. L., Herman, D. S., & Stein, M. D. (2013). Perceived Relapse Risk and Desire for Medication Assisted Treatment among Persons Seeking Inpatient Opiate Detoxification. *Journal of Substance Abuse Treatment, 45*(3), 302–305. https://doi.org/10.1016/j.jsat.2013.04.002

Balhara, Y., & Mathur, S. (2014). Bhang - beyond the purview of the narcotic drugs and psychotropic substances act. *Lung India, 31*(4), 431. https://doi.org/10.4103/0970-2113.142109

Beletsky, A., Liu, C., Lochte, B., Samuel, N., & Grant, I. (2024). Cannabis and Anxiety: A critical review. *Medical Cannabis and Cannabinoids, 7*(1), 19–30. https://doi.org/10.1159/000534855

City of Dearborn. (2025, March 26). *Dearborn sees major drop in overdoses following public health interventions.* https://dearborn.gov/government/news-communication/Dearborn-sees-major-drop-in-overdose-following-public-health-interventions

Degenhardt, L., Clark, B., Macpherson, G., Leppan, O., Nielsen, S., Zahra, E., Larance, B., Kimber, J., Martino-Burke, D., Hickman, M., & Farrell, M. (2023). Buprenorphine versus methadone for the treatment of opioid dependence: a systematic review and meta-analysis of randomised and observational studies. *The Lancet Psychiatry, 10*(6), 386–402. https://doi.org/10.1016/s2215-0366(23)00095-0

Doukas N. (2016). Centre for Addiction and Mental Health. Substance use among Muslims residing in the United States: A literature review. *Alcohol Drug Abuse Subst Depend.* 2016;2(1):1-4. doi:10.24966/adsd-9594/100006

Feingold, D., & Weinstein, A. (2020). Cannabis and depression. *Advances in Experimental Medicine and Biology,* 67–80. https://doi.org/10.1007/978-3-030-57369-0_5

Ghiabi, M., Maarefvand, M., Bahari, H., & Alavi, Z. (2018). Islam and cannabis: Legalisation and religious debate in Iran. *International Journal of Drug Policy, 56,* 121–127. https://doi.org/10.1016/j.drugpo.2018.03.009

Haffajee, R. L., & Mello, M. M. (2017). Drug companies' liability for the opioid epidemic. *New England Journal of Medicine, 377*(24), 2301–2305. https://doi.org/10.1056/nejmp1710756

Hasan, A., Von Keller, R., Friemel, C. M., Hall, W., Schneider, M., Koethe, D., Leweke, F. M., Strube, W., & Hoch, E. (2019a). Cannabis use and psychosis: a review of reviews. *European Archives of Psychiatry and Clinical Neuroscience, 270*(4), 403–412. https://doi.org/10.1007/s00406-019-01068-z

Hasan, S. S., Shaikh, A., Ochani, R. K., Ashrafi, M. M., Ansari, Z. N., Abbas, S. H., Abbasi, M. K., Ashraf, M. A., & Ali, W. (2019b). Perception and practices regarding cannabis consumption in Karachi, Pakistan: A cross-sectional study. *Journal of Ethnicity in Substance Abuse, 20*(3), 471–489. https://doi.org/10.1080/15332640.2019.1667287

Herndon, D. (2020). American Human Rights Council. Opioid crisis in Muslim community focus of community meeting in Dearborn. Press and Guide. https://businessdirectory.pressandguide.com/news/opioid-crisis-in-muslim-community-focus-of-community-meeting-in-dearborn/article_a707d806-540f-11ea-8d40-bf58c4c2b440.html.

Hjorthøj, C., Posselt, C. M., & Nordentoft, M. (2021). Development over time of the Population-Attributable Risk Fraction for Cannabis Use disorder in schizophrenia in Denmark. *JAMA Psychiatry, 78*(9),

1013. https://doi.org/10.1001/jamapsychiatry.2021.1471

Hunter, G. (2016, March 14). Arab-American community comes to grips with drugs. *The Detroit News*. https://www.detroitnews.com/story/news/local/wayne-county/2016/03/14/arab-american-drug-abuse/81749192/

Institute for Social Policy and Understanding. (2021, October 12). *Substance Abuse and Addiction in the Muslim Community: Stigma and Support - ISPU*. ISPU. https://ispu.org/substance-abuse-and-addiction-in-the-muslim-community/

Khalid, A., Haseeb, A., Mushtaq, G., & Kamal, M. A. (2022). Medicinal and economic benefits of legalization of marijuana in Pakistan. *PubMed, 21*, 1304–1305. https://doi.org/10.17179/excli2022-5477

Kolodny, A. (2020). How FDA failures contributed to the opioid crisis. *The AMA Journal of Ethic, 22*(8), E743–750. https://doi.org/10.1001/amajethics.2020.743

LeFevre, N., St Louis, J., Worringer, E., Younkin, M., Stahl, N., & Sorcinelli, M. (2023). The end of the X-waiver: excitement, apprehension, and opportunity. *The Journal of the American Board of Family Medicine, 36*(5), 867–872. https://doi.org/10.3122/jabfm.2023.230048r1

Mallik, S., Starrels, J. L., Shannon, C., Edwards, K., & Nahvi, S. (2020). "An undercover problem in the Muslim community": A qualitative study of imams' perspectives on substance use. *Journal of Substance Abuse Treatment, 123*, 108224. https://doi.org/10.1016/j.jsat.2020.108224

Mattingly, D. T., Richardson, M. K., & Hart, J. L. (2024). Prevalence of and trends in current cannabis use among US youth and adults, 2013–2022. *Drug and Alcohol Dependence Reports, 12*, 100253. https://doi.org/10.1016/j.dadr.2024.100253

Mead, A. (2019). Legal and regulatory issues governing cannabis and Cannabis-Derived Products in the United States. *Frontiers in Plant Science, 10*. https://doi.org/10.3389/fpls.2019.00697

Michalak, L., Trocki, K., & Katz, K. (2009). "I Am a Muslim and My Dad is an Alcoholic—What Should I Do?" Internet-Based Advice for Muslims About Alcohol. *Journal of Muslim Mental Health, 4*(1), 47–66. https://doi.org/10.1080/15564900902771325

Minhas, F. A., & Nizami, A. T. (2006). Somatoform disorders: Perspectives from Pakistan. *International Review of Psychiatry, 18*(1), 55–60. https://doi.org/10.1080/09540260500466949

Nahas, G. G. (1982, December 1). *Hashish in Islam 9th to 18th century*. PubMed. https://pubmed.ncbi.nlm.nih.gov/6762898/

National Institutes of Health (NIH). 2021, October 5). *Trends in U.S.*

methamphetamine use and associated deaths. https://www.nih.gov/news-events/nih-research-matters/trends-us-methamphetamine-use-associated-deaths

Power, E., Sabherwal, S., Healy, C., Neill, A. O., Cotter, D., & Cannon, M. (2021). Intelligence quotient decline following frequent or dependent cannabis use in youth: a systematic review and meta-analysis of longitudinal studies. *Psychological Medicine*, *51*(2), 194–200. https://doi.org/10.1017/s0033291720005036

Qatanani, A., Umar, M., & Padela, A. I. (2021). Bioethical insights from the Fiqh Council of North America's recent ruling on medical cannabis. *International Journal of Drug Policy*, *97*, 103360. https://doi.org/10.1016/j.drugpo.2021.103360

Ragheb, H., Ahmed, S., Uddin, S., Foll, B. L., & Hassan, A. N. (2023). The prevalence and treatment utilization of substance use disorders among Muslims in the United States: A national epidemiological survey. *American Journal on Addictions*, *32*(5), 497–505. https://doi.org/10.1111/ajad.13443

Rosenthal, F. (1971). *The Herb. Hashish versus Medieval Muslim Society*. Google Books. https://books.google.com/books/about/The_Herb_Hashish_Versus_Medieval_Muslim.html?hl=&id=5ArazwEACAAJ

Schoeler, T., Ferris, J., & Winstock, A. R. (2022). Rates and correlates of cannabis-associated psychotic symptoms in over 230,000 people who use cannabis. *Translational Psychiatry*, *12*(1). https://doi.org/10.1038/s41398-022-02112-8

Shakil, S. S. M., Gowan, M., Hughes, K., Azam, M. N. K., & Ahmed, M. N. (2021). A narrative review of the ethnomedicinal usage of Cannabis sativa Linnaeus as traditional phytomedicine by folk medicine practitioners of Bangladesh. *Journal of Cannabis Research*, *3*(1). https://doi.org/10.1186/s42238-021-00063-3

Substance Abuse and Mental Health Services Administration. (2020). Key Substance Use and Mental Health Indicators in the United States: Results from the 2019 National Survey on Drug Use and Health. In *Substance Abuse and Mental Health Services Administration*. https://www.samhsa.gov/data/sites/default/files/reports/rpt29393/2019NSDUHFFRPDFWHTML/2019NSDUHFFR1PDFW090120.pdf

The White House (2023). https://www.whitehouse.gov/ondcp/briefing-room/2023/08/21/readout-of-white-house-meeting-with-faith-leaders-on-president-bidens-unity-agenda-efforts-to-beat-the-overdose-epidemic/. Accessed November 15, 2024

Van Zee, A. (2008). The promotion and marketing of OxyContin: commercial triumph, public health tragedy. *American Journal of*

Public Health, *99*(2), 221–227. https://doi.org/10.2105/ajph.2007.131714

Vaziri, A., Esmaeilinasab, M., Hamdieh, M., Farahani, H. (2022) Pseudo Relationships: An Interpersonal Characteristic of Patients with Somatic Symptom Disorder in an Iranian Sample. *International Journal of Behavioral Sciences,15*(4):268-274. doi:10.30491/ijbs.2022.289652.1580

Wazir, M. N. K., Kakakhel, S., Gul, A. N., Awan, Q., Khattak, A. F., Yousaf, N., & Wahid, F. (2023). Psychiatric Illnesses, somatic complaints, and Treatments in a tertiary care hospital in Khyber Pakhtunkhwa, Pakistan: a Cross-Sectional study. *Cureus.* https://doi.org/10.7759/cureus.43151

West, M. L., & Sharif, S. (2022). Cannabis and psychosis. *Child and Adolescent Psychiatric Clinics of North America, 32*(1), 69–83. https://doi.org/10.1016/j.chc.2022.07.004

SECTION FIVE

CONTEMPORARY ISSUES

CHAPTER FIFTEEN

FIRST AND SECOND-GENERATION IMMIGRANTS IN NORTH AMERICA: PERSPECTIVES FROM THEORY AND LIVED EXPERIENCES

Hanan Hashem, Waleed Sami, Somer Saleh

The acculturation process is a defining experience for first and second-generation Muslim immigrants in North America. In this chapter, we utilize the Multidimensional Model of Acculturation (Schwartz et al., 2010) to highlight the unique and dynamic aspects of cultural reconciliation that impact the mental health of both first and second-generation Muslims in North America. We will begin with a brief overview of the model, followed by a discussion on how acculturation intersects with mental health processes, behaviors, and outcomes. By applying the Multidimensional Model of Acculturation to the experiences of first- and second-generation Muslim immigrants, we describe the nuances of heritage and receiving culture, highlighting the negotiation of practices, values, and identity between cultures, and framing the acculturation experience through the "context of reception." After providing a narrative of the lived experiences of acculturation of the authors of this chapter, showcasing our positionality by reflecting on our acculturation processes and contexts, and reconciling identities through time and place, we end the chapter with research, clinical, and policy recommendations.

Introduction

Acculturation is the process by which individuals reconcile their heritage culture with the culture of the new environment they have immigrated to. This process is significantly influenced by the stage of life in which a person migrates, as it can affect individuals in various overlapping ways, as discussed throughout this chapter. The acculturative process of a first-generation Malaysian Muslim living in Vancouver, Canada, may have factors that are different and overlapping with the experiences of a second-generation Lebanese Muslim living in Torreón, Mexico. In addition to the impact of Islamophobia in global, national, and local politics across the world, Muslim migrants may also face specific challenges depending on their relationship with their religious heritage and culture, as separate or intertwined with their ethnic heritage culture. This is especially true for Muslim immigrants who have the desire to maintain their ethnic and religious cultural traditions while living in North America, which is largely shaped by post-colonial Christian cultures. The interaction of cultures can strongly predict mental health attitudes, behaviors, and outcomes, such as help-seeking tendencies, resiliency strategies, perceptions of stigma, and the likelihood of accessing formal or informal mental health services in their community. Additionally, the immigration process can also result in experiences of loss, trauma, and discrimination, impacting mental health outcomes and cultural identity development (Tummala-Narra, 2014).

We use the term immigrants to include individuals and family systems across the developmental lifespan who have traveled and settled in North American land for various reasons, including but not limited to improved economic and educational opportunities, as well as fleeing political turmoil and violence in their native countries as refugees or asylum seekers. Teasing apart the difference between first and second-generation immigrants has been a worthy pursuit among academics and clinicians. In this chapter, we define first-generation Muslims as individuals who were not born in North America but immigrated to North America during their lifetime, while second-generation Muslims are those born in the country to which their family immigrated. Understanding the acculturation process can help professionals and community advocates invested in the mental health and well-being of this population create and implement prevention and intervention strategies to build healthy adaptive systems in which Muslim immigrants can thrive.

Much of the academic literature exploring the experience of first and second-generation Muslims in North American countries strongly represents the experiences of those who migrated to the United States of America, followed by Muslim immigrants to Canada. Relatively little is known about the immigrant experience in Central American, Caribbean, and Bahama countries and territories (i.e., Belize, Guatemala, El Salvador, Honduras, Jamaica, Nicaragua, Costa Rice, and Cuba). The migration history and patterns of Muslims in North America are beyond the scope of this chapter, so we encourage readers to engage with *Becoming American.: The Forging of Arab and Muslim Identity in Pluralist America* by Yvonne Haddad (2011) and *The Muslim Question in Canada: A Story of Segmented Integration* by Abdolmohammad Kazemipur (2014) to understand the migration history and patterns of Muslims to the United States and Canada. Some literature describes the experiences of the African, Arab, and South Asian Muslim diaspora that exist in other parts of North America, such as Central American and Caribbean countries and territories (Chitwood, 2017; Mustapha, 2012). Throughout the chapter, we will attempt to highlight the ways that acculturation experiences can impact the relationships that immigrant Muslim communities have with mental health outcomes and systems across North American countries.

Multidimensional Model of Acculturation

To understand the complex intersections of mental health and generational experiences and differences within the Muslim community, it is crucial to ground our analysis in models that capture the community's heterogeneous dynamism. The study of acculturation began in Western-based literature from a unidimensional approach to acculturation (Gordon, 1964), transitioning to a strategy approach to acculturation by Berry (2005), and is currently understood by some as a Multidimensional Model of Acculturation posited by Schwartz and colleagues (2010). We frame our discussion of generational dynamics through the lens of the Multidimensional Model of Acculturation (Schwartz et al., 2010). The Multidimensional Model offers a more nuanced and dynamic framework, critiquing the traditional, unilateral understanding of acculturation as overly reductive.

Early research on acculturation framed it as a linear and unilateral process, wherein immigrants and minorities were expected to assimilate fully into the dominant mainstream culture over successive generations (Berry, 2005; Ward & Geeraert, 2015). This Eurocentric model, developed around European immigrant waves of the 18th and 19th centuries, overlooked the distinct challenges faced by post-World War II immigrants from Asia, Africa, and Latin America (Schwartz et al., 2010). Berry (2005) later proposed a more nuanced framework with four acculturation strategies: *integration*, where individuals maintain their original culture while engaging with the new one; *assimilation*, where the original culture is relinquished in favor of adopting the dominant culture; *separation*, where individuals avoid engagement with the dominant culture and cling to their own; and *marginalization*, where individuals lose connection to both cultures, resulting in identity fragmentation. While integration is considered the most conducive to well-being, these strategies are shaped by societal pressures and individual agency (Safdar et al., 2021).

As the U.S. becomes increasingly diverse, however, these early theories have been critiqued as overly simplistic, leading to the emergence of a Multidimensional Model of Acculturation, which highlights the interplay between personal agency and contextual influences in several ways (Ward & Geeraert, 2015; Schwartz et al., 2010).

First, *acculturation is not a zero-sum process*; minorities and immigrants can integrate into aspects of mainstream culture while retaining their native cultural identity (Ward & Geeraert, 2015). Acculturation is thus bidirectional, involving a complex negotiation between one's native culture and the dominant mainstream. Second, *acculturation varies across different domains of life*. For example, some individuals may feel more acculturated in professional settings within the mainstream yet prefer to socialize with those who share their linguistic or cultural heritage (Schwartz et al., 2010; Ward & Geeraert, 2015). Others may align with political and social movements in the host country that reflect the values of their native culture. This suggests that acculturation in one domain may be more pronounced than in others.

Third, *context plays a critical role*. Social and political environments often shape the opportunities for and pressures against acculturation (Schwartz et al., 2010; Ward & Geeraert, 2015). The role of context includes historical and political events that profoundly influence how cohorts navigate cultural adaptation. For instance, immigrants who arrived in the U.S. during the Great Depression faced a starkly different social and economic environment compared to those arriving during the prosperity of the 1960s. Muslim Americans, particularly from immigrant backgrounds, have had their identities shaped by events such as 9/11, the war on terror, and the legal and social marginalization that followed. Thus, acculturation within the multidimensional model is dynamic, with individual choices shaped by broader socio-political contexts and constraints.

Acculturative patterns and strategies also vary across the lifespan. Younger individuals may find it easier to integrate or assimilate, while older adults may focus more on cultural preservation (Juang & Syed, 2019). For instance, younger individuals may feel more acculturated when they express values related to individualism, compared to familism and interdependence expressed by older generations (Schwartz et al., 2010). Sensitive periods during childhood and young adult development can explain the generational difference in acculturative processes, where younger Muslims are more susceptible to cultural adaptations than their older counterparts (Cheung et al., 2011). This generational divergence significantly impacts family dynamics and mental health. For example, older adults may prioritize cultural maintenance to ensure their children inherit their traditions.

In comparison, younger adults may lean toward integration or assimilation to pursue social and economic mobility. These contrasting goals can create familial conflicts and identity struggles, which often affect mental well-being. Although these differences can be more distinctively studied through first-generation versus second-generation immigrants, it is important to note that first-generation immigrants can include individuals who immigrated to North America as young children, paralleling some of the processes a second-generation Muslim immigrant born to recently immigrated parents may experience. Healthy development across generations requires supportive systems and open communication through shared language, enabling individuals from different generations to articulate their experiences and needs in shared cultural expressions (Schwartz et al., 2010).

The Multidimensional Model posits that biculturalism or ethnogenesis may reflect the most adaptive approach to acculturation and well-being (Schwartz et al., 2010). Biculturalism, where individuals integrate aspects of their heritage and the new culture, can promote better mental health outcomes. The authors describe that biculturalism can occur through two processes: integrating both cultures to create a new "blended" culture or integrating both cultures by embodying the two cultures distinctively. The "blended" process has been linked to enhanced self-confidence and reduced emotional strain (Chen et al., 2008). Biculturalism allows individuals to maintain a strong sense of identity and values from their original culture while adapting to and benefiting from the new culture. Over time, attitudes toward mental health may improve, with increased awareness and acceptance in both generations.

Acculturative Stress & Mental Health

Understanding acculturation is crucial, especially within the context of Muslim migration to America, as it significantly impacts health behaviors and outcomes for first and second-generation immigrants. Acculturation refers to the process of cultural change and psychological adaptation that occurs when individuals from one culture come into continuous contact with another (Schwartz et al., 2010). This process can lead to acculturative stress, which encompasses the psychological and social challenges of adapting to a new cultural environment.

For Muslim immigrants, acculturative stress may arise from experiencing discrimination, cultural and religious conflicts, and the pressures of balancing native values with the norms of American society (Zia & Mackenzie, 2024). First-generation immigrants often face challenges adapting to the new environment, while second-generation individuals might experience stress from navigating dual cultural identities. This stress can manifest in various ways, impacting mental health, such as increased anxiety, depression, and identity confusion, as well as physical health through psychosomatic symptoms (Schwartz et al., 2010).

Intergenerational Stressors

Cultural gaps between generations can further complicate these dynamics. First-generation immigrants who immigrated at a later time in their lifespan may have different attitudes toward mental health, often viewing it through the lens of the cultural background in which they were raised, which might stigmatize mental health issues or prioritize different coping mechanisms (Schwartz et al., 2010). In contrast, first and second-generation immigrants who grow up exposed to American cultural norms may have a more open attitude toward mental health and a greater willingness to seek professional help. This disparity can lead to family misunderstandings and conflicts, affecting family cohesion and support structures.

Migration Stressors

The immigration process itself may cause additional stressors, such as any pre-migration stressors that can include forced displacement, loss of community and livelihood, or exposure to trauma; stressors during migration, such as separation from family members, encountering detention or border control issues, or dangerous travel conditions; or post-migration stressors, such as language, culture, legal, economic, and social adjustments. Muslims migrating to North America may be directly negatively impacted by these stressors, resulting in mental health issues that are further complicated by cultural barriers to seeking help. For example, children of parents who struggle with mental health issues due to these acculturative stressors often face additional challenges, as evident by the impact of adverse childhood experiences. They may take on caregiving roles prematurely or feel pressured to succeed academically and socially to compensate for their parents' struggles, potentially leading to burnout and their own mental health issues (Schwartz et al., 2010). However, these children can also develop resilience and adaptive skills from navigating complex cultural landscapes, often sharing these adaptive strategies with their peers and the generations younger than them experiencing similar struggles.

Stigma and Barriers to Care

Understanding acculturation is crucial in the context of mental health, especially for groups like Western Muslims facing internalized stigma regarding psychological help (Zia & Mackenzie, 2024). Acculturation involves navigating between the stigma and cultural attitudes towards mental health that exist in both heritage and host cultures, impacting help-seeking behaviors and other health outcomes. Culturally sensitive approaches in mental health care services and systems can tackle this unaddressed stressor. A nuanced cultural understanding can help create targeted interventions that consider cultural and religious contexts, thereby improving the willingness and comfort of individuals to seek help. The study on internalized stigma among Western Muslims underscores this by illustrating how cultural and religious factors, alongside stigma, can influence mental health help-seeking behaviors.

The Multidimensional Model of Acculturation for Muslim Immigrants in North America

To evaluate the mental health of first—and second-generation Muslim immigrants in North America more closely, we describe the nuances of Muslim immigrants' receiving and heritage cultures, highlight the negotiation of practices, values, and identity between cultures, and frame the acculturation experience through the "context of reception."

Heritage Culture, Receiving Culture, and Being Muslim

The heritage culture that Muslim immigrants embody from their native countries, the receiving culture of the community that Muslims migrate into, and the similarity/dissimilarity between the receiving and heritage cultures, can provide context to the lived experiences of first and second-generation Muslim immigrants in North America. Each of these components can heavily impact the relationship an individual, family system, or cultural community has on the expression of distress, the conceptualization of distress, attitudes towards formal and informal support, adherence to a treatment plan, and motivation towards healing. A clinician looking to understand the impact of culture can take time in the intake session with their clients to speak about the client's connection to their family's heritage culture and the culture in which they currently reside.

While the focus on the ethnic culture of the native country and the dominant culture of the receiving culture is critical, an analysis of the acculturative experience of first and second-generation Muslims must also highlight the *religious-cultural acculturation* that is inextricable from *ethnic-cultural acculturation*. Namely, some Muslims may have heritage cultures with overlapping religious and ethnic cultures and traditions. The interaction between religious and ethnic cultures in an individual's heritage country can vary greatly, influencing how immigrants embody and understand their Muslim identity. For example, consider Muslims who settle in North America may come from Muslim-majority countries or communities (e.g., Bosnia, Senegal, or Pakistan) compared to the experiences of Muslims who immigrate from non-Muslim majority countries or communities (e.g., India, Uganda, or France). Individuals and families who want to maintain their Muslim traditional and spiritual practices must undergo an additional process of reconciling and teasing apart religious and spiritual culture and traditions (e.g., praying the daily *salah* or attending the Friday sermon at the mosque) from ethnic culture and tradition (e.g., food or clothing), mainly if their experience in a Muslim-majority country may not have prompted this interrogation. On the other hand, some Muslims migrate from countries where they lived as a religious minority (e.g., India, Uganda, South Africa) before resettling. Their experience as a religious minority in their ancestral country can result in culturally embedded strategies of coping as a religious minority.

Due to Western European colonization, North American countries and territories are primarily Christian nations, which has particular implications for Muslim immigrants. More specifically, the receiving culture of Muslim immigrants in North America is shaped by Christian traditions and customs, such as the celebration of Christian holidays and the influence of Christian values in political and social life. Muslims in Christian countries must often advocate for practicing and expressing their religious culture and tradition, such as prayer spaces or time off from school and/or work for Friday sermons and Eid celebrations. As receiving cultures, the United States and Canada are heavily influenced by White Anglo-Saxon Protestant, or WASP, culture (Kaufmann, 2004). These contexts are shaped by White supremacist strategies of racial and economic stratification that affect Muslim immigrant acculturation experiences, as well as their experiences of Islamophobia. Later in this chapter, the "Context of Reception" section further expands on how this context impacts Muslim mental health processes and outcomes. Alternatively, as receiving cultures, Central American, Caribbean, and Bahama countries and territories may have more overlapping ethnic cultural values with the heritage culture of Muslim immigrants who come from more collectivistic societies and traditions due to the integration of Indigenous and Black cultures in the dominant culture. This cultural similarity may heavily impact the acculturation process for Muslim immigrants.

Ethnic enclaves

While no country in North America is Muslim majority, many Muslim majority communities have maintained their ethnic expression of culture and faith, often termed *ethnic enclaves* within these countries and territories (Qadeer et al., 2010). Many Muslims settle in ethnic enclaves, which can make the acculturative process different from a Muslim family who settles in a neighborhood with a dominant culture that is dissimilar to their heritage culture. To be more specific, a Muslim family settling in the rural Midwest may interact with a dominant monoculture with established norms and distinct assimilation pressures than a Muslim family settling in New York City, which hosts dozens of ethnic enclaves.

Converts

Islam is the second-largest religion in the world, attracting converts from all backgrounds. Thus, individuals from various cultural backgrounds and recent immigrants may choose to convert and face dual challenges and opportunities of acculturation and faith development within a new religion and community. The cultural expression of being Muslim may shift across individuals and generations within a family or community system, resulting in opportunities and tensions between systems. A more detailed discussion of these interactions can be found later in this chapter.

Cultural Reconciliation of Practices, Values, and Identity

Muslim immigrants in North America experience acculturation in distinct ways, exhibiting different approaches to managing cultural adaptation. Understanding the multidimensionality of acculturation—specifically behavioral, value, and identity-based acculturation—helps illuminate how both first- and second-generation Muslim immigrants navigate their cultural and religious lives within the context of North American society.

Behavioral Acculturation

Behavioral acculturation refers to how immigrants adjust their daily behaviors and practices in response to the host society's norms and expectations (Berry, 2005). Some Muslim immigrants may strongly emphasize maintaining traditional religious practices, such as observing Islamic dress codes, dietary laws (halal), and religious obligations like prayer and fasting. They may engage in these practices within private spaces or among their Muslim communities while adopting Western behaviors in public spaces to ease their integration into North American society. Other

Muslim immigrants may have more fluid and hybrid behavioral acculturation patterns across various settings. They may more easily blend the cultural norms of their ancestral homeland with those of host society. For instance, while they might continue to observe their ethnic culture's expression of Islamic dress codes and dietary practices (i.e., hijab, beards, avoiding pork consumption), they may adopt Western communication styles, entertainment, and social interactions. Muslims raised in North America may be generally more proficient in the local language and embrace Western values of individualism and independence more readily than their parents. Muslims raised in their native culture may feel motivated to preserve their cultural and religious practices. At the same time, the second generation may experience a sense of "cultural tug-of-war," trying to maintain a connection to their Muslim heritage while integrating more seamlessly into the host society (Berry, 2005). Both groups may experience tension in balancing cultural expectations.

Value Acculturation

Value acculturation involves internalizing and negotiating societal norms and values from the immigrant's culture of origin and the host society (Schwartz et al., 2010). Some Muslim immigrants often adhere to the traditional values of their countries of origin, including collectivism, family cohesion, respect for elders, and a strong emphasis on religious values. These values often conflict with more individualistic values prevalent in North America, such as personal autonomy, freedom of choice, and culturally bound gender equality. Muslims raised in North America may experience a shift in values due to their exposure to Western education, media, and social norms. They may be more likely to adopt liberal attitudes on topics such as gender roles, marriage, and civic participation by reinterpreting Islamic principles in ways that align with North American values, such as promoting gender equity, diversity, and social justice within the framework of their faith. For instance, Muslim women may advocate for wearing the hijab as a personal choice and seek professional success in public spheres. This negotiation of values can sometimes create generational tensions. First-generation parents may worry that their children are losing touch with core Islamic or cultural values. At the same time, second-generation Muslims may feel a need to balance the expectations of their parents with the societal norms of the receiving culture.

Identity-Based Acculturation

According to Schwartz et al. (2010), acculturation also encompasses identity-based dynamics. First-generation Muslim immigrants can sometimes maintain a strong identification with their homeland and may even define themselves primarily in terms of their national, ethnic, or religious identity. They may experience challenges in reconciling this with the need to adapt to North American cultural norms. This tension can lead to identity bifurcation, where individuals oscillate between their heritage identity and the pressures to conform to the host culture, potentially resulting in a fragmented or dual identity. Muslims raised in North America face a different set of identity challenges. Having been raised in two cultures, they are more likely to experience a bicultural identity, identifying as both Muslim and their host identity. This hybrid identity can be empowering, providing a sense of belonging to the Muslim ummah and the broader North American society. However, they may also face challenges such as Islamophobia, discrimination, or feeling "othered" due to their visible markers of Muslim identity, such as the hijab. These external pressures can shape their self-perception and lead to identity-based conflicts, where they feel they have to choose between their Muslim identity and being fully accepted by the wider society. While many Muslims work to reconcile their bicultural identities, others may struggle with a sense of belonging, feeling caught between the expectations of the Muslim community and the broader Western society.

Digital Platforms and Biculturalism

As an example, Muslim immigrants in Mexico face their unique challenges as they navigate cultural and religious identity in a predominantly Catholic society. According to Hasif (2023), Muslim immigrants in Mexico often turn to digital platforms like YouTube to express and negotiate their identities, just like their North American counterparts, who blend Islamic traditions with local societal norms. This digital space serves as a site of identity negotiation, where immigrants can address the marginalization, they experience as religious minorities in a predominantly Catholic society. Muslim immigrants in Mexico engage in a form of biculturalism through social media, blending their Islamic identity with local cultural norms. These digital narratives help foster a sense of belonging and community, even as immigrants navigate their marginalization and acculturation in physical and virtual spaces. In this way, platforms like YouTube provide an outlet for both preserving Islamic identity and adapting to new societal contexts, reflecting the broader themes of acculturation found among Muslim immigrants worldwide.

Navigating Hyphenated Identities

The multidimensionality of acculturation highlights the complexity of the immigrant experience for Muslims in North America. For some Muslims, embracing a "hyphenated identity" (e.g., Muslim-American or Somali-Canadian) becomes a source of pride. They work to create a space where they can be both authentically Muslim and fully integrated members of

North American society. Others may struggle with a sense of belonging, feeling that they are neither fully accepted in the Muslim community nor in the broader Western context.

"Context of Reception"

One of the strengths of the Multidimensional Model lies in its dynamism and sensitivity to context. Acculturation patterns occur based on the sociopolitical environment and its influence across life stages. The rise of bigotry and xenophobia against Muslims—prevalent before 9/11 but dramatically escalating afterward—has significantly shaped the acculturation strategies of Muslim Americans (Williams, 2016). While attitudes toward Muslims are complex, with factors such as political affiliation and personal relationships sometimes mitigating the impact of bigotry, widespread suspicion and hostility remain pervasive (Helbling & Traunmüller, 2018). Geopolitical events, including the rise of the Islamic State of Iraq and Syria (ISIS) and Israel's ongoing oppression of Palestinians, have further fueled discrimination and xenophobia against Muslim Americans, as well as those who are racially coded as Muslim (Kumar, 2021). This underscores the critical importance of context in shaping how individuals navigate their acculturation strategies.

Generational Differences

Young children growing up in this environment may be driven toward assimilation as a defense against intense peer bullying and prejudice from school staff. To minimize differences and avoid stigma, children and teens may abandon their primary culture and religion, viewing them as burdens. Alternatively, many feel marginalized—unable to fully identify with the older generation's culture while also facing rejection and bigotry from the majority culture (Juang & Syed, 2019; Rivas-Drake et al., 2014). This sense of exclusion can lead to pervasive emptiness, leaving individuals struggling to form a healthy identity. In their search for belonging, some may turn into unhealthy peer groups (e.g., gangs), engage in hedonistic behaviors as a coping mechanism, or withdraw from society altogether (Bogaerts et al., 2021). This alienation can manifest as *double consciousness*, where individuals feel divided between different parts of themselves, unable to integrate these elements into a cohesive identity (Walsh & Ferazzoli, 2023).

For older adults, prejudice and xenophobia have a different impact. While they may have a stronger sense of identity to help cope with bigotry, their concerns often focus on cultural preservation, which can lead to authoritarian parenting styles that alienate younger generations (Yaman et al., 2010). They may also adopt a separation strategy, isolating themselves from the dominant culture, thereby creating further disconnection with the younger generation. As a result, bigotry and discrimination tend to polarize generational acculturation strategies, exacerbating conflicts between generations.

It is important to recognize that this model is not deterministic. As a heterogeneous group, Muslim immigrants possess many strengths and resources that enable them to choose healthier acculturation strategies throughout their lifespan. Resistance, advocacy, and activism against societal bigotry and xenophobia can paradoxically foster a sense of belonging (Haim-Litevsky et al., 2023). When individuals fight to reform society, even as recent arrivals, they inevitably develop a psychological connection to that society, as they have a vested interest in its future. Activism and solidarity against prejudice, therefore, improve one's sense of identity but also help foster integration across the lifespan by creating a psychological stake in society (Haim-Litevsky et al., 2023).

Regional Context

Regional differences also significantly shape the context of acculturation. Different areas within a nation vary in history, demographics, and ethnic diversity, leading to diverse acculturation experiences. For example, in the United States, the majority of Muslim immigrants are concentrated in large metropolitan areas such as Detroit, New York City, Washington D.C., Chicago, and Houston. These larger communities offer greater opportunities for building social capital, engaging with varied acculturation models, and connecting with peers at similar developmental stages. In contrast, many rural or suburban regions of the U.S. have few Muslims and limited ethnic or religious diversity, which can impact acculturation patterns. Understanding the local context is thus essential for grasping the range of acculturation strategies available to Muslim immigrants.

Narrative as Case Studies

The following sections provide our narratives as authors to elucidate the applicability of the Multidimensional Mode of Acculturation to first and second-generation Muslims in North America. Below, we describe our relationship with our heritage and receiving culture, the acculturation patterns we witnessed in our family and communities, and specific areas of our respective professional fields. These narratives also serve to describe our positionality as authors of this chapter. As authors, we collectively engage in research, teaching, clinical, and community work efforts to strengthen Muslim individuals, families, and communities shaped by the factors within our acculturation experiences. While we share our stories of being raised and currently living within the context of the United States, we also share how our stories are embedded in our professional actions to improve the mental health outcomes of first and second-generation Muslim immigrants.

Somer

The Multidimensional Model of Acculturation resonates deeply with my experience as a Yemeni-American, as it captures how individuals engage with their heritage and host cultures. Navigating these cultural intersections often feels like a constant balancing act, where one is expected to choose one identity over the other. As an Arab American Muslim woman, I constantly moved between two cultural worlds—Arab and American. Yet, this doesn't even touch on the additional intersections of my identity that were sometimes overlooked, such as being Muslim or a woman.

Growing up in the United States, my parents—who immigrated at very young ages (12 and 2)—struggled with adapting and shaping my worldview. My family strived for the "All-American Dream," doing things that many immigrant families were not. English was the dominant language in our home, and our meals often consisted of French fries, pizza, and burgers. It was only when extended family visited that Yemeni culture became more present, which often confused me and my siblings. Though proud of his roots, my father criticized aspects of Yemeni culture, while my mother, seemingly more assimilated, would make remarks that hinted at her deep connection to our heritage. This delicate dance of adaptation and cultural maintenance was a constant feature of my upbringing, highlighting how families navigate acculturation along multiple dimensions.

Despite these efforts, I struggled to find my place. Having never been to Yemen and speaking English at home, I was labeled "too American" or "whitewashed" in Arab spaces, while in Western settings, I was seen as "Muslim," "Arab," or "other." Even at my Islamic school, I was questioned about my heritage, which only reinforced the feeling of not fully belonging to either culture. This tension added to the complexity of my identity, leading to acculturative stress in multiple environments. My classmates' judgment of my Arabic skills or my lack of connection to Yemen became sources of exclusion and anxiety, further complicating my sense of belonging.

When I entered college, professors commended my English proficiency, subtly reinforcing that I did not quite fit into American culture. This interplay between biculturalism and bicultural stress became a recurring theme in my life. I often felt that I was not "American enough" for my peers nor "Arab enough" for the Arab community. This dissonance left me in constant negotiation between the two worlds, never fully anchored in either. The Multidimensional Model of Acculturation allows me to understand this process as more than just fitting into one culture or the other. It reflects an ongoing negotiation—between adapting to American life, maintaining elements of Yemeni heritage, and navigating the cultural divides within my community. This model offers a more nuanced understanding of acculturation, framing it not as a binary choice but a continuous balancing act between multiple cultural forces.

These formative experiences navigating between cultures have deeply informed me of my professional work today. As a therapist, professor, and community leader, I am deeply aware of the intersectional gaps between mental health and the Muslim community. The cultural tensions I experienced growing up fuel my passion for advocating for culturally sensitive mental health care. Whether I am creating programs on mental wellness, facilitating workshops, or providing therapy, the lens through which I operate will always be informed by the need to honor the cultural and mental health needs of Muslim individuals, ensuring that care is empathetic and contextually grounded.

Waleed

Navigating the gauntlet of acculturation experiences and challenges between generations is daunting for anyone and their family system. I grew up as a first-generation Pakistani-American with parents who had recently immigrated from Pakistan. Our family experienced a lot of stress and precarity. Growing up in a working-class family, the additional acculturation challenges, along with the context of where I grew up (a deeply conservative part of the country that had few, if any, Muslims present) during 9/11, challenged our resources and shaped my early development stage.

Our area had only a few Muslims, needing us to gather from all corners of the region just to find peers, with one or two mosques supporting the nascent community. After 9/11, the backlash against Muslims was immense, with the school system and our local political leaders galvanizing revenge against Muslims. When not openly bigoted, many in the local community had very little knowledge or interest in Islam and Muslims, outside of a few exceptions. With so few Muslim peers and increasingly hemmed in by bigotry and economic stress, I found myself isolated from my identity and grappling with feelings of marginalization, a potential acculturative dimension. The political context and the regional dynamics, made the context of my reception ambivalent, and thus, the choices for acculturation felt like complete assimilation or marginalization. A few of my peers who came from middle-class and intact families (our family had divorced, and life had become even more precarious) found ways to focus on academics as a path to social mobility, supported by a family system that kept them somewhat buffered against the stressors in our environment. My path was more circuitous, I worked minimum wage jobs, focused on athletics (as I felt more equal to my non-Muslim peers there), and did poorly at my local state college. Generationally, there were immense challenges within my immediate family, as class and gender-based stressors collided in an environment that held folks with our identity with ambivalence or hostility. Thus, my story encapsulates the crucial nature of context and systemic stressors as profoundly influencing acculturation dynamics. It is easy to see how, through the vehicle of fate and random luck, my experiences may have been different if I had grown up in a more diverse area with more Muslim peers, or if I had grown up in a time when the politicization of Muslims was not so salient in the culture. Lastly, economic and social class stressors profoundly influence acculturation options (Wilczewska, 2023), making inequality and stratification an important unit of analysis as well.

Hanan

I often reflect on my parents' acculturation experience living in Saudi Arabia with Yemeni parents. All of my grandparents were born and raised in Yemen. At 11, my mother's nuclear family moved to Saudi Arabia. My father was born and raised in Yemen until moving to Saudi Arabia for medical school. I wonder how both of their acculturation experiences in Saudi Arabia may have prepared our family unit to navigate cultural differences in the United States while maintaining a cultural connection to our Arab culture. My acculturation process continues to unfold as contemporary global wars and conflict have made even more evident the United States' imperialist relationship with the Middle East, profoundly shaping my lived experiences of physical and psychological safety. Imperialism requires a foreign threat, and to be attributed as a threat in the country I call home has brought lifelong existential reflections of identity, belonging, and liberation.

My parents migrated from Saudi Arabia to a Yemeni ethnic enclave in Detroit, Michigan, in 1994. I was exclusively surrounded by a community that was mostly Yemeni and completely Muslim - at least, that is how I remember it. For all of my childhood, I was immersed in Arab and Muslim cultures in several different communities across the metropolitan Detroit area. My experiences within diverse racial and ethnic Muslim communities in the United States were formative in shaping my identity as a pan-Arab Muslim woman. My move to Texas for my doctoral study in my early twenties was my first experience living in a community where I was one of the only Muslim or Middle Eastern persons around. I continue to uncover the impact of my family's arrival in a Yemeni enclave in the U.S. This space provided a cushion for my development against the acculturative stress I inevitably faced as an adult in Texas, navigating the full force of the marginalized experiences of being Arab and Muslim in the United States.

My family's immigration story has allowed me to have a home on multiple lands. Our yearly summer trips to Yemen and Saudi Arabia, and oft international trips across the globe, have made me aware of my privileges as a citizen of the United States, which has allowed me opportunities for freedom of movement across the globe, as well as an understanding of the power of the Global North. Throughout most of my life, I was acutely aware of the systemic injustices that prioritized particular groups of people at the expense of others. All I had to do was look around. I continue to witness it within the Muslim and Arab communities in which I am embedded, in particular with the ways Anti-Blackness is expressed, gender-based violence is normalized, and White supremacy standards are idealized. I also witness it within the broader United States' political and economic systems, where Indigenous, Black, Muslim, and other minority communities bear the weight of disparities and oppression. My vocational path served as an opportunity to tackle the different forms of systemic oppression my community and I were battling against through education, clinical work, and community consultancy. Although I am early in my professional career, through years of community service work, I have learned that building sustainable spaces, programs, and systems that meet the needs of the people while centering their voices and strengths can heavily promote wellness.

Recommendations

Academia and Research

The next generation of social scientists may obtain much value from interacting with Muslim acculturation dynamics in North America. As noted above, Muslims in North America are incredibly heterogeneous across race/ethnic origin, linguistic background, generational challenges, and social class. Thus, Muslims in North America provide unique insights into rapidly diversifying nations. Researchers can test validity, and replication claims across various models and survey instruments to see if the population changes or nuances results. Specifically related to acculturation, researchers may be interested in seeing how religious identity and meaning-making play another role in shaping acculturation challenges or opportunities. For instance, do strong Islamic identities determine an acculturation outcome? Secondly, researchers should examine how different stratifications (i.e., race and social class) influence acculturation dynamics within the Muslim communities in North America, further extending the literature on the multidimensional model. Researchers may also focus on specific histories of various Muslim immigrant groups through the lens of history and anthropology to explore how the context of reception shaped and influenced acculturation challenges and opportunities.

Practice and Interventions

Embedded within acculturative stressors for Muslim immigrants to North America are intergenerational cultural conflicts, often serving as a significant and common challenge in immigrant family systems. Families are adaptive systems that can foster resiliency across the lifespan; clinicians are responsible for providing culturally attuned care to support and address different parts of the family system. Practitioners can explore and be mindful of the acculturative stressors that impact family systems, given their clients' specific intersectional cultural experiences. In addition to cultural background, factors ranging from broader socio-political climate to regional and local contexts shape the acculturation strategies available to Muslims (Schwartz et al., 2010). Generational conflicts over acculturation are likely influenced by the unique circumstances each experience within these contexts. Practitioners can work to provide a shared language to articulate these universally experienced challenges as a step toward fostering productive dialogue between generations (Ward & Geeraert, 2015).

Policy and Community Systems

One way effective policy and community systems can address the structural challenges that first and second-generation Muslim immigrants face in navigating their dual identities is by emphasizing culturally responsive support services, such as accessible mental health resources tailored to the unique needs of this population (Berry, 2005). Schools, workplaces, and community organizations should adopt frameworks that promote inclusivity, enabling immigrants to preserve their cultural practices while actively participating in broader societal structures. At a systemic level, funding should prioritize initiatives that foster community building, including cultural exchange programs and mentorship opportunities for youth (Schwartz et al., 2010). Additionally, local and federal policies must tackle structural barriers like discrimination and xenophobia by implementing anti-bias training and establishing pathways for reporting and addressing systemic inequities. Building strong partnerships between Muslim-led organizations and public institutions can further enhance trust and ensure that policies are informed by lived experiences, ultimately creating a supportive environment for successful acculturation.

Conclusion

In this chapter, we used the Multidimensional Model of Acculturation (Schwartz et al., 2010) to illustrate the unique and dynamic characteristics of cultural reconciliation that affect the mental health of first and second-generation Muslims in North America. We examined how Muslim immigrants navigate the complexities of integrating heritage and receiving cultures, focusing on the distinct and overlapping interplay of practices, values, and identity. We explored how acculturation impacts mental health, discussing processes, behaviors, and outcomes shaped by the "context of reception" within their environments. The chapter included a personal narrative from the authors, reflecting on our acculturation journeys and offering insight into the lived realities of reconciling identities over time. Finally, we concluded with actionable recommendations for research, clinical practice, and policy aimed at better supporting the mental health and well-being of Muslim immigrants.

References

Berry, J. W. (2005). Acculturation: Living successfully in two cultures. *International Journal of Intercultural Relations, 29*(6), 697–712. https://doi.org/10.1016/j.ijintrel.2005.07.013

Bogaerts, A., Claes, L., Buelens, T., Verschueren, M., Palmeroni, N., Bastiaens, T., & Luyckx, K. (2021). Identity synthesis and confusion in early to late adolescents: Age trends, gender differences, and associations with depressive symptoms. *Journal of Adolescence, 87*(1), 106–116. https://doi.org/10.1016/j.adolescence.2021.01.006

Chen, S. X., Benet-Martínez, V., & Harris Bond, M. (2008). Bicultural Identity, bilingualism, and psychological adjustment in multicultural societies: immigration-based and globalization-based acculturation. *Journal of Personality, 76*(4), 803-838.

Cheung, B. Y., Chudek, M., & Heine, S. J. (2011). Evidence for a sensitive period for acculturation: Younger immigrants report acculturating at a faster rate. *Psychological Science, 22*(2), 147-152.

Chitwood, K. (2017). The study of Islam and Muslim communities in Latin America, the Caribbean, and the Americas: The state of the field. *International Journal of Latin American Religions, 1*(1), 57–76.

Gordon, M. M. (1964). Assimilation in American Life: The Role of Race, Religion, and National Origins. Oxford: Oxford University Press on Demand.

Haddad, Y. Y. (2011). *Becoming American? The forging of Arab and Muslim identity in pluralist America.* Baylor University Press.

Haim-Litevsky, D., Komemi, R., & Lipskaya-Velikovsky, L. (2023). Sense of Belonging, Meaningful Daily Life Participation, and Well-Being: Integrated Investigation. *International Journal of Environmental Research and Public Health, 20*(5), 4121. https://doi.org/10.3390/ijerph20054121

Helbling, M., & Traunmüller, R. (2018). What is Islamophobia? Disentangling Citizens' Feelings Toward Ethnicity, Religion and Religiosity Using a Survey Experiment. *British Journal of Political Science, 50*(3), 811–828. https://doi.org/10.1017/s0007123418000054

Hasif, N. (2023). Muslim Immigrant Identifications in Mexico's YouTube Sphere. *International Journal of Latin American Religions, 7*(2), 482–520.

Juang, L. P., & Syed, M. (2019). The evolution of acculturation and development Models for understanding immigrant children and Youth adjustment. *Child Development Perspectives, 13*(4), 241–246. https://doi.org/10.1111/cdep.12346

Kaufmann, E. P. (2004). The decline of the 'WASP' in Canada and the United States. In: Kaufmann, Eric P. (ed.) *Rethinking Ethnicity: Majority Groups and Dominant Minorities.* Abingdon, UK: Routledge, pp. 61–83.

Kazemipur, A. (2014). *The Muslim question in Canada: A story of segmented integration.* UBC Press.

Kumar, D. (2021, September 22). *Anti-Muslim racism began centuries before 9/11, according to newly revised book.* School of Communication and Information | Rutgers

University. https://comminfo.rutgers.edu/news/anti-muslim-racism-began-centuries-911-according-newly-revised-book

Mustapha, N. (2012). Muslims in the Caribbean. In R. L. Hangloo (Ed.), *Indian diaspora in the Caribbean: History, culture and identity* (pp. 43–54). Primus Books.

Qadeer, M., Agrawal, S. K., & Lovell, A. (2010). Evolution of ethnic enclaves in the Toronto Metropolitan Area, 2001–2006. *Journal of International Migration and Integration/Revue de l'integration et de la migration internationale, 11*, 315-339.

Rivas-Drake, D., Seaton, E. K., Markstrom, C., Quintana, S., Syed, M., Lee, R. M., Schwartz, S. J., Umaña-Taylor, A. J., French, S., & Yip, T. (2014). Ethnic and Racial Identity in Adolescence: Implications for psychosocial, academic, and health outcomes. *Child Development, 85*(1), 40–57. https://doi.org/10.1111/cdev.12200

Safdar, S., Ray-Yol, E., Reif, J. A., & Berger, R. (2021). Multidimensional Individual Difference Acculturation (MIDA) model: Syrian refugees' adaptation into Germany. *International Journal of Intercultural Relations, 85*, 156–169. https://doi.org/10.1016/j.ijintrel.2021.09.012

Schwartz, S. J., Unger, J. B., Zamboanga, B. L., & Szapocznik, J. (2010). Rethinking the concept of acculturation: Implications for theory and research. *American Psychologist, 65*(4), 237–251. https://doi.org/10.1037/a0019330

Tummala-Narra, P. (2014). Cultural identity in the context of trauma and immigration from a psychoanalytic perspective. *Psychoanalytic Psychology, 31*(3), 396.

Walsh, J., & Ferazzoli, M. T. (2023). The Colonised self: the politics of UK asylum practices, and the embodiment of colonial power in lived experience. *Social Sciences, 12*(7), 382. https://doi.org/10.3390/socsci12070382

Ward, C., & Geeraert, N. (2015). Advancing acculturation theory and research: the acculturation process in its ecological context. *Current Opinion in Psychology, 8*, 98–104. https://doi.org/10.1016/j.copsyc.2015.09.021

Wilczewska, I. T. (2023). Examining the relationship between acculturation and socioeconomic status and their role in the first-generation Polish immigrants' well-being. *Journal of International Migration and Integration / Revue De L Integration Et De La Migration Internationale, 24*(3), 1337–1355. https://doi.org/10.1007/s12134-023-01006-y

Williams, J (2016). *Donald Trump's speech scared me as an American Muslim. It should scare you, too.* Donald Trump's speech scared me as an American Muslim. It should scare you, too. | Vox

Yaman, A., Mesman, J., Van IJzendoorn, M. H., Bakermans-Kranenburg, M. J., & Linting, M. (2010). Parenting in an Individualistic Culture with a Collectivistic Cultural Background: The Case of Turkish Immigrant Families with Toddlers in the Netherlands. *Journal of Child and Family Studies, 19*(5), 617–628. https://doi.org/10.1007/s10826-009-9346-y

Zia, B., & Mackenzie, C. S. (2024). Internalized stigma negatively affects attitudes and intentions to seek psychological help among Western Muslims:

Testing a moderated serial mediation model. *Stigma and Health, 9*(1), 71–80. https://doi.org/10.1037/sah0000314

CHAPTER SIXTEEN

ISLAMOPHOBIA & MENTAL HEALTH IN NORTH AMERICA

Rania Awaad, Kubra Tor-Cabuk, Maram Saada

This chapter discusses the historical underpinnings of Islamophobia as well as the psychological costs. The socio-political impact of Islamophobia cannot be overstated, as it has impacted all spheres of life, from schools to workplaces and even policy. However, more pertinently, it has devastating mental health costs as well. Its pervasive impact on Muslim communities has impeded the community's psychological development as they face challenges to their identities. The intersectionality of the North American Muslim population places them at a higher risk of experiencing psychological harm, underscoring the importance of identifying risk and protective factors within the community to foster resilience. Implications for theory and practice are also discussed to highlight the importance of work needed to support the Muslim community's psychological health.

Introduction

There is a growing number of Muslims living in North America, including native-born, immigrants, and converts. There are about 3.45 million Muslims in the US alone, and the community is expected to exceed 2% of the US population by 2050 (Pew Research Center, 2018); however, the exact number is unknown due to the exclusion of religious affiliation in US census data. Islam was Canada's second most commonly reported religion in 2021, with the Muslim population increasing from 2% in 2001 to 4.9% in 2021 (Statistics Canada, 2022). Despite the increasing Muslim presence, there is a noticeable gap in health-related research addressing this population (Samari et al., 2018). A critical issue faced by Muslims is the widespread discrimination they encounter (Husain & Howard, 2017). Muslim Americans report higher rates of religious discrimination than any other religious group in the country (Ikramullah, 2024). Anti-Muslim hate incidents have increased by 56% compared to the previous year (Council on American-Islamic Relations [CAIR], 2024), underscoring the need for further exploration of this topic. Although the number of reported hate crimes provides some insight into the issue, it only scratches the surface of the broader discrimination-based challenges faced by Muslims in North America. These numbers should also be read with caution, as Muslim Americans underreport these incidents because of desensitization and feeling that nothing can be done (Matias & Newlove, 2017).

With the increasing number of hate incidents and the need for research in the field of mental health, this chapter aims to present how Islamophobia manifests itself in varied settings among diverse communities of Muslims living in North America and, more importantly, how it affects their mental health. We also aim to delineate the risk and protective factors associated with Islamophobia, outline ways researchers can help combat Islamophobia, and how clinicians can help patients who struggle with its effects.

Definition and History of Islamophobia

Islamophobia and Anti-Muslim racism

The term "Islamophobia," introduced by Said (1978), describes the discriminatory attitudes and practices directed toward the Muslim population. In his usage, the term reflects how Western societies have historically constructed a fearful image of Muslims, often conflating them with the "Arab Other" (Said, 1978). Oxford Dictionary (2006) describes it as a 'dislike of or prejudice against Islam or Muslims, especially as a political force.' The term has been used interchangeably with anti-Muslim bigotry and anti-Muslim prejudice in research, with its limitation to address hostility towards Muslims by only implying fear.

Anti-Muslim racism is another term used in research and is defined as 'Racialized "othering" of people based on historical and ongoing social, political, and religious antipathy toward Islam. It is not limited to religious discrimination' (Ford & Sharif, 2020). This term highlights how the religious identities of Muslims have been racialized and how Muslims are intersectionally marginalized in Western populations. However, categorizing anti-Muslim prejudice and discrimination as a form of racism not only limits its usage in terms of excluding the unique role of religious identity but further perpetuates the idea of Muslims as a monolith, ignoring the differential experiences of Muslims in North America by race-ethnic background. In particular, this verbiage reduces the intersectional and compounded racial and religious discriminatory experiences of Black Muslims in North America to a singularity.

History of Islamophobia

Evidence of Islamophobia can be traced to medieval Europe, as anti-Muslim attitudes underpinned the Crusades and later the imperialist conquest of Africa and Asia. Support for the Crusades was garnered by portraying Muslims as the distinct enemy of Christians and the West (i.e., Europe). Pope Urban II heralded Muslims as "the enemies of the Lord" in his speech at the Council of Clermont (McNeal & Thatcher, 1908). This demonization of Muslims continued through the 1400s with the Christian Reconquista of Spain. The constant demographic changes brought by conflict led to the Spaniards wanting to encode qualities and customs that define their culture and heritage. One such rule was *Impreza de sangre*, or 'purity of blood,' a hierarchical system that classified individuals depending on genealogy and religious affiliation (Kaplan, 2012). During this time, racial and religious purity became a preoccupation, leading to widespread public suspicion of individuals not of pure Christian lineage. Those with "impure blood" were excluded from various organizations, and this statute hindered their advancement in society (Kaplan, 2012). The preoccupation with Muslims as culturally inferior continued throughout European colonialism.

The cultural superiority advanced by the West was a hallmark feature of European imperialism. European colonial power depicted Islam as uncivilized and in need of European intervention. Colonialism illuminated the racial attitudes of Europeans, who described Muslims as religious fanatics. Said (1978), in his seminal work *Orientalism,* writes that the historical construction of the 'Orient,' which encompassed Islamic traditions, was part of a broader agenda that justified Western superiority and colonial control. Orientalism, which was viewed as a scholarly curiosity toward Muslim-majority societies, was a form of imperialism as it positioned Islam as antithetical to modernity, thereby shaping Western society's views of Islam. This was seen in Winston Churchill's (1899) "The River War," in which he writes about Sudanese society during the British colonial campaign. He likens Islamic devotion to "hydrophobia in a dog" and describes Muslims as irrational and prone to having "fatalistic apathy." His description paints Islamic practices as resistant to development, necessitating Western society to civilize them. Justifications such as these helped perpetuate European imperialism and led to Muslims being portrayed as cultural outsiders and later as security threats.

Major global events have also affected the severity of Islamophobia in North America. The 2015 terrorist attacks in Paris paved the way for increased discrimination, where the French public vilified Muslims as terrorists (Samari et al., 2018). Muslims have been held accountable for the crimes of religious extremists, and people placed the responsibility for these crimes on those who identify themselves as Muslims- or even on those perceived as Muslim (e.g., Arab Americans; Alsaidi et al., 2021, and Sikh men; Ahluwalia & Pellettiere, 2010). Muslim Americans also stated that the 2017 Muslim Ban, in which former President Trump banned travel from seven Muslim-majority countries to the US, has made being Muslim in the US much harder than before and caused an increase in hate crimes against Muslims (Agrawal et al., 2019; Pew Research Center, 2017).

Recent events also affected the Muslim community and increased the mental toll of Islamophobia, including COVID-19 and the war in Palestine. COVID-19 has played a catalyst role in the increase of existing prejudices towards ethnic communities, especially Asian communities (Ho & Çabuk, 2023). Muslim healthcare workers were also subjected to instances of discrimination during COVID-19 (Awaad et al., 2022). Thirty percent of healthcare workers reported experiencing discrimination outside of their workplaces, and 19% reported experiencing it within the workplace. Studies have shown that the pandemic has not only intensified existing prejudices but has also led to increased mental health challenges for Muslim communities facing discrimination. The experiences of Muslim women, particularly those who wear hijabs, have demonstrated increased anxiety and fear due to rising anti-Muslim sentiments exacerbated by the pandemic (Saleh et al., 2023).

After the 2023 war began in Palestine, the severity of Islamophobia and incidents towards Muslims has escalated. Several harassment cases were reported, including receiving death threats, hijabs being torn off, and being spat at (CAIR, 2024). A stark reminder of Islamophobia's consequences was seen in the murder of six-year-old Palestinian-American Wadea Al-Fayoume in Illinois, where his landlord stabbed him twenty-six times because he was Muslim (Awaad, 2023b). Additionally, seven-year-old Yemeni-American Saida Mashra was playing in a park when a man assaulted her and sliced her neck in Detroit (Ortega, 2024). The primary escalation of these Islamophobic incidents is the Gaza War, as CAIR (2024) reported a 56% increase in reported complaints following the start of the war, with nearly half of the complaints occurring in the last three months of 2023. Although research has yet to show the deleterious effects of these actions, it is evident that they are affecting the young generations of Muslims (Awaad et al., 2023a). Along with these severe actions against the Muslim population, the helplessness and witnessing of a genocide taking place has left Muslim people feeling helpless and guilty. The reports emphasize the role of positive religious coping, including turning to Quranic verses and sayings of Prophet Muhammad, peace be upon him, seeking solace through prayer and worship, prioritizing self-care, and connecting with the Muslim community (Awaad et al., 2023a).

Manifestations of Islamophobia in Different Settings

In today's society, people's perceptions of Islam and Muslims are greatly influenced by the media, as it controls how non-majority populations are understood. The media have the power to characterize groups through the language they use . The increase in sensational news around acts of terror has only fueled this cycle. This dominance in media coverage was corroborated by a study by Kearns et al. (2019), which found that media coverage of attacks by Muslim perpetrators received 357% more coverage than other attacks. This aggressive coverage shows that the media highlights and labels certain acts of terror. Religious terrorism is not a response solely committed by Muslims, as there are examples, especially in recent years, of Christian religious terrorism. The perpetrators of the 2019 Christchurch mosque shooting in New Zealand and the Oslo and Utoya Attacks in Norway in 2011 both wrote manifestos that indicated their motives for the killing were based on the Bible (Coaston, 2019). However, even if their actions were religiously motivated, they are not labeled the moniker of a Christian terrorist but rather called right-wing extremists or "lone wolves" in the media (Tavkhelidze, 2021). The language surrounding Islam in the media has consistently associated Muslims with negative terms. Alzyoud (2022) examined *The New York Times* coverage of Islam and Muslims during six months in 2014 and found that most stories focused on topics related to terrorism and extremism. The newspaper failed to establish a difference between Islam and terrorist groups, further shaping the negative image of Islam for the public.

Islamophobia manifests itself in different settings in the form of prejudice, discrimination, hate crimes, and microaggressions. Schools are one place where discrimination occurs through bullying. Almost half of Muslim female students reported being bullied by another student due to their religious identity (CAIR, 2023). The rates are higher for students who wear hijab, with 64% reporting that they feel unsafe, unwelcome, or uncomfortable at school because of their religious identity (CAIR, 2023). Research also shows that seven out of nine interpersonal discrimination cases narrated by adolescents happened in school settings (Aroian, 2012). Discrimination in the workplace is also a common form of Islamophobia. Employment-related abuse is the third most common issue among Muslim Americans, including denial of work, lack of promotion, and harassment by the staff (Abdelhadi, 2017). Discrimination toward Muslims also appears in housing; Gaddis and Ghoshal (2015) revealed that women with Arab-origin names received 40% fewer replies than women with White names in their roommate-wanted advertisements. Discrimination is observed in medical settings, as Muslim women who wear hijabs report higher perceived discrimination compared to women who do not wear hijabs (Martin, 2015).

Islamophobia in Policy

Islamophobia has also been entrenched in American policies, with local and federal authorities promoting procedures aimed at discriminating against Muslims. In the aftermath of 9/11, many domestic policies were introduced that were aimed at surveilling Muslims and relied on discriminatory profiling practices. One such policy was the National Security Entry-Exit Registration System (NSEERS), introduced as a counter-terrorism policy. The policy required nonimmigrant and non-citizen males sixteen years or older to register with local immigration offices, which would include invasive interviews and fingerprinting (The NSEERS effect, 2012). Of the twenty-five countries listed as countries of interest, only one, North Korea, was not a Muslim-majority country (The NSEERS effect, 2012). The policy was ultimately unsuccessful as it did not result in a single terrorism-related conviction (The NSEERS effect, 2012). O'Connor and Jahan (2014) highlighted the mental health cost of these discriminatory policies, finding that American Muslims often experience heightened anxiety due to government surveillance. This study also found that American Muslims engaged in self-censorship, avoiding discussing contentious topics as they worry about the possibility of surveillance (O'Connor & Jahan, 2014). Thus, such policies' emotional and behavioral consequences can affect the community's mental health.

Islamophobia and Mental Health Outcomes

Identifying the impacts of Islamophobia on mental health is challenging due to the multifaceted nature of the discrimination faced by Muslims. To gain a comprehensive understanding, we will examine the effects of Islamophobia on mental health through the lenses of race and ethnicity, gender, age, immigration status, and socioeconomic background to emphasize the unique role of each of these identities on Muslim experiences. However, it is crucial to recognize that these identities often overlap, making the experience of Islamophobia more complex. The diversity within Muslim communities in North America requires a nuanced discussion that considers how these various identities interact with and are impacted by Islamophobia.

Race and Ethnicity

Muslims are America's most ethnically diverse religious community, with 28% Black, 23% Asian, 19% White, 14% Arab, and 8% Hispanic (Institute for Social Policy and Understanding [ISPU], 2017). Canadian Muslims are also a diverse community, with 30% from West Central Asian and Middle Eastern backgrounds, 18% African, 15% South Asian, and 13% East Indian (Shah, 2019a). Islamophobia presents an additional challenge for minority ethnic groups within the Muslim community in North America. For example, African American Muslims face a double burden of minority effect (Adam, 2019). Studies have shown that African/Black Americans experience higher levels of medical discrimination compared to their Arab American and South Asian American counterparts, highlighting the impact of multiple minority effects on the experiences of Muslims (Murrar et al., 2024).

Additionally, Black Muslims report anti-Black racism in non-Black immigrant Muslim religious communities (Ahmed & Abdallah, 2023) and a lack of belonging within non-Black Muslim spaces of worship (Elsayed et al., 2024). These findings further demonstrate that Black Muslims experience layers of discrimination, both within and outside the Muslim-American community. The adverse mental health effects of religious discrimination among African/Black American Muslims are demonstrated through limited research on these communities. One study found a significant association between discrimination and worsening symptoms of depression, anxiety, and post-traumatic stress among Somali immigrants (Lincoln et al., 2021). Nearly half (46%) of the participants in the study listed religion as a reason for discriminatory experiences, further highlighting the compounding impact of racism and Islamophobia on these communities.

The Arab American population, often considered an "invisible" public health population in the US (Alsaidi et al., 2021), reported increased rates of anxiety and depression following the events of 9/11 (Amer & Hovey, 2012). Research on Arab Americans indicates that Arab Muslims reported significantly more experiences of ethnic discrimination compared to their non-Muslim counterparts, with higher levels of discrimination being associated with greater psychological stress (Ikizler & Szymanski, 2018). Another study also highlights how Arab American women's well-being was impacted by the discrimination that they face from other Arab Americans based on colorism and socioeconomic status, with lighter skin and "Westernized" cultural norms being valued, which contributes to feelings of devaluation (Alsaidi et al., 2021).

South Asians make up a significant portion of the Muslim population in North America, and their experiences with Islamophobia and its impact on mental health also require focused attention. Among South Asians, experiences of discrimination were associated with higher depressive symptoms, anxiety, and anger (Nadimpalli et al., 2016). Other research also highlighted the lower mental health utilization rates of this population, although they experience several challenges to their mental health, including acculturative stress, intergenerational conflict, and discrimination (Ahmed & Islam, 2023). Research is needed to understand healthcare utilization and the specific relationship between Islamophobia and mental health among this population.

Gender

The term 'gendered Islamophobia' underlines the experiences of discrimination among Muslim women and how their experiences differ from those of Muslim men. This form of Islamophobia involves stereotypes that characterize Muslim women as oppressed or submissive, making them targets of both individual harassment and systemic discrimination (Zine, 2006). Muslim women are more likely to experience discrimination due to visible religious markers such as hijab and veil, and they are at higher risk of developing worse mental health outcomes (Ali et al., 2022). However, it is also important to note that although being visibly Muslim was associated with higher rates of discrimination, it also moderated women's well-being and was associated with positive psychological outcomes when coupled with behavioral aspects of Muslim identity like engaging in Islamic practices (Jasperse et al., 2012).

Research also shows that the association between discrimination and psychological distress was stronger for Arab American men (Assari & Lankarani, 2017). The authors attributed their findings to the stereotypes regarding Muslim men being portrayed as oppressive and 'terrorists.' Muslim men and women also exhibit different responses to trauma. Muslim women report avoiding public spaces out of fear for their safety. In contrast, Muslim men frequently experience fatigue and emotional exhaustion as they attempt to manage ongoing stress from perceived harassment by law enforcement or public scrutiny (Abu-Ras & Suarez, 2009).

Taken together, although Muslim women have the advantage of not being targeted as the "bearded terrorist" and are perceived as more passive and oppressed in society, they face the disadvantage of intersectional invisibility, further exacerbating their exclusion from discourses around gender and social movements meant to empower them (Ghani et al., 2024). Zakaria (2021) also highlights this issue in her book, stating that Muslim women need to be relatable to White women to fit into their agenda (i.e., Western/White feminism) or be included in their discussion.

Age

Muslims are the youngest faith community in America, with nearly a quarter of Muslim Americans between the ages of 18 and 24 (ISPU, 2017). This age group is in a crucial stage of identity formation, making them particularly vulnerable to the effects of Islamophobia. Studies show that younger Muslims report higher levels of discrimination than their older counterparts; 69% of Muslims aged 18-29 experience discrimination, compared to 58% of those aged 30-49. For Muslim youth, Islamophobia is closely linked to various mental health challenges (Abu-Khalaf et al., 2023). As previously mentioned, schools are among the most common environments where young Muslims encounter Islamophobia, often in the form of bullying and exclusion. These experiences disrupt their learning experience and can lead to the internalizing and externalizing of problems, including depression, anxiety, hopelessness, and low self-esteem (Abu-Khalaf et al., 2023; Balkaya-Ince , 2020; Lowe et al., 2019). Experiencing discrimination during these critical developmental years can hinder young Muslims' ability to form a positive sense of civic and religious identity, underscoring the need for safe and supportive school environments (Saada, 2024).

Abu Khalaf et al. (2023) also noted in their meta-analysis that Muslim students face an onslaught of discrimination from multiple spheres, including peers, teachers, and educational institutions. When authority figures like teachers and administrations do not intervene when Muslim students face issues, they become discriminatory actors. School policies like experiencing discriminatory curriculum or anti-Islamic guest speakers, as well as not having a dedicated space to pray on campus, all create challenges for students as they perceive the school environment as unwelcoming of their religious identity. These experiences further led to negative outcomes like decreased academic achievement, stress, anxiety, and an unwillingness to go to school (Abu Khalaf et al., 2023).

Research indicates that a strong sense of religious identity and belonging to a larger community can provide resilience against these negative impacts among Muslim youth (Tahseen et al., 2019). In one study, Muslim students in grades 6-8 shared that their Muslim identity "provided a means to serve God and, in this process, to serve the community" (Elkassem et al., 2018). This sense of belonging can foster resilience and hope, helping counteract feelings of isolation and low self-esteem (Elkassem et al., 2018). To support Muslim youth, it is vital to encourage community involvement and create spaces where they can contribute to the community. Such involvement may enhance their self-esteem, reinforce positive identity formation, and support their well-being.

Immigration Status

Eighty-six percent of Muslims in the United States are either US-born or naturalized citizens. Yet, immigration remains a central part of the community's identity, with more than half of Muslims born outside the US (ISPU, 2017). This diversity in immigration status shapes how Muslims experience Islamophobia and its impact on mental health. For immigrant Muslims, the challenges of adapting to a new country compound the effects of Islamophobia. Everyday microaggressions, such as being labeled "exotic" or told to "go back to their country," can make immigrant Muslims feel unwelcome and othered in American society (Nadal et al., 2012). Xenophobia, when combined with Islamophobia, creates a uniquely challenging experience that can lead to issues like depression, anxiety, and a heightened sense of fear and isolation. Immigrant Muslims often face additional stressors, including the pressure to navigate cultural differences, fear for their safety, and the strain of adapting to Western norms, all of which can impact mental health (Nasir et al., 2024).

Interestingly, US-born Muslims report higher levels of discrimination than their immigrant counterparts (Gecewicz & Mohamed, 2017). This discrepancy may be influenced by factors such as cultural visibility or the differing ways each group perceives and copes with discrimination. For US-born Muslims, who might be more embedded in American society, discrimination can feel more personal and confrontational, intensifying its mental health effects (Abu-Ras et al., 2018). Additionally, research suggests that the length of time immigrant Muslims spend in the US affects their experiences; those who have been in the country longer often perceive greater impacts of religious discrimination and experience more Islamophobia-related stress (Abu-Ras et al., 2018).

Muslim American well-being can also be affected by how much they simultaneously identify themselves as both Muslims and Americans (Hakim et al., 2018). Identity formation is a primary issue concerning Muslim-American youth; how they identify themselves affects how they perceive discrimination: people with strong group identification tend to characterize themselves more as targets of discrimination (Operario & Fiske, 2001). One study termed this formation "hyphenated selves" (Sirin & Fine, 2007), whereby those affiliated suffer from the need to be both Muslim and American simultaneously. Moreover, Muslim Americans who are most acculturated into "American life" face criticism from their Muslim community, blaming them for being too American to be Muslim (Casey, 2018). Although the Muslim community can be a supportive environment for most Muslims in the US, some experience this in-group stigmatization because of their identity process.

Socioeconomic Background

Muslims have similar levels of education compared to the general American population but report lower incomes (Pew Research Center, 2017). They are the faith community most likely to report low income, with approximately a third at or slightly under the poverty line (ISPU, 2017). In the United States, income disparities exist between immigrant Muslims, who are more likely to have a higher income, and US-born Muslims, who are mainly from the Black community and have disproportionately lower incomes (Pew Research Center, 2017). In Canada, Muslims also report lower incomes compared to the general population, indicating that economic challenges affect Muslims across North America (Statistics Canada, 2022).

Economic difficulties, coupled with Islamophobia, present unique challenges to the mental health of Muslims across North America. Although research on the socioeconomic diversity of Muslim communities is limited since most studies recruit college students, representing only a small portion of the community (Amer & Bagasra, 2013), there is evidence that income disparities, unemployment, and workplace discrimination contribute to the mental health impact of Islamophobia (el-Aswad & el-Aswad, 2019). For instance, research shows that less educated participants reported higher stress related to perceived discrimination than highly educated participants (Abu-Ras et al., 2018). This finding suggests that socioeconomic status intensifies the stress associated with Islamophobia. Aroian's (2012) study also mentioned the socioeconomic background of the neighborhood as a factor affecting the likelihood of bullying among adolescents. Together, these findings indicate that the socioeconomic background of Muslims and the neighborhood that they reside in are important determinants in terms of how they experience Islamophobia and its associated mental health impacts.

Risk and Protective Factors Associated with Islamophobia

Research examining the relationship between religious discrimination and mental health has found that those who viewed religion as a significant part of their identity were more likely to report psychological distress (Hashem & Awad, 2021). Interpersonal and community factors often converge to act as either buffers or risk factors depending on the population served. For instance, fear of stigma often negatively affects how Muslims engage with others in the public arena. Anticipation of harassment has been found to result in internalizing Islamophobic stereotypes and may even lead to identity concealment (Samari, 2016). On a community level, the instance of a hate crime may act as a deterrent to engaging in one's community as a consequence of insecurity. Islamophobia stereotype threat can also impair Muslims' access to health care, as the provider-client relationship may produce impaired communication or make them feel misunderstood (Hammoud et al., 2005). Consequently, Muslim community centers have come to play an important role in the provision of psychosocial services. Many studies have highlighted the role of religious leaders, such as Imams, in providing psychological support or acting as a means to promote access to mental health support (Abu-Ras et al., 2008). Mental health services can subsequently buffer the adverse effects of Islamophobia, further emphasizing the need for an integrated model for providing mental health support within the Muslim community. Shah (2019b) further corroborated this point as she found that attending religious services moderately buffered discrimination for Muslims. She argued that the social inequality faced by Muslims as a result of their minority status in the community prompts religion to become more valuable for marginalized populations and religious institutions to become access points for social resources. These resources are a means to bridge the gap between healthcare professionals, as congregants may be more willing to utilize resources if endorsed by the Muslim community centers. Religiosity also acts as a psychological buffer against Islamophobia. Ahmed et al. (2011) found that adolescents who used more religious coping strategies and had stronger ethnic identity and religious support reported less psychological distress.

Implications for Theory

Research on Muslim Americans must recognize the diversity within the Muslim community and include individuals with varied identities in their studies. As highlighted in the mental health outcomes section, the intersecting identities of Muslims significantly impact their mental health. It is essential to understand the subtleties these identities introduce and offer recommendations for enhancing the mental health of Muslim Americans, all framed within the appropriate theoretical context. Thus, a thorough framework enables a deeper understanding of the distinct experiences of Muslim Americans.

The term anti-racism is increasingly used to characterize prejudices against Muslims and to analyze the racialization of Muslim identity, shedding light on how Muslims are classified as a group and perceived differently within society. In their study, Jones and Unsworth (2024) explore two aspects of Islamophobia: the racial dimension, suggesting that anti-Muslim racism shares characteristics with other forms of group prejudice, and the religious dimension, which highlights the specific hostility directed at Islam. Despite criticism of framing Islamophobia as a form of racism, they argue that integrating discussions of race and religion can enhance the understanding of anti-Muslim sentiments.

Another framework that allows a comprehensive examination of the Muslim American experience is the theory of intersectionality (Crenshaw, 1989). Intersectionality points out that the experiences of Black women, who navigate both race and gender identities, cannot be equated with those of Black men or White women. This framework serves as a valuable lens for understanding the experiences of Muslims in North America as they navigate their lives at the intersection of race, gender, immigration status, class, and more.

Based on the literature review on Muslims' diverse identities, future research should incorporate Muslims of lower socioeconomic backgrounds and non-college students into its work to better understand the overall Muslim experience in North America. Researchers should also work towards creating more holistic frameworks to grasp the realities of Muslims in Western societies.

Conclusion

Although Islamophobia has been associated with the political after-effects of 9/11, it has historical roots that date back to medieval times. Islamophobia has a multifaceted impact on the Muslim community, impacting the community's mental health and affecting various spheres of their lives. Challenges are further exacerbated as a result of the Muslim community's intersectional identities, as their race, immigration status, socioeconomic background, and age compound their experience of Islamophobia, creating unique challenges. Risk factors like visibility, being a woman, Arab, and the youth were the most vulnerable and often exacerbate the impact of Islamophobia. However, research has found protective factors that buffer the impact of Islamophobia, like Muslim community centers and religiosity. Thus, mental health professionals who work within the Muslim community must be cognizant of these factors to provide culturally humble interventions to best support the population.

References

Abdelhadi, E. (2017). Religiosity and Muslim Women's Employment in the United States. *Socius: Sociological Research for a Dynamic World*, *3*, 1–17. https://doi.org/10.1177/2378023117729969

Abu Khalaf, N., Woolweaver, A. B., Reynoso Marmolejos, R., Little, G. A., Burnett, K., & Espelage, D. L. (2023). The Impact of Islamophobia on Muslim Students: A Systematic Review of the Literature. *School Psychology Review*, *52*(2), 206–223. https://doi.org/10.1080/2372966X.2022.2075710

Abu-Ras, W. M., & Suarez, Z. E. (2009). Muslim men and women's perception of discrimination, hate crimes, and PTSD symptoms post 9/11. *Traumatology*, *15*(3), 48–63. https://doi.org/10.1177/1534765609342281

Abu-Ras, W. M., Suárez, Z. E., & Abu-Bader, S. (2018). Muslim Americans' safety and well-being in the wake of Trump: A public health and social justice crisis. *American Journal of Orthopsychiatry*, *88*(5), 503–515. https://doi.org/10.1037/ort0000321

Abu-Ras, W., Gheith, A., & Cournos, F. (2008). The imam's role in mental health promotion: a study at 22 mosques in New York City's Muslim community. *Journal of Muslim Mental Health*, *3*(2), 155–176. https://doi.org/10.1080/15564900802487576

Adam, B. (2019). Addressing the Mental Health Needs of African American Muslims in an Era of Islamophobia. In *Islamophobia and Psychiatry*, 257–266. https://doi.org/10.1007/978-3-030-00512-2_22

Agrawal, P., Yusuf, Y., Pasha, O., Ali, S. H., Ziad, H., & Hyder, A. A. (2019). Interpersonal stranger violence and American Muslims: An exploratory study of lived experiences and coping strategies. *Global Bioethics*, *30*(1), 28–42. https://doi.org/10.1080/11287462.2019.1683934

Ahmed, S., & Abdallah, K. (2023). Young, Black, Muslim American: An intersectional lens to understanding emerging adult religious experiences. *Psychology of Religion and Spirituality*, *15*(2), 319.

Ahmed, N., & Islam, N. S. (2023). The Health Implications of Perceived Anti-Muslim Discrimination Among South Asian Muslim Americans. *AJPM focus*, *2*(4), 100139. https://doi.org/10.1016/j.focus.2023.100139

Ahmed, S. R., Kia-Keating, M., & Tsai, K. H. (2011). A Structural Model of Racial Discrimination, Acculturative Stress, and Cultural Resources Among Arab American Adolescents. *American Journal of Community Psychology*, *48*(3–4), 181–192. https://doi.org/10.1007/s10464-011-9424-3

Ahluwalia, M. K., & Pellettiere, L. (2010). Sikh men post-9/11: Misidentification, discrimination, and coping. *Asian American Journal of Psychology*, *1*(4), 303–314. https://doi.org/10.1037/a0022156

Ali, S., Elsayed, D., Elahi, S., Zia, B., & Awaad, R. (2022). Predicting rejection attitudes toward utilizing formal mental health services in Muslim women in the US: Results from the Muslims' perceptions and attitudes to mental health study. *International Journal of Social Psychiatry*, *68*(3), 662-669.

Alsaidi, S., Velez, B. L., Smith, L., Jacob, A., & Salem, N. (2021). "Arab, brown, and other": Voices of Muslim Arab American women on identity, discrimination, and well-being. *Cultural Diversity and Ethnic Minority Psychology.* https://doi.org/10.1037/cdp0000440

Alzyoud, S. (2022). The US Media Coverage of Islam and Muslims in the Wake of the ISIS Emergence [Review of *The US Media Coverage of Islam and Muslims in the Wake of the ISIS Emergence*]. *Eximia Journal, 4,* 195–208. https://eximiajournal.com/index.php/eximia/article/view/123/68

Amer, M. M., & Bagasra, A. (2013). Psychological research with Muslim Americans in the age of Islamophobia: Trends, challenges, and recommendations. *American Psychologist, 68*(3), 134.

Amer, M. M., & Hovey, J. D. (2012). Anxiety and depression in a post-September 11 sample of Arabs in the USA. *Social psychiatry and psychiatric epidemiology, 47,* 409–418.

Aroian, K. J. (2012). Discrimination Against Muslim American Adolescents. *The Journal of School Nursing, 28*(3), 206–213. https://doi.org/10.1177/1059840511432316

Assari, S., & Lankarani, M. M. (2017). Discrimination and psychological distress: gender differences among Arab Americans. *Frontiers in psychiatry, 8,* 23.

Awaad, R. (2015). A Journey of Mutual Growth: Mental Health Awareness in the Muslim Community. In: Roberts, L., Reicherter, D., Adelsheim, S., Joshi, S. (eds) Partnerships for Mental Health. Springer, Cham. https://doi-org.umasslowell.idm.oclc.org/10.1007/978-3-319-18884-3_11

Awaad, R. (2023a, November). *How to support the Palestinian cause when feeling overwhelmed.* TRT World. https://www.trtworld.com/opinion/how-to-support-the-palestinian-cause-when-feeling-overwhelmed-16044578

Awaad, R. (2023b, November 16). *The Devastating Mental Health Effects of Islamophobia.* TIME. https://time.com/6335453/islamophobia-mental-health-effects-essay/

Awaad, R., Suleiman, K., Mogahed, D., Abdole, L., Ali, A. & Hammami, N. (2022, April 20). *Mental Health of Muslim Healthcare Workers During Covid-19.* ISPU (Institute for Social Policy and Understanding). https://www.ispu.org/mental-health-muslim-healthcare-workers/

Balkaya-Ince, M. (2020). *A Multi-Method Approach to Examine Predictors and Outcomes of Muslim American Adolescents' Social Identities.* [Doctoral dissertation, University of Maryland].

Bartlett, A., Faber, S., Williams, M., & Saxberg, K. (2022). Getting to the Root of the Problem: Supporting Clients With Lived-Experiences of Systemic Discrimination. *Chronic stress (Thousand Oaks, Calif.), 6,* 24705470221139205. https://doi.org/10.1177/24705470221139205

Casey, P. M. (2018). Stigmatized Identities: Too Muslim to Be American, Too American to Be Muslim. *Symbolic Interaction, 41*(1), 100–119. https://doi.org/10.1002/symb.308

Churchill, W. S. (1899). *The River War.* Longmans, Green and Co. Coaston, J. (2019, March 15). *New Zealand mosque shooting: The shooter's manifesto shows how white nationalist rhetoric spreads.* Vox; Vox. https://www.vox.com/identities/2019/3/15/18267163/new-zealand-shootingchristchurch-white-nationalism-racism-language

Coaston, J. (2019, March 15). New Zealand mosque shooting: the shooter's manifesto shows how white nationalist rhetoric spreads. Vox; Vox. https://www.vox.com/identities/2019/3/15/18267163/new-zealand-shooting-christchurch-white-nationalism-racism-language

Council on American-Islamic Relations (CAIR). 2023. 2023 Bullying Report. Available online: http://ca.cair.com/updates/bullying-report-2023/

Council on American Islamic Relations. (2024). *Fatal: The Resurgence of Anti-Muslim Hate* (pp. 1–70) [Review of *Fatal: The Resurgence of Anti-Muslim Hate*]. Council on American Islamic Relations. https://islamophobia.org/wp-content/uploads/2024/04/2024_Fatal_The_Resurgence_of_Anti-Muslim_Hate-1.pdf

Crenshaw, K. (1989). Demarginalizing the Intersection of Race and Sex: Black Feminist Critique of Antidiscrimination Doctrine, Feminist Theory and Antiracist Politics. University of Chicago Legal Forum, 1989, 139–168.

El-Aswad, E. S., & el-Aswad, E. S. (2019). Indicators of Quality of Life and Well-being in the Middle East and North African Region: A Comparative Analysis. *The Quality of Life and Policy Issues among the Middle East and North African Countries*, 45-80.

Elkassem, S., Csiernik, R., Mantulak, A., Kayssi, G., Hussain, Y., Lambert, K., ... & Choudhary, A. (2018). Growing up Muslim: The impact of Islamophobia on children in a Canadian community. Journal of Muslim Mental Health, 12(1), 3-18.

Elsayed, D., Mirnajafi, Z., Manjra, H., Al-Alusi, D., McBryde-Redzovic, A., Mohammad, I., & Awaad, R. (2024). Believing Without Belonging? The Effects of Racial Discrimination at the Mosque on Religiosity and Mosque Attendance Through Belonging for Black Muslims. [Manuscript submitted for publication].

Ford, C. L., & Sharif, M. Z. (2020). Arabs, whiteness, and health disparities: the need for critical race theory and data. *American Journal of Public Health*, *110*(8), e2.

Furqan, Z., Malick, A., Zaheer, J., & Sukhera, J. (2022). Understanding and addressing Islamophobia through trauma-informed care. *CMAJ: Canadian Medical Association journal = journal de l'Association medicale canadienne*, *194*(21), E746–E747. https://doi.org/10.1503/cmaj.211298

Gaddis, S. M., & Ghoshal, R. (2015). Arab American Housing Discrimination, Ethnic Competition, and the Contact Hypothesis. *The ANNALS of the American Academy of Political and Social Science*, *660*(1), 282–299. https://doi.org/10.1177/0002716215580095

Gecewicz, C., & Mohamed, B. (2017). *American-born Muslims more likely than Muslim immigrants to see negatives in US society*. Pew Research Center. https://www.pewresearch.org/short-reads/2017/09/26/american-born-muslims-more-likely-than-muslim-immigrants-to-see-negatives-in-u-s-society/

Ghani, A., Hudson, S. K. T., Rumaney, H., & Sidanius, J. (2024). Of Christians, Jews, and Muslims: When gender is unspecified, the default is men. *Psychology of Religion and Spirituality, 16*(2), 251.

Hakim, N. H., Molina, L. E., & Branscombe, N. R. (2018). How Discrimination Shapes Social Identification Processes and Well-being Among Arab Americans. *Social Psychological and Personality Science, 9*(3), 328–337. https://doi.org/10.1177/1948550617742192

Hammoud, M. M., White, C. B., & Fetters, M. D. (2005). Opening cultural doors: Providing culturally sensitive healthcare to Arab American and American Muslim patients. *American Journal of Obstetrics and Gynecology, 193*(4), 1307–1311. https://doi.org/10.1016/j.ajog.2005.06.065

Hashem, H. M., & Awad, G. H. (2021). Religious identity, discrimination, and psychological distress among Muslim and Christian Arab Americans. *Journal of Religion and Health, 60*(2), 961–973. https://doi.org/10.1007/s10943-020-01145-x

Haque, A., Tubbs, C. Y., Kahumoku-Fessler, E. P., & Brown, M. D. (2019). Microaggressions and Islamophobia: Experiences of Muslims across the United States and clinical implications. Journal of marital and family therapy, 45(1), 76–91.

Ho, I. K., & Çabuk, K. (2023). The impact of racial discrimination on the health of Asian Americans during the COVID-19 pandemic: A scoping review. *Ethnicity & Health, 28*(7), 957–982. https://doi.org/10.1080/13557858.2023.2208312

Hodge, D. R., Zidan, T., & Husain, A. (2023). How to Work with Muslim Clients in a Successful, Culturally Relevant Manner: A National Sample of American Muslims Share Their Perspectives. *Social work, 69*(1), 53–63. https://doi.org/10.1093/sw/swad048

Husain, A., & Howard, S. (2017). Religious Microaggressions: A Case Study of Muslim Americans. *Journal of Ethnic and Cultural Diversity in Social Work, 26*(1–2), 139–152. https://doi.org/10.1080/15313204.2016.1269710

Ikizler, A. S., & Szymanski, D. M. (2018). Discrimination, religious and cultural factors, and Middle Eastern/Arab Americans' psychological distress. *Journal of Clinical Psychology, 74*(7), 1219-1233.

Ikramullah, E. (2024, July 25). *American Muslims, especially students, most likely to experience religious discrimination*. ISPU. https://ispu.org/ceasefire-poll-3/ Institute for Social Policy and Understanding (ISPU; 2017). *American Muslims 101 Resources for Interfaith Leaders, Community Educators + Allies*. [PowerPoint slides]. https://ispu.org/american-muslims-101/

Jasperse, M., Ward, C., & Jose, P. E. (2012). Identity, Perceived Religious Discrimination, and Psychological Well-being in Muslim Immigrant Women. *Applied Psychology, 61*(2), 250–271. https://doi.org/10.1111/j.1464-0597.2011.00467.x

Jones, S. H., & Unsworth, A. (2024). Two Islamophobias? Racism and religion as distinct but mutually supportive dimensions of anti-Muslim prejudice. *The British Journal of Sociology, 75*(1), 5–22.

Kaplan, G. B. (2012). The Inception of Limpieza de Sangre (Purity of Blood) and its Impact in Medieval and Golden Age Spain. In *BRILL eBooks* (pp. 19–41). https://doi.org/10.1163/9789004222588_003

Kearns, E. M., Betus, A. E., & Lemieux, A. F. (2019). Why Do Some Terrorist Attacks Receive More Media Attention Than Others? *Justice Quarterly*, *36*(6), 985–1022. https://doi.org/10.1080/07418825.2018.1524507

Lincoln, A. K., Cardeli, E., Sideridis, G., Salhi, C., Miller, A. B., Da Fonseca, T., Issa, O., & Ellis, B. H. (2021). Discrimination, marginalization, belonging, and mental health among Somali immigrants in North America. *The American journal of orthopsychiatry*, *91*(2), 280–293. https://doi.org/10.1037/ort0000524

Lowe, S. R., Tineo, P., & Young, M. N. (2019). Perceived discrimination and major depression and generalized anxiety symptoms: In Muslim American college students. *Journal of religion and health*, *58*, 1136–1145.

Martin, M. B. (2015). Perceived discrimination of Muslims in health care. *Journal of Muslim Mental Health*, *9*(2), 41–69. https://doi.org/10.3998/jmmh.10381607.0009.203

Matias, C. E., & Newlove, P. M. (2017). Better the devil you see, than the one you don't: Bearing witness to emboldened en-whitening epistemology in the Trump era. *International Journal of Qualitative Studies in Education*, *30*(10), 920–928. https://doi.org/10.1080/09518398.2017.1312590

McLaughlin, M. M., Ahmad, S. S., & Weisman de Mamani, A. (2022). A mixed-methods approach to psychological help-seeking in Muslims: Islamophobia, self-stigma, and therapeutic preferences. *Journal of consulting and clinical psychology*, *90*(7), 568–581. https://doi.org/10.1037/ccp0000746

McNeal, E., & Thatcher, O. (1908). A Source Book of Mediaeval History: Documents Illustrative of European Life and Institutions from the German Invasion to the Renaissance. *The American Historical Review*. https://doi.org/10.1086/ahr/14.1.187

Murrar, S., Baqai, B., & Padela, A. I. (2024). Predictors of perceived discrimination in medical settings among Muslim women in the USA. *Journal of racial and ethnic health disparities*, *11*(1), 150-156.

Nadal, K. L., Griffin, K. E., Hamit, S., Leon, J., Tobio, M., & Rivera, D. P. (2012). Subtle and overt forms of Islamophobia: Microaggressions toward Muslim Americans. *Journal of Muslim Mental Health*, 6(2), 15–37, DOI: http://dx.doi.org/10.3998/jmmh.10381607.0006.203.

Nadimpalli, S. B., Cleland, C. M., Hutchinson, M. K., Islam, N., Barnes, L. L., & Van Devanter, N. (2016). The association between discrimination and the health of Sikh Asian Indians. Health psychology: official journal of the Division of Health Psychology, American Psychological Association, 35(4), 351–355. https://doi.org/10.1037/hea0000268

Nasir, N., Hand, C., & Rudman, D. L. (2024). Aging Muslim immigrants transitioning from Muslim majority countries to Muslim minority countries: A scoping review addressing dynamics of occupation, place, and identity. *Journal of Occupational Science*, *31*(3), 606-626.

O'Connor, A. J., & Jahan, F. (2014). Under Surveillance and Overwrought: American Muslims' emotional and behavioral responses to government surveillance. *Journal of Muslim Mental Health, 8*(1). https://doi.org/10.3998/jmmh.10381607.0008.106

Omar, I. (2021, December 15). H.R.5665 - 117th Congress (2021-2022): Combating International Islamophobia Act. Www.congress.gov. https://www.congress.gov/bill/117th-congress/house-bill/5665

Omar, I. (2023). H.R.3985 - 118th Congress (2023-2024): Combating International Islamophobia Act. Congress.gov. https://www.congress.gov/bill/118th-congress/house-bill/3985

Operario, D., & Fiske, S. T. (2001). Ethnic identity moderates perceptions of prejudice: Judgments of personal versus group discrimination and subtle versus blatant bias. *Personality and Social Psychology Bulletin, 27*(5), 550–561. https://doi.org/10.1177/0146167201275004

Ortega, V. (2024, October 11). *Mother of 7-year-old girl attacked with knife in Detroit speaks out: "Why her?"* Cbsnews.com; CBS Detroit. https://www.cbsnews.com/detroit/news/mother-of-7-year-old-attacked-in-detroit-speaks-out/

Oxford University Press. (2006). Islamophobia. In *Oxford English dictionary*. Retrieved November 4, 2024, from https://www.oxfordlearnersdictionaries.com/us/definition/english/islamophobia#:~:text=%E2%80%8Bdislike%20or%20unfair%20treatment%20of%20Islam%20or%20Muslims

Pew Research Center. (2017, July 26). Demographic portrait of Muslim Americans. *Pew Research Center's Religion & Public Life Project*. https://www.pewresearch.org/religion/2017/07/26/demographic-portrait-of-muslim-americans/

Pew Research Center. 2018. New estimates show US Muslim population continues to grow. January 3. https://www.pewresearch.org/fact-tank/2018/01/03/new-estimates-show-u-s-muslim-population-continues-to-grow/

Qadeer, A., Tor-Cabuk, K., McBryde-Redzovic, A., Mahoui, I. & Awaad, R. (in press). Perceptions of Muslim Americans on the Role of Mental Health Professionals in Supporting Muslims With Mental Illness: A Community-Based Participatory Research (CBPR) Study. *Spirituality in Clinical Practice*.

Saada, N. (2024). Teaching Against Islamophobia: Educational Interventions. *Multicultural Perspectives, 26*(1), 14–26.

Said, E. W. (1978). Orientalism. New York, Pantheon Books.

Saleh, N., Clark, N., Bruce, A., & Moosa-Mitha, M. (2023). Using narrative inquiry to understand anti-Muslim racism in Canadian nursing. *Canadian Journal of Nursing Research, 55*(3), 292–304.

Samari G. (2016). Islamophobia and Public Health in the United States. *American Journal of Public Health, 106*(11), 1920–1925. https://doi.org/10.2105/AJPH.2016.303374

Samari, G., Alcalá, H. E., & Sharif, M. Z. (2018). Islamophobia, health, andpublic health: A systematic literature review. *American Journal of Public Health, 108*(6), e1–e9. https://doi.org/10.2105/AJPH.2018.304402

Shah, S. (2019a). (rep.). *Canadian Muslims: Demographics, discrimination, religiosity, and voting* (pp. 1–80). Institute of Islamic Studies Occasional Paper Series.

Shah, S. (2019b). Does Religion Buffer the Effects of Discrimination on Distress for Religious Minorities? The Case of Arab Americans. *Society and Mental Health, 9*(2), 171–191. https://doi.org/10.1177/2156869318799145

Sirin, S. R., & Fine, M. (2007). Hyphenated selves: Muslim American youth negotiating identities on the fault lines of global conflict. *Applied Developmental Science, 11*(3), 151–163. https://doi.org/10.1080/10888690701454658

Statistics Canada. *(2022, October 26). The Canadian Census: A rich portrait of the country's religious and ethnocultural diversity. The Daily* -. https://www150.statcan.gc.ca/n1/daily-quotidien/221026/dq221026b-eng.htm

Tahseen, M., Ahmed, S. R., & Ahmed, S. (2019). Muslim youth in the face of Islamophobia: Risk and resilience. In *Islamophobia and psychiatry: Recognition, prevention, and treatment*, 307-319.

Tavkhelidze, T. *(2021).* Historical Origins of European Islamophobia. *Journal of the Contemporary Study of Islam, 2*(2), 142–162. https://doi.org/10.37264/jcsi.v2i2.64

Tervalon, M., & Murray-García, J. (1998). Cultural humility versus cultural competence: a critical distinction in defining physician training outcomes in multicultural education. *Journal of health care for the poor and underserved*, 9(2), 117–125. https://doi.org/10.1353/hpu.2010.0233

The NSEERS effect: a decade of racial profiling, fear, and secrecy. (2012). Penn State Law eLibrary. https://elibrary.law.psu.edu/irc_pubs/11/

The White House. (2024). The US National Strategy to Counter Islamophobia and Anti-Arab Hate [Review of The US National Strategy to Counter Islamophobia and Anti-Arab Hate]. In https://www.whitehouse.gov (pp. 1–64). The White House. https://bidenwhitehouse.archives.gov/wp-content/uploads/2024/12/National-Strategy-Doc.pdf

Zakaria, R. (2021). *Against white feminism: Notes on disruption*. WW Norton & Company.

Zine, J. (2006). Unveiled sentiments: Gendered Islamophobia and experiences of veiling among Muslim girls in a Canadian Islamic school. *Equity & Excellence in Education, 39*(3), 239–252.

CHAPTER SEVENTEEN

MEDIA AND MUSLIM MENTAL HEALTH

Anisah Bagasra, Burton Speakman

This chapter examines various forms of media, especially news media, film, and social media, and how the portrayal of Muslims in the media (with a focus on North America and Europe) impacts the health and wellbeing of Muslims. Negative framing of Muslims through selective news coverage, associating Muslims with terrorism, and painting Islam and Muslims as an existential threat to Western values has led to an increase in bias, discrimination, and hate crimes toward Muslims. The media influences public opinion of Islam and Muslims, leading to greater acceptance of policies that are unfair or discriminatory. The media's role in situating Muslims as a targeted religious minority contributes to mental health impacts, including higher rates of anxiety and depression and lower rates of healthcare service utilization. The authors outline the media framing of Muslims, its mental health implications, and how mental health professionals can effectively work with Muslim clients impacted by negative media exposure.

Introduction

Overall concern at an international level about Islamophobia is a recent development, with documents about racism and prejudice not mentioning Islamophobia until the late 1990s (Kathawalla et al., 2024; Zúquete, 2016). After the September 11, 2001 attacks, media framing of Muslims changed significantly, with politicians and news media using discourse to connect Islam to violence, terrorism, and death both physically and metaphorically and as the antithesis to the Christian way of life (Al-Azami, 2021; Zúquete, 2016). News journalists are struggling to adapt to the information environment where other means of receiving information are spreading faster and to wider audiences (Bhatia & Arora, 2024; Farkas & Schousboe, 2024). This comes at a time when online disinformation influences individuals and larger-scale public opinion and, ultimately, political decision-making (Rodríguez-Pérez & García-Vargas, 2021). Disinformation, along with strategic racism, is often used to convince segments of the population to support policies that target and disenfranchise marginalized groups (MacLean, 2020). The role of the media in creating and maintaining negative stereotypes of Islam and Muslims is a significant challenge. For this chapter, the media is broadly defined as journalism, popular culture such as movies and television, partisan media, and social media. How the media impacts attitudes, stereotypes, and imagery of Muslims, and in turn, how this influences the mental health of Muslim Americans will be discussed.

What is Media framing?

Framing represents how human consciousness influences communication (Entman, 1993), involving a process of selection resulting in salience where some elements of reality are going to be emphasized in communication and others ignored (Entman, 1993, 2007; Entman et al., 2009). Media framing can result in bias where one side is mistreated in a political debate (Entman, 2007). This form of presentation represents the media's role in power distribution by determining whose arguments are heard, read, or seen. The media can influence the public by telling them what topics to think about, which impacts what they think about those topics (Entman, 2007). The mainstream media often engage in this framing unintentionally: "Frames do more than make certain considerations accessible; they suggest which of the many, possibly conflicting, considerations should predominate when forming opinions on an event or issue" (Entman et al., 2009 p. 153). The media within every nation helps to create a collective language through its framing choices, which can result in rhetoric that is attributed to stereotypes (Anderson, 2006; Billig, 2017; Castelló, 2016). These frames often revolve around a sense of place, who traditionally belongs, and maybe, more importantly, who does not (Powers, 2011).

The Framing of Muslims in the Media

In this section, we will discuss the framing of Muslims in the media pre and post 9/11, with a focus on US Media. Framing, generally, and in the media in particular, provides an understanding of problems and cultural and moral ideas (Entman, 1993). Media framing, in general, tends to support hegemonic ideas, which in the United States are represented by capitalism, patriarchy, heterosexism, individualism, consumerism, and White privilege, along with other elements of entrenched values (Budd et al., 1999). "Despite some efforts by Western mainstream media to provide fair and objective portrayals of Muslims, the dominant portrayals tend to be negative" (Eid, 2014, p. 99). The result of these portrayals in various forms of media is extenuating the idea of Muslims as others in Western culture (Eid, 2014).

The media, in general, since September 11, 2001, have framed Muslims as a dangerous 'Other' whose existence is a risk to Western culture (Celermajer, 2007). This trend exists in the United States, Australia, and Western Europe (Celermajer, 2007; Morey & Yaqin, 2011; Rane & Ewart, 2012). The general tenor is one in which Muslims, as a whole, are simply incompatible with Western society to live within a secular nation (Celermajer, 2007). The overarching theme is one of Muslims as being religious primitives: "The association of Islam with terrorism has come to be accepted as part of the discourse on security and terrorism, so much so that the terms "Muslim" and "terrorist" have become almost synonymous," (Eid & Karim, 2011, p. 4).

Framing of Muslims in the News

Media framing of Islam in Western media serves as a representation of content bias since content typically only represents one side (Entman, 2007). They do this through shaping attitudes and often confirming prejudices against Muslims (Morey & Yaqin, 2011). For example, when the United States and Britain engaged in war in Iraq, the media in both nations used framing emphasizing national unity and fear utilizing terms like the "War on Terror" (Karatzogianni, 2013). These press frames linked Islam to terrorism, which aided in creating fear and Islamophobia in the West (Iqbal, 2010; Ramji, 2008).

Far-right groups in the Western world have become increasingly willing to tolerate and utilize blatantly racist language (Hawley, 2017; Mondon & Winter, 2020; Sanchez, 2018). In particular, far-right groups sought to make Islamophobic ideas mainstream with considerable success within conservative media through manipulation of both mainstream and conservative media (Hawley, 2017; Mondon & Winter, 2020; Woods & Hahner, 2019). For example, conservative media played on the fears of Muslims when reporting on a "Ground Zero Mosque" as part of misleading messaging to otherize Muslims (Mayer, 2017). Additionally, conservative religious leaders such as Jerry Falwell have falsely stated for decades that Islam teaches adherents to hate all non-Muslims (Swain, 2002). Muslims are not the only non-White group that experienced these campaigns designed to divide and mislead (Mayer, 2017). Therefore, while it is not just conservatives who frame Muslims as being the "other," they are the most frequent and vocal offender (Mondon & Winter, 2020). Additionally, Muslims who choose not to assimila by wearing a hijab or otherwise asserting religious or religious-ethnic identity create opportunities for convenient targeting by groups already engaged in racist and xenophobic rhetoric (Alimahomed-Wilson, 2017).

The media also struggle when covering issues such as "honor killings," linking them to other cultural elements perceived as negative by the Western majority (Morey & Yaqin, 2011). At times, cases that are simply examples of patriarchal dominance within another culture are referred to as honor killings when committed by Muslim men (Morey & Yaqin, 2011).

Framing of Muslims in Film and Television

The overarching framing of Muslims and Islam prior to September 11, 2001, was one of Orientalism (Sardar & Davies, 2010). This was presented through depictions of deserts, magic carpets, loud city markets as part of cities that overall are ancient and opulent, stock of evil characters, and harems of scantily clad women (Sardar & Davies, 2010)

Television has a mixed record in its framing of Muslims because, in some cases, shows present effective multicultural presentations of Muslims, but in other cases, they reiterate stereotypical tropes that are easily duplicated (Morey & Yaqin, 2011). There have been several television series that have shown Muslims engaged in terrorist activities, including *24, Sleeper Cell,* and *Dirty War*, among others (Morey & Yaqin, 2011). Overall, television has been known to produce characters and programming that are hostile to Muslims and mosques, presenting both using negative stereotypes:

> "In post-9/11 dramas, the stereotype tends to be articulated through an implicit distance posited between the viewer (the normalized subject) and the Muslim object of the gaze, whose difference is always in view. This differentiation process— also heavily marked by racial value judgments—we have called ethnonormativity. The ethnonormative space is the viewing space called into being by the

narrative tension between the contending groups depicted (host community versus alien wedge)." (Morey & Yaqin, 2011, pp. 113–114)

Television makes Muslims appear different by putting female characters in hijabs, making the men bearded and praying, suggesting they do not conform to a secular society (Morey & Yaqin, 2011). However, studies focused on other Western nations have suggested that television shows have moved away from framing that connects Muslims to terrorism (Rane & Ewart, 2012). Despite some thoughtful portrayals of Muslims on television, representations of Muslim women, in particular, remain primarily stereotypical (Eid, 2014). Following September 11, 2001, Hollywood has more frequently presented Muslims as dangerous and uncivilized, as a group to be feared (Aguayo, 2009). Since September 11, the goal of framing Muslims within popular culture is to synonymize Muslims and Arabs, then presenting those Arabs as being backward-looking, violent, and barbaric people (Fatima, 2016, p. 60).

Women are often presented as being oppressed by the dangerous males in their lives, with white women helping to remove their covering and introduce them to modern society (Aguayo, 2009). Aguayo states,

> "My analysis of various scenes, accompanied by verbal and visual narratives within the film, have elucidated how the dangerous Muslim man is scripted as lecherous, premodern, and uncivilized; and when he is not, as is the case with Col. Al-Ghazi, he is at odds with himself, given that his limited character is fixed in a rigid binary system. The 'imperiled' Muslim woman, although representationally disembodied throughout the film, is, in fact, hyperinvisible through Mayes, thus shaping public discourse about Muslim women on and offscreen." (pg. 53)

The goal seems to be to offer binary presentations of Muslims, with most being violent terrorists, who are uncivilized fundamentalists living within a totalitarian country (Fatima, 2016). Part of this is included in the idea presented that Muslims are the enemy in many forms of Western popular culture (Kiran et al., 2021). The overall goal seems to be one of creating fear of Muslim characters, and fear is one of the prerequisites for Islamophobia (Kiran et al., 2021). Yet overall, "After 9/11, it is observed that the films have increased the sympathetic portrayal of Muslims. Even if a movie is based on Islamic terrorism, other positive Muslim characters are added to offset the negative depiction" (Kiran et al., 2021, p. 1133).

Muslims are overwhelmingly presented in popular culture as extremist, violent, or militant, which could include portrayals as assassins, kidnappers, or terrorists who are allegedly acting in the name of Islam (Eid, 2014; Karim, 2003). This negative framing existed well before September 11, 2001, (Noureen & Paracha, 2019). However, the shift might be more geared toward terrorism and danger after September 11 and less about the exotic foreign culture stereotypes, yet it should be noted that Muslims as terrorists is a frame that has existed in television and film for decades prior to 2001 (Noureen & Paracha, 2019). Overall, there is some belief that Muslims were transitioned to be the new enemy du jour in Western popular culture to take the role left by the fall of the Soviet Union (Fatima, 2016).

Framing of Muslims in Social Media

The framing that people see in the media is often reused in social media situations (Billig, 2017; Castelló, 2016). On right-wing media posts on Facebook about Muslims, the sites' followers would post images of Muslim politicians as snakes or terrorists (Speakman & Bagasra, 2022). In most instances, these posts were not condemned but instead supported and added by other users (Speakman & Bagasra, 2022). One of the commonly used social media posts about Muslims is to attack them over their alleged hatred of the United States for various reasons but often centered around freedom (Awan, 2014; Ogan et al., 2014; Speakman & Bagasra, 2022). There is also extensive conversation about Muslims wanting to convert the United States to Sharia law, which is often linked to terrorism (Morey & Yaqin, 2011; Speakman & Bagasra, 2022). One of the acceptable frames used by some segments within social media is to attack at least some Muslims over an alleged hatred of America (Awan, 2014; Ogan et al., 2014).

People share content on social media primarily to attain or maintain connections (Hermida, 2016). Self-representation is one of the primary drivers for people to post on Facebook, and it includes the display of their selected identity (Hawley, 2017). In some ways, social media allows the worst impulses to thrive because the algorithm of the site is designed to make people less likely to see content that is displeasing to them, therefore removing people from their "friends" and driving them to content that agrees with their political worldview (Vaidhyanathan, 2018; Valenzuela et al., 2017)

The framing of Muslims on social media often takes away the agency of the individual; it presents Islam as being an agency, and it engages in negative actions, including making "war" against Western culture (Nixon, 2019). Even atheists who critique some behaviors and beliefs associated with Islam will often generalize and end up supporting far-right rhetoric on social media sites (Nixon, 2019). The goal of much of social media framing is the dehumanization of Muslims (Abdalla et al., 2021). One of the dehumanizing measures used is the depiction of Muslim individuals as snakes, which serves a double purpose of making them seem less than human and tying into metaphors about snakes being untrustworthy (Abdalla et al., 2021; Speakman & Bagasra, 2022). The dehumanizing rhetoric and imagery are often tied to politicians or political issues (Abdalla et al., 2021; Speakman & Bagasra, 2022).

Islamophobic Rhetoric and Imagery

Though this section will focus primarily on social media, it remains important to understand that Islamophobic images have appeared in the media prior to the advent of social media. One notable incident was the cartoons that ran in the Danish Newspaper Jyllands Posten in 2005, with much of the coverage focused on the Muslim reaction to the images, which included death threats (Christensen, 2006). However, the cartoons themselves contained images that portrayed the prophet Mohammed as a terrorist, alluded to Muslim terrorists receiving virgins upon becoming martyrs, and extensive other Islamophobic content (Christensen, 2006).

How social media sites are created does not privilege honest or helpful information; the goal of these sites is to create engagement through interactions (Karpf et al., 2020). This functionally rewards individuals for bad behavior on social media (Karpf et al., 2020). This creates a location ripe for the unscrupulous to use existing fear and prejudice to attain reactions. Social media sites allow enumerable conversations that present Muslims as different, backward, and unable to conform to the standards of Western culture (Evolvi, 2018). Social media serves as a haven for those who wish to make Islamophobic content, at times encouraged by media outlets seeking to provoke them (Speakman & Bagasra, 2022). "In expressing Islamophobic statements, many tweets also defend discrimination. The exclusion of Muslims from mainstream society is indeed seen as a necessary precaution against Islam and seldom recognized as being problematic" (Evolvi, 2018, p. 307). Islam is the only major religion that is frequently discussed negatively on social media (Ittefaq & Ahmad, 2018). The sites that post this content do so frequently, not daily, but often every hour (Ittefaq & Ahmad, 2018).

News coverage and high-profile events seem to trigger Islamophobic rhetoric on social media (Awan, 2014; Speakman & Bagasra, 2022). However, it must be noted that certain people use social media to engage in constant efforts to stereotype Muslims (Awan, 2014). These are often far-right figures who use social media to stir up tension between groups (Vidgen et al., 2022). While there is sizable rhetoric on social media that is openly Islamophobic, much more of the content is nuanced and designed to skirt any regulations against offensive posts (Vidgen et al., 2022). One of the challenges with social media is that anti-Muslim groups have become able to disseminate hateful content rapidly (Ghasiya & Sasahara, 2022; Vidgen et al., 2022). Social media sites do a poor job of preventing or even in the removal of misinformation regarding Muslims (Ghasiya & Sasahara, 2022). This is at least partially due to social media algorithms designed to detect profanity and other more direct negative portrayal (Abdalla et al., 2021). Many groups have become experts at circumventing those algorithms through lightly veiled rhetoric and the use of imagery, including memes (Woods & Hahner, 2019). This ability to understand the rules of social media also helps in the spread of anti-Islam misinformation (Bhatia & Arora, 2024). One of the major issues with social media is that it allows for those seeking to provide misinformation to micro-target their content to make sure it meets a potentially receptive audience, one that might be less likely to complain, another method of getting around social media's enforcement efforts (Starr, 2020).

Doctored Images, Misinformation and Propaganda

Those who engage in misinformation have developed detailed practices to not just present misinformation but to make that disinformation effective by tying into existing prejudices and themes of commonality (Bhatia & Arora, 2024). The news diet of many people is shifting to the point where they receive as much disinformation as legitimate news (Cea & Palomo, 2021). Misinformation relating to Muslims is not simply an issue in English-language and Western social media sites. The issue with the current social media misinformation is that it is effective in building conviction among a segment, sometimes a sizable segment, of the population (Bhatia & Arora, 2024).

Other research suggests that social media sites such as Twitter serve as a way for Muslims to combat misinformation and be influential in discourse (Downing & Dron, 2020). Social media can be a fluid process where discourse can quickly vary. One of the challenges with misinformation is that it is often attractive to lower-educated individuals, who are also more likely to share that information (Ahmed & Gil-Lopez, 2022). Partisanship and preexisting prejudices against Muslims also result in believing misinformation about prominent Muslims and more likely to rely on social media algorithms to deliver additional information (Ahmed & Gil-Lopez, 2022).

Islamophobia in the Media: Direct Impacts

Few studies have sought to examine the impact Islamophobia in the media has on public opinions of Islam and Muslims or the impact on Muslims themselves. In this section, we discuss how the framing of Muslims has a direct impact on public opinion of Islam and Muslims broadly, including increased prejudicial attitudes and support for policies that discriminate against Muslims (Lajevardi, 2021). Then, two specific direct impacts of negative framing are discussed: the media's role in framing Muslim political candidates and elected officials and the media framing of mosque buildings and other projects.

Islamophobia and Mental Health Outcomes

Identifying the impacts of Islamophobia on mental health is challenging due to the multifaceted nature of the discrimination faced by Muslims. To gain a comprehensive understanding, we will examine the effects of Islamophobia on mental health through the lenses of race and ethnicity, gender, age, immigration status, and socioeconomic background to emphasize the unique role of each of these identities on Muslim experiences. However, it is crucial to recognize that these identities often overlap, making the experience of Islamophobia more complex. The diversity within Muslim communities in North America requires a nuanced discussion that considers how these various identities interact with and are impacted by Islamophobia.

The impact of Islamophobia in media on public attitudes towards Islam and Muslims

Post 9/11, we have seen negative attitudes toward Islam and Muslims increase among the general public, often in direct correlation with media coverage that focuses on negative portrayals or incidents involving Muslims (Ogan, Willnat, Pennington & Bashir, 2014). In Canada, findings suggest that in almost all regions, Muslims are viewed unfavorably compared to other ethnic, religious, or sexual minority groups (Wilkins, 2018). Similar findings have been documented in New Zealand (Sibley et al., 2020; Shaver, Sibley, Osborne, & Bulbulia, 2017). In Europe, political advertising has been found to have a direct impact on both implicit and explicit attitudes towards Muslims (Schmuck & Matthes, 2019), demonstrating the direct role of anti-Muslim media can shift public attitudes toward a targeted community. Similarly, news coverage explicitly linking Islam and Muslims to terrorism had a similar impact on negative attitudes toward Muslims (von Sikorski, Schmuck, Matthes & Binder, 2017). Political rhetoric among U.S. politicians has fueled the anti-Sharia law movement, increased public perceptions of Muslims as a threat, and contributed to the delegitimization of Islam as a religion (Uddin, 2019). Research suggests that hate speech by politicians targeting minorities helps to garner support for discriminatory policies (Grillo, 2014) and increases attitude polarization (Schmuck, Heiss, & Matthes, 2020). In these ways, the rhetoric of politicians, who use the media as a platform to share their messages, has a significant impact on local and national perceptions of Muslim Americans and their status as religious minorities. The "otherization" of Muslims continues to shape attitudes and opinions in the United States (Boydstun, Feezell & Glazier, 2018; Kalkan, Layman & Uslaner, 2009; Pal & Wellman, 2022). Negative public opinions, in turn, lead to increased anti-Muslim prejudice and discrimination toward Muslims in various forms (Aranguren, Madrisotti, & Durmaz-Martins, 2023; Taras, 2024).

The impact of media on Muslim political candidates and elected officials

Media framing can hurt Muslim politicians and political candidates and indirectly impact how other Muslims view their place in the public sphere. In the United States, Congresswomen Ilhan Omar and Rashida Tlaib were the first prominent Muslim women to be covered in news media for their elections (Bashri, 2019). They have often been vilified, especially on social media platforms. The two congresswomen are the most visible examples of the impact of negative media attention on the health and safety of Muslim political candidates and elected officials, and the use of hate speech on platforms such as Twitter (Pintak, Bowe & Albright, 2022). Several lesser-known politicians have faced considerable negative media campaigns, impacting individuals who have decided to run for political positions. Saffiya Khalid was the first Somali-American and youngest to be elected to Lewiston City Council in Lewiston, Maine in 2019 despite facing negative attacks online, threats received by email, and doxing with her home address posted online. Similarly, Ghazala Hashmi ran for the Virginia State Senate, winning as the first Muslim State Senator in 2019. News stories on social media announcing her election were met with hundreds of racist comments. A study analyzed 3,000 comments on five news stories about her election in 2019, finding that many of the comments utilized the "enemy within" trope, accusing Muslim Americans of being enemies of the United States (Eason & Gannavarapu, 2019). Muslims who view this negative content may be less likely to engage in civic engagement, such as running for elected office or engaging in social activism, out of fear of being trolled or doxed. Attacks on Muslim politicians in the media perpetuate the image that Muslims are not truly American or can be trusted and may impact a sense of belongingness. Isolation and alienation can lead to detrimental mental health impacts.

The impact of media framing on mosque building and other projects

Media framing has had a direct impact on the presence of Muslims in public spaces, especially since September 11, continuing to rise with the start of the anti-Sharia political movement (Beydoun, 2021). Negative media coverage and misinformation designed to target mosque building projects, Muslim cemeteries, and other visible Muslim spaces within the greater landscape can hurt acculturation and sense of belongingness among Muslim communities in Muslim minority countries, including the United States, Canada, European countries, and Australia. The most prominent example of the media's role in shaping public opinion and opposition to a mosque building project is the Park51 project, which was labeled by the media as the "Ground Zero Mosque" (DeFoster, 2015). In 2010, as part of a larger multicultural center, a mosque was proposed to be built. The location was two blocks from Ground Zero. The media contributed to framing the project as insensitive, which resulted in public opinion being swayed toward opposition to the project. Petitions opposing the mosque's construction were circulated (Boulahnane,2018; Yang & Self, 2015; Kilde, 2011). The media encouraged opposition to the mosque building project to assert nationalism and an American identity (Pierce, 2014; Schaffner, 2013).

Additionally, rhetoric and language referencing the mosque building project were often divided along political ideologies (Dehghani, Sagae, Sachdeva, & Gratch, 2014). However, Kumar (2014) argues that liberals played an enabling role in the controversy created over the project. Opposition to the Park51 Islamic Community Center highlights the struggle of Muslims to be viewed as genuinely American and accepted as a part of U.S. public space (Takim, 2011). This can lead to a further sense of alienation and psychological distress. Despite massive strides in the construction of Muslim community spaces, media framing and political rhetoric have led to a number of high-profile battles, creating barriers that take a psychological toll on members of the Muslim community who have to navigate public zoning hearings through media misinformation or negative coverage.

Media and Health Outcomes of Muslims

In this section, we discuss how media exposure, especially exposure to negative framing of Muslims and Islam, has an effect on Muslims themselves and the implications of this for mental health professionals. Most of the research thus far focuses on forms of discrimination towards Muslims, which may be related to media framing, political rhetoric, as well as direct acts of discrimination. Islamophobia and anti-Muslim discrimination have been associated with depression, generalized anxiety, hypervigilance, and subclinical paranoia in Muslim Americans, especially for individuals with a strong Muslim identity (Hodge, Zidan & Husain, 2016; Lowe et al., 2019; Rippy & Newman, 2006).

The literature on physical health outcomes and health care utilization associated with Islamophobia is limited but growing. Early studies have focused on maternal and child outcomes. One study focused on preterm birth and low birth weight among women with Arabic names from pre- to post-9/11, and one on preterm birth among women from countries targeted in the Muslim Ban (Executive Order 13669) (Lauderdale, 2006; Samari et al., 2020). Both studies found that preterm birth increased after the implementation of the Muslim ban, and the Lauderdale study found that low birth weight increased (Lauderdale, 2006; Samari et al., 2020). Another study focusing on the impact of the Executive Order compared healthcare utilization from pre- to post-implementation among patients from Muslim-majority counties in Minnesota (Samuels et al., 2021). Researchers found that emergency department (ED) visits increased after the Executive Order was issued for patients from countries targeted by the EO. In examining the mental health of Muslim Americans in the face of microaggressions, Haque and colleagues (2019) found that participants experienced stress created by bias in various forms of media, including misrepresentation of Islam and frequent news, film, and social media associations of Islam with violence. The inability to counteract the frequent posts of misinformation and reading bigoted comments by colleagues or friends of friends on social media was seen as frustrating and overwhelming.

Mental Health Outcomes and Social Media Usage

A small number of studies have sought to examine the impact online Islamophobia has on Muslims' mental health. A study of Muslim social media users during the 2016 U.S. presidential election (Eckert, Metzger-Riftkin, Kolhoff & O'Shay-Wallace, 2019) examined emotional reactions to encountering Islamophobia online and face-to-face. Participants noted that though they encountered more Islamophobia online, it was less upsetting and frustrating than face-to-face encounters as social media could be ignored, and friendships could be cultivated to avoid anti-Muslim messaging. Though emotionally fatiguing, most of the participants felt unable to quit social media and engaged in countering online Islamophobia through educating or coping by avoiding or ignoring sources of Islamophobia on Snapchat, Instagram, Facebook, and Twitter. Research has also found that many bystanders reduce the likelihood that a person will attempt to counter hate speech on Facebook (Leonhard, Rueß, Obermaier, & Reinemann, 2018).

In a study conducted by the authors in 2023 (manuscript in preparation), eight hundred and thirty (M=466, F=364) Muslim Americans who use at least one form of social media completed an anonymous survey on their experiences with Islamophobia on social media. The majority of participants were in the 18-44 age range, had at least a bachelor's degree, were most active on Facebook (followed by Instagram and Twitter), and used social media two or more times per day. The social media sites they reported encountering the most Islamophobia were Facebook (54%), followed by Twitter (15%) and Instagram (13.5%). In describing personal encounters with Islamophobic posts on social media, the majority fell into the themes of associating Islam or Muslims with terrorism and violence, Muslims/Islam as foreign, gender oppression, or Muslims as generally evil. The data suggests that Muslim American adults encounter negative comments and posts on social media frequently (14%) or often (18%), with 17% stating they frequently report Islamophobic posts they see. Thirty-seven percent indicated that seeing anti-Islam or anti-Muslim content on social media often or frequently impacted their mood, and 31% reported it often or frequently impacted their mental health (See Table 1). Twenty-seven percent have deactivated or deleted a social media account because of anti-Islam/Muslim content. Avoidance behaviors include avoiding displaying Muslim identity in social media posts, avoiding supporting a Muslim political candidate on social media and avoiding sharing religious content or videos. This type of self-reporting provides some insight into how Muslims perceive social media impacts their mental health. However, it does not provide clear data on whether high social media use is tied to rates of diagnosable mental health disorders.

Table 1: Mental Health Impacts of Islamophobia on Social Media

	Very Frequently	Often	Sometimes	Rarely	Never
Negative Posts about Islam and Muslims on social media have impacted my mental health	13%	19%	27%	22%	20%
Negative posts about Islam and Muslims have impacted my view of my Muslim identity	14%	14%	24%	21%	27%
The negative posts about Islam and Muslims have impacted my self-esteem.	14%	18%	23%	21%	24%
Viewing anti-Muslim/anti-Islam posts on social media has impacted my mood.	17%	20%	28%	21%	15%

Impact of Islamophobic Media on Help-seeking and Service Utilization

There is an increasing body of evidence suggesting that exposure to Islamophobic imagery and rhetoric can contribute to a fear that mental health professionals will be biased toward Muslim clients. A study in Germany found that exposure to negative coverage of Muslims increased perceptions that the public would have negative opinions of Muslims (Zerback & Karadas, 2023). One study found that viewing negative representations of Muslims in the media caused Muslim college students to avoid interaction with members of the dominant culture (Saleem & Ramasubramanian, 2019). Similarly, viewing negative news coverage of Muslims also reduced trust in the U.S. government among Muslim Americans. The erosion of trust directly impacts broader help-seeking behaviors. Perceived and real experiences of discrimination, which can be amplified through media consumption, significantly impact help-seeking behaviors within marginalized communities. Additionally, there remain few interventions or health promotions that directly address the Muslim community or model Muslim people in their advertisement of services.

Implications for Helping Professionals

Individuals working with Muslim clients must be aware of the potential for heightened distress among their clients during times when the media may increase negative coverage of Islam and Muslims. This often occurs following terrorist attacks and during major election seasons, as politicians tend to increase anti-immigrant, Xenophobic, and anti-Muslim rhetoric during campaigning. Experiencing discrimination or viewing media content where Muslims are experiencing discrimination may be traumatic and have long-lasting effects on identity, self-image, perceived stigma, and a sense of safety and security. This type of vicarious trauma is more prevalent now than ever before, as individuals are exposed to global violence and hate crimes through their social media feeds (Ashraf & Nassar, 2018). Assessing how much time a client may be spending on social media or watching the news may help understand if frequent exposure to anti-Muslim rhetoric and imagery is contributing to personal distress. One may need to recommend that a client take breaks from their phone or limit time spent on social media when experiencing heightened distress. Additionally, refugee, asylum-seeking, and immigrant populations may be more susceptible to negative media coverage that dehumanizes them. Helping professionals must be aware of the many layers of trauma experienced by these populations.

It is important to help professionals to assess their levels of bias and potential exposure to negative media frames that could shape their perceptions of a Muslim client. The CE Workshop that one of the authors of this chapter offers includes a section of the workshop aimed at this self-assessment. Asking oneself questions such as: "What imagery of Islam and Muslims do I have from the media?" "How do I respond to news stories featuring Islam and Muslims?" "What stereotypes or hidden prejudices about Islam and Muslims may I be harboring as a result of my own media exposure?" can help reflect on potential beliefs or attitudes that may impact successfully working with Muslim clients. Many Muslim women report therapists not being able to look past their hijab or attributing their problems automatically to religion or culture (Bagasra, 2023). This leads many Muslims to stop using therapy or avoid seeking out help when needed. The development of several training courses that focus on reducing bias and increasing religious and spiritual competencies can help to increase service utilization and retention of clients.

As more Muslims are entering the field of counseling and psychology, we are seeing an increase in the development of Islamically integrated therapies. Practitioners should assess the level of religiosity of clients and determine if these therapies may be helpful as well for clients experiencing vicarious trauma, distress over portrayals of their religion, low self-esteem, or are direct victims of cyberbullying or harassment.

Conclusion

A growing body of evidence demonstrates the role of the media in creating and contributing to negative and often dangerous depictions of Islam and Muslims. Organizations like the Council on American Islamic Relations (CAIR), elected Muslim officials, and some within the entertainment industry have attempted to counteract negative imagery and stereotypes through education and producing shows that portray ordinary Muslims. Muslim presence in mainstream media as actors, news anchors, and writers is still considerably smaller than for other minority groups. The constant focus since 9/11 associating Muslims with terrorism has led to dehumanization, fear, and skewed public perceptions. This, in turn, has increased hate crimes and support for policies that have a detrimental effect on the ability of Muslims living in Muslim-minority countries to integrate and feel a sense of belonging. Collectively, this can have a detrimental impact on the health and wellbeing of Muslims. Hate speech is legally protected unless it calls for violence, and even direct calls for violence have been interpreted differently (Guiora & Park, 2017). Social media has provided a space where hate speech often goes unchecked and amplifies misinformation. Improved definitions of what constitutes hate speech, better automotive detection on social media, and increased removal of speech violating community standards could reduce some of the current effects. Counselors, social workers, health professionals, and others in related fields should be aware of the potential role the media can play in chronic stressors. Additionally, perceptions of how the dominant majority may view one's identity may impact help-seeking and healthcare utilization, as many Muslims worry about experiencing bias or a lack of understanding from physical and mental healthcare providers.

References

Abdalla, M., Ally, M., & Jabri-Markwell, R. (2021). Dehumanisation of 'Outgroups' on Facebook and Twitter: Towards a framework for assessing online hate organisations and actors. *SN Social Sciences, 1*, 1–28.

Abrahamian, E. (2003). The US media, Huntington, and September 11. *Third World Quarterly, 24*(3), 529–544.

Aguayo, M. (2009). Representations of Muslim bodies in the Kingdom: Deconstructing discourses in Hollywood. *Global Media Journal, 2*(2), 41.

Ahmed, S., & Gil-Lopez, T. (2022). Engaging with vilifying stereotypes: The role of YouTube algorithmic use in perpetuating misinformation about Muslim congresswomen. *Journalism & Mass Communication Quarterly*, doi: 10776990221110113.

Al-Azami, S. (2021). Language of Islamophobia in right-wing British newspapers. *Journal of Media and Religion, 20*(4), 159–172. https://doi.org/10.1080/15348423.2021.1972667

Alimahomed-Wilson, S. (2017). Invisible Violence: Gender, Islamophobia, and the Hidden Assault on U.S. Muslim Women. *Women, Gender, and Families of Color, 5*(1), 73–97

Anderson, B. (2006). *Imagined communities: Reflections on the origin and spread of nationalism.* Verso books.

Aranguren, M., Madrisotti, F., & Durmaz-Martins, E. (2023). Anti-Muslim behaviour in everyday interaction: evidence from a field experiment in Paris. *Journal of Ethnic & Migration Studies, 49*(3), 770–794. https://doi.org/10.1080/1369183X.2021.1953378

Ashraf, A., & Nassar, S. (2018). American Muslims and vicarious trauma: An explanatory concurrent mixed-methods study. *American Journal of Orthopsychiatry, 88*(5), 516–528. https://doi.org/10.1037/ort0000354

Awan, I. (2014). Islamophobia and Twitter: A Typology of Online Hate Against Muslims on Social Media. *Policy & Internet, 6*(2), 133–150. https://doi.org/10.1002/1944-2866.POI364

Bagasra, A. (2023). Religious interpretations of mental illness and help-seeking experiences among Muslim Americans: Implications for clinical practice. *Spirituality in Clinical Practice, 10*(1), 20–31. https://doi.org/10.1037/scp0000299

Bashri, M. (2019). Elections, Representations, and Journalistic Schemas: Local News Coverage of Ilhan Omar and Rashida Tlaib in the US Mid-term Elections. *Essachess, 12*(24), 129–146.

Beydoun, K. A. (2021). On Sacred Land. *Minnesota Law Review, 105*(4), 1803–1885.

Bhatia, K. V., & Arora, P. (2024). Discursive toolkits of anti-Muslim disinformation on Twitter. *The International Journal of Press/Politics, 29*(1), 253–272.

Billig, M. (2017). Banal nationalism and the imagining of politics. In *Everyday Nationhood* (pp. 307–321). Springer.

Boydstun, A. E., Feezell, J. T., & Glazier, R. A. (2018). In the wake of a terrorist attack, do Americans' attitudes toward Muslims decline? *Research and Politics, 5*(4). https://doi.org/10.1177/2053168018806391

Boulahnane, S. (2018). Ground Zero mosque in the context of America's post-9/11 religious pluralism: CDA of mainstream news media's coverage of the discursive event. *Indonesian Journal of Islam and Muslim Societies, 8*(2), 253–280. https://doi.org/10.18326/ijims.v8i2.253-279

Bowe, B. J. (2018). Permitted to Build? Moral Foundations in Newspaper Framing of Mosque- Construction Controversies. *Journalism & Mass Communication Quarterly, 95*(3), 782–810. https://doi.org/10.1177/1077699017709253

Budd, M., Craig, S., & Steinman, C. M. (1999). *Consuming environments: Television and commercial culture.* Rutgers University Press.

Burke, S., Diba, P., & Antonopoulos, G. A. (2020). 'You sick, twisted messes': The use of argument and reasoning in Islamophobic and anti-Semitic discussions on Facebook. *Discourse & Society, 31*(4), 374–389.

Cashin, S. (2010). To be Muslim or Muslim-looking in America: A comparative exploration of racial and religious prejudice in the 21st century. *Duke FL & Soc. Change, 2,* 125.

Castelló, E. (2016). Anderson and the Media. The strength of "imagined communities." *DEBATS. REVISTA DE CULTURA, PODER Y SOCIEDAD, 1.*

Cea, N., & Palomo, B. (2021). Disinformation matters: Analyzing academic production. *Politics of Disinformation: The Influence of Fake News on the Public Sphere,* 5–22.

Celermajer, D. (2007). If Islam is our other, who are 'we '? *Australian Journal of Social Issues, 42*(1), 103–123.

Christensen, C. (2006). Islam in the media: Cartoons and context. *Screen Education, 43,* 27–33.

DeFoster, R. (2015). Orientalism for a New Millennium: Cable News and the Specter of the "Ground Zero Mosque."*Journal of Communication Inquiry, 39*(1), 63–81. https://doi.org/10.1177/0196859914536577

Dehghani, M., Sagae, K., Sachdeva, S., & Gratch, J. (2014). Analyzing political rhetoric in conservative and liberal weblogs related to the construction of the "ground zero mosque". *Journal of Information Technology & Politics, 11*(1), 1-14.

Downing, J., & Dron, R. (2020). Tweeting Grenfell: Discourse and networks in critical constructions of British Muslim social boundaries on social media. *New Media & Society, 22*(3), 449–469.

Eason, H. & Gannavarapu, S. (2019). *Election of Virginia's first Muslim state senator draws racist comments on Facebook.* Prince William Times, https://www.princewilliamtimes.com/news/election-of-virginias-first-muslim-state-senator-draws-racist-comments-on-facebook/article_fed659e8-0240-11ea-a0ae-cf3538cc4924.html

Eckert, S., Metzger-Riftkin, J., Kolhoff, S., & O'Shay-Wallace, S. (2019). A hyper differential counter public: Muslim social media users and Islamophobia during the 2016 US presidential election. *New Media & Society, 23*(1), 78-98. https://doi.org/10.1177/1461444819892283

Eid, M. (2014). Perceptions about Muslims in Western societies. In *Re-imagining the Other: Culture, media, and Western-Muslim intersections* (pp. 99–

119). Springer.
Eid, M., & Karim, K. H. (2011). Ten years after 9/11—What have we learned ?*Global Media Journal–Canadian Edition*, *4*(2), 1–12.
Entman, R. M. (1993). Framing: Toward clarification of a fractured paradigm. *Journal of Communication*, *43*(4), 51.
Entman, R. M. (2007). Framing Bias: Media in the Distribution of Power. *Journal of Communication*, *57*(1), 163–173.
Entman, R. M., Matthes, J., & Pellicano, L. (2009). Nature, sources, and effects of news framing. In *The handbook of journalism studies* (pp. 195–210). Routledge.
Evolvi, G. (2018). Hate in a tweet: Exploring internet-based Islamophobic discourses. *Religions*, *9*(10), 307.
Farkas, J., & Schousboe, S. (2024). Facts, values, and the epistemic authority of journalism: How journalists use and define the terms fake news, junk news, misinformation, and disinformation. *Nordicom Review*, *45*(1), 137–157.
Fatima, S. (2016). Muslim in movies: The Hollywood construction. *Pakistan Journal of Society, Education and Language (PJSEL)*, *2*(1), 54–75.
Fiske, S. T., & Taylor, S. E. (1991). *Social cognition*. McGraw-Hill Book Company.
Ghasiya, P., & Sasahara, K. (2022). Rapid sharing of Islamophobic hate on Facebook: The case of the Tablighi Jamaat controversy. *Social Media+ Society*, *8*(4), 20563051221129151.
Grillo, M. C. (2014). The Role of Emotions in Discriminatory Ethno-Religious Politics: An Experimental Study of Anti-Muslim Politics in the United States. *Politics, Religion & Ideology*, *15*(4), 583–603. https://doi.org/10.1080/21567689.2014.959504
Guiora, A., & Park, E. (2017). Hate Speech on social media. *Philosophia*, *45*(3), 957–971.
Haque, A., Tubbs, C. Y., Kahumoku-Fessler, E. P., & Brown, M. D. (2019). Microaggressions and Islamophobia: Experiences of Muslims Across the United States and Clinical Implications. *Journal of Marital and Family Therapy*, *45*(1), 76–91. https://doi.org/10.1111/jmft.12339
Hawley, G. (2017). *Making Sense of the Alt-Right*. Columbia University Press.
Hermida, A. (2016). *Tell everyone: Why we share and why it matters*. Anchor Canada.
Hodge, D. R., Zidan, T., & Husain, A. (2016). Depression among Muslims in the United States: Examining the Role of Discrimination and Spirituality as Risk and Protective Factors. *Social Work*, *61*(1), 45–52. https://doi.org/10.1093/sw/swv055
Iqbal, Z. (2010). *Understanding Islamophobia: Conceptualizing and Measuring the Construct*. *13*(4), 17.
Ittefaq, M., & Ahmad, T. (2018). Representation of Islam and Muslims on social media: A discourse analysis of Facebook. *Journal of Media Critiques [JMC]*, *4*(13).
Jasperse, M., Ward, C., & Jose, P. E. (2012). Identity, perceived religious discrimination, and psychological wellbeing in Muslim immigrant

women. *Applied Psychology, 61*(2), 250–271. https://doi.org/10.1111/j.1464-0597.2011.00467.x

Kathawalla, U., Gulamhussein, Q., Chan, F. B., Riegelman, A., & Syed, M. (2024). Conceptualization and measurement of Islamophobia: A systematic review. *Analyses of Social Issues & Public Policy*, 1. https://doi.org/10.1111/asap.12426

Karatzogianni, A. (2013). *Violence and War in Culture and the Media*. Routledge.

Karim, K. H. (2003). Making sense of the "Islamic peril": Journalism as cultural practice. In *Journalism after September 11* (pp. 119–134). Routledge.

Kalkan, K. O., Layman, G. C., & Uslaner, E. M. (2009). "Bands of Others"? Attitudes toward Muslims in Contemporary American Society. *Journal of Politics, 71*(3), 847–862. https://doi.org/10.1017/S0022381609090756

Karpf, D., Bennett, W., & Livingston, S. (2020). How digital disinformation became dangerous. *The Disinformation Age: Politics, Technology, and Disruptive Communication in the United States*, 153–168.

Kilde, J. H. (2011). The Park 51/Ground Zero Controversy and Sacred Sites as Contested Space. *Religions, 2*(3), 297–311. https://doi.org/10.3390/rel2030297

Kiran, U., Qamar, A., Adnan, M., & Youssef, E. Y. M. (2021). Muslims depiction in Hollywood movies: A qualitative study. *PalArch's Journal of Archaeology of Egypt/Egyptology, 18*(08), 1126–1136.

Kumar, D. (2014). Mediating Racism: The New McCarthyites and the Matrix of Islamophobia. *Middle East Journal of Culture & Communication, 7*(1), 9–26. https://doi.org/10.1163/18739865-00701001

Lauderdale D. S. (2006). Birth outcomes for Arabic-named women in California before and after September 11. *Demography, 43*(1), 185–201. https://doi.org/10.1353/dem.2006.0008

Lajevardi, N. (2021). The Media Matters: Muslim American Portrayals and the Effects on Mass Attitudes. *Journal of Politics, 83*(3), 1060–1079. https://doi.org/10.1086/711300

Leonhard, L., Obermaier, M., Rueß, C., & Reinemann, C. 2018. Perceiving threat and feeling responsible. How severity of hate speech, number of bystanders, and prior reactions of others affect bystanders' intention to counter argue against hate speech on Facebook. Studies in Communication and Media 7(4): 555-579. https://doi.org/10.5771/2192-4007-2018-4-555

Lowe, S. R., Tineo, P., & Young, M. N. (2019). Perceived discrimination and major depression and generalized anxiety symptoms: in Muslim American college students. *Journal of Religion and Health, 58*(4), 1136–1145. https://doi.org/10.1007/s10943-018-0684-1

MacLean, N. (2020). "Since we are greatly outnumbered." In *Cambridge University Press eBooks* (pp. 120–150). https://doi.org/10.1017/9781108914628.005

Mayer, J. (2016). *Dark money: The Hidden History of the Billionaires Behind the Rise of the Radical Right*. Doubleday Books.

Mondon, A., & Winter, A. (2020). *Reactionary Democracy: How Racism and the Populist Far Right Became Mainstream*. Verso Books.

Morey, P. (2010). Strangers and stereotypes: The Spooks controversy and the framing of Muslims. *Journal of Postcolonial Writing, 46*(5), 529–539.

Morey, P., & Yaqin, A. (2011). *Framing Muslims: Stereotyping and representation after 9/11*. Harvard University Press.

Nixon, A. G. (2019). Public Atheism and 'Islamophobia on Twitter. In *The Digital Social* (pp. 153–177). DeGuyter.

Noureen, A., & Paracha, S. A. (2019). Muslims and Islam: Freeze Framed Discourses in Hollywood during 1978-2013. *Global Regional Review, 4*(4), 37–43.

Ogan, C., Willnat, L., Pennington, R., & Bashir, M. (2014). The rise of anti-Muslim prejudice: Media and Islamophobia in Europe and the United States. *International Communication Gazette, 76*(1), 27–46. https://doi.org/10.1177/1748048513504048

Pal, S., & Wellman, J. D. (2022). Threat, fundamentalism, and Islamophobia: Assessing the factors associated with negative attitudes toward Muslims. *Psychology of Religion and Spirituality, 14*(4), 635–638. https://doi.org/10.1037/rel0000347

Pierce, L. (2014). A Rhetoric of Traumatic Nationalism in the Ground Zero Mosque Controversy. *Quarterly Journal of Speech, 100*(1), 53–80. https://doi.org/10.1080/00335630.2014.888461

Pintak, L., Bowe, B. J., & Albright, J. (2022). Influencers, Amplifiers, and Icons: A Systematic Approach to Understanding the Roles of Islamophobic Actors on Twitter. *Journalism & Mass Communication Quarterly, 99*(4), 955–979. https://doi.org/10.1177/10776990211031567

Powers, J. L. (2011). Reimaging the imagined community. *American Behavioral Scientist, 55*(10), 1362–1378. https://doi.org/10.1177/0002764211409380

Ramji, R. (2008). Muslims and the news media. In *Contemporary Islam* (pp. 195–196). I.B. Taurus and Co.

Rane, H., & Ewart, J. (2012). The framing of Islam and Muslims in the tenth-anniversary coverage of 9/11: Implications for reconciliation and moving on. *Journal of Muslim Minority Affairs, 32*(3), 310–322.

Rippy, A. E., & Newman, E. (2006). Perceived religious discrimination and its relationship to anxiety and paranoia among Muslim Americans. *Journal of Muslim Mental Health, 1*(1), 5–20. https://doi.org/10.1080/15564900600654351

Rodríguez-Pérez, C., & García-Vargas, G. R. (2021). Understanding which factors promote exposure to online disinformation. *Politics of Disinformation: The Influence of Fake News on the Public Sphere*, 173–186.

Saleem, M., & Ramasubramanian, S. (2019). Muslim Americans' responses to social identity threats: Effects of media representations and experiences of discrimination. *Media Psychology, 22*(3), 373–393. https://doi.org/10.1080/15213269.2017.1302345

Saleem, M., Wojcieszak, M. E., Hawkins, I., Li, M., & Ramasubramanian, S. (2019). Social identity threats: How media and discrimination affect Muslim Americans' identification as Americans and trust in the U.S.

government. *Journal of Communication, 69*(2), 214–236. https://doi.org/10.1093/joc/jqz001

Samari, G., Catalano, R., Alcalá, H. E., & Gemmill, A. (2020). The Muslim Ban and preterm birth: Analysis of US vital statistics data from 2009 to 2018. Social Science & Medicine, 265, 113544.

Samari, G., Alcalá, H. E., & Sharif, M. Z. (2018). Islamophobia, health, and public health: a systematic literature review. *American Journal of Public Health, 108*(6), 1-9. doi:10.2105/AJPH.2018.304402

Samuels, E. A., Orr, L., White, E. B., Saadi, A., Padela, A. I., Westerhaus, M., ... & Gonsalves, G. (2021). Healthcare utilization before and after the "Muslim Ban" executive order among people born in Muslim-majority countries and living in the US. *JAMA Network Open, 4*(7), e2118216-e2118216.

Sanchez, J. C. (2018). Trump, the KKK, and the Versatility of White Supremacy Rhetoric. *Journal of Contemporary Rhetoric, 8*(1/2), 44–56.

Sardar, Z., & Davies, M. W. (2010). Freeze framing Muslims: Hollywood and the slideshow of Western imagination. *Interventions, 12*(2), 239–250.

Schaffner, B. F. (2013). Support at Any Distance? The Role of Location and Prejudice in Public Opposition to the "Ground Zero Mosque." *PS: Political Science and Politics, 46*(4), 753–759.

Schmuck, D., Heiss, R., & Matthes, J. (2020). Drifting Further Apart? How Exposure to Media Portrayals of Muslims Affects Attitude Polarization. Political Psychology, 41(6), 1055–1072. https://doi.org/10.2307/45379088

Schmuck, D., & Matthes, J. (2019). Voting "Against Islamization"? How Anti-Islamic Right-Wing, Populist Political Campaign Ads Influence Explicit and Implicit Attitudes Toward Muslims as Well as Voting Preferences. *Political Psychology, 40*(4), 739–757. https://doi.org/10.1111/pops.12557

Shaver, J. H., Sibley, C. G., Osborne, D., & Bulbulia, J. (2017). News exposure predicts anti-Muslim prejudice. *PLoS ONE, 12*(3), e0174606. https://doi.org/10.1371/journal.pone.0174606

Sibley, C. G., Afzali, M. U., Satherley, N., Ejova, A., Stronge, S., Yogeeswaran, K., Grimshaw, M., Hawi, D., Mirnajafi, Z., Barlow, F. K., Milojev, P., Greaves, L. M., Kapeli, S., Zubielevitch, E., Hamley, L., Basabas, M. C., Wu, M. H., Howard, C., Lee, C. H. J., & Yanshu Huang. (2020). Prejudice toward Muslims in New Zealand: Insights from the New Zealand Attitudes and Values Study. New Zealand Journal of Psychology, 49(1), 48–72.

Speakman, B., & Bagasra, A. (2022). Reinforcing Islamophobic Rhetoric Through the Use of Facebook Comments: A Study of Imagined Community. *Journal of Communication & Religion, 45*(1).

Starr, P. (2020). The Flooded Zone: How we became more vulnerable to disinformation in the digital age. In *The Disinformation Age*. Cambridge University Press. 2020.

Swain, C. M. (2002). *The new white nationalism in America: Its Challenge to Integration*. Cambridge University Press.

Takim, L. (2011). The Ground Zero Mosque Controversy: Implications for

American Islam. *Religions*, *2*(2), 132-144. https://doi.org/10.3390/rel2020132

Taras, R. (2024). Xenophobia, Islamophobia, and the Media: When Prejudice Runs Amok. *Medya ve Din Araştırmaları Dergisi*, *7*(1), 1–13. https://doi.org/10.47951/mediad.1497590

Uddin, A. (2019). *When Islam is not a religion: Inside America's fight for religious freedom.* New York: Pegasus Books.

Vaidhyanathan, S. (2018). *Antisocial media: How Facebook disconnects us and undermines democracy.* Oxford University Press.

Valenzuela, S., Piña, M., & Ramírez, J. (2017). Behavioral effects of framing on social media users: How conflict, economic, human interest, and morality frames drive news sharing. *Journal of Communication*, *67*(5), 803–826.

Vidgen, B., Yasseri, T., & Margetts, H. (2022). Islamophobes are not all the same! A study of far-right actors on Twitter. *Journal of Policing, Intelligence and Counter Terrorism*, *17*(1), 1–23.

von Sikorski, C., Schmuck, D., Matthes, J., & Binder, A. (2017). "Muslims are not Terrorists": Islamic State Coverage, Journalistic Differentiation Between Terrorism and Islam, Fear Reactions, and Attitudes Toward Muslims. *Mass Communication & Society*, *20*(6), 825–848. https://doi.org/10.1080/15205436.2017.1342131

Wilkins, L. S. (2018). Islamophobia in Canada: Measuring the Realities of Negative Attitudes Toward Muslims and Religious Discrimination. *Canadian Review of Sociology*, *55*(1), 86–110. https://doi.org/10.1111/cars.12180

Woods, H. S., & Hahner, L. A. (2019). *Make America meme again: The rhetoric of the Alt-right.* Peter Lang New York.

Yang, A., & Self, C. (2015). Anti-Muslim prejudice in the virtual space: A case study of blog network structure and message features of the "Ground Zero mosque controversy." *Media, War & Conflict*, *8*(1), 46–69.

Zerback, T., & Karadas, N. (2023). They will hate us for this: effects of media coverage of Islamist terror attacks on Muslims' perceptions of public opinion, perceived risk of victimization, and behavioral intentions. *Human Communication Research* *49*(3), 227–237. https://doi.org/10.1093/hcr/hqac030

Zúquete, J. P. (2016). The European extreme-right and Islam: New directions? In *The Populist Radical Right* (pp. 121–141). Routledge.

CHAPTER EIGHTEEN

WORKPLACE MENTAL HEALTH IN NORTH AMERICA WITH MUSLIM EMPLOYEES

Raymond H. Hamden, Aysha Mazoon

Mental health challenges in the workplace significantly affect employee well-being and productivity. This chapter explores the unique mental health issues Muslim employees face in Western countries, including psychological strain, burnout, and discrimination. These challenges hinder performance and emphasize the need for effective coping mechanisms.

The text highlights forms of religious and racial discrimination that increase stress and worsen mental health, stressing the importance of targeted support and inclusive practices. It also discusses the rise of research on Islamophobia and its mental health impacts since September 11, coupled with ongoing cultural misunderstandings. Statistical data showcases the mental health disparities experienced by Muslim individuals, highlighting the urgent need for inclusive policies and supportive environments. The chapter concludes by offering solutions to promote workplace inclusivity and better support Muslim employees.

Overview of Mental Health Challenges in the Workplace

Mental health issues permeate all aspects of life, with the World Health Organization (2022) (WHO) reporting one in four individuals experiencing these challenges at some point. The WHO describes mental health as a state of well-being where people can fulfill their potential, manage everyday life stress, perform effectively at work, and are able to contribute positively to their community. Unlike physical ailment or diagnosed mental illness, mental health problems often manifest through less obvious symptoms, such as stress and burnout, which can significantly impact employee well-being.

Psychological strain is characterized by prolonged distress and tension, leading to deteriorating mental health and well-being. Although not classified as a diagnosable mental illness in the DSM-5, it falls within the 'injured' or 'struggling' categories of the mental health continuum, with symptoms including anxiety, poor sleep quality, diminished performance, and depressive signs (Delphis, 2020). In organizational contexts, psychological strain arises from sustained stress responses due to continuous stressors, leading to physiological changes and heightened psychological and physical arousal.

Burnout, similarly, is an occupational phenomenon marked by emotional exhaustion, cynicism, and detachment (Kelloway, Dimoff & Gilbert, 2023). Burnout can result from a lack of control, unclear job expectations, dysfunctional workplace dynamics, mismatched values, poor job fit, and extreme activities (Hamden, 2016, 2018). Mental health issues can lead to decreased job performance, slower productivity, and increased errors. Effective coping mechanisms are crucial, with positive strategies including acknowledging one's condition, taking breaks, seeking medical help, engaging in mindfulness practices, fostering open communication, using humor, and adopting compensatory measures.

Topical Importance within the Context of Muslim Employees in Western Countries

Muslim employees in Western countries face unique and heightened mental health challenges. The COVID-19 pandemic has exacerbated stress levels, with over 80% of American Muslim healthcare workers reporting increased stress and around 60% feeling anger daily. Discrimination is a significant factor, with 47% experiencing workplace discrimination, 19% facing Islamophobia, and 22% encountering racial discrimination (Institute for Social Policy and Understanding [ISPU] & the Stanford Muslim Mental Health & Islamic Psychology Lab, 2022). These discriminatory experiences correlate with significantly higher risks of psychological distress, emphasizing the need for targeted mental health support for Muslim employees. The subsequent sections of this chapter, titled "Workplace Mental Health in North America with Muslim Employees," will delve deeper into these specific challenges. The further sections will explore historical and current instances of discrimination, examine the impact of mental health on job performance, and propose effective strategies and solutions to mitigate these challenges. This chapter aims to provide meaningful insights and actionable recommendations to enhance workplace inclusivity and, thereby, help improve overall performance for Muslim employees.

Historical Context

Early Instances and Patterns of Discrimination Against Muslims in Western Workplaces

In an increasingly interconnected world, the contrast between the peaceful teachings of Islam and the harsh realities of religious supremacy and fear has become stark. The discrimination against Muslims in Western societies has been exacerbated by events such as the 9/11 attacks and other global terror incidents. These events have fueled Islamophobia, overshadowing Islam's core message of peace and leading to distorted perceptions of religious supremacy. While all major religions advocate for peace and harmony, the extremist groups within these communities often propagate hostility to assert dominance. Movements from different religious fundamentalists and political and ideological factions have instigated violence across religious lines, posing significant threats to global peace for political gains (Cesari, 2015).

The hijab controversy, which began in France in 1989, gained momentum in 2010 and rapidly spread to other parts of the West, including the USA, particularly after events like 9/11 (Diallo, 2018). This escalation has given rise to "Hijabophobia," a specific form of Islamophobia that targets Muslim women who wear the hijab or veil. Hijabophobia represents religious, social, and cultural discrimination and hatred against these women, who often become targets due to the hijab being a clear, visible symbol of their Muslim identity (Ussif, Ussif & Yussif, 2020).

After 9/11, the hijab, which is a noticeable part of Muslim women's clothing, has often been wrongly viewed in Western countries as a barrier to social integration and national unity, as well as a symbol of gender oppression and inequality (Paz & Kook, 2021). Studies have highlighted the negative impact of wearing the hijab on Muslim women, revealing that those who wear it more frequently are more likely to experience religious discrimination (Hodge, Zidan & Husain, 2023).

Another study specifically examined the relationship between discrimination and psychological distress among Muslim women in the United States, focusing on the concept of "solo status"—being the only Muslim in various settings. The study found that for women who always wear the hijab, high solo status exacerbated the effects of discrimination, leading to increased symptoms of anxiety, somatization, and paranoia. Conversely, for Muslim women who do not wear the hijab, low solo status amplified the impact of discrimination on these psychological symptoms (Hashem & Awad, 2024). However, such stereotypes and inaccuracies regarding the hijab arise partly due to a lack of knowledge on the subject within Western society. This lack of understanding can lead to further negative consequences for Muslim women who choose to wear the hijab (Marzouk, 2021).

Globalization has also contributed to the spread of Islamophobia by promoting concepts such as modernism, consumer culture, democratic governance, and human rights, which contrast with the ideology of political Islam. This has facilitated the spread of Islamophobia as a seemingly rational outcome of globalization in affected countries and societies (Bordbar et al., 2020). For instance, a study examining the discrimination experienced by Arab and Muslim children and families as a direct consequence of the events of September 11, 2001, and the subsequent war on terror, found that these communities faced increased prejudice, social exclusion, and heightened surveillance, negatively affecting their social integration and mental health (Sirin, Choi & Tugberk, 2021). These findings underscore the profound and lasting impact of national and global security measures on the mental health of the Arab and Muslim populations, emphasizing the need for policies that address these challenges while safeguarding their rights and well-being.

Evolution of Awareness Regarding Mental Health Issues Among Muslim Population

The twentieth century witnessed relatively little research on Islamophobia compared to the significant increase seen in the first two decades of the twenty-first century. A meta-analysis on Islamophobia found minimal research in the 20th century, with only 43 articles published between 1901 and 2000. However, after September 11, 2001, interest in this area surged dramatically. From 2001 to 2020, the number of articles rose to 7,601, showing how these events not only raised concerns about Islamophobia but also significantly increased academic attention to it (Sufi & Yasmin, 2022).

Power distance refers to the extent to which a culture recognizes and accepts the unequal distribution of power within society (Lin, Wang & Chen, 2013). In today's globalized world, where cultures increasingly intermingle, individuals are more apt to form intercultural friendships. While these friendships can present challenges, they also offer opportunities for mutual growth and steps toward social justice.

An autoethnographic study examines the interplay between interculturality and friendship amid the Israeli-Palestinian conflict, a setting generally unfavorable for Arab-Jewish friendships. In this study, a Jewish Israeli of Dutch descent investigates his friendship with a Palestinian Bedouin, navigating through the complexities delineated by Hofstede's cultural dimensions: individualism versus collectivism, uncertainty avoidance, power distance, and the spectrum of masculinity to femininity. Despite stark contrasts in their cultural frameworks, their relationship presents significant challenges and unique opportunities for bridging these gaps. The analysis reveals how cultural differences emerge in their interactions, affecting them on emotional, cognitive, and behavioral levels. The research advocates refining the 'uncertainty avoidance' dimension into two more precise categories, 'tradition' and 'discipline,' to address inconsistencies with Hofstede's original theory.

Concluding with a reflection on the broader ramifications of their intercultural friendship, the study highlights the profound influence of power distance on such relationships, underscoring its implications for personal growth, professional development, and the pursuit of social justice (Weishut, 2020).

Understanding the historical context and the evolution of awareness regarding mental health issues among minority groups, particularly Muslims in Western workplaces, provides a foundation for addressing these challenges. The following sections will delve deeper into the specific challenges faced by Muslim employees, exploring historical and current instances of discrimination and examining the impact of mental health on their job performance.

It will also consider effective strategies and solutions to mitigate these challenges, enhance workplace inclusivity, and improve overall performance. This comprehensive analysis aims to provide meaningful insights and actionable recommendations to foster a more inclusive and supportive work environment for Muslim employees.

Research on Muslims Who Exhibit Islamophobia and its Impact on Mental Health

In the realm of psychological and sociological research, the study of Muslims who exhibit Islamophobic attitudes presents a unique and intricate paradox. Islamophobia, by definition, denotes prejudice or discrimination against Muslims, making it seemingly contradictory for a Muslim to harbor such sentiments (Pratt & Woodlock, 2016). However, various instances have revealed that individuals who identify as Muslim can indeed express or internalize negative attitudes toward their religion or community. This phenomenon can arise from multiple underlying factors, each contributing to a deeper understanding of this complex issue.

Internalized Islamophobia

One significant factor is the internalization of negative stereotypes about Islam and Muslims. Societal pressures, pervasive media portrayals, or adverse personal experiences can drive this internalization. When individuals are constantly exposed to negative depictions of their faith, they may begin to absorb these views, leading to a form of self-directed Islamophobia (Suleiman, 2017).

Political or Ideological Motivations

Another dimension involves political or ideological motivations. In some instances, individuals who identify as Muslim may adhere to strong nationalist, secular, or even extremist ideologies that conflict with their religious beliefs (Hibbard, 2015). These ideological stances can lead them to criticize or disparage Islam or other Muslims as part of a broader political or ideological agenda.

Cultural Influences

Cultural influences also play a crucial role in shaping attitudes towards Islam. Within some communities, cultural norms or practices may diverge from Islamic teachings, prompting individuals to reject aspects of the religion. This cultural dissonance can manifest as hostility towards Islam, mainly when cultural identity precedes religious identity (Wani, Abdullah & Chang, 2015).

Rejection of Identity

The struggle with religious identity is another contributing factor. Individuals facing personal challenges or grappling with their religious identity may distance themselves from Islam (Voas & Fleischmann, 2012). This distancing can evolve into negative attitudes towards religion, especially if they perceive it as a source of conflict or difficulty.

Such attitudes portrayed by Muslim Americans have significantly impacted their mental health, affecting their overall well-being and sense of self. These internalized negative beliefs, stemming from widespread Islamophobic rhetoric, have influenced their daily and personal perceptions, leading to a range of psychological and emotional challenges. For instance, a study aimed at understanding the lived experiences of Muslim Americans with Islamophobia revealed that many participants specifically struggled with internalizing Islamophobic rhetoric throughout their lives. This internalization led to profound psychological effects, with several participants reporting feelings of insecurity and self-worth. For example, one participant shared that Islamophobia had hindered her identity development and confidence during her upbringing, illustrating the profound and lasting impact of such experiences (Ali, 2021).

Imam Suleiman (2017) suggests that internalized Islamophobia often operates on a subconscious level and is particularly prevalent among younger individuals. These young people frequently report experiencing feelings of indifference, identity crisis, fear, and feelings of oppression when associated with visibly portraying their Muslim identity, such as wearing a hijab. This internalization of islamophobia attitudes leads them to struggle with their cultural and religious identity, making them fearful of expressing their faith openly and feeling oppressed by societal expectations and prejudices and as a result, resulting in lower self-esteem and overall well-being as a result from subconsciously accepting the prevailing society's stereotypes on one's ethnic group.

Research in this field delves into the intersections of identity, social context, and personal beliefs to elucidate how these factors influence attitudes toward Islam and Muslims. It is an evolving area of study that demands a nuanced understanding of individual psychology and broader social dynamics. By exploring these multifaceted influences, researchers aim to uncover the underlying mechanisms that lead some Muslims to adopt Islamophobic views, ultimately contributing to a more comprehensive understanding of the complexities of identity and prejudice within religious communities.

Current Media Propagation of Discrimination and Its Impact on Identity Management

Currently, discrimination continues to be extensively propagated through media channels, significantly influencing societal norms and individual behaviors. It is the primary source of perpetuating negative stereotypes of Muslims and spreading fear of Islam. Widespread feelings of fear and apprehension regarding hate crimes have become prevalent among Muslim Americans, particularly following negative media portrayals of Islam (Haque, Tubbs, Kahumoku-Fessler & Brown, 2019). Such experiences are found to be associated with poor psychological health, social well-being (Samari, Alcalá & Sharif, 2018), and identity crisis (Saleem & Ramasubramanian, 2019). A survey conducted among Muslim young adults in Genesee County, Michigan—where Muslims constitute 2.6% of the population—revealed that certain discriminatory experiences significantly impacted their identification as solely Muslim or both Muslim and American. The study found that being accused or suspected of wrongdoing because of their Muslim identity was a strong predictor of this identity choice. Specifically, the probability of a young Muslim identifying only as Muslim increases to 43.1% when they sometimes experience such accusations, compared to 32.8% for those who never face this form of discrimination (Hummel, Daassa, Alshabani & Felo, 2020). This profound impact of media portrayals on the experiences of discrimination among Muslim Americans.

Furthermore, numerous participants also reported that media coverage of attacks on individuals who appear to be Muslim and on Muslim places of worship instills fear and apprehension about leaving the safety of their homes. Additionally, they expressed concerns about potential retaliatory attacks by right-wing individuals or groups (Haque, Tubbs, Kahumoku-Fessler & Brown, 2019).

These results underscore the profound influence of media and personal experiences of discrimination on the social identities of minority group members, exacerbating the challenges in intergroup relations between minority and majority groups.

Research has increasingly shown that internalized Islamophobia can lead Muslims to question their religion as they internalize widespread discrimination against Muslims (Gil-Benumeya, 2023). A comprehensive study reviewing 87 journal articles from 2002 to 2021 focused on Islamophobia and its impact on young Muslims, particularly in Western countries like the UK, USA, and Australia. This descriptive analysis highlighted a significant increase in empirical studies over the last five years, especially within educational contexts. The findings revealed four recurrent themes: Islamophobia, identity, school experiences, and gender-specific issues. These themes showed that young Muslims from minority backgrounds are often compelled to negotiate and navigate their identities in response to external pressures and discrimination. This process involves altering their behaviors and potentially questioning their religious beliefs to conform to the prevailing social identities. The studies particularly highlighted 'identity negotiation strategies' as a critical area of concern, illustrating how these young individuals feel pressured to reshape their identities. This identity negotiation is often a response to trying to fit into a society where they face religious bullying and gendered discrimination, which are predominant in educational settings (Farooqui & Kaushik, 2022).

As this exploration into the history of Muslim discrimination concludes, it is evident that this issue is deeply rooted in complex socio-political dynamics spanning centuries. From early confrontations during the

Crusades to the profound impact of the 9/11 attacks, Islamophobia has evolved and intensified, driven by global events and shaped by cultural and media portrayals. This historical context underscores the challenges inherent in reconciling the peaceful teachings of Islam with the harsh realities of discrimination and prejudice perpetuated in various forms. Fostering understanding and dialogue across cultures is crucial to address and mitigate these deep-seated issues, promoting a more inclusive and just global society.

Current Issues and Concerns

Specific Mental Health Challenges Faced by Muslim Employees

Muslim employees encounter unique mental health challenges that are intertwined with their cultural and religious identities. These challenges often arise from discrimination, cultural misunderstandings, and power distancing in the workplace. For instance, hijab-wearing Muslim women face significant employment discrimination compared to their non-hijab-wearing counterparts. A meta-analysis of seven studies from 2010 to 2020 revealed that hijab-wearing Muslim women are 40% less likely to be hired than Muslim women who do not wear the hijab (Ahmed & Gorey, 2023). This discrimination is likely driven by employer prejudices towards the hijab, highlighting the need for policy reevaluation and future research to address these biases.

Role of Politicians on Islamophobia and its Effect on the Workplace Environment for Muslims

Islamophobia has been an ongoing issue in the United States, particularly within its political sphere, including Congress. Over recent years, the actions and rhetoric of certain politicians have contributed to an environment where Muslims, along with their workplaces and organizations, continue to be subjected to mass surveillance and discrimination. According to the Pew Research Center from NBCUniversal News Group (2022, January 7), Muslims are consistently ranked unfavorably in public opinion surveys, often alongside atheists, and political polarization has further intensified negative perceptions of Islam, especially among Republicans who are more likely to associate the religion with violence. This political climate has profound effects on Muslim employees in the workplace. As they navigate their professional environments, many are confronted with colleagues who harbor prejudice, fear, and mistrust towards them solely based on their religious identity.

The atmosphere can become toxic, with some Muslim employees knowing that lies and negative stereotypes are being spread about them and their community. The lack of human resources and management support exacerbates this situation, leaving these individuals without resources to address their concerns or improve the hostile work environment. Recent inflammatory remarks by politicians, such as those by Rep. Borbert, have only heightened this climate of Islamophobia, leading to increased anxiety and fear among Muslim staff, their families, and communities (NBCUniversal News Group, 2022, January 7). This situation underscored the urgent need for stronger support from leaders and organizations to counteract the harmful effects of such political rhetoric on the well-being of Muslim employees.

Statistical Overview of Mental Health Disparities Affecting Muslims in the Workplace

The American Psychiatric Association (2018) reports that Muslim Americans, a diverse community originating from various parts of the world, face significant mental health disparities due to religious discrimination.

Data from the Council on American-Islamic Relations [CAIR]

According to CAIR reports from 2023, which constitute 20% of all complaints, 15% of Muslim Americans experienced employment discrimination, and 8.5% faced education discrimination. Additionally, hate crimes and incidents were among the most frequently reported categories. The reports also indicated that anti-Muslim incidents have increased by 56% compared to previous years (Allison, 2023, April 2). This type of discrimination contributes to mental health conditions such as depression and anxiety (American Psychiatric Association, 2018). Moreover, Muslim career women have reported that workplace discrimination significantly impacts their mental health, leading to increased stress and anxiety levels, which hinder their professional growth and deteriorate their psychological well-being (Hankir, Carrick & Zaman, 2015).

This highlights the pressing need for further research to better understand the unique challenges faced by Muslim women in the workplace. This can help explore the extent of discrimination, its specific effects on mental health, and the mechanisms through which it impacts professional development. Such research could inform the development of targeted interventions and policies to create more inclusive and supportive work environments for Muslim career women, ultimately promoting their well-being and professional success.

Impact of Cultural Misunderstandings and Discrimination

Cultural misunderstandings and discrimination in the workplace exacerbate mental health issues for Muslim employees. These experiences often stem from ignorance or misconceptions about Islamic practices and beliefs. The stereotype and stigma associated with Muslims, especially post-9/11, contribute to a hostile work environment. However, faith in Islam can act as a resilience factor. A longitudinal study by Abdul Aziz & Ahmad (2021) found that despite facing religious discrimination, Muslim women's strong belief in Islam positively influenced their well-being and career outcomes, demonstrating that faith can mitigate the negative impact of discrimination on mental health.

Power Distancing

Power distance, or the extent to which less powerful members of organizations accept unequal power distribution, plays a significant role in the workplace experiences of Muslim employees. High power distance cultures reinforce hierarchical structures, exacerbating feelings of exclusion and discrimination among minority groups (Trzebiatowski & Triana, 2020). Understanding and addressing power distance is crucial in creating a more inclusive workplace environment where Muslim employees feel valued and respected.

Case Studies or Recent Incidents Highlighting Current Challenges

Recent incidents and studies provide insight into the ongoing challenges faced by Muslim employees. For instance, the discrimination faced by hijab-wearing Muslim women in employment processes underscores the broader issue of religious bias in hiring practices. Additionally, personal accounts and studies highlight how discrimination impacts mental health and identity management among Muslim employees. The experiences of Muslim American students, who report withdrawing from seeking acceptance and avoiding interactions with majority members due to negative media portrayals and personal experiences of discrimination, illustrate the profound influence of societal biases on minority groups (Saleem & Ramasubramanian, 2019).

As this exploration into the current issues and concerns facing Muslim employees concludes, it is clear that systemic discrimination has profound impacts on their mental health and workplace experiences. With a significant portion of the Muslim American community facing discrimination, it is crucial to transition toward discussing the developments and positive changes that can mitigate these challenges. The following section will explore the existing initiatives and potential strategies to improve inclusivity and equality, promoting a healthier and more equitable workplace environment for all.

Development and Positive Changes

Mental Health Programs and Workplace Inclusion

In recent years, Western workplaces have increasingly recognized the importance of mental health, developing various initiatives and programs designed to support employees' well-being. These include Employee Assistance Programs (EAPs), which offer confidential counseling and support services for employees dealing with personal or work-related issues (Attridge, 2023). Mental Health Training programs provide managers and employees with the skills to recognize and respond to mental health issues, such as Mental Health First Aid (Carleton et al., 2020). Wellness Programs incorporate yoga, mindfulness sessions, and stress management workshops to promote overall well-being (Jones, Molitor & Reif, 2019). Flexible Work Arrangements allow for remote work, flexible hours, and additional leave to help employees manage their mental health better. Mental Health Days encourage employees to take time off specifically for mental health, reducing stigma and promoting self-care (Shifrin & Michel, 2022).

Successful Inclusion Strategies in Western Workplaces

Various Western workplaces have implemented inclusive strategies to ensure diversity is viewed as an asset. Cultural Competence Training educates employees about different cultures, religions, and practices to foster a more inclusive environment (Shepherd et al., 2019). Diversity and Inclusion Policies establish clear guidelines and expectations for inclusive behavior and practices within the organization (Tamtik & Guenter, 2019). Employee Resource Groups (ERGs) support networks for employees from diverse backgrounds, including religious groups, providing a sense of community and advocacy within the workplace (Foldy, 2019). Inclusive Recruitment Practices ensure that job postings, hiring processes, and promotional opportunities are accessible and fair to all candidates, regardless of background (Coleman, Dossett & Dimick, 2021). Open Dialogues and Discussions encourage conversations about diversity, inclusion, and personal experiences to build understanding and empathy among employees (Al-Hadrawi, 2023).

Policy Changes and Management Practices in Promoting Mental Health

Policy changes and management practices are crucial in fostering a supportive organizational climate. Inclusive Policies that explicitly support mental health and diversity must be communicated and implemented effectively. Leadership Commitment involves leaders demonstrating a commitment to mental health and inclusion by modeling supportive behaviors and prioritizing these values in decision-making (Abdullah, Ling,

& Ping, 2017). Regular assessments, such as surveys to gauge employee well-being and the effectiveness of mental health and inclusion initiatives, can help organizations make necessary adjustments based on feedback (Van der Schaaf et al., 2017). Resource Allocation ensures that sufficient resources are dedicated to mental health and inclusion programs, making them sustainable and impactful. Transparent communication maintains open lines of communication about mental health and inclusion efforts, fostering trust and encouraging employee engagement.

Impact of Inclusive Organizational Climates on Muslim Employees

An exploratory study examined the impact of inclusive organizational climates on Muslim diaspora members within Western workforces. Key findings from interviews with 30 Muslim employees across industries in Australia, New Zealand, the United States, and Canada include positive employee outcomes, where inclusive environments contribute positively to employee well-being, job satisfaction, and overall organizational goals. Muslim employees preferred workplaces that encouraged open discussions about faith, values, and practices, enhancing personal interactions. The study is grounded in social exchange theory and underscores the importance of personal-level coworker interactions in fostering inclusion (Khan, Afroze & Zaman, 2022).

Social Exchange Theory in Workplace Inclusion

Social exchange theory focuses on reciprocal resource exchanges and is crucial in understanding workplace behavior. This theory provides a framework for understanding how relationships and exchanges impact workplace dynamics. Psychological Transactions, or further exploring psychological perspectives on social exchange theory, can advance its application and relevance in workplace inclusion (Cropanzano et al., 2017). Addressing critiques about the lack of precise theoretical grounding can enhance the practical application of social exchange theory in fostering inclusive environments.

Advancements in mental health initiatives and inclusive strategies in Western workplaces pave the way for more supportive and diverse environments. By addressing mental health concerns, promoting inclusive practices, and understanding the role of policy changes and management practices, organizations can create climates that benefit all employees, including those from diverse backgrounds, like the Muslim diaspora.

Effective Job Performance and Productivity

Link Between Mental Health and Job Performance Among Muslim Employees

Mental health plays a critical role in job performance, particularly among Muslim employees. Research indicates that religiosity significantly impacts work engagement and job performance. For instance, a study examined the impact of Islamic work ethics on employee performance and counterproductive work behavior, with job satisfaction being a moderator between Islamic work ethics and employee performance and counterproductive work behavior. Results found that Islamic work ethic positively affects employee performance while negatively impacting Counterproductive Work Behavior (Naeem & Rashid, 2023). Consequently, the study suggests that management and relevant authorities should promote Islamic work ethics among employees to improve their job satisfaction and performance.

Research on How Mental Well-being Influences Productivity and Work Relationships

Mental well-being significantly influences productivity and work relationships. Key findings from the research include enhanced engagement, where religiosity enhances employee engagement, boosting job performance (Nwachukwu, Chládková, Agboga & Vu, 2021). Engaged employees are more involved and enthusiastic about their tasks, contributing positively to organizational success. Personal religiosity moderates the effects of job strain on well-being. A study involving 117 Muslim academic and administrative employees in Malaysian universities showed that personal religiosity significantly mitigates job strain and enhances well-being (Achour, Mohd Nor & Mohd Yusoff, 2016). Teachers' job satisfaction, well-being, and emotional intelligence positively influence their engagement at work, demonstrating that employee engagement significantly enhances job performance regardless of religiosity (Sudibjo & Sutarji, 2020).

Barriers to Effective Performance Due to Mental Health Issues

Mental health issues can undermine job performance through various mechanisms, such as reduced work quality, slower pace, and increased errors. Negative coping strategies, such as substance abuse, hiding symptoms, and overworking when unwell, can worsen job performance outcomes (Hennekam, Richard & Grima, 2020). Muslim employees may face additional workplace discrimination and stressors not experienced by non-Muslim peers, magnifying the challenges to their mental health and work output.

Coping Strategies and Their Impact

Coping strategies can have mixed effects on job performance. Negative approaches, such as substance abuse and hiding symptoms, often worsen mental health and job performance (Frone, 2015). Positive approaches, such as acknowledging one's condition, taking breaks, engaging in therapy, practicing mindfulness, maintaining open communication, utilizing humor, and applying compensatory techniques, can enhance job performance (López-Cabarcos, Vázquez-Rodríguez & Quiñoá-Piñeiro, 2022).

The research underscores the significant impact that mental health has on job performance. Mental well-being directly influences the quality and efficiency of work, with effective coping strategies potentially enhancing performance (Hennekam, Richard & Grima, 2020). For Muslim employees who may face additional stressors and discrimination, addressing mental health concerns is crucial to improving their job performance and overall well-being.

Given the complexity of these issues, the following section will explore strategies to improve workplace inclusivity and support for Muslim employees. This will include discussions on effective programs and resources, recommendations for employers, policymakers, and mental health professionals, and directions for future research. This comprehensive approach aims to foster a more supportive and productive workplace environment for all, acknowledging Muslim employees' unique challenges.

Solutions and Recommendations for Workplace Inclusivity and Support for Muslim Employees

Individual-Level Interventions and Recommendations

In a bustling modern workplace, the journey towards inclusiveness and mental health support begins with small yet significant steps at the individual level. For Muslim employees, sharing personal information highlighting their unique characteristics, traits, and skills becomes a powerful tool in breaking down stereotypes. When colleagues learn about their interests, hobbies, and professional achievements, they see a fuller picture, reducing reliance on group categorizations (Singletary & Hebl, 2009). This nuanced understanding fosters a more inclusive atmosphere where everyone is seen for who they are beyond their religious identity.

Providing positive counter-stereotypical information further reshapes perceptions. Imagine a workplace where the success stories of Muslim employees are highlighted, showcasing their contributions and altering preconceived notions. This strategy effectively improves customer satisfaction, changes views about various groups and helps create a more favorable and accurate image (Lindsey, King, McCausland, Jones, & Dunleavy, 2013). Highlighting these positive examples can transform a workplace into a more welcoming environment.

Small actions make a big difference, too. Verbal and nonverbal cues like frequent smiling and affirmative language help shape perceptions positively (Ryan & Gardner, 2021). These gestures convey friendliness and openness, representing individuals distinctly from negative group stereotypes. Through radiating positivity, Muslim employees challenge and change the often unfair assumptions held about them, paving the way for better interpersonal connections.

Allies from dominant or majority groups play a crucial role in this transformation. These allies support and advocate for better organizational policies and create a more inclusive workplace environment (Sabat et al., 2014). Whether it is standing up against discrimination or promoting the inclusion of diverse voices, allies help amplify the efforts of marginalized groups. Building these alliances is essential for creating a supportive network where everyone feels valued and understood.

Organizational-Level Interventions and Recommendations

At the organizational level, the implementation of religious accommodation is key. For many Muslim employees, practicing their faith is integral to their lives. Policies that accommodate religious practices, such as designated prayer spaces and flexible scheduling for religious observances, support them in maintaining their spiritual commitments without conflict (Garcia-Yeste, Mara, de Botton & Duque, 2022). These accommodations signal respect and recognition of diverse religious needs, fostering a more inclusive and respectful workplace.

Adopting learning and access perspectives on diversity management recognizes diversity as a strategic advantage. Implementing diversity audits and fostering open dialogues about religious and cultural differences create a more inclusive environment (Roberson, 2006; McKay et al., 2009). These practices encourage continuous learning and adaptation, ensuring that diversity is acknowledged, actively celebrated and integrated into the organizational culture.

Promoting minority representation in leadership roles is another crucial step. Techniques like adopting counter-stereotypical exemplars and implementing affirmative action programs reduce implicit biases (FitzGerald, Martin, Berner & Hurst, 2019). When employees see diverse leaders, it challenges stereotypes and demonstrates that the organization values and practices inclusion at all levels. This representation inspires and motivates all employees, creating a more equitable and dynamic workplace.

Facilitating meaningful interactions between diverse groups within the workplace can reduce prejudice and promote understanding. Structured intergroup contact, supported by organizational policies, significantly improves leadership diversity and workplace harmony (Ensari & Riggio, 2023). These interactions help break down barriers and build empathy, creating a more cohesive and collaborative work environment.

Programs and resources currently available in workplaces also play a vital role. Employee Resource Groups (ERGs) for Muslim employees provide support networks and advocacy within the organization (Casey, 2021). These groups foster a sense of community and belonging, offering a platform for members to share experiences, seek support, and advocate for their needs. The presence of ERGs greatly enhances the workplace's inclusivity and supportiveness.

Cultural competence training programs educate employees about different cultures and religions, enhancing understanding and reducing biases (Brottman, Char, Hattori, Heeb & Taff, 2020). These programs contribute to a more inclusive workplace by equipping employees with the knowledge and skills to interact respectfully and effectively with colleagues from diverse backgrounds. Mental health and wellness programs that include mindfulness, stress management, and counseling support employee well-being and productivity (Waddell et al., 2023). These programs recognize the importance of mental health and provide resources to help employees manage stress and maintain a healthy work-life balance.

Offering flexible work hours and remote work options helps employees better manage their personal and professional lives, reducing stress and improving performance (Vyas, 2022). These arrangements demonstrate the organization's commitment to accommodating diverse needs and promoting work-life balance.

Employers, policymakers, and mental health professionals each have a role in fostering an inclusive and supportive workplace. Employers should develop and enforce policies that support religious diversity and mental health. Encouraging open dialogues about diversity, inclusion, and mental health builds a supportive work environment. Providing training and resources on cultural competence and mental health is essential for creating an informed and supportive workplace (Flynn et al., 2020).

Policymakers can enact laws protecting employees from discrimination based on religion and mental health conditions and incentivize organizations to implement diversity and inclusion programs (Wu et al., 2021). Mental health professionals should ensure that mental health services are accessible to all employees, including those from diverse backgrounds. Training mental health professionals on cultural sensitivity and the specific needs of Muslim employees enhances the effectiveness of mental health care.

By taking these individual and organizational-level steps and providing supportive programs and resources, workplaces can become more inclusive and supportive environments for all employees, including those from diverse backgrounds like the Muslim community. Through these efforts, employers, policymakers, and mental health professionals can work together to create workplaces where everyone feels valued and empowered.

Future Directions and Conclusion

As we conclude this exploration into the mental health and workplace inclusion of Muslim employees, it is clear that while significant strides have been made, there remains much ground to cover. Looking ahead, several key future directions emerge, providing a roadmap for fostering a more inclusive and supportive environment.

Firstly, the development and implementation of comprehensive anti-discrimination policies are crucial. These policies must prohibit discrimination and harassment based on religion, ensuring they are clearly communicated and regularly reviewed. Additionally, organizations should create and enforce policies that accommodate religious practices, such as prayer times, dietary requirements, and religious holidays, demonstrating a commitment to inclusivity.

Cultural competence training plays a vital role in this journey. Regular training programs should be implemented for all employees, focusing on religious diversity and inclusion. Specialized training for managers and leaders is equally important, equipping them with the skills needed to support and manage a diverse workforce effectively.

Mental health support is another critical area. Ensuring that mental health services are accessible to all employees, including culturally competent counselors who understand the specific needs of Muslim employees, is essential. Enhancing Employee Assistance Programs (EAPs) to include support for religious and cultural issues will provide confidential counseling and resources, contributing to a healthier work environment.

Employee Resource Groups (ERGs) offer a valuable platform for fostering inclusion. Encouraging the formation and active support of ERGs for Muslim employees can create safe spaces for sharing experiences and advocating for their needs. Promoting interfaith networks within the organization will further understanding and collaboration among employees of different religious backgrounds.

Inclusive workplace practices must be prioritized. Implementing flexible work schedules that allow for religious observances, such as prayer times and fasting during Ramadan, is vital.

Additionally, providing facilities that cater to the needs of Muslim employees, such as prayer rooms and halal food options in cafeterias, demonstrates a commitment to inclusivity.

Awareness campaigns are essential for educating the broader workforce about the importance of religious diversity and inclusion. Sharing stories and testimonials from Muslim employees can highlight their experiences and contributions, fostering a more inclusive environment.

Continuous research and feedback mechanisms are necessary to understand Muslim employees' evolving needs and challenges. Establishing anonymous feedback mechanisms will allow organizations to gather insights regularly and assess the effectiveness of inclusion initiatives.

Another vital direction is engaging with the broader community through external partnerships and corporate social responsibility (CSR) activities. By supporting Muslim communities and addressing issues of discrimination and mental health, organizations can extend their commitment to inclusivity beyond the workplace.

Finally, visible leadership support and accountability measures are essential. Organizational leaders must visibly champion diversity and inclusion initiatives, setting the tone from the top. Implementing accountability measures to track progress and hold leaders responsible for fostering an inclusive workplace culture will ensure sustained efforts toward inclusion.

This chapter has outlined the impact that mental health issues and discrimination can have on Muslim employees in Western workplaces. It has underscored the importance of recognizing and addressing these challenges through thoughtful, well-informed strategies that enhance inclusivity and support. The findings and discussions presented call for a combined effort by stakeholders at all levels - employers, policymakers, and mental health professionals - to commit to ongoing education, policy reform, and culturally sensitive practices.

By addressing these areas, organizations can create a more inclusive and supportive environment for Muslim employees, enhancing their well-being and enabling them to thrive in the workplace. This commitment to inclusivity benefits Muslim employees and enriches the entire organization, fostering a culture of understanding, respect, and unity.

US Government Policies and Laws Governing Workplace Mental Health for Muslim Employees

In North America, particularly the United States, the intersection of mental health, religion, and workplace rights is shaped by a tapestry of laws, policies, and cultural practices. The US legal framework provides protections designed to ensure that all employees, including religious minorities like Muslims, can work in environments free from discrimination, with accommodations that meet both their religious and mental health needs. While these laws set the foundation, emerging trends are pushing for more comprehensive, culturally sensitive approaches to workplace mental health, particularly in addressing issues such as Islamophobia and religious discrimination.

The current laws and policies govern workplace mental health for Muslim employees while also suggesting new laws and regulations that could enhance protections and support.

Federal Anti-Discrimination Laws (US): Ensuring Mental Health Protection

One of the cornerstones of workplace protection in the US is Title VII of the Civil Rights Act of 1964, which explicitly prohibits discrimination based on race, color, religion, sex, or national origin. For Muslim employees, this law provides a vital shield, ensuring that religious practices such as daily prayers, fasting during Ramadan, or wearing religious attire like the hijab are respected. Any failure to accommodate these practices may lead to increased stress or anxiety, contributing to a hostile work environment.

Beyond Title VII, the Americans with Disabilities Act (ADA) broadly addresses mental health accommodations. This law mandates that employers provide reasonable accommodation for employees with disabilities, which include mental health conditions such as anxiety or depression. In the case of Muslim employees, religious discrimination or workplace Islamophobia may exacerbate these conditions. Under the ADA, Muslim employees facing mental health challenges related to religious bias are entitled to accommodations that support their mental well-being, as long as these do not impose an undue burden on the employer.

Workplace Mental Health Policies: Addressing the Impact of Islamophobia

Mental health in the workplace is not just a matter of legal compliance; it is a critical component of a safe and productive work environment. The Occupational Safety and Health Administration (OSHA) mandates that workplaces be free from hazards that can affect employees' physical and mental health. While OSHA focuses primarily on physical safety, the mental health implications of a hostile work environment cannot be overlooked. Workplace Islamophobia, harassment, or bias can lead to significant mental health problems such as stress, anxiety, or depression among Muslim employees. Employers have a duty to actively prevent these issues by fostering an environment of inclusivity and respect.

Employers must also make reasonable religious accommodations, ensuring that Muslim employees can perform their religious duties without added stress. This might mean allowing flexible work schedules for prayer, accommodating fasting during Ramadan, or providing private spaces for worship. When these accommodations are denied or minimized, it can lead to heightened levels of stress, contributing to deteriorating mental health.

Anti-Discrimination Policies and Mental Health Support

One of the most effective ways to prevent mental health issues stemming from religious discrimination is to implement comprehensive anti-discrimination policies in the workplace. These policies should specifically address religious biases, including Islamophobia. Mandatory training on unconscious bias and cultural sensitivity helps reduce the likelihood of discriminatory behavior, ensuring that Muslim employees feel valued and respected. An inclusive culture promotes mental well-being by reducing the anxiety and stress that often accompanies religious discrimination.

Moreover, under the Family and Medical Leave Act (FMLA), employees are entitled to take unpaid leave for serious health conditions, including mental health crises. This provision allows Muslim employees who are facing workplace-related stress or mental health challenges to take the time they need to recover without risking their employment. The FMLA provides a safety net, ensuring that mental health care remains a priority for all employees, regardless of their religious background.

Emerging Trends in Workplace Mental Health: DEI Initiatives

As the United States workforce becomes increasingly diverse, many employers are implementing Diversity, Equity, and Inclusion (DEI) initiatives to address the unique needs of minority employees, including Muslims. DEI programs aim to create a culture of belonging, which is essential for the mental health and well-being of Muslim employees. These initiatives often include mental health awareness campaigns, support services like Employee Assistance Programs (EAPs), and telehealth options that provide confidential access to mental health professionals.

For Muslim employees, telehealth services offer an added layer of privacy and security, particularly in cases where cultural stigma around mental health may prevent them from seeking help in person. The availability of culturally competent mental health professionals is key to ensuring that Muslim employees receive care that acknowledges their religious and cultural background, thereby improving outcomes.

New Laws and Policies: Strengthening Mental Health Protections for Muslim Employees

While existing laws provide a strong framework for protecting the mental health of Muslim employees, there is still room for improvement. Several new laws and regulations could be suggested to enhance these protections:

1. Mandatory Mental Health Training with Cultural Sensitivity: A proposed law requiring employers to implement mental health training that includes cultural and religious sensitivity, with a specific focus on Islamophobia, would foster greater understanding and reduce discrimination. This would alleviate workplace stress for Muslim employees, promoting a more inclusive environment.

2. Enhanced Religious Accommodation Laws: Amending Title VII to explicitly address the mental health implications of denying religious accommodation could strengthen the legal framework. This would ensure that employers consider the mental health consequences of failing to accommodate Muslim employees' religious practices.

3. Paid Mental Health Leave: Introducing legislation for paid mental health leave, separate from regular sick leave, would provide Muslim employees the necessary time to recover from workplace stress or discrimination without financial hardship. Recognizing the mental health impact of Islamophobia and religious bias would reduce stigma and encourage timely care.

4. Anti-Islamophobia Workplace Law: A law explicitly targeting Islamophobia in the workplace would provide Muslim employees with stronger protections. This law would include preventive measures, such as mandatory cultural sensitivity training and corrective actions for instances of religious discrimination.

5. Confidential Religious Discrimination Reporting Mechanism: Implementing a confidential reporting system for religious discrimination would allow Muslim employees to report incidents without fear of retaliation. This would encourage a more open dialogue about religious bias and its impact on mental health, ensuring timely intervention.

6. Workers' Compensation for Mental Health Issues Stemming from Religious Discrimination: Including religious discrimination under workers' compensation laws would ensure that Muslim employees suffering from mental health issues like anxiety, depression, or

PTSD due to harassment or bias can access the necessary mental health resources.

7. Telehealth Services with Religious and Cultural Expertise: Requiring companies to provide telehealth services staffed by mental health professionals trained in cultural and religious sensitivity would ensure Muslim employees receive appropriate care.

8. Public Accountability for Inclusivity and Mental Health Initiatives: Mandating public reporting on inclusive practices, including mental health initiatives for religious minorities, would hold employers accountable and encourage proactive measures to foster inclusive work environments.

Toward a More Inclusive Workplace

The mental health of Muslim employees in the United States is protected through a combination of federal laws, workplace policies, and emerging DEI initiatives. While progress has been made, there is still work to be done to create truly inclusive workplaces free from religious bias and supportive of the mental well-being of all employees.

By implementing new laws and strengthening existing ones, employers and policymakers can ensure that Muslim employees, and indeed all employees, are protected from discrimination, fostering workplaces that promote mental health, productivity, and harmony.

APPENDIX

US government policies and laws governing workplace mental health for Muslim employees:

Title VII of the Civil Rights Act of 1964: This cornerstone of US anti-discrimination law prohibits workplace discrimination based on religion, race, sex, or national origin. It protects Muslim employees' religious practices, including daily prayers, wearing religious attire like the hijab, and fasting during Ramadan, by requiring employers to make reasonable accommodations. Failing to accommodate these religious practices may contribute to a hostile work environment and increase stress, negatively affecting mental health (US Equal Employment Opportunity Commission, "Religious Discrimination").

Americans with Disabilities Act (ADA): This law mandates reasonable accommodations for employees with disabilities, including mental health conditions such as anxiety and depression. It covers Muslim employees whose mental health is impacted by religious discrimination or Islamophobia, ensuring they receive workplace adjustments to maintain their well-being, provided it does not create undue hardship for the employer (US Department of Justice, "ADA: Know Your Rights").

Occupational Safety and Health Act (OSHA): OSHA requires employers to provide a safe work environment free from hazards, including mental health risks arising from workplace harassment or hostility, such as Islamophobia. These standard underscores the employer's responsibility to foster an environment that promotes the mental well-being of all employees (Occupational Safety and Health Administration, "OSHA Standards and Regulations")

Family and Medical Leave Act (FMLA) allows employees to take unpaid leave for serious health conditions, including mental health crises. This provision helps Muslim employees cope with workplace stress or religious discrimination by giving them time to recover without risking job security (US Department of Labor, "FMLA Fact Sheet").

Emerging Diversity, Equity, and Inclusion (DEI) Initiatives: DEI initiatives in the workplace aim to support the mental health of minority groups, including Muslims. These initiatives promote an inclusive environment through mental health programs, Employee Assistance Programs (EAPs), and telehealth services tailored to culturally sensitive care (Forbes, "DEI in the Workplace").

Proposed Legislative Measures: Recent discussions highlight the need for stronger protections, such as mandatory mental health training with a focus on cultural sensitivity, paid mental health leave, and laws targeting workplace Islamophobia. These efforts aim to enhance support systems and create more inclusive work environments

References

Abdul Aziz, N. I., & Ahmad, F. A. (2021). Mental health among Muslim career women. *International Journal of Academic Research in Business and Social Sciences*, *11*(12). https://doi.org/10.6007/ijarbss/v11-i12/11863

Abdullah, A. G. K., Ling, Y. L., & Ping, C. S. (2017). Workplace happiness, transformational leadership and affective commitment. *Advanced Science Letters*, *23*(4), 2872-2875.

Achour, M., Mohd Nor, M. R., & Mohd Yusoff, M. Y. Z. (2016). Islamic personal religiosity as a moderator of job strain and employee's well-being: The case of Malaysian academic and administrative staff. *Journal of Religion and Health*, *55*, 1300-1311.

Ahmed, S., & Gorey, K. M. (2023). Employment discrimination faced by Muslim women wearing the hijab: Exploratory meta-analysis. *Journal of Ethnic & Cultural Diversity in Social Work*, *32*(3), 115–123.

Ali, H. (2021). *The Experiences and Mental Health Impact of Islamophobia on Muslim Americans Following the 2016 US Presidential Election: A Hermeneutic Phenomenological Study* (Doctoral dissertation, University of Denver).

Al-Hadrawi, B. K. (2023). Promoting Productive Dialogue in the Workplace: The Profound Influence of Civility. *Journal of Production & Industrial Engineering (JPIE)*, *4*(2).

Allison, I. (2023, April 2). *New Cair Civil Rights Report reveals highest number of complaints in group's 30-year history*. CAIR. https://www.cair.com/press_releases/new-cair-civil-rights-report-reveals-highest-number-of-complaints-in-groups-30-year-history/

American Psychiatric Association. (2018). *Mental health disparities: Muslim Americans*. APA. Retrieved from https://www.psychiatry.org/File%20Library/Psychiatrists/Cultural-Competency/Mental-Health-Disparities/Mental-Health-Facts-for-Muslim-Americans.pdf

Attridge, M. (2023). The current state of Employee Assistance Programs in the United States: A research-based commentary. *International Journal of Scientific and Research Publications*.

Bordbar, A., Mohammadi, S., Parashi, P., & Butenko, V. (2020). Globalization and Islamophobia: Critical view at globalization's impact on expansion of Islamophobia. *J. Pol. & L.*, *13*, 72.

Brottman, M. R., Char, D. M., Hattori, R. A., Heeb, R., & Taff, S. D. (2020). Toward cultural competency in health care: a scoping review of diversity and inclusion education literature. *Academic Medicine*, *95*(5), 803-813.

Carleton, R. N., Afifi, T. O., Turner, S., Taillieu, T., Vaughan, A. D., Anderson, G. S., ... & Camp, R. D. (2020). Mental health training, attitudes toward support, and screening positive for mental disorders. *Cognitive Behaviour Therapy*, *49*(1), 55-73.

Casey, J. C. (2021). Employee Resource Groups: A strategic business resource for today's workplace.

Cesari, J. (2015). Religion and politics: What does God have to do with it? *Religions*, *6*(4), 1330–1344.

Coleman, D. M., Dossett, L. A., & Dimick, J. B. (2021). Building high performing teams: opportunities and challenges of inclusive recruitment practices. *Journal of Vascular Surgery, 74*(2), 86S-92S.

Cropanzano, R., Anthony, E. L., Daniels, S. R., & Hall, A. V. (2017). Social exchange theory: A critical review with theoretical remedies. *Academy of Management Annals, 11*(1), 479-516.

Delphis (2020, June 30). *The Mental Health Continuum is a Better Model for Mental Health.* https://delphis.org.uk/mental-health/continuum-mental-health/

Diallo, R. (2018, April 4). *Hijab: A very French obsession.* Al Jazeera. https://www.aljazeera.com/opinions/2018/4/4/hijab-a-very-french-obsession

Ensari, N., & Riggio, R. E. (2023). Muslimophobia: Overcoming Religious Discrimination and Exclusion in the Workplace. In *Inclusive Leadership: Equity and Belonging in Our Communities* (Vol. 9, pp. 221-232). Emerald Publishing Limited.

Farooqui, J. F., & Kaushik, A. (2022). Growing up as a Muslim youth in an age of Islamophobia: A systematic review of literature. *Contemporary Islam, 16*(1), 65-88.

FitzGerald, C., Martin, A., Berner, D., & Hurst, S. (2019). Interventions designed to reduce implicit prejudices and implicit stereotypes in real-world contexts: a systematic review. *BMC Psychology, 7,* 1–12.

Flynn, P. M., Betancourt, H., Emerson, N. D., Nunez, E. I., & Nance, C. M. (2020). Health professional cultural competence reduces the psychological and behavioral impact of negative healthcare encounters. *Cultural Diversity and Ethnic Minority Psychology, 26*(3), 271.

Foldy, E. G. (2019). Employee resource groups: What we know about their impact on individuals and organizations. In *Academy of Management Proceedings* (Vol. 1, p. 10633). Briarcliff Manor, NY 10510: Academy of Management.

Frone, M. R. (2015). Relations of negative and positive work experiences to employee alcohol use: testing the intervening role of negative and positive work rumination. *Journal of Occupational Health Psychology, 20*(2), 148.

Garcia-Yeste, C., Mara, L. C., de Botton, L., & Duque, E. (2022). Building a More Inclusive Workplace for Religious Minorities. *Religions, 13*(6), 481.

Gil-Benumeya, D. (2023). The consent of the oppressed: An analysis of internalized racism and Islamophobia among Muslims in Spain. *Sociological Perspectives, 66*(6), 1146-1164.

Hamden, Raymond H. (2016, 2018). Balanced-4-Life: Before BurnOut, WestBow Press, 50.

Hankir, A., Carrick, F. R., & Zaman, R. (2015). Islam, mental health, and being a Muslim in the West. *Psychiatria Danubina, 27*(suppl 1), 53–59.

Haque, A., Tubbs, C. Y., Kahumoku-Fessler, E. P., & Brown, M. D. (2019). Microaggressions and Islamophobia: Experiences of Muslims across the United States and clinical implications. *Journal of marital and family therapy, 45*(1), 76–91.

Hashem, H. M., & Awad, G. H. (2024). Hijab, Solo Status, Discrimination, and Distress among Muslim Women in the US. *The Counseling*

Psychologist, 52(5), 773–801.
Hennekam, S., Richard, S., & Grima, F. (2020). Coping with mental health conditions at work and its impact on self-perceived job performance. *Employee Relations: The International Journal, 42*(3), 626-645.
Hibbard, S. (2015). Religion, Nationalism, and the Politics of Secularism. In *The Oxford Handbook of Religion, Conflict, and Peacebuilding* (p. 100). Oxford University Press.
Hodge, D. R., Zidan, T., & Husain, A. (2023). Are females who wear the hijab more likely to experience discrimination? A national study of perceptions among American Muslim women. *Journal of Ethnic & Cultural Diversity in Social Work*, 1-12.
Hummel, D., Daassa, M., Alshabani, N., & Felo, L. (2020). Identifying as Muslim and American: The role of discrimination. *Review of Religious Research, 62*(3), 465–483.
Institute for Social Policy and Understanding (ISPU) and the Stanford Muslim Mental Health & Islamic Psychology Lab. (2022, April). *Mental Health of Muslim Healthcare Workers: ISPU.* Institute for Social Policy and Understanding. https://www.ispu.org/mental-health-muslim-healthcare-workers/
Jones, D., Molitor, D., & Reif, J. (2019). What do workplace wellness programs do? Evidence from the Illinois workplace wellness study. *The Quarterly Journal of Economics, 134*(4), 1747-1791.
Kelloway, E. K., Dimoff, J. K., & Gilbert, S. (2023). Mental health in the workplace. *Annual Review of Organizational Psychology and Organizational Behavior, 10*, 363–387.
Khan, S., Afroze, R., & Zaman, L. (2022). Inclusive climate and the performance of employees from Muslim diaspora in the Western organisations.
Lindsey, A., King, E., McCausland, T., Jones, K., & Dunleavy, E. (2013). What we know and don't: Eradicating employment discrimination 50 years after the Civil Rights Act. *Industrial and Organizational Psychology, 6*(4), 391–413.
Lin, W., Wang, L., & Chen, S. (2013). Abusive supervision and employee well-being: The moderating effect of power distance orientation. *Applied Psychology, 62*(2), 308-329.
López-Cabarcos, M. Á., Vázquez-Rodríguez, P., & Quiñoá-Piñeiro, L. M. (2022). An approach to employees' job performance through work environmental variables and leadership behaviours. *Journal of Business Research, 140*, 361-369.
Marzouk, H. O. (2021). *The Hijab in the Quran and its Effects on Muslim Women in the Western Society.* Honors Theses. 1591. Retrieved March 19, 2025, from https://egrove.olemiss.edu/hon_thesis/1591
McKay, P. F., Avery, D. R., & Morris, M. A. (2009). A tale of two climates: Diversity climate from subordinates' and managers' perspectives and their role in store unit sales performance. Personnel Psychology, 62(4), 767–791.
Naeem, A., & Rashid, M. (2023). the Effect of Islamic Work Ethics on Employee Performance and Counterproductive Work Behavior: Examining the Role of Job Satisfaction. *International Journal of Business Reflections, 3*(2).

NBCUniversal News Group. (2022, January 7). *Islamophobic remarks by members of Congress betray American values*. MSNBC. https://www.msnbc.com/opinion/islamophobic-remarks-members-congress-betray-american-values-n1287120

Nwachukwu, C., Chládková, H., Agboga, R. S., & Vu, H. M. (2021). Religiosity, employee empowerment, and employee engagement: An empirical analysis. *International Journal of Sociology and Social Policy, 41*(11/12), 1195-1209.

Paz, A., & Kook, R. (2021). 'It reminds me that I still exist'. Critical thoughts on intersectionality; refugee Muslim women in Berlin and the meanings of the hijab. *Journal of Ethnic and Migration Studies, 47*(13), 2979-2996.

Pratt, D., & Woodlock, R. (2016). Introduction: Understanding Islamophobia. *Fear of Muslims? International Perspectives on Islamophobia*, 1–18.

Roberson, Q. M. (2006). Disentangling the meanings of diversity and inclusion in organizations. Group & Organization Management, 31(2), 212-236.

Ryan, A. M., & Gardner, D. M. (2021). Religious harassment and bullying in the workplace. *Dignity and inclusion at work*, 463–487.

Sabat, I. E., Lindsey, A. P., Membere, A., Anderson, A., Ahmad, A., King, E., & Bolunmez, B. (2014). Invisible disabilities: Unique strategies for workplace allies. *Industrial and Organizational Psychology, 7*(2), 259–265.

Saleem, M., & Ramasubramanian, S. (2019). Muslim Americans' responses to social identity threats: Effects of media representations and experiences of discrimination. *Media Psychology, 22*(3), 373-393.

Samari, G., Alcalá, H. E., & Sharif, M. Z. (2018). Islamophobia, health, and public health: a systematic literature review. *American Journal of Public Health, 108*(6), e1-e9.

Shepherd, S. M., Willis-Esqueda, C., Newton, D., Sivasubramaniam, D., & Paradies, Y. (2019). The challenge of cultural competence in the workplace: perspectives of healthcare providers. *BMC health services research, 19*, 1-11.

Shifrin, N. V., & Michel, J. S. (2022). Flexible work arrangements and employee health: A meta-analytic review. Work & Stress, 36(1), 60–85.

Singletary, S. L., & Hebl, M. R. (2009). Compensatory strategies for reducing interpersonal discrimination: The effectiveness of acknowledgments, increased positivity, and individuating information. *Journal of Applied Psychology, 94*(3), 797.

Sirin, S. R., Choi, E., & Tugberk, C. (2021). The impact of 9/11 and the war on terror on Arab and Muslim children and families. *Current Psychiatry Reports, 23*(8), 47.

Sudibjo, N., & Sutarji, T. (2020). The roles of job satisfaction, well-being, and emotional intelligence in enhancing the teachers' employee engagement. *Management Science Letters, 10*(11), 2477-2482.

Sufi, M. K., & Yasmin, M. (2022). Racialization of public discourse: portrayal of Islam and Muslims. *Heliyon, 8*(12).

Suleiman, O. (2017). Internalized Islamophobia: Exploring the faith and identity crisis of American Muslim youth. *Islamophobia Studies Journal, 4*(1), 1–12.

Tamtik, M., & Guenter, M. (2019). Policy analysis of equity, diversity and inclusion strategies in Canadian universities–How far have we come? *Canadian Journal of Higher Education, 49*(3), 41-56.

Trzebiatowski, T., & Triana, M. D. C. (2020). Family responsibility discrimination, power distance, and emotional exhaustion: When and why are there gender differences in work-life conflict? *Journal of Business Ethics, 162*(1), 15-29.

Ussif, R., Ussif, R., & Yussif, U (2020). Challenges Muslim Women and Converts Faced in Wearing Hijab. *International Journal of Academic Multidisciplinary Research, 4(8)* 36-44.

Van der Schaaf, M., Donkers, J., Slof, B., Moonen-van Loon, J., van Tartwijk, J., Driessen, E., & Ten Cate, O. (2017). Improving workplace-based assessment and feedback with an e-portfolio enhanced with learning analytics. *Educational Technology Research and Development, 65*, 359-380.

Voas, D., & Fleischmann, F. (2012). Islam moves west: Religious change in the first and second generations. *Annual review of sociology, 38*(1), 525-545.

Vyas, L. (2022). "New normal" at work in a post-COVID world: work-life balance and labor markets. *Policy and Society, 41*(1), 155–167.

Waddell, A., Kunstler, B., Lennox, A., Pattuwage, L., Grundy, E. A., Tsering, D., & Bragge, P. (2023). How effective are interventions in optimizing workplace mental health and well-being? A scoping review of reviews and evidence map. *Scandinavian Journal of Work, Environment & Health, 49*(4), 235.

Wani, H., Abdullah, R., & Chang, L. W. (2015). An Islamic perspective in managing religious diversity. *Religions, 6*(2), 642-656.

Weishut, D. J. (2020). Challenges and Opportunities. In *Intercultural Friendship: The Case of a Palestinian Bedouin and a Dutch Israeli Jew* (pp. 211-242). Brill.

World Health Organization. (2022, July 8). *Mental Health*. World Health Organization. https://www.who.int/news-room/facts-in-pictures/detail/mental-health

Wu, A., Roemer, E. C., Kent, K. B., Ballard, D. W., & Goetzel, R. Z. (2021). Organizational best practices supporting mental health in the workplace. *Journal of Occupational and Environmental Medicine, 63*(12), e925-e931.

Yasmin, M., Masso, I. C., Bukhari, N. H., & Aboubakar, M. (2019). Thespians in print: Gender portrayal in Pakistani English print media. *Cogent Arts & Humanities, 6*(1), 1661647.

CHAPTER NINETEEN

DIGITAL FRONTIERS
IN MUSLIM MENTAL HEALTH

Aurra Startup, Omar Khan, Iqra Ashfaq, Wadud Hassan, Subhaan Ashrafi, Athraa Fakier

This chapter explores the transformative potential of digital tools in addressing the unique mental health needs of Muslim communities by examining the role of technology and the intersections with developing platforms that are culturally responsive and spiritually aligned. While mental health apps and AI technology offer unprecedented opportunities for personalized care, they often lack frameworks to adequately support Muslim populations, who might experience mental health concerns within specific religious, cultural, and social contexts. Through exploring case studies and critical analyses, this chapter highlights the potential for key innovations, such as culturally and religiously tailored AI, integrating Islamic principles, and collaborative platforms to connect trusted community leaders and mental health professionals. Additionally, this chapter addresses contemporary challenges, including the digital divide, the need for regulatory oversight, and the importance of building digital trust. Addressing these realities calls for collaborative efforts from academics, policymakers, and mental health professionals to bridge current gaps, reduce stigma, and establish effective, accessible care for Muslim communities. Ultimately, this chapter envisions a future where technology and spiritual competence come together to support holistic mental health care across diverse Muslim populations.

Introduction

As Muslims in North America continue to face increasing stigma, discrimination, and social exclusion impacting psychological distress, there is an urgent need for culturally and religiously aligned mental health solutions. Yet, many Muslims are underserved by the current mental health system, partly due to fears of stigma and a lack of religiously appropriate resources. There is a strong preference for integrating Islamic practices, such as prayers and Qur'an recitations, into mental health care, which research shows can be more effective than conventional treatments. Digital technology, including meditation apps and online therapy platforms, offers scalable solutions to help Muslims manage stress and anxiety while reinforcing their faith.

Since the COVID-19 Pandemic, the usability of video calling services, including Zoom, Microsoft Teams, and WhatsApp, has increased significantly, creating increased opportunities to connect people globally over virtual platforms. As the world shifts towards more technological integrations, there is a place for digital tools like mindfulness apps and virtual therapy platforms to propel mental health services and reach those who have been previously underserved. At the same time, digital solutions offer greater accessibility and inclusivity, and ethical considerations arise, especially regarding Artificial Intelligence (AI) and user data storage. It is essential to balance the benefits and harms of AI for Muslim users by addressing bias in AI models and ensuring cultural sensitivity. Robust data protection is also critical to safeguard privacy and maintain the rights and integrity of users.

Innovations in digital mental health services for Muslims are transforming how mental health care is delivered, with several successful interventions demonstrating the potential of digital tools to facilitate positive wellbeing. Despite scalability challenges and the digital divide, these tools offer the potential to complement existing mental health services, with the advantage of wider-reaching impact through social media and marketing strategies tailored to the reality of the Muslim American.

The future of digital mental health in the Muslim community is promising to be transformative. As AI advances, concerns arise about replacing traditional therapists, with AI tools offering hyper-personalized interventions tailored to individual needs. However, traditional therapists offer an interpersonal approach that AI currently cannot achieve. Thus, AI must complement therapists' work and facilitate more time-effective, accessible, and quality support. Challenges that may arise include ensuring that these tools align with Islamic principles and maintaining digital trust amid concerns like deep fake therapists and hackers. End-to-end encryption, firewalls, and various validation tools will be needed to protect the service user and provider.

Empowering Imams and community leaders with digital tools can enhance their role in mental health support, but scalability remains a hurdle. Training practitioners in these technologies and integrating them into the broader mental health ecosystem, including oversight by a governing body for Muslim-based mental health applications, will be essential for ensuring quality and accessibility. Additionally, future research must focus on the unique needs of Muslim populations, exploring the potential of AI and digital tools while addressing ethical considerations and the risks of digital shortcomings.

Understanding the Landscape

Digital Evolution and the Muslim Mental Health Paradigm

In the current context, Muslims are facing a global mental health crisis, and the stigma and social injustices faced by the Muslim community continue to increase at an alarming rate. Since the 9/11 attacks, Muslim Americans have experienced heightened psychological distress. However, they continue to be underserved by the mental health care system (Ahmed & Reddy, 2007). As a result of cultural and religious identities, Muslim communities continue to experience social exclusion, a factor closely linked to mental health challenges (Rassool, 2015). Muslim individuals often experience intense stigma, resulting in rejection and isolation of both them and their families due to mental health issues, addiction, and experiences around suicide.

The digital revolution continues to face notable advancements in recent years, especially regarding digital mental health platforms (Bucci et al., 2019). Mental health challenges remain a growing public health concern and among the leading contributors to the global and societal burden, which intensifies the urgent need for mental health care solutions. As the rapid expansion of digital technology continues, Muslim populations within Western contexts Islamically align with mental health solutions.

Research shows that the experiences of Muslims' mental health challenges are either overlooked by secular mental health services or are addressed at later stages. Data also shows that Muslims are less likely to seek support for their mental health than the general population (Latif et al.,

2020). Mental health issues are stigmatizing in many Muslim communities, which is a significant barrier to accessing services. The stigma is relevant in Muslim communities due to, but not limited to, the following: misconceptions or limited awareness about mental health services, fears that treatment will be disclosed to others, and specifically for addictions, due to the beliefs that the addiction is shameful and should not be discussed outside of families (Hassan et al., 2021).

For the small subset of Muslims that do seek services, they find it challenging to find religiously appropriate resources, as they are scarce or inaccessible (Shoib et al., 2022). More specifically, Muslims who live in Muslim-minority countries often experience anti-Muslim sentiments, including microaggressions, and face stigmatization, discrimination, prejudice, hate crimes, social exclusion, and life stressors on a day-to-day basis, impacting their psychological wellbeing (Rassool, 2015; Shoib et al., 2022). Moreover, the misrepresentation of Muslims in the media significantly contributes to their mistreatment and sustains the ongoing nature of this issue (Rassool, 2015). These challenges can inevitably lead Muslims to develop mental illnesses and even lead to suicide attempts (Shoib et al., 2022). Furthermore, Muslims can begin to have inner conflicts and can even start to question their faith.

Muslims have expressed concerns that secular counseling may not respect their Islamic values and beliefs (Rassool, 2015). Recently, there has been a move towards integrating culturally and religiously responsive training into mental health counseling. Evidence shows that religious psychotherapy can be more effective than conventional treatments for Muslims dealing with anxiety, depression, and grief (Malviya, 2023). Additionally, many Muslims prefer therapists who are knowledgeable about Islamic values and principles. In order to scale such treatments, a digital therapy platform dedicated to Muslims, such as Ruh Care, Muraqabah, the Sabr App, Noor Meditation, and many others, can be highly beneficial in addressing these barriers.

Furthermore, Muslims strongly prefer integrating spiritual methods into counseling, such as prayers, fasting, repentance, supplications, and Qur'an recitations (Rassool, 2015). Hamdan (2008) suggests that several essential cognitive aspects of the Islamic faith can be applied in counseling Muslims. These include acknowledging the temporary nature of this world, emphasizing the afterlife, understanding the purpose and impact of trials, placing trust and reliance on Allah, believing that ease follows hardship, focusing on Allah's blessings, engaging in dhikr (remembrance of Allah), reading the Qur'an, and making supplications (Hamdan, 2008). Furthermore, when a therapist lacks the Islamic knowledge a patient seeks, a collaborative care team, including an Imam and a trained counselor, can be assembled. Additionally, digital technology can be utilized to enhance and streamline this collaborative approach.

Islamic values and principles provide essential insights for managing psychological stress (Hassan, 2024). Alongside religious and culturally based therapy, there is a growing need for digital tools to design platforms to support Muslims in managing stress and anxiety on a broader scale. These resources can emphasize reliance on Allah, gratitude, patience, and balance to tackle anxiety and stress. By offering practical tools, Muslims can take a proactive approach to mental health rather than merely responding to issues as they arise. For example, mindfulness-based therapies could be adapted into informative meditation, motivational, and dhikr sessions rooted in Islamic values and principles. Islamic-oriented apps such as Noor Meditation, Ruh, Sabr, and Muraqaba can help Muslims manage their psychological stress proactively. Research shows that Islam-inspired meditation is more effective than Western meditation in reducing anxiety for Muslims (Gul & Jehangir, 2019) and that participating in dhikr can help improve one's mental health.

Ethical, Spiritual, and Cultural Considerations in Digital Mental Health for Muslim Communities

Spiritual and Cultural Sensitivity

Digital mental health solutions have become increasingly popular, offering convenient and accessible supplements or alternatives to traditional in-person therapy. However, for Muslim communities, adopting these technologies requires careful consideration of ethical, spiritual, and cultural factors. The rapid growth of artificial intelligence in mental health applications brings benefits but also presents challenges related to inclusivity, privacy, and bias. Focusing on how Muslim users can navigate the intersection of technology, spirituality, and culture while ensuring mental wellbeing is essential in facilitating users' safety and trust. Digital tools that provide faith-based solutions, such as Islamic counselling apps, are gaining popularity. These apps offer features like guided Muraqaba (meditation), dua (supplications), contemplative Quranic verses of healing or affirmation, and access to Muslim mental health professionals who understand users' religious and cultural backgrounds. When spiritually aligned, these solutions can effectively offer culturally appropriate care.

In Islamic tradition, mental health is viewed holistically, encompassing emotional, psychological, and spiritual wellbeing. The concept of nafs (the self), ruh (the soul), and qalb (the heart) play a crucial role in understanding human behavior and mental health. Digital mental health solutions must, therefore, align with these spiritual values. Spiritual responsiveness in mental health services acknowledges that spiritual distress or imbalance can contribute to psychological challenges, and thus, spiritual healing practices, such as prayer, reflection, and religious counseling, should be integrated into mental health care. Additionally, cultural sensitivity, particularly in Islamic contexts, requires understanding religion's role in shaping community values, family dynamics, and coping mechanisms. Mental health professionals, including those offering digital services, must be trained to work with the cultural nuances of Muslim patients. For instance, family support, modesty, and privacy must be respected when delivering mental health care through apps, teletherapy, or AI-powered platforms.

The availability of Islamically aligned mental health solutions is growing, but questions about their effectiveness remain. These platforms strive to integrate Islamic teachings with mental health or emotional wellness education, offering faith-based and culturally responsive solutions. The effectiveness of these solutions often depends on user testing and feedback and how well they integrate religious counseling and evidence-based therapeutic practices like Cognitive behavioral Therapy (CBT) or mindfulness techniques. An example of effective integration is using Qur'anic reflections during therapy sessions to help users manage anxiety or depression. This can enhance both spiritual growth and emotional wellbeing. However, collecting more empirical data to guide this work remains challenging. Funding and global partnerships are other challenges to ensure that effective solutions developed by local experts can be globally known and accessible. Although these emerging efforts focusing on digital tools are starting to address the need for culturally competent mental health care, they may not always have the resources or reach to serve all Muslim communities globally, particularly in rural or underserved areas.

Mindfulness, a practice that has gained popularity in secular and clinical settings, deeply resonates with traditional Islamic spiritual tools such as muraqabah (experiential meditation and self-awareness) and tafakkur (contemplation). Digital mindfulness tools, such as guided meditation apps or breathing exercises, can be adapted for Muslim users by incorporating Islamic spiritual tools into their content. Integrating mindfulness in digital platforms can greatly benefit emotional and spiritual wellbeing. When paired with Islamic practices like prayer and reflection, mindfulness has been observed to cultivate a deep connection with Allah, promoting inner peace and emotional resilience. Apps that remind users to pause and engage in dhikr (remembrance of Allah) or encourage gratitude practices aligned with Islamic values can positively impact mental, spiritual, and physical health. However, digital mindfulness tools must be designed to be sensitive to religious and cultural nuances. For example, a mindful pause for a Muslim user might involve reciting a short prayer or reflecting on the names of Allah rather than engaging in generic meditation practices that might not resonate culturally. The key is to create balance, allowing users to cultivate self-awareness and emotional regulation while staying rooted in their spiritual identity.

The stigma around mental health remains a significant barrier in many Muslim communities, often preventing individuals from seeking help, whether through digital platforms or traditional in-person therapy. Mental health struggles may be perceived as a weakness of faith or a lack of trust in Allah, leading to reluctance in accessing care. Digital mental health solutions have the potential to reduce this stigma by offering private, anonymous access to mental health support. Many individuals may feel more comfortable using apps or teletherapy services, as these platforms allow them to seek help discreetly without fearing judgment from their community. Furthermore, digital platforms can offer culturally sensitive resources that encourage seeking help as part of a holistic approach to wellbeing rather than framing mental health issues as solely spiritual deficiencies. Despite these advantages, stigma can still impact the effectiveness of digital mental health solutions. Some individuals may not trust digital platforms due to concerns over privacy or the fear that using these services will be viewed negatively by others in their community. Therefore, digital mental health providers must address cultural stigma and privacy concerns to encourage broader use of these services.

Ensuring that digital mental health solutions are accessible and inclusive for all members of the Muslim community is essential. This includes overcoming language, technological literacy, and socioeconomic status barriers. Inclusivity also means addressing the needs of diverse groups within the Muslim community, including women, children, refugees, and those with disabilities. Efforts to improve accessibility include developing multilingual platforms, offering teletherapy services for those in remote areas, and creating low-cost or free options for underserved populations. Ensuring that digital mental health solutions are both inclusive and accessible will broaden their reach and impact within Muslim communities worldwide.

Ethical Considerations in Digital Mental Health

The rise of digital mental health solutions raises ethical questions, particularly regarding informed consent, data security, and the quality of care provided. Muslim users may be concerned about religious ethics, such as whether the advice aligns with Islamic principles or how personal data is used. One of the primary ethical concerns is ensuring that users are fully informed about how their data is collected, stored, and used. For many Muslim users, there is an added layer of sensitivity regarding personal information, as privacy is a deeply held value in Islamic culture. Safeguarding sensitive information and ensuring that digital platforms adhere to strict privacy protocols is critical to maintaining trust. Another ethical concern is the potential for exploitation or misinformation. Some platforms may not provide qualified mental health professionals, offering generic or non-licensed advice. Ensuring digital mental health services are held to the same ethical standards as in-person care is essential for protecting users.

Privacy is a fundamental concern for Muslims using digital mental health services, as Islamic teachings emphasize the importance of safeguarding personal information. Digital platforms must prioritize robust data security measures to protect sensitive information from misuse or unauthorized access. This includes implementing end-to-end encryption, anonymizing user data, and ensuring that users have complete control over how their information is shared and stored. Digital mental health providers must also consider the ethical implications of using data for AI development. While anonymized data can be valuable for improving AI models, it is essential that users provide informed consent and are aware of how their information may be used in research or development.

AI-powered mental health tools have the potential to revolutionize care, offering personalized, on-demand support. However, these technologies also raise ethical challenges, particularly bias and cultural insensitivity. AI algorithms are often trained on data that may not represent the diversity of global populations, leading to models that do not adequately serve Muslim users. Balancing the benefits and harms of AI in mental health care for Muslim users requires ongoing evaluation of how these technologies are developed and implemented. Muslim scholars, mental health professionals, and technologists should collaborate to ensure that AI tools align with Islamic ethical principles and effectively serve the needs of Muslim communities. To address bias in AI models, developers must ensure that their algorithms are trained on diverse datasets that include Muslims and other underrepresented groups. Promoting cultural sensitivity in AI models involves actively incorporating cultural and religious values into the design of mental health tools. By addressing bias and promoting cultural sensitivity, AI-powered digital mental health tools can better serve Muslim users, offering practical solutions aligned with their values.

Innovations and Interventions

Case Studies: Digital Tools in Action

The rise of digital tools rooted in Islamic values has unveiled new possibilities for delivering mental health support to Muslim communities and other underserved populations. These platforms aim to address unique barriers, including cultural stigma, the underrepresentation of culturally competent professionals, and the complex interplay between faith and mental health (Friis-Healy et al., 2020; Ibrahim & Mojab, 2023). Research indicates that Muslim individuals often seek mental health support from providers who understand their religious and cultural contexts, as this alignment fosters trust and effective therapeutic relationships (Tanhan & Francisco, 2019; Ciftci et al., 2013). Faith and culture play a central role in how Muslims perceive, and address matters related to mental health, underscoring the importance of culturally and spiritually aligned supports for effective user engagement (Abu-Raiya & Ayten, 2019; Altalib et al., 2019). As such, culturally responsive digital platforms offer a faith-based alternative to traditional therapy, which many Muslims may view as inaccessible or misaligned with their values (Alharbi et al., 2023). Platforms such as Ruh Care, the Noor Meditation App, and the Sabr App demonstrate the effectiveness of digital mental health solutions, highlight the potential of digital mental health tools to deliver responsive care at scale, ensuring these resources are inclusive and accessible to meet the needs of diverse Muslim communities (Alharbi et al., 2021; Tanhan & Young, 2022).

Ruh Care

Ruh Care is a digital therapy platform designed to meet the unique needs of Muslim communities by offering Islamically aligned, culturally responsive, and accessible mental health care services (Ruh Care, 2024). A digital tool that began as a mindfulness app has quickly evolved into a comprehensive mental health support toolkit, now including a Muslim therapist directory, various therapy options, clear pathways to partner with masjids and religious centers globally, and specialized support for individuals in crisis. Since October 2023, the platform has mobilized nearly 560 mental health professionals, facilitated over 550 free therapy sessions, and offered 65 free healing circles for individuals impacted by the ongoing crisis in Palestine. This scale of mobilization is a key example of how virtual platforms can overcome barriers such as geographical limitations. As such, virtual therapy options provide users with the option to engage in therapeutic processes without the fear of judgment that can come with being seen visiting a therapist by other community members. Thus, these tools create opportunities for privacy, reducing cultural stigmas towards seeking counseling (Tanhan, 2019; Alhomaizi et al., 2018). The digital format allows for scalability without needing physical offices, making mental health care more accessible for marginalized Muslim communities with limited resources. This technological approach also enables data collection, providing valuable insights into the efficacy of service delivery and the mental health needs of Muslim populations, which is a gap often left unaddressed in mainstream mental health services (Firth et al., 2017). By integrating Imams and community leaders into the mental health support system, Ruh Care strengthens therapeutic alliances and builds trust, using culturally relevant communication methods like chat tools and smart phrases, which facilitate effective digital engagement.

The Sabr App

The Sabr App is a mindfulness platform rooted in Islamic values, offering resources that blend spirituality with mental wellbeing. Key features of the app include guided meditations, Quranic recitations, nasheeds, and soothing soundscapes designed to equip users with the tools to address experiences including anxiety or stress through Islamic practices such as *muraqabah*, a form of Islamic mindfulness (Ciftci et al., 2013). The guided meditations, developed with guidance from Muslim therapists and scholars, integrate faith into meditation practice, ensuring the content is culturally and spiritually relevant, which allows users to engage deeply with mental health topics in a way that resonates with their core values (Abu-Raiya & Ayten, 2019). This alignment with Islamic values is crucial, as research indicates that many Muslims are hesitant to use mindfulness apps unless they reflect their faith's core principles (Abu-Raiya & Ayten, 2019; Abdulkerim & Li, 2022). One of the app's distinguishing features is its vocals section, which includes Quranic recitations and nasheeds that adhere to Islamic guidelines, avoiding instrumental music, thereby making these resources more accessible to Muslims who prioritize faith-compliant content (Alhomaizi et al., 2018; Ibrahim & Mojab, 2022). The app's user-friendly design and faith-based content reduce barriers to accessing mental health support, encouraging the development of consistent self-care practices that are in harmony with Islamic beliefs. By offering resources that are both accessible and aligned with Islamic values, Sabr bridges the gap between faith and mental health, demonstrating the effectiveness of culturally tailored digital tools in engaging Muslim communities (Gan et al., 2022; Firth et al., 2017). This faith-oriented approach not only supports mental wellness but also addresses the gaps left by mainstream mindfulness apps, which often do not resonate with Muslim users.

Noor Meditation

Noor Meditation is an innovative digital app that integrates Islamic teachings with mental and spiritual wellness, designed to meet the unique mindfulness needs of Muslims. The app's foundation rests on the founders' research regarding the physiological benefits of mindfulness and listening to Qur'anic recitation, creating meditative experiences that cater to Muslim users (Naslund et al., 2016). Its advanced Noor-AI is an intelligent virtual assistant; the app responds to users' inquiries about Islam, suggests personalized meditation sessions, and even detects patterns that indicate when users might benefit from professional support. For cases involving potential self-harm, Noor-AI can recommend Muslim therapists through platforms like Ruh Care or alert emergency services, ensuring timely and culturally competent intervention (Keshavarzi & Haque, 2013; Tanhan & Francisco, 2019). The app's collaboration with the Centre for Addiction and Mental Health (CAMH) further highlights its commitment to evidence-based practice, as ongoing studies assess Noor's real-world efficacy (Alharbi et al., 2023). Features such as a digital dhikr board allow users to reflect on calming phrases without needing extra tools, fostering both convenience and spiritual engagement. User testimonials praise Noor Meditation's effectiveness in helping users manage stress and achieve spiritual calm. This case underscores the potential of culturally sensitive digital tools to bridge the gap in mental health resources for Muslims, providing a trusted, accessible platform that meets both mental and spiritual needs comprehensively (Alhomaizi et al., 2018).

The Muraqabah App

The Muraqaba app delivers Islamically integrated mindfulness, spiritual, and emotional wellbeing tools to Muslims in the US, Canada, South Africa, and Australia. Recognizing the unique mental health needs of the Muslim community, the app combines evidence-based psychological practices with faith-centered guidance, helping users manage emotional dysregulation, stress, obsessive thoughts, and overwhelm. Inspired by strong user feedback, Muraqaba launched in September 2024, offering customized wellness resources that resonate with Islamic values and meet the demand for accessible mental health tools aligned with users' cultural and spiritual identities. What sets Muraqaba apart is its foundation in neuroscience and Prophetic teachings, making it a comprehensive resource for mental health rooted in faith. The app's personalized emotional check-ins allow users to receive tailored guidance, creating a supportive digital environment. Muraqaba's suite of tools includes faith-based guided audio and video practices designed to enhance mental health, productivity, and personal growth. By encouraging practices such as mindfulness and emotional awareness, Muraqaba equips users with practical tools for everyday challenges while also fostering a supportive community rooted in Islamic values. This case study demonstrates how culturally responsive, faith-based digital platforms can transform the mental wellness landscape for Muslims globally.

The Digital Divide: Addressing Supply and Demand between Digital Tools and Traditional Support

The digital divide presents a significant challenge in the context of Muslim mental health, particularly when attempting to bridge the gap between digital tools and traditional support systems. This divide encompasses challenges concerning access, literacy, and cultural relevance with digital tools best suited as complements to existing services rather than replacing conventional treatment (Aryana & Brewster, 2019). While Islamically oriented apps provide innovative solutions to the unique mental health challenges of Muslim communities, significant disparities remain due to socioeconomic factors, varying levels of digital literacy, and a lack of culturally sensitive digital infrastructure (Tanhan & Young, 2022). One of the primary challenges in addressing Muslim mental health needs is the shortage of culturally and spiritually competent professionals (Alhomaizi et al., 2018; Al Uqdah, Hamit, & Scott, 2019). For many Muslim users, mental health care is most effective when it incorporates Islamic values, beliefs, and practices. However, mainstream mental health platforms are not designed with Islamic ethical principles in mind, creating a disconnect between the tools available and the community's needs. This gap can lead to Muslims seeking mental health support, feeling that their spiritual needs are either not acknowledged or dismissed entirely (Keshavarzi & Haque, 2013). The lack of readily accessible resources means that Muslims cannot access services that align with their values, resulting in increased rates of untreated mental health challenges, isolation, and overall diminished wellbeing (Al Uqdah et al., 2019).

Scalability remains a significant challenge in adapting digital mental health tools to be effective in supporting individuals from diverse Muslim communities. Research highlights that the digital divide, including disparities in access to technology and internet connectivity, mainly affects lower socioeconomic and rural areas, limiting the accessibility and usability of these platforms for many users (Friis-Healy et al., 2020; Gan et al., 2022). To address these barriers, digital mental health tools must prioritize cultural adaptability, with features such as multilingual support, user-friendly interfaces that accommodate varying access to technology, and content aligned with cultural and religious values (Batterham et al., 2021). This adaptability can extend the reach of these platforms without the need for physical infrastructure, offering advantages and opportunities for care in underserved regions where access to culturally competent in-person services is limited (Friis-Healy et al., 2020). Digital tools also offer opportunities to enhance access for populations in remote or socioeconomically disadvantaged areas by pairing digital tools with in-person services to streamline intake processes, such as using tools for initial mental health assessments and offering ongoing services through video or phone appointments. These features offer users access to culturally and spiritually informed therapists, regardless of the physical location of clients (Kaveladze et al., 2022). However, despite these adaptations and possibilities, retention challenges remain, as tailored apps often struggle to maintain user engagement beyond initial interactions, indicating a need for ongoing improvements in digital support models (Batterham et al., 2021).

Integrating digital tools alongside traditional mental health services presents a valuable approach to enhancing mental health care within Muslim communities, offering the flexibility and accessibility many patients seek. Despite this promise, significant barriers remain: skepticism toward digital tools among mental health professionals and community members alike. There is a prevailing belief that online therapy cannot fully replicate the depth and nuance of in-person interactions (Lukka et al., 2023). This hesitancy is particularly strong within Muslim communities, where effective mental health interventions often rely on an understanding of Islamic values and cultural sensitivity (Keshavarzi & Haque, 2013). However, research suggests that culturally tailored digital tools grounded in frameworks like Islamic psychology can help address these concerns by aligning therapeutic interventions with Islamic ethical principles, thus easing stigmas associated with mental health care (Mitha, 2020).

Digital mental health tools offer promising therapeutic benefits when paired with in-person care, primarily through faith-based content. For example, an advising psychiatrist from the Muraqaba team noted the value of a customized, post-clinic digital curriculum that promotes focus, calmness, and resilience between therapy sessions. This continuous support enhances patient care by providing a consistent and faith-aligned layer of mental wellness. Many Muslim patients report comfort and meaning in Islamically integrated mindfulness and wellness tools, which incorporate God-centered practices into mental health interventions. Hybrid models combining digital assessment tools and ongoing support with in-person sessions for deeper engagement offer a culturally resonant, spiritually fulfilling, and clinically comprehensive approach to mental health care (Stawarz et al., 2020; Tanhan & Young, 2022). By bridging traditional and digital resources, these hybrid models can address complex mental health needs through an inclusive, holistic care experience that respects both spiritual and clinical dimensions, making them an effective and meaningful layer of initial support for Muslim patients, especially those with busy lifestyles.

While digital tools are meaningful, they may not always suit all patients. Without guidance from experts in mental health and Islamic psychology, digital tools risk offering content that may not suit all users, especially those with unique needs like trauma, demonstrating the importance of these tools to consider these individual challenges. Supervision is essential to ensure digital platforms provide safe, relevant, and beneficial resources to meet users' needs. Additionally, the field lacks empirical research on the efficacy of these tools for Muslim mental health, emotional wellness, or peak performance to fully understand the efficacy of these current and emerging tools, highlighting a need for data-driven insights by Muslim mental health researchers. Addressing these gaps could foster informed improvements in digital resources tailored to the community. Islamically integrated digital wellness and mental health education can play a crucial role in boosting awareness and literacy within the Muslim community. Initiatives like online Mental Health First Aid training have successfully equipped educators, counselors, imams, and chaplains to identify and refer community members for appropriate mental health interventions. However, many community leaders remain untrained in these readily available resources, which are often offered at no cost to nonprofits and community organizations. Digital courses and a train-the-trainer approach could further empower leaders to share these skills through workshops, halaqas, and khutbahs. Platforms with a global directory of mental health practitioners and educators can connect service providers with patients based on individualized needs, addressing challenges such as finding Islamic-integrated mental health counseling for students and individuals with diverse requirements. This train-the-trainer model and directory approach can help establish culturally competent mental health support, providing personalized, faith-aligned care for the community.

Building Trust and Therapeutic Alliances Online

Building trust in online therapeutic relationships is important for the success of digital mental health tools, particularly within Muslim communities where skepticism towards therapy, in general, is compounded by a hesitancy towards online counseling as a result of confidentiality concerns, perceived impersonality of digital interactions, and doubts about the efficacy of online interventions (Borghouts et al., 2021; Tanhan & Young, 2022). Addressing these issues requires attention to education and transparency on the purpose and efficacy of digital interventions, as well as the ongoing development of culturally and spiritually congruent platforms by Muslim mental health platforms that seek to prioritize user privacy and integrity.

Research has shown that digital mental health tools can produce therapeutic outcomes similar to traditional in-person therapy for specific conditions such as anxiety and depression (Andersson & Titov, 2014).

However, for these tools to gain acceptance by Muslim communities, they must incorporate elements of Islamic teachings, provide content in multiple languages, and ensure that the platforms are accessible to individuals with varying levels of digital literacy (Borghouts et al., 2021). Culturally responsive education campaigns and the visibility of success stories in Muslim communities can support the process of challenging stigmas and normalizing online therapy in the hopes of cultivating a sense of safety and efficacy toward digital mental health care.

Spiritual Design Principles for Muslim Mental Health Digital Tools

For digital tools to address the needs of Muslim mental health users effectively, they must be rooted in Islamic principles and values (Al-Karam, 2018). This means that the design of these tools should reflect the values of the communities they seek to support, including respect for privacy, promoting spiritual wellbeing, and avoiding content that could be considered haram (forbidden) (Albar, 2007). Developers of these tools must engage with Islamic scholars and mental health professionals to ensure their products are culturally and religiously appropriate (Albar, 2007; Borghouts et al., 2021). Integrating Islamic values authentically into digital mental health platforms builds trust by ensuring that the tools reflect the cultural context of the community and to address concerns related to utilizing these services.

Designing digital tools for Muslim mental health requires carefully considering the user experience. This includes ensuring the tools are easy to navigate, visually appealing, and culturally relevant. The use of Islamic art and symbols, such as calligraphy-based designs and Islamic geometric patterns, is a visually appealing way to honor the historical traditions of Islamic art. In addition, including Quranic verses and Hadiths (sayings of the Prophet Muhammad PBUH), push notifications for prayer times, and reminders for dhikr can enhance user engagement by enhancing a sense of user familiarity with religious concepts. Studies highlight that culturally resonant visual and interactive elements can significantly reduce resistance and enhance user engagement, particularly in communities with specific spiritual needs (Ciftci et al., 2013).

Additionally, incorporating translations and culturally relevant content, such as Quranic and Hadith-based wellness tools and soothing audio recitations, can create a spiritually uplifting experience rooted in the Islamic principle of Ihsaan (excellence). Ensuring compatibility with various devices, especially mobile, is critical for accessibility, as mobile access allows broader reach, including younger users and those in regions with limited infrastructure (D'Adamo et al., 2023). Visual appeal and ease of navigation are critical to creating an environment where users feel understood and respected.

Incorporating Islamic teachings and practices into digital mental health tools can enhance effectiveness. Features such as guided prayers, reminders for daily Salah (prayers), guidance with practicing muraqabah (mindfulness), and modules that teach Islamic coping strategies for dealing with stress and anxiety (Alharbi et al., 2021). By aligning the tools with the spiritual practices of the community, developers can create interventions that resonate more deeply with cultural and religious practices they already rely on and provide them with a sense of spiritual support alongside their mental health care in a way that resonates. This approach may support attracting users who are hesitant to engage with mental health resources that lack a spiritual component (Abu-Raiya & Ayten, 2019).

Finally, the issue of digital permanence must be considered as long-term sustainability, which is vital to maintaining the relevance and ongoing development of these tools. As digital tools become more widespread, it is important to consider how these resources will be maintained and updated over time. This includes regular updates responsive to technological advancements, community feedback, and evolving security to ensure these tools remain functional, relevant, and congruent with Islamic values with time (Borghouts et al., 2021). By addressing these issues, developers can ensure that their products leave a lasting presence and continue to operate as a dependable platform for ongoing support to serve the needs of the Muslim community for years to come.

Future Directions

The Future of Digital Mental Health in the Muslim Community

The future of digital mental health care in Muslim communities, particularly in Western contexts such as the United States and Canada, holds immense promise with advancements in artificial intelligence and digital tools, where responsive services have been historically limited. These technologies are projected to play a significant role in overcoming existing barriers Muslims face in accessing mental health services in response to the complex and unique needs within these diverse communities (Tanhan & Francisco, 2019). AI systems, in particular, are well-equipped to analyze vast amounts of data, allowing for targeted and efficient identification of symptoms and the development of personalized treatment plans based on individual needs (Nusland et al., 2016; Schueller et al., 2019). While AI in mental health has the potential to offer clients access to personalized care and access to ongoing monitoring, assessments, and responsive support, concerns persist regarding its ability to replace human therapists fully. Given the emotional, cultural, and spiritual nuances entrenched in mental health care in Muslim communities, AI tools may lack the depth required to address the unique aspects in an effective way (Naslund et al., 2016; Tanhan & Francisco, 2019). Therefore, while AI can serve as a valuable tool for practitioners to rely on for initial assessments or supplementary care, it is unlikely to replicate or replace the comprehensive care of person-to-person therapeutic relationships essential to address the cultural and spiritual dimensions involved with supporting Muslim clients (Nusland et al., 2016; Keshavarzi & Haque, 2013).

Digital tools offer unique potential to empower community leaders, such as imams, in supporting mental health within Muslim communities, particularly given the cultural preference to seek initial guidance from religious leaders rather than mental health professionals (Keshavarzi & Haque, 2013; Alhomaizi et al., 2018). In Muslim communities, religious leaders such as Imams often serve as the first point of contact for individuals experiencing mental health issues (Alharbi et al., 2023). By integrating digital tools that can offer community members access to mental health resources and education, digital tools enable imams and community leaders to guide individuals towards culturally and religiously aligned services and supports without needing to be the community's sole resource for all matters. This approach reduces the pressure on leaders to act as the all-encompassing support figures, allowing them to shift towards serving the community as connectors rather than primary health care and other service providers by leveraging resources that allow them to offer initial mental health guidance, refer individuals to professional care and collaborate with licensed practitioners to determine steps forward as necessary (Albar, 2007; Keshavarzi & Haque, 2013; Tanhan & Francisco, 2019). As such, digital tools also expand access to support for individuals when community leaders are unavailable, thus fostering an accessible support system that complements in-person spiritual support that religious and other community leaders can continue to offer. These figures can better support their community's mental health needs while reducing the stigma associated with seeking help from formal mental health services (Alhomaizi et al., 2018). By positioning trusted figures such as imams as bridges to these digital resources, this approach supports the process of destigmatizing mental health care by framing these services through religious and cultural contexts to enhance community acceptance, reduce barriers, and increase accessibility to supports (Ibrahim & Mojab, 2022; Tanhan & Francisco, 2019). Digital interventions enhance the accessibility and sustainability of mental health services by empowering community leaders to connect individuals with culturally and spiritually competent professionals, allowing leaders to focus on broader community efforts.

Challenges and Opportunities

As digital mental health tools become increasingly prevalent, there is a parallel need to train mental health practitioners in effectively using these platforms, especially regarding technology's role in supporting culturally diverse populations such as Muslim clients. Research highlights the importance of equipping practitioners with both technical skills and cultural competency, as this dual approach supports clinicians in better understanding how digital tools can support monitoring, assessment, and treatment in ways that enhance rather than replace traditional therapeutic relationships and processes (Gan et al., 2022; Schuller et al., 2022). However, many therapists are unfamiliar with digital platforms, mobile apps, and AI-based interventions, highlighting the need for targeted training in these areas (Naslund et al., 2016; Tanhan & Francisco, 2019). Additionally, digital competency should extend to understanding cultural sensitivities and religious frameworks, as studies show that culturally aligned approaches in digital tools lead to greater engagement and treatment efficacy among Muslim clients (Keshavarzi & Haque, 2013; Alhomaizi et al., 2018). By integrating technical and cultural competencies, practitioners can more effectively bridge digital tools with in-person care, creating a balanced system that respects technological advancements and the cultural nuances critical to providing meaningful mental health care for Muslim communities (Al-Karam, 2018).

The development of Muslim-based mental health apps, such as those rooted in Islamic psychology, raises important questions about governance and consumer trust. There are few formal processes for approving mental health apps through regulatory health organizations, leading to consumer concerns over their safety and reliability. However, consumer reviews can provide some insight into the quality and effectiveness of these apps. Research by Schuller et al. (2017) highlights that many digital health products lack oversight, resulting in inconsistent quality and efficacy. Given the unique spiritual and psychological needs of Muslim communities, Islamic mental health apps must adhere to both the Islamic ethical principles and best practices in mental health care to ensure reliable and responsive care. However, without regulatory guidelines, consumers lack a reliable process to assess these apps' effectiveness. As such, establishing transparent approval processes through governing bodies would enhance consumer trust and ensure that Muslim-based mental health apps consistently meet high ethical and psychological care standards.

Future Research Needs

While digital tools are increasingly integrated into mental health care in general and for Muslim populations, there remains a significant gap in research that addresses the specific cultural, religious, and social contexts of these communities. Existing digital mental health tools often overlook these unique contexts, resulting in tools that may not fully resonate with or meet the needs of Muslim users. Research by Kaveladze et al. (2022) highlights the need for more inclusive and interdisciplinary approaches to research to develop further frameworks, processes, and standards for ensuring that current and future mental health resources are culturally and religiously responsive. Additionally, a study by Tanhan and Francisco (2019) highlights the unique psychosocial challenges many Muslim populations face in Western contexts, including experiences of Islamophobia, immigration-related stress, and religious discrimination, which can all affect one's mental health outcomes. Addressing these specific challenges requires digital tools sensitive to Muslim users' unique cultural and religious experiences. By involving Muslim communities in the co-creation and testing these tools, future digital mental health resources can be better tailored to provide effective and accessible support. This approach enhances the relevance and usability of these tools. It ensures they align more closely with Muslim communities' values and lived experiences, as suggested by Alharbi et al. (2021).

AI and digital tools offer unprecedented opportunities to create hyper-personalized mental health care where interventions are tailored to the individual's needs, behaviors, and preferences. The capacity of AI to process and analyze vast amounts of data enables therapists to have access to precise assessments, accurate diagnoses, and personalized treatment plans (Naslund et al., 2016). For Muslim populations, for instance, AI-driven mental health tools could be designed to consider and take into account religious practices, cultural norms, and spiritual values in addition to standard psychological metrics, thereby supporting and creating a more holistic approach to mental health care (Naslund et al., 2016). This process of personalization is especially useful and applicable in making mental health care more accessible and relevant, especially in communities where mental health issues are often stigmatized or misunderstood (Naslund et al., 2016). However, the automation of these processes requires the support of human practitioners to address the potential biases and incorrect assessments digital tools make due to limited access to diverse data representative of the populations these tools serve (Schuller et al., 2022).

As AI and digital technologies evolve, new challenges are emerging, particularly around digital trust in mental health care. One such concern is the potential rise of "deepfake" therapists, also understood as AI-generated avatars that can mimic human therapists but may lack the empathy, cultural sensitivity, and spiritual guidance essential for the mental health care of Muslim populations. Using deepfake technology in therapy raises significant ethical questions around authenticity, trust, and the quality of care. Deepfake therapists may undermine clients' trust in mental health services, mainly if users are unaware that their service provider is AI-generated (Schueller et al., 2019). While these digital services might initially attract users with high ratings, maintaining long-term trust and engagement could be challenging due to lacking human connection and empathy (Kaveladze et al., 2022). The challenge is particularly significant within Muslim communities where trust in healthcare systems may already be limited due to past experiences of cultural insensitivity or religious discrimination (Nusland et al., 2016; Alharbi et al., 2023). To mitigate these risks, it is essential for future research to explore ways to build and maintain digital trust, ensuring that AI-driven tools are transparent, ethical, and distinguishable from human therapists to uphold the ethical and religious expectations in Muslim communities of transparency and authenticity (Albar, 2007). Additionally, governing bodies and regulatory frameworks will need to evolve to address these emerging challenges, ensuring that digital mental health solutions are safe, effective, and trusted by the communities they serve (Torous & Roberts, 2017).

Conclusion

In the evolving landscape of digital mental health tools, there lies immense potential to transform the quality of mental health support available to Muslim communities. This chapter emphasizes the critical need for digital solutions responsive to the cultural, religious, and spiritual needs to address existing gaps in traditional mental health services. Muslim populations hold unique psychological, cultural, and religious needs in mental health services, recognizing the integral role that faith plays in the mental wellbeing of these communities. Digital tools, when ethically designed and developed in alignment with Islamic principles, offer a path to increased accessibility and culturally competent care for a variety of underserved populations, including Muslim communities that historically have avoided the use of such tools. Culturally responsive and faith-based tools rooted in Islamic values, such as Ruh Care, the Sabr App, and Noor Meditation, demonstrate how mental health resources can be enriched through the integration of Islamic values within the initial development of these platforms to foster holistic wellness of the mind, body, and spirit.

The future of digital mental health care in Muslim communities necessitates a collaborative and interdisciplinary approach. First, ongoing research and data collection are important elements for assessing the effectiveness and inclusivity of these tools and understanding the remaining gaps within the realm of digital tools. Academics and mental health practitioners should actively collaborate with Muslim communities to co-create and refine mental health tools that reflect and are rooted in the lived experiences of those they seek to support. Policymakers and technology developers are also crucial in addressing privacy, ethical, and regulatory concerns to protect user data and enhance long-term trust.

The potential for digital mental health tools extends beyond the immediate treatment of clients but allows us to envision the potential for broader social impact. For instance, engaging imams, educators, and community leaders as trusted figures within the community can break down existing stigmas and hesitations, fostering more supportive attitudes toward seeking mental health support. Additionally, with the advancements in AI technology, developers can personalize interventions that consider the overlapping needs of users to advance access to resources to support underserved communities.

Ultimately, digital mental health care for Muslim communities is not only about delivering services but, rather, about building a holistic system of support that seeks to honor and uplift the psychological and spiritual components of health. With intentional development and ongoing research through community collaboration, digital mental health tools can become beacons of hope, offering accessible, compassionate, and faith-based mental health support for Muslims worldwide.

References

Abe-Kim, J., Takeuchi, D. T., Hong, S., Zane, N., Sue, S., Spencer, M. S., & Alegría, M. (2007). Use of mental health-related services among immigrant and US-born Asian Americans: Results from the National Latino and Asian American study. *American journal of public health, 97*(1), 91-98.

Abdulkerim, N., & Li, C. (2022). How applicable are mindfulness-based interventions to Muslim clients in the US *Professional Psychology: Research and Practice, 53*(3), 253-265. https://doi.org/10.1037/pro0000454

Abu-Raiya, H., Ayten, A., Tekke, M., & Agbaria, Q. (2019). On the links between positive religious coping, satisfaction with life and depressive symptoms among a multinational sample of Muslims. *International journal of psychology: Journal international de psychologie, 54*(5), 678–686. https://doi.org/10.1002/ijop.12521

Abu-Raiya, H., & Sulleiman, R. (2021). Direct and indirect links between religious coping and posttraumatic growth among Muslims who lost their children due to traffic accidents. *Journal of Happiness Studies, 22*(5), 2215-2234.

Ahmed, S., & Reddy, L. A. (2007). Understanding the mental health needs of American Muslims: Recommendations and considerations for practice. *Journal of Multicultural Counseling and Development, 35*(4), 207–218.

Al-Karam, C. Y. (2018). Islamic psychology: Towards a 21st century definition and conceptual framework. *Journal of Islamic Ethics, 2*(1-2), 97-109.

Albar, M. A. (2007). Seeking remedy, abstaining from therapy and resuscitation: An Islamic perspective. *Saudi Journal of Kidney Diseases and Transplantation, 18*(4), 629–637.

Alharbi, H., Farrand, P., & Laidlaw, K. (2023). Understanding the beliefs and attitudes towards mental health problems held by Muslim communities and acceptability of cognitive behavioral therapy as a treatment: Systematic review and thematic synthesis protocol. *BMJ open, 11*(6), 1-4.

Alhomaizi, D., Alsaidi, S., Moalie, A., Muradwij, N., Borba, C. P., & Lincoln, A. K. (2018). An exploration of the help-seeking behaviours of Arab-Muslims in the UUS A socio-ecological approach. *Journal of Muslim Mental Health, 12*(1), 19–48.

Altalib, H. H., Elzamzamy, K., Fattah, M., Ali, S. S., & Awaad, R. (2019). Mapping global Muslim mental health research: analysis of trends in the English literature from 2000 to 2015. *Global Mental Health, 6*(e6), 1-10.

Al Uqdah, S. N., Hamit, S., & Scott, S. (2019). African American Muslims: Intersectionality and cultural competence. *counseling and Values, 64*(2), 130-147.

Amri, S., & Bemak, F. (2013). Mental health help-seeking behaviors of Muslim immigrants in the United States: Overcoming social stigma and cultural mistrust. *Journal of Muslim Mental Health, 7*(1), 43-63.

Andersson, G., & Titov, N. (2014). Advantages and limitations of Internet-based interventions for common mental disorders. *World Psychiatry, 13*(1), 4-11.

Aryana, B., Brewster, L., & Nocera, J. A. (2019). Design for mobile mental health: An exploratory review. *Health and Technology, 9*, 401–424.

Ashfaq, I. (2016). *An exploration of stress reactivity, stress recovery, mindfulness meditation, and prayer with the use of heart rate variability.* [Doctoral dissertation].

Basit, A., & Hamid, M. (2010). Mental health issues of Muslim Americans. *The Journal of IMA, 42*(3), 106-110.

Batterham, P. J., Calear, A. L., McCallum, S. M., Morse, A. R., Banfield, M., Farrer, L. M., Gulliver, A., Cherbuin, N., Rodney Harris, R. M., Shou, Y., & Dawel, A. (2021). Trajectories of depression and anxiety symptoms during the COVID-19 pandemic in a representative Australian adult cohort. *The Medical journal of Australia, 214*(10), 462–468. https://doi.org/10.5694/mja2.51043

Bhattacharyya, S., Ashby, K. M., & Goodman, L. A. (2014). Social justice beyond the classroom: Responding to the marathon bombing's Islamophobic aftermath. *The Counselling Psychologist, 42*(8), 1136–1158.

Borghouts, J., Eikey, E., Mark, G., De Leon, C., Schueller, S. M., Schneider, M., & Sorkin, D. H. (2021). Barriers to and facilitators of user engagement with digital mental health interventions: Systematic review. *Journal of Medical Internet Research, 23*(3), 1-29. https://www.jmir.org/2021/3/e24387/

Bucci, S., Schwannauer, M., & Berry, N. (2019). The digital revolution and its impact on mental health care. *Psychology and Psychotherapy: Theory, Research, and Practice, 92*(2), 277–297.

Chaudhry, S., & Li, C. (2011). Is solution-focused brief therapy culturally appropriate for Muslim American counselees? *Journal of Contemporary Psychotherapy, 41*, 109–113.

Ciftci, A., Jones, N., & Corrigan, P. W. (2013). Mental health stigma in the Muslim community. *Journal of Muslim Mental Health, 7*(1). https://doi.org/10.3998/jmmh.10381607.0007.102

D'Adamo, L., Paraboschi, L., Grammer, A. C., Fennig, M., Graham, A. K., Yaeger, L. H., & Fitzsimmons-Craft, E. E. (2023). Reach and uptake of digital mental health interventions based on cognitive-behavioral therapy for college students: A systematic review. *Journal of Behavioral and Cognitive Therapy, 33*(2), 97-117.

Firth, J., Torous, J., Nicholas, J., Carney, R., Pratap, A., Rosenbaum, S., & Sarris, J. (2017). The efficacy of smartphone-based mental health interventions for depressive symptoms: a meta-analysis of randomized controlled trials. *World Psychiatry, 16*(3), 287–298. https://doi.org/10.1002/wps.20472

Friis-Healy, E. A., Nagy, G. A., & Kollins, S. H. (2021). It is time to REACT: Opportunities for digital Mental health apps to reduce mental health disparities in racially and ethnically minoritized groups. *JMIR Mental Health, 8*(1), e25456. https://doi.org/10.2196/25456

Gul, L., & Jehangir, S. F. (2019). Effects of mindfulness and Sufi meditation on anxiety and mental health of females. *Pakistan Journal of Psychological Research, 34*(3), 583–599.

Hamdan, A. (2008). Cognitive restructuring: An Islamic perspective. *Journal of Muslim Mental Health, 3*(1), 99–116.

Hassan, M. (2024). Finding peace: Islamic approaches to managing stress. *Research Journal Ulūm-e-Islāmia, 31*(1), 1–11.

Hassan, A. N., Ragheb, H., Malick, A., Abdullah, Z., Ahmad, Y., Sunderji, N., & Islam, F. (2021). Inspiring Muslim minds: Evaluating a spiritually adapted psycho-educational program on addiction to overcome stigma in Canadian Muslim communities. *Community Mental Health Journal, 57,* 644–654.

Ibrahim, M., & Mojab, F. (2023). Healing through Faith: The role of spiritual healers in providing psychosocial support to Canadian Muslims. *Journal of Muslim Mental Health, 17*(1), 72–79.

Kaveladze, B. T., Wasil, A. R., Bunyi, J. B., Ramirez, V., & Schueller, S. M. (2022). User experience, engagement, and popularity in mental health apps: Secondary analysis of app analytics and expert app reviews. *JMIR human factors, 9*(1), 1-11. https://doi.org/10.2196/30766

Keshavarzi, H., & Haque, A. (2013). Outlining a psychotherapy model for enhancing Muslim mental health within an Islamic context. *International Journal for the Psychology of Religion, 23*(3), 230-249.

Latif, R., Rodrigues, S., & Galley, A. (2020). *Muslim Women's Mental Health.* Canadian Mental Health Association, 1–27.

Lukka, L., Karhulahti, V. M., & Palva, J. M. (2023). Factors affecting Digital tool use in client interaction according to mental health professionals: Interview study. *JMIR Human Factors, 10(e44681), 1-19.*

Malviya, S. (2023). The need for integration of religion and spirituality into the mental health care of culturally and linguistically diverse populations in Australia: A rapid review. *Journal of religion and health, 62*(4), 2272–2296.

McLaughlin, M. M., Ahmad, S. S., & Weisman de Mamani, A. (2022). A mixed-methods approach to psychological help-seeking in Muslims: Islamophobia, self-stigma, and therapeutic preferences. *Journal of Consulting and Clinical Psychology, 90*(7), 568–581.

Mitha, K. (2020). Conceptualizing and addressing mental disorders amongst Muslim communities: Approaches from the Islamic Golden Age. *Transcultural Psychiatry, 57*(6), 763–774.

Naslund, J. A., Aschbrenner, K. A., Marsch, L. A., & Bartels, S. J. (2016). The future of mental health care: Peer-to-peer support and social media. *Epidemiology and psychiatric sciences, 25*(2), 113-122.

Phillips, D., & Lauterbach, D. (2017). American Muslim immigrant mental health: The role of racism and mental health stigma. *Journal of Muslim Mental Health, 11*(1), 39-56.

Rassool, G. H. (2015). Cultural competence in counseling the Muslim patient: Implications for mental health. *Archives of Psychiatric Nursing, 29*(5), 321–325.

Ruh Care. (2024). *About.* Ruh Care. https://www.ruhcare.com/about

Schueller, S. M., Hunter, J. F., Figueroa, C., & Aguilera, A. (2019). Use of digital mental health for marginalized and underserved populations. *Current Treatment Options in Psychiatry, 6*(1), 243-255.

Shoib, S., Armiya'u, A. Y. U., Nahidi, M., Arif, N., & Saeed, F. (2022). Suicide in the Muslim world and the way forward. *Health Science Reports, 5*(4), 1-3.

Stawarz, K., Preist, C., Tallon, D., Thomas, L., Turner, K., Wiles, N., & Coyle, D. (2020, April). Integrating the digital and the traditional to deliver therapy for depression: Lessons from a pragmatic study. In *Proceedings of the 2020 CHI Conference on Human Factors in Computing System*s. [Presentation]. (pp. 1-14). https://dl.acm.org/doi/abs/10.1145/3313831.3376510

Subandi, M. A., Chizanah, L. L., & Subhan, S. (2022). Psychotherapeutic dimensions of an Islamic-Sufi-based rehabilitation center: A case study. *Culture, Medicine, and Psychiatry*, 1–20.

Tanhan, A. (2019). Acceptance and commitment therapy with ecological systems theory: Addressing Muslim mental health issues and wellbeing. *Journal of Positive Psychology and Wellbeing, 3*(2), 197–219.

Tanhan, A., & Francisco, V. T. (2019). Muslims and mental health concerns: A social-ecological model perspective. *Journal of Community Psychology, 47*(4), 964-978.

Tanhan, A., & Young, J. S. (2022). Muslims and mental health services: A concept map and a theoretical framework. *Journal of religion and health, 61*(1), 23-63.

Torous, J., & Roberts, L. W. (2017). Needed innovation in digital health and smartphone applications for mental health: Transparency and trust. *JAMA psychiatry, 74*(5), 437-438.

SECTION SIX

HUMANITARIAN AND SOCIAL SERVICE ORGANIZATIONS

CHAPTER TWENTY

MENTAL HEALTH SERVICES IN MUSLIM NGOS: CHALLENGES AND SOLUTIONS

Somer Saleh, Sarah Murad, Danyal Khan

Muslim NGOs in North America have evolved to meet the diverse needs of their communities, with a growing focus on mental health. This chapter discusses the historical development of these organizations, the increasing demand for culturally competent and Islamically integrated mental health services, and the unique stressors facing Muslim populations, such as cultural alienation and discrimination. Despite their vital role, these NGOs face funding instability, insufficient visibility, and a lack of professional mental health infrastructure. The reliance on imams for mental health support, coupled with limited training, highlights the gap in culturally appropriate care. Gender disparities in leadership and the high demand for underfunded services further complicate these issues. This chapter offers practical solutions based on interviews with leaders from key Muslim NGOs. Recommendations include building organizational capacity, professionalizing services, leveraging technology, fostering collaborations, and adopting sustainable funding models. By addressing these barriers, Muslim NGOs can better serve their communities' mental health needs, promoting resilience and a holistic approach to well-being in North America.

Introduction

History of Muslim Organizations: Addressing Concerns & Creating Spaces

Muslim NGOs in North America have a rich history that dates back to the early 20th century, evolving significantly over the decades to meet the changing needs of Muslim communities. Early Muslim immigrants to North America, often from the Middle East, South Asia, and Africa, established some of the first Islamic centers and mosques, which served as community hubs for worship, social gatherings, and cultural preservation. These early organizations primarily focused on providing a sense of community and belonging in a foreign land, addressing their members' immediate social and religious needs.

As the Muslim population in North America grew and diversified, so did the scope and scale of Muslim organizations. By the mid-20th century, organizations like the Islamic Society of North America (ISNA) and the Muslim Student Association (MSA) were established, focusing on education, advocacy, and community development. These organizations played a pivotal role in unifying Muslim voices, promoting interfaith dialogue, and advocating for civil rights and social justice.

In recent decades, the increasing visibility and integration of Muslims in North American society have led to the emergence of specialized Muslim NGOs addressing various aspects of community life, including healthcare, education, and humanitarian aid. The need for mental health services became particularly pronounced as communities recognized the unique cultural and religious challenges faced by Muslims in accessing mainstream mental health care. This need is underscored by research that highlights how Muslim communities face distinct mental health stressors, including cultural alienation, discrimination, and misconceptions about Islam (Haque, 2004). Amber Haque's study on American Muslims highlights stressors, such as negative media portrayals, post-9/11 prejudice, and a lack of culturally sensitive counseling, contribute to an increasing demand for mental health services that are integrated with Islamic principles. Haque emphasizes the importance of having culturally competent therapists who can incorporate Islamic values into their treatment methods. To address this gap, Muslim-focused mental health organizations have been established, aiming to provide culturally competent and Islamically integrated mental health services.

The evolution of these organizations reflects the growing understanding of the multifaceted needs of Muslim communities, from spiritual and social support to professional and psychological services. However, the journey has not been without challenges. Muslim organizations have had to navigate issues related to professionalization, funding, and maintaining the balance between religious principles and contemporary practices. Despite these challenges, they continue to play a crucial role in fostering resilience, empowerment, and well-being within Muslim communities across North America.

In order to provide a comprehensive understanding of the challenges Muslim NGOs face, we interviewed individuals in leadership positions from a diverse range of Muslim organizations across North America. This includes organizations such as the Muslim American Society (MAS), ICNA Relief, the Family and Youth Institute (FYI), Naseeha Mental Health, Wafa House, Islamic Social Services Association (ISSA), ADAMS Center, and other notable entities. These organizations have been pivotal in advocating for civil rights, providing humanitarian aid, and offering educational programs within the Muslim community. Additionally, we explored the efforts of Muslim tech organizations, such as RUH, which have been instrumental in expanding digital platforms to create more accessibility around Muslim mental health services. For a detailed discussion on the role of technology in this context, please refer to the chapter on digital tools.

To further enrich our understanding, we interviewed leadership experts from Oaktree Institute, a nonprofit organization specializing in leadership training and organizational development for Muslim nonprofits. Their insights highlighted the importance of capacity building and professional development in overcoming operational challenges and enhancing the effectiveness of Muslim NGOs. These perspectives have allowed us to gain a nuanced view of Muslim NGOs' multifaceted challenges and opportunities, ranging from funding and resource mobilization to the need for culturally competent mental health services and technology integration in outreach and service delivery. This comprehensive approach underscores these organizations' vital role in addressing the unique needs of Muslim communities across North America.

Importance in the Muslim Community

Research on the mental health of North American Muslims is limited; however, several studies have highlighted the prevalence of mental health issues within the Muslim community. For instance, Ahmad et al. (2023) found that the rates of psychiatric disorders among Muslim Americans were often comparable to those of their American counterparts. However, the likelihood of seeking help with these issues was disproportionately low. This is particularly concerning because, on average, Americans can delay seeking help for a mental health condition for up to 11 years after the onset of symptoms. By that time, a crisis often occurs as a result (Wang et al., 2004).

The Muslim community has faced numerous devastating crises. Research indicates that American Muslims are twice as likely to report a history of suicide attempts compared to other faith groups (Awad et al., 2021). Generally, faith and spirituality act as protective factors for mental health (Lucchetti et al., 2021). Awaad et al. (2021) conducted research indicating that, despite the protective aspects of faith, there exists a significant gap between this protection and the actual risk of suicide, which disproportionately affects American Muslims. It is well-known within the general Muslim population that suicide is prohibited in Islam. This awareness suggests that the suicide attempts reported by American Muslims are made with the understanding that they conflict with their beliefs and values. Research shows that mental health conditions such as depression, substance use, psychosis, and anxiety often contribute significantly to suicidality (Bachmann, 2018). The presence of these conditions may help explain how individuals reach a level of pain or hopelessness that drives them to contemplate or attempt to end their own lives, even when such actions contradict their beliefs. Furthermore, Awaad et al. found that the suicide attempt rates among American Muslims are higher than those of their counterparts in other Muslim-majority countries (2021), highlighting the reality of a mental health crisis within the American Muslim community.

To further emphasize this point, we have documented cases of tragic murder-suicides, such as that of Sania Khan in Chicago. She was killed by her ex-husband, who likely had untreated mental health issues that contributed to the breakdown of their marriage. This turmoil ultimately led to his violent decision to pursue and murder her in cold blood (Cabral, 2022).

In another instance, two brothers in Allen, Texas, made a devastating pact to kill their entire family before taking their own lives, resulting in the deaths of all six family members. Both brothers had been struggling with severe depression for years (Stengle, 2021).

These tragic examples highlight the severe consequences that can arise from untreated mental health concerns—unfortunately, these are just two among countless others. The stigma surrounding help-seeking behaviors for mental health issues runs very deep, leaving many problems unaddressed. This not only causes significant distress for individuals and their families but often leads to crises that are far more challenging to resolve, even if they don't result in the most tragic outcomes like those mentioned above. Furthermore, when Muslims manage to overcome the stigma and are ready to seek help, they often encounter difficulties in finding suitable care. The context of their concerns can be very different from what is typically understood by the average American therapist or social agency (Ahmed & Reddy, 2007).

In many Muslim organizations, imams or sheikhs, due to their respected positions, often take on the role of mental health advisors for community members. This is further complicated by the fact that Muslims experiencing mental health challenges may initially seek help from their local imams, who can provide spiritual guidance but typically lack the specialized training necessary for effective mental health care (Ciftci et al., 2013; Ali et al., 2005). When staff members are expected to fulfill multiple roles within an organization, it can lead to conflicts of interest and breaches of confidentiality. This undermines community trust and poses risks to clients. The dual role of imams can blur the boundaries between religious counseling and therapeutic intervention, making it difficult to distinguish between the two.

A common perception within the community views mental health struggles through an "Islamic lens," attributing these challenges to a "low level of faith" or insufficient worship. While faith can be a protective factor, this misconception may discourage individuals from seeking the necessary mental health support, leading to potential harm from untreated issues (Bagasra & Mackinem, 2014). Furthermore, untrained religious leaders who provide mental health support might inadvertently reinforce these misconceptions. This highlights the need for appropriate mental health training for individuals in advisory roles within the community.

These points emphasize the significant need for resources to support Muslim Americans in addressing their mental health concerns. It is crucial for the community to have access to education, support, and treatment for mental health issues in order for it to thrive. The demand for mental health services within the American Muslim community is recognized, as evidenced by the numerous organizations working to meet this need from various perspectives. While there has been a recent increase in the number of Muslim mental health professionals, this growth is still insufficient to fully address the community's needs. For instance, the Khalil Center, which provides Islamically Integrated Psychotherapy services, often has long waiting lists that can take months to navigate. Similarly,

Naseeha.org, the first Muslim Mental Health Helpline available 24/7, has a year-long waitlist for its free therapy services (anonymous, personal communication, September 19, 2024). Muslim mental health providers frequently experience high demand, leading to overflowing caseloads and insufficient time or staff to adequately meet the diverse needs of the community requires (anonymous, personal communication, September 16, 2024; anonymous, personal communication, October 2, 2024).

Challenges and Solutions in Providing Mental Health Services

Institutional Focus

Determining an Organization's Limits and Scope

The mental health field is extensive, making it essential to understand the scope of the services offered. This includes preventive care, early intervention, clinical treatment, and ongoing support. By incorporating these elements, systemic mental health services can provide a structured and multifaceted approach to mental health care that is both inclusive and effective.

Mohammad Hasan from the Oaktree Institute highlighted that many Muslim nonprofits in the U.S. (including mosques, relief organizations, Islamic schools, and community and civic organizations) tend to cast too wide a net regarding the services they aim to provide or promote. This approach often spreads their resources too thin, resulting in fragmented efforts and a lack of focus on delivering quality, sustainable services. Without clear objectives and adequate infrastructure to support long-term programming, these organizations face rapid burnout among staff and volunteers.

Furthermore, a lack of specialized training, funding instability, and the failure to establish strategic partnerships exacerbate these challenges. Consequently, many initiatives collapse under the weight of their ambitious goals before they can gain traction or effectively address the community's needs. Without a focused effort on building capacity and sustainable frameworks, these organizations struggle to make a lasting impact on mental health services (M. Hasan, personal communication, July 11, 2024).

This presents a significant challenge because when an organization tries to do everything, its resources become stretched thin, leading to surface-level solutions. Muslim NGOs have historically faced the challenge of defining their service boundaries. They often find themselves torn between the desire to help their community comprehensively and the reality of their actual capacity. Interviews with leaders from various NGOs reveal that the services they provide are often based on anecdotal evidence and reactive strategies, rather than on a predetermined methodology, such as a needs assessment. Conversely, some organizations in the Muslim community have demonstrated the benefits of narrowing their focus and making evidence-based decisions. A notable example is Wafa House, located in North Jersey, which specializes in providing support to survivors of domestic violence. Over time, they have refined their approach, allowing them to secure grant funding and collaborate effectively with other organizations.

Simon Sinek introduced the concept of the "Golden Circle," which emphasizes the importance of understanding your organization's "why" the core purpose behind its existence (2009). This purpose should clearly explain why the organization does what it does, reflecting its mission and cause. A well-defined "why" fosters loyalty among beneficiaries and investors, including clients and donors in the context of Muslim organizations. Without clear organizational boundaries, leadership often faces multiple challenges. Some of these challenges include a lack of alignment among internal stakeholders regarding the organization's direction, difficulties in collaborating with similar organizations due to concerns about competition and struggles in recruiting talent that aligns with the organization's core culture.

To establish clear organizational boundaries and reap the associated benefits, Muslim NGOs can take several steps. First, they should refine their core purpose using Sinek's framework. This involves reviewing and clarifying the organization's mission and vision. Once this foundation is set, organizations can focus on enhancing their internal company culture. Leadership should explore the core values they wish to promote within the organization. This process can be challenging, particularly when legacy stakeholders are resistant to change. Therefore, it may be beneficial to engage a professional facilitator who can guide the conversation toward a more innovative and forward-thinking approach.

Defining Your Service Approach

Once an organization has established its "why," the next step is to explore the "how" and "what." When defining a service approach for NGOs, it is crucial to consider setting up programs and developing a clear identity. The struggle to take on too much while needing direction often leads to unrealistic expectations. A well-defined service approach ensures that the organization remains aligned with its core mission. Without a clear identity, NGOs risk overlapping with other organizations, which can result in redundant services. Similar to a town with various interconnected parts, NGOs must understand exactly which piece of the pie they intend to occupy. This clarity allows others to step in and use their resources more collaboratively and effectively.

Wafa House enhances its effectiveness by carefully selecting who they serve and how they provide their services. This process involves examining their mission and vision, as well as assessing the needs of their beneficiaries and the resources available to them. This approach is known as a Gap Analysis, a framework that evaluates the difference between an organization's current status and its desired goals. The findings from this analysis inform an action plan, allowing the organization to clearly define its service approach and envision its future direction. Dr. Hasnaa Mokhtar, the Executive Director of Wafa House, explained that by clearly identifying their service strategy, they are better equipped to determine whom to assist directly and whom to refer to other resources. This clarity has opened many collaborative opportunities and established them as a leading authority in their local area.

The Social Location of an Organization

Without a strong institutional focus, mental health programs may not reach their full potential. Issues like poor coordination, inadequate staff training, and limited accountability can diminish the effectiveness and availability of these essential services. Understanding the social context of an organization is crucial for addressing the challenges faced by Muslim organizations regarding mental health. The term "social context" refers to the various social and cultural factors that shape an organization's identity and experiences, such as community demographics, cultural norms, religious beliefs, and socioeconomic conditions. Acknowledging these factors enables organizations to tailor their services to better meet the needs and preferences of their target population, ensuring greater relevance and effectiveness.

This understanding also promotes stronger community trust and engagement, as services are seen as culturally sensitive and responsive. By aligning their strategies with their social context, organizations can develop more focused and sustainable mental health programs that are better equipped to address the unique challenges and opportunities within their specific environments. During a conversation with a director from the Muslim American Society (MAS), several key challenges faced by the organization were highlighted. These challenges include time constraints, the necessity of wearing multiple hats, and a lack of training. The director, who wished to remain anonymous, noted that they often have only partial solutions and frequently jump from one task to another, leading to programs that are either not fully developed or executed to their potential (anonymous, personal communication, June 25, 2024). This situation exemplifies the difficulties that arise when organizations do not closely adhere to their social context, resulting in a diffusion of focus and resources that hampers their ability to effectively address their core mission and community needs.

Hasan from the Oaktree Institute notes that many Muslim organizations are relatively young and still in development, often lacking uniformity and systematic processes. Most operate in a manner similar to startups run by a small group of individuals, which contributes to ongoing challenges. Operationally, there is often a lack of formal processes and standards, particularly because these organizations differ significantly from one another. Some are started by individuals without prior organizational experience, often due to their immigrant backgrounds or careers unrelated to organizational management. Even those with corporate experience may find it challenging, as they might lack the know-how to run community-based or nonprofit organizations. Additionally, these organizations frequently encounter financial constraints, necessitating continuous fundraising efforts and limiting the time available to establish more effective processes. The challenges described by Hasan are closely linked to the organization's social context, as they typically stem from the specific cultural, social, and economic environments in which these organizations operate (M. Hasan, personal communication, July 11, 2024).

Lack of Funding, Education, and Visibility

One of the most pressing challenges that Muslim NGOs face in delivering mental health services is financial stability. This concern has been echoed by leaders from organizations such as ICNA Relief, FYI, Naseeha Mental Health, ISSA, MAS, and the ADAMS Center during our interviews. There is often insufficient funding available to support their work, which hinders the growth and effectiveness of these organizations. Despite having valuable resources and significant potential for development, they struggle due to this multifaceted issue. Part of the funding shortfall stems from a lack of awareness in the community about the importance of mental health, the reasons for securing funding, and the different levels and methods of support needed. Additionally, each organization tends to operate independently, which limits collaboration. When the community does not recognize or understand the valuable contributions these organizations make, their achievements and available resources often go unnoticed.

The FYI follows a public health model; they do not offer direct services but instead conduct community participant research focused on mental health issues specific to the Muslim community. They then work to transform this research into resources that can be shared across all areas of the community. One of their challenges is helping the community understand what they do and why it is important. Explaining their logic model can be difficult and complex, as it requires the community to be sufficiently informed about why they should care about this issue. This process demands effort and time to build relationships with stakeholders, which necessitates having staff who understand the work and can dedicate the time to foster those connections. Additionally, many Muslim organizations are often understaffed and overworked, which makes achieving these goals even more challenging (anonymous, personal communication, September 16, 2024).

Hiring qualified personnel for various roles within a robust organization that provides multiple services can be challenging. For direct services like counseling, it is essential to hire licensed therapists and counselors, who typically hold at least a master's degree, if not a doctorate. However, attracting qualified individuals with nonprofit-level salaries is incredibly difficult. ICNA Relief has made significant efforts to expand its counseling team over the past few years, but few of their counselors are full-time employees. The hiring process remains challenging due to the inability to offer competitive salaries. Additionally, offering lower salaries may result in hiring less qualified candidates, which could compromise the quality and effectiveness of the services provided.

Most NGOs primarily rely on private donors for funding; however, some organizations, like ISSA Canada, have transitioned to a grant funding model, though this approach is not widely adopted. While many Muslim organizations utilize grants for supplemental funding, their main source of financial support usually comes from a dedicated base of grassroots donors.

Organizations that operate locally in North America often face challenges in securing donations, as the Muslim donor mindset tends to emphasize sending money abroad rather than investing in local initiatives. Consequently, global relief efforts in Muslim-majority countries are typically prioritized over local spending. This focus on international aid can lead to fluctuating funding sources, particularly in response to global events. For instance, since the onset of the genocide in Gaza in October 2023, there has been a significant shift in the community's priorities, with many Muslims understandably directing their financial support towards relief efforts in that region. While this cause is important and deserves the community's attention, one unintended consequence of the shift in focus has been the struggle of many local organizations to survive. Naseeha Mental Health faced a significant risk of bankruptcy in the months following the Covid-19 pandemic. Although they are no longer at risk of financial collapse, they continue to face challenges in sustaining their organization. The current donor-funded system lacks sustainability and consistency, leaving organizations vulnerable to various external factors beyond their control.

One potential solution to address fluctuations in donations while engaging the donor base is to shift towards a focused crowdfunding effort. The idea is to gather as many donors as possible and encourage them to make small, consistent contributions on a monthly or quarterly basis. Many organizations have adopted this model to better plan their finances according to expected donations throughout the year. The challenge lies in attracting people who can commit to this initiative. However, the more individuals who commit, the lower the individual amounts become. For example, if we can secure commitments from 10,000 donors to contribute just $15 each month, this would establish a steady base budget of $150,000 per month, totaling up to $1,800,000 a year. While 10,000 may seem like a large number, it represents only 0.47% of the estimated 2.15 million adult Muslims in the U.S. as of 2017, according to PEW Research. This population is expected to grow at a significant rate (Mohamed, 2018), but the key is to gain buy-in from the community. Another advantage of the crowdfunding model is its inclusivity; it invites participation from all members of the community. The term 'donor' often implies wealth and large contributions, but this approach does not have to be limited to wealthy individuals. Everyone can give according to their means. Some may be able to contribute more than the suggested $15, while others might only manage $1 or $5. This inclusive practice aligns perfectly with Islamic values of giving, as everyone is encouraged to contribute in a way that is comfortable for them.

Abu Hurairah narrated that the Messenger of Allah (ﷺ) said: "Take on only as much as you can do of good deeds, for the best of deeds is that which is done consistently, even if it is little." Sunan Ibn Majah 4240.

The two main obstacles to achieving this goal are the lack of awareness within the Muslim community about mental health initiatives and their importance, as well as the challenge of securing and implementing a crowdfunding model from donors. Addressing this issue requires significant manpower, highlighting the initial problem of inadequate funding.

Another challenge with this funding model is that most donors tend to focus on immediate, tangible results; they want to see their money in action as quickly as possible. For instance, ICNA Relief has strong Hunger Prevention and Disaster Relief programs that address immediate needs during a crisis. When these programs are highlighted, fundraising efforts are more successful, and people are willing to contribute quickly and without much persuasion. However, promoting counseling services presents a challenge because the impact is gradual, affecting individuals over weeks and months rather than providing immediate results. This makes it difficult to measure and promote to the public. Furthermore, confidentiality is a key aspect of counseling, so unless clients choose to share their experiences—which is rare—much of the progress made remains behind closed doors and inaccessible to the public and donors.

Additionally, many donors prefer to ensure that most of their contributions are "going directly to the people most in need," which translates to funding direct services for clients. The lower the overhead costs an organization can document and the greater the focus on direct services, the more appealing they become to donors. Due to this mindset, organizations like FYI face significant challenges as they do not provide direct services. However, their work is essential for enabling those direct services, a fact that the community sometimes struggles to understand (anonymous, personal communication. September 16, 2024).

The emphasis on funding direct services creates a challenging cycle, even within organizations like ICNA Relief. For example, their Chicago office provides a rigorous transitional housing program for single women aimed at building self-sufficiency. However, due to limited staffing, they are unable to handle crisis situations. Given the prevalence of crises and domestic violence in the Muslim community, mosques often serve as the first point of contact for these urgent cases. They have communicated to ICNA Relief employees the need for a women's shelter, in addition to transitional housing, to support the many emergency cases rather than referring them to non-Muslim shelters that may struggle to meet specific cultural needs (anonymous, personal communication, April 12, 2022).

Establishing a shelter requires 24-hour staff for security, sanitation, and case management, which significantly increases overhead costs. However, donors often resist higher funding for overhead expenses, perpetuating the cycle of inadequate resources to address critical community needs. The lack of visibility can hinder organizations from effectively reaching potential clients and target populations, leaving individuals in need unaware of the services available to them. The natural vulnerability associated with mental health crises, coupled with the stigma surrounding these issues, means that many remain hidden from the majority of the Muslim community. This is why it is crucial to educate the community in order to continue reducing stigma. Moreover, this lack of visibility is compounded by the confidentiality requirements that direct service providers must adhere to by law. As a result, organizations must be creative in advertising their impact and successes. This situation exacerbates the challenge of educating the Muslim community on the importance of mental health initiatives; while the issues are present, they often go unseen. For instance, Naseeha has relied completely on word-of-mouth to promote its 24/7 helpline services and considers it a luxury to be able to hire a specialized social media and marketing position (anonymous, personal communication, September 19, 2024). However, when organizations do successfully advertise their services and begin to receive requests for help, they struggle to meet the rising demand. "We have to be careful about how we expand," one representative expressed (anonymous, personal communication, August 25, 2024). This ongoing challenge underscores the difficulty of building trust and visibility within the community while also striving to meet its needs.

Many organizations we interviewed have proposed and adopted the practice of applying for grants to address their funding deficits. This approach has met with mixed success, but most agree that with more time and effort, it can make a positive difference (anonymous personal communication, September 19, 2024; anonymous personal communication, August 25, 2025; anonymous personal communication, October 2, 2024). Another recommendation is for organizations to explore creative ways to implement a social enterprise model, which can help fund and sustain their operations (anonymous personal communication, September 19, 2024).

The Gender Dilemma

There is a significant concern regarding funding in the mental health field, particularly highlighting a gender divide. Mental health providers and leaders within these organizations are often women, many of whom face challenges in securing support from male community members. Numerous women working in this area report feeling overlooked or unheard when advocating for funding, which presents a critical barrier to advancing mental health initiatives. This gender disparity not only affects funding but also extends to the provision and seeking of services. For instance, 70% of Naseeha's helpline service users are female, while 30% are male (anonymous, personal communication, September 19, 2024). In the U.S. overall, 77.1% of all mental health counselors are female, whereas 22.9% are male (Census Bureau Data USA, 2022). Moreover, Muslim women leaders have taken a prominent role in mental health initiatives within their communities. Notable figures include Dr. Aneesah Nadir, the founder and President of the Islamic Social Services Association (ISSA-USA); Dr. Farha Abbasi, co-editor of this book, who founded the Muslim Mental Health Conference and Consortium; Dr. Sameera Ahmed, founder and first director of the Family and Youth Institute (FYI); Dr. Rania Awaad, director of the Stanford Muslim Mental Health & Islamic Psychology Lab and Co-Founder and President of Maristan; and Arshia Wajid, Founder &

Development Director of American Muslim Health Professionals, among many others. These women have paved the way in Muslim mental health advocacy, research, and services.

Considering how challenging it is for Muslim women to attain leadership positions in other Muslim spaces, these trailblazers in Muslim mental health are remarkable. While men are involved in the field, women represent the majority of the workforce, illustrating that Muslim women often spearhead initiatives in American Muslim mental health. A cause for concern is the small number of men participating in these areas, especially given that they typically dominate leadership roles in other Muslim NGO spaces, such as masjid boards. This lack of male involvement can lead to diminished importance and reduced funding for mental health initiatives (anonymous, personal communication, September 19, 2024).

The Boys Club of NGOs

In recent years, the term "boys' club" has been used to describe informal, male-dominated networks that often restrict the participation and influence of women and individuals outside the inner circle, whether consciously or unconsciously. This dynamic is particularly evident in Muslim spaces, affecting leadership positions within mosques and Islamic organizations, decision-making processes, and social gatherings. Men frequently have greater access to resources and opportunities, leading to gender imbalances in leadership roles and the marginalization of women's voices. Reinforced by traditional gender norms, the "boys' club" effect makes it challenging for women to attain leadership positions or be regarded as equals in shaping the community.

Dr. Aneesah Nadir shares her experiences of this exclusion as an African American woman. She notes that she is often not invited to speak or present at community events and emphasizes how her lack of wealthy connections further contributes to her invisibility (personal communication, June 13, 2024). Dr. Nadir's experience exemplifies intersectional invisibility, where individuals at the intersection of multiple marginalized identities—such as race, gender, and socioeconomic status—are more likely to be overlooked.

In Muslim spaces, traditional power structures often favor specific ethnic, racial, or socioeconomic groups, leading to the exclusion of women like Dr. Nadir. Her African American identity, combined with her gender and lack of access to affluent networks, increases her invisibility in environments where influence is closely tied to privilege. This intersectional invisibility goes beyond mere representation and has significant implications for integrating mental health care within Muslim

NGOs. When decision-makers and leaders do not reflect the full diversity of the Muslim community—especially those from marginalized backgrounds—the mental health needs of the entire community may be overlooked. Individuals like Dr. Nadir, who offer important perspectives from underrepresented groups, often lack equal opportunities to shape discussions around mental health services, advocacy, or resource allocation.

For instance, if the leadership of Muslim NGOs remains mostly male or consists of individuals from affluent, well-connected communities, there is a risk of overlooking mental health issues that particularly affect African American Muslims, women, and low-income families. These groups encounter unique challenges, such as racial discrimination, financial hardship, and gender-specific obstacles, but their experiences may not be fully addressed in mental health initiatives. Consequently, efforts to destigmatize mental health or provide culturally competent care may lack the depth and nuance necessary to meet the needs of these marginalized subgroups.

To create inclusive and effective mental health services, it is crucial to involve diverse voices and dismantle the intersectional barriers that limit the participation of individuals like Dr. Nadir. Failing to do so risks perpetuating the "boys' club" mentality that has historically marginalized women in leadership roles, creating a cycle where both gender and racial biases hinder meaningful progress in Muslim spaces.

Accountability and Professional Management

Supervision, Liability & HIPAA Compliance

Understanding supervision, liability, and HIPAA compliance is essential for anyone in mental health care. These standards help protect the organization and its clients from legal and ethical violations. Failing to address liability and compliance can lead to serious legal consequences, including fines and lawsuits, which can drain resources and harm the organization's reputation. Additionally, breaches of confidentiality can undermine trust within communities that are already hesitant to seek mental health care, ultimately hindering the organization's mission.

To tackle these challenges, Muslim organizations should collaborate with qualified mental health professionals while also acknowledging the valuable spiritual support provided by imams and sheikhs. Proper supervision ensures that only trained professionals manage therapeutic roles, maintaining ethical boundaries and protecting client confidentiality. By integrating the strengths of both religious leaders and mental health providers, organizations can offer comprehensive, culturally sensitive care while upholding high standards of professionalism and compliance.

In a conversation with Suheir Kafri, a social worker in the ADAMS Center's social services department, she mentioned that each time leadership changes, she often has to renegotiate the importance of her department. One significant challenge she encounters is navigating these discussions while upholding client confidentiality (S. Kafri, personal communication, September 5, 2024).

Lack of Management Structure

One of the challenges NGOs faces when providing mental health services is the lack of investment in organizational management infrastructure. Many of these organizations were founded by a small group of passionate individuals who were driven by a vision but often lacked a solid structural foundation. Without a clear management structure, defined roles, accountability frameworks, and systematic oversight, programs and services can quickly become disorganized, which may affect the longevity of key contributors.

Institutionalizing an organization offers clear benefits when it comes to scaling. Historically, Muslim NGOs have struggled to expand their reach due to various factors. One significant issue is the tendency to "working in the business instead of working on the business." Due to insufficient resources, one of the priority hires for NGOs tends to be service providers. However, these service providers often do not receive adequate administrative or operational support. As a result, they end up handling tasks that go beyond their designated job descriptions. While such working conditions may be justifiable in the short term or during the early stages of an NGO's existence, they typically do not sustain well over time. Organizations that spread too thin and individuals who do the same are likely to maintain the status quo at best. This situation can hinder how teams respond to challenges; without sufficient bandwidth, no one has the time to assess the root causes of problems. When combined with unrealistic expectations from leadership, the outcome is often a burned-out service provider on the verge of leaving.

Taking a top-down approach, let us review some common challenges Muslim NGOs face in institutionalizing themselves. The Board of Directors or members are at the nonprofit sector's highest level. Board members have historically struggled to understand their scope of work about the team's day-to-day operations. Common issues within the board include a lack of expertise, accountability, commitment to engagement, overdependence on founders, and confusion surrounding governance and management (Bradshaw & Fredette, 2013). Executive leadership operates under the board and typically includes roles such as the Executive Director or C-suite positions.

Executives in the nonprofit sector must skillfully balance their organization's mission and strategy with day-to-day operations. A common pitfall for these executives is becoming overly involved in operational details, which can distract them from achieving key organizational objectives. Additional challenges include developing middle management and other executive roles, establishing two-way accountability with the board, managing limited funding, and dealing with the frequent turnover of staff and volunteers (Drucker, 2006). Directly beneath the executive team, nonprofits typically have middle management that translates organizational objectives into actionable tasks. Managers are responsible for navigating upward communication with executive supervisors and downward management of individual contributors. However, many Muslim NGOs invest little in middle management, leading to role ambiguity. These organizations often struggle with establishing authority and managing expansion projects (Yukl, 2012). Ultimately, managers are tasked with overseeing the on-ground team and the individual contributors.

The team includes counselors, therapists, and administrative personnel who work on the front lines. A significant portion of employee turnover is attributed to compassion fatigue and burnout. There is often a disconnect between the on-ground team and executive leadership, which can lead to misalignment in goals and expectations. Many staff members face limited opportunities for career development and growth unless they are willing to pursue a management position, which rarely becomes available (Maslach & Leiter, 2016).

These challenges have also been observed within organizations like Wafa House, which actively use strategic objectives to address concerns. Dr. Mokhtar has shared recommendations to improve the situation, such as ensuring that the board does not become a mere social club, providing a long-term strategic plan for reference, and offering accommodations to support on-ground staff. She expressed her concerns about the high turnover of talented staff, attributing it to a lack of institutionalization in the past (H. Mokhtar, personal communication, September 20, 2024). These challenges are more prevalent than one might expect and affect various sectors within the NGO space.

Recommendations

Strengthening Partnerships

Mohamed Hasan explains that the challenge of building stronger networks and alliances among Muslim NGOs is deeply rooted in the complexities of achieving unity within the Muslim ummah. The community is often fragmented along sectarian lines, differing beliefs, interpretations of Islamic law (Fiqh), and ethnic backgrounds. This division can hinder collaboration among organizations, as many feel little motivation to join forces (M. Hasan, personal communication, July 11, 2024).

To effectively address this challenge, a multifaceted approach should be tailored to the unique characteristics and dynamics of each borough or state. First, organizations should facilitate dialogue and foster understanding through regular inter-organizational forums and community gatherings, encouraging open discussions about shared goals and values. For instance, local mosques, community centers, and nonprofit organizations could host quarterly town hall meetings to bring together various stakeholders from different backgrounds, promoting intercultural understanding and collaboration.

Training programs focused on collaboration skills and leadership development are essential for equipping individuals with tools for effective engagement. Additionally, establishing a framework for joint initiatives with transparent processes and clear expectations can help overcome practical barriers to collaboration. By implementing these strategies at the community, city, borough, or state level, Muslim NGOs can enhance their collective impact, navigate existing divisions, and work together to address shared challenges within the community. These initiatives will strengthen individual organizations and contribute to the broader goal of unity and collaboration within the Muslim ummah.

Collaboration can also be challenging outside of the Muslim community space. Muslim NGOs are fewer and newer compared to their non-Muslim counterparts. Dr. Mokhtar from Wafa House mentioned that no resources are available for outreach initiatives when navigating these spaces. She has often had to take the initiative herself, knocking on doors and exploring different forums to identify opportunities for Muslim NGOs to leverage and their potential contributions to the larger community. She discovered that personally reaching out to executive leadership in these organizations has helped her build rapport and directed her to the right resources.

A notable example of successful collaboration is Isaiah in Minnesota, where a coalition of over 20 mosques has been organized and mobilized for civic and social change (ISAIAH MN, n.d.). The coalition has successfully advocated for initiatives such as Paid Family and Medical Leave, a $1 billion investment in affordable housing, and many other significant achievements. Organizers at Isaiah credit much of their success to the support from the Muslim community in Minnesota (ISAIAH MN. 2023, June 24).

Leveraging Technology

RUH is an online therapy platform dedicated to enhancing individuals' mental and spiritual well-being worldwide. In a conversation with Omar Khan, the Co-Founder and CEO, he emphasized the significance of leveraging technology to support the Muslim community. RUH provides three main services: an online therapy platform, a directory of resources, and a mindfulness app. Khan recognized the necessity for a space where Muslims can see themselves reflected and feel safe when seeking mental health care (personal communication, May 30, 2024). For more information about the importance of technology in Muslim mental health care, check out their chapter.

Utilizing technology can greatly improve the integration of mental health services within Muslim NGOs through several strategies. First, offering telehealth services—such as virtual counseling and mobile apps like RUH and SABR specifically designed for the Muslim community—can enhance accessibility for those hesitant to seek in-person help. For Muslims in various fields who are not mental health professionals, online training sessions and resource libraries can provide essential knowledge about mental health awareness and cultural competency, as seen in AMHP's Mental Health First Aid Training. Additionally, leveraging social media and online forums can encourage community engagement by spreading information, sharing success stories, and creating spaces for open discussions.

Technology can significantly enhance the outreach and awareness of organizations. One simple step is to transition from physical copies of annual reports to digital flipbooks hosted on the organization's website, which can improve visibility. In the short term, organizations may also consider outsourcing administrative functions to alleviate budget concerns while achieving positive results in often-overlooked areas. Platforms like Upwork, Fiverr, and TaskRabbit can connect organizations with contractors who specialize in various services, particularly in creative fields. Outsourcing marketing, design, and other digital components to fully remote and agile creative agencies is a common practice among startups with limited funding. Additionally, setting up a Calendly account for each executive can streamline scheduling by syncing their availability with their calendars. Human Resources has also become more accessible through platforms like BambooHR, which offer packages that include an HR representative to assist with onboarding and other essential processes. These tools provide nonprofits with flexible options instead of hiring full-time staff in the short term. Another suggestion from the interview is to use artificial intelligence (AI) to compensate for limited human resources. AI can manage initial contact stages, helping to sort and prioritize clients and their needs (anonymous, personal communication, September 19, 2024).

Training and Capacity Building

During a conversation with Imam Abdul Malik Merchant, the lead chaplain at the ADAMS Center, he expressed concerns about volunteer retention, as well as the lack of community engagement and growth (A. Merchant, personal communication, August 19, 2024). Imam Merchant is not alone in pointing out the need for training and capacity building within organizations. He discussed the Islamic concept of Ihsan (excellence), emphasizing that while the push for professionalization can enhance effectiveness, it often leads to a corporate mindset that neglects the community's genuine needs.

To address this issue, Muslim NGOs should implement targeted training programs focused on community engagement, volunteer management, and cultural competency. These programs should involve all levels of management to ensure shared accountability and that leaders model values of service and community connection. By fostering a culture of continuous learning and development, organizations can better align their objectives with the needs of the community, thereby improving volunteer retention and engagement.

When speaking with Hasan, he emphasizes that while providing services and programs for the community is essential, it is equally important to support and develop the organization's internal members. This focus should be reflected at all levels of the organization. To foster a culture of growth, systems need to be put in place to support mentorship and leadership development, allowing younger leaders to take on more significant roles. Succession planning is critical for ensuring organizational continuity and creating an environment where individuals feel empowered to advance.

Professionalizing these processes can greatly enhance the organization's capabilities. For example, properly documenting roles, responsibilities, and donor lists will facilitate knowledge transfer and create opportunities for new talent to emerge (M. Hasan, personal communication, July 11, 2024). By prioritizing training and capacity building, organizations can cultivate a culture that nurtures existing members while attracting and retaining new talent, ultimately strengthening their ability to serve the community effectively.

Conclusion

As we move forward, we encourage Muslim NGOs to thoroughly explore the various challenges they face, consider implementing the solutions outlined in this chapter, and continue the conversation to foster meaningful improvements in the mental health of the North American Muslim community. Organizational leaders and contributors in the Muslim NGO sector have carefully examined the issues and recommendations identified here. By following the suggested recommendations, NGO representatives will have a clearer direction to study further and tailor solutions specific to their needs. Most NGOs operate under certain limitations and face challenges similar to those discussed in this chapter. As a result, NGO representatives must be creative when seeking solutions. Fortunately, there are many opportunities that most NGOs have yet to explore, such as outsourcing marketing and operational functions or automating processes through technology. Another positive development is the notable increase in the number of professionals actively working to enhance the quality of service within the Muslim NGO space. Through our interviews, the co-authors of this chapter have had the privilege of meeting and speaking with various pioneers in the field, who not only identified gaps in the industry but are also advocating for change and introducing solutions that could potentially be replicated across the Muslim NGO sector. This is a pivotal moment for Muslim NGO service providers and beneficiaries alike as we observe a shift in priorities. We hope this chapter inspires leaders to critically assess their organizational practices and invest in solutions that align with their missions while effectively addressing community needs. By collaborating on these initiatives, we can enhance individual well-being and advance the vision of comprehensive community care.

References

Ahmad, F., AlZeben, F., Kattan, W., Alyahyawi, H. Y., & Hassan, A. N. (2023). Prevalence, correlates, and impact of psychiatric disorders and treatment utilization among Muslims in the United States: Results from the National Epidemiological Survey of Alcohol and Related Conditions. *Community Mental Health Journal*, 59(8), 1568–1577. https://doi.org/10.1007/s10597-023-01145-7

Ahmed, S., & Reddy, L. (2007). Understanding the mental health needs of American Muslims: Recommendations and considerations for practice. *Journal of Multicultural Counseling and Development*, 35(4), 207–219.

Ali, O. M., Milstein, G., & Marzuk, P. M. (2005). The imam's role in meeting the counseling needs of Muslim communities in the United States. *Psychiatric Services*, 56, 2–5. http://dx.doi.org/10.1176/appi.ps.56.2.202

Awaad, R., El-Gabalawy, O., Jackson-Shaheed, E., Zia, B., Keshavarzi, H., Mogahed, D., & Altalib, H. (2021). Suicide attempts of Muslims compared with other religious groups in the US. *JAMA Psychiatry*, 78(9), 1041. https://doi.org/10.1001/jamapsychiatry.2021.1813

Bachmann, S. (2018). Epidemiology of suicide and psychiatric perspective. *International Journal of Environmental Research and Public Health*, 15(7), 1425. https://doi.org/10.3390/ijerph15071425

Bagasra, A., & Mackinem, M. (2014). An exploratory study of American Muslim conceptions of mental illness. *Journal of Muslim Mental Health*, 8(1), 57–76. https://doi.org/10.3998/jmmh.10381607.0008.104

Bradshaw, P., & Fredette, C. (2013). Determinants of the range of nonprofit governance responsibilities. *Nonprofit and Voluntary Sector Quarterly*, 42(5), 902–927.

Cabral, S. (2022, August 8). Sania Khan: She tiktoked her divorce, then her husband killed her. BBC. Retrieved 2024, from https://www.bbc.com/news/world-us-canada-62427084

Ciftci, A., Jones, N., & Corrigan, P. (2013). Mental health stigma in the Muslim community. *Journal of Muslim Mental Health*, 7, 17–32.

Drucker, P. (2006). The effective executive: The definitive guide to getting the right things done. *Harper Business*.

Haque, A. (2004). Religion and mental health: The case of American Muslims. *Journal of Religion and Health*, 43(1), 45–58.

ISAIAH MN. (2023, June 24). Power belongs to those who show up together. ISAIAH. https://isaiahmn.org/2023/06/24/power-belongs-to-those-who-show-up-together/

ISAIAH MN. (n.d.). Muslim Coalition. ISAIAH. https://isaiahmn.org/project/muslim-coalition/

Lucchetti, G., Koenig, H. G., & Lucchetti, A. L. G. (2021). Spirituality, religiousness, and mental health: A review of the current scientific evidence. *World Journal of Clinical Cases*, 9(26), 7620–7631. https://doi.org/10.12998/wjcc.v9.i26.7620

Maslach, C., & Leiter, M. P. (2016). Understanding the burnout experience: Recent research and its implications for psychiatry. *World Psychiatry*, 15(2), 103–111.

Mohamed, B. (2018, January 3). New estimates show US Muslim population continues to grow. Retrieved October 15, 2024.

Sinek, S. (2009). *Start with why: How great leaders inspire everyone to take action.* Penguin.

Stengle, J. (2021, April 26). 6 family members dead in apparent murder-suicide at Texas home, police say. *USA Today.* Retrieved 2024, from https://www.usatoday.com/story/news/nation/2021/04/06/six-family-members-murder-dallas/7103936002/

Wang, P. S., Berglund, P. A., Olfson, M., & Kessler, R. C. (2004). Delays in initial treatment contact after first onset of a mental disorder. *Health Services Research,* 39(2), 393–415. https://doi.org/10.1111/j.1475-6773.2004.00234.x

Yukl, G. (2012). *Leadership in organizations.* Pearson Education.

www.ingramcontent.com/pod-product-compliance
Lightning Source LLC
Chambersburg PA
CBHW020452030426
42337CB00011B/83